Handbook of Research on Multi–Agent Systems:
Semantics and Dynamics of Organizational Models

Virginia Dignum
Utrecht University, The Netherlands

INFORMATION SCIENCE REFERENCE

Hershey · New York

Director of Editorial Content:	Kristin Klinger
Director of Production:	Jennifer Neidig
Managing Editor:	Jamie Snavely
Assistant Managing Editor:	Carole Coulson
Typesetter:	Jeff Ash
Cover Design:	Lisa Tosheff
Printed at:	Yurchak Printing Inc.

Published in the United States of America by
 Information Science Reference (an imprint of IGI Global)
 701 E. Chocolate Avenue, Suite 200
 Hershey PA 17033
 Tel: 717-533-8845
 Fax: 717-533-8661
 E-mail: cust@igi-global.com
 Web site: http://www.igi-global.com

and in the United Kingdom by
 Information Science Reference (an imprint of IGI Global)
 3 Henrietta Street
 Covent Garden
 London WC2E 8LU
 Tel: 44 20 7240 0856
 Fax: 44 20 7379 0609
 Web site: http://www.eurospanbookstore.com

Library of Congress Cataloging-in-Publication Data

Handbook of research on multi-agent systems : semantics and dynamics of organizational models / Virginia Dignum, editor.
  p. cm.

Includes bibliographical references and index.

Summary: "This book provide a comprehensive view of current developments in agent organizations as a paradigm for both the modeling of human organizations, and for designing effective artificial organizations"--Provided by publisher.

ISBN 978-1-60566-256-5 (hardcover) -- ISBN 978-1-60566-257-2 (ebook)

1. Intelligent agents (Computer software)--Handbooks, manuals, etc. 2. Self-organizing systems--Handbooks, manuals, etc. I. Dignum, Virginia.

QA76.76.I58H335 2009
006.3--dc22
                    2008033935

British Cataloguing in Publication Data
A Cataloguing in Publication record for this book is available from the British Library.

All work contributed to this book set is original material. The views expressed in this book are those of the authors, but not necessarily of the publisher.

Editorial Advisory Board

List of Contributors

Table of Contents

Introduction

Section I
Methodologies and Frameworks for
Agent Organizations

Section IV
Norms and Institutions

Section V
Organizational Dynamics

Section VI
Applications

Detailed Table of Contents

Introduction

Chapter I

Virginia Dignum, Utrecht University, The Netherlands

Agent Organization can be understood from two perspectives: organization as a process and organization as an entity. That is, organization is considered both as the process of organizing a set of individuals, or as an entity in itself, with its own requirements and objectives. In fact, agent organizations demand the integration of both perspectives and rely for a great extent on the notion of openness and heterogeneity of MAS. Practical applications of agents to organizational modeling are being widely developed, however, formal theories are needed to describe interaction and organizational structure. Furthermore, it is necessary to get a closer look at the applicability of insights and theories from organization sciences to the development of agent organizations. In this chapter, current approaches to agent organizations are discussed. Agent Organizations bring concepts and solutions from sociology and organizational theory into agent research, integrating organizational and individual perspectives, and aim at the dynamic adaptation of models to organizational and environmental changes, both of which are impacted by the notion of openness and heterogeneity. The chapter also presents a promising application of agent organizations to the area of human-agent teams.

In this chapter, the authors discuss the concepts of agent organization, organizational model, and review some existing organizational models. Before the review, the authors discuss how to classify the diverse aspects of agent organizations currently captured by organizational models. These aspects are named "modelling dimensions". The authors show that there are at least four basic dimensions: the structural dimension mainly composed of roles and groups, the interactive dimension characterized by dialogical interaction structures, the functional dimension formed by goal/task decomposition and, the normative dimension in which the authors find the concepts of norms, rights, rules, and so forth. Apart from the basic dimensions, the authors also identify four other complementary dimensions: environment, evaluation, evolution, and ontology. These are related to the aspects of situatedeness, measurement, adaptation, and domain specific semantics of agent organizations. Finally, the authors compare the organizational models reviewed and describe how the idea of modelling dimension can help in finding correspondences between organizational models.

Chapter III

In this chapter, the authors stress the importance of thinking a MAS in all its aspects (agents, environment, interactions, organizations, and institutions), using a more integral vision. The authors show that a genuine organizational approach has to take into account both the environment and the institutional part of MAS societies. Then, the authors propose the MASQ (Multi-Agent System based on Quadrants) meta-model, which constitutes an abstraction of the various aspects of an OCMAS (Organization Centered Multi-Agent Systems), extending AGR (Agent/Group/Role). MASQ is based on a four-quadrant framework, where the analysis and design of a system is performed along two axes: an interior/exterior dimension and an individual/collective dimension. The authors give a conceptual definition of this approach and the authors will show that it is possible to apply it to practical models.

Chapter IV

This chapter introduces a suite of technologies for building complex, adaptive systems. It is based in the multi-agent systems paradigm and uses the Organization Model for Adaptive Computational Systems (OMACS). OMACS defines the knowledge needed about a system's structure and capabilities, to allow it to reorganize at runtime in the face of a changing environment and its agent's capabilities. However, the OMACS model is only useful if it is supported by a set of methodologies, techniques, and architectures that allow it to be implemented effectively on a wide variety of systems. To this end, this chapter presents a suite of technologies including (1) the Organization-based Multi-agent Systems Engineering (O-MaSE) methodology, (2) a set of policy specification techniques that allow an OMACS system to remain flexible while still providing guidance, and (3) a set of architectures and algorithms used to implement OMACS-based systems. The chapter also includes the presentation of a small OMACS-based system.

Chapter V

  Christopher Cheong, RMIT University, Melbourne, Australia
  Michael Winikoff, RMIT University, Melbourne, Australia & University of Otago,
   Dunedin, New Zealand

Although intelligent agents individually exhibit a number of characteristics, including social ability, flexibility, and robustness, which make them suitable to operate in complex, dynamic, and error-prone environments, these characteristics are not exhibited in multi-agent interactions. For instance, agent interactions are often not flexible or robust. This is due to the traditional message-centric design processes, notations, and methodologies currently used. To address this issue, the authors have developed Hermes, a goal-oriented design methodology for agent interactions which is aimed at being pragmatic for practicing software engineers. Hermes focuses on interaction goals, that is, goals of the interaction which the agents are attempting to achieve, and results in interactions that are more flexible and robust than message-centric approaches. This chapter presents the design and implementation aspects of Hermes. This includes an explanation of the Hermes design processes, notations, and design artifacts, along with a detailed description of the implementation process which provides a mapping of design artifacts to goal-plan agent platforms, such as Jadex.

Section II
Formal Approaches for Agent Organizations

Chapter VI

  Viara Popova, De Montfort University, UK
  Alexei Sharpanskykh, Vrije Universiteit Amsterdam, The Netherlands

This chapter introduces a formal framework for modeling and analysis of organizations. It allows representing and reasoning about all important aspects of artificial and human organizations structured in a number of views, including performance-oriented, process-oriented, power- and interaction-related aspects. The framework provides means to model formal (pre)defined organizational structures and dynamics, informal relations, and behavior of organizational actors. The meaning attached to the modeling concepts is specified based on the literature from Social Science. Unlike many existing organization modeling approaches the proposed framework has formal foundations based on the order-sorted predicate logic, which enables different types of analysis of organizational specifications of particular views and across views. The framework allows scalability of modeling and analysis of complex organizations, by considering them at different aggregation levels. Furthermore, the framework provides support for real-time management of organizational processes. The framework was applied in several case studies, one of which is discussed here.

In this chapter, the author proposes a declarative language designed specifically for describing, in an expressive way, a variety of social interactions. The author attempts to avoid the fallacies of artificial restriction, and similarly, confounding under-specification of the design domain, yet constructing a rigorous, machine-interpretable semantics. The author intends to introduce such a semantic, in that it will lead to a constructive dialogue between communities of agent-based social modeling and agent-based software design, and lead to a greater integration of agent development toolkits and agent-based modeling toolkits.

In this chapter, the authors investigate how organizations can be represented as graphs endowed with formal semantics. They distinguish different dimensions of organizations, each with a dimension that leads to a different structure in the organizational graph. By giving the graphs a formal semantics in Description Logic, the authors show that it is possible to formalize the effect of the organization on the activities of the agents playing the roles of the organization. Such perspective, which combines quantitative (graph-theory) and qualitative (logic) methods is shown to provide a formal ground for the study and analysis of properties of organizations which are commonly addressed only informally.

Organization concepts and models are increasingly being adopted for the design and specification of multi-agent systems. Agent organizations can be seen as mechanisms of social order, created to achieve common goals for more or less autonomous agents. In order to develop a theory on the relationship between organizational structures, organizational actions, and actions of agents performing roles in the organization, a theoretical framework is needed to describe and reason about organizations. The formal model presented in this chapter is sufficiently generic to enable the comparison of different existing organizational approaches to Multi-Agent Systems (MAS), while having enough descriptive power to describe realistic organizations.

Section III
Interactions in Organizations

Chapter X

Cristiano Castelfranchi, ISTC-CNR, Italy

This chapter presents organizations as a macro-micro notion and device; they presuppose autonomous proactive entities (agents) playing the organizational roles. Agents can have their own powers, goals, and relationships (of dependence, trust, etc.). This opens important issues to be discussed: Does cooperation require mentally shared plans? Which is the relationship between individual powers and role powers; personal dependencies and role dependencies; personal goals and assigned goals; personal beliefs and what we have to assume when playing our role; individual actions and organizational actions? What about possible conflicts, deviations, power abuse, given the agents' autonomy? Multi-Agent Systems discipline should both aim at scientifically modeling human organizations, and at designing effective artificial organizations. The author's claim is that for both those aims, one should model a high (risky) degree of flexibility, exploiting autonomy and pro-activity, intelligence, and decentralized knowledge of role-players, allowing for functional violations of requests and even of rules.

Chapter XI

Paolo Torroni, University of Bologna, Italy
Pınar Yolum, Boğaziçi University, Turkey
Munindar P. Singh, North Carolina State University, USA
Marco Alberti, University of Ferrara, Italy
Federico Chesani, University of Bologna, Italy
Marco Gavanelli, University of Ferrara, Italy
Evelina Lamma, University of Ferrara, Italy
Paola Mello, University of Bologna, Italy

In this chapter, the authors present and discuss two declarative, social semantic approaches for modeling interaction. The first approach takes a state-oriented perspective, and models interaction in terms of commitments. The second adopts a rule-oriented perspective, and models interaction in terms of logical formulae expressing expectations about agent interaction. The authors use a simple interaction protocol taken from the e-commerce domain to present the functioning and features of the commitment- and expectation-based approaches, and to discuss various forms of reasoning and verification that they accommodate, and how organizational modeling can benefit from them.

Chapter XII

Gita Sukthankar, University of Central Florida, USA
Katia Sycara, Carnegie Mellon University, USA
Joseph A. Giampapa, Carnegie Mellon University, USA
Christopher Burnett, University of Aberdeen, Scotland

This chapter discusses the problem of agent aiding of ad-hoc, decentralized human teams so as to improve team performance on time-stressed group tasks. To see how human teams rise to the challenge, the authors analyze the communication patterns of teams performing a collaborative search task that recreates some of the cognitive difficulties faced by teams during search and rescue operations. The experiments show that the communication patterns of successful decentralized ad-hoc teams performing a version of the task that requires tight coordination differ both from the teams that are less successful at task completion and from teams performing a loosely coupled version of the same task. The authors conclude by discussing (1) what lessons can be derived, from observing humans, to facilitate the development of agents to support ad-hoc, decentralized teams, and (2) where can intelligent agents be inserted into human teams to improve the humans' performance.

Bob van der Vecht, Utrecht University, The Netherlands & TNO Defense,
Security and Safety, The Netherlands
Frank Dignum, Utrecht University, The Netherlands
John-Jules Ch. Meyer, Utrecht University, The Netherlands

This chapter discusses how autonomous agents can adopt organizational rules into their reasoning process. Agents in an organization need to coordinate their actions in order to reach the organizational goals. Organizational models specify the desired behaviour in terms of roles, relations, norms, and interactions. The authors have developed a method to translate norms into event-processing rules of the agents. They propose a modular reasoning model that includes the organizational rules explicitly. Since the agents are autonomous, they will have their own reasoning rules next to the organizational rules. The modular approach allows for meta-reasoning about these rules. The authors show that this stimulates bottom-up dynamics in the organization.

Section IV
Norms and Institutions

Nicoletta Fornara, Università della Svizzera italiana, Switzerland
Marco Colombetti, Università della Svizzera italiana, Swtizerland & Politecnico di Milano,
Italy

The specification of open interaction systems is widely recognized to be a crucial issue, which involves the problem of finding a standard way of specifying: a communication language for the interacting agents, the entities that constitute the context of the interaction, and rules that regulate interactions. An approach to solve these problems consists in modeling open interaction systems as a set of artificial institutions. In this chapter, the authors address this issue by formally defining, in the Event Calculus, a repertoire of abstract concepts (like commitment, institutional power, role, norm) that can be used to specify every artificial institution. The authors then show how, starting from the formal definition of these concepts and of application-dependent concepts, it is possible to obtain a formal specification of a system. By using a suitable tool, it is then possible to simulate and monitor the system's evolution through automatic deduction.

Chapter XV

Francesco Viganò, Università della Svizzera italiana, Switzerland

Marco Colombetti, Università della Svizzera italiana, Swtizerland & Politecnico di Milano, Italy

Institutions have been proposed to explicitly represent norms in open multi-agent systems, where agents may not follow them and therefore require mechanisms to detect violations. In doing so, they increase the efficiency of electronic transactions carried out by agents, but raise the problem of ensuring that such institutions are not characterized by contradictory norms, and provide agents with all the needed powers to fulfill their objectives. In this chapter the authors present a framework to verify organizations regulated by institutions, which is characterized by a precise formalization of institutional concepts, a language to describe institutions, and a tool to model check them. Finally, to evaluate and exemplify our approach, the authors model and verify the Chaired Meeting Institution, showing that the verification of institutional rules constitutes a necessary step to define sound institutions.

Chapter XVI

Mehdi Dastani, Utrecht University, The Netherlands

Nick A.M. Tinnemeier, Utrecht University, The Netherlands

John-Jules Ch. Meyer, Utrecht University, The Netherlands

Multi-agent systems are viewed as consisting of individual agents whose behaviors are regulated by an organizational artifact. This chapter presents a programming language that aims at facilitating the implementation of norm-based organizational artifacts. The programming language is presented in two steps. The authors first present a programming language that is designed to support the implementation of non-normative organizational artifacts. Such artifacts are specified in terms of non-normative concepts such as the identity of participating agents, the identity of the constituting environments in which individual agents can perform actions and the agents' access relation to the environments. The programming language is then modified and extended to support the implementation of norm-based artifacts. Such artifacts are specified in terms of norms being enforced by monitoring, regimenting and sanctioning mechanisms. The syntax and operational semantics of the programming language are discussed and explained by means of a conference management system example.

Section V
Organizational Dynamics

Chapter XVII

Antônio Carlos da Rocha Costa, Universidade Católica de Pelotas, Brazil

Graçaliz Pereira Dimuro, Universidade Católica de Pelotas, Brazil

This chapter presents the Population-Organization model, a formal tool for studying the organization of open multi-agent systems and its functional and structural dynamics. The model is minimal in two senses: it comprises a minimal set of extensional concepts able of adequately accounting for the notion of dynamic organization; and, it is a core organization model upon which a certain kind of dynamical rules can be defined, to account for the action of intentional organizational elements like prestige, power, morality, and so forth. This chapter gives a detailed presentation of the core model, in a version adapted for describing organizations where interactions have a periodic character. The authors also illustrate how the model supports intentional organizational processes, by introducing a sample set of moral rules for agents playing roles in informal organizations.

Chapter XVIII

This chapter presents an adaptive organizational policy for multi-agent systems called TRACE. TRACE allows a collection of multi-agent organizations to dynamically allocate tasks and resources between themselves in order to efficiently process an incoming stream of tasks. The tasks have deadlines and their arrival pattern changes over time. Hence, at any instant, some organizations could have surplus resources while others could become overloaded. In order to minimize the number of lost requests caused by an overload, the allocation of resources to organizations is changed dynamically by using ideas from microeconomics. The authors formally show that TRACE has the ability to adapt to load variations, reduce the number of lost requests, and allocate resources to computations on the basis of their critical-ity. Furthermore, although the solution generated by TRACE is not always Pareto-optimal, TRACE has the properties of feasibility and monotonicity that make it well suited to time-constrained applications. Finally, the authors present experimental results to demonstrate the performance of TRACE.

Chapter XIX

The authors of this chapter have been developing a framework for executable specification of norm-gov-erned multi-agent systems. In this framework, specification is a design-time activity; moreover, there is no support for run-time modification of the specification. Due to environmental, social, or other condi-tions, however, it is often desirable, or even necessary, to alter the system specification during the system execution. In this chapter the authors extend our framework by allowing for "dynamic specifications", that is, specifications that may be modified at run-time by the members of a system. The framework extension is motivated by Brewka's "dynamic argument systems" — argument systems in which the rules of order may become the topic of the debate. They illustrate the framework for dynamic specifica-tions by presenting: (i) a dynamic specification of an argumentation protocol, and (ii) an execution of this protocol in which the participating agents modify the protocol specification.

    Marco Lamieri, Institute for Scientific Interchange Foundation, Italy
    Diana Mangalagiu, Management and Strategy Department, Reims Management
    School, France, & Institute for Scientific Interchange Foundation, Italy

This chapter's authors present a model of organization aimed to understand the effect of formal and informal structures on the organization's performance. The model considers the interplay between the formal hierarchical structure and the social network connecting informally the agents emerging while the organization performs a task-set. The social network creation and evolution is endogenous, as it doesn't include any function supposed to optimize performance. After a review of the literature, the authors propose a definition of performance based on the efficiency in allocating the task of a simulated organization that can be considered as a network-based problem-solving system. They analyze how the emergence of a stable process in decomposing tasks under different market conditions can alleviate the rigidity and the inefficiencies of a hierarchical structure and compare the performance of different hierarchical structures under variable environment conditions.

Section VI
Applications

    Steven Okamoto, Carnegie Mellon University, USA
    Katia Sycara, Carnegie Mellon University, USA
    Paul Scerri, Carnegie Mellon University, USA

Intelligent software personal assistants are an active research area with the potential to revolutionize the way that human organizations operate, but there has been little research quantifying how they will impact organizational performance or how organizations will or should adapt in response. In this chapter, the authors develop a computational model of the organization to evaluate the impact different proposed assistant abilities have on the behavior and performance of the organization. By varying the organizational structures under consideration, they can identify which abilities are most beneficial, as well as explore how organizations may adapt to best leverage the new technology. The results indicate that the most beneficial abilities for hierarchical organizations are those that improve load balancing through task allocation and failure recovery, while for horizontal organizations the most beneficial abilities are those that improve communication. The results also suggest that software personal assistant technology will facilitate more horizontal organizations.

    Sachin Kamboj, University of Delaware, USA
    Keith S. Decker, University of Delaware, USA

This chapter presents an approach to organizational-self design (OSD), a method of designing organizations at run-time in which the agents are responsible for generating their own organizational structures. OSD is especially suitable for environments that are dynamic, albeit slowly changing. Such environments preclude the use of static, design-time generated, organizational structures, and yet contain certain characteristics and conditions that change slowly, if at all; these characteristics can be harnessed for the purposes of creating stable organizational structures. This chapter extends the existing approaches to OSD by applying them to worth-oriented domains – that is, domains in which problems are represented using TÆMS based task structures. The authors present the editor's OSD primitives and framework, and discusses some interesting future lines of research.

Chapter XXIII

This chapter focuses on a Petri Net-based model for team organization and monitoring. The applications considered are missions performed by several robots that cooperate in different ways according to the goals to be achieved. Formal operations on the Petri Net representing the mission plan allow the dynamic hierarchy of subteams to be revealed and the agents' individual plans – including the relevant cooperation context – to be calculated. The model also allows several failure propagation ways within the team to be highlighted and local plan repair to be considered. Moreover Petri Nets allow direct implementation and monitoring and control of the plan at each level of the organization: team, subteams, and individual robots.

Foreword

Fifty years after the publication of the influential book on human organizations by March and Simon (1958) this new publication presents an overview of current work in agent organizations. Researchers have been attempting to use our understanding of human organizations to inform our appreciation of artificial organizations for over 50 years and this volume clearly illustrates a maturing of those investigations. It is also of note that the varied perspectives presented by the internationally diverse author panel demonstrates that the field is still at a formative stage.

To start with, the notion of "organization" in artificial intelligence is anything but crisp, and several of the early chapters discuss models and dimensions that can be seen as complementary attempts to capture the essence of the concept. Just as one can choose to describe a light switch as an "agent," but it is generally not fruitful to do so (Shoam, 1993), the study of organizations is indeed intended to capture more than just the presence of multiple, interacting entities. The contributions in Sections I, IV, and VI provide the reader with a selection of analyses that point to the richness of organizations as a way of capturing complex "macro" phenomena in an integrated model. In contrast, the chapters in Section III adopt a "micro" perspective where interactions between agents are the focus of attention. Bridging these views, the material presented in Section II, can be seen as an attempt to ensure that the theory is supported by semantics, or, as McDermott (1978) puts it, "No notation without denotation". The chapters in Section VI, by providing a trio of practical applications, can then be viewed as a response to the exhortation "No notation without exploitation" (Shoam, 1993).

This book presents a journey through a complex landscape. The editor, Virginia Dignum, has built on the tradition of contributions from the Utrecht group to the agent research community by bringing together a panel of highly credentialed authors. These researchers, who have already made individually significant contributions to the study of agent organizations, are well placed to influence the direction of the field. While the route taken in the book is shaped by the choice of authors, not simply by navigating to agreed signposts of the field, readers can be sure that they will have been taken to some of the most interesting landmarks, and are then well prepared to appreciate the opportunities for future research on agent organizations.

Liz Sonenberg
University of Melbourne
July 2008

REFERENCES

March, J. G., & Simon, H. A. (1958). *Organizations*. Wiley.

Mc Dermott, D. V. (1978). Tarskian Semantics, or no notation without denotation! *Cognitive Science* 2(3), 277-282.

Shoam, Y. (1993). Agent-oriented programming. *Artificial Intelligence, 60,* 51-92.

Liz Sonenberg is professor of Information Systems and currently Dean of the Faculty of Science at the University of Melbourne, Australia. Her research expertise includes reasoning machinery as may be useful for the design of systems that exhibit complex collaborative behaviours and she has received funding from government and industry sources. Liz Sonenberg was a member of the Board of the International Foundation for Autonomous Agents and Multiagent Systems from 2002 to 2008, and in 2004 was program co-chair of the Third International Joint Conference on Agents and Multi Agent Systems hosted in New York.

Preface

The main topic of this book is agent organization. Organizations in Multi-Agent Systems (MAS) can be understood as complex entities where a multitude of agents interact, within a structured environment aiming at some global purpose. Agent organizations are often associated with the idea of openness and heterogeneity in MAS. Open and heterogeneous environments pose new demands on MAS design and implementation including the integration of global and individual perspectives and the dynamic adaptation of systems to environmental changes. As systems grow to include hundreds or thousands of agents, there is a need to move from an agent-centric view of coordination and control to an organization-centric one to cope with the complexity of interaction in an environment. The view of coordination and control central to MAS needs to be expanded to enable a societal-centric focus. MAS design languages provide structures for developing organizational models, but can also enable the analysis of how natural organizations may be augmented or enhanced. That is, the tools needed for modeling, simulating agent organizations will provide new insights into organization theory.

The term agent organization, of multi-agent organization, has become common-place within the Multi-Agent Systems (MAS) community, but is used to mean different, often incompatible, issues. On the one side, organization is taken as the process of organizing a set of individuals, whereas the other side sees organization as an entity in itself, with its own requirements and objectives. As it is often the case in such situations, this leads to a fragile sense of understanding causing interpretation and integration problems when trying to compare, merge, or analyze different models and frameworks. Practical applications of agent organizations and of agent principles for organizational modeling are being widely developed; however, formal theories are needed to describe interaction and organizational structure. Furthermore, it is necessary to understand the relation between organizational roles and the agents that fulfill them. Without attempting to merge different views into one general whole, this book presents a comprehensive overview of the different perspectives, such that the reader will be able to better understand and judge the differences.

The intent of this book is simple – to provide an overview of current work in agent organizations, from several perspectives, and focus on different aspects of the organizational spectrum. It is the hope that the work presented here will provoke additional thought, research attention and concern, for the concept of organization in and for multi-agent systems.

The book is divided in 6 sections, each focusing on a different aspect of multi-agent organizations. The first section "*Methodologies and Frameworks for Agent Organizations*" sets the tone of the book by presenting state-of-the-art developments on integrated models for MAS where the notion of organization is central.

Chapter I, "*The Role of Organization in Agent Systems*" provides an introduction to the volume, focusing on the use of organization concepts in MAS and discusses the differences between organizing MAS and MAS for organizations.

Chapter II, "*Modelling Dimensions for Agent Organizations*" by Coutinho, Sichman, and Boissier, discusses how to classify diverse aspects, or modelling dimensions, of agent organizations currently captured by different organizational models. Four basic dimensions are proposed: the structural dimension, mainly composed of roles and groups; the interactive dimension, characterized by dialogical interaction structures; the functional dimension, formed by goal/task decomposition; and, the normative dimension, defining norms, rights, rules, and so forth. Apart from the basic dimensions, four complementary dimensions are discussed: environment, evaluation, evolution, and ontology. These are related to the aspects of situatedeness, measurement, adaptation, and domain specific semantics of agent organizations.

Chapter III, "*Towards an Integral Approach of Organizations in Multi-Agent Systems*" by Ferber, Stratulat, and Tranier, posit that a genuine organizational approach has to take into account both the environment and the institutional part of MAS societies. As in Chapter I, they also stress the importance of integrating different dimensions (agents, environment, interactions, organizations, and institutions) into an integral vision. A meta-model, MASQ (Multi-Agent System based on Quadrants), is proposed and constitutes an abstraction of the various aspects of an organization centred MAS, extending the well known AGR (Agent/Group/Role) model.

Chapter IV, "*OMACS: A Framework for Adaptive, Complex Systems*", DeLoach introduces a suite of technologies for building complex, adaptive systems that includes a set of methodologies, techniques, and architectures that allow it to be implemented effectively on a wide variety of systems. It uses the organization model for adaptive computational systems (OMACS) to define the knowledge needed about a system's structure and capabilities to allow it to reorganize at runtime in the face of a changing environment and its agent's capabilities.

Another concrete example of an organization-oriented methodology for MAS is given in **Chapter V**, "*Hermes: Designing Flexible and Robust Agent Interactions*" by Cheong and Winikoff. Hermes is a goal-oriented design methodology for agent interactions which is aimed at being pragmatic for practicing software engineers. Hermes focuses on interaction goals, such as goals of the interaction which the agents are attempting to achieve, and results in interactions that are more flexible and robust than message-centric approaches.

Section II is about formalisms for agent organizations. In **Chapter VI**, "*A Formal Framework for Organization Modeling and Analysis*" by Popova and Sharpanskykh is a formal framework for modeling and analyzing organizations is proposed and allows representing and reasoning about all important aspects of artificial and human organizations structured in a number of views, including performance-oriented, process-oriented, power- and interaction-related aspects.

Chapter VII, "*Describing Agent Societies: A Declarative Semantics*" by Tsvetovat, proposes a declarative language designed specifically for describing in an expressive way a variety of social interactions.

Chapter VIII, "*Structural Aspects of Organizations*" by Grossi and F. Dignum, investigates how organizations can be represented as graphs endowed with formal semantics. They distinguish different dimensions of organizations leading to different graph structures. By giving the graphs a formal semantics using Description Logic, the chapter shows that it is possible to formalize the effect of the organization on the activities of the agents playing the roles of the organization.

Chapter IX, "*A Logic for Agent Organizations*" by Virginia and Frank Dignum, posits that in order to develop a theory on the relation between organizational structures, organizational actions, and actions of agents performing roles in the organization, a theoretical framework to describe and reason about organizations is needed. The Language for Agent Organization (LAO) proposed in this chapter is sufficiently generic to enable the comparison of different existing organizational approaches to Multi-Agent Systems (MAS), while having enough descriptive power to describe realistic organizations.

In *Section III* the individual agent and their interactions in organizations are central. In **Chapter X**, *"Grounding Organizations in the Minds of the Agents"*, by Castelfranchi, presents organizations as a macro-micro notion and device. Organizations presuppose autonomous proactive entities (agents) playing the organizational roles. However, agents may have their own powers, goals, and relationships (of dependence, trust, etc.), which opens up important issues to be discussed. In order to model human organizations, and designing effective artificial organizations, models that exhibit a high degree of flexibility, exploiting autonomy and pro-activity, intelligence, and decentralized knowledge of role-players are needed; allowing for functional violations of requests and even of rules.

Chapter XI, *"Modelling Interactions via Commitments and Expectations"* by Torroni, Yolum, Singh, Alberti, Chesani, Gavanelli, Lamma, and Mello, presents and discusses two declarative, social semantic approaches for modeling interaction. The first one takes a state-oriented perspective, and models interaction in terms of commitments. The second one adopts a rule-oriented perspective, and models interaction in terms of logical formulae, expressing expectations about agent interaction.

Chapter XII, *"Communications for Agent-Based Human Team Support"*, by Sukthankar, Sycara, Giampapa, and Burnett, discusses the problem of agent aiding of ad-hoc, decentralized human teams so as to improve team performance on time-stressed group tasks. To see how human teams rise to the challenge, communication patterns of teams performing a collaborative search task are analyzed using empirical experiments.

The focus of **Chapter XIII**, *"Autonomous Agents Adopting Organizational Rules"*, by Van der Vecht, F. Dignum, and Meyer is agent autonomy. In particular, it discusses the adoption of organizational rules into the reasoning process of autonomous agents. It proposes a modular reasoning model that explicitly includes organizational rules and shows that this stimulates bottom-up dynamics in organization models.

Section IV presents the institutional view on organizations in which they are taken as highly regulated environments governed by norms. In **Chapter XIV**, *"Specifying Artificial Institutions in the Event Calculus"*, by Fornara and Colombetti, communication in open interaction systems is central. An approach to the standardization of communication is formally defined in the Event Calculus, which consists in modeling open interaction systems as a set of artificial institutions.

Chapter XV, *"Verifying Organizations Regulated by Institutions"*, by Viganò and Colombetti, proposes institutions to explicitly represent norms in open multi-agent systems, where agents may not follow them and which therefore require mechanisms to detect violations. A framework to verify organizations regulated by institutions is presented, which is characterized by a precise formalization of institutional concepts, a language to describe institutions, and a tool to model-check them.

In **Chapter XVI**, *"A Programming Language for Normative Multi-Agent Systems"*, by Dastani, Tinnemeier, and Meyer, views MAS as consisting of individual agents whose behaviors are regulated by an organizational artifact. The chapter presents a programming language that aims at facilitating the implementation of norm-based organizational artifacts for MAS.

Section V introduces several approaches to organizational dynamics and adaptation. In **Chapter XVII**, *"A Minimal Dynamical MAS Organization Model"*, by Rocha Costa and Pereira Dimuro, the Population-Organization model is presented as formal tool for studying the organization of open multi-agent systems and its functional and structural dynamics. The model is minimal in two senses: it comprises a minimal set of extensional concepts capable of adequately accounting for the notion of dynamic organization; and, it is a core organization model upon which a certain kind of dynamical rules can be defined to account for the action of intensional organizational elements like prestige, power, morality, and so forth.

Chapter XVIII, *"A Framework for Dynamic Agent Organizations"*, by Fatima and Wooldridge, presents an adaptive organizational policy for multi-agent systems called TRACE. TRACE allows a collection of multi-agent organizations to dynamically allocate tasks and resources between themselves in order to efficiently process an incoming stream of tasks.

Chapter XIX, "*Dynamic Specifications for Norm-Governed Systems*", by Artikis, Kaponis, and Pitt, a framework for executable specification of norm-governed multi-agent systems, is extended to allow for "dynamic specifications", that is, specifications that may be modified at run-time by the members of a system. The framework extension is motivated by Brewka's "dynamic argument systems"—an argument systems in which the rules of order may become the topic of the debate.

Chapter XX, "*Interactions Between Formal and Informal Organizational Networks*", by Lamieri and Mangalagiu, presents a model of organization aimed to understand the effect of formal and informal structures on the organization's performance. The model considers the interplay between the formal hierarchical structure and the social network connecting informally the agents emerging while the organization performs a task-set.

Finally, in *Section VI*, practical applications of MAS organizations are presented. **Chapter XXI**, "*Personal Assistants for Human Organizations*" by Okamoto, Sycara, and Scerri, focus on intelligent software personal assistants The chapter describes the development of a computational model of organization to evaluate the impact that different proposed assistant abilities have on the behavior and performance of the organization. By varying the organizational structures under consideration, is possible to identify which abilities are most beneficial, as well as explore how organizations may adapt to best leverage the new technology.

Chapter XXII, "*Organizational Self-Design in Worth-Oriented Domains*", by Kamboj and Decker, presents an approach to Organizational-Self Design (OSD), a method of designing organizations at run-time in which the agents are responsible for generating their own organizational structures. OSD is applied to worth-oriented domains – that is, domains in which problems are represented using TÆMS-based task structures.

Chapter XXIII, the final chapter, "*A Formal Petri Net-Based Model for Team Monitoring*" by Bonnet-Torrès, and Tessier, focuses on a Petri Net-based model for team organization and monitoring. The applications considered are missions performed by several robots that cooperate in different ways according to the goals to be achieved. The model allows several failure propagation ways within the team to be highlighted and local plan repair to be considered.

We have attempted to provide a comprehensive view of current developments in agent organizations as a paradigm for both the modeling of human organizations, and for designing effective artificial organizations. This book is intended to inspire and stimulate further research in the topic.

Virginia Dignum
Utrecht University, The Netherlands
July 2008

Acknowledgment

It is appropriate to conclude by acknowledging all the *agents* that together made this book possible. First, I want to thank all authors for their excellent work. Without their contributions, representative of the high standard of the research in the field, this volume would not have been possible. Thanks are also due to the members of the editorial advisory board for their excellent reviewing work and their detailed suggestions to the authors that have directly contributed to the high quality final result presented here. Special thanks to Liz Sonenberg for her kind foreword to this book, for her contribution to the idea of this volume, born during my sabbatical at the University of Melbourne in 2006, and for the continued interchange of ideas, students, and projects. Hopefully, it will continue for many years. Thanks also to Heather Probst at IGI Global for her never failing efficiency on answering all mine and the author's questions and for her management of the editing process. Thanks to Laura Dignum for the organization and verification of all camera ready materials.

This work was made possible by the support of The Netherlands Organization for Scientific Research (NWO), through the Veni-fellowship project "Supporting Knowledge Sharing in Organizations".

Finally, I dedicate this book to Frank, Martyn, and Laura, my home *organization*.

Virginia Dignum

Introduction

Chapter I
The Role of Organization in Agent Systems

Virginia Dignum
Utrecht University, The Netherlands

ABSTRACT

Agent Organization can be understood from two perspectives: organization as a process and organization as an entity. That is, organization is considered both as the process of organizing a set of individuals, or as an entity in itself, with its own requirements and objectives. In fact, agent organizations demand the integration of both perspectives and rely for a great extent on the notion of openness and heterogeneity of MAS. Practical applications of agents to organizational modeling are being widely developed, however, formal theories are needed to describe interaction and organizational structure. Furthermore, it is necessary to get a closer look at the applicability of insights and theories from organization sciences to the development of agent organizations. In this chapter, current approaches to agent organizations are discussed. Agent Organizations bring concepts and solutions from sociology and organizational theory into agent research, integrating organizational and individual perspectives, and aim at the dynamic adaptation of models to organizational and environmental changes, both of which are impacted by the notion of openness and heterogeneity. The chapter also presents a promising application of agent organizations to the area of human-agent teams.

INTRODUCTION

The main topic of this book is Agent Organization. Since their coming out in the 80's, Multi-Agent Systems (MAS) have often been defined as organizations or societies of agents, i.e. as a set of agents that interact together to coordinate their behavior and often cooperate to achieve some collective goal (Ferber et al., 2003). The term agent organization has become common-place within the MAS community, but is used to mean different, often incompatible, issues. In short, one class of views takes organization as the process of organizing a set of individuals, whereas the other sees organization as an entity in itself, with its own requirements and objectives. These differences are for a great part due to the diverse world views and backgrounds of different research fields, namely Sociology and Organization Theory (OT) on the one hand, and distributed Artificial Intelligence (AI) on the other hand. From a sociologic perspective, agent organization is specified independently from its participants and relates the structure of a system to its externally observable global behavior. The artificial intelligence view on MAS is mostly directed to the study of the mental state of individual agents and their relation to the overall behavior. As it is often the case in such situations, such differences can lead to a fragile sense of understanding causing interpretation and integration problems when trying to compare, merge or analyze different models and frameworks. Without attempting to merge different views into one general whole, this book presents a comprehensive overview of the different perspectives, such that the reader will be able to better understand and judge the differences.

The stance in this chapter, and in the rest of this book is that agent organizations demand the integration of organizational and individual perspectives, the dynamic adaptation of models to organizational and environmental changes, and rely for a great extent on the notion of openness and heterogeneity of MAS. Practical applications of agents to organizational modeling are being widely developed but formal theories are needed to describe interaction and organizational structure. Furthermore, it is necessary to get a closer look at the applicability of insights and theories from organization sciences to the development of agent organizations. All these issues are becoming increasingly recognized and researched within the MAS community, as can be seen by the growing number of publications and workshops on the subject, of which COIN[1] (International Workshop Series on Coordination, Organization, Institutions and Norms in MAS) is the most known example.

A first main issue to be discussed in this chapter is dialectic: is agent organization synonym with organization of agents? Such a question identifies a possible difference of perspective between the entity, an agent organization, and a process, the act of organizing agents. It also illustrates the two perspectives: that of agent-centric MAS and that of organization-centric MAS, as proposed by (Ferber et al., 2003). From an organizational perspective, the main function of an individual agent is the enactment of a role that contributes to the global aims of the organization. That is, organizational goals determine agent roles and interaction norms. Agents are then seen as the actors that perform role(s) described by the organization design. However, the very notion of agent autonomy refers to the ability of individual agents to determine their own actions, plans and believes. From the agent's perspective, its own capabilities and aims determine the reasons and the specific way an agent will enact its role(s), and the behavior of individual agents is motivated from their own goals and capabilities (Weigand & Dignum, 2004).

Agent organization models will play a critical role in the development of larger and more complex MAS. As systems grow to include hundreds or thousands of agents, it is necessary to move from an agent-centric view of coordination and control to an organization-centric one. The overall problem of analyzing the social, economic and technological dimensions of agent organizations, and the co-evolution of agent and human social and personal structures in the organization, provide theoretically demanding, interdisciplinary research questions at different levels of abstraction.

Another important aspect is that of performance. In Organization Theory it is commonly accepted that different types of organizational structure are suitable for particular environmental conditions (Burns & Stalker, 1961). In case of a dynamic environment, this implies that organizations must be able to reorganize its design. This may seem somewhat contradictory with the aspiration to stability associated with the concept of organization. One of the main reasons for creating organizations is to provide stable means for coordination that enable the achievement of global goals. In particular, a distinguishing factor between organizations and other groups of people is "… *a commitment to achieving members' goals by means of an explicit and stable structure of task allocations, roles, and responsibilities.*" (Starbuck, 1965). As Blau and Scott state, the design of formal organizations stresses this aspect by fixing "… *the goals to be achieved, the rules the members of the organization are expected to follow, and the status structure that defines the relations between them*" as a conscious a priori activity to anticipate and guide interaction and activities (Blau & Scott, 1962, p.5).

This chapter is organized as follows. In the next two sections the agent-centric and the organizational-centric views on organization are presented, after which the design and performance of organizations in dynamic environments is discussed. The last section is about the interactions in organizations, in particular on the collaboration between human and artificial agents, their autonomy and the control over it by the organization. The chapter ends with conclusions and directions for further research.

ORGANIZING AGENTS

According to the most accepted definition of software agents, an agent is "*an encapsulated computer system that is situated in some environment and that is capable of flexible, autonomous action in that environment in order to meet its design objectives*" (Wooldridge, Jennings, 1995). MAS contribute to the Software Engineering discipline as a way to simplify the design of complex software systems (Jennings, 2000). Currently, many models and frameworks for MAS that have been proposed stress the autonomy and encapsulation characteristics of agents. In this view, interactions between agents are mostly seen as speech acts whose meaning may be described in terms of the mental states of an agent.

Characteristics of traditional MAS are: (a) each agent has bounded (incomplete) resources to solve a given problem, (b) there is no global system control, (c) data is decentralized, and (d) computation is asynchronous [18]. Social and mentalistic metaphors used to describe agents – such as the Beliefs-Desires and Intentions (BDI) model proposed by Bratman (cf. Wooldridge, 2000) - lead to highly abstract design models. From a software engineering perspective, this means that the development of MAS is not straightforward. Even though, one of the most important characteristics of MAS is that the final set of agents is not given at design time, traditional MAS systems often only allow participation of agents that fully comply to a predefined agent type or class. Permitted agent types in a MAS are described in the agent architecture (containing the interaction rules, goals and reasoning mechanism of the agent). Agent types and their descriptions are specified by grouping system functionalities [22]. The definition of coordination mechanisms between different agent types is a major part of the MAS model, resulting in implementations where social aspects, goals and behaviors are part of the architecture of the specific individual agents. Such architectures exhibit neat theoretical properties that enable the specification of elegant formalisms and design and implementation tools. The disadvantage is that systems are then closed for agents that are not able to use the same type of coordination and behavior, and that all global characteristics and requirements are implement *in* the individual agents and not *outside* them.

Another common view on agent-centric MAS is that of emergence, following the assumption that MAS require no real structure, patterns and outcome of interaction being unpredictable. Emergent MAS are typically made up of a population of simple agents interacting locally with one another and with their environment. Communication is based on modification of the environment (stygmergy). There is no centralized control structure dictating how individual agents should behave, meaning that local interactions between such agents are expected to lead to the emergence of global behavior. Emergent agent systems are mostly used in the domains of social simulation, adaptive planning, logistics and Artificial Life. The main drawback with this approach is how to design them when a specific global behavior is desired. In fact, "*some way of structuring the society is typically needed to reduce the system's complexity, to increase the system's efficiency, and to more accurately model the problem being tackled.*" (Jennings, Wooldridge, 2000).

Moreover, in many situations, individuals do not share nor necessarily pursue the same aims and requirements as the global system, or society to which they belong. In these cases, the view of coordination and control needs to be expanded to consider not only an agent-centric perspective but mostly take a societal focus. In the programming and design of MAS, the concept of role is often used to indicate how different agent (types) relate to each other and form design patterns, or social structures that can be reused, or as placeholders in a conceptual structure (Wooldridge et al., 2000). Based on the role it is enacting, an agent is allowed to perform only certain actions in the environment and issue only certain communicative actions.

AGENT ORGANIZATIONS

Organizations in Multi-Agent Systems can be understood as complex entities where a multitude of agents interact, within a structured environment aiming at some global purpose. The view of coordination and control has to be expanded to consider not only an agent-centric perspective but mostly take a societal and organization-centric focus. Agent organizations demand the integration of organizational, intermediate level and individual perspectives, the dynamic adaptation of models to organizational and environmental changes, and rely for a great extent on the notion of openness and heterogeneity of MAS. MAS design languages can provide structures for developing organizational models, but will also provide insight on how natural organizations may be augmented or enhanced. The tools needed for modeling, simulating organizations and work practices and developing intelligent agent systems will provide new insights into organization theory.

Organizations are inherently computational (Carley, 2002) which explains the choice for agent based models to simulate and formally capture and understand organizations. Such models yield positive results and promise further tremendous potential (Davidsson, 2002). Also, in the Multi-Agent Systems (MAS) research area there is an increased realization that concepts from Organization Theory are well applicable to understand and structure MAS in ways that extend and complement traditional agent-centric approaches. Agent organizations can be understood as complex entities where a multitude of agents interact, within a structured environment aiming at some global purpose.

In organization-centric MAS, interaction is not designed in terms of the mental states of individual agents, but in terms of organizational concepts such as roles (or function, or position), groups (or communities), tasks (or activities) and interaction protocols (or dialogue structure), that is, on what relates the structure of an organization to the externally observable behavior of its agents.

From an organizational perspective, the main function of an individual agent is the enactment of a role that contributes to the global aims of the organization. That is, organizational goals determine the agent roles and interaction aims and rules. Agents are then seen as actors that perform the role(s) described by the organization design. However, the very notion of agent autonomy refers to the ability of individual agents to determine their own actions, plans and beliefs. From the agent's perspective, its own capabilities and aims determine the reasons and the specific way an agent will enact its role(s), and the behavior of individual agents is motivated from their own goals and capabilities (Dastani et al., 2003, Weigand & Dignum, 2004). That is, agents bring in their own ways into the society as well. Role-oriented approaches to agent systems that assume this inherent dichotomy between agent interests and global aims are increasingly popular in MAS research (Castelfranchi, 1995, Dignum, 2004, Zambonelli et al., 2001, Artikis et al., 2001).

The considerations above indicate the need for models that integrate two levels of autonomy:

- **Internal autonomy:** interaction and structure of the society must be represented independently from the internal design of the agents
- **Collaboration autonomy:** activity and interaction in the society must be specified without completely fixing in advance the interaction structures.

Models for the assessment of organizational design must be able to separate organizational from individual concerns. Agent organization models provide an abstract representation of organizations, their environment, objectives and participating agents that enables the analysis of their partial contributions to the performance of the organization. In this sense, the organization is a set of mechanisms of social order that regulate autonomous actors to achieve common goals (Dignum, 2004). The performance of an organization in such framework is determined both by the structures of interactions between agents, and by the individual characteristics of the agents. Organizational structures define the formal lines of communication, allocation of information processing tasks, distribution of decision-making authorities, and the provision of incentives.

That is, agent organizations describe roles, interactions and rules in an environment. Social conventions are the way people provide order and predictability in their environment (Geertz, 73), which have resulted in complex normative and organizational systems that regulate interaction. Roles describe rights and obligations together with the capabilities and objectives of different parties. By knowing one's role, expectations can be defined and plans established. Organizational theory and sociology research have since long studied structure, dynamics and behavior of human organizations and human interactions, based on the concept of role and relationships between roles. Research on Agent Organizations translates normative, social and organization solutions coming from *human societies* into electronic distributed computational mechanisms for the design and analysis of distributed systems. Systems are viewed as collections of heterogeneous computational entities called *agent organizations*. These approaches often include means to describe acceptable behaviour specification and define the social structure that establishes the (accepted) relations among agents or roles. Roles define the restrictions to be followed by the agents that enact such roles. Examples of such approaches are described in this book, particularly in Parts I and III.

At least four paradigms in organization science speak about the potential impact of smart agents on new organizational form – structuralism, contingency theory, information processing theory, and social networks. Work on organizational design suggests that different architectures influence performance and there is no one right organizational design for all tasks (Mintzberg, 1983, Donaldson, 2001, Burton et al., 2006). However, independent of the task, the organizational form can be characterized in terms of networks describing the linkages among agents that influence both agent behavior and organizational performance. Basically, three types of coordination in organizations can be identified (Nouwens & Bouwman, 1995): hierarchy, market and network. Hierarchies limit interaction between agents to direct superior/subordinate relations. Interaction between and among all agents is encouraged in networks, and in markets, interaction reflects supplier/consumer relations and are determined by transaction costs. Intuitively, it seems that hierarchical style of dependency requires less reasoning power from the agents performing children roles: they just take their 'orders' from above. Hierarchical coordination is therefore well suited for directive organization styles. On the other extreme, in network relations all agents must be able to reason about the why and how of role performance, which requires more intelligence on the agents' side.

Conform to contingency theory (Donaldson, 2001), the effectiveness of the three coordination types (hierarchy, market, network) is not the same in all situations. For instance, hierarchies perform well in familiar, repetitive situations, where many resources are shared, and communication is reliable. On the other hand, networks seem to perform better in unfamiliar situations, where few resources need to be shared, and parallelism can be exploited. In order to establish adaptation strategies for organizations the characteristics and adequacy of different coordination types must be considered. In the following section, we describe the characteristics and requirements for reorganization.

ORGANIZATION DYNAMICS: DESIGN AND PERFORMANCE

One of the main reasons for having organizations is to achieve stability. However, organizations and their environments are not static. Agents can migrate, organizational objectives can change, or operational behavior can evolve. That is, as circumstances change, organizational structures must also be able to change, disappear or grow. In fact, organizations are active entities, capable not only of adapting to the environment but also of changing that environment, which leads to the question of how and why change decisions are made in organizations (Gazendam & Simons, 1998). Models for organizations must therefore be able to describe dynamically adapting organizations to changes in the environment. Such models will enable to understand how different organizations can be designed from different populations of agents, performing different tasks in changing environments, to meet various performance goals (So & Durfee, 1998).

As discussed in the previous sections, one of the main reasons for creating organizations is efficiency, that is, to provide the means for coordination that enable the achievement of global goals in an efficient manner. Such global objectives are not necessarily shared by any of the individual participants but can only be achieved through combined action. In order to achieve its goals, it is thus necessary that an organization employs the relevant agents, and assures that their interactions and responsibilities enable an efficient realization of the objectives. In its most simple expression, an organization consists of a set of agents and a set of objectives in a given environment. Contingency theory states that organizational performance can be seen as a dependent variable on these factors.

In many situations, agent organizations operate under uncertainty, in dynamically changing environments, and often unreliable communication. The need for techniques to make agent systems more flexible and adaptive is therefore high. Changes in the environment lead to alterations on the effectiveness of the organization and therefore to the need to reorganize, or in the least, to the need to consider the consequences of that change to the organization's effectiveness and efficiency. On the other hand, organizations are active entities, capable not only of adapting to the environment but also of changing that environment. This means that organizations are capable, to a certain degree, to alter environment conditions to meet their aims and requirements, which leads to the question of how and why reorganization decisions should be reached. Dynamic adaptation, during operation, often results in better performance, and more robust systems. The first step in the development of a model for dynamic reorganization of agent societies is to identify and classify situations of change in organizations.

The flexibility of an organization is defined as the combination of the changeability of an organizational characteristic (structure, technology, culture) and the capabilities of management to change that characteristic (Gazendam & Simons, 1998). Chapter VIII in this volume, "Structural Aspects of Organizations", by Grossi and F. Dignum, discusses organizational characteristics in more detail and presents models for analysis.

In Organizational Theory, the concept of *adaptation* can mean different things, ranging from strategic choice to environmental determinism. Strategic choice refers to the planned pursuit of ends based on a rational assessment of available means and conditions, resulting in an explicit decision to change the organization. Deterministic views on adaptation, on the other hand, explain organizational change as (involuntary) response to environmental requirements. In this section, we consider adaptation as a design issue that requires an (explicit) decision which results in the modification of some organizational characteristics. Such decisions can be of two kinds: proactive, preparing the organization in advance for an expected future, and reactive, making adjustments after the environment has changed (Dignum et al., 2004).

As reorganization is somehow contrary to stability, the question is then: under which conditions is it better to reorganize, knowing that stability will be (momentarily) diminished, and when to maintain stability, even if that means loss of response success. In order to answer this question, it is necessary to define the *performance* of an organization. Organizational success means the organization's ability to bring all its information and assets to bear, and the ability to recognize and take advantage of fleeting opportunities. Success is one way to measure the performance of a system. Reorganization is desirable if it leads to increased success of the system. That is, the reorganized instance should perform better in some sense than the original situation. Given the assumption of agent autonomy, the success of an organization is dependent not only on its global success but also on the perceived success of its participants. Performance is thus evaluated differently from the global and individual perspectives.

- **Global performance:** is defined in terms of interaction, role and structure success. Performance depends also on the cost of the reorganization. Reorganization decisions must take into account the success of a given organizational structure, as the cost of any change needed to achieve that structure from the current situation (Glasser & Morignot, 1997).

- **Individual performance:** success is measured differently for each agent, taking in account issues such as its own goals, resource production and consumption. Basically, we can assume that rational agents will participate in a society if its individual utility increases. Furthermore, different social attitudes will result in different evaluations of individual utility. That is, the utility function of a social agent may take in account some measure of society utility, whereas for a selfish agent only individual concerns matter.

Modeling Reorganization

Why do organizations change? It is evident that environment changes are the obvious triggers to reorganization, but when does one decide that a role should be added/deleted from the current structure, or that interactions should have different aims or follow modified patterns. Section VI in this volume (Chapters XVII to XX) presents different views and approaches to organizational change. There are different gradations of change, from a slight adaptation of an interaction instance to drastic changes in the social structure of the organization. Organizational studies often relate reorganization to flexibility. Flexibility can be defined as *"ability to do something other than that which was originally intended"* (Evans, 1991). In human societies, reorganization maneuvers have both a temporal and an intentional aspect. The timing of reorganization can be either *proactive* - preparing in advance for an unpredictable future change - or *reactive* – making adjustments after an event has occurred. The intentional aspect of a reorganization, may be *offensive*, in which case the organization aims at gaining competitive advantage, or *defensive*, aiming at organizational survival. Combined, these result in the following four maneuvers (Eardly et al., 1997, Evans, 1991):

- *pre-emptive* (proactive, offensive): allows to take advantage of possible future events and is most useful where the future is unpredictable and where the exploitation of innovation is a tool of competition.
- *protective* (proactive, defensive): applied before unpredictable events attempt to limit the damage caused by an unknown future.
- *exploitive* (reactive, offensive): taken after an event, in order to capitalize on existing opportunities.
- *corrective* (reactive, defensive): taken to prevent more damage, and usually used when other tactics fail, to ensure continuing existence.

This list, originating from OT research, can be applied to classify the reorganization in agent organizations. However, the full deployment of such reasoning is for a great deal dependent on the capabilities of the agents enacting organizational roles. The proactive situations require high-level reasoning capabilities. That is, in order to make a proactive reorganization decision, agents must be endowed with mechanisms to reason and evaluate current and desired behavior and utility. Reactive reorganization, on the other hand, requires agents to be able to sense and react to environment events, and therefore simpler agents are sufficient. Moreover, proactive situations often imply a modification of behavior: agents dynamically change their behavior, that is, the way they enact their roles, can change the patterns of interaction, or even the definition of the roles or their relationships. That is, the expected effects of change can be evaluated without drastic structure changes. In this way, organizations can test 'what-if' situations and reason whether a more permanent, structural change, should be required. Reactive reorganization will often result in modifications of the structure of the organization.

Types of Reorganization

In early work on adaptation in MAS, restructuring was only possible in the initialization phase of the system. During the actual problem solving phase, the structure was fixed. One of the first attempts to approach dynamic adaptation of the system structure is that described in (Hannebauer, 2002). Other implementations of organizational adaptation include approaches based on load balancing (Shaerf et al., 1995) or dynamic task allocation (Shehory & Kraus, 1998). The latter is often the case in organizational self-design in emergent systems that, for example, include composition and decomposition primitives that allow for dynamic variation of the organizational structure (macro-architecture) while the system population (micro-architecture) remains the same. Another common approach is dynamic participation. In this case, agent interaction with the organization is modeled as the enactment of some roles, and adaptation occurs as agents move in and out of those roles (So & Durfee, 1998, Glasser and Morignot, 1997, Dignum, 2004). However, few of these systems allow agents to change the problem-solving framework of the system itself (Barber and Martin, 2001). In (Dignum et al., 2004), we have identified the following reorganization situations:

Behavioral change. In this case the organizational structure stays the same but the agents currently enacting roles, decide (collectively or individually) to use different protocols for the same abstract interaction described in the structure. This is the case when:

1. *A new agent joins the MAS.* In this case, a new agreement should be made specifying e.g. the expectations and obligations of the society towards role enactment, and possibly incorporating some of the agent's own requirements.
2. *An agent leaves the MAS.* In this case, it is necessary to determine whether organizational operation is still completely or partially possible.
3. *Interaction pattern instantiation.* In this case, the agents currently enacting an interaction pattern agree on a specific protocol that complies with the pattern specification. Such protocols can be different, depending on the agents' current evaluation of the environment and/or their own goals and behavior rules.

Structural change. In this case a decision is made concerning the modification of one or more structural elements.

1. *Organizational Self Design*: that is, dynamic variation in emergent societies, resulting from changes in the interaction between agents.
2. *Structural Adaptation*: In this case, designed societies are adapted to environment changes by adding, deleting or modifying its structural elements (e.g. roles, dependencies, norms, ontologies, communication primitives).

Intuitively, behavioral changes have a more temporary character, and do not influence future activity of the organization, whereas structural change is meant to accommodate permanent modification, and as such direct the activity of future instantiations of the organization. This raises the question of reorganization decision. That is, how does a decision for (structural) reorganization is taken, by whom and based on what knowledge?

Requirements for Reorganization

Change is a result of observation of the environment. Making sense of a situation begins by identifying relevant patterns and access current response possibilities. Sense-making is however more than sharing information and identifying patterns. It involves the ability to generate options, predict outcomes and understand the effect of particular courses of action. These are capabilities that few software agents are endowed with. Hence, enabling dynamic reorganization has consequences for the capabilities required from the agents involved, and it therefore makes sense to identify which reorganization type is most appropriate for a given situation, and what is then needed from the agents. Sense-making furthermore, requires to keep a system history, also across different role enactors.

A characteristic of reorganization is *timeliness*, that is, adequate response at the appropriate time (not to be confused with speed). This implies the need to access when and how often, and at which level to change. When change occurs too often and to quick, the predictability of the system will decrease, but too slow and too late change results in rigidness of the system. Both situations are usually not desirable. The aim is *resiliency*, that is, flexible but durable and consistent with its (meta) norms and objectives. An interesting study by Carley et al, 2002, explores the resiliency of organizations by studying their performance when key leaders were removed. Different domains will have different appreciations of timeliness and resiliency. For instance, in rescue operations, timeliness is often directly related to speedy response. That is, a quick, even if sub-optimal, adaptation will be preferred over the optimal solution if that one only arrives after it is too late (e.g. the house has already burned down). On the other hand, in institutions (such as a university department), timeliness is often related to consensus. That is, the good time to change is when all parties are conscious of the need to change and agree on the changed model.

WORKING TOGETHER IN ORGANIZATIONS

What happens when human and artificial agents interact together in organizations? Cooperation between humans and machines is happening at an increasingly quick pace[2]. It is particularly well suited in situations where reaction speed is important (such as emergency response), where knowledge is diffuse, where a high level of connectivity is necessary, or where operation in constantly changing environments is needed. Nevertheless, the reach and consequences of coordinated activity between people and machines working in close and continuous interaction is not well understood. Planning technologies for intelligent systems often take an *autonomy-centered* approach, with representations, mechanisms, and algorithms that have been designed to accept a set of goals, and to generate and execute a complete plan in the most efficient and sound fashion possible. The *teamwork-centered autonomy* approach takes as a premise that people are working in parallel alongside one or more autonomous systems, and hence adopts the stance that the processes of understanding, problem solving, and task execution are necessarily incremental, subject to negotiation, and forever tentative (Bradshaw et al., 2007). That is, autonomy in teams requires a close adjustment to the current work of other team members and one's perception of the team's goals.

In order to achieve the vision of *the right information at the right time in the right format to the right person*, significant consideration must be given to the way in which automated systems are used to enhance the capability of the individual and to design effective interfaces such that true interaction is achieved (Carver et al., 2006). These situations require people and systems to act autonomously while keeping close interaction on the maintenance of shared understanding of the situation and the results of each other's actions. Human-agent teams are networks where both intelligent systems (agents) and people cooperate effectively within one group, creating synergy by reinforcing each other's strong points and anticipate on each other's weak points (Payne et al., 2000).

By definition, teamwork implies interdependence between participants and therefore requires some management work to be carried out to manage the coordination, such as communication and maintenance of some level of visibility of each other's actions and shared situation awareness. In (Klein et al., 2004) the following requirements for effective coordination have been described, which can be answered by agent organization models:

- *Interpredictability* refers to the need for accurate prediction of others' actions in order to be able to plan one's actions. In human teams, this is achieved through experience, skilled knowledge, or explicit predesigned structures and procedures.
- *Shared awareness*, or common ground, requires mutual knowledge and assumptions concerning the state and evolution of the surrounding environment. Shared histories and explicit agreements on goals and requirements for joint activity are means to support shared awareness.
- *Directability* refers to the capacity to assess and modify actions of other parties as conditions and priorities change. This is commonly achieved in human teams by the establishment of power and control relationships.

Organizational concepts are relevant for human-agent teams for two main reasons. On the one hand, successful teams require the distribution of tasks between team members according to their roles and capabilities. An appropriate structure for goal distribution together with clear command and control chains are essential for teamwork. On the other hand, knowledge about role goals and their relation to the overall team goal is necessary in order to be able to recover from unsuccessful situations and adapt to unforeseen cases. Collaboration in decision-making processes where agents are active peers in the team, require adjustable autonomy, that all team members must be able to decide when to follow orders and when to take their own decisions (Sierhuis et al., 2003), (van der Vecht et al, 2008).

Human-agent teams are social structures where members commit to jointly achieve goal(s). In order to enable collaboration with humans and other agents, social deliberating agents are needed that provide helpful behaviour in a reliable manner (Castelfranchi, Falcone, 1998) which must also be able to plan and act in the real world. Currently, there is a large amount of research done on human-robot teams (Hoffman, Brazeal, 2004) and on simulation systems for training of crisis teams (Schurr et al., 2005). In most cases, research focuses on the single agent approach, which does not work well in a complex environment where the requirements of large amounts of information, heterogeneity of supported functions, and high performance make the single agent solution impracticable. Collaboration is a complex type of behaviour and several formal theories have been introduced (e.g. Dunin, Verbrugge, 2003), which provide abstract guidelines for building collaborative agents. However, they leave many formal issues unresolved, namely concerning the link between reactive and deliberative behaviour, and ignore pragmatic implementation concerns. Even if to date, there are no formal models that provide generic and comprehensive computationally grounded formal models for engineering mixed societies of intelligent agents and people work in this direction is presented in this book, e.g. Chapters XII - "An Analysis of

Salient Communications for Agent Support of Human Teams", by Suktankar et al., XIII -"Autonomous Agents Adopting Organizational Rules", by van der Vecht et al. and XXI - "Software Assistants for Human Organizations" by Okamoto et al.

As domain complexity increases, decision making often involves various kinds of expertise and experiences, which are typically distributed among a group of decision makers. In such cases, it is crucial to do what is needed to get the most out of the information available to the team. Information needs anticipation and proactive information sharing are certainly key factors to enhancing decision making under time pressure. Organizational Theory and sociology research have since long studied structure, dynamics and behaviour of human organisations and human interactions, such studies are mostly descriptive in nature and cannot be easily used to develop formal models and frameworks.

CONCLUSION

Agent Organization can be understood from two perspectives: organization as a process and organization as an entity. That is, organization is considered both as the process of organizing a set of individuals, or as an entity in itself, with its own requirements and objectives. In MAS, both perspectives have been used in parallel and results are for a great part due to the diverse world views and backgrounds of different research fields. From a sociologic perspective, agent organization relates the structure of MAS to its externally observable behavior, whereas the distributed artificial intelligence view on MAS is mostly directed to the study of the mental state of individual agents and their relation to the overall behavior. As it is often the case in such situations, such differences can lead to a fragile sense of understanding causing interpretation and integration problems when trying to compare, merge or analyze different models and frameworks. Without attempting to merge different views into one general whole, this book presents a comprehensive overview of the different perspectives, such that the reader will be able to better understand and judge the differences.

We proposed that Agent Organization demands the integration of organizational and individual perspectives, the dynamic adaptation of models to organizational and environmental changes, and rely for a great extent on the notion of openness and heterogeneity of MAS. Practical applications of agents to organizational modeling are being widely developed but formal theories are needed to describe interaction and organizational structure. Furthermore, it is necessary to get a closer look at the applicability of insights and theories from organization sciences to the development of agent organizations. There is a need for a theoretic model to describe organizations and their environments that enables the formal analysis of the fit between organizational design and environment characteristics. This enables the a priori comparison of designs and their consequences and therefore supports the decision making process on the choice of design. The approaches presented in this book (cf. Section I and II) provide both practical as formal representation of organizations, their environment, objectives and agents in a way that enables to analyze their behavior and compare different solutions.

Another important issue is that of organizational adaptation. Reorganization is needed in order to enable systems to enforce or adapt to changes in the environment. This issue has been discussed by many researchers in both Organizational Theory and Distributed Systems, resulting mostly in domain-oriented empiric solutions. The lack, in most cases, of a formal basis makes it difficult to develop theories about reorganization, prevents the comparison of approaches and results, and makes it difficult to adapt models to other domains or situations.

The research on Agent Organisations presented in this book brings concepts and solutions from OT into agent research integrating organisational and individual perspectives, and aims at the dynamic adaptation of models to organisational and environmental changes, both of which are impacted by the notion of openness and heterogeneity. A promising application of agent organizations is in the area of human-agent teams as discussed in the previous section.

ACKNOWLEDGMENT

The author is grateful to Liz Sonenberg and Frank Dignum for the many discussions on the topic of organization, reorganization and MAS. This research is funded by the Netherlands Organization for Scientific Research (NWO), through Veni-grant 639.021.509.

REFERENCES

Artikis, A., & Pitt, J. (2001). A formal model of open agent societies. In *Proc. International Conference on Autonomous Agents,* Montreal, Quebec, Canada, ACM Press, pages 192—193.

Barber K., & Martin, C. (2001). Dynamic reorganization of decision making groups. In *Proceedings of the 5th Autonomous Agents Conference.*

Blau, P. M., & Scott, W. R. (1962). *Formal Organizations.* Chandler, San Francisco, CA.

Bradshaw, J., Feltovich, P., Johnson, M., Bunch, L., Breedy, M., Jung, H., Lott, J., & Uszok A. (2007). Coordination in Human-Agent-Robot Teamwork. In *Proceedings of the AAAI Fall Symposium on Regarding the "Intelligence" in Distributed Intelligent Systems*, AAAI.

Burns, T., & Stalker, G. (1961). *The Management of Innovation*, Tavistock, London.

Burton, R., DeSanctis, G., & Obel, B. (2006). *Organizational Design: A step by step approach.* Cambridge University Press.

Carley, K. (2002). Computational organization science: a new frontier. *PNAS*, 99(3), 7257-7262.

Carley, K., Lee, J., & Krackhardt, D. (2002). Destabilizing Networks. *Connections*, 24(3) 79-92.

Carver, E., Hinton, J., Dogan, H., & Dawson, B. (2006). Enhancing communication in rescue teams. In *Proceedings of ISCRAM 2006*: 3rd International Conference on Information Systems for Crisis Response and Management, Newark, NJ.

Castelfranchi, C. (1995). Guarantees for autonomy in cognitive agent architecture. In *ATAL'94, LNAI* 980. Springer.

Castelfranchi, C., & Falcone, R. (1998). Principles of Trust for MAS: Cognitive Anatomy, Social Importance, and Quantification. *Proceeding of ICMAS*, pages 72-79.

Davidsson, P. (2002). Agent based social simulation: A computer science view. *Journal of Artificial Societies and Social Simulation*, 5(1).

Dastani, M., Dignum, V., & Dignum, F. (2003). Role Assignment in Open Agent Societies. In *Proceedings of AAMAS'03, Second International Joint Conference on Autonomous Agents and Multi-agent Systems*, Melbourne, Australia.

Dignum, V., & Weigand, H. (2002). Towards an Organization-Oriented Design Methodology for Agent Societies. In V. Plekhanova (Ed.) *Intelligent Agent Software Engineering*. Idea Group Publishing, pages 191-212.

Dignum, V. (2004). *A Model for Organizational Interaction: Based on Agents, Founded in Logic*. SIKS Dissertation Series 2004-1. Utrecht University. PhD Thesis.

Dignum, V., Dignum, F., & Sonenberg, L. (2004). Towards dynamic organization of agent societies. In Vouros, G. (Ed.) *Proceedings of Workshop on Coordination in Emergent Agent Societies*, ECAI 2004, pages 70-78.

Donaldson, L. (2001). *The Contingency Theory of Organizations*, Sage.

Dunin, B., & Verbrugge, R. (2003). Evolution of Collective Commitment during Teamwork. *Fundamenta Informaticae, 56*(4), 329-371.

Eardley, A., Avison, D., & Powell, P. (1997). Strategic information systems: An analysis of development techniques which seek to incorporate strategic flexibility. *Journal of Organizational Computing, 7*(1), 5777.

Evans, J. (1991). Strategic flexibility for high technology maneuvers: A conceptual framework. *Journal of Management Studies*.

Ferber, J., Gutknecht, O., & Michel, F. (2003). From Agents to Organizations: an Organizational View of Multi-Agent Systems. In P. Giorgini, J. Müller, J. Odell (Eds.) *Agent-Oriented Software Engineering (AOSE) IV*. LNCS 2935, pp. 214-230, Springer.

Gazendam, H., & Simons, J. (1998). An analysis of the concept of equilibrium in organization theory. In *Proceedings of the Computational and Mathematical Organization Theory Workshop*.

Glasser N., & Morignot, P. (1997). The reorganization of societies of autonomous agents. In *Proceedings of MAAMAW*, pp. 98-111.

Hannebauer, M. (2002). *Autonomous Dynamic Reconfiguration in Multi-Agent Systems*. LNAI 2427, Springer.

Hoffman, G., & Breazeal, C. (2004). Collaboration in Human-Robot Teams. *Intelligent Systems*.

Jennings, N. R. (200) On Agent-Based Software Engineering. *Artificial Intelligence, 117*(2), 277-296.

Jennings, N. R., & Wooldridge, M. (2000). Agent-Oriented Software Engineering. In Bradshaw, J. (Ed.) *Handbook of Agent Technology*, AAAI/MIT Press.

Nouwens, J., & Bouwman, H. (1995). Living Apart Together in Electronic Commerce: The Use of Information and Communication Technology to Create Network Organisations. In C. Steinfield (Ed.) Special Issue in Electronic Commerce. *Journal of Computer Mediated Communication, 1*(3).

Payne, T. R., Lenox, T. L., Hahn, S., Sycara, K., & Lewis, M. (2000). Agent-based support for human/agent teams. In *CHI '00: Extended Abstracts on Human Factors in Computing Systems*, The Netherlands, ACM.

Schurr, N., Marecki, J., Scerri, P., Lewis, J., & Tambe, M. (2005). The DEFACTO system: Coordinating Human-Agent Teams for the Future of Disaster Response. *Programming Multi-Agent Systems*, LNAI 3346. Springer.

Shaerf, A., Yoav Shoham, Y., & Tennenholz, M.(1995). Adaptive load balancing: A study in multi-agent learning. *Journal of Artificial Intelligence Research, 2.*

Shehory, O., & Kraus, S. (1998). Methods for task allocation via agent coalition formation. *Artificial Intelligence, 101*(1-2), May 1998, pages 165-200.

Sierhuis, M., Bradshaw, J., Acquisiti, A., van Hoof, R., Jeffers, R., & Uszok, A. (2003). Human-agent teamworks and adjustable autonomy in practice. In *Proceedings of the 7th International Symposium on Artificial Intelligence, Robotics and Automation in Space*: i-SAIRAS, Japan.

So, Y., & Durfee, E. (1998). Designing organizations for computational agents. In Carley, K., Pritula, M., and Gasser, L. (Eds.) *Simulating Organizations*, pages 47-64.

Starbuck, W. (1965). Organizational growth and development. In J. G. March (Ed.) *Handbook of Organizations*; Rand McNally, pages 451-583.

van der Vecht, B., Dignum, F., Meyer, J.-J., & Neef, M. (2008). A Dynamic Coordination Mechanism Using Adjustable Autonomy. In Sichman et al. (Eds): *Coordination, Organization, Institutions and Norms in MAS*, (COIN 2007), LNAI 4870. Springer.

Weigand, H., & Dignum, V. (2004). I am Autonomous, You are Autonomous. In M. Nickles, M. Rovatsos & G. Weiss (Eds.) *Agents and Computational Autonomy*, LNAI 2969. Springer, pages 227-236.

Wooldridge, M. (2000). *Reasoning About Rational Agents*. The MIT Press

Wooldridge, M., Jennings, N., & Kinny, D. (2000). The Gaia methodology for agent-oriented analysis and design. *Autonomous Agents and Multi-Agent Systems, 3*(3), 285-312.

Zambonelli, F., Jennings, N., & Wooldridge, M. (2001). Organizational abstractions for the analysis and design of multi agent systems. In P. Ciancarini and M. Wooldridge (Eds.). *Agent-Oriented Software Engineering*, LNAI 1957, pages 235- 251. Springer.

KEY TERMS

Agent Organization: Comparable to human organizations, agent organizations are characterized by global goals and formalized social structures representing the stakeholder desired results. Can be seen as the structural setting in which agent interactions occur.

Environment: The forces outside the organization that can impact it. Include marketplace, regulatory and legal situation, opportunities and threats of the context in which the organization operates.

Human-Agent Team: A network where both intelligent systems (agents) and people cooperate effectively within one group, creating synergy by reinforcing each other's strong points and anticipate on each other's weak points.

Organization Design: (viewed as entity) The complete specification of strategy, structure, processes, actors (people or agents), coordination and control components of the organization.

Organization Design: (viewed as process) Is the process of determining and implementing goals, roles and rules that define interaction. It involves both the partition of global organization goals into specific tasks to be executed by smaller units, and the coordination of such smaller units so that they fit together and enable efficient realization of the larger goal.

Organizational Structure: Represents the relations between entities of an agent organization that are taken to be invariant through time. The main constructs found in it are roles, groups, and relationships between them.

Performance: Comprises the actual output or results of an organization as measured against its intended outputs (that is, its goals and objectives). Performance depends on how well the organization fits with its environment.

ENDNOTES

[1]   See http://www.pcs.usp.br/~coin

[2]   Recently the South Korean government has predicted that by 2020, every Korean household will have a robot (De Volkskrant, 31-03-2007, http://www.volkskrant.nl/wetenschap/article411675.ece, in Dutch)

Section I
Methodologies and Frameworks for Agent Organizations

Chapter II
Modelling Dimensions for Agent Organizations

Luciano R. Coutinho
University of São Paulo, Brazil

Jaime S. Sichman
University of São Paulo, Brazil

Olivier Boissier
ENS Mines Saint-Etienne, France

ABSTRACT

In this chapter, we discuss the concepts of agent organization, organizational model, and review some existing organizational models. Before the review, we discuss how to classify the diverse aspects of agent organizations currently captured by organizational models. These aspects are named "modelling dimensions". We show that there are at least four basic dimensions: the structural dimension mainly composed of roles and groups, the interactive dimension characterized by dialogical interaction structures, the functional dimension formed by goal/task decomposition, and the normative dimension in which we find the concepts of norms, rights, rules, and so forth. Apart from the basic dimensions, we also identify four other complementary dimensions: environment, evaluation, evolution, and ontology. These are related to the aspects of situatedeness, measurement, adaptation, and domain specific semantics of agent organizations. Finally, we compare the organizational models reviewed and describe how the idea of modelling dimension can help in finding correspondences between organizational models.

INTRODUCTION

In the last few years, a broad agreement in the area of *Multi-Agent Systems* (MASs) has been to consider the *human organizations* as a suitable metaphor to effectively assemble computational systems from a dynamic collection of heterogeneous autonomous agents (Ferber, Gutknecht & Michel, 2004; Zambonelli, Jennings & Wooldridge, 2003; Gasser, 2001). In such computational systems – often called "open MASs" –, the defining characteristics are both a variable number of autonomous agents at runtime (i.e., agents can enter and leave the system when it is in production), and the presence of agents with different interests and/or designs (i.e., agents representing different stakeholders, conceived by several designers, and/or built using different agent architectures). To cope with these characteristics, the organizational perspective proposes that the joint activity inside the MAS be explicitly regulated (moulded, constrained) by a consistent body of norms, plans, mechanisms and/or structures formally specified to achieve some definite global purpose. And this, in essence, is what "human organization" means when the autonomous agents are human beings – a dynamical collection of persons that accept to have their joint activity formally patterned and controlled, given some global goals (Scott, 1998). Inspired by the metaphor, in this chapter, we will use the term "agent organization" to denote an open MAS, or one of its sub-systems, that was designed and operates in a way similar to human organizations.

This broad agreement around agent organizations has led to the proposal of different *organizational models* for their engineering (incomplete list of proposals is: Ferber, Gutknecht & Michel, 2004; Lesser et al., 2004; Hübner, Sichman & Boissier, 2002; Esteva, Padget & Sierra, 2002; Dignum, 2004; Horling & Lesser, 2004; Tambe et al., 1999; Parunak & Odell, 2002; Silva, Choren & Lucena, 2004). An organizational model provides the designer with a conceptual framework and a syntax in which she can write *organizational specifications* for agent organizations. From an organizational specification, an agent organization can be implemented on a traditional agent platform or, more realistically, by using some *organizational middleware* or *platform* (Hübner, Sichman & Boissier, 2005; Esteva et al., 2004; Gutknecht & Ferber, 2000). In general, these organizational middleware or platforms take the organizational specifications as input, interpret them, and provide the agents with an organizational environment (agent organization) according to the specification. In order to enter, to work inside or to leave the agent organization, the agents are supposed to know how to access the services of the middleware/platform and to make requests according to the available organizational specification.

While there has been a strong emphasis on agent organizations, as shown by the number and diversity of proposed organizational models, there is not in the literature any work whose explicit aim is to review the proposals and to assess their modelling capabilities. To our knowledge there is related work that reviews and compares *organizational paradigms* – i.e., general types of organizational structures like hierarchies, teams, markets, matrix organizations, etc. (Horling & Lesser, 2005; Dignum & Dignum, 2001). Some other work proposes *taxonomies* of organization and social concepts for the engineering of agent organizations (Mao & Yu, 2005). However, none addresses a representative collection of existing organizational models and tries to describe in a coherent view their commonalities and differences regarding the type of modelling constructs offered to create organizational specifications.

The aim of this chapter is to try to fill this gap. Firstly, we present in more detail the notions of agent organizations and organizational models. Secondly, we discuss in general terms how we can classify the diverse aspects of agent organizations currently captured by organizational models. These aspects are named "modelling dimensions". Thirdly, we review existing organizational models taking into account the identified modelling dimensions. Fourthly, we summarize the review by presenting a comparative table of the organizational models analysed.

Before proceeding, the reader should to be warned that in the text she will not find answers to pragmatic questions such as: given an application domain, what organizational model to choose? Or, given an organizational model, what is its domain of applicability? We acknowledge that these are highly important questions. However, they are outside the scope of this chapter. This is due to the fact that our treatment is geared towards finding points of similarities among different organizational models to promote *organizational interoperability* (i.e., means to enable agents to flexibly work in several agent organizations that were specified with different, but comparable, organizational models). Our vision is that to interconnect agent organizations in the context of larger open systems (e.g., formed by federating open MAS), not only issues of domain model and communication language interoperability (Erdur, Dikenelli, Seylan & Gürcan, 2004), but also issues of organizational model interoperability must be handled (Coutinho, Brandão, Sichman & Boissier, 2007).

Thus, after the analysis and comparison of organizational models, we outline how the modelling dimensions can be used as the starting point to a detailed alignment of different organizations models. Finally, we comment on related work and present our final conclusions.

AGENT ORGANIZATIONS AND MODELS

Let us begin by clarifying the central notions of *agent organization* and *organizational model*. Through the rapid analysis of these concepts, we will position and define the basic vocabulary used in the chapter.

Agent Organizations

We hold the premise that concrete systems in general, not only agent organizations, exhibit some fundamental traits that are natural candidates to be represented in models, not only organizational models. The basic traits are:

- the *system structure* – i.e., the elements that form the system and the relationships that interconnect these elements; and,
- the *system functions* – i.e., the input/output relations that couple the system to external elements from the environment in which the system is situated.

Also, we submit that these basic traits can be regarded under two complementary points of view:

- the *static* perspective – when we describe them in a time independent manner; or,
- the *kinetic* perspective – when we consider the time in their descriptions.

These fundamental traits and perspectives form the point of departure of our analyses and comparison of organizational models for agent organizations. In the sequel, we further detail the notions of structure and function, both under the static and the kinetic perspectives. We illustrate the concepts by showing how they occur in agent organizations. This discussion will serve the double purpose of refining the concept of agent organization and providing the basis for justifying the modelling dimensions presented in the next sections.

Structure

In general, a *system* can be defined as a complex entity resultant from two or more basic entities of some kind that influence each other in such a way that the whole possess some features that its components lack. According to Bunge[1] (1979), all systems are formed by a definite *composition*, a definite *environment* and a definite *structure*. The composition delimits the boundaries of the system by stating the collection of all entities that are parts of the system. The environment determines the immediate outside of the system by defining the collection of entities that directly influence or are influenced by the composition of the system. The **structure** is the collection of *influence relations* that interconnect all the elements from the composition and the environment of the system.

In the case of agent organizations, its composition is formed primarily by autonomous agents, and these can possibly be heterogeneous. By heterogeneous, we mean that the agents, when seen as smaller systems, are not supposed to have a pre-established type of structure. All that is required from the agents is that they meet some functional requirements, i.e., are able to perform some functions (or goals as discussed in the sequel). The environment of agent organizations may consist in other agents or computational resources. For an illustration, see the Figure 1. Looking at the figure, we see that an agent organization can be a *sub-system* (i.e., a subset of the structure and environment) of an entire MAS. And, we admit that it is possible to have both computational and human agents inside the boundaries of an agent organization – however, our primarily concern is with agent organization composed of only computational agents.

Regarding the structure of agent organizations, it is mainly moulded following the human organizations metaphor. From this metaphor, an agent organization is viewed as a *social system* and the autonomous

Figure 1. Static description of the agent organization σ: composition $C_\sigma = \{a2, a4, a5, a6\}$; environment $E_\sigma = \{a1, a3, a7\} \cup \{computational\ resources\}$; structure $S_\sigma^{comm} = \{a1 \rightarrow a4, a2 \leftrightarrow a4, a4 \leftrightarrow a3, a4 \leftrightarrow a5, a4 \leftrightarrow a6, a2 \rightarrow a7\}$; $S_\sigma^{auth} = \{a4 \rightarrow a2, a4 \rightarrow a5\}$, where, $x \rightarrow y$ denotes the pair (x,y), and $x \leftrightarrow y$ the pairs (x,y) and (y,x).

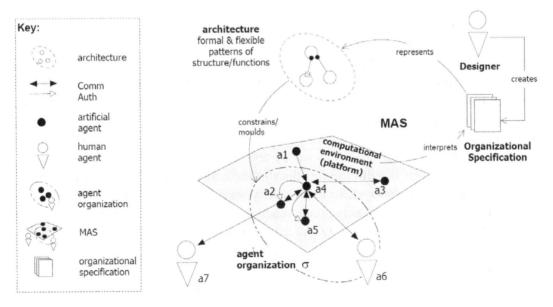

agents are conceived as being capable not only of *material action* (action between agents and non-autonomous entities), but also of *social action* (action influencing other autonomous agents). Examples of material actions are *production, consumption*, etc. Examples of social action are *communication, authority, delegation, power, coordination, control*, etc. (Grossi, Dignum, Datani & Royakkers, 2005; Castelfranchi, 1998). Each one of these types of action gives rise to an influence relation and these form the total structure of the agent organization. In Figure 1, we illustrate the structure of an agent organization formed by two influence relations S_σ^{comm} and S_σ^{auth} representing the social actions of communication and authority, respectively.

From the example presented, and adopting a *static* point of view (time independent), any complex entity characterized by a mathematical structure $\langle C_\sigma, E_\sigma, S_\sigma^1, \ldots, S_\sigma^n \rangle$ (where, C_σ denotes composition, E_σ environment and each $S_\sigma^{1 \leq i \leq n}$ represents an influence relation over $C_\sigma \cup E_\sigma$) that forms a connected graph (where, $C_\sigma \cup E_\sigma$ are the vertices and $S_\sigma^1 \cup \ldots \cup S_\sigma^n$ are the edges) fulfils the basic conditions and can be considered a system. When the elements in C_σ and E_σ are themselves mathematical abstractions such as numbers, sets, functions, etc., the system will be called an *abstract system*. If the elements in C_σ and E_σ are concrete entities like people, computer process, etc., the system will be named a *concrete system*.

In concrete systems the components and the environment undergo change over time. In this context, we say that an entity *acts upon* another one when the first causes or prevents the occurrence of changes in the second. *Interaction* occurs when the action is mutual. Action and interaction are special classes of influence relations forming the structure of concrete systems. They are the effective cause of the overall behaviour and properties of any concrete system.

If we take time into account and attempt to describe step by step the actions and interactions occurring among the components and the environment of a system we then provide a *kinetic* description of the system. In such a description, the structure of the system is seen as actions and interactions unfolding over time; actions and interactions producing and being produced by structure. Being given T (an ordered set of time steps), the kinetic description of a system σ can be formalized by a function f_σ which produces static instantaneous descriptions $f_\sigma(t) = \langle c_\sigma(t), e_\sigma(t), s_\sigma^1(t), \ldots, s_\sigma^n(t) \rangle$ of the system σ, for each time step $t \in T$.

Functions

The **functions** (or goals) performed by a system can be conceived as a definite relation between *input actions* and *output actions* of a system. An input action is an action of some element of the environment upon some element of the composition of the system. Conversely, an output action represents some composition element acting upon some environment element.

When systems are decomposed into sub-systems, we can think of identifying not only the functions of the entire system, but also the functions of its sub-systems. Also, we hope to be able of composing the functions of the sub-systems to fulfil the functions of the entire system. Moreover, this process may be applied recursively to the sub-systems of the sub-systems, and so on. When this happens, i.e., when we have some recursive way of breaking some functions into smaller functions and combine the pieces to achieve the original functions, we say that the functions of the system form a *functional (or goal) decomposition hierarchy*. In general, functional decompositions are inherently time dependent (kinetic) descriptions of the functions of a system. When decomposing a function into smaller functions, there will always be some topological sort guiding the expected sequence of performance of the smaller functions to achieve the decomposed function; and the very presence of sequences represents indirectly the notion of time.

In the case of agent organizations, the functions represent the purpose of the system (the goals or objectives for which the agent organization was assembled). They can be decomposed in sub-goals and allocated to groups of agents (sub-systems), or to individual agents. The set of goals allocated to a group or an individual agent will form the *functional requirements* imposed on the structure of the group or the agent. As noted above, heterogeneous agents will meet the same functional requirements with different structures. In the case of groups, the allocated functions will be realized by means of sequences of actions and interactions involving the agents of the group. In a static description, the sequences of actions and interactions that actually occur inside a group to realize some function is abstracted into time-invariant relations that compose the description. Only by resorting to a kinetic description, we can uncover the time-dependent aspects of the actions and interactions geared towards some function; so to speak, only kinetic descriptions revels us the structure in motion while performing some function.

Concluding, we quote a definition of human organizations by Scott (1998) which clearly synthesize our discussion: **agent organizations** are *"collectivities oriented to the pursuit of relatively specific goals and exhibiting relatively highly formalized social structures"* (p. 26).

Organizational Models

Looking more closely, we see in the definition of Scott (1998) the term "highly formalized" applied to structure. A social structure is formal when "the social positions and the relationships among them have been explicitly specified and are defined independently of the ... characteristics and relations of the participants occupying these positions" (Scott, 1998, p. 19). This idea of formal structure makes us to posit that, apart from the static and kinetic descriptions, we can also regard the structure and functions of a system from the perspectives of:

- the *realization* (or *materialization*) of the system – this happen when we pin-point a particular structure and/or functions of the system;
- the *architecture* (or *formalization*) of the system – when we represent the formal (independent of particular components) and flexible (allowing some degree of deviance) patterns that mould or constrain the structure and/or functions of the system.

In essence, an **organizational model** is a vehicle to express formalizations for agent organizations. In other words, by using an organizational model we can represent the architecture (i.e., patterns in the structure and functions) of agent organizations. At least, we can think of using an organizational model to formalize the structure and the functions of an agent organization, both from the static and the kinetic perspectives. What else can be done in terms of formalization of agent organizations, and how this has been specifically tackled by the existing organizational models is the subject of the rest of the chapter.

Taking a MAS engineering orientation, we interpret organizational models as modeling languages (in the sense of a definition of a class of models). In order to avoid confusion, we call a specific model created by using and organizational model (an instance of an organizational model) by the name "organizational specification". Organizational specifications are created to implement agent organizations (see Figure 1).

Modelling Languages

In general, a modelling language provides two elements: a *conceptualization* and a *syntax* (Guizzardi, 2007). The conceptualization is a world view, a body of general concepts (*modelling constructs*) that we instantiate to produce abstractions of some system under study. For example, if we regard the set theory as a general modelling language, its conceptualization is composed of modelling constructs such as *Element*, *Set*, the ∈ relation, etc. Another example is the Unified Modelling Language (UML[2]) commonly used in Software Engineering. Using UML we create abstractions of systems based on the concepts of *Class*, *Attribute*, *Association*, etc.

The syntax of a language is a collection of rules of composition and symbols that are used to write down an abstraction in a particular form. For example, a standard syntax for set theory consists in denoting elements of sets by letters "a", "b", etc. and using certain rules to write sets by using braces "{}", etc. In UML, a common syntax is to use shapes like rectangles, lines, etc. to designate the basic concepts and to structure these shapes in diagrams giving rise to a model.

A model is then an abstraction – the instantiation of a given conceptualization that captures some system under study – materialized by a syntactic representation. Both abstraction and syntactic representation are produced by using a modelling language. In this case, abstraction and syntactic representation are said to conform respectively to the conceptualization (world view) and to the syntax of the modelling language used.

Metamodels

The conceptualization underlying a modelling language can be conceived as an abstract system. Being a system, this leads us to consider representing the composition and structure of a conceptualization. For this, we can build models; i.e., propose representations that can be used in the place of the conceptualization w.r.t. some purpose. Such a model is often called a *metamodel*. Then, a metamodel is a model that represents the conceptualization behind a modelling language. Normally, a metamodel is constructed with the aim of providing a formal specific structure to interpret the syntax of a modelling language w.r.t. the supported conceptualization. In this case, the metamodel is said to capture the *abstract syntax* of the language. A metamodel can also be constructed with the aim of providing a representation of the conceptualization of a modelling language not committed to the syntax of the language. In (Guizzardi, 2007), this is called the *domain ontology* of the language.

In this perspective, we can notice that there are two types of models. On the one hand, there are regular models, i.e., models of systems other than languages (*modelling level*). On the other hand, there are metamodels, i.e., models of modelling languages (*meta-modelling level*). A metamodel can represent either the conceptualization of a given modelling language w.r.t. the language syntax (*abstract syntax model*) or the conceptualization of some domain without regard to syntax (*domain ontology model*).

Organizational Models, Specifications and Metamodels

Summing up, we collect the ideas discussed above in the diagram presented in Figure 2. The diagram tries to convey in a single picture a comprehensive view of the possible meanings for the notion of organizational model. A regular model written with an organizational model is called an "organizational

Figure 2. Elements of an organizational model

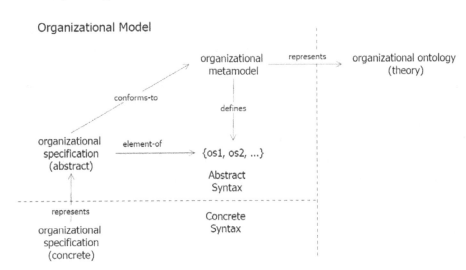

specification". The metamodel that conveys the abstract syntax of an organizational model is called an "organizational metamodel". The domain ontology model behind an organizational model is named an "organizational ontology" (or "organizational theory"). Combining the terms we have: an organization specification conforms to an organizational metamodel; an organizational metamodel represents some organizational ontology (theory) and defines a class of possible organizational specifications. Finally, an organizational specification conforming to the abstract syntax (metamodel) of an organization model is concretely represented by using a particular concrete syntax defined for the organizational model. All of these elements compose the idea of an organizational model.

ORGANIZATIONAL MODELLING

In this section, we propose a general classification for the modelling constructs present in the metamodels of existing organization models. We classify the modelling constructs in what we call *modelling dimensions*. Also, we present the meta-modelling language we have used to describe the metamodel of organizational models. The modelling dimensions and the meta-modelling language form the basic framework for the analysis and comparison of organizational models presented in the next sections.

Modelling Dimensions

Recalling the previous section, an organizational model may provide constructs to represent formal patterns in the structure and functions of an agent organization, these patterns being either static or kinetic.

Basic Dimensions

This general analysis (complemented by the review of organizational models in the next section) leads us to posit four basic cohesive categories of modelling constructs in an organizational model:

- *Organizational Structure* – constructs to represent what aspects of the structure of the agent organization have to be invariant through time;
- *Organizational Functions* – constructs that represent global goals and goal decompositions to be accomplished by the agent organization;
- *Organizational Interactions* – constructs to represent time-dependent aspects of standardized actions and interactions involving the elements from the organizational structure and organization function;
- *Organizational Norms* – constructs to further regulate and show how organizational structure (time-independent relations), organizational interaction (time-dependent functioning) and organizational functions are interrelated.

We call these basic categories of modelling constructs the "basic modelling dimensions" of organizational models. Here, the qualifier "basic" refers to the fact that these dimensions appear both in our analysis presented in the previous section and in research on organizational models reported in the MAS literature, as we will present in the next sections. Alternatively, we will also refer to them as the *structural*, the *functional*, the *interactive* and the *normative* dimensions, respectively.

It is illustrative to mention that in more traditional languages for modelling software systems, like UML, at least the first three basic dimensions appear explicitly. In UML, for instance, modelling constructs such as class, package and component diagrams are structural, i.e., represent basic constraints over possible static object structures; interaction and collaboration diagrams represent orchestrated functioning over a given structure; finally, the use case and activity diagrams capture functional aspects.

Regarding normative constructs, they are not explicit in traditional software modelling. In UML, we can regard realization relationships between use cases and collaborations (i.e., relations stating that a use case will be implemented by a given collaboration) as a kind of "rule" relating interactive constructs to functional constructs. However, in traditional software architectures, the underlying components are not viewed as entities capable of autonomous action. In this way, normative aspects in traditional software systems are not the focus of modelling because we can rigidly fix beforehand how structural and interactive constructs lead to functional aspects. Moreover, at run-time there will be no autonomous actions and interactions deviating from what was prescribed in design. Therefore, our conclusion is that normative constructs have to appear more explicitly in organizational models than in traditional modelling languages because they will be the necessary mechanism to flexibly couple the agents to the prescribed organization; i.e., to balance the needs of the autonomous agents and the constraints imposed by the organization.

Also, these four basic modelling dimensions traditionally appear in Social Sciences research as it is shown in a review of some early work in Sociology made by Timasheff (1952):

"The works studied exhibits several common general qualities. ... in the construction of the basic conceptual scheme, three main trends are discernible. Relationism ... emphasizes social relations and social

interactions; normativism ... emphasizes norms, ideal patterns, or institutions; and functionalism ...lays stress on function;" (p. 177)

Later on, the author makes a further connection between *social relationships* and *social interaction*, distinguishing them from *function*:

"If one agrees with the authors ... social relationships and social interaction are two views on the same element of social reality, one static, that is, structural, and the other kinetic. The latter term is preferable to the often used "functional," since the term "function" and its derivatives must be reserved to connote another element of social reality." (Timasheff, 1952, p. 177)

Concluding, we can say that this analysis of Timasheff, made in the context of social human groups, when used as metaphor to model agent organizations also drives us towards the basic dimensions we have identified above.

Complementary Dimensions

Beyond the basic dimensions, organizational models have also explored other complementary traits of agent organizations. In general, agent organizations can also present:

- *Organizational Evaluation* – constructs to measure the performance of the formal structure and norms of an agent organization w.r.t. specific goals;
- *Organizational Evolution* – constructs to model changes in the organization (formal structure, norms and goals) at some points in the time in order to adapt the functioning of the agent organization to new demands from the environment;
- *Organizational Environment* – constructs to represent a collection of resources in the space of the agent organization formed by non-autonomous entities that can be perceived and acted upon (manipulated, consumed, produced, etc.) by the components agents;
- *Organizational Ontologies* – constructs to build conceptualizations regarding the application domain of the agent organization that must be consistently shared by the component agents. These global conceptualizations are important to maintain the coherence of the activity inside the agent organization.

These will be called the "complementary dimensions" of organizational modelling. They are related to the notions of *measurement, adaptation, situatedeness*, and *semantics* of agent organizations, respectively. Despite calling them complementary, these are quite important; they are called complementary just because they appear less frequently as explicit organizational elements in the available organizational models, as we will see in the sequel.

Meta-Modelling Language

The approach we will use to analyze and compare the organizational models w.r.t. the modelling dimensions is based on the construction of object oriented organizational metamodels. In the original proposals, the organizational models (their organizational metamodels) are generally defined using a mathematical formalism based on set theory or logic. Such definitions are then associated to concrete notations. In our research, however, we have found more convenient to translate these abstract organizational

Figure 3. Ecore syntax

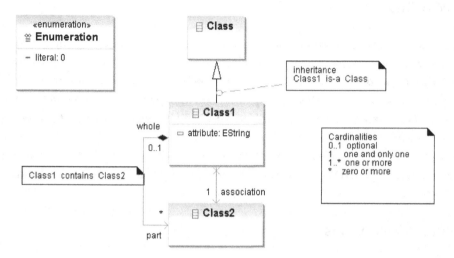

metamodels into an explicit object oriented structure based on a single meta-modelling language. There are two main reasons for making this option. Firstly, this permits to homogenize the definitions of the abstract syntax of the several organizational models. Secondly, this enables a further application of a *Model Driven Engineering* (Schimidt, 2006) approach to formalize possible mappings and integrations among organizational models (Coutinho, Brandão, Sichman & Boissier, 2008).

The particular object oriented meta-modelling language we will use to represent the organizational metamodels is Ecore[3], a class based meta-modelling language. Using Ecore, we will represent the main abstractions (and their interrelationships) found in the organizational models by means of classes, attributes, relationships (inheritance, composites and associations) and enumeration (lists of literal values)[4]. A summary of the notation we will use to draw organizational metamodels written in Ecore is depicted in Figure 3. We have chosen to use Ecore to represent the organizational metamodels for three reasons. Firstly, it is expressive enough to represent the abstract syntax of the different organization metamodels. Secondly, a metamodel written in Ecore can be automatically translated to other meta-modelling languages like MOF[5] and KM3[6]. Thirdly, it has a practical and free modelling environment based on the Eclipse platform[7].

ORGANIZATIONAL MODELS REVIEW

We turn now to illustrate how some of the existing organizations models cover the space of possible modelling constructs identified in the previous section. We will describe the central modelling constructs of five organizational models – AGR (Ferber, Gutknecht & Michel, 2004), TAEMS (Decker, 1996; Lesser et al., 2004), MOISE+ (Hübner, Sichman & Boissier, 2002), ISLANDER (Esteva, Padget & Sierra, 2002) and OperA (Dignum, 2004). Other organizational models – ODML (Horling & Lesser, 2004), STEAM (Tambe et al., 1999), AUML (Parunak & Odell, 2002) and MAS-ML (Silva, Choren & Lucena, 2004) – will be briefly outlined in the end of the section.

We have chosen to describe AGR (an essentially structural model), TAEMS (essentially functional, but also encompassing the evaluation and environment dimensions), MOISE+ (encompassing the structural, functional and normative dimensions), ISLANDER (emphasizing the structural, interactive, normative and ontology dimensions) and OperA (encompassing the structural, interactive, functional, normative and ontology dimensions) in more detail because we think of these as good exemplars to introduce and show the interplay among the modelling dimensions. Also, three of them (AGR, MOISE+ and ISLANDER) have associated implementation platforms and frameworks that have enabled us to practically conduct experiments with them (Hübner, Sichman & Boissier, 2006; Esteva et al., 2004; Gutknecht & Ferber, 2000). In the descriptions, first we will briefly explain the basic concepts (organizational ontology) found in each organizational model; after, we will present an example of an organizational specification (concrete syntax); finally, we will show an organizational metamodel (abstract syntax) written in Ecore that convey the basic concepts found in the organizational model.

AGR

AGR (Agent, Group, Role) (Ferber, Gutknecht & Michel, 2004) is the evolution of the AALAADIN model (Ferber & Gutknecht, 1998). In AGR *agent*, *group* and *role* are the primitive modelling concepts. An agent is an active, communicating entity playing one or more roles within one or more groups. No constraints are placed upon the architecture of an agent or about its mental capabilities. According to the authors, "an agent may be as reactive as an ant, or as clever as a human" (Ferber, Gutknecht & Michel, 2004, p. 220). A group is a set of agents sharing some common characteristics. A group is the context for a pattern of activities and is used for partitioning organizations. An agent can participate at the same time in one or more groups. Agents may communicate if and only if they belong to the same group. A role is the abstract representation of a functional position (expected behaviour) of an agent in a group. Roles are local to groups, and a role must be requested by an agent.

Figure 4. AGR concrete organization and organizational specification

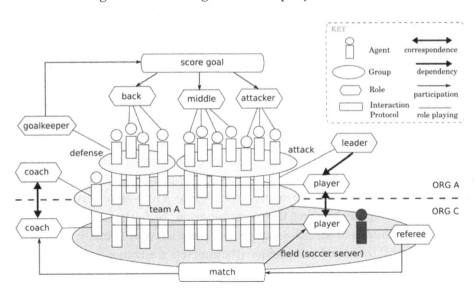

Figure 5. AGR metamodel

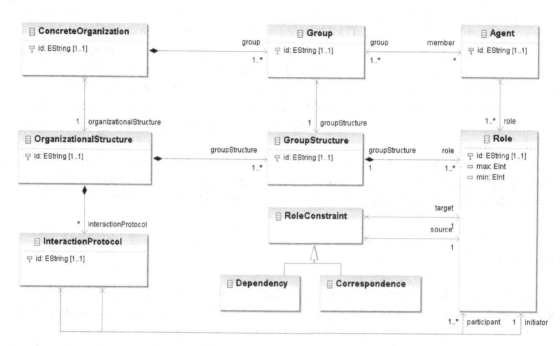

Given the three primitive concepts, in AGR the organization of an agent organization is conceived as a structure of groups and roles. In order to specify an organization, we have to define *group structures* composed of roles. Roles may be described by *cardinality attributes* (how many agents may play that role) and *role constraints*. There are two kinds of role constraints: *correspondence*, which states that an agent playing one role will automatically play another role; and *dependency*, which tells the previous role an agent has to play to be able to play another role. Finally, the organizational specification can indicate interaction protocols involving the roles of group structures, but the primitives and the sequence of their use are not defined in the organization level.

In Figure 4, AGR is applied to the modelling of a simulated soccer game. In the example, we see represented a team as a group of eleven "players" plus a "coach". The players are divided in two sub-groups, the "defense" and "attack" sub-groups. Besides being part of the team, the eleven players plus coach are also described as playing correspondent roles in a bigger group called "field". Completing the field, there is an agent playing the role of a "referee". The group structures, roles, interaction protocols and interrelationships comprise an organizational specification. The agents and group instances compose a description of concrete agent organization shaped by the organizational specification.

Another example of an agent organization specified in AGR is presented in Chapter III "Towards an Integral Approach of Organizations in Multi-Agent Systems" by Ferber et al. in this collection. In Figure 5, it is shown the AGR metamodel to which the organizational specification of Figure 4 conforms.

Discussion. The main characteristic of the AGR model is its minimalist structural-based view of organizations. In an AGR model an organization is specified as a role-group structure imposed on the agents. AGR also says that agents can have their joint behaviour orchestrated by interaction protocols, but the nature and the primitives to describe such protocols are left open. Finally, AGR provide modelling constructs to represent the actual composition (the concrete realization) of an agent organization.

Figure 6. TAEMS metamodel

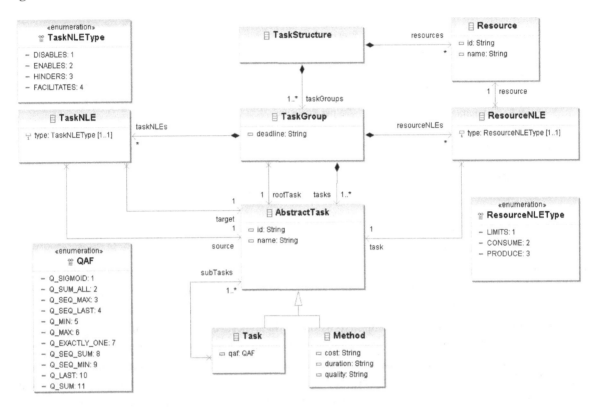

TAEMS

TAEMS (Task Analysis, Environment Modeling, and Simulation) is an organizational model whose basic modelling primitive is the concept of *task* (Decker, 1996, Lesser et al., 2004). In essence, TAEMS is a modelling language to specify *tasks structures*. A task structure is specified by defining tasks, *resources*, *tasks relationships*, and *task groups*. A task group is an independent collection of inter-related tasks. Interrelating the tasks, there are two kinds of task relationships: *sub-task* and *non-local effects* relationships. The sub-task relationship links a parent task to child task explicitly defining a task decomposition tree. Individual tasks that do not have child tasks are called *methods*. Methods are primitive tasks that agents should be able to perform. Methods can be associated to discrete probability distributions describing expected *duration*, *quality* and *costs*. These values are used to evaluate the organization performance. The total quality of a task group, for instance, can be calculated by combining the qualities of the methods in a recursive way by means of *quality accumulation functions*. Non-local effects are task relationships that have positive or negative effects in the quality, costs or duration of the related tasks. Examples of possible non-local effects are: *facilitates*, *enables*, *hinders*, *limits*, etc. Finally, non-local effects can also relate tasks to *resources*, i.e., environmental elements necessary to their realizations.

In Figure 6, the conceptual framework of TAEMS is represented in an explicit metamodel. In Figure 7, a partial specification that conforms to the TAEMS metamodel is shown. The specification shows how an agent is supposed to proceed to buy a product inside an e-market MAS. To buy a product, the agent

Figure 7. TAEMS task group specification (adapted from Lesser et al., 2004, p. 110)

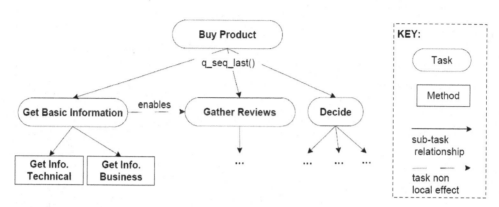

has to follow a task structure composed of three sub-tasks: "Get Basic Information", "Gather Reviews" from other customers and "Decide" to buy. These will be done in sequence and the total quality of the task group (denoted by the quality assurance function q_seq_lat()) will be the quality of the last task (i.e., the task "Decide"). Each sub-task can be further decomposed. For instance, the task "Get Basic Information" is decomposed in "Get Info. Technical" and "Get Info. Business" methods.

Discussion. Unlike AGR whose emphasis is on static structural aspects of an organization (roles, groups, etc.), TAEMS is geared towards the description of functional aspects. The basic unity of analysis is the task or goal. This in essence describes what should be accomplished by an agent (method) or a group of agents (task group). Besides functional aspects, TAEMS also provides constructs for representing task evaluation and resources from the environment of the agent organization.

MOISE+

MOISE+ (Model of Organization for multI-agent SystEms) (Hübner, Sichman & Boissier, 2002) is an organizational model that explicitly distinguishes three aspects in the modelling of an organization: the *structural specification*, the *functional specification* and the *deontic specification*.

The structural specification defines the agents' static relations through the notions of *roles*, *roles relations* and *groups*. A role defines a set of constraints the agent has to accept to enter in a group. There are two kinds of constraints: structural and functional. Structural constraints are defined by means of links and compatibilities that a source role has in relation to a target role. The links are sub-divided in communication, acquaintance and authority links. The communication links enable message exchange between related roles. Acquaintance links enable agents playing one role to get information about agents playing another role. The authority links represent power relation between roles. All the links define constraints that an agent accepts when it enters a group and begins to play a role. By its turn, the compatibility relation constrains the additional roles an agent can play given the roles it is already playing. A compatibility between a role A and a role B means that an agent playing role A is also permitted to play role B. In the structural specification, a group is defined by a group specification. A group specification consists in group roles (roles that can be played), sub-group specifications (group decomposition), links and compatibilities definitions, role cardinalities and sub-group cardinalities.

In Figure 8(a), we present part of a MOISE+ structural specification for a simulated soccer game; the example is similar to the one used to illustrate AGR (Figure 4). We can notice the definition of three

Figure 8. MOISE+ organizational specification

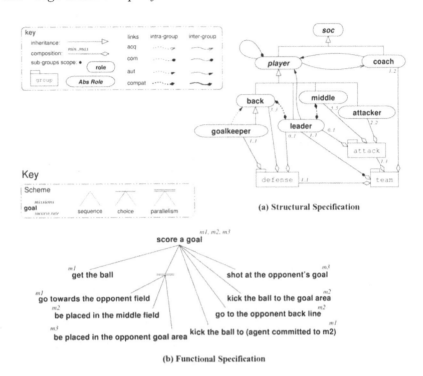

(a) Structural Specification

(b) Functional Specification

groups: "team", "defense" and "attack". The group "defense" gathers the roles "goalkeeper", "leader" and "back". The "attack" group gathers the roles "leader", "middle" and "attacker". The group "team" gathers the groups "attack" and "defense" as sub-goups, and the role "coach"; the role "leader" is in-directly (sub-group scope) part of "team" and in the context of a "team" there must be only one agent in the role of "leader". All the roles are *specializations* (inheritance relation) of the role "soc" (the root of the role hierarchy). "Player" is an *abstract role* (no agent can play it directly) used to impose com-munication and authority constraints to all roles that inherit from it. Intra-group constraints have only one group as scope; inter-group constraints are valid to different groups. In this way, a "player" can communicate with players inside his group and players of other groups; and, a "goalkeeper, has authority over a "back" agent only if both are on the same group. Finally, the agent that plays "leader" can also play either "middle" or "back" roles.

The functional specification describes how an agent organization usually achieves its *global goals*, i.e., how these goals are decomposed (by *plans*) and distributed to the agents (by *missions*). Global goals, plans and missions are specified by means of a *social scheme*. A social scheme can be seen as a goal decomposition tree, where the root is a global goal and the leaves are goals that can be achieved by an individual agent. In a social scheme, an internal node and its children represent a plan to achieve a sub-goal. The plan consists in performing the children goals according to a given plan operator. There are three kinds of plan operators: sequence (to do the sub-goal in sequence), choice (to choose and do only one sub-goal) and parallel (to do all the sub-goals in parallel).

In Figure 8(b), it is presented a social scheme that is part of the MOISE+ functional specification for the simulated soccer example. There is a social scheme named "score a goal". In order to perform this scheme it is necessary to have agents that have committed to missions "m1", "m2" and "m3". Missions

Figure 9. MOISE+ metamodel

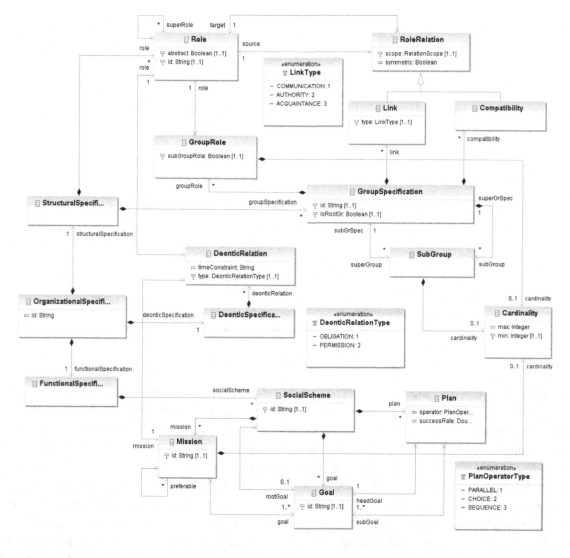

are coherent sets of goals or sub-goals. An agent that is committed to a mission is responsible for the satisfaction of all components goals. The agent with mission "m1" initiates the scheme. After, in parallel, agents with missions "m1", "m2" and "m3" will perform certain actions. Finally, an ordered sequence of actions finishes the social scheme.

The deontic specification associates roles to missions by means of *permissions* and *obligations*. In the simulated soccer example, this specification could state that agents playing the role of "attacker" are obliged to commit to mission "m3", while those playing the role of "middle" are allowed to commit to "m2". In Figure 9, we show the MOISE+ organization metamodel.

Discussion. On the one hand, comparing MOISE+ with AGR we can see that an AGR specification corresponds only to the structural elements of MOISE+; however, one may notice that the representation of concrete agents is not possible in MOISE+. The structural aspect of MOISE+ also extends the concepts found in AGR adding the ideas of *abstract roles*, role *inheritance* and *group hierarchies*. On the other hand, comparing MOISE+ with TAEMS we can see that the MOISE+ functional elements (social schemes) correspond to the idea of task groups in TAEMS. However, the task hierarchical decomposition present in TAEMS is more elaborated having concepts such as non-local effects and quality accumulation functions not encountered in MOISE+. Finally, in MOISE+, the structural and functional aspects are independent of each other. The deontic specification links these two aspects specifying permissions and obligations (normative elements) for roles with respect to missions.

ISLANDER

ISLANDER is a declarative language for specifying *electronic institutions* (Esteva, Padget & Sierra, 2002). Electronic institutions are the computational counterpart of human institutions. *"Institutions establish how interactions of a certain sort will and must be structured within an organization. ... Human institutions not only structure human interactions but also enforce individual and social behavior by obliging everybody to act according to the norms"* (Esteva, Padget & Sierra, 2002, p. 348).

In ISLANDER, an electronic institution is composed of four basic elements: (1) *dialogic framework*, (2) *scenes*, (3) *performative structure*, and (4) *norms*. In the dialogic framework the valid *illocutions* that agents can exchange are defined, as well as which are the participant *roles* and their *relationships*. The valid illocutions are those that respect a common *ontology*, a common *communication language and knowledge representation language*. Each role defines a pattern of behaviour within the institution and any agent within an institution is required to adopt some of them. A scene is a collection of agents playing different roles in interaction with each other in order to realize a given activity. Every scene

Figure 10. ISLANDER e-Institution specification (adapted from Esteva, Padget & Sierra, 2002)

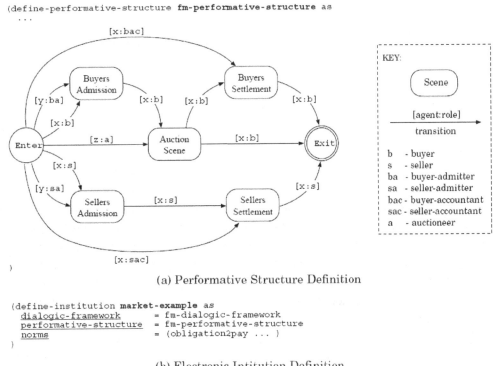

(a) Performative Structure Definition

```
(define-institution market-example as
    dialogic-framework      = fm-dialogic-framework
    performative-structure  = fm-performative-structure
    norms                   = (obligation2pay ... )
)
```

(b) Electronic Intitution Definition

Figure 11. ISLANDER metamodel

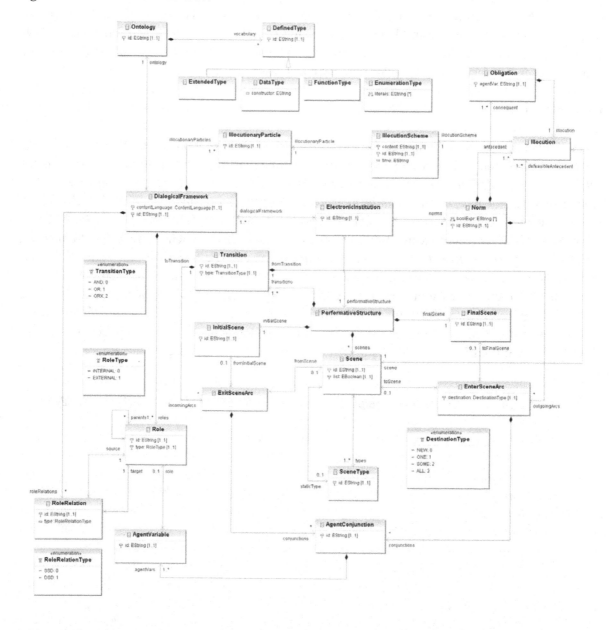

follows a well-defined *communication protocol*. The performative structure establishes relationships among scenes. The idea is to specify a network of scenes that characterizes more complex activities. The connections among the scenes define which agents playing a certain role can move from one scene to other(s) subject to given constraints. The norms of an electronic institution define the commitments, obligations and rights of participating agents.

In the Figure 10, we see a fragment of an ISLANDER specification for an electronic market. In the market, products are sold by means of auctions. Buyer and seller external agents come to the market, are admitted, take part in auctions, follow an exit protocol and finally get out from the market. All this process is orchestrated by a performative structure (Figure 10(a)). The performative structure is one piece of the entire e-institution specification (Figure 10(b)). In Figure 11, a metamodel detailing the main abstractions of ISLANDER is shown.

Discussion. When we compare ISLANDER with AGR, TAEMS and MOISE+ the first thing we notice is the terminological shift from organization to institution. Despite this terminological difference, we can see that what the ISLANDER authors' calls institution is in several senses very similar to our notion of agent organization. The second point of difference of ISLANDER with respect to AGR, TAEMS and MOISE+ is that instead of structural and functional aspects, ISLANDER focus is on normative aspects (norms that enforce behaviour) and interactive aspects (dialogic structures). A third point that deserves mention is the nature of the dialogic structures of ISLANDER when compared to the goal-driven interactions of TAEMS and MOISE+. In Figure 8, we have specified a MOISE+ scheme to score a soccer-goal. The scheme describes a plan to achieve a goal. In the plan we can specify some indirect interactions, that is, interactions that can occur by means of perception and action in the environment. In ISLANDER this indirect kind of interaction is difficult, if not impossible to describe. This is due to the fact that all interacting activity taking place in an electronic institution, like the one shown in Figure 10, is purely dialogical; that is, interactions are restricted to direct communication between the agents. However, ISLANDER is the first model analysed to provide modelling constructs to explicitly describe in detail patterns of direct dialogical interactions among agents.

OperA

OperA (Organizations per Agents) (Dignum, 2004) is a framework for the specification of multi-agent systems consisting of three interrelated models: (1) the *Organizational Model* (OM), which describes the organizational structure of the society by means of roles and interactions; (2) the *Social Model* (SM), which specifies how individual agents agree to enact roles; and (3) the *Interaction Model* (IM), describing the possible interaction between agents. A main characteristic of OperA is that it explicitly acknowledges and proposes constructs to represent both the concerns of the agent organizations (in the OM) and the interests of individual agents (in the SM and IM). In this review, we concentrate on the OM component of OperA.

The organizational model of OperA is used to specify an agent organization in terms of four structures: the *social*, the *interaction*, the *normative* and the *communicative* structures. In the social structure are defined *roles*, *objectives*, *groups* and role *dependencies*. Roles identify activities and services necessary to achieve social objectives and enable to abstract from the specific individuals that will eventually perform them. Roles are described in terms of objectives (what an actor is expected to achieve), norms (how is an actor expected to behave), rights (capabilities that actors receive when enacting the role) and the type of enactment (institutional or external role). Groups provide means to collectively refer to a set of roles. Groups are used to specify norms that hold for all roles in the group. Role dependencies describe how the roles are related in terms of objective realization. There are three types of role dependencies, related to the *hierarchy* (delegation), *market* (bidding) and *network* (request) general coordination mechanisms (Dignum & Dignum, 2001).

The interaction structure defines how the main activity of an agent organization is supposed to happen. This definition is done in terms of *scenes, scene scripts, scene transitions and role evolution* relations. Scenes are representations of specific interactions involving actors. Scenes follow abstract scene scripts. A scene script is described by its players (roles or groups), scene norms (expected behavior of actors in a scene) and a desired interaction pattern (ordering of *landmarks* – i.e., expressions involving

Figure 12. OperA metamodel

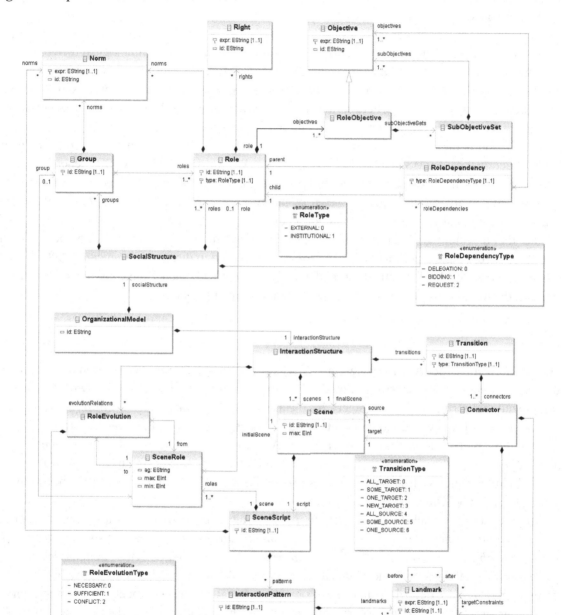

objectives – that must be respected by any protocol eventually used to realize the scene). Scene transitions are used to coordinate scenes by defining the ordering and synchronization of the scenes. Role evolution relations specify the constraints that hold for the role-enacting agents as they move from scene to scene respecting the defined transitions.

The normative structure of the OM of OperA gathers all the norms that are defined during the specification of roles, groups, and scene scripts. Norms are specified as expressions following the LCR

Figure 13. OperA organizational specification (adapted from Dignum, 2004)

(a) Social Structure: Role Dependencies.

(b) Interaction Structure: Scene and Transitions.

formalism introduced in (Dignum, 2004). Finally, the communicative structure describes the set of performatives and the domain concepts used in the interaction structure by the role enacting agents.

In Figure 12, we depict an organization metamodel for OperA. In Figure 13, we show a fragment of an organizational specification written in conformance to the OperA metamodel. The example is an agent organization for the realization of conferences. In Figure 13(a), we have a role dependency graph depicting some of the roles found in the conference organization. In Figure 13(b), we see the main interaction structure for the conference realization composed of scenes and transitions. In this collection, another example of an agent organization specified by means of OperA is presented in the Chapter XIII "Autonomous Agents Adopting Organizational Rules" by van der Vecht et al.

Discussion. We can notice that the OM of OperA copes with several organization modelling dimensions. Looking closely, we can perceive a vision of organizational modelling that resembles AGR and MOISE+ in structural aspects and ISLANDER in interactive and normative aspects. On the one hand, notions like role, groups and role relations are integral parts of AGR and MOISE+. On the other hand, the concepts of scenes, scenes scripts, ontology definitions, communicative acts and norms, all are presented in ISLANDER. Regarding functional aspects of organizations, OperA has the concept of objective that resembles the goal and task concepts of MOISE+ and TAEMS, but it is less developed than these.

Other Models and Extensions

The literature on organizational models is vast. Extensions to the models discussed in the previous sections plus other models are briefly mentioned below:

- AGRE (Agent, Group, Role, Environment) (Ferber, Michel & Baez, 2005) - an extension of AGR that takes into account physical and social environments. The main idea is that agents are situated in domains called *spaces*. The spaces can be physical (areas) or social (groups). In this collection, AGRE is also described in the Chapter III "Towards an Integral Approach of Organizations in Multi-Agent Systems" by Ferber, Statulat & Tanier.

- MOISE[Inst] (Gateau et al., 2005) - an extension of MOISE+ that allows for *Contextual Specifications* (*contexts* and transitions between contexts) and *Normative Specifications* (*norms* set) in the modelling of an MAS organization.

- ODML - *Organizational Design Modelling Language* (Horling & Lesser, 2004) - a minimalist organizational model that provides elements to model and evaluate structural aspects of organizations.

- STEAM - a *Shell for TEAMwork* (Tambe et al., 1999) - an organizational model in the context of teamwork. A MAS organization is modelled by means of two hierarchies: a role hierarchy composed of teams and sub-teams, and a hierarchy of plans and joint activities.

- AUML - *Agent UML* (Parunak & Odell, 2002) - an effort to extend the UML to cope with MAS development. Regarding organizational modelling the used meta-model is based on the AGR meta-model.

- MAS-ML - *MAS Modelling Language* (Silva, Choren & Lucena, 2004) - a modelling language that extends UML with elements of the TAO conceptual framework (Silva et al., 2003). Regarding organizational modelling, one of the distinguishing features of MAS-ML is that agent organizations technically are an extension of an *AgentClass* classifier. This means that agent organizations are conceived as kinds of agents.

Table 1. Organizational models comparison

Model	Modelling Dimensions							
	Structure	Interaction	Function	Norms	Environment	Evolution	Evaluation	Ontology
AGR	7	1	-	-	-	-	-	-
TAEMS	-	-	21	-	5	-	11	-
MOISE+	12	-	9	4	-	+	-	-
ISLANDER	6	20	-	2	-	-	-	6
OperA	11	19	3	3	-	-	-	+
AGRE	+	+	-	-	+	-	-	-
MOISE[Inst]	+	-	+	+	-	+	-	-
ODML	+	-	-	-	-	-	+	-
STEAM	+	-	+	-	-	-	-	-
AUML	+	+	+	-	+	-	-	-
MAS-ML	+	+	+	+	+	-	-	-

ORGANIZATIONAL MODELS COMPARISON

Given the modelling dimensions and the organizational models review, we summarize the discussion by showing the dimensions covered by each organizational model discussed in the previous section in a comparison table. After, we outline how this comparison table based on the dimensions can help us to proceed to a detailed comparison of the models based on the correspondence between their meta-models.

Dimensions-Based Comparison

In Table 1, we show how the modelling constructs found in organizational models reviewed are distributed among the modelling dimensions. The table is divided in two parts. In the first part, we have the organizational models that were reviewed in more detail. Below, there are the organizational models we have briefly mentioned at the end of the previous section. The columns represent the modelling dimensions. In the first part of the table, the numbers in the cells of the organizational models represent how many classes[8] we have found in the respective metamodels relative to a given dimension. This counting reveals approximately[9] the emphasis given by the organizational model for a particular modelling dimension. If the organizational model does not provide constructs in a given modelling dimension then we represent this fact by a minus sign '-'.

In the case of the organizational models in the inferior part of the table, we have not produced an explicit metamodel. Therefore, we are not able to provide an objective counting of the modelling constructs for each dimension. However, we have examined if the organizational model does support or not the modelling dimensions. This is represented in the table respectively by a plus sign '+' or by a minus sign '-'[10].

Given this picture, a first thing to remark is that the first four dimensions concentrate indeed the modelling constructs found in organizational models. Another remark is that the structural dimension is more frequent than the others, almost a consensus as a defining aspect of organization, being addressed in all organizational models reviewed but TAEMS. Regarding the four last dimensions, these have received less attention. Below, we further comment the coverage of each modelling dimension:

- *Organizational Structure* - in almost all models this is the primary modelling concern. The main modelling elements found were roles, groups, and relationships between them. The structure of roles and groups defines a system of possible positions where the agents should find a place to become a member of an agent organization.
- *Organizational Interactions* - found mainly in ISLANDER and OperA. In this respect, the models provide constructs to express the dynamic of communicative interactions between the agents (positioned in the social structure). Some constructs are interaction protocols, scenes and scene structures.
- *Organizational Function* - appeared with more emphasis in TAEMS, STEAM and MOISE+. In these models, (one of) the main concern is to provide means to specify procedures to achieve goals. In order to model this feature, we find in the models conceptual elements such as tasks or goals, missions and plans.
- *Organizational Norms* - described in term of deontic norms (regulate the behaviour of social entities: what they are allowed to do - direct or indirectly -, what they are obliged to do, etc.).

ISLANDER, OperA and MOISE[Inst] are representative examples of organizational models that provide mechanisms to specify normative structures.

- *Organizational Environment* - here the models provide means to describe elements lying in the topological space occupied by the agent organization and the way agents (positioned in the social structure, performing some task and/or in the course of some dialogical interaction, respecting some norms) are related to these elements. AGRE and MAS-ML are examples of organizational models (modelling techniques) that provide constructs to represent organization environment elements.

- *Organizational Evolution* - this is related to modelling the way organizations can change (their social, task decomposition, dialogical, and normative structures) in order to cope with changes in its purpose and/or environment. Among the organizational models reviewed, only MOISE+ and its extension MOISE[Inst] explicit address organization evolution issues.

- *Organizational Evaluation* - in order to modify some organization (re-organization) it is important to know how well the present organization is performing. Thus, some models have elements to specify means to assess some properties of an organization. Among these we have found TAEMS and ODML.

- *Organizational Ontology* - here we find ontologies used to ground the elements of the other dimensions as can be seen in the organizational models ISLANDER and OperA.

Correspondences-Based Comparison

A main trust in this chapter is that we can compare organizational models by analysing their coverage with regard to eight modelling dimensions. However, this is not enough when we want to know to what extent one organizational specification written in one organizational model can be expressed

Figure 14. Correspondences between AGR and MOISE+

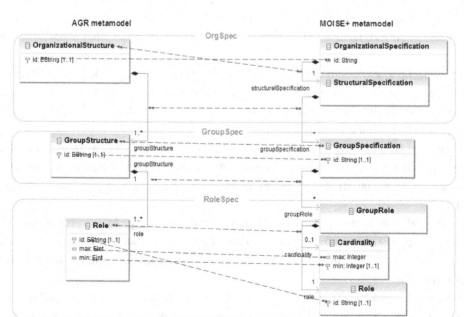

in another organizational model. As noted in the introduction, this is an important issue regarding the interoperability between two agent organizations with different underlying organizational models. In the sequence, we sketch our current work in this area.

Our main idea is that we can use some results from *Model Driven Engineering* and *Ontology Engineering* (Coutinho, Brandão, Sichman & Boissier, 2007) to formally analyse the correspondences between different organizational models and automate the process of translation between organizational specifications, when this translation is feasible (Coutinho, Brandão, Sichman & Boissier, 2008). Then, the correspondences between organizational models, or the actual translation between organizational specifications, can be used by the agents working in the context of different organizational models to interoperate (organizational interoperability).

In order to make the discussion more concrete, let us analyse a case where we can make correspondences between organizational models. If we look at Table 1, we can see that AGR and MOISE+ both address the structural dimension to a certain degree. Then, we can look further and see if their underlying conceptualizations can be put in correspondence. Taking into account the metamodels presented in the previous sections, we can make the correspondence model between AGR and MOISE+ as presented in Figure 14.

In Figure 14, we can see three main correspondence clusters between AGR and MOISE+ w.r.t. the structural dimension. Firstly, the concept of *Organizational Structure* in AGR corresponds to *Organizational Specification* and *Structural Specification* in MOISE+. The rationale is that AGR is committed with a structural view of organization while MOISE+ consider more dimensions; this makes AGR treat two concepts that are separate in MOISE+ (the specification of the organization as a whole and the specification of only the structural dimension of the organization) as only one concept (the specification of the structure of the organization). Secondly, the idea of *Group Structure* in AGR is similar to the concept of *Group Specification* in MOISE+. Both concepts aggregate the concept of *Role*. However, in MOISE+ the notion of role is more detailed. This leads us to the third cluster of correspondences: in MOISE+ there are the notions of *Group Role* (role that can be played in a group) and of *Role* (role independent of any group that helps to define a general hierarchy of constraints that further is associated to specific groups). In AGR there is only the definition of role inside a group, i.e., roles are always defined inside groups. In conclusion, we can assert that the structural view of AGR, to some extent, is encompassed by the structural view of MOISE+.

This type of analysis can be formalized in *correspondence models* (Bernstein, 2003) that can be used to automate the process of translation of organizational specifications. Also, correspondence models serve as the basic input for proposing *integrations* between organizational models (Potinger & Bernstein, 2003). Then, being given these correspondence models, or integrations of organizational models, the idea is that they can be used by the agents to interoperate. However, one important question regarding the correspondences is to assess how reliably they reflect the real semantics of the organizational models. This is a very difficult problem. In our research we are trying to ground the mappings taking into account their formal definitions and operational semantics of the models w.r.t. their reference implementations. Another important question is how to cope with models that address different modelling dimensions. This problem will limit the interoperation between existing agents working in different organizational settings. However, by knowing that organizations can be specified along different modelling dimensions we can think in building agent architectures that tries to flexibly operate in the various organizational contexts.

RELATED WORK

Some related research (Mao & Yu, 2005; Horling & Lesser, 2005; Grossi et al., 2005) present reviews of organizational concepts, paradigms and dimensions that can be to some extend compared to the modelling dimensions presented in this chapter.

In (Mao & Yu, 2005), the authors propose a taxonomy of organizational and social concepts found in the literature about methodologies and models for Agent Oriented Software Engineering (AOSE). The taxonomy is divided in four *construct levels*: the "single agent", the "two agents", the "two or more agents acting in a coordinated way", and the "all agents" levels. In the "single agent" level, the concepts are: *role*, *position* and *actor* (abstract characterizations of agents in an organizational context); *responsibility* and *goal* (functionalities of a role); *permission*, *right* and *resource* (requirements of a role); *activity*, *plan* and *task* (behaviours of a role). In the "two agents" level, the authors cite the concepts of *dependency* and *interaction protocol* (structural and behavioural relationships between individual agents). In the "two or more agents acting in a coordinated way" level the concepts presented are: *group* and *group structure* (decomposition of organizations); *common goal*, *joint intention* and *commitment* (behavioural information of a group). Finally, in the "all agents" level, the authors describe the concepts of *organization* (collection of roles, relationships, and institutionalized interaction patterns); *organization rule*, *social rule* and *interaction rule* (global constraints); *organization structure* and *organization pattern* (classes of organization and control regime). Compared with the organizational modelling dimensions presented in the previous sections, this four level taxonomy is (nearly) an orthogonal way of classifying organizational modelling abstractions regarding MAS. The four levels of Mao & Yu (2005) stress aggregation stages inside organizations (one agent, two agents, group of agents, all agents) as the categorization framework. In another perspective, our eight organizational dimensions divide organizational abstractions according to their intended modelling purpose. For example, the concepts of role (one agent), dependency (two agents), group (several agents), organization structure (all agents) comprise the structural dimension discussed in the previous section. Another example is the permission and right (one agent), organization rule, social rule and interaction rule (all agents) as concepts of the normative dimension.

In (Horling & Lesser, 2005), the authors make a survey of organizational paradigms applied to MAS. They identify *hierarchies*, *holarchies*, *coalitions*, *teams*, *congregations*, *societies*, *federations*, and *matrix organizations* as the major organizational strategies presented in the research literature. Comparing with the organizational modelling dimensions, we believe that the organizational paradigms of (Horling & Lesser, 2005) are general patterns of existing/proposed agent organizations. On the other hand, the modelling dimensions are different aspects or perspectives in which organizations can be represented. This being the case, one agent organization that follow some paradigm (e.g., team or society) can possibly be represented in regard to the eight organization modelling dimensions identified in the previous section.

In (Grossi et al., 2005) and also in Chapter VIII, "Structural Aspects of Organizations" by Grossi & Dignum, in this collection, the authors argue that organizational structures in MAS should be seen along at least three dimensions, namely the *power*, *coordination*, and *control dimensions*. In their analysis, the authors conceive an organizational structure as the necessary product of task decomposition to pursue global objectives. Global objectives are decomposed in sub-objectives, and these define agent roles within the organization. Agent roles are conceived in terms of three basic notions: *objectives*, *norms* and *information*. The power dimension describes how agent roles are related regarding delegation of goals (goals that come from the objectives that define the role). Delegation consists in the possibility for an agent enacting a role to transfer a given goal to a subordinate one. In the control dimension, agent roles are related by means of control relations. A control relation states monitoring activities that triggers appropriate reactions to objectives failures and norms violations. The coordination dimension, in a simple way, is reduced to the question: who informs whom? In other words, the coordination dimension describes relations between agent roles regarding information (actual state of the organization) access and sharing. Given this brief description, the power, coordination and control dimensions can be regarded as an alternative, more restricted and fine-grained way of classifying organizational structures. The power dimension can be seen as contained in the structural dimension of the previous section. The control dimension is something that mixes aspects from the dimensions we call functional and normative. Finally, the coordination dimension can be compared to the interactive dimension.

CONCLUSION AND PERSPECTIVES

In this chapter, we have discussed the notions of agent organization and organizational model w.r.t. open computational MASs. An agent organization was defined as a system composed of autonomous agents bounded by actions and interactions. In this context, organization refers to patterns of actions and interactions towards some global purpose. An organizational model is the conjunction of both a conceptualization of organization and syntax used to write organizational specifications prescribing desired agent organizations behaviour. Along these lines, we have identified eight modelling dimensions that can be useful to analyse and compare the expressive power of organizational models. The modelling dimensions were identified after an analysis of the notion of system in general and a review of eleven organizational models proposals reported in the literature.

Regarding the modelling dimensions, the main conclusion is that structure (based on roles and group hierarchies), interaction (described as networks of scenes and protocols), function (goals decomposed in plans) and norms (obligations, permissions) are the organizational aspects that have received more emphasis in the models analysed in this work. These aspects are followed by organizational environment (non-autonomous resources), ontology (conceptualizations), evolution (organization change) and evaluation (performance measurement).

Among all dimensions, the organizational structure has appeared as one of the core aspects in the organizational models. All models (except TAEMS that emphasizes function) provide concepts to model organizational structure. A tentative explanation we offer to this pattern is the following. There are basically two ways of analysing a system: as a white box and as a black box. Seeing a system as a white box leads us to basic notion of system structure (influence relations between its components); we need structure to define the other aspects. On the other hand, if we initially regard a system as a black box, the basic notion is then the idea of function and function decomposition. In this way, function hides structure. However, at some level of function decomposition some structure has to show up to perform the tasks. This structure can be explicitly represented, or not (as is the case of TAEMS).

By their turn, environment and evolution (related to the notions of situatedness and adaptiveness, respectively) are among the dimension less explored in the organizational models reviewed.

Finally, we visualize two main directions for future research. First, we need to study the interplay among the modelling dimensions. Along this line, an important question is how to delimit the scope of organizational modelling: should an organizational model span the whole spectrum of dimensions we have identified or it has to be restricted to some core interconnected dimensions? What are these dimensions? Second, we also need to deepen our understanding about the concepts and mechanisms composing each dimension. In reality, this is already being done by complementary research efforts receiving diverse names such as coordination, normative systems, electronic institutions, etc. The challenge is then to integrate these efforts with the comprehensive view provided by organizational models.

ACKNOWLEDGMENT

Luciano R. Coutinho was supported by FAPEMA, Brazil, grant 127/04 and CAPES, Brazil, grant 1511/06-8. Jaime S. Sichman was partially supported by CNPq, Brazil, grants 304605/2004-2, 482019/2004-2, 506881/2004-0 and USP-COFECUB, grant 98/-4. Olivier Boissier was partially supported by USP-COFECUB, grant 98/-4.

REFERENCES

Ackoff, R. (1999). *Ackoff's best, His classic writings on management*. New York, USA: John Wiley & Sons, Inc.

Bernstein, P. (2003). Applying model management to classical meta data problems. *Proceedings of the 2003 CIDR Conference* (pp. 209-220), Asilomar, CA: Retrieved April 30, 2008, from http://www-db.cs.wisc.edu/cidr/2003Proceedings.zip

Bunge, M. (1977). *Treatise on basic philosophy, Ontology I: The furniture of the world*. Dordrecht-Holland: D. Reidel.

Bunge, M. (1979). *Treatise on basic philosophy, Ontology II: A world of systems*. Dordrecht-Holland: D. Reidel.

Bunge, M. (2004). How does it work? The search for exploratory mechanisms. *Philosophy of the Social Sciences, 34*(2), 182-210.

Castelfranchi, C. (1998). Modelling social action for AI agents. *Artificial Intelligence, 103*, 157-182.

Coutinho, L., Brandão, A., Sichman, J., & Boissier, J. (2007). Organizational interoperability in open multiagent systems – an approach based on metamodels and ontologies. In Guizzardi, G. & Farias, C. (Eds.), *Anais II Workshop on Ontologies and Metamodeling in Software and Data Engineering, WOMSDE 2007* (pp. 109-120). João Pessoa, Brasil.

Coutinho, L., Brandão, A., Sichman, J. & Boissier, J. (2008). Model-driven integration of organizational models. *Paper presented at the Ninth International Workshop on Agent Oriented Software,* held at AAMAS 2008, Estoril, Portugal.

Decker, K. (1996). TAEMS: A framework for environment centered analysis & design of coordination mechanisms. In O'Hare, G. & Jennings, N. (Eds), *Foundations of Distributed Artificial Intelligence* (pp. 429-448). Wiley Inter-Science.

Dietz, J. (2006). *Enterprise ontology.* Berlin: Springer.

Dignum, V., & Dignum, F. (2001). Modelling agent societies: co-ordination frameworks and institutions. In Brazdil, P. & Jorge, A. (Eds.), *Progress in Artificial Intelligence, 10th Portuguese Int. Conf. on Artificial Intelligence, EPIA'01,* LNAI 2258 (pp. 191–204). Berlin: Springer.

Dignum, V. (2004). *A model for organizational interaction: based on agents, founded in logic.* Doctoral dissertation, Utrecht University, Utrecht.

Erdur, R. C., Dikenelli, O., Seylan, I., & Gürcan, O. (2004). Semantically federating multi-agent organizations. In Gleizes, M-P., Omicini, A. & Zambonelli, F. (Eds.), *Engineering Societies in the Agents World V, ESAW 2004,* LNCS 3451 (pp. 74-89). Berlin: Springer.

Esteva, E., et al. (2004). AMELI: An agent-based middleware for electronic institutions. In *Third Inter. Joint Conference on Autonomous Agents and Multiagent Systems, AAMAS 2004* (pp. 236–243). New York: IEEE Press.

Esteva, M., Padget, J., & Sierra, C. (2002). Formalizing a language for institutions and norms. In Meyer, J-J. C. & Tambe, M. (Eds.), *Intelligent Agents VII, ATAL 2001,* LNAI 2333 (pp. 348–366). Berlin: Springer.

Ferber, J., & Gutknecht, O. (1998). A meta-model for the analysis and design of organizations in multi-agent systems. In *Third Inter. Conference on Multi Agent Systems, ICMAS'98* (pp. 128-135). IEEE Press.

Ferber, J., Gutknecht, O., & Michel, F. (2004). From agents to organizations: an organizational view of multi-agent systems. In Giorgini, P., Müller, J. P. & Odell, J (Eds.), *Agent Oriented Software Engineering IV,* LNCS 2935 (pp. 443-459). Berlin: Springer.

Ferber, J., Michel, F.. & Baez, J. (2005). AGRE: Integrating environments with organizations. In Weyns, D., Parunak, H.; Michel, F. (Eds.), *Environments for Multi-Agent Systems, E4MAS 2004,* LNCS 3374 (pp. 48–56). Berlin: Springer.

Gasser, L. (2001). Perspectives on organizations in multi-agent systems. In *Multi-Agent Systems and Applications, 9th ECCAI Advanced Course ACAI 2001 and Agent Link's 3rd European Agent Systems Summer School, EASSS 2001,* LNAI 2086 (pp. 1-16). Berlin: Springer.

Gâteau, B. et al. (2005). MOISE[Inst]: an organizational model for specifying rights and duties of autonomous agents. In *1st International Workshop on Coordination and Organisation, CoOrg'05,* Namur, Belgium.

Grossi, D., et al. (2005). Foundations of organizational structures in multiagent systems. In *Forth Inter. Joint Conference on Autonomous Agents and Multiagent Systems, AAMAS 2005* (pp. 690–697). Utrecht: ACM Press.

Guizzardi, G. (2007). On Ontology, ontologies, conceptualizations, modeling languages, and (meta)models. In Vasilecas, O., Eder, J & Caplinskas, A (Eds.), *Databases and Information Systems IV - Selected Papers from the Seventh International Baltic Conference DB&IS'2006* (pp. 18-39). Amsterdam: IOS Press.

Gutknecht, O., & Ferber, J. (2000). The MADKIT agent platform architecture. In Wagner, T. & Rana, O. (Eds.), *Revised Papers from the International Workshop on Infrastructure for Multi-Agent Systems:*

Infrastructure for Agents, Multi-Agent Systems, and Scalable Multi-Agent Systems, LNCS 1887 (pp. 48–55). Berlin: Springer.

Horling, B., & Lesser, V. (2004). Quantitative organizational models for large-scale agent systems. In Ishida, T., Gasser, L. & Nakashima, H. (Eds.), *Massively Multi-Agent Systems I,, MMAS 2004*, LNCS 3446 (pp. 121–135). Berlin: Springer.

Horling, B., & Lesser, V., (2005). A Survey of Multi-Agent Organizational Paradigms. *The Knowledge Engineering Review*, 19(4), 281-316.

Hübner, J., Sichman, J. & Boissier, O. (2002). A model for the structural, functional, and deontic specification of organizations in multiagent systems. In Bittencourt, G. & Ramalho, G. L. (Eds.), *Advances in Artificial Intelligence, 16th Brazilian Symposium on AI, SBIA'02*, LNAI 2507 (pp. 118–128). Berlin: Springer.

Hübner, J., Sichman, J. & Boissier, O. (2006). S-MOISE+: A middleware for developing organised multi-agent systems. In Boissier, O., et al. (Eds.), *Coordination, Organizations, Institutions, and Norms in Multi-Agent Systems*, LNCS 3913 (pp. 64-78). Springer: Berlin.

Lesser, V., et al. (2004). Evolution of the GPGP/TAEMS domain independent coordination framework. *Journal of AAMAS*, 9, 87–143.

Mao, X., & Yu, E. (2005). Organizational and social concepts in agent oriented software engineering. In Odell, J., Giorgini, P. & Müller, J. (Eds.), *Agent Oriented Software Engineering V, AOSE 2004*, LNCS Vol. 3382 (pp. 1–15). Berlin: Springer.

Parunak, H., & Odell, J. (2002). Representing social structures in UML. In Wooldridge, M. J., Weiß, G. & Ciancarini, P. (Eds.) *Agent-Oriented Software Engineering II, AOSE 2001*, LNCS 2222 (pp. 1–16). Berlin: Springer.

Pickel, A. (2004). Systems and mechanism, A symposium on Mario Bunge's philosophy of Social Science. *Philosophy of the Social Sciences*, 34(2), 169-181.

Pottinger, R., & Bernstein, P. (2003). Merging models based on given correspondences. Freytag, J. C. et al. (Eds.), *VLDB 2003, Proceedings of 29th International Conference on Very Large Data Bases*, (pp. 862-873). Berlin, Germany: Morgan Kaufmann.

Schmidt, D. C. (2006). Model-driven engineering. *IEEE Computer*, February, 25–31.

Scott, W. R. (1998). *Organizations: rational, natural and open systems*. Upper Saddle River, NJ: Prentice Hall.

Silva, V. et al. (2003). Taming agents and objects in software engineering. In Garcia, A. et al. (Eds.), *Software Engineering for Large-Scale MAS*, LNCS 2603 (pp. 1–26). Berlin: Springer.

Silva, V., Choren, R. & Lucena, C. (2004). A UML based approach for modeling and implementing multi-agent systems. In *Third Inter. Joint Conference on Autonomous Agents and Multiagent Systems, AAMAS 2004* (pp. 914–921). New York: IEEE Press.

Tambe, M. et al. (1999). Building agent teams using an explicit teamwork model and learning. *Artificial Intelligence*, 110, 215–239.

Timasheff, N. (1952). The basic concepts of sociology. *The American Journal of Sociology, 58*(2), 176-186.

Wand, Y., & Weber, R. (1990). *An ontological model of an information system. IEEE Transactions on Software Engineering, 16*(11), 1282-1292.

Zambonelli, F., Jennings, N.. & Wooldridge, M. (2003). Developing multiagent systems: the Gaia methodology. *ACM Trans. Software Engineering and Methodology, 12*(3) 317–370.

KEY TERMS

Agent Organization: A Multi-Agent System (computational system), or one of its sub-systems, possibly open and which was designed and operates in a way similar to human organizations. Compared to human organizations, agent organizations are characterized by specific goals and formalized social structures.

Modelling Dimension: A coherent class of modelling constructs found in a modelling language. The modelling dimensions are defined taking into account the main aspects in which a subject can be modelled. In the case of organizational models, we can identify four commonly occurring modelling dimensions: organizational structure, organizational interaction, organizational functions and organizational norms.

Organizational Functions: Also called "functional dimension", it is a modelling dimension composed of constructs to represent global goals and goal decompositions (plans) to be accomplished by an agent organization.

Organizational Interaction: Also called "interactive dimension", it is a modelling dimension that is formed by constructs to represent standardized actions and interactions involving the elements from the structural and functional dimensions. Some constructs found in this dimension are interaction protocols, scenes and scene structures.

Organizational Model: Modelling languages used to formally specify agent organizations. Organizational models provide a conceptualization of organizations for Muti-Agent Systems and a syntax to write specific models. In an abstract way, the syntax can be expressed by means of an organizational metamodel.

Organizational Norms: Also called "normative dimension", it is composed of constructs to further regulate and show how organizational structure (time independent relations), organizational interaction (standardized functioning) and organizational functions are interrelated. The name "normative" is due to the fact that in the existing organizational model the concepts in this dimension are described in term of deontic norms (i.e., statements that regulate the behaviour of social entities: what they are allowed to do - direct or indirectly -, what they are obliged to do, etc.).

Organizational Structure: Also called "structural dimension", it is a modelling dimension that gathers constructs to represent what aspects of the structure of an agent organization have to be invariant through time. The main constructs found in it are roles, groups, and relationships between them.

ENDNOTES

[1] All system concepts discussed are defined taking into account the *systemism* philosophy proposed by Bunge (1977, 1979, 2004). Specifically, we follow *systemism* by the fact that it has been used both in *Information Systems Engineering* (Wand & Weber, 1990) and in *Social Sciences* (Dietz, 2006; Pickel 2004) as a basic ontology of reality when analysing and design computational systems and human social systems (including organizations), respectively. An alternative (but compatible in general lines) conceptualization of systems is found in (Ackoff, 1999).

[2] http://www.omg.org/technology/documents/formal/uml.htm (last access April 30, 2008).

[3] http://www.eclipse.org/modeling/emf/ (last access: April 29, 2008)

[4] In a complete organizational metamodel, we can also have contextual constraints written is some declarative constraint language like OCL (http://www.omg.org/technology/documents/formal/ocl.htm ; last access: April 29, 2008). In order to simplify the discussion, we omit any constraint expressions in the organizational metamodels presented.

[5] http://www.omg.org/technology/documents/formal/mof.htm (last access: April 29, 2008)

[6] http://wiki.eclipse.org/index.php/KM3 (last access: April 29, 2008)

[7] http://www.eclipse.org/ (last access: April 29, 2008)

[8] In the case of Enumerations that represent sub-types of a given class, we have counted every literal as a new class. For example, in the metamodel of TAEMS (Figure 6), the enumeration QAF denotes sub-types of Tasks; in this case each literal of QAF was counted as an element of the functional dimension. Also, QAF denotes a concept that can be classified as pertaining to evaluation; the each literal was counted as an element of the evaluation dimension.

[9] This is not the best approach but it permits the reader to have a numerical idea of how each organizational model cover the dimensions. One important weakness of the approach of counting the classes is that there are some classes having textual attributes that hide structural complexity. For example, in the case of the normative dimension, the numbers gives us an impression that MOISE+ is more elaborated in this dimension. However, this is not the case. The normative classes in OperA and ISLANDER permit norm expressions in textual form and this implicit structure is not captured in the metamodels. Thus, in the specific case of the normative dimension the reader must take this fact into account.

[10] A plus signal also occurs in the cells MOISE+/evolution and OperA/ontology because the models provide modelling constructs in these dimensions but the constructs are not present in the metamodels we have showed.

Chapter III
Towards an Integral Approach of Organizations in Multi–Agent Systems

Jacques Ferber
LIRMM – University of Montpellier II, France

Tiberiu Stratulat
LIRMM – University of Montpellier II, France

John Tranier
LIRMM – University of Montpellier II, France

ABSTRACT

In this chapter, we stress the importance of thinking a MAS in all its aspects (agents, environment, interactions, organizations, and institutions), using a more integral vision. We show that a genuine organizational approach has to take into account both the environment and the institutional part of MAS societies. Then, we propose the MASQ (Multi-Agent System based on Quadrants) meta-model, which constitutes an abstraction of the various aspects of an OCMAS (Organization Centered Multi-Agent Systems), extending AGR (Agent/Group/Role). MASQ is based on a four-quadrant framework, where the analysis and design of a system is performed along two axes: an interior/exterior dimension and an individual/collective dimension. We give a conceptual definition of this approach and we will show that it is possible to apply it to practical models.

1. INTRODUCTION

Multi-agent systems (MAS) are often considered as collections of agents that interact together to co-ordinate their behavior to achieve some individual or collective goal. The research in MAS domain focuses therefore on the study of the agent-based interaction, which roughly could be divided in agent-centered interaction and mediated interaction. Agent-centered interaction is the most known and well understood as the works of FIPA (2005), the standardizing body of the MAS domain, reflect it. The interaction is considered from the perspective of a single agent communicating with another agent in isolation. The research in mediated interaction tries to complement this perspective and concentrates rather on distributed and social aspects, when many agents are in interaction. Mediated interaction is based on the idea of structuring the interaction by adding a sort of middleware responsible to manage the complexity of the interactions between many agents[1]. Depending on the kind of interaction, we can further have two types of mediated interaction: environment-based interaction and organization-centered MAS (OCMAS) interaction.

In the case of environment-based interaction research has concentrated on the physical distributed aspects of interaction. The environment is considered as a first-class abstraction at the same level as the agents, and has its own state and laws of change (Weyns, Omicini & Odell, 2007). The main reason of using an environment as a medium of interaction is to control (independently of the agents) the effects of external events or parallel actions produced simultaneously by two or more agents (Ferber & Müller, 1996). The works on environment-based interaction concentrate mainly on how to represent objects in an environment, how to specify the actions of agents and the various laws of change, and how to execute the overall system dynamics. The other problems in environment–based interaction are similar then to those of distributed systems: openness, security, coherence, load-balancing, etc.

In the case of OCMAS, an emphasis has been put on the social aspects of interaction and inspiration comes from human forms of organization. It becomes more and more accepted that the interaction can be specified and structured in terms of organizations, roles, groups and norms (Dignum, 2004; Ferber & Gutknecht, 1998; Ferber, Gutknecht & Michel, 2004). In this view, an organization is seen as a collection of agents that can be considered together in groups, playing roles or regulated by organizational rules. For instance, in AGR model (Ferber & Gutknecht, 1998) the agents can interact only inside a group in which they play roles. An agent can play one or many roles and enter into one or many groups. A role is a general concept to which a MAS architect can associate various semantics (i.e. rights, obligations, norms, powers, patterns of behaviour, etc.). Similarly, in the family of MOISE models (Hübner, Sichman & Boissier, 2007) an organization is considered coherently under its functional, structural and deontic dimensions (for all these aspects, see also Chapter II, *Modelling Dimensions for Multi-Agent Systems Organizations,* by Coutinho et al.).

Although the initial studies of organizational interaction have not suggested explicitly the use of an organizational environment, the specification of an organization is made however independently of the participating agents and therefore at the execution time it is necessary to introduce a way to handle it. For instance, an organization could be designed architecturally as an organizational layer to keep trace of the events and information that are organizationally important. In MadKit (2004) the core layer (kernel) which implements the organizational environment has as basic functionalities to let agents join groups, associate roles to agents and let only members to the same group to interact. Another way to represent an organization is to reify it at the same level with other agents within a socially constructed agent (Boella & Van der Torre, 2004). The concept of organization becomes then a first class abstraction with a representation on its own (i.e. an organization can have its own goals and beliefs).

In addition to organizational concepts, recent researches have shown the importance of other social concepts to MAS. The works on electronic institutions (Noriega, 1997; Esteva, Rosell, Rodrıguez-Aguilar & Arcos, 2004), similarly to those in OCMAS, reflect the same idea of passing through a middleware to structure the social interaction, the term institution referencing the works of North (1990) in economics. In Islander, agents can enter into "dialogical" interactions which are grounded in institutions. An institution is designed architecturally as an independent layer. Inside an institution, to each agent corresponds a governor and the interaction is defined through protocols that are called *scenes*. An institution is characterized by a set of states and the scenes characterize the transitions between states when some conditions are satisfied. Norms are also used to define some deontic states and identify their violation.

Another stream of research that makes use of the term institution takes its inspiration from the philosophical work of Searle. According to (Searle, 1995) an institution establishes the rules of how commonly a human society attributes a social meaning to what happens in the physical reality. More precisely, an institution is defined as a set of *count-as* rules (also known as constitutive rules) that link facts from the brute reality to institutional facts. Jones and Sergot (1996) formalized the count-as operator within the perspective of institutionalized power, where agents acting in specific roles are "empowered" to create or modify institutional facts. In (Artikis, Pitt & Sergot, 2002) the concept of institutionalized power is adapted to what the authors call "electronic" or "computational" societies. For instance, they propose to associate to each member of a society a social state describing its institutional powers, permissions, obligations, sanctions, and roles. Then, according to the social laws governing the institution, the initial social state and the externally observable events, they propose a computational framework, based on event calculus, to compute the social state at a certain moment of time (see also Chapter XIV, *Formal Specification of Artificial Institutions Specification Using Event Calculus*, by Fornara and Colombetti). More recent works try to clarify the various aspects of the constitutive rules (procedural, declarative, normative) and use them to implement normative agent systems (Boella & Van der Torre, 2004; Cardoso & Oliveira, 2007) and show the connection to social commitments (Grossi, D., Dignum, F., Dastani, M. & Royakkers, 2005; Fornara, Viganò, Verdicchio & Colombetti, 2007)

However, these works on institutions seem to ignore the importance of environment and actions (Weyns, Van Dyke Parunak, Michel, Holvoet, & Ferber, 2005), apart from the communications (Fornara, Vigano, & Colombetti, 2007). On the other part, researches on action in environments did not grant much attention to organizational and institutional issues. Consequently, it seems that both organizations and environments should be reconciled in a general framework in order to be able to design MAS in all their dimensions.

In this chapter, we will describe a general framework and an abstract model of what constitutes a first step towards an integral view of multi-agent systems. This approach, that is called MASQ (Multi-Agent Systems based on Quadrants) is based on a four-quadrant approach and is derived from the AQAL model of Wilber (2001), which is a comprehensive map of (human) social systems. MASQ as we will see considers equally the concepts of actions, environments, organizations and institutions and propose to integrate them in the same conceptual framework.

2. AGR AND BEYOND: ADDING ENVIRONMENTS TO ORGANIZATION

In this section we present the AGR family of models, which have been thoroughly used to design organization centered MAS.

2.1. Organization Centered MAS

Organization centered MAS, or OCMAS for short, contrary to standard MAS which are oriented towards agents, are built according to the following principles (Ferber, Gutknecht & Michel, 2004):

- **Principle 1:** The organizational level in MAS describes the "what" and not the "how". The organizational level should impose a structure into the pattern of agents' activities, but does not describe how agents behave.
- **Principle 2:** No agent description and therefore no mental issues at the organizational level. The organizational level should not say anything about the way agents would interpret this level. Thus, reactive agents as well as intentional agents may act in an organization.
- **Principle 3:** An organization provides a way for partitioning a MAS, each partition (or groups, spaces, etc.) constitutes a context of interaction for agents. Thus, a group is an organizational unit in which all members are able to interact freely.

Therefore, an organization may be seen as a dynamic framework where agents may be considered a kind of autonomous components. Designing systems at the organizational level may leave open some implementation issues such as the choice of building the right agent to play a specific role.

2.2. From AGR to AGRE: Adding Environments to Organizations

In order to show how these principles may be actualized in a computational model, we have proposed the Agent-Group-Role model, or AGR for short (Ferber, 2004) also known as the Aalaadin model (Ferber & Gutknecht, 1998) for historical reasons, which complies with the organization centered general principles that we have proposed in the previous section. The AGR model is based on three primitive concepts, *agent*, *group* and *role*, which are structurally connected and cannot be constructed from other primitives.

- **Agent:** an agent is an active, communicating entity playing *roles* within *groups*. An agent may hold multiple roles, and may be member of several groups. An important characteristic of the AGR model is that no constraints are placed upon the architecture of an agent or about its mental capabilities. Thus, an agent may be as reactive as an ant, or as clever as a human being.
- **Group:** a group is a set of agents sharing some common characteristics. A group is used as a context for a pattern of activities, and is used for partitioning organizations. Two agents may communicate if and only if they belong to the same group, but an agent may belong to several groups. This feature will allow us to give the definition of organizational structures.
- **Role:** the role is the abstract representation of a functional position of an agent in a group. An agent must play a role in a group, but an agent may play several roles. Roles are local to groups, and a role must be requested by an agent. A role can be played by several agents.

Figure 1. A simplified UML representation of AGR

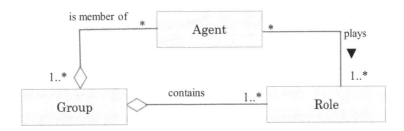

The simplicity of the AGR model comes from its minimalism and its generic aspect. There is only a minimal set of concepts to describe the main aspects of organizations. In AGR, by defining its groups, its roles and their relations, an organization may be seen as a framework for activities and interactions. By avoiding the strictly "agent-centered" approach, and by focusing on the organization, it may be possible to describe an application at an abstract level. Organizations can be seen as dynamic frameworks (where 'framework' is used in its object-oriented meaning), where agents may be placed in the 'holes' of the framework, where roles of the organization stand for the 'holes'. An organization can then be described only from its structure, i.e. the way groups and roles are arranged to form a whole. Several diagrams may be used to describe an organization in the AGR context.

The AGR meta-model is represented in Figure 1 in UML (to see a view of the complete metamodel, see Chapter II, *Modelling Dimensions forAgent Organizations*, by Coutinho et al.). A group type (or group structure), situated at the organizational level describes a particular type of group, how a group is constituted, what are its roles, its communication language, and the possible norms that apply to this type of group. A group is thus a kind of instance of a group type. A role type is part of the description of a group structure and describes the expected behavior of an agent playing that role. Role types may be described as in (Zambonelli, Jennings & Wooldridge, 2003) by attributes such as the cardinality (how many agents may play that role). It is also possible to describe interaction protocols and structural constraints between roles. A structural constraint describes a relationship between roles that are defined at the organizational level and are imposed to all agents. A role, which is part of a group, is an instance of a role type defined for an agent. We can see the role as a representative of an agent or as a kind of social body that an agent plays when it is a member of a group, the interface by which an agent is able to communicate and more generally to perform actions in a group.

Several notations may be used to represent organizations. In (Ferber, Gutknecht & Michel, 2004) we have proposed a set of diagrams to represent both static and dynamic aspects of organizations, such as the "cheese-board" diagram where a group is represented as an oval that looks like a board. Roles are represented as hexagons. Agents are represented as skittles that stand on the board and sometimes go through the board when they belong to several groups. Figure 2 represents a classical organization of a program committee for a conference. It can be noted that the "submission group" is composed of authors and of one submission receiver, which happens to be also the program chairman. Members of the program committee may define reviewers groups that they coordinate. It is clear from this diagram that agents may belong to different groups: a committee member may be a reviewing manager of an evaluation group *and* an author submitting a paper.

However, another very important concept, usually absent from the models described in section 2.1, and more generally in most OCMAS (see for instance the MOISE family of models in (Hübner, Sichman

Figure 2. The cheese-board diagram for describing organizations in AGR

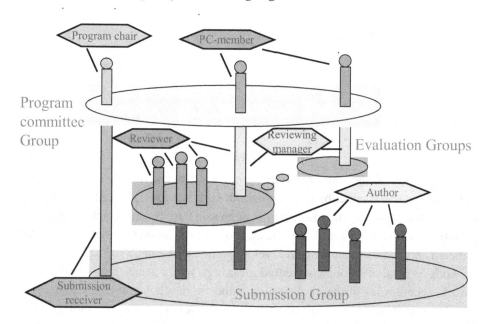

& Boissier, 2007)), is the concept of environment, which is the corner stone of interactions between agents, and more specifically situated agents. Several extensions of AGR have been proposed to integrate the environment. For instance, the model proposed in (Odell et al, 2002) consists in directly associating environments to groups, as it is shown on Figure 3. However, this extensions did not really solve all questions related to the integration of environments with organizations. Several issues about the relation that exists between an agent and its environment remain unsolved. For instance, the concept of body, i.e. the part of the agent that performs an action in an environment, is not properly analyzed.

This is why it is important to go further in defining what an agent is. An agent should be thought as having two parts: a mind (or brain) and a body which may be either a "physical body" in an environment, or a "social body" (a role) in an organization. This is what has been proposed in (Ferber, Michel, & Baez, 2005) with the AGRE model, an extension of AGR (E stands for 'Environment'), which integrates the physical and the social aspects of agents (fig. 4). In AGRE, an agent possesses a set of bodies[2]. Social

Figure 3. AGR extension with environment proposed by Parunak and Odell

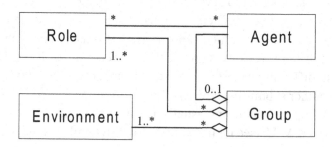

Figure 4. UML diagram of the AGRE model

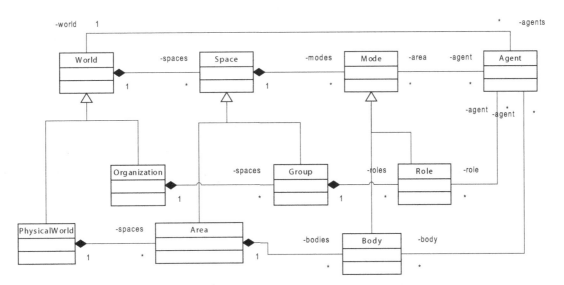

bodies, which may be considered as social interfaces to act in groups, are called *roles*, to be congruent with AGR. Likewise, *physical bodies* are seen as physical interfaces to act in an *area*. More generally *bodies* are social interfaces to act in *spaces*.

In AGRE, a *world* proposes the required primitives that are necessary for an agent to enter a space and get its bodies.

2.3. Limits of the AGR Family of Models

Approaches such as AGR and AGRE have shown their interest for designing MAS and building agent-based development frameworks such as MadKit (2004). While providing an important structuring framework for describing and designing MAS organizations, AGR and AGRE, lack to integrate norms and institutions in a simple and clean way. On the organizational aspect, AGRE has abstracted the concept of groups by introducing spaces, thus providing for a neat abstraction of both physical and social spaces. However, AGRE does not provide an action theory which would take into account concurrent actions. In both AGR and AGRE, it has always been clear that these models are based on OCMAS principles (see above) that do not say anything about mental issues. Still, without contradicting these principles, it is important to be able to take into account agent's mental states into a general framework, in order, not to impose a specific architecture for agents, but to be able to integrate agents with actions and their environment.

We will overcome these limits by proposing a new framework which will extend AGR and its family of models.

3. MASQ AS A FOUR-QUADRANT APPROACH

We propose a new framework for designing OCMAS, called MASQ, which provides a two-dimensional heuristic description of the complex relationships within social systems (Phan & Ferber, 2007; Tranier

Figure 5. The four-quadrant map

Interior-Individual (I-I)	Exterior-Individual (E-I)
Subjectivity	*Objectivity*
<mental states, emotions, beliefs, desires, intentions,...>	<agent behavior, object, process, physical entities >
Interiority	Exteriority
Interior-Collective (I-C)	**Exterior-Collective (E-C)**
intersubjectivity	*Interobjectivity*
<shared knowledge, social norms, conventions, ontologies, collective representations>	< Environment, organizations, reified social structures, social facts>
Noosphere	Sociosphere (social structures)

2007). This approach, which is loosely based on the work of Wilber (2001), resides on a decomposition along two axes: the *individual vs. collective* perspectives on one side, and the *interior* (i.e. mental states, representations) *vs. exterior* (i.e. behaviour, objects, organizations) perspectives on the other side. These two axes taken together provide for a four-quadrant map where each quadrant must be seen as a perspective by which individuals, situations and social systems may be understood, as it is shown on Figure 5.

The I-I (*Interior-Individual*, upper left) quadrant is about emotions, beliefs, desires, intentions, drives, etc., of an individual, i.e. about its mental states, its subjectivity. The E-I (*Exterior-Individual*, upper right) quadrant describes physical bodies, concrete objects, and also behaviours of individuals. The I-C (*Interior – Collective*, lower left) quadrant is about shared knowledge and beliefs, collective representations, ontologies, social norms, and represents the inter-subjective part of a set of individuals, what could be called their *culture* or the *noosphere*. The E-C (*Exterior-Collective, lower right*) quadrant is about material or formal social structures such as organizations, i.e. collective forms and structures of groups and systems, what could be called the *sociosphere*.

The MASQ meta-model is based on the following assumptions:

a. **Separation between mind and body:** an agent is assumed to be composed of an interior aspect, its 'mind', and an exterior aspect, its 'bodies'. A mind corresponds to the internal structure of an agent or to its decision-making component. Bodies, either 'physical' or 'social' are parts of the environment and are connected to minds. This principle is intended to separate the cognitive (e.g. representations, plans, maps, reasoning) and conative (e.g. decisions, goals, intentions, drives) parts of an agent from its environmental part. See a mobile robot for instance: all of its physical parts (chassis, wheels, legs, motors, etc.) and even hardware controls are parts of the physical world, but not its software which resides in the 'information processing' domain. This dualistic view allows MAS designers to not mix up what is relevant to the mind of agents, i.e. their representation and decision process, and what refers to their ability to act in a specific domain. Thus, the body of an agent determines the agent's existence in the environment: it gives the agent the abilities to act and perceive the environment. A body is also the manifestation of an agent in the environment and allows others to perceive it. It is subject to environmental constraints and it forms the basis of the "incarnation" of an agent in an environment because bodies are treated as special kind of objects, i.e. entities that are situated in spaces. Mind and bodies are connected through the influence/reaction principle.

b. **The agent integrity principle:** the mind of an agent (i.e. its internal structure) is not public and cannot be accessed from outside. Neither the environment nor any other agent can go into the mind of an agent. It is only the behavior displayed in the environment (through its body) that can be used to reason about an agent. This principle allows us to preserve the autonomy and heterogeneity of agents.

c. **Actions as reactions to influences:** in order to take concurrent actions into account, we use the influence-reaction model (Ferber & Müller, 1996; Helleboogh, Vizzari, Uhrmacher, & Michel, 2007). This principle is based on the idea that an agent cannot directly change the state of the world, but it can only "influence" its dynamics. An agent decides what action to do next, but it is the environment that determines its consequences. For instance, an agent "wants" to mail messages and do the operation to send them, but it is the environment which actually transmits and delivers messages. In the same vein, a robot decides to move but it is the environment (both its body and the external surrounding) that performs the displacement. Thus, the environment reacts to influences produced by agents to determine its dynamics, through a set of "laws", which in the physical world, are the laws of physics and dynamics. Influences represent the transformation of mind elements into physical aspects, and may be seen as a generalization of both the "command" and "sensory" concepts in robotics (see Chapter XIV, *Formal Specification of Artificial Institutions Specification Using Event Calculus*, by Fornara and Columbetti, for another formalism that takes into account parallel and concurrent actions).

This assumption, in connection with the previous one, prohibits any direct interaction between agents, which means that it cannot exist any "telepathic" connection between them. The activity of an agent is made possible only through the environment and through influences and reactions. Consequently, everything that is not provided by the environment is simply not possible for an agent.

Integration of a), b) and c) allows for a simple definition of an agent through its mind/body decomposition: a mind is a process, independent of the environment, but in interaction with it through

Figure 6. Separation between "mind" and "body"

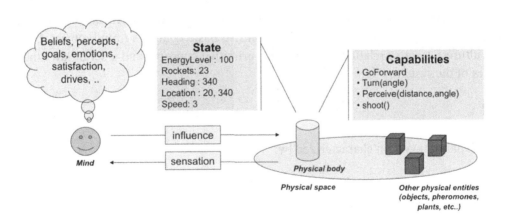

its bodies. It has its own life cycle, and it maintains a permanent asynchronous communication with the environment. The communication is made under the form of an exchange of influences (issued by the mind) and sense data (issued by the environment). The result of the deliberation phase determines the operations that will generate influences on the environment. Figure 6 shows this distinction between mind and body in an influence-reaction model.

d. **Groups and physical spaces:** Groups (i.e. social spaces) and physical spaces are seen as different varieties of 'spaces', in which agents (i.e. minds) may have bodies. Thus, agents may possess social bodies as well as physical bodies. Social bodies are the active parts of roles. It is then possible to generalize and extend the AGR and AGRE models (Ferber, Gutknecht, & Michel, 2004; Ferber, Michel, & Baez, 2005) by mapping groups and roles into social spaces.

e. **Brute environment vs. culture.** This principle stems from Searle's work on the construction of social reality (Searle, 1995). It provides a clear distinction between what constitutes a brute reality, i.e. its objective part of what happens in a world, and the collective knowledge and subjective values that can be made by a society of agents to describe and interpret that "objective" world. We use the term *culture* to denote this collective and subjective realm which is situated in the I-C quadrant. A culture is made of collective subjective elements such as social norms, social commitments, ontologies or more generally common knowledge. Following Searle, institutions are produced by "count as" functions of the form X count as Y in C, where Y are elements of cultures and X are elements of both cultural and brute spaces. Thus, cultures may be seen as interpretive domains giving values to sensations, i.e. brute perceptions.

Different interpretations of the brute reality may exist at the same time for an agent. They depend on the various societies that an agent accepts to belong to. A society of agents can influence the agents in their decisions, particularly in terms of social pressure, but it has no direct impact on the brute reality. The interpretation of the brute reality does not impose any physical constraint on an agent. As we will see below, these concepts are all linked together. An agent makes decisions with its mind and acts in the brute space through its body where it will be possible to enter into interaction with various other objects. Then the interpretation of the brute space interaction will be used as support for the construction of the culture in which the agent is immersed.

4. DESCRIPTION OF MASQ

Given the above principles we can now describe in more details the main elements on which the MASQ model is based. The meta-model MASQ is built on five basic concepts (mind, object, bodies, brute space and cultures), a set of relations among these primitive concepts and a set of laws that describe the dynamics of the system.

4.1. Mind

A mind is a dynamical system characterized by:

1. an internal state,
2. a mechanism of state change that determines how the state evolves over time, given the sensation information the mind receives. It should be noted that the execution of a mind is not synchronized

with that of the environment. Therefore, in one loop the input on the agent side can be composed by a (possibly empty) set of senses data issued by the environment at different times. This mechanism can be modeled by a state transition function.

3.   an influence production mechanism that determines the influences produced by the mind according to its internal state. This mechanism can be modeled by a production function.

The last two points are grouped under the term *internal dynamics*. The internal state of an agent corresponds to the individual internal reality, in the sense of four quadrants, and its internal dynamics expresses the agent's cognitive abilities, i.e. how its internal state can evolve.

The mind definition we propose is intentionally left very generic. It allows someone to integrate various agent models and let co-exist heterogeneous agents in the same system. The only requirement that we impose on this definition is that the mind should be able to receive sense data from its environment and issue influences back on it.

Objects

In MASQ, the concept of object is used to describe individual entities that compose the environment. Unlike minds, objects are neither proactive, nor autonomous. Their evolution is entirely determined by the laws of the environment and the different activities that occur in it. Objects are considered as passive entities because the environment controls completely their evolution. However, they are not inert because they can have their own activities such as rolling for a ball or changing periodically of color for a traffic light. An object is characterized by a dynamic state, which describes at a given instant t both the state of the object (state variables) and its activity (dynamic variables).

In a "natural" environment (e.g. the movement of a ball moving in the "real" world) the evolution of an object can be determined if one has sufficient knowledge of the laws of physics. In the case of a virtual environment, the laws that govern its evolution should be described explicitly. Thus, we introduce the concept of instantaneous evolution law (or *internal activity*) that allows one to describe the dynamic state of an object in isolation. An instantaneous evolution law is a function Φ that associates two dynamic states δ and δ', where Δ_o the set of all possible dynamic states of the object o:

$$\Phi : \Delta_o \to \Delta_o : \delta \to \delta' = \Phi(\delta)$$

Obviously, objects are not isolated. The future state of an object depends also on the activities of other objects. For example, an arrow may encounter an obstacle during its flight, which stops its movement. Thus, the evolution of an object cannot be determined by considering only the object itself. We will see later that it is the role of the environment to completely compute the evolution of the objects that compose it[3].

When describing objects we make use of the concept of object type, so that an object is always the instance of a certain object type. An object type contains the description of the set of dynamic or state variables and the instantaneous evolution law. For each variable we provide also the corresponding domain that gives the set of all possible dynamic states for the objects of that type.

Agents: Embodiment of Minds into Objects

Some objects have the distinction of being connected to a mind, and in such a case we speak of *bodies*. A body plays the role of mediator between the mind and the environment. A body allows the mind to act on its environment, perceive it and be perceived by other minds. A body is also the manifestation of an agent in its environment; it allows its very existence in it.

We stated previously that a mind could only influence and perceive the environment. We can now specify that a mind can do this only because it has a body into that environment. We note *HoldBody* the relationship between a body and a mind. It should be noted that a mind may have several bodies and a body is associated to a unique mind. To describe how a mind can intervene on the evolution of a dynamic state of its body we use the notions of influence and reaction. A reaction law indicates how a set of influences may modify the dynamic state of a body. A reaction law of an object type T is a function:

$$RLaw : \Delta_T \times 2^\Gamma \rightarrow \Delta_T$$

$$(\delta, \{\gamma_1, \gamma_2, \ldots, \gamma_i\}) \rightarrow \delta'$$

where γ_1 are influences produced by a connected mind. A reaction law is always linked to a type of object T. It is a function that computes the new dynamic state of a body from its current dynamic state and the influences that it receives from its mind. For a given dynamic state and a set of influences, a law of reaction can return the initial dynamic state, which means that the influences issued by the mind will not necessarily produce a transformation of its body. A mind can potentially send all kinds of influences to its body, but only certain types of influences will have a real effect on it. We will then call these influences valid. Since bodies are not synchronized with their minds, issuing an influence by a mind does not lead to an immediate transformation of body's dynamic state. Influences are simply queued for later computation. It is the environment that manages the dynamics of its objects and determines the timing of the reaction of a body according to the body type reaction law and queued influences.

The concept of body that we define in MASQ is very general. This usually suggests a physical nature, as it is the case in the example of a mobile robot. But this concept should be seen only as any means to perceive and act in an environment, whatever its nature. The notion of body introduced here is identical with the concept of *mode* presented in (Báez-Barranco, Stratulat & Ferber, 2007) and the concept of agent-in-role as in (Pacheco, Carmo 2003).

In MASQ, the relationship between body and mind is dynamic. As we already mentioned previously, a mind could have multiple bodies, and over time it can acquire new bodies or lose bodies it currently possesses. Therefore, the material capabilities available to an agent on the environment are not frozen: they can change depending on the bodies that are acquired or released by the mind. We will give more details on this later in the next section.

4.2. Brute Space

We introduce the concept of brute space to describe the environment. The environment represents for a MAS the brute reality that corresponds to the quadrants E-I and E-C. It maintains a state of affairs that is objective, independent of agents' points of view. From a conceptual point of view, the environment is composed of objects and has as main role to manage how these objects interact. A brute space is composed of objects (where some of these objects are bodies), and forms a boundary between its objects and the rest of the environment. Objects are dynamically interconnected inside a brute space. Motions (i.e. how objects can move in a space) and communications (i.e. how information can be exchanged between objects) are examples of such connections. An object cannot belong to several brute spaces.

Physical Spaces vs. Social Spaces

The nature of brute spaces can be very diverse, but two categories of brute spaces are usually distinguished: physical spaces and social spaces.

A physical space is used to model a portion of the physical world (e.g. a football field). It may be equipped with a particular topology that allows someone to locate objects and to establish topological relations between objects (e.g. distance, collision and contact detection). Reaction laws implement the dynamics of the physical space (gravity, mass, dynamics forces, etc.).

A social space is used to model specific and deterministic social structures of interaction. For instance, message transfer and routing is accomplished in a space where agents are located through their email address. To send and receive messages an agent must possess a communicative body (e.g. in an email system, an address and a queuing mechanism for storing incoming and outgoing messages) situated in a communicative environment (e.g. an infrastructure for message delivery). These communicative capabilities are associated to specific rights (what kind of communications the agent is allowed to perform) which refer to its status (e.g. administrators often have more rights than simple users). A good way to understand what is a social space is to see it as an abstraction of most community related web systems, such as forums, wiki, meeting systems, etc. In those systems, each participant has a pseudonym, related to a status, which gives the participants their specific capabilities for acting in this space. The pseudonym, with all the capabilities associated to it, may be seen as a social body, and the web system as an interaction space. Like in physical spaces, it is also possible to define a topology for social spaces (Zambonelli, Jennings & Wooldridge, 2003). For example, an organization that uses the

Figure 7. Diagrams of brute spaces, whether physical or social and the HoldBody *function between minds and bodies. Thus minds may be seen as being embodied in brute space through their bodies.*

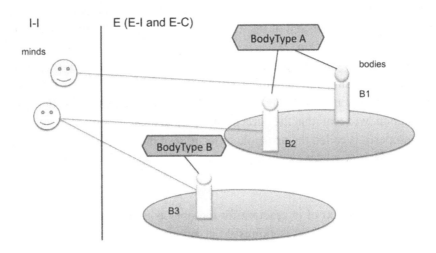

Figure 8. Evolution of brute spaces results of a cycling process of 1) reaction of bodies to mind's influences, 2) interference management, 3) local evolution of objects

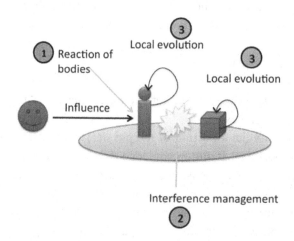

roles of master and slave defines a hierarchical topology. Note that the concept of group from AGR is absorbed in MASQ as a social space and the concept of role as a social body.

We have shown that from an abstract point of view, social and physical spaces may be seen as two forms of the same concept of space. A brute space, whether physical or social, contains bodies that are able to perceive and act, and its dynamics is described by reaction laws.

Therefore, we have reused the diagrams of AGR that represent groups and roles to represent spaces and bodies, as it is shown on Figure 8. Note that, for drawing simplicity, we have merged the quadrants E-I (Exterior-Individual) and E-C (Exterior-Collective) in just one zone called E (Exterior). But bodies belong to E-I and spaces to E-C.

Relation to Minds

Minds are connected to objects by the relationship *HoldBody* and objects are linked to brute spaces by the relationship *BelongTo*. Therefore we can transitively define the relationship between minds and brute spaces by introducing the concept of incarnation or embodiment: a mind is embodied in a body, which is situated in a brute space (Fig. 7).

A mind can have several bodies in different brute spaces. Note also that a mind can have many bodies in the same brute space, although in many cases a unique body per space is the common scenario. A brute space is also used to limit the scope of the perception and the possible actions for a mind in the brute reality. In addition, we recall that the perception remains local; a body does not perceive an entire brute space. This property is called the principle of locality of perception.

Brute Interaction

A brute space defines the context of interaction for the objects that compose it. Each object taken individually has an internal activity that is expressed at any moment by its dynamic state. The various activities that are carried out within a brute space may interfere with each other as, for example, when two moving objects come into collision. The conditions under which an interference may occur and its corresponding effects are described at the level of brute spaces.

As in (Helleboogh, Vizzari, Uhrmacher & Michel, 2007) interferences can result in a transformation of activities of the corresponding objects. For example, when two objects come into collision, their speed and direction of movement can change. Such a transformation in activities is expressed in MASQ by a change in the objects' dynamic state using the influence/reaction model (Fig. 8).

4.3. Cultures

Cultures[4] have been introduced to capture the perspective of the I-C quadrant, i.e. inter-subjectivity. A *culture* represents the subjective elements that are shared by a group of minds, i.e. collective interpretations, social norms, ontologies, common or shared knowledge, Schank's scripts, etc.

The main interest of cultures is to provide a context that allows agents to reach a common understanding. From the perspective of an agent, the culture is used to interpret communications, understand events and anticipate the behavior of other agents. Conversely, from the perspective of a society, a culture is a tool that helps the society to control the behavior of its members while preserving their integrity and heterogeneity. Thus, a culture induces a form of social pressure to obtain better coordination between the members of a society while reducing and/or solving possible conflicts.

In MASQ, a mind can have access to shared knowledge by being embedded in one or more cultures. To express the relationship between a mind and a culture we say that a mind *m* is *immersed* in at least a culture *CS*. A mind may be immersed in several cultures. Coherence of a mind between several cultures is left to the mind's developer.

For a culture, here are three important types of common knowledge:

1.   **Shared knowledge and ontologies:** information expressed in the form of concepts and relations between concepts that gives a culture its conceptual basis.

Figure 9. A driver interpretation of a red light as an obligation to stop through the interpretation function of his or her culture

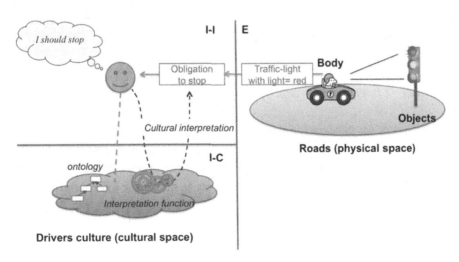

Figure 10. A policeman sends a message to the drivers that should stop to a signal

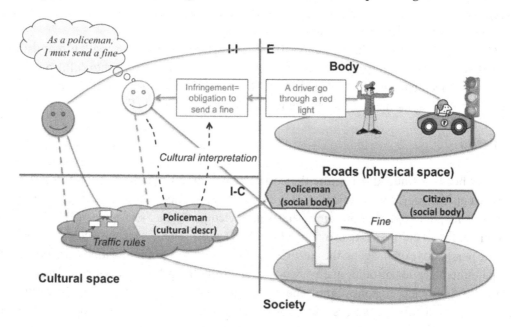

2. **Shared patterns of behaviors** that are displayed by all individuals of the same culture in similar situations, i.e. his or her role in a specific context. These patterns of behavior may be represented as deontic elements (obligation, interdiction, authorization), shared plans, protocols, Schank's scripts, etc.

3. **Collective interpretation:** interpretations of phenomena occurring in brute spaces that are not specific to a single mind but are collectively accepted in a culture.

An important issue of cultures is the notion of interpretation of brute space events. A body in a brute space acquires information through its senses, and gets a sensation which is a kind of brute percept. This has to be transformed into a percept, i.e. a representation of something through the cultural filter. For instance, an electric plug may be seen by a robot as a kind of food resource for its own purpose. But in a different context, the same plug may be considered as a way to power devices. We say that the same plug may have different *interpretations* depending on its culture, which constitutes a context of interpretation. A collective interpretation of a brute event in a culture *cs* is a function which maps a sensation to a percept:

Interpret$_{cs}$: Sensation → InterpretedPercept

where *InterpretedPercept* (or *percept* for short) are descriptions represented with the ontology of the culture *cs*. This means, that an interpretation function takes a sensation and delivers a percept described in terms of the cultural ontology. For instance: a car driver which sees a red light interprets it as a road signal which means that she has to stop, as shown on figure 9, due to the interpretation function defined in her "driver's culture".

Cultures contain also plans, protocols and scripts, i.e. patterns of behavior that one is supposed to apply in a specific circumstance with a specific role. Let us suppose that our driver of the previous example does not stop and goes through the traffic light, and let us suppose that a policeman watches the scene. Because he plays the role of the policeman, he interprets the behavior of the driver as an infringement and then as the obligation to send a fine to the driver. But sending a fine is associated to both the rights *and* the effective power to send it, the latter being possible in MASQ through a social body. Thus, the policeman has the capability to send a mail containing a fine (Fig. 10). Then the driver, when receiving the fine will interpret it, with regard to her culture, as an obligation to pay, etc.

We can see that there is still a possibility of "free will" for the policeman. The obligation to send a fine is determined by its role in a culture, but he may circumvent it. This is due to the fact that the culture produces deontic elements such as obligations and interdictions, but does not execute minds. Thus the decision process is still an autonomous quality of agents in MASQ.

MASQ captures the main ideas behind the concept of institution as in (Searle, 1995) where institutions are defined as a set of constitutive rules and regulative rules. According to Searle, an institution can be used to build a social reality from the brute reality and/or other social realities. *Constitutive* rules can give a meaning to a brute fact or a fact from another social reality. They are of the form "$X \Rightarrow_c Y$" which is read "X count as Y in the context C" and they put a brute fact X in relation with an institutional fact.

For instance the "driving culture" which contains the traffic rules is an institution built from rules of the form:

$$going\text{-}through\text{-}red\text{-}light(driver) \Rightarrow_{driving} infringement(driver)$$

R*egulative* rules give a characterization of the institutional facts showing "how things should be". The distinction between these two types of rules is essential. The constitutive rules are used to create a social reality, whereas the regulative rules regulate the activities in an already existent social reality.

A regulative rule is an expression that associates a deontic description to an institutional fact. Since we do not think of a specific representation for regulative rules, our proposal is intentionally very generic. One can see rules, as it is often done, as formulas of the form : $\beta \Rightarrow OPI\alpha$ where $OPI\alpha$ is a deontic characterization (*OPI* – obligation, permission or interdiction) of a property or action α, and β is a conditional boolean expression. But our goal is not to explicitly describe how rules should be expressed, but merely to show how normative aspects may be linked to other aspects of MAS. In practice someone will obviously need to be very explicit on the details of the integration of such a deontic formalism, that is application dependent.

Roles, Groups and Organizations in MASQ

We have seen that MASQ integrates the environmental, social and cultural perspectives. One may ask how groups, roles and organizations are now handled in this meta-model.

We have shown that AGR groups are now represented as social spaces, i.e. as special kinds of brute spaces, more akin to message passing and status position. However, we propose that descriptions of groups and roles be situated in cultures as shared knowledge. Thus, minds can access this information if they are immersed in the corresponding culture.

In MASQ, groups and roles have now two aspects: a brute and a cultural one. Since a group corresponds to a space, a group is formed at the cultural level from a brute aggregation of agents, according to some constitutive rules. A social group could be seen like in AGR as a collection of social bodies subject to some brute (physical or social) causal laws.

As for roles, as it has been shown previously in the MAS literature (see for instance Odell et al. 2003), they may have several meanings. In MASQ the cultural aspect is related to the normative behavioral repertoire of an agent, and the social and physical aspects concern the powers and abilities that an agent acquires in a space when playing a role. A role in MASQ contains also the link between these aspects by indicating how social bodies are related to collective representations at the cultural level (e.g. through constitutive laws).

4.4. How to Represent Institutions?

The work of Searle (Searle, 1995) is fundamental in our approach because it allows someone to understand how an institutional reality can be constructed from the brute reality by using institutions. However, Searle has not fully addressed the relationship between individuals and the institutional reality, that is, how people become aware of the facts that are institutionally established. This becomes more obvious if we condition that the knowledge that an agent may have of an institutional reality is directly dependent on its perception of the brute reality. In practice, an agent has only a partial representation of the environment in which it operates and hence it can not have a complete representation of the institutional reality even that it has full knowledge about the constitutive rules. Therefore, we believe that the institutional rules, both constitutive and regulative, should be considered and handled as common knowledge, but their application or the interpretation of the brute reality is something that happens at individual internal level (mind).

By representing an institution as a set of institutional rules leads to similar problems as when representing common knowledge. Therefore, in our proposal we make a distinction between two kinds of constitutive rules, formal and informal. Intuitively, a *formal* rule is similar to a written law such as the civil code, code of conduct in an organization, etc. It has a representation in the brute world. An *informal* rule corresponds to a shared knowledge or custom, accepted by the members of a culture, but that is not described in a formal way, for instance how to greet each.

In MASQ a formal rule is an institutional rule that is reified in a brute space. It means that the rule will be expressed in a certain language and will be encapsulated in a particular object. All the formal rules can be accessed by minds through the mechanism of bodies and percepts. Instead, the informal rules since they have no counterpart in brute spaces, they have an existence only in cultures. To be aware of informal rules, a mind must belong to the culture that they establish. For a mind ignorant of a specific culture, a learning process is required to incorporate the rules of this culture. This learning can be achieved in various ways: by imitating others, observing and generalizing the behavior of others, being informed of the practice by members of this culture, or in terms of rewards and penalties received.

The acquisition process is hence different for formal rules and informal rules. In the case of formal rules it is sufficient to consult the "official records" whereas in the case of informal rules it is necessary to discover or adopt them through interaction.

Whether the rules are formal or informal, it is necessary that a mind internalize them in order to be able to have a representation of an institutional reality. The process of internalization is the adoption of institutional rules as beliefs. By considering the institutional constraint operator $D_s \alpha$, introduced by Jones & Sergot (1996) to describe that α is an institutional fact, a constitutive rule of the form $X \Rightarrow_s Y$ could be internalized by an agent i within a belief of the form $B_i(X \Rightarrow D_s Y)$.

In our proposal, there is no explicit representation of an institutional reality that is external to minds. Instead, every mind can have its own representation according to the internalized rules and its perception of the brute space.

Figure 11. A snapshot of Warbot in progress

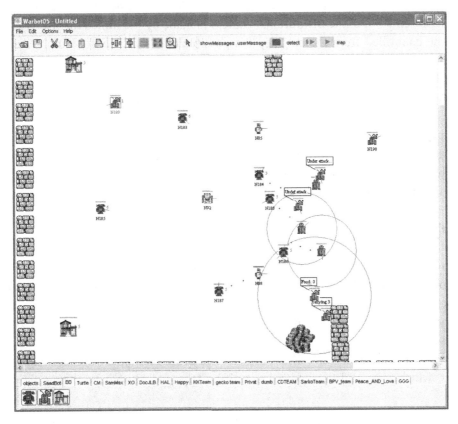

Figure 12. The Warbot example described within the MASQ approach

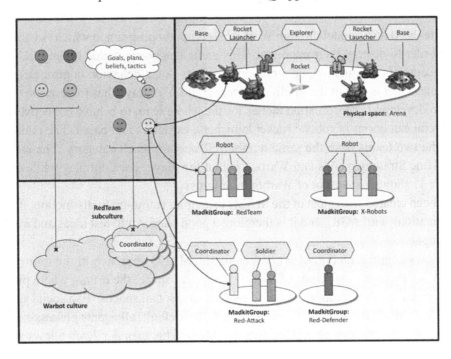

As a consequence, every mind may have a partial and inaccurate representation of an institutional reality, which is the price to pay to preserve the principle of locality of perception. In addition, the construction of a representation of the institutional context is made by the minds themselves, and because minds cannot be controlled from the outside, it is possible that some do not simply create any such representations.

4.5. Culture vs. Brute Space

In MASQ, the distinction between a culture and a brute space is essential. A brute space allows the realization of an action while a culture allows the interpretation of a collective activity. In the environment, that is, brute spaces, things are as they are. The environment provides no judgment on the elements it contains. The culture, through cultures, gives a meaning to the phenomena occurring in the environment.

The rules that govern a brute space and correspondingly a culture are of very different natures. Rules in a brute space determine its evolution, what an agent can do and what consequences of its actions are. These rules are given to agents. Rules in a culture are descriptive in nature and they have no direct impact on the brute reality. They have no impact on the capabilities of an agent in a brute space. For instance, considering an action as "good" or "bad" is performed at the cultural level and does not alter the ability for an agent to execute it, nor does it change its consequences in the environment, i.e. in brute spaces.

However, while a culture does not affect directly the brute reality, it influences agents' minds in their decisions, which may lead them to behave differently, and ultimately change the brute reality indirectly.

5. EXAMPLE: WARBOT, A VIRTUAL WAR OF ROBOTS

We will illustrate the MASQ model through Warbot[5], a computer program in which two teams of virtual robots fight in order to destroy their opponent. This game has been created to help MAS students to understand concepts of coordination, cooperation, conflicts, local behavior, communications, beliefs, organizations, etc. and it is part of the MadKit platform (2008). A player has to describe the "minds" of its robots and to develop his coordination tactics for the whole team to behave collectively. The player disposes of several categories of robots: rocket launchers, explorers and bases. The number of each is not fixed, but the two teams have the same number of robots in each category. The main difference between Real Time Strategy games and Warbot, is that the player does not play while the game is in progress. Figure 11 shows a snapshot of Warbot in progress.

Warbot has been created with most of the MASQ principles (mind-body distinction, influence-reaction, and organizations with AGR), and it is therefore a good platform to test ideas and implementation of MASQ concepts.

Figure 12 shows a representation of Warbot using the MASQ approach in the four-quadrant map. In terms of MASQ, there are two kinds of spaces: a physical space, the *arena*, where physical bodies may move, perceive their environment and send rockets, and social spaces. Two social spaces, inheriting from the default MadKit group, represent the teams. By default, all agents possess a *member body*, which inherits from the default role of MadKit (and AGR). This *member body* allows agents to send messages to each other, to know who is the member of a group and to broadcast messages.

There are other groups that correspond to tactical coordination units (e.g. assailants, defenders, etc.). Reaction rules and local evolution of objects are parts of the MadKit (for the groups) and of Warbot (for the arena and the robots bodies).

Robots can perceive objects in the environment: they receive sensory data (brute percepts) through the sensors of their bodies, and these sensations will be interpreted relative to their culture.

For instance, a mind connected to an explorer body *b* will perceive the environment through a combination of sensation and interpretation:

```
Set<Percept> p = WarbotCulture.interpret(b.getSenseData())
```

will return a set of percepts as they are interpreted in the `WarbotCulture` (the default culture in which all robots are immersed).

Specific cultures, such as team subcultures, may easily be represented in MASQ as cultures which contain new concepts, new rules and add new interpretations. For instance, a RedTeam may define a notion of danger, which could be expressed with the following pseudo-code:

```
when a rocket-launcher with team = other
  and with distance(Base) < security-distance
then the team-is-in-danger
```

If the `team-in-danger` concept is considered as a cultural element for the RedTeam, all members of the group may use this item as if it was a simple percept. It is part of their culture, part of the way they reason. Thus, they know that they may send messages using this item because it has some meaning for all members of the team.

6. DISCUSSIONS AND CONCLUSION

We have briefly presented a new meta-model, called MASQ, which is able to take into account both actions in an environment and cultures (norms, institutions) in an integrated way. We have shown that it is possible to represent several aspects of OCMAS systems in this framework.

Actually, MASQ may be used in different ways. It can be used as an operational framework, and the next MadKit platform will use MASQ as its core. But it can also be used as a methodological tool to take into account the various perspectives of OCMAS.

In the case of natural systems the role of physical and institutional reality is rather clear, if we suppose that there is such thing as an objective reality, but when modeling artificial systems it is necessary to determine precisely what is in the brute reality and what forms the cultural reality. For example, to set up a voting system, humans must establish an institution so that raising a hand may count for a vote. But, in an artificial system, we can choose to use the environment and its brute spaces to give the agents the capability to vote. It is not necessary to represent minds in such systems.

The choice to model a certain aspect of the system at the brute level or at the cultural level depends on the properties we want to obtain for that system. By using brute spaces we have more control on how things happen, e.g. to promote security issues or guarantee a certain result. Problems that are modeled with such approaches have fixed solutions that may be "hardwired". The way to solve them is mostly implemented within evolution and interference laws at the brute level. Thus, brute spaces are rather used to model well-defined causal interaction such as physical interaction (e.g. a rolling ball) and social organized interaction (e.g. playing a role in an organization with fixed protocols).

The choice to model a system at the cultural level gives a new alternative that promotes the adaptability, by promoting culture and agents' autonomy in detriment of causal determinism. Agents have many possibilities to act and to adapt their behavior to world events, and the way to control them may be given in terms of institutional laws, both constitutive and regulative. However, in a cultural approach it is nearly impossible to guarantee that a satisfactory solution will finally be obtained.

A mix of brute and cultural approaches should be used diligently. For instance, in the case of agents that exchange goods on the Internet, trust in others is important. We may let trust be built only at the cultural level, but it is clear that we can improve its construction by using protocols of interaction described at the brute level (keep trace of exchanged messages, force agents to identify themselves, make payments through third-party organisms, etc.). One of our future efforts will be to propose a methodology based on MASQ that will help a designer to decide how to model a system in terms of culture and brute spaces.

REFERENCES

Artikis, A., Pitt, J., & Sergot, M. (2002). Animated Specifications of Computational Societies. *Proceedings of Autonomous Agents and Multi-Agent Systems (AAMAS)*, (pp. 1053-1062).

Báez-Barranco, J.-A., Stratulat, T., & Ferber, J. (2007). A Unified Model for Physical and Social Environments. In D. Weyns, H. Van Dyke Parunak & F. Michel (Eds.), *Environments for Multi-Agent Systems III* (pp. 41-50). LNAI 4389, Springer.

Boella, G., & Van der Torre, L. (2004). Organizations as socially constructed agents in the agent oriented paradigm. *Engineering Societies in the Agent World, ESAW'04* (pp 1–13). LNAI 3451, Springer.

Cardoso, H. L., & Oliveira, E. (2007). Institutional Reality and Norms: Specifying and Monitoring Agent Organizations. *International Journal of Cooperative Information Systems*, *16*(1), 67-95.

Dignum, V. (2004). *A Model for Organizational Interaction. Based on Agents, Founded on Logic*. SIKS Dissertation Series.

Esteva, M., Rosell, B., Rodrıguez-Aguilar, J. A., & Arcos, J. L. (2004). AMELI: An agent-based middleware for electronic institutions. Proceedings of the *Third International Joint Conference on Autonomous Agents and Multiagent Systems*, *1*, 236–243.

Ferber, J., & Müller, J.-P. (1996). Influences and Reaction: A Model of Situated Multi-agent Systems. *Proceedings of the 2nd International Conference on Multi-agent Systems (ICMAS'96)* (pp. 72–79). The AAAI Press.

Ferber, J., & Gutknecht, O. (1998). A Meta-Model for the Analysis and Design of Organizations in Multi-Agent Systems. *Proceedings of the 3rd International Conference on Multi Agent Systems (ICMAS'98)* (pp. 128-135). IEEE Computer Society.

Ferber, J. (1999). *Multi-Agent System: An Introduction to Distributed Artificial Intelligence.* Addison-Wesley.

Ferber, J., Gutknecht, O., & Michel, F. (2004). From Agents to Organizations: An Organizational View of Multi-Agent Systems. In P. Giorgini, J. Müller, J.Odell (Eds.), *Agent-Oriented Software Engineering (AOSE) IV* (pp. 214-230). LNCS 2935, Springer.

Ferber, J., Michel, F., & Baez, J. (2005). AGRE: Integrating Environments with Organizations. In D. Weyns, V. D. Parunak, F. Michel (Eds). *Environments for Multi-Agent Systems* (pp. 48-56). LNAI 3374, Springer.

FIPA (2005). The Foundation of Intelligent Physical Agents. www.fipa.org

Fornara, N., Vigano, F., & Colombetti, M. (2007). Agent Communication and Artificial Institutions. *Journal of Autonomous Agents and Multi-Agent Systems, 14*(2), 121-142.

Grossi, D., Dignum, F., Dastani, M., & Royakkers, L. (2005). Foundations of organizational structures in multiagent systems. *Proceedings of the International Conference on Autonomous Agents,* (pp. 827 – 834).

Helleboogh, A., Vizzari G., Uhrmacher, A., & Michel, F. (2007). Modeling Dynamic Environments in Multi-Agent Simulation. *Journal of Autonomous Agents and Multi-Agent Systems, 14*(1), 87-116.

Hübner, J. F., Sichman, J. S., & Boissier, O. (2007). Developing organised multiagent systems using the MOISE. *International Journal of Agent-Oriented Software Engineering, 1*(3/4), 370-395.

Jones, A. J. I., & Sergot, M. J. (1996). A Formal Characterization of Institutionalized Power. *Journal of the IGPL 4(3),* 429-445.

MadKit (2004). *A Multi-Agent Development Kit.* www.madkit.org

Noriega, P. (1997). *Agent-Mediated Auctions: The Fishmarket Metaphor.* PhD thesis. IIIA Monograph Series, Number 8.

North, D. C. (1990). *Institutions, Institutional Change and Economic Performance.* Cambridge University Press.

Odell, J., Van Parunak H., Fleischer M., Brueckner S. (2002). Modeling Agents and their Environment. In *AOSE III,* F. Giunchiglia, James Odell, Gerhard Weiss, (eds.), LNCS vol. 2585, Springer, 2002.

Odell, J., Van Parunak H., & Fleischer M. (2003). The Role of Roles in Designing Effective Agent Organizations. In *Software Engineering for Large-Scale Multi-Agent Systems,* Garcia, A.; Lucena, C.; Zambonelli, F.; Omicini, A.; Castro, J. (eds.), LNCS Vol. 2603, Springer.

Pacheco O., Carmo J. (2003) A role-based model for the normative specification of organized collective agency and agents interaction. JAAMAS, *6*(2), 145-184.

Phan, D., & Ferber, J. (2007). Thinking the Social Dimension of the Artificial World: Ontological Status of Collective Beliefs. *International Transactions on Systems Science and Applications.* Forthcoming.

Searle, J. R. (1995). *The Construction of Social Reality.* Free Press.

Tranier J. (2007). *Vers une vision intégrale des systèmes multi-agents. Contribution à l'intégration des concepts d'agent, d'environnement, d'organisation et d'institution.* PhD thesis, Univ. de Montpellier II. (in French) 154 p.

Vigano, F., Fornara, N., & Colombetti, M. (2006). An Event Driven Approach to Norms in Artificial Institutions. In Boissier, O., Padget, J., Dignum, V., Lindemann, G., Matson, E., Ossowski, S., Simao Sichman, J. & Vazquez-Salceda, J., eds.: *Co-ordination, Organization, Institutions and Norms in Multi-Agent Systems I* (pp. 142–154). LNAI 3913, Springer.

Weyns, D., Van Dyke Parunak, H., Michel, F., Holvoet, T., & Ferber, J. (2005). Environments for Multiagent Systems. State-of-the-Art and Research Challenges. in V. D. Parunak, F. Michel (Eds). *Environments for Multi-Agent Systems* (pp. 3-52). LNAI 3374, Springer.

Weyns, D., Omicini, A., & Odell, J. (2007). Environment as a first-class abstraction in multiagent systems. *JAAMAS, 14*(1), 5-30.

Wilber, K. (2001). *A Theory of Everything: An Integral Vision for Business, Politics, Science and Spirituality.* Shambhala Publications.

Zambonelli, F., Jennings, N., R. & Wooldridge, M. (2003). Developing Multi-agent Systems: The Gaia Methodology. *ACM Transactions on Software Engineering and Methodology* (pp. 317–370). ACM Press.

KEY TERMS

Agent-Group-Role (AGR): A generic model of multi-agent organizations which does not impose any constraints on the architecture of agents. AGR conforms to the OCMAS principles.

Agent-Group-Role-Environment (AGRE): Adds the concept of environment to AGR.

Body: The interface between a mind and a brute space. Social bodies, i.e. bodies which are situated in organizational spaces, are called 'roles'.

Brute Spaces: The environmental domains in which action takes place and where objects (and bodies) are objectively situated.

Culture: In MAS, we use the term "culture" to denote the subjective elements that are shared by a group of minds, i.e. collective interpretations, social norms, ontologies, common or shared knowledge, etc.

Influence-Reaction: A model of action which allows for concurrent activities.

Mind: The reasoning, decision-making and cognitive part of an agent. Minds are associated to bodies in order to act in brute spaces.

Multi-Agent Systems based on Quadrants MASQ): An approach in which multi-agent systems are seen from four perspectives: the subjective and personal perspective of minds, the objective and personal perspective of behaviors, the objective and collective perspective of environments and their structuring in terms of objective organizations, the subjective and collective perspective of culture.

Organization Centered Multi-Agent Systems (OCMAS): A set of principles to design multi-agent systems based on organizations. In OCMAS, organizations neither describe how tasks are carried out, nor impose any constraints on the cognitive aspects of agents.

ENDNOTES

[1] In the agent-centered case, interaction goes also through a middleware whose main function is to provide a message transport mechanism between any two agents.

[2] Bodies are called "modes" in AGRE. But because this word was not well understood, we have decided to use the most understandable word "body" in MASQ, which is both an extension and a redefinition of AGRE.

[3] This idea is very often applied in the physical engines that are used in video games for simulating the laws of physics and animate bouncing objects.

[4] In MASQ, we distinguish between the objective aspect of society, and we call it social, and its intersubjective (or interior) aspect and we call it cultural. Thus 'social' has here a different meaning than in the work of Searle. Thus most of the use of "social reality" in Searle should be translated here as "cultural reality". For instance a father-son relation is social, because it is a fact, but what is associated to it in a specific culture is called "cultural" and here "social" refers to aggregates and relations that belong to the brute space.

[5] www.warbot.fr

Chapter IV
OMACS:
A Framework for Adaptive, Complex Systems

Scott A. DeLoach
Kansas State University, USA

ABSTRACT

This chapter introduces a suite of technologies for building complex, adaptive systems. It is based in the multi-agent systems paradigm and uses the Organization Model for Adaptive Computational Systems (OMACS). OMACS defines the knowledge needed about a system's structure and capabilities to allow it to reorganize at runtime in the face of a changing environment and its agent's capabilities. However, the OMACS model is only useful if it is supported by a set of methodologies, techniques, and architectures that allow it to be implemented effectively on a wide variety of systems. To this end, this chapter presents a suite of technologies including (1) the Organization-based Multiagent Systems Engineering (O-MaSE) methodology, (2) a set of policy specification techniques that allow an OMACS system to remain flexible while still providing guidance, and (3) a set of architectures and algorithms used to implement OMACS-based systems. The chapter also includes the presentation of a small OMACS-based system.

INTRODUCTION

Multiagent systems have become popular over the last few years for building complex, adaptive systems in a distributed, heterogeneous setting. The problem is that many multiagent systems are typically designed to work within a limited set of configurations. Even when the system possesses the resources and computational power to accomplish its goal, it may be constrained by its own structure and knowledge of its member's capabilities. To overcome these problems, we have developed a framework that allows the system to design its own organization at runtime. The key component of our framework is the Organization Model for Adaptive Computational Systems (OMACS). OMACS defines the knowledge needed about a system's structure and capabilities to allow it to reorganize at runtime in the face of a changing environment and its agent's capabilities. Thus, as is also pointed out in Chapter III "Towards an Integral Approach of Organizations in Multi-Agent Systems", by Ferber et al. the environment plays an critical role in the specification of adaptive organizations. The OMACS model is based on the assumption that agents accept certain limitations on their autonomy; if assigned a role to play in order to achieve a goal, the agents must agree to attempt to play that role in the organization and pursue the assigned goal. The OMACS model also assumes no specific architecture (although one appropriate example is presented later in the chapter). It is assumed that the "organization" reasons based on the knowledge described in OMACS.

That being said, the OMACS model is only useful if it is supported by a set of methodologies, techniques, and architectures that allow it to be implemented effectively on a wide variety of systems. To this end, this chapter also presents a suite of technologies developed to support OMACS-based system development. After discussing the OMACS model, we present the Organization-based Multiagent Systems Engineering (O-MaSE) methodology. O-MaSE is a framework for creating O-MaSE compliant processes that support the development of OMACS-based systems. Next, we discuss an area of vital importance to reorganizing systems, policy specification. Since it is often desirable to constrain how a system can reorganize, we have investigated the notion of system-level policies. In this section we introduce the notion of *guidance policies* that allow us to specify policies that must be followed except when absolutely necessary. Finally, we present an architecture and a set of algorithms that can be used to implement OMACS-based systems.

BACKGROUND

Computational organization theory uses mathematical and computational techniques to study both human and artificial organizations (Carley 1999). While organizational concepts are not exclusive to computational organization theory, results from the field are illuminating. Specifically, they suggest that organizations tend to adapt to increase performance or efficiency, that "the most successful organizations tend to be highly flexible" (Carley 1998), and that the best organizational designs are highly application and situation dependent (Carley, 1995). Recently, the notion of separating the agents populating a multiagent system from the system organization (Zambonelli, Jennings, & Woodridge, 2001) has become well-accepted. While agents play roles *within* the organization, they do not constitute the organization. The organization itself is part of the agent's environment and defines the social setting in which the agent must exist. An organization includes *organizational structures* as well as *policies,* which define the requirements for system creation and operation.

There have been several attempts at formalizing the concepts of teamwork within an organization in the area of multiagent systems. While efforts such as Teamwork (Cohen & Levesque, 1991), Joint Intentions (Jennings, 1995), Shared Plans (Grosz & Kraus, 1996) and Planned Team Activity (Kinny, Ljungberg, Rao, Sonenberg, Tidhar & Werner, 1992), have been proposed and even implemented (Tambe, 1997), they fail to provide straightforward and easily adaptable concepts for wide spread development of such systems. In addition, these approaches require all agents to be capable of sophisticated reasoning about their organization, which tends to get intertwined with reasoning about the application, thus increasing the complexity of the agents.

While there have been several organization models proposed, none have been specifically targeted towards providing a general mechanism that allows the system to reorganize in order to adapt to its environment and changing capabilities. One of the first models of agent organizations was given by Ferber and Gutknecht in the AALAADIN model (Ferber & Gutknecht, 1998) and extended in the AGR model (Ferber, Gutknecht & Michel, 2003).The AALAADIN/AGR model used agents, groups, and roles as its primitive concepts and they are now found in almost all other organization models in one form or another. There have also been other attempts to extend the basic AGR model such as that proposed by Peng and Peng (2005) to provide some behavioral definition of roles. The MOISE+ model greatly extended the notion of an organization model by including three aspects: structural, functional, and deontic (Hübner, Sichman & Boissier, 2002). The structural aspect of MOISE+ is similar to the AGR model, defining the organizational structure via roles, groups, and links. The function aspect describes how goals are achieved by plans and missions while the deontic aspect describes the permissions and obligations of the various roles. One of the most complete organization models is the Organizational Model for Normative Institutions (OMNI) (Dignum, Vázquez-Salceda & Dignum, 2004), which is a framework that caters to open multiagent systems. OMNI allows heterogeneous agents to enter the organization with their own goals, beliefs, and capabilities and does not assume cooperative agents. OMNI combines two previous organization models: OperA (Dignum, 2004) and HarmonIA (Vázquez-Salceda & Dignum, 2003). An excellent overview of existing organizational models and dimensions of organizational modeling is found in Chapter II "Modelling Dimensions for Multi-Agent Systems Organizations" by Coutinho et al.

While almost all multiagent methodologies have an underlying metamodel that describes their basic modeling concepts, most are not explicitly defined. One exception is the ROADMAP method, whose metamodel is defined in Juan and Sterling (2004). ROADMAP defines a nice clean metamodel that includes the basic modeling concepts of roles, protocols, services, agents, knowledge, and the environment. Likewise, the Multiagent Systems Engineering (MaSE) methodology metamodel was defined in part based on the implementation of agentTool, a tool that supports the MaSE modeling process (DeLoach & Wood, 2001). The MaSE metamodel defines the main modeling concepts of goals, roles, agents, conversations, and tasks. Bernon et. al., combined the metamodels from three well-known methodologies – ADELFE, Gaia, and PASSI – into a common metamodel that they hoped would provide interoperability between the methods (Bernon, Cossentino, Gleizes, Turci & Zambonelli, 2005). While the unified metamodel contains many more concepts than those of single methodologies, the unified metamodel is very complex and it is not clear how many of the concepts are actually related. Based on his experience in trying to combine existing multiagent method fragments using the OPEN process framework, Henderson-Sellers has concluded that a single standard metamodel is required before fragments can be combined successfully on a large scale (Henderson-Sellers, 2005). OMACS provides the foundation for organization-based multiagent metamodel in which the analysis and design concepts are directly related to run-time concepts.

OMACS MODEL

The OMACS model grew from the MaSE metamodel, which was based on the original AGR model (Ferber, Gutknecht & Michel, 2003). We realized that while we could define multiagent systems in terms of agent playing roles in order to achieve system goals, we did not have to limit the flexibility of agents by predefining the roles they could and could not play. Noting that agents could be assigned to roles based on the capabilities required to play various roles and the capabilities possessed by the agents, we figured the agents could adapt their assignments based on the current set of goals required to be achieved by the system. This basic idea led to the OMACS model as defined in DeLoach, Oyenan, and Matson (2007) and shown in Figure 1.

General Organization Definition

OMACS defines an organization as a tuple O=⟨G, R, A, C, Φ, P, Σ, *oaf, achieves, requires, possesses*⟩ where

- G — goals of the organization
- R — set of roles
- A — set of agents
- C — set of capabilities
- Φ — relation over G × R × A defining the current set of agent/role/goal assignments
- P — set of constraints on Φ
- Σ — domain model used to specify environment objects and relationships

Figure 1. OMACS model

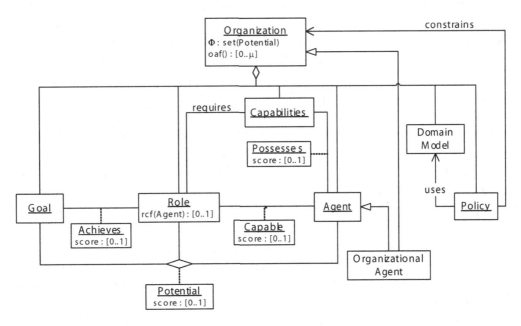

Equation 1.

$$
\mathrm{rcf}(a,r) = \begin{cases} if & \prod_{c \in requires(r)} possesses(a,c) = 0 & 0 \\ \\ else & & \dfrac{\sum_{c \in requires(r)} possesses(a,c)}{|requires(r)|} \end{cases}
$$

- oaf — function P(G × R × A) → [0.. ∞] defining quality of a proposed assignment set
- achieves — function G × R → [0..1] defining how effective the behavior defined by the role could be in the pursuit of the specified goal
- requires — function R → P(C) defining the set of capabilities required to play a role
- possesses function A × C → [0..1] defining the quality of an agent's capability

OMACS also includes two additional derived functions to help compute potential assignment values: capable and potential.

- capable — function A × R → [0..1] defining how well an agent can play a role (computed based on requires and possesses)
- potential — function A × R × G → [0..1] defining how well an agent can play a role to achieve a goal (computed based on capable and achieves)

Main Elements

The first eight elements in the organization tuple defined above – G, R, A, C, Φ, P, Σ, and *oaf* – constitute the main elements of the OMACS model as depicted in Figure 1. *Goals* are generally defined as a desirable situation (Russell & Norvig, 2003) or the objective of a computational process (van Lamsweerde, Darimont & Letier, 1998). In OMACS, each organization has a set of goals, G, that it seeks to achieve. OMACS makes no assumptions about these goals except that they can be assigned and achieved by one, and only one agent playing an appropriate role in the organization (i.e., agents do not share goals).

Each OMACS organization also has a set of roles (R) that it can use to achieve its goals. A *role* defines a position within an organization whose behavior is expected to achieve a particular goal or set of goals. These roles are analogous to roles played by actors in a play or by members of a typical corporate structure. Each OMACS role has a *name* and a function that defines how well an agent can play the role based on the capabilities possessed by that agent. This function is termed the role capability function, $rcf : A \times R \rightarrow [0..1]$. The rcf is defined at design time for each role and computed in terms of the capabilities required to play that role. A default rcf (as shown in Equation 1) would assume that all the capabilities required to play a role r are equally important, essentially taking the average of all the required possesses values ($possesses(a,c)$) (with the stipulation that none of those possesses scores are 0).

Each OMACS organization also has a set of heterogeneous *agents* (A), which are assumed to be computational systems (human or artificial) that sense and act autonomously in a complex dynamic environment in order to realize a set of assigned goals. Thus, we assume that agents exhibit the attributes of autonomy, reactivity, pro-activity, and social ability (Russell & Norvig, 2003). To be part of an OMACS organization, agents must have the ability to communicate with each other (which requires a share ontology and communication language at the organizational level), accept assignments to play roles that match their capabilities, and work to achieve their assigned goals.

OMACS uses the capabilities possessed by an agent to determine whether or not it can play a specific role. In OMACS, *capabilities* are atomic entities used to define a skill or capacity of agents. Capabilities can be used to capture *soft* abilities such as the ability to access certain resources or the knowledge of algorithms, or *hard* abilities such as sensors and effectors that are often associated with hardware agents such as robots. The set of capabilities, C, known to an organization is the union of all the capabilities required by roles or possessed by agents in the organization.

$$\forall \ c:C \ (\exists \ a:A \ possesses(a,c){>}0 \ \lor \ \exists \ r:R \ c{\in}requires(r)) \tag{2}$$

An *assignment set* Φ is the set of agent-role-goal tuples $\langle a, r, g \rangle$, that indicate that agent a has been assigned to play role r in order to achieve goal g. Φ is a subset of all the *potential assignments* of agents to play roles to achieve goals. This set of potential assignments is captured by the *potential* function (see equation (8)), which maps each agent-role-goal tuple to a real value ranging from 0 to 1 representing the ability of an agent to play a role in order to achieve a specific goal. If $\langle a, r, g \rangle {\in} \Phi$, then agent a has been assigned by the organization to play role r in order to achieve goal g. The only inherent constraints on Φ is that it must contain only assignments whose potential value is greater than zero (Equation 3) and that only one agent may be assigned to achieve a goal at a time (Equation 4).

$$\Phi \subseteq \{\langle a,r,g \rangle \mid a{\in}A \land r{\in}R \land g{\in}G \land potential(a,r,g) > 0\} \tag{3}$$

$$\forall \ a1,a2:A \ r1,r2:R \ g1,g2:G \ \langle a1,r1,g \rangle{\in}\Phi \land \langle a2,r2,g \rangle{\in}\Phi \land a1{=}a2 \tag{4}$$

In order to select the best set of assignments to maximize an organization's ability to achieve its goals, OMACS defines an *organizational assignment function*, or oaf, which is a function over the current assignment set, $oaf: \ \Phi \ \to \ 0..\infty$. As with the rcf, the selection of assignments may be application specific. Thus, each organization has its own application specific organization assignment function, oaf, which computes the *goodness* of the organization based on Φ. As with the rcf, we can define a default oaf, which is simply the sum of the potential scores in the current assignment set Φ.

$$oaf = \sum_{<a,r,g>\in\Phi} potential(a,r,g) \tag{5}$$

In general, *policies* are a set of formally specified rules that describe how an organization may or may not behave in particular situations. In OMACS, we distinguish between three specific types of policies: *assignment* policies (P_Φ) *behavioral* policies (P_{beh}), and *reorganization* policies (P_{reorg}). A more detailed discussion of policies is given later.

An OMACS *domain model*, Σ, is used to define object types in the environment and the relations between those types. The domain model is based on traditional object oriented class and relation concepts[1]. Specifically, an OMACS domain model includes a set of object classes, each of which is defined by a set of attribute types. The relations between object classes include general purpose associations as well as generalization-specialization and aggregation. Relations may also include multiplicities to constrain the number of object classes participating in any given relation.

Relations and Functions

There are three major relations/functions and two derived functions between the eight main elements that provide the power of the OAMCS model: *achieves*, *requires*, *possesses*, *capable*, and *potential*. The *achieves* function (although somewhat confusingly named) actually defines how effective an agent could be while playing that role in the pursuit of a specific goal. For instance, if one role requires more resources or better capabilities, it can use a different approach and thus yield better results than a second role that requires fewer resources or capabilities. Providing two different roles to achieve the same goal may provide the organization flexibility in deciding how to actually achieve a given goal. The value of achieves can be predefined by the organization designer or learned before or during system operation (Odell, Nodine & Levy, 2005). Thus, the OMACS `achieves` function formally captures the effectiveness of a role in achieving a specific goal by defining a total function from the R x G to a real value in the range of 0 to 1, `achieves: G × R → [0..1]`. Thus, by definition, a role that cannot be used to achieve a particular goal must have an `achieves` value of 0, while a role that can achieve a goal would have an `achieves` value greater than zero.

The key in assigning agents to roles is determining which agents are capable of playing which roles. In order to play a given role, agents must possess a sufficient set of *capabilities* that allow the agent to carry out the role and achieve its assigned goals. Thus OMACS defines the *requires* function, `re-quires: R → P(C)`, which allows an organization designer to define the minimal set of capabilities agents must possess in order to play that role.

In order to determine if some agent has the appropriate set of capabilities to play a given role, OMACS defines a similar relation, the `possesses` relation, that captures the capabilities a specific agents actually possesses. The possesses relation is formally captured as a function over agents and capabilities that returns a value in the range of 0 to 1, `possesses: A × C → [0..1]`. The real value returned by the possesses function indicates the quality of each capability possessed by the agent; 0 indicates no capability while a 1 indicates a high quality capability.

Using the capabilities required by a particular role and capabilities possessed by a given agent, we can compute the ability of an agent to play a given role, which we capture in the *capable* function. The capable function returns a value from 0 to 1 based on how well a given agent may play a specific role, `capable: A × R → [0..1]`. Since the capability of an agent, a, to play a specific role, r, is application and role specific, OMACS provides the `rcf` defined in the previous section that controls how this value is computed. Thus, the *capable score* of an agent playing a particular role is defined via the designer defined `rcf` of each role.

$$\forall \ a{:}A \ r{:}R \ capable(a,r) = r.rcf(a) \tag{6}$$

While the *rcf* is user defined, it must conform to one OMACS constraint. To be *capable* of playing a given role in the current organization, an agent must *possess* all the capabilities that are *required* by that role.

$$\forall \ a{:}A, \ r{:}R \ capable(a,r) > 0 \Leftrightarrow requires(r) \subseteq \{c \mid possesses(a,c) > 0\} \tag{7}$$

The main goal of OMACS is to provide a mechanism to assign goals to agents in such a way that agents cooperate toward achieving some top-level goal. Intuitively, this mechanism should provide a way to assign the best agents to play the best roles in order to achieve these goals. Thus, OMACS has defined a *potential* function that captures the ability of an agent to play a role in order to achieve a specific goal. The potential function maps each agent-role-goal tuple to a real value ranging from 0 to 1, `potential: A × R × G → [0..1]`. Here, a 0 indicates that the agent-role-goal tuple cannot be used to achieve the goal while a non-zero value indicates how well an agent can play a specific role in order to achieve a goal. The potential of agent a to play role r to achieve goal g is defined by combining the capable and achieves functions.

$$\forall \ a{:}A \ r{:}R \ g{:}G \ potential(a,r,g) = achieves(r,g) * capable(a,r) \tag{8}$$

Organizational Agents

Organizational agents (OA) are organizations that function as agents in a higher-level organization. In OMACS, OAs enable hierarchical organizations, providing OMACS with scalability while supporting software engineering principles such as modularity. As agents, OAs may possess capabilities, coordinate with other agents, and be assigned to play roles. OAs represent an extension to the traditional Agent-Group-Role (AGR) model developed by Ferber and Gutknecht (1998) and are similar to concepts in the organizational metamodel proposed by Odell, Nodine, and Levy (2005). While OAs are an integral part of OMACS, they are not discussed further in the chapter and the reader is referred to DeLoach, Oyenan and Matson (2007) for more information.

ORGANIZATION-BASED MULTIAGENT SYSTEMS ENGINEERING (O-MASE)

In order to create OMACS-based systems, we have defined a methodology that allows us to use modern multiagent design approaches. This process is part of the O-MaSE Process Framework (Garcia-Ojeda, DeLoach, Robby, Oyenan & Valenzuela, 2007) as shown in Figure 2. The O-MaSE Process Framework is based on the OPEN Process Framework (OPF) (Firesmith & Henderson-Sellers, 2002) and uses the OPF metamodel in level M2, which defines processes in terms of Work Units (Activities, Tasks, and Techniques), Producers, and Work Products. Level M1 contains the definition of O-MaSE in the form of the O-MaSE metamodel, method fragments, and guidelines. Customized processes are instantiated at the M0 level for specific projects (a *process instance*).

The goal of the O-MaSE Process Framework is to allow process engineers to construct custom agent-oriented processes using a set of method fragments, all of which are based on a common metamodel. To achieve this, we define O-MaSE in terms of a metamodel, a set of method fragments, and a set of guidelines. The O-MaSE *metamodel* defines a set of analysis, design, and implementation concepts and a set of constraints between them. The *method fragments* define how a set of analysis and design products may be created and used within O-MaSE. Finally, *guidelines* define how the method fragment may be combined to create valid O-MaSE processes, which we refer to as O-MaSE compliant processes.

Figure 2. O-MaSE Process Framework (Garcia-Ojeda, et al., 2007)

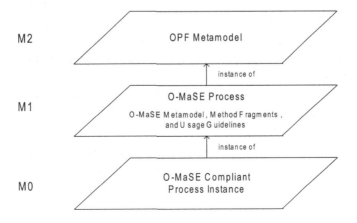

Figure 3. O-MaSE Metamodel

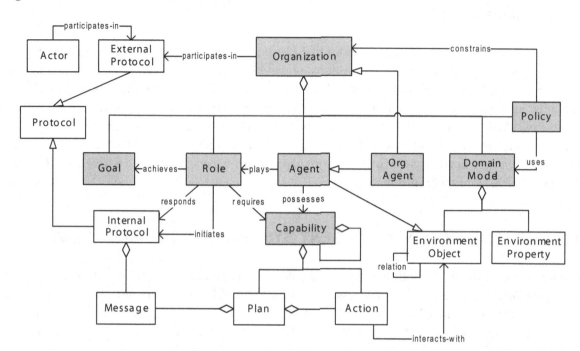

The O-MaSE methodology is supported by the agentTool III development environment[2], which is designed as a set of Eclipse plug-ins. agentTool includes a plug-in for each O-MaSE model and the agentTool Process Editor (APE), which was developed to support the design and definition of O-MaSE compliant processes. The APE plug-in is based on the Eclipse Process Framework and provides a process designer the ability to (1) extend O-MaSE with new tasks, models, or usage guidelines and (2) create new process instances by composing tasks, models, and producers from the O-MaSE method fragment library and then verifying that they meet process guidelines.

Metamodel

The metamodel defines the main concepts used in O-MaSE to design multiagent systems. It encapsulates the rules (grammar) of the notation and depicts those graphically using object-oriented concepts such as classes and relationships (Firesmith & Henderson-Sellers, 2002). The O-MaSE metamodel is based on the OMACS metamodel as shown in Figure 3, with the common parts of OMACS and O-MaSE shown in grey. This commonality allows us to easily create O-MaSE compliant process that can be used to develop OMACS systems.

Additional O-MaSE concepts include external actors, protocols, messages, plans, actions, and environment objects and properties. *External actors* are used to represent any agent, system, or user that lies outside the system being designed. *Protocols* define a set of allowable *message* sequences that may exist between external actors and an organization (external protocols) or between agents roles within an organization (internal protocols). *Plans* are a type of agent capability that define a sequence of *actions* or *messages* that can be used to achieve an agent's goal. The O-MaSE domain model consists of

Table 1. O-MaSE method fragments

Work Units					
Activity	**Task**	**Technique**	**Work Products**	**Producer**	**Language**
Requirement Engineering	Model Goals	AND/OR Decomposition	AND/OR Goal Tree	Goal Modeler	Natural languages, for textual documents
	Goal Refinement	Attribute-Precede-Trigger Analysis	Refined GMoDS		
Analysis	Model Organizational Interfaces	Organizational Modeling	Organization Model	Organizational Modeler	
	Model Roles	Role Modeling	Role Model	Role Modeler	UML, for specific models
	Define Roles	Role Description	Role Description Document		
	Model Domain	Traditional UML notation	Domain Model	Domain Expert	Agent-UML
Design	Model Agent Classes	Agent Modeling	Agent Class Model	Agent Class Modeler	O-MaSE specific notation
	Model Protocol	Protocol Modeling	Protocol Model	Protocol Modeler	
	Model Plan	Plan Specification	Agent Plan Model	Plan Modeler	Formal Language, for formal specification of properties of the system.
	Model Policies	Policy Specification	Policy Model	Policy Modeler	
	Model Capabilities	Capability Modeling	Capabilities Model	Capabilities Modeler	
	Model Actions	Action Modeling	Action Model	Action Modeler	

a set of environment objects that describe the objects in the system's domain and a set of environment properties that specify the principles and processes that govern the environment.

Method Fragments

As described above, the OPF metamodel defines Stages, Work Units, Work Products, Producers, and Languages for use in creating tailorable processes. In O-MaSE, the method fragments were derived from an extended version of the MaSE methodology (DeLoach, Wood & Sparkman, 2001). Currently, we have focused our efforts on the analysis and design and thus, we have defined three main activities in O-MaSE (1) requirements engineering, (2) analysis, and (3) design. As shown in Table 1, each Activity is decomposed into a set of Tasks with a corresponding set of Techniques that can be used to accomplish them. Each task also has an associated set of Work Products, Producers, and Languages.

In the Requirement Engineering activity, we seek to translate systems requirement into system level goals by defining two tasks: *Model Goals* and *Goal Refinement*. The first focuses on transforming system requirements into a system level goal tree while the second refines the relationships and attributes for the goals. The goal tree is captured as a Goal Model for Dynamic Systems (GMoDS) (Miller, 2007). The Goal Modeler must be able to: (1) use AND/OR Decomposition and Attribute-Precede-Trigger Analysis (APT) techniques, (2) understand the System Description (SD) or Systems Requirement Specification (SRS), and (3) interact with domain experts and customers. The result of these two tasks are an AND/OR Goal Tree and GMoDS tree.

Table 2. Work product states

No.	State	Definition
1	inProcess()	True if the work product is in process.
2	completed()	True if the work product has been finished.
3	exists()	exists() = inProcess() ∨ completed()
4	previousIteration()	True if the work product's iteration is any previous one.
5	available()	This state applies to producers and not to work products.

The objective of the *Model Organizational Interfaces* task is to identify the organization's interfaces with external actors. There are three steps in modeling organizational interfaces including (1) identifying each external actor that may interact with the organization (system), (2) identifying how those actors interact with the organization, and (3) identifying the system level goals achieved by the organization.

Guidelines

Guidelines are used to describe how the method fragments can be combined in order to obtain O-MaSE compliant processes and are specified as a set of Work Unit pre and postconditions over Work Products (WP), Producers (P), Work Products states (see Table 2), and Work Product iterations (n) and versions (m). We formally specify guidelines as a tuple ⟨Iνπυτ, *Output, Precondition, Postcondition*⟩, where *Input* is a set of Work Products that may be used in performing a work unit, *Output* is a set of Work Products that may be produced from the Work Unit, *Precondition* specifies valid Work Product/Producer states, and *Postcondition* specifies the Work Product State that is guaranteed to be true after successfully performing a work unit (if the precondition was true).

Figure 4 shows the guidelines for the Model Goals task. Inputs include the Systems Description (SD), the Systems Requirement Specification (SRS), the Role Description Document (RD), or a previous version of the Goal Model (GM). Actually, only one of these inputs is required, although as many as are available may be used. The inputs are used by the Goal Model Producer (GMP) to identify organization goals. As a result of this task, the GM work product is obtained.

Figure 4. Model goal task constraints

TASK NAME: Model Goals			
Input	Output	Precondition	Postcondition
SD,SRS, RD,GM	GM	((exists(<SD,n,m>) ∨ exists(<SRS,n,m>) ∨ exists(<RD,n,m>) ∨ previousIteration(<GM>)) ∧ available(GMP)	completed(<GM,n,m>)

POLICIES FOR OMACS-BASED SYSTEMS

Harmon, DeLoach and Robby (2007) define the notion of policies for controlling the adaptiveness of OMACS systems. While this work is similar to the more general specification of institutional norms using concepts from deontic logic (Vázquez-Salceda, et. al. 2004), it is more narrowly focused towards controlling the adaptive processes of closed multiagent organizations such as those supported by OMACS. For our work, we define *policies* as specifications of desired system behavior that can be used to specify either (1) what the system should do or (2) what the system should not do, which essentially equate to liveness and safety properties (Lamport, 1977). These policies are essential in designing adaptive systems that are both predictable and reliable (Robby, DeLoach & Kolesnikov, 2006). In early multiagent research, policies (or laws) were described as *social laws* that must always hold (Shoham and Tennenholtz, 1995); we refer to these as *law policies*. This concept is similar to *regimented norms*, which is one approach to the operationalization of norms that cannot (as opposed to should not) be violated (van der Torre, et. al. 2005). An example of a law policy for a multiagent conference management system might be that no agent (representing a committee member) may review more than five papers as represented in (1).

$$\forall a{:}A, \mathcal{L} : \Box \, (sizeOf(a.reviews) \leq 5) \qquad (1)$$

The $\mathcal{L}$ in the policy denotes that this is a law policy and the $\Box$ is the temporal logic operator that declares that this property must always hold. Intuitively, this policy states that no legal run of the system may be in a state where any agent is assigned to review more than five papers-. While the policy is helpful in ensuring no agent overworked, it restricts, possibly unnecessarily, the flexibility of the system to deal with unforeseen situations. Consider the case where more papers are submitted than were expected. If there are not enough agents, the entire system will fail. This is a common problem when using only law policies.

The more traditional use of the term policies in human organizations refers to a normative guidance as opposed to strict laws. Interpreting policies as laws in multiagent systems can lead to inflexibility and poor overall system performance. In contrast, human policies are often suspended to achieve the organization goals. To overcome the inflexibility of law policies, we created a weaker policy type called *guidance policies*, which are defined as policies that the system must adhere to *when possible*. An example of policy (1) converted to a guidance policy is shown in (2).

$$\forall a{:}A, \mathcal{G} : \Box \, (sizeOf(a.reviews) \leq 5) \qquad (2)$$

The $\mathcal{G}{:}$ in the policy indicates that it is a guidance policy. Thus, while the specification for both types of policies is identical save the $\mathcal{L}$ or $\mathcal{G}$, the difference lies in the interpretation. Law policies ensure some property is *always* true (e.g. for safety or security), while guidance policies are used when the policy should remain true, when possible. With a guidance policy (2) in effect instead of law policy (1), the system can still achieve its goals when it gets more submissions than expected since it can assign more than five papers to an agent. However, when there are sufficient agents, however, policy (2) ensures that each agent performs five or fewer reviews.

In our research, the phrase *when possible* means that a system may only violate a guidance policy when there is no way the system can achieve its goal without violating the policy. This condition is easy to determine when the system only has to worry about violating a single guidance policy at a time. However, it is often the case that we have multiple guidance policies and the system may be forced to choose between two (or more) guidance policies to violate. To solve this dilemma in a non-random way, we define a partial ordering of guidance policies that allows the system designer to set precedence relationships between guidance policies. This partial order forms a lattice, such that a policy that is a parent of another policy in the lattice, is more-important-than its children. When there is clear precedence relation between the guidance policies being analyzed for violation, the least important policy is violated. However, when there is no clear precedence between policies (due to it only being a partial ordering), then one of the policies is chosen at random. Again, there is similar work related to conflict detection and resolution for norms (Kollingbaum et. al. 2007), which is more complex than our problem of guiding the adaptivity of organizations.

Harmon, DeLoach, and Robby (2007) showed that the guidance policies provide the best of both worlds. When applied in two multiagent systems, they resulted in systems with the same flexibility as similar systems with no policies while providing the improved performance of systems with comparable law policies. Essentially you get the benefit of law policies with none of the drawbacks.

REORGANIZATION ALGORITHMS AND ARCHITECTURES

During the development of several OMACS-based systems, we have developed several reorganization algorithms, most of which have been centralized. These algorithms range from sound and complete total reorganization algorithms to greedy algorithms (Zhong, 2006). As expected, sound and complete total reorganization algorithms are extremely slow, especially when the organization lacks any policies that limit the number of legal combinations of agents, roles, and goals (Zhong & DeLoach, 2006). The greedy algorithms also perform as expected, giving low computational overhead and producing generally adequate organizations. However, greedy algorithms typically must be tailored to the system being developed. We have also looked at learning reorganization algorithms (Kashyap, 2006).

Figure 5. General reorganization algorithm

```
function reorganize(oaf, G_w, A_w)
    1.    for each g ∈ G_w
    2.     for each role r ∈ R
    3.       if achieves(r,g) > 0 then m ← m ∪ ⟨r,g⟩
    4.     ps ← P_Φ(powerset(m))
    5.    for each agent a ∈ A_w
    6.     for each set s ∈ ps
    7.       if capable(a,s.r) then pa ← pa ∪ ⟨a,s⟩
    8.     pas ← powerset(P_Φ(pa))
    9.    for each assignment set i from c
    10.    for each assignment x from pa
    11.       Φ ← Φ ∪ ⟨x.a,x.s_i⟩
    12.    if P_Φ(Φ) is valid
    13.      if oaf(Φ) > best.score then best ← ⟨oaf(Φ),Φ⟩
    14.    return best.Φ
```

A general purpose reorganization algorithm that produces an optimal solution with OMACS is shown in Figure 5. By *optimal*, we refer to the organization with the highest score as returned by the *oaf*. Therefore, finding the optimal organization score requires going through every potential assignment (every combination of goals, roles, and agents) and computing the organization score for each combination. In the algorithm, G_w refers to the goals that the organization is currently pursuing while A_w refers to the current set of agents that are available to be assigned. Lines 1 – 3 create all valid goal–role pairs from goals in G_w and the roles that are able to achieve that goal. Line 4 creates a powerset of all possible sets of goal–role pairs and then removes invalid sets using the assignment policies. Lines 5 – 7 create all the possible assignments pa between the agents from A_w and the goal–role pairs in each set in ps. Line 8 removes invalid assignments from pa based on the assignment policies and then creates the set of all possible assignment sets, pas. Lines 10 – 13 go through each possible assignment set to find the one with the best *oaf* score. Finally, line 14 returns the best (optimal) set of assignments.

Assignment policies can have significant effects on the time complexity of reorganization algorithms. With the simple policy that *agents can only play one role at a time*, algorithmic complexity can be reduced by an order of magnitude as described in Zhong (2006).

While this centralized reorganization algorithm is optimal, its performance makes it impractical in real systems. Therefore, we generally use application specific reorganization algorithms that have been tuned to include application-specific policies. For example, in many cases, we do not always want to do a complete reorganization every time a new goal appears. It is also often the case that we only want to assign a single goal to an agent at a time. These two application specific modifications make most realistic reorganization algorithms run extremely quickly and generally perform close to optimal.

Team Level Architecture

Our current Team-level Architecture is shown in Figure 6. There are two components in each agent: the Control Component (CC) and the Execution Component (EC). The CC performs all organization-level reasoning while the EC provides all the application specific reasoning.

To reason about the team's organizational state, each agent has an instance of the organization model and an appropriate set of reasoning algorithms and coordination protocols to work within their team to organize and reorganize as needed. The model and algorithms perform the organization-level reasoning

Figure 6. Organization-level architecture

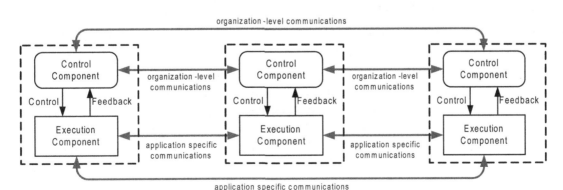

Figure 7. Organization-based agent architecture

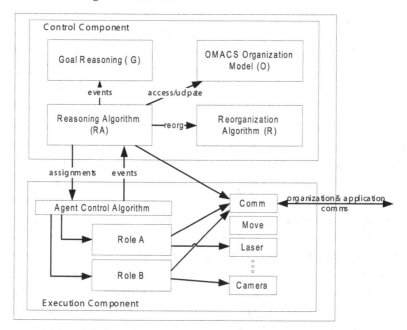

via interaction between the individual CCs as shown in Figure 6. In essence, the combined organizational level of the individual agents forms a distributed organizational control mechanism. The agents cooperate to share organizational knowledge and define the appropriate team organization. In this scheme, the CC provides *control* to the agent about the roles it should be playing, the set of goals it is trying to satisfy, and other agents with which it may coordinate. The EC provides *feedback* based on possible events that are of interest to the organization (goal failure, goal completion, or application specific events that may trigger new goals, etc.). The agents also communicate at the application-specific level, which includes the coordination between agents that allows them to carry out their assigned roles.

Organization-Based Agent Architecture

Our current version of the internal architecture of our agents is called the Organization-based Agent (OBA) architecture, as shown in Figure 7. In the *Control Component*, there are four basic components:

Figure 8. Generic OMACS reasoning algorithm

```
loop
    e = getEvent()
    <G_a, G_additions, G_deletions> = G.occurred(e)
    O.setActiveGoalSet(G_a)
    O.removeAssignments(G_deletions)
    assignSet = R.reorg(O.A, G_a)
    O.addAssignmetns(assignSet)
    sendUpdates(assignSet)
end loop
```

Goal Reasoning, Organization Model, Reorganization Algorithm (RA), and the overall Reasoning Algorithm. The Reasoning Algorithm ties the other three components together. First, the RA gets an event from either another agent or the Application Specific Roles/Behavior component. This event is passed to the Goal Reasoning component, which updates the goal instance tree and returns a tuple that include the new set of active goals, the additions to the active goal set, and the deletion from it. The RA then sets the active goal set in the Organization Model component and removes any assignments related to the goals deleted from the active goal set. If we need to do a total reorganization (via some undetermined process), we compute the new assignment set by calling the Reorganization Algorithm; if not, then we only ask for a reorganization using the unassigned agents and the new goals. The new assignment set is updated in the Organization Model and these assignment updates are sent to either other agents or to the Application Specific Roles/Behavior component.

One of the main design goals of the OBA architecture was enable as much reuse as possible. Since in an OMACS based system, much of the reasoning has standard forms (e.g., goal reasoning, reorganization, etc.), much of the code in the CC is in fact reusable. Knowledge about the OMACS entities can be inserted into standard implementations of both G and O, while a set of standard reorganization algorithms (R) are being developed for plug-and-play compatibility; these algorithms include centralize as well as distributed versions. While much of the EC is application specific, the Agent Control Algorithm can be reused and use of standard capabilities can make the job of developing the application specific roles much simpler.

Reasoning Algorithm

A high-level algorithm for the Reasoning Algorithm (RA) component is shown in Figure 8. Again, this algorithm is often tuned to the application being developed and thus we simply show it as a notional

Figure 9. WMD goal model

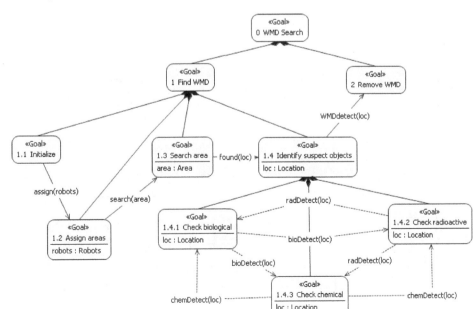

algorithm. When RA receives an event (which include organization events such as goal achievement/failure or the modification of agent capabilities as well as application specific events such as goal triggers) from either an external agent or from its Execution Component, it calls the *occurred* method of the Goal Reasoning component in order to get the new active goal set G_a, along with the set of additions to and deletions from G_a. The RA updates the active goal set and assignment set in the OMACS Organization Model. The RA then calls the *reorg* method of the Reorganization Algorithm to get a new set of assignments, which is then updated in the Organization Model. Finally, updates of the assignments are sent to other agents (if this is the centralized reorganization agent) and to its Execution Component.

In the Execution Components, the assignments (which include the role to be played to achieve a specific goal) are received by the Agent Control Algorithm, which invokes the appropriate roles and for execution. When a role achieves its assigned goal, fails to achieve its assigned goal, or recognizes an application-specific event that impacts the goal model, the role passes the event to the Agent Control Algorithm, who in turns passes that back to the RA. In the OBA architecture, the various capabilities possessed by an agent are encoded in separate components and invoked directly by the roles.

EXAMPLE

To illustrate the use of O-MaSE to develop OMACS systems, we show the development of a Weapons of Mass Destruction (WMD) Cooperative Robotic Search system. While we do not have space to discuss the creation of the O-MaSE compatible process that we used to develop this system, suffice it to say that we took a very simple approach and developed only four models: a Goal Model, a Role Model, a set of Plan Models, and an Agent Class Model. To completely define the system, we probably should have included Capability-Action Models and a Domain Model as well. The four models we did develop are presented below.

The GMoDS Goal Model for the system is shown in Figure 9. The top goal is decomposed into two subgoals: *Find WMD* and *Remove WMD*. The *Find WMD* goal is decomposed further into four subgoals:

Figure 10. WMD role model

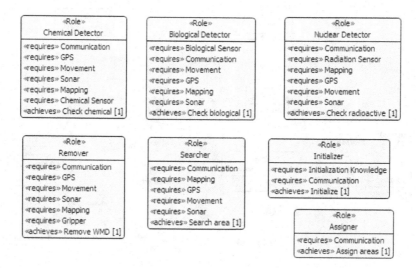

Initialize, *Assign areas*, Search *area*, and *Identify suspect objects*. The solid arrows between goals represent events that occur during achievement of the first goal, which triggers the instantiation of the second goal. Thus, for example, the *Initialize* goal will be assigned to some agent at system initialization. Essentially, each robot must register with the agent performing the *Initialize* goal. Once enough robots register or enough time has elapsed, that robot triggers, via the assign trigger with the list of robots, a new goal, *Assign areas*. A new robot is assigned to achieve the *Assign* areas goal using the list of robots. This robot divides the predefined search area into subareas based on the robots available to search. For each subarea, the robot triggers a new *Search area* goal (parameterized by subarea) via the search event. Each *Search area* goal is then assigned to a robot to be achieved. During the search, if one of the searching robots finds a suspicious object, it triggers a new Iden*t*ify suspect object goal by raising the event found with a specific loc (location) parameter. The *Identify* suspect object goal is actually decomposed into three subgoals, thus, when a found event is raised, the three subgoals – *Check biological*, *Check radioactive*, and *Check chemical* – are actually triggered. Anytime these three goals are triggered, they are assigned to robots with the appropriate sensors to be able to achieve the goals. The dashed arrows between the three subgoals represent *negative triggers*, which actually remove existing goal instances from the system. Thus, if the robot assigned to the goal *Check biological* determines that the object is actually a biological weapon, not only does it raise a *WMDdetect* event with the loc parameter, but it also raises a *bioDetect* event as well. The *bioDetect* event negatively triggers both the *Check radioactive* and *Check chemical* goals whose parameter, loc, matches the event. In essence, it tells the other robots assigned to check out the WMD that they no longer need to check that location. Finally, when a *WMDdetect* event is raised, it triggers a *Remove WMD* goal.

Once the GMoDS Goal Model is defined, a set of roles are identified for achieving the individual leaf goals. A Role Model for the WMD system is shown in Figure 10. Essentially, we have mapped each leaf goal to a single role that is responsible for achieving it as annotated by the «achieves» keyword; the value of the achieves function for the associated role-goal pair is shown in square brackets, which in this case are all 1's as there is only a single role capable of achieving each goal. The «requires» keyword in the role boxes indicate the capabilities that are required to play that role. This maps directly the notion of roles and required capabilities in the OMACS model. In a typical Role Model, it is often the case that there

Figure 11. Searcher plan model

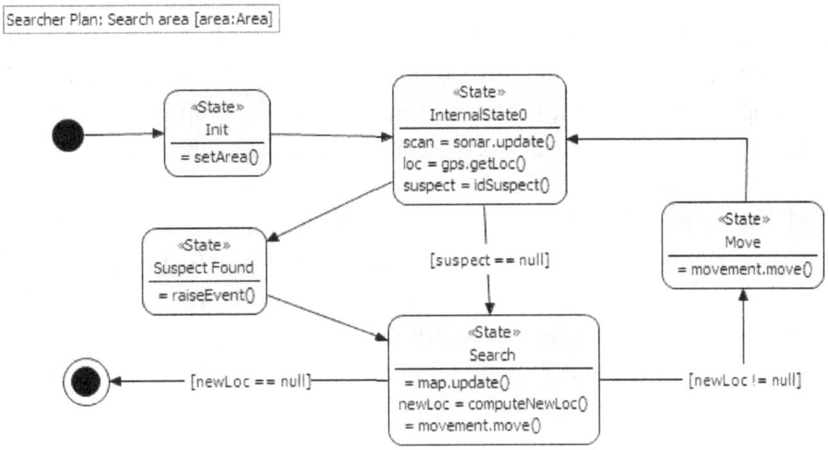

Figure 12. WMD agent class model

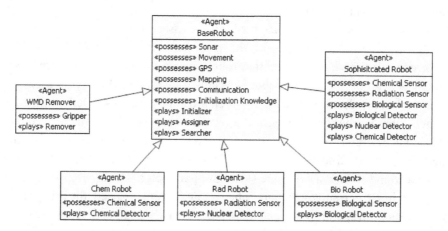

would be directed relations between roles indicating that a protocol, and thus information sharing exists between two roles. However, the lack of explicit protocols between roles is not uncommon in OMACS-based systems as most of the information required for collaboration between roles is embedded in the goals that are instantiated. For instance, in Figure 9, when a search event triggers to *Search area* goal, it carries a parameter that defines the area to be searched. Thus, when an agent is assigned to play the *Searcher* role in order to achieve that goal, the goal is given to the agent and no explicit communication is required. The same thing happens when a suspicious object is found or a WMD is detected.

Once a role and its required capabilities have been identified, plans can be developed that define exactly how the capabilities are used to achieve a specific goal. In O-MaSE, a Plan Model is defined in terms of a finite state machine with sequentially executed actions in each state. The box in the upper left hand corner of Figure 11 shows that the Searcher Plan was developed in order to achieve the *Search area* goal, which has a parameter that specifies the search area. If there were explicit communication required, this communication would be shown on the state transitions as explicit *send* and *receive* actions. The actions called inside the states are either lower level function calls or direct calls to capability actions. Capability actions are denoted by the form `capabilityName.actionName(parameters)`.

After the roles and their required capabilities are identified, the types of agents, or agent classes, must be defined. In a cooperative robotic system, this corresponds to defining the types of robots that will be available along with their capabilities. The Agent Class Model for the WMD system is shown in Figure 12. There is a *BaseRobot* type, which defines a standard robot. By analyzing the capabilities it possesses, we can tell that the *BaseRobot* is capable of playing the *Searcher, Initializer,* and *Assigner* roles. The other five agent types inherit the capabilities (and thus the ability to play those three roles) from the *BaseRobot* class. Except for the *Sophisticated Robot* class, the other four specialized agent classes are designed to play a single specific role. However, because the *Sophisticated Robot* has all three types of WMD sensors, it can play *Chemical, Biological,* and *Nuclear Detector* roles.

At this point, we have defined all the basic OMACS elements except for policies and a domain model, which are not included due to space limitations. It would also be helpful to use the Capability-Action Model to define the effects of the actions, as used in the plans, on domain model elements. We implemented this system in our Cooperative Robotic Simulator (CROS) to demonstrate the effectiveness of the OMACS and GMoDS models. The simulation worked as expected and showed how the team of robots could effectively assign and reassign robots to play specific roles to achieve goals as they were instantiated based on the events that occurred in the environment. In the next section, we walk through a small part of a scenario to illustrate the details of OMACS operation.

Scenario

To illustrate the basic operation of OMACS, we walk through a simple scenario using the WMD system defined above. For this example, we have four agent types: two *BaseRobots* (BR1, BR2), one *Sophisticated Robot* (SR), one *Chem Robot* (CR), and one *WMD Remover Robot* (RR). We assume each agent is designed using the OBA architecture, although the exact reorganization algorithm used does not need to be specified. For simplicity, the reader may wish to assume that a centralized version of the algorithm is being used where all agents forward events and receive assignments directly from the central decision maker. In this case, the term *the organization* refers to the central decision maker. Since we only have a single role capable of be used to achieve each goal, we assume that the `achieves` value of each role-goal pair is either 0 or 1, depending on whether or not the role can be used to achieve a goal. Also, for simplicity, we assume that capabilities do not degrade and all robots (with a single exception) possess the same quality of capabilities. The exception is that the CR's *Chemical Sensor* capability is better than the SR's *Chemical Sensor* and thus `possesses(CR,Chemical Sensor)=1` while `possesses(SR,Chemical Sensor)=0.5`. Using the default `rcf` as defined in equation (1) and the `potential` function as defined in (8), we see that the potential of all agent, role, goal triples are either 0 or 1 with the exception that `potential(SR, Chemical Detector, Check chemical) = .917` (the `rcf` averages the possesses of the six required capabilities for the *Chemical Detector* role).

When the system starts, some leader election algorithm decides which robot becomes the central decision maker and all robots in the organization register with it. Then, the *Initialize* goal is instantiated by the organization (as it is not triggered by an application specific event) and placed in the active goal set (G_A). The organization's reorganization algorithm is invoked to decide which robot is assigned the *Initialize* goal. While all robots could play the *Initializer* role in order to achieve the *Initialize* goal (since all have robots have *Initialization Knowledge* and *Communication* capabilities), we assume it is assigned to robot RR and the initial state of the organization is:

G_A = {Initialize}
Φ = {<RR, Initializer, Initialize>}

RR follows the plan associated with the *Initializer* role to determine the number of robots available who are capable of playing the *Searcher* role. Then, RR raises the *assign* event (parameterized with a list of the available robots) to the organization. The organization uses the Goal Reasoning component (G) to determine that an *Assign areas* goal (parameterized with the list of robots) should be instantiated and placed in G_A. At that point, RR has achieved the *Initialize* goal and raises an *achieved* event. At this point, the organization again calls its reorganization algorithm to determine how to assign the *Assign areas* goal. Since the only role capable of being used by an agent to achieve the *Assign areas* goal is the *Assigner* role and all robots are capable of playing it with equal capability, one is chosen at random. We assume the assignment is given to SR and the state of the organization is

G_A = {Assign Areas(robots)}
Φ = {<SR, Assigner, Assign Areas(robots)>}

SR performs the *Assigner* role resulting in the division of the search area into five separate search areas (based on the number of robots that can play the *Searcher* role). The SR raises a *search(area)* event to the organization for each of the five search areas a1, a2, a3, a4, and a5. These five events cause the instantiation of five *Search area* goals, each having a unique parameter based on the unique search areas. At this point, SR has successfully completed playing the *Assigner* role and raises an *achieved* event resulting in the removal of the *Assign areas* goal from G_A and the assignment of SR from Φ. At this point, the organization runs its reorganization algorithm and produces the following set of assignments.

G_A = {Search area(a1), Search area(a2), Search area(a3), Search area(a4), Search area(a5)}
Φ = {<BR1, Searcher, Search area(a1)>, <BR2, Searcher, Search area(a2)>,
<SR, Searcher, Search area(a3)>, <CR, Searcher, Search area(a4)>,
<RR, Searcher, Search area(a5)>}

The robots perform their assignments until a new event occurs; possible events include a goal being achieved, a change in capability, or the discovery of a suspicious object. First, we assume that BR1's sonar fails and it can no longer play the *Searcher* role and thus cannot achieve the *Search area*(a1) goal. BR1 raises a *failed* event for goal *Search area*(a1) and the organizer runs its reorganization algorithm to reassign that goal. Depending on the actual reorganization algorithm in used, a robot could be picked at random, or application specific knowledge such as the physical relationship of the areas to be searched could be used to make the assignment. For our purposes, we assume BR2 is assigned to this goal resulting in the following organizational state.

G_A = {Search area(a1), Search area(a2), Search area(a3), Search area(a4), Search area(a5)}
Φ = {<BR2, Searcher, Search area(a1)>, <BR2, Searcher, Search area(a2)>,
<SR, Searcher, Search area(a3)>, <CR, Searcher, Search area(a4)>,
<RR, Searcher, Search area(a5)>}

Notice that BR2 is assigned to search two areas since we have not specified any policies that restrict the assignment. If we had a policy that a robot could play a single role at a time, then the goal *Search area(a1)* could not be assigned to any robot and it would have to wait until a robot became free. Next, assume BR2 finds a suspicious object, resulting in it raising a *found(loc)* event, where loc represents the x,y location of the object. This event causes the organization to instantiate the three sub-goals of the *Identify suspect object* goal, which are *Check biological*, *Check chemical*, and *Check radioactive*. The only two robots that can achieve these goals are SR and CR. As far as the *Check biological* and *Check radioactive* goals, either of the two robots are equivalent in that their possesses score for five required capabilities (Communication, Movement, GPS, Mapping, Sonar and either Biological or Radiation Sensor) for the associated roles (Biological Detector and Nuclear Detector) yield identical potential values. However, for the *Check radioactive* goal, the difference in the Chemical Sensor capability produces a potential value of .917 for SR and 1.0 for CR. Therefore, while the reorganization algorithm may assigned either SR or CR to the *Check biological* and *Check radioactive* roles, it will always assign CR to play the Chemical Detector role in order to achieve the *Check chemical* goal since its potential value shows that it is the most capable robot. One possible state of the organization is shown below.

$G_A =$ {Search area(a1), Search area(a2), Search area(a3), Search area(a4), Search area(a5)}
$\Phi =$ {<BR2, Searcher, Search area(a1)>, <BR2, Searcher, Search area(a2)>,
    <SR, Searcher, Search area(a3)>, <CR, Searcher, Search area(a4)>,
    <RR, Searcher, Search area(a5)>, <SR, Biological Detector, Check biological>,
    <CR, Radioactive Detector, Check radioactive>,
    <CR, Chemical Detector, Check chemical>,
    }

CONCLUSION

In this chapter, we presented the OMACS model as a metamodel for designing complex, adaptive systems that can reorganize at runtime in the face of a dynamic environment. While the OMACS model itself is a useful tool, we believe that in order to make its application more straightforward, a suite of technologies that support its use must also be available. Specifically, the O-MaSE framework is a key element of this support suite. Using O-MaSE, developers have a set of models and techniques they can use to design the key elements of an OMACS-based system. The fact that O-MaSE was designed to be tailorable to a large number of situations makes its especially useful for OMACS as well as other multiagent approaches.

The use of policies in adaptive systems will be necessary in order to provide some level of control over the system adaptation. Experience has shown that emergent behavior is often detrimental as opposed to being useful. However, the use of strict law policies often has the effect of limiting the flexibility (and thus emergent behavior) too much. We have attempted to overcome this limitation by introducing the formal notion of guidance policies which provides the performance enhancing effects of law policies while not unnecessarily restricting the ability of the system to adapt.

Finally, we presented the OBA architecture, which we use to implement OMACS-based systems. While this is not the only architecture that can be used to implement OMACS-based systems, we have been able to demonstrate its effectiveness on several multiagent and cooperative robotic systems. The goal of the architecture is to provide a modular framework that can reuse as much OMACS-specific code as possible.

FUTURE WORK

There are several areas where additional work is needed. We will highlight three: architecture and algorithm development, software engineering for complex, adaptive systems, and integration of humans into artificial agent teams. While the architectures and algorithms presented in this chapter have been shown to be effective in developing OMACS-based systems, additional work needs to be done toward creating a component-based, plug-and-play agent architecture. While we have used the GMoDS, other goal reasoning models can be used. The same is true for reorganization algorithms. Due to the algorithmic complexity of a general-purpose optimal reassignment algorithm, algorithms that use general or application specific policies to prune the search area would be beneficial. In fact, it is common to have the general policy that an agent may only play one role at a time. Simply embedding this into the reorganization algorithm reduces the algorithm complexity significantly. We are also investigating algorithms that look at local reorganization techniques to reduce the effect of a total reorganization. Having the ability to choose reorganization algorithms from a library would be extremely helpful.

A second area of future work is continued work in the area of software engineering of agent-oriented systems. Specifically, O-MaSE needs to continue its evolution in terms of the number and diversity of models and techniques for designing OMACS-based systems. Because it is impossible to test all possible configurations of OMACS-based systems, developers will need help in trying to get a handle on all the possibly ways the system can reconfigure and how that might affect system performance. We have started working on *predictive metrics*, where we have applied model checking techniques to determine the effectiveness of design and their impact on system adaptivity. In Robby, DeLoach and Kolesnikov (2006), we developed two metrics used to predict system flexibility: Covering Percentage and Coarse Redundancy. Each metric computes the increase or decrease in the flexibility of a design as compared to the maximum flexibility inherent in the system Goal Model. We are currently investigating metrics that tell us about the criticality of individual goals, roles and agents; however, more work needs to be done.

While completely autonomous teams of agents are one possible solution to complex, adaptive systems, we believe that it is much more likely that a mix of humans, hardware agents, and software agents will be necessary to achieve the results that will be expected of future systems. Therefore, there is research needed into how to include human agents into OMACS organizations. When determining the proper human personnel to deploy, many factors are considered such as training, expertise, and current work cycles, etc. While these factors can be looked at as OMACS capabilities, exactly how we might do that is open to speculation. On approach would be to develop specific functions for *human performance shaping factors* that can be employed to determine the team organization and predict human performance degradations. A second area requiring research is to develop interaction techniques to allow humans and artificial agents to work together.

ACKNOWLEDGMENT

This work was supported by grants from the US National Science Foundation grant number 0347545 and by the US Air Force Office of Scientific Research grant number FA9550-06-1-0058.

REFERENCES

Bernon, C., Cossentino, M., Gleizes, M., Turci, P., & Zambonelli, F. (2005). A study of some multi-agent meta-models. In J. Odell, P. Giorgini, J. Müller (Eds.) *Agent-Oriented Software Engineering V: 5th Intl. Workshop*, Lecture Notes in Computer Science 3382, Springer: Berlin, (pp. 62-77).

Carley, K. M. (1995). Computational and mathematical organization theory: perspective and directions. *Computational and Mathematical Organization Theory, 1*(1), 39-56.

Carley, K. M. (1998). Organizational adaptation. *Annals of operations research, 75*, 25-47.

Carley, K. M., & Gasser, L. (1999). Computational organization theory. In G. Weiss (ed.), *Multiagent systems: A modern approach to distributed artificial intelligence.* MIT Press: Cambridge, MA.

Cohen, P. R., & Levesque, H. J. (1991). Teamwork. *Nous, 25*(4), 487-512.

DeLoach, S. A., & Wood, M. F. (2001). Developing multiagent systems with agentTool. In C. Castelfranchi, Y. Lesperance (Eds.). *Intelligent agents vii. Agent theories architectures and languages, 7th international workshop.* Lecture Notes in Computer Science 1986. Springer: Berlin.

DeLoach, S. A., Oyenan, W., & Matson, E. T. (2008). A capabilities-based theory of artificial organizations. *Journal of Autonomous Agents and Multiagent Systems, 16*(1), 13-56.

DeLoach, S. A., Wood, M. F., & Sparkman, C. H. (2001). Multi-agent systems engineering. *The International Journal of Software Engineering and Knowledge Engineering, 11*(3), 231-258.

Dignum, V. (2004). *A model for organizational interaction: Based on agents, founded in logic.* PhD thesis, Utrecht University.

Dignum, V. Vázquez-Salceda, J., & Dignum, F. (2004). Omni: Introducing social structure, norms and ontologies into agent organizations. In *Programming multi-agent systems: 2nd international workshop,* Lecture Notes in Computer Science 3346, Springer: Berlin. (pp.181–198).

Ferber, J., & Gutknecht, O. (1998). A meta-model for the analysis and design of organizations in multi-agent systems, in *Proceedings of the third international conference on multiagent systems,* IEEE Computer Society: Washington D.C. 128-135.

Ferber, J., & Gutknecht, O., & Michel, F. (2003). From agents to organizations: An organizational view of multi-agent systems. In P. Giorgini, J.P. Muller, J. Odell (Eds.), *Software engineering for multi-agent systems IV: Research issues and practical applications series,* Lecture Notes in Computer Science 2935, Springer: Berlin. 214-230. 10.1007/b95187.

Firesmith, D. G., & Henderson-Sellers, B. (2002). *The OPEN process framework: An introduction.* Harlow, England: Addison-Wesley.

Garcia-Ojeda, J. C., DeLoach, S. A., Robby, Oyenan, W. H., & Valenzuela, J. (2008). O-MaSE: A customizable approach to developing multiagent development processes. In Michael Luck (eds.), *Agent-Oriented Software Engineering VIII: The 8th International Workshop on Agent Oriented Software Engineering (AOSE 2007),* Lecture Notes in Computer Science 4951, Springer: Berlin, 1-15.

Grosz, B. J., & Kraus, S. (1996). Collaborative plans for complex group action. *Artificial intelligence, 86*(2), 269-357.

Harmon, S. J., DeLoach, S. A., & Robby. (2007, October). Trace-based specification of law and guidance policies for multiagent systems. *Paper presented at The Eighth Annual International Workshop Engineering Societies in the Agents World,* Athens, Greece.

Henderson-Sellers, B. (2005). Evaluating the Feasibility of Method Engineering for the Creation of Agent-Oriented Methodologies. In M. Pechoucek, P. Petta, L.Varga (eds) *Multi-agent systems and applications iv: 4th international central and eastern European conference on multi-agent systems.* Lecture Notes in Computer Science 3690, Springer: Berlin. (pp. 142-152).

Hübner, J., Sichman, & Boissier, J. O. (2002). MOISE+: Towards a Structural, Functional and Deontic Model for MAS Organization. In *Proceedings of the 1st international joint conference on autonomous agents and multi-agent systems* (pp. 501-502).

Jennings, N. R. (1995). Controlling cooperative problem solving in industrial multi-agent systems using joint intentions. *Artificial intelligence, 75*(2), 195-240.

Juan, T., & Sterling, L. (2004). The roadmap meta-model for intelligent adaptive multi-agent systems in open environments. In *Proceedings 2nd international conference on autonomous agents and multi-agent systems* (pp. 53-68), Lecture Notes in Computer Science 2935, Springer: Berlin.

Kashyap, S. (2006). *Reorganization in multiagent systems*, Master's Thesis, Kansas State University.

Kinny, D., Ljungberg, M., Rao, A. S., Sonenberg, L., Tidhar, E., & Werner, G. E. (1992). Planned team activity. In C. Castelfranchi, E. Werner (eds.), *Artificial social systems - Selected papers from the fourth European workshop on modeling autonomous agents in a multi-agent world* (pp. 226-256), Lecture Notes in Artificial Intelligence 830, Springer: Berlin.

Kollingbaum, M. J., Norman, T. J., Preece, A., & Sleeman, D. (2007). Norm Conflicts and Inconsistencies in Virtual Organisations. In J. G. Carbonell and J. Siekmann (Eds.) *Coordination, Organizations, Institutions, and Norms in Agent Systems II*. Lecture Notes in Computer Science 4386, Springer: Berlin, 245-258.

Lamport, L. (1977). Proving the correctness of multiprocess programs. *IEEE Transactions on Software Engineering, 3*(2), 125-143.

Miller, M. A. (2007). *Goal model for dynamic systems*. Master's Thesis, Kansas State University.

Odell, J., Nodine, M., & Levy, R. (2005). A metamodel for agents, roles, and groups, In J. Odell, P. Giorgini, Müller, J. (Eds.), *Agent-oriented software engineering V: The fifth international workshop* (pp. 78-92). Lecture Notes in Computer Science 3382 Springer: Berlin. 10.1007/b105022.

Peng, Z., & Peng, H. (2005) An improved agent/group/role meta-model for building multi-agent systems. In *Proceedings of the 2005 international conference on machine learning and cybernetics* (pp. 287-292).

DeLoach, S. A., & Kolesnikov, V. A. (2006). Using design metrics for predicting system flexibility, in L. Baresi, R. Heckel (eds.), *Proceedings of the 9th International Conference on Fundamental Approaches to Software Engineering*, Lecture Notes in Computer Science 3922, (pp. 184-198). Springer: Berlin. 10.1007/11693017_15.

Russell, S., & Norvig, P. (2003). *Artificial intelligence a modern approach*. Upper Saddle River, NJ: Pearson Education.

Shoham, Y., & Tennenholtz, M. (1995). On social laws for artificial agent societies: off-line design. *Artificial Intelligence, 73*(1-2), 231-252.

Tambe, M. (1997). Towards flexible teamwork. *Journal of AI research, 7*, 83-124.

van der Torre, L., Hulstijn, J., Dastani, M., Broersen, J. (2005). Specifying Multiagent Organizations. In J. G. Carbonell, J. Siekmann (Eds.) *Proceedings of the Seventh Workshop on Deontic Logic in Computer Science (Deon'2004)*. Lecture Notes in Computer Science 3065, Springer: Berlin, (pp. 243-257).

van Lamsweerde, A., Darimont, R., & Letier, E. (1998). Managing conflicts in goal-driven requirements engineering. *IEEE Transactions on Software Engineering, 24*(11), 908-926.

Vázquez-Salceda, J., Aldewereld, H., & Dignum, F. (2004). Implementing norms in multi-agent systems in J. G. Carbonell and J. Siekmann (Eds.) *Multiagent System Technologies*, Lecture Notes in Artificial Intelligence 3187, Springer: Berlin, 313-327.

Vázquez-Salceda, J., & Dignum, F. (2003). Modelling electronic organizations. In V. Marik, J. Muller, M. Pechoucek (eds.), *Multi-agent systems and applications iii* (pp. 584–593). Lecture Notes in Artificial Intelligence 2691, Springer: Berlin, 584-593..

Zambonelli, F., Jennings, N. R., & Wooldridge, M. J. (2001). Organisational Rules as an Abstraction for the Analysis and Design of Multi-Agent Systems. *International Journal of Software Engineering and Knowledge Engineering, 11*(3), 303-328.

Zhong, C. (2006). *An investigation of reorganization algorithms*. MS Thesis, Kansas State University, 2006.

Zhong, C., & DeLoach, S. A. (2006). An Investigation of Reorganization Algorithms, In Hamid R. Arabnia (Ed.): *Proceedings of the International Conference on Artificial Intelligence*, 2 (pp. 514-517). CSREA Press.

ADDITIONAL READING

Aldewereld, H. Dignum, F. Garcia-Camino, A. Noriega, P. Rodriguez-Aguilar, J.A. and Sierra, C. (2006). Operationalisation of norms for usage in electronic institutions. In Proceedings of the fifth international joint conference on Autonomous agents and multiagent systems. 223—225.

Artikis A. Sergot M. and Pitt J. (2007). Specifying Norm-Governed Computational Societies. ACM Transactions on Computational Logic (in press).

Bergenti F., Gleizes M.P., & Zambonelli F. (Eds.). (2004). *Methodologies and software engineering for agent systems: The agent-oriented software engineering handbook*. Kluwer Academic Publishers: Norwell, MA.

Bernon C., Cossentino M., & Pavón J. (2005). Agent oriented software engineering. *The Knowledge Engineering Review*. 20, 99–116.

Beydoun G., Gonzalez-Perez C., Henderson-Sellers B., Low G. (2005). Developing and evaluating a generic metamodel for MAS work products. In: Garcia, A., Choren, R., Lucena, C. Giorgini, P., Holvoet, T., and Romanosky, A. (eds.): *Software Engineering for Multi-Agent Systems IV*. Lecture Notes in Computer Science, 3194. Springer-Verlag: Berlin, 126–142.

Cossentino M., Gaglio S., Henderson-Sellers B., and Seidita V. (2006). A metamodelling-based approach for method fragment comparison. In J. Krogstie, T.A. Halpin, H.A. Proper (Eds.) *Proceedings of the 11th international workshop on exploring modeling methods in systems analysis and design*, Namur University Press: Namur, Belgium, 419-432.

Coutinho, L., Sichman, J., Boissier, O. (2005). Modeling Organization in MAS: A Comparison Of Models, in *Proceedings of the 1st.Workshop on Software Engineering for Agent-Oriented Systems* Uberlândia, Brazil.

DeLoach S.A., Valenzuela J.L. (2007). An agent-environment interaction model. In L. Padgham, F. Zambonelli (Eds): *Agent oriented software engineering VII*. Lecture Notes in Computer Science, 4405. Springer-Verlag, 1-18.

DeLoach, S.A. (2001). Analysis and Design using MaSE and agentTool, In *Proceedings of the 12th Midwest Artificial Intelligence and Cognitive Science* Conference. Oxford, Ohio.

DeLoach, S.A., (2006). Multiagent systems engineering of organization-based multiagent systems. In A. Garcia, et. al. (Eds). *Software engineering for multi-agent systems IV: Research issues and practical applications series*. Lecture Notes in Computer Science 3914, Springer: Berlin, 109-125.

European Institute for Research and Strategic Studies in Telecommunications. (2000). *MESSAGE: Methodology for engineering systems of software agents, EURESCOM project P907-GI*. Heidelberg, Germany: R. Evans, P. Kearney, J. Stark, G. Caire, F.J. Garijo, J.J Gomez Sanz, J. Pavon, F. Leal, P. Chainho, P. Massonet.

Henderson-Sellers, B., Giorgini P. (Eds.). (2005). *Agent-oriented methodologies*. Idea Group: New York.

Horling, B., Lesser, V. (2005). Using ODML to model multi-agent organizations. In *Proceedings of the IEE/WIC/ACM international conference on intelligent agent technology*. 72-80, DOI: 10.1109/IAT.2005.139.

Hübner, J. Sichman, J. & Boissier, O. (2002). MOISE+: Towards a structural, functional and deontic model for MAS organization. In *Proceedings of the 1st international joint conference on autonomous agents and multi-agent systems*. ACM Press: Bologna, Italy. 501-502.

Jennings, N.R., (1993). Commitments and conventions: The foundation of coordination in multiagent systems. *Knowledge Engineering Review*, 8(3), 223-250.

Knottenbelt, J.A. (2001). Policies for Agent Systems. MS Thesis. Department of Computing, Imperial College London.

Matson, E., DeLoach, S.A. (2004). Integrating robotic sensor and effector capabilities with multi-agent organizations. *Proceedings of the international conference on artificial intelligence*. CSREA Press, 481-488.

Matson, E., DeLoach, S.A., (2003). An organization-based adaptive information system for battlefield situational analysis. In *Proceedings of the international conference on integration of knowledge intensive multi-agent systems*. 46-51. DOI: 10.1109/KIMAS.2003.1245020.

Nair, R. Tambe, M. & Marsella, S. (2002). Team formation for reformation. In *Proceedings of the AAAI spring symposium on intelligent distributed and embedded systems.*

Robby, Dwyer, M.B. & Hatcliff, J. (2003). Bogor: An extensible and highly-modular model checking framework. In *Proceedings of the 4th joint meeting of the European software engineering conference and ACM sigsoft symposium on the foundations of software engineering.* ACM: New York. 267 – 276.

Seidita, V., Cossentino, M., Gaglio, S. (2006). A repository of fragments for agent systems design. In F. De Paoli, A. Di Stefano, A. Omicini, C. Santoro (Eds.) *Proceedings of the 7th workshop from objects to agents.* Catania, Italy. 130–137.

Sycara, K. (1998). Multiagent Systems, *AI Magazine*, 19 (2). 79-93.

Turner, R.M. & Turner, E.H. (2001). A two-level, protocol-based approach to controlling autonomous oceanographic sampling networks. *IEEE Journal of Oceanic Engineering*, 26(4), 654-666.

Uszok, A. and Bradshaw, J. and Jeffers, R. and Suri, N. and Hayes, P. and Breedy, M. and Bunch, L. and Johnson, M. and Kulkarni, S. and Lott, J. (2003). KAoS policy and domain services: toward a description-logic approach to policy representation, deconfliction, and enforcement. In POLICY 2003: IEEE 4th International Workshop on Policies for Distributed Systems and Networks. IEEE, 93-96.

Wagner, G. (2001). Agent-oriented analysis and design of organisational information systems. In J. Barzdins, A. Caplinskas (Eds.). *Databases and Information Systems.* Kluwer Academic Publishers: Norwell, MA. 111-124.

Vasconcelos W. Kollingbaum M. and Norman T. (2007). Resolving conflict and inconsistency in norm-regulated virtual organizations. In AAMAS '07: Proceedings of the 6th international joint conference on Autonomous agents and multiagent systems. ACM Press : New York, NY, USA. 1-8.

Wooldridge, M. Jennings, N.R., D. Kinny. (2000). The gaia methodology for agent-oriented analysis and design. *Journal of Autonomous Agents and Multi-Agent Systems.* 3(3), 285-312.

Zambonelli, F. Jennings, N.R., Wooldridge, M.J. (2001). Organisational abstractions for the analysis and design of multi-agent systems. In P. Ciancarini, M.J. Wooldridge (Eds.) *Agent-oriented software engineering – Proceedings of the first international workshop on agent-oriented software engineering.* Lecture Notes in Computer Science 1957, Springer: Berlin. 207-222.

Zambonelli, F., Jennings, N.R., Omicini, A., Wooldridge, M.J. (2001). Agent-oriented software engineering for internet applications. In A. Omicini, F. Zambonelli, M. Klusch, R. Tolksdorf (Eds.) *Coordination of internet agents: models, technologies, and applications.* Springer: Berlin. 326-346.

KEY TERMS

Agent: An entity that perceives and can perform actions upon its environment, which includes humans as well as artificial (hardware or software) entities.

Capability: An atomic entities used to define a skill or capacity of agents.

Goal: A desirable state of the world or the objective of a computational process.

Goal Model for Dynamic Systems (GMoDS): a set of models for capturing system level goals and for using those goals at runtime to allow the system to adapt to dynamic problems and environments.

Organization Model for Adaptive Computational Systems (OMACS): A model that defines the knowledge needed about a system's structure and capabilities to allow it to reorganize at runtime in the face of a changing environment and its agent's capabilities.

Organization-Based Agent (OBA) Architecture: an architecture for implementing agents capable of reasoning within an OMACS organization.

Organization-Based Multiagent Systems Engineering (O-MaSE): A framework for creating compliant processes that support the development of OMACS-based systems

Policy: A specification of desired system behavior that can be used to specify either (1) what the system should do or (2) what the system should not do.

Reorganization: The transition from one organizational state to another.

Role: Defines a position within an organization whose behavior is expected to achieve a particular goal or set of goals.

Chapter V
Hermes:
Designing Flexible and Robust Agent Interactions

Christopher Cheong[1]
RMIT University, Melbourne, Australia

Michael Winikoff
RMIT University, Melbourne, Australia
University of Otago, Dunedin, New Zealand

ABSTRACT

Although intelligent agents individually exhibit a number of characteristics, including social ability, flexibility, and robustness, which make them suitable to operate in complex, dynamic, and error-prone environments, these characteristics are not exhibited in multi-agent interactions. For instance, agent interactions are often not flexible or robust. This is due to the traditional message-centric design processes, notations, and methodologies currently used. To address this issue, we have developed Hermes, a goal-oriented design methodology for agent interactions which is aimed at being pragmatic for practicing software engineers. Hermes focuses on interaction goals, i.e., goals of the interaction which the agents are attempting to achieve, and results in interactions that are more flexible and robust than message-centric approaches. In this chapter, we present the design and implementation aspects of Hermes. This includes an explanation of the Hermes design processes, notations, and design artifacts, along with a detailed description of the implementation process which provides a mapping of design artifacts to goal-plan agent platforms, such as Jadex.*

INTRODUCTION

Our ever-evolving and technologically advanced world is a place that is complex, dynamic, and failure-prone. Intelligent agents are steadily accruing purchase as a technology which is intrinsically able to address the aforementioned real world issues (Jennings, 2001). Currently, intelligent agents are used in a range of real world applications spanning a number of different domains. These include telecommunication systems (Chaib-draa, 1995; Jennings 2001), process control (Sycara 1998; Jennings et al. 1998), air traffic control (Sycara, 1998), business process management (Jennings, 2001), logistics (Benfield et al., 2006), production scheduling (Munroe et al., 2006), and many more.

A key issue in developing and using agents is how to systematically analyse and design multi-agent systems. This issue has resulted in the development of the field of *Agent Oriented Software Engineering*. This field has seen the development of a number of *methodologies* which provide the developer with guidance, processes, and notations for the analysis and design of agent systems.

The systems in the previous examples all employ multiple agents as "there is no such thing as a single agent system" (Wooldridge, 2002). In such multi-agent systems, agent interactions are the crux of the matter, as the agents will need to interact in various ways in order to achieve their goals. Consequently, the design of agent *interactions* is a crucial part of a design methodology.

Current approaches to interaction design are message-centric as the design process is driven by messages that are exchanged during the interaction and is focused on the information passed within the messages. For example, in the Prometheus methodology (Padgham and Winikoff, 2004), as part of its interaction design process, the designers are advised to think about messages and alternatives. This is not restricted to Prometheus, but is also the norm in other methodologies such as Gaia (Zambonelli et al., 2004), MaSE (DeLoach et al., 2001) and Tropos (Bresciani et al., 2004).

Using current message-centric approaches to create interactions results in a number of problems. The main problem is that designs resulting from message-centric approaches tend to be overly, and sometimes unnecessarily, constrained. For example, using the interaction protocol of Figure 1, the interaction must begin with the Customer agent enquiring about the price of a laptop. It cannot, for example, enquire about the availability of a laptop first. Similarly, if a laptop is out of stock, the Vendor cannot proactively send a "Laptop Out of Stock" message to the Customer agent before or after replying with the price.

This lack of flexibility and robustness in interactions is problematic for intelligent agents. By following such limited designs, key intelligent agent characteristics, such as autonomy and proactivity, are greatly subdued and the fundamental concept of goal-orientation is ignored. Thus, current approaches to interaction design are not congruent with the agent paradigm.

More abstractly, the problem with message-centric approaches results from the general design process where the designer begins by creating a desirable but rigid message sequence and then "loosens it", i.e. improves flexibility and robustness by adding alternatives. The problem with this is that the "default" result is an interaction that has not been sufficiently "loosened", and is more constrained than it needs to be. A number of alternative approaches for specifying agent interactions have been explored. These alternative approaches avoid overly restricting interactions by starting with completely unconstrained interactions and then adding constraints so that the protocols are restricted and lead only to desirable interactions.

In this chapter we describe one such alternative approach: the *Hermes* methodology. Hermes provides a way of designing agent interactions that results in flexible and robust interactions. A key design aim of Hermes was that it had to be *pragmatic*, that is, easily usable by designers. In particular, we wanted Hermes to include processes, notations, and guidance, not just a means for representing interactions. Furthermore, Hermes had to be usable by software engineers, not just agent researchers.

Hermes is intentionally limited to the design and implementation of agent *interactions* and not of entire agent systems as there are already many good methodologies for such in existence. Instead

Figure 1. Message-centric protocol example

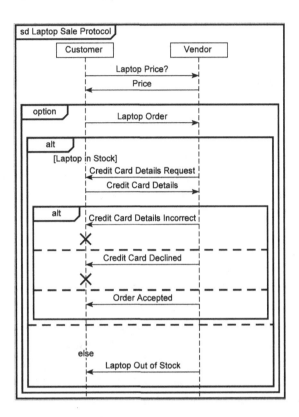

of competing with those methodologies, Hermes should be integrated with existing methodologies. Although not covered in this chapter, Hermes has been integrated with the Prometheus methodology (Cheong and Winikoff, 2006b). In the integrated methodology Hermes replaces the interaction design part of Prometheus, leaving the rest of the methodology unchanged.

The work, as currently presented, is intended for closed agent systems[2]. However, during the development of this methodology, the applicability of this work to open systems[3] was kept in mind. Although not specifically designed for such systems, the methodology should be able to be adapted to work with open systems.

Thus the aim of this work, which has a software-engineering flavour, is to provide a practical *solution* to designing flexible and robust interactions between agents (primarily) in *closed* systems (where agents have more limited autonomy). By contrast, Chapter X, 'Grounding Organizations into the Minds of Agents', by Castelfranchi has more of a philosophical flavour, and is concerned with posing *questions* about the nature of organizations, roles, agents, goals, and their relationships, including the process of goal adoption and delegation.

The remainder of this chapter is structured as follows. A background section reviews some background covering both traditional and alternative approaches to designing interactions. The following section presents the Hermes methodology, covering a process and design notations. We then present guidelines for implementing Hermes designs, and finally conclude and discuss future research directions.

BACKGROUND: INTERACTION DESIGN

There are a number of ways in which agent interactions can be modeled and designed. The most obvious and simplest approach is to focus on information exchanged between interacting agents, i.e. the messages, and to specify and design interactions in terms of possible sequences of messages. This is indeed the approach that many current design methodologies use, and we refer to such approaches as "traditional" or "message-centric".

Although simple and obvious, the problem with this approach is that it only captures the interaction at a superficial level. Focussing only on the communicative acts means that important information, such as the reason for uttering the communication, is not considered in the interaction design process. Furthermore, the interactions tend to be more restricted in terms of the range of possible interactions that are supported (termed "flexibility"), and in their ability to recover from failure (termed "robustness"). These shortcomings have motivated researchers to investigate a range of "alternative" approaches for agent interaction.

In addition to work that aims to make interactions (in closed systems) more flexible and robust, there is also work on designing (open) societies of agents. Rather than focusing on enabling the social ability of intelligent agents, this body of work is about defining societal-level mechanisms, such as norms, obligations and social laws, to provide rules of interactions for intelligent agents.

Two approaches to societal design of agent interactions are Islander and OperA. Islander (Vasconcelos et al., 2002; Esteva et al., 2002), an approach to electronic institutions, focuses on the macro-level (societal) aspects of multi-agents systems, rather than the micro-level (agent level). Electronic institutions are similar to their human counterparts in that they regulate what interactions can occur between agents. More specifically, an electronic institution defines a number of interaction properties, such as what interactions can occur, which agents can and cannot interact and under what circumstances these interactions can take place. In Islander, this is achieved by a global protocol which constrains the interactions between all components of the system.

Similarly to Islander, OperA (*Organizations per Agents*) (Dignum, 2004; Dignum and Dignum, 2003) takes a macro-level view of agent systems and focuses on agent societies rather than individual agents. The motivation for OperA is that most existing agent-oriented methodologies design agents from the individual agent perspective, however, a wider perspective, such as a societal-level one, is required to design agent societies as a society, i.e. not just a collection of individual agents interacting together. Furthermore, some societal-level goals cannot be captured as a collection of individual agent goals. Capturing societal-level goals allows for the analysis of societal characteristics, which is a motivation for OperA. OperA is a model and a design methodology for creating such agent societies.

The remainder of this section describes the traditional message-centric approach, and then surveys a number of alternative approaches.

Traditional Message-Centric Approaches to Agent Interactions

Agent interactions have traditionally been specified in terms of interaction protocols expressed in notations which focus on the message exchanges between the agents. Common notations for expressing such agent interactions are Agent UML (AUML) (Odell et al., 2000; Huget and Odell, 2004), Petri nets (Reisig, 1985), and finite state machines. AUML sequence diagrams (Huget et al., 2003) are quite often used to specify agent interactions, and has been adopted by methodologies, such as Gaia, MaSE,

Prometheus, and Tropos, and is commonly used. It should be noted that the AUML sequence diagram has developed from its original version (Bauer et al., 2000 & 2001) to a more recent version (Huget et al., 2003; Huget and Odell, 2004) which is influenced by UML 2.0.

In relation to our goal of designing flexible and robust agent interactions we observe that although the AUML sequence diagram is frequently used to represent agent interactions, it has a number of problems associated with it. In theory, it is possible to have an unlimited number of alternative message sequences; thus, it is possible, in theory, to create a very flexible and robust design in which all alternatives are catered for. However, in practice, this is impractical and cumbersome, and would result in an AUML sequence diagram which is difficult to read, understand, and manage. This practical limitation is attributed to the fact that the notation for AUML sequence diagrams focuses on the sequences of messages exchanged between agents in the interactions.

Furthermore, although AUML itself is a notation and not a design process, the design processes often employed with AUML sequence diagrams lead to designs that exhibit limited flexibility and robustness. For example, when developing interaction protocols using Prometheus, the interaction designer is focused on identifying alternative out-going messages in response to incoming messages and, thus, does not have the autonomy and proactivity of intelligent agents foremost in mind when designing these interactions.

These processes typically start with a desired set of message exchanges between agents in an interaction and then are generalized by the addition of alternative message sequences. That is, the design begins with a very restricted interaction and then proceeds to "loosen" or "relax" it by adding alternatives. This tends to result in designs that have a limited number of alternatives as it is a cumbersome process to add many alternatives and it is also impractical to add many alternatives using the AUML sequence diagram notation. By contrast, Hermes is somewhat better able to capture alternatives, and its design process leads the designer to explicitly consider failure points, resulting in a more flexible and robust design (see the evaluation discussed in the conclusion section of this chapter).

Thus, the AUML sequence diagram notation, in concert with message-centric design processes, leads to designs that have limited alternatives. As the agents are bound to follow the designed interactions, they are restricted to the limited number of alternatives that the interaction designers have allowed.

For example, using the interaction protocol of Figure 1, the interaction must begin with the Customer agent enquiring about the price of a laptop. It cannot, for example, enquire about the availability of a laptop first. This is inflexible since the Customer may be more concerned about availability (e.g. if the price is standard and they need the machine quickly). Similarly, if a laptop is out of stock, the Vendor cannot proactively send a "Laptop Out of Stock" message to the Customer agent before or after replying with the price. Furthermore, this protocol does not allow for an alternative credit card to be used, should the provided card be declined.

A better approach to interaction design is to start at the opposite end of the spectrum. That is, to begin with a completely unconstrained interaction and then proceed by adding constraints to restrict the agents so that they produce desirable interactions. Because the design is by default unconstrained, rather than constrained, this tends to lead to a greater number of alternatives, resulting in greater flexibility and robustness in interactions. Such alternative approaches to the traditional message-centric approach are discussed in the following section.

Alternative Approaches to Traditional Agent Interactions

There are various alternative approaches to the traditional message-centric interaction design. These alternative approaches, in contrast to message-centric approaches, diverge from focusing on the messages to design the interaction. Instead, they focus on various other elements of the interaction, such as social commitments or the states of the interaction which guide the agents to communicate (i.e. exchange messages). Thus, these alternative approaches are at a higher level of abstraction than message-centric approaches.

Although the end product is still agent interactions in which agents communicate through exchanges of messages, designing these interactions at a higher level of abstraction has a number of advantages. The foremost of which is that valid message sequences *emerge* from the interaction in a less constrained manner, which increases the flexibility of the interaction. This is quite different to message-centric interaction design in which, as explained in the previous section, valid message sequences must be *explicitly specified* and are often too constrained.

Alternatives to message-centric design includes commitment- and landmark-based approaches, along with a number of other alternative approaches. In commitment-based interactions, agents are guided by social commitments to communicate and progress through the interactions.

There are a number of approaches based on the notion of social commitments (Singh, 1991; Castelfranchi, 1995). Also see Chapter XI 'Modelling Interactions via Commitments and Expectations' by Torroni et al., which also considers using *expectations* as an alternative approach to defining the semantics of interactions. One reason for the popularity of social commitment-based approaches is that social commitments are *verifiable*. That is, social commitments are independent from an agent's internal structure and mental states and are observable by other agents. These are two important properties, as the first allows the social commitment to be utilized by heterogeneous agents and the second allows all agents involved in the interaction to determine if a commitment has been violated or not.

In commitment machines (Yolum and Singh, 2002 & 2004), a (social) commitment between two agents represents one agent's responsibility to bring about a certain condition for the other agent. There are two types of commitments in commitment machines: base-level and conditional commitments. A base-level commitment is denoted as $C(x, y, p)$, which states that a debtor, x must bring about a condition, p, for creditor, y. A conditional commitment is denoted as $CC(x, y, p, q)$ and states that if a condition p is brought about, then debtor x will be committed to creditor y to bring about condition q.

For example, consider an e-commerce example based on a simplified version of the NetBill protocol, taken from (Yolum and Singh, 2002), in which a *customer* is attempting to purchase a product from a *vendor*. One possible action is for the vendor to send a quote to the customer. This action has the effect of creating two conditional commitments: the first is an offer that, should the customer accept the offer, the vendor will then be committed to delivering the product[4]; the second commitment is for the vendor to provide a receipt conditional on the customer having paid. Formally these commitments are $CC(vendor, customer, agree, productDelivered)$ and $CC(vendor, customer, paid, receiptSent)$ where *agree* is itself the commitment $CC(customer, vendor, productDelivered, paid)$.

The interaction is driven by the (base-level) commitments of the agents. In this example, once the customer accepts the offer from the vendor, the first commitment above becomes a base-level commitment to ensure that products are delivered. Once this is done the customer's agreement becomes the base-level commitment to pay, and once payment is received the vendor's second commitment becomes a base-level commitment to send a receipt.

A key point in the approach is that this particular sequence is only one of many possible sequences. For example, another, equally valid, interaction begins with the vendor shipping the goods (this may make good sense if the goods are "zero cost", e.g. software) and the customer may then decide whether to pay for the goods. Another interaction sequence begins with the customer accepting (i.e. committing to pay for goods should they be provided).

The work of Flores and Kremer (2004b, 2004a), is another approach based on social commitments, however, their notion of commitment is slightly different to that of commitment machines. They view a social commitment as an agreement between two agents in which one agent is responsible for the *performance* of a certain action for the other agent. Note that the debtor does not necessarily have to perform the action itself; it is only responsible for that action being performed, whether it performs it itself or employs another agent to perform it. As with commitment machines, the agents progress through the interaction through the attainment, manipulation, and discharge of commitments.

A third commitment-based approach to agent interactions is the work of Fornara and Colombetti (2002, 2003). As with the previous approaches, the social commitments are utilized to drive the interaction. However, in this body of work, the commitments are defined as an abstract data type, the *commitment class*, which can be instantiated into a *commitment object*. The commitment abstract data type consists of a number of fields (such as debtor, creditor, state, content, and condition) which describe the properties of a commitment and a number of methods (such as make, cancel, reject) which are used to manipulate it.

Chapter XIV, 'Specifying Artificial Institutions in the Event Calculus' by Fornara and Colombetti, provides an analysis of commitments and their life-cycle using the event calculus, and relates commitments to the larger picture of institutions.

Although a social commitment approach is suitable for creating more flexible and robust interactions than current message-centric approaches, it has a number of disadvantages. Commitment-based approaches have only been applied to a few small examples and it is not clear whether they are applicable to larger or more realistic interactions. Additionally, it is unclear what software tool support exists for the facilitation of creating interactions based on commitment machines.

Another disadvantage is the lack of mature design processes for creating agent interactions using social commitments. That is, given a particular interaction, it is not obvious what commitments are required to create a commitment-based interaction. The work in (Yolum, 2005) describes a number of protocol conditions to be checked and provides algorithms to check these conditions. A methodology for the design of commitment machines has been recently presented (Winikoff, 2006) (along with a process for mapping commitment machine designs to a collection of plans (Winikoff, 2007)). However, this is only an initial methodology and it has not been applied to a wide range of examples. Furthermore, this methodology begins interaction design with a Prometheus-style scenario, which is a sequence of ordered steps. This tends to result in designs that are constrained and do not exploit well the flexibility and robustness that commitment machines are able to achieve.

Thus, although promising, designing flexible and robust interactions using social-commitments does not yet seem to be a usable and pragmatic approach for practicing software engineers. In contrast, this work aims to provide a pragmatic methodology for the design of flexible and robust agent interactions. This methodology has been applied to a larger range of interaction than the initial commitment machine methodology presented in (Winikoff, 2006).

In the landmark-based approach (Kumar et al., 2002a; Kumar et al., 2002b; Kumar and Cohen, 2004), a *landmark* represents a particular state of affairs and agent interactions are represented by a set of partially ordered landmarks, which can be initial (the start of the interaction), essential intermediate landmarks, optional intermediate landmarks, or final landmarks where the interaction terminates. Agents navigate through the landmarks to reach a final desired landmark, that is, a desired state of affairs, proceeding from one landmark to another by communicating with one another. The landmarks and their partial ordering can be depicted as a graph.

In this work the states of affairs are more important than the actions (i.e. communicative acts) that bring them about. Thus, as with the commitment-based approaches, the message sequences are not explicitly defined, but rather, they emerge as the agents communicate in an attempt to reach a final desired state of affairs.

The landmarks approach is theoretical in nature and has a heavy reliance on expertise in modal and temporal logics, which practicing software engineers typically will not have. Although an implementation, *STAPLE*, has been mentioned, there have been no further details apart from the publication of two posters (Kumar et al., 2002b; Kumar and Cohen, 2004).

More closely related to the research in this chapter is the goal-plan approach of Hutchison and Winikoff (2002), in which interactions are realized using the plans and goals of Belief-Desire-Intention (BDI) agents. The work proposed a process to translate a message-centric protocol to a set of goals and plans. The work can be seen as a predecessor to this research. However, although a design process was outlined, it was not detailed and there is no mapping from design to implementation. Further to lacking a clear design process, as with the aforementioned approaches, the goal-plan approach has not been integrated with any existing full agent system design methodologies.

Although this section describes alternative approaches to traditional message-centric design, there is not much discussion about how to *design* agent interactions in the presented approaches. The approaches focus on novel ways in which more flexible and robust agent interactions can be represented and achieved, but as yet, they do not focus on how the interactions can be *designed* using these novel approaches. In the previously described approaches, the lack of design processes and methodologies is a recurring disadvantage and limitation. In fact, this lack of design processes is one of the key motivation for the research described in this document.

HERMES DESIGN PROCESS

In this section, we present the design aspect of the Hermes methodology. The contributions of this section are:

- A design process that guides the designer to create goal-oriented interactions from an initial high level description of an interaction through to a design which can be implemented on goal-plan agent platforms, including steps for identifying and handling failure.
- Failure handling mechanisms which increase the flexibility and robustness of the goal-oriented interactions.
- Notation[5] for capturing and modeling key goal-oriented design artifacts.

We begin with an overview of the Hermes methodology, and then progress through the design process in subsequent sections. Note that Hermes is not a full design methodology. It focuses solely on aspects relating to designing interactions, and is missing other aspects such as identifying agent types, defining the internals of agents, or delineating the boundary between the agents and their environment.

Figure 2. Hermes methodology overview diagram

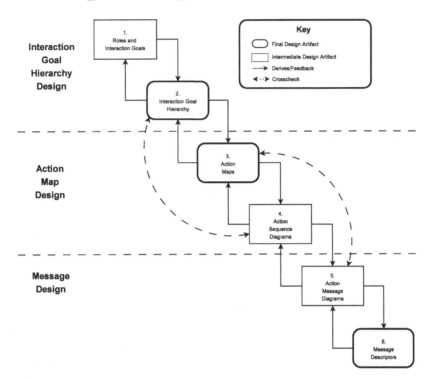

Methodology Overview

An overview of the Hermes methodology is shown in Figure 2. The methodology is divided into three phases which are performed in an incremental iterative manner.

The first two steps fall into the first phase, the *Interaction Goal Hierarchy Design* phase, in which the designer is focused on the overall design of the interaction. The designer is concerned with *what* the interaction is to achieve and *who* (i.e. which roles) are involved in the interaction. Thus, Hermes begins by identifying roles and interaction goals as they are required before one can develop actions in the second phase. The identified roles and interaction goals are simply captured in a list. Afterwards, in the second step, these interaction goals are organized into an *Interaction Goal Hierarchy* (see the next section), which is the final[6] artifact produced by this phase.

The second phase, the *Action Map Design* phase, requires the designer to think about *how* the roles involved can achieve the interaction goals identified in the previous phase. As such, actions which the interacting roles will need to carry out are identified in step 3 and are organized into appropriate execution sequences. In step 4, these execution sequences are checked. The final artifacts produced by this phase are the *Action Maps* (resulting from step 3), which define possible sequences of actions executed by the roles to achieve the interaction goals. There may also be intermediate *Action Sequence Diagram* artifacts (resulting from step 4), which are used to ensure that the sequences in the action maps are sufficient to allow the roles to achieve the interaction.

In the last phase, the *Message Design* phase, the designer's attention shifts from actions to communications between the roles, i.e. messages, as they are required to complete the interaction definition.

Step 5 requires the designer to identify where messages are required to be exchanged between roles, while step 6 calls for the designer to define what information the messages will contain. The final artifacts from this phase are the message definitions, which will vary depending on whether the designer is using platform-specific message types or standards, such as KQML, FIPA or SOAP. The message definitions are recorded in *message descriptors*.

The following sections explain each of the phases and steps of the design process in detail and provides an example of how a design is created in Hermes.

Interaction Goal Hierarchy

The first step in creating the interaction goal hierarchy is to determine the roles involved in the interaction and the interaction goals which they are attempting to achieve. Consider an agent type, *Academic Agent*. This agent can take on a number of different roles in different interactions. For example, in an academic paper reviewing interaction, the *Academic Agent* can undertake any of the following roles: *Author, Reviewer, Editor*, etc.

Therefore, a role usually represents a subset of what an agent can do and one agent is able to assume other roles in other interactions. Although possible, it is not usual for one agent to assume multiple roles in the same interaction. In fact, there may be rules preventing an agent from undertaking multiple roles in the same interactions. For example, in the aforementioned academic paper reviewing interaction, an agent cannot play both the roles of *Reviewer* and *Author* on the same paper.

The second step of developing the interaction goal hierarchy is to refine and organize the interaction goals identified in the previous step. Where possible, the interaction goals are broken down into smaller sub-interaction goals and are organized into a hierarchy. The hierarchy should only have one interaction goal at its apex, which captures the overall goal of the entire interaction.

As an example, consider a scenario in which four agent roles, *Sales Assistant, Customer Relations, Delivery Manager*, and *Stock Manager*, are interacting to fulfil an *Order Book* request in an online store[7]. The *Sales Assistant* is the main interface to the customer who places the online order whilst the *Customer Relations* maintains customer details, such as customer records. The *Delivery Manager* fulfils deliveries to the customer and the *Stock Manager* keeps track of inventory levels. In general, the steps of the interaction involve retrieving the customer's details, accepting payment, and shipping the book to the customer. Logs and records will also need to be updated as required.

As the top-most goal of the interaction goal hierarchy is usually the most abstract goal and is meant to capture the overall intent of the interaction, *Order Book* is placed at the apex of the hierarchy.

To continue developing the interaction goal hierarchy, more interaction goals are identified from the textual description of the interaction and are placed into the interaction goal hierarchy using decomposition relationships, that is, interaction goals are placed into parent-child relationships. Some of these interaction goals that will need to be added will be obvious to the designer. The remaining goals can be identified using either a top-down or bottom-up approach (or a mixture). In the top-down approach, the designer analyzes each existing interaction goal and determines if it can be decomposed into smaller, more concrete goals. Decomposition should stop before producing goals that do not require interaction between roles (i.e. that can be achieved by a single role). Taking a bottom-up approach requires the designer to identify and aggregate bottom-level, concrete interaction goals into abstract ones and progress up the interaction goal hierarchy.

Figure 3. Intermediate interaction goal hierarchy

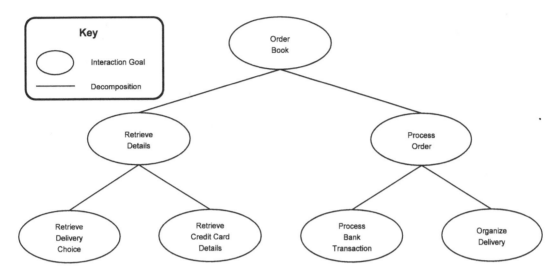

An example interaction goal hierarchy is shown in Figure 3 in which the undirected lines denote parent-child or sub-goal relationships. The lines from *Order Book* to *Retrieve Details* and *Order Book* to *Process Order* state that for the *Order Book* interaction goal to be achieved, the *Retrieve Details* and *Process Order* interaction goals must be achieved. Furthermore, the *Retrieve Details* and *Process Order* interaction goals are achieved when their sub-goals are achieved.

The interaction goal hierarchy is, in actuality, a goal-tree, similar to those used in methodologies such as MaSE (DeLoach et al., 2001; DeLoach 2006) or Prometheus (Padgham and Winikoff, 2004). Leaves in the tree (i.e. goals with no children) are termed *atomic* interaction goals. Achieving the other interaction goals in the hierarchy, which are named *composite* interaction goals, is done by achieving the atomic interaction goals.

Once the designer has settled on an appropriate interaction goal hierarchy, temporal dependencies[8] (depicted as directed lines in Figure 4) are added. The temporal dependencies provide an effective way for the designer to place *constraints* on the sequence of the interaction and, thus, restrict the order in which certain interaction goals can be achieved. For example, in Figure 4, the directed line between *Retrieve Details* and *Process Order* depicts a temporal dependency between the two interaction goals and states that the *Retrieve Details* interaction goal must be achieved (successfully) before the *Process Order* interaction goal can start.

While temporal constraints are useful to restrict certain undesirable sequences of interaction goal achievement from occurring, they should be used loosely as the more temporal constraints are used, the less flexible the interaction. For example, the particular design shown in Figure 4 is a strongly constrained design, however, alternative designs could, for instance, retrieve the delivery choice and credit card details simultaneously, thus, relaxing some of the temporal constraints.

The placement of temporal dependencies will depend on the designer and the interaction itself. In general, they are placed to ensure that interaction goals are achieved in a sensible sequence. For example, it does not make sense for the roles to achieve the *Process Order* interaction goal before achieving the *Retrieve Details* interaction goal.

Figure 4. Final interaction goal hierarchy

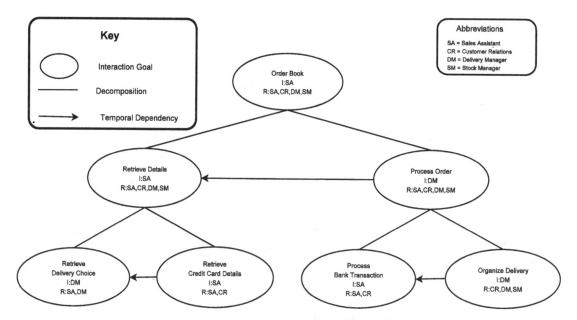

As part of developing the interaction goal hierarchy, the designer should also assign to each interaction goal the roles that are involved in that interaction goal. Typically, all roles involved in the interaction will be involved in each interaction goal, however, there may be situations in which only a subset of the roles are involved in particular interaction goals. The roles involved are shown in Figure 4 as (e.g.) *R: SA, CR, DM, SM* (short for Roles: Sales Assistant, Customer Relations, Delivery Manager, and Stock Manager).

The designer must also identify for each interaction goal which role is the *initiator*. The initiator can be one of the roles involved in the interaction goal, or the symbol ↑ indicating that the initiator is *inherited*, i.e. the initiator for the interaction goal is the same as the initiator of its parent. In Figure 4 there are no inherited intiators, however, in other interactions it might be desirable to be able to state that the agent that began the interaction is responsible for initiating a particular interaction goal (i.e. an inherited initiator) (Cheong and Winikoff, 2006a). This provides more flexibility in the design of interactions.

In some cases it may not be clear which role should initiate a given interaction goal. In such cases an inherited initiator can be used initially and later on, in the action map design, the designer can use the initial actions (see the following section on developing initial action maps) to determine which role should be the initiator. However, this approach is only suitable for atomic interaction goals since only atomic interaction goals have associated action maps.

The interaction goal hierarchy provides an overview of the interaction and depicts what the interacting roles need to achieve in order to achieve the interaction. Up to this point, only the common and coordination aspects of the interaction have been designed. The next step in developing a Hermes interaction is to consider how the interaction will be realised. This is done by creating an action map for each atomic interaction goal. Each action map shows *how* its corresponding interaction goal is to be achieved. The development process of action maps is described in the following section.

Action Maps

For ease of explanation, the action map development process is described in three[9] distinct steps, however, it is not intended that designers rigidly follow these steps.

The steps are as follows:

1. Develop the initial action maps.
2. Add data to the action maps and consider data flow issues.
3. Generalize the action maps.

Typically, one action map is created for each atomic interaction goal, however, due to space limitations, we explain the development of only one action map in this document.

Develop Initial Action Maps

The initial development of action maps is broken down into three steps:

A. Identify actions and assign them to roles involved in the interaction;
B. Establish action sequences by use of causality links; and
C. Identify the type of each action.

The first step in developing an action map is to identify actions and assign them to the roles involved by placing them into the appropriate role's swim lane. To identify what actions are required, the designer will need to consider the abilities of the relevant roles and what interaction goals they have to achieve.

For example, consider the *Organize Delivery* interaction goal in Figure 4. All four roles are involved, and, thus, all four are present in the corresponding action map, shown in Figure 5. To achieve the *Organize Delivery* interaction goal, a number of actions, such as *Place Delivery Request*, and *Log Outgoing Delivery* will need to be identified and allocated to roles as in Figure 5.

Once actions have been identified and assigned to the involved roles, the action execution order must be established, which is achieved by placing causality links between the actions. The causality links impose temporal restrictions and indicate the *action flow* of the action map, i.e. which actions can be attempted after an action has been executed. Causality links[10] are not necessarily inter-agent; they can also be intra-agent. Furthermore, causality links are able to be labeled with conditions or states. This is useful to clarify the causality paths on the action map.

Where to place causality links will depend on the designer and the interaction, and is usually common sense. For example, in the online book store, the *Delivery Manager* firstly places the delivery request and then logs the outgoing delivery, hence, a causality link is placed between the two actions. To ensure that all causality links have been identified, the designer should check each action against all other actions and ensure that the established sequence is sensible. This will involve checking that dependencies are correct (e.g. *Send Email* cannot occur until the records have been updated) and that all actions are reachable (i.e. all actions are connected by causality links).

The last part of the initial development of the action maps is to determine the action type of each action. The action types are needed to indicate which actions start and terminate the action maps, because it is necessary to allow for multiple start and end points. The different action types are:

Figure 5. Initial action map

Organize Delivery (Initial without data stores)

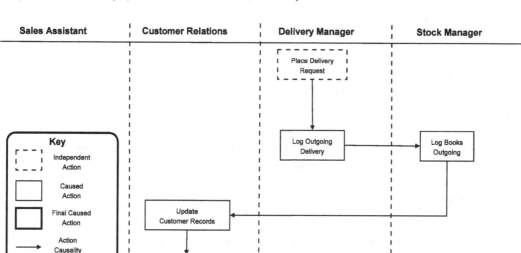

- *Independent Actions*, denoted as a rectangle with dashed border, which can start without being triggered by another action (although they also can be triggered). Typically independent actions are used as entry points to the action map.
- *Caused Actions* which *must* be triggered by another action and are denoted as a rectangle with solid line.
- *Final Caused Actions*, denoted by a rectangle with thick solid line, which are caused actions which terminate an interaction goal, i.e. once done, no further actions will be executed in that action map.
- *Final Independent Actions*, denoted by a rectangle with a thick dashed line, which are independent actions which terminate an interaction goal. This action type is rarely used since it corresponds to a situation where the action is both the initial and final action, i.e. it is the only action used.

At the end of this step, a rudimentary action map is created, for example see Figure 5. The consequent steps will refine it into a more flexible, robust and complete action map.

Adding Data to Action Maps

This step involves identifying and adding data stores to the action maps. This is important as particular actions will require appropriate data. The designer must also ensure that data which the roles require is accessible. To identify the necessary data stores, the designer analyzes the actions carefully and considers what data is required for the actions to execute successfully. It is also useful to determine what data needs to be passed from one action to another. Once the data has been identified, data stores are placed in the swim lane of the role to which they belong. Note that only relevant data stores are displayed on an action map; not all the data stores that a role contains. This avoids unnecessarily cluttering the action maps.

For example, in Figure 6, the *Customer Relations* role will need to store customer records somewhere. This is captured by its *Customer DB* data store. Similarly, the *Delivery Manager* will need to keep track of customer orders and the *Stock Manager* will need to manage inventory. These are represented by their *Customer Orders* and *Stock DB* data stores respectively.

Simply adding data stores is not sufficient, the designer must ensure that actions which read and write data have *direct* access to the data stores. The designer must also ensure that all actions will have access to data even if the data store resides in another role. This may mean that required data is read from a data store and is passed along through multiple actions to reach a particular action that requires the data. In order to ensure all these, the designer should consider for each action what data is needed, where the data will be obtained from, and where the data will (finally) end up.

For example, the *Store Manager*'s *Log Books Outgoing* action might need details from the customer records located in the *Delivery Manager*'s *Customer Orders* data store. Thus, the customer order record is passed along the causality link between the *Delivery Manager*'s *Log Outgoing Delivery* and the *Stock Manager*'s *Log Books Outgoing* actions. This is denoted in Figure 6 by use of the *Note Indicator*.

Dashed lines were chosen to represent the data flow as they differentiate the data flow from the control flow, i.e. the causalities, which are represented with solid lines. Furthermore, this also avoids cluttering the action maps with solid lines.

In this step, data stores have been added and the correctness of data flow between actions has been ensured by checking that actions have access to data. The next step will generalize the action map to make it more flexible and more complete.

Figure 6. Action map with data stores

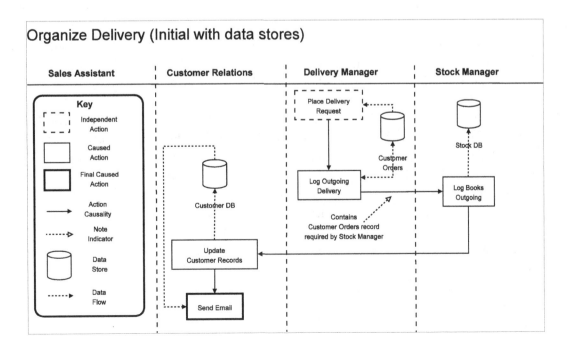

Generalizing Action Maps

In this step, the designer seeks to improve the action map by generalizing it, i.e. providing multiple ways in which the action map can be followed to achieve its corresponding interaction goal. There are two ways in which this can be done. The first is for the designer to add alternative paths to success in the action map. The second is for the designer to identify where problems can occur in the action map (i.e. an action fails) and provide failure handling for the foreseen problem.

Identifying appropriate places for adding alternative paths can be difficult as it is dependent on the domain, the roles involved and the actual interaction. However, although there are no set guidelines for identifying where alternative paths can be added, the designer can systematically analyze each action and determine if the action can be achieved in a different manner or if additional useful actions can be added.

For example, in the online book store, the *Delivery Manager* does not determine if the book to be delivered is currently in stock (refer to Figure 6). Placing a delivery request can be achieved in two ways. Firstly, the availability of stock is to be checked, then, if available, the book is delivered as per the current action map (Figure 6). However, if the book is unavailable, the book can be ordered from the publisher and once it arrives, it is then delivered to the customer.

Note that in the current action map (refer to Figure 6), the availability of the ordered book is never explicitly queried; it is assumed to be part of the delivery options. In order to clarify matters, querying for the ordered book's availability needs to be made explicit. This is done by adding two new actions at the start of the action map: *Check Book Availability* and *Check Stock* (refer to Figure 7). These two actions are used to determine how to arrange the delivery. *Check Book Availability* is used to query the *Stock Manager* about the availabilty of the ordered book. *Check Stock* is the action in the *Stock Manager* that replies to the query. If the ordered book is available, the delivery order is placed and processed. If the ordered book is not available, the *Add Pending Order* action is used to order the book (from the publishing firm). Once the book comes in (from the publishing firm), *Process Newly Received Stock* is triggered, the pending order is filled and the delivery is processed. The result of this step is shown in Figure 7.

The remainder of this section focuses on failures and how to attend to them. Failure handling is of crucial importance as it is what gives the action maps, and thus Hermes, the majority of their robustness[11]. By being able to handle foreseeable failures, the roles are able to persevere through these failures in order to complete the interaction.

The different types of failures possible in Hermes are firstly described. Then, the available Hermes failure recovery mechanisms which can be used to address these failures are presented, after which follows an explanation of how to determine and add failure handling to the action maps.

There are two types of failures in Hermes: *action failure* and *interaction goal failure*. An action failure is when an action fails to achieve its interaction goal or intended purpose. For example, *Place Delivery Request* may fail because the customer's address is invalid. An interaction goal failure is more dire. In such failures, the roles are unable to achieve the interaction goal. For example, because of incorrect credit card details, payment is unable to be processed. In this case, the *Process Bank Transaction* interaction goal fails (refer to Figure 4).

In Hermes, an *action retry* can be used to handle action failures. The concept of an action retry is simple: it allows a failed action to be recovered from by retrying that, or another, action. For example, if the *Place Delivery Request* fails because the customer's address is invalid, the customer can be asked

Figure 7. Generalized action map

Organize Delivery (Generalized)

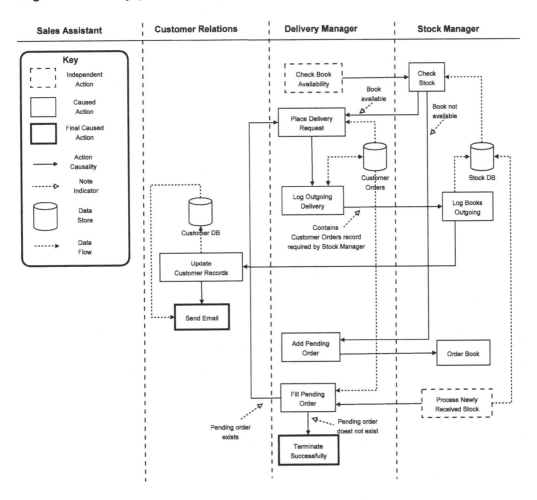

for another address and the *Place Delivery Request* action can be retried instead of the interaction goal failing at this point.

If an action fails and is not able to be handled by action retries, this can lead to interaction goal failure. When this occurs, the interaction can be either terminated or rolled back to a previous interaction goal. The main notion of rollback is that if an interaction is returned to a previous interaction goal and the interaction goal is re-achieved in a different manner (which leads to a different intermediate result than previously acquired), the failed interaction goal may then be successfully re-achieved. For example, in the case of payment processing failing due to incorrect credit card details (i.e. *Process Bank Transaction* failing, refer to Figure 4), instead of terminating the interaction, the interaction can be rolled back to the *Retrieve Credit Card Details* interaction goal. That interaction goal can be re-achieved in a different manner, e.g. the customer provides the correct details of the credit card, and the *Process Bank Transaction* interaction goal will then be able to be achieved. Whereas action retry is used *within* a single interaction goal, rollback is used *between* interaction goals.

Interaction goals at which rollbacks can be issued and which interaction goals can be rolled back to is both domain- and application-specific. Therefore, it is up to the designer to determine this. The designer must thus indicate whether rollbacks are permissible for each interaction goal, and if so, which interaction goal should the interaction be allowed to roll back to.

Determining where rollbacks can be issued from can sometimes be challenging. The designer should analyze each action individually and consider whether it is sensible to issue a rollback from it if it fails. The designer should pay careful consideration to termination actions as they can often be substituted with roll backs. As a test, the designer should be able to clearly explain the purpose of issuing a rollback from a particular action and what advantages it brings to the interaction. Once a potential rollback has been identified, the designer will need to determine what interaction goal the rollback will roll back to.

One constraint of rollbacks is that in order to be able to roll back to a previous interaction goal, the current interaction goal must be dependent on the interaction goal which it desires to roll back to. That is, for interaction goal B to roll back to interaction goal A, B must depend on A (as A must occur before B in order for the roll back to make sense).

Similarly to rollbacks, where and when an interaction can be terminated is also domain- and application-specific. As with the rollbacks, the designer will have to carefully analyze and consider each action map and determine whether it is sensible to terminate an interaction at that point. For example it is not sensible for the online book store interaction to terminate after the payment has been taken but before the book has been delivered[12].

Terminations can be identified at points in the interaction where no alternatives are possible (i.e. all possible alternatives have been exhausted) and essential particulars of the interaction cannot be agreed upon. Terminations are usually placed at points that "make or break" the interaction. If the roles involved cannot agree on a particular of the interaction and there are no alternatives, then the interaction simply cannot proceed.

Terminating in response to failure provides a graceful exit from an interaction which cannot be successfully achieved. As such, when a termination occurs, all roles involved in the interaction should leave the interaction in a desirable state. For example, in the online book store interaction, when a termination occurs, all parties should leave the interaction without incurring any loss. It would be undesirable for the customer to have made payment and for the online book store not to transfer the book.

There are three parts to adding failure handling to action maps:

1. Failure Identification
2. Adding Action Retries
3. Adding Rollbacks

In order to identify where possible failures might occur, the designer should think about each action and determine whether it can fail or not. If the action can fail, the designer should determine what types of failures can result from it. Once failures have been identified, the designer should determine ways in which the failures can be addressed.

For each action map, the designer should create a table to summarize all the possible failures and ways to rectify them as shown in Table 1. For example, it has been identified that the *Order Book* action could fail if a book is out of print, and the suggested remedial action is to suggest an alternative title.

Table 1. Possible failures and remedial actions for Organize Delivery

#	Action	Possible Failures	Remedial Actions
1	Order Book	Book out of print	Suggest alternative title or edition
2	Place Delivery Request	Invalid address	Get details from user and validate
3	Send Email	Email bounces	Use different medium to contact user (e.g. send mail via post)

To further enhance flexibility and robustness, the designer can also analyse each action and determine different ways in which they can succeed (i.e. determine alternative success paths). This will further increase flexibility and robustness in the interactions.

Once failures have been identified and remedial actions determined, the designer can then update action maps with action retries and rollbacks. Adding action retries to action maps is relatively straightforward. In the case of the *Order Book* action failing, the suggested remedial action of suggesting an alternative title is achieved by the *Process Book Out Of Print Message* action, which leads to the *Suggest Alternative or Similar Title* action (refer to Figure 8). The other two identified failures and remedial actions from Table 1 have also been incorporated into Figure 8.

An effect of adding action retries is that it can lead to loops between actions. Note that a loop has now formed between *Place Delivery* and *Get User Address*. It is important to ensure that there are no endless loops in action maps. This is done by providing an exit condition: if *Get User Address* fails (i.e. the customer cannot or does not want to provide a valid address), the interaction is terminated. Experienced designers will be able to immediately add such exit conditions but novice designers may not realize that they are required. However, novice designers should be able to identify, in a second iteration through the action maps, that the *Get User Address* action could fail. As such, this failure should be handled. In this case, it is handled by providing an action which will terminate the interaction.

Adding rollbacks to action maps is quite simple once they have been identified. If the desired book is unavailable and the customer wishes to purchase a suggested title, it is necessary to roll back the interaction to adjust the payment amount[13]. Thus, a rollback action, *Rollback to Process Bank Transaction*, is provided on the action map (refer to Figure 8) to return the interaction to the *Process Bank Transaction* interaction goal.

After the final iteration of this step, the action map is now in a completed state. It is also more flexible and robust than the initial action map developed in Figure 5.

Messages

In this phase of the interaction design, messages need to be identified. These messages are necessary to realize inter-agent triggering of action/causality links as defined in action maps. To identify the messages, the designer will need to analyze the action maps and determine where one role needs to trigger an action of another role or where data needs to be transmitted from one role to another.

Consider the causality link between the *Delivery Manager*'s *Log Outgoing Delivery* action and the *Stock Manager*'s *Log Books Outgoing* action (refer to Figure 8). For this causality to be realized, there will need to be a message sent from the *Log Outgoing Delivery* action to the *Log Books Outgoing* action.

Figure 8. Finalized action map

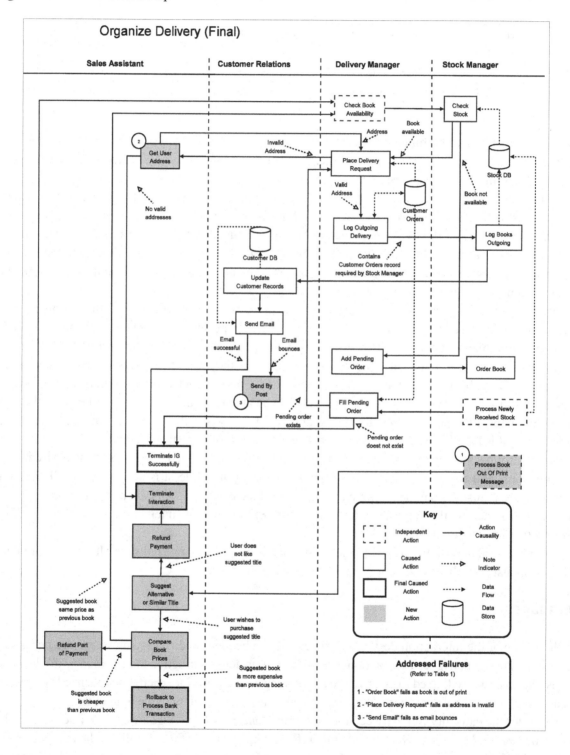

Part of defining messages will also involve determining the data carried by the messages. The message between the *Delivery Manager*'s *Log Outgoing Delivery* action and the *Stock Manager*'s *Log Books Outgoing* action will need to carry information from the customer's records. The way the data is represented will depend on the message standards being used, which, in turn, will depend on the intent of the implemented interaction. For example, if the implemented interaction is to be used in open systems, then standards such as KQML, FIPA, or SOAP might be appropriate. If the implemented interaction is to be used in a closed system, then the default message type of the agent platform being implemented upon might suffice.

Messages are defined in *message descriptors* which specify the message's name, type and data, as well as a description.

Action Sequence and Action Message Diagrams

Action sequence diagrams and action message diagrams are simple and minor Hermes artifacts which can be used to check that action maps allow for desired interactions to occur. These artifacts are optional and are to be used at the designer's discretion.

An action sequence diagram follows a specific trace from an action map. It is different from action maps, which show all possible execution sequences, as an action sequence diagram shows *one* specific sequence of actions being executed. An action sequence diagram (which is similar to a UML sequence diagram) shows a lifeline for each role with the actions performed by that role placed on its lifeline. The actions are depicted using the same notation as action maps (e.g. a thick border indicates a final action). Actions that are carried out to achieve a particular interaction goal are enclosed in a shaded box which represents that interaction goal (see Figure 9).

Figure 9. Action message diagram

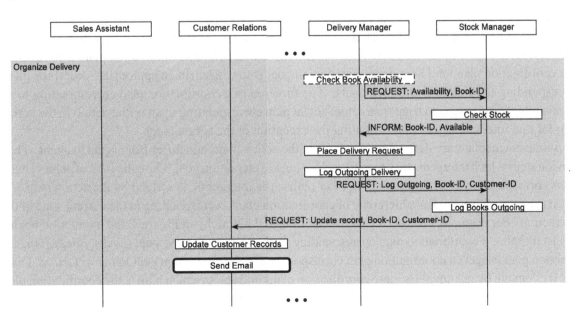

To develop an action sequence diagram, the designer traces through the action maps and interaction goal hierarchy, and makes appropriate choices of what action is executed at particular points. That is, the designer simulates an execution of the action map.

The purpose of an action sequence diagram is to check that identified actions from the action maps are sufficient to allow for complete and successful interactions. It also allows the designer to ensure that specifically desired interactions can be generated by the interaction goal hierarchy and its associated actions.

Messages are added to action sequence diagrams to give action message diagrams. These can be useful in identifying what data needs to be carried in the message. When the messages are placed between the actions, the designer can consider what data needs to be communicated between the roles. For example, in Figure 9, the request message between the *Delivery Manager*'s *Check Book Availability* action and the *Stock Manager*'s *Check Stock* action will need to carry across data such as the Book-ID.

IMPLEMENTING HERMES DESIGNS

In this section, we explain how Hermes designs are implemented by mapping design artifacts to collections of goals and plans. As Hermes is goal-oriented, the implementation platform needs to be one that defines agents in terms of goals and plans. These platforms include those based on the Belief-Desire-Intention (BDI) model, such as JACK™ [14], Jadex, JAM, Jason, and others. Although Hermes designs have only been currently implemented using Jadex, it is possible to implement Hermes on any of the aforementioned platforms. This is possible since the implementation scheme does not use any platform-specific features.

Implementation Overview

An overview of the implementation is shown in Figure 10, including the different plan types and their inter-connections.

Interaction goals are directly mapped to coordination plans, which are used to coordinate participating agents through the interaction. These plans are common to all agents involved in the interaction. Each interaction goal in the interaction goal hierarchy is mapped to a coordination plan. The function of a coordination plan for a non-atomic interaction goal is to trigger (in an appropriate order) the plans corresponding to its child interaction goals. The function of a coordination plan corresponding to an atomic interaction goal is to trigger an achievement plan corresponding to an initial action in the action map for that interaction goal (thus initiating the execution of the action map).

Achievement plans are derived from actions in the action maps and differ from agent to agent. They provide steps which the agents take towards achieving an interaction goal. The collection of achievement plans corresponding to an action map together realise the interaction described by the action map.

At runtime each agent has a hierarchy of coordination plans corresponding to the current state of the interaction. For example, considering the interaction goal hierarchy in Figure 4, the interaction begins by instantiating a coordination plan corresponding to the root interaction goal (*Order Book*). This interaction goal triggers a coordination plan corresponding to the interaction goal *Retrieve Details*. Once this is complete (which involves more coordination plans and achievement plans), the coordination plan for *Order Book* triggers the coordination plan for *Process Order* which in turn results in coordination

Figure 10. Implementation overview

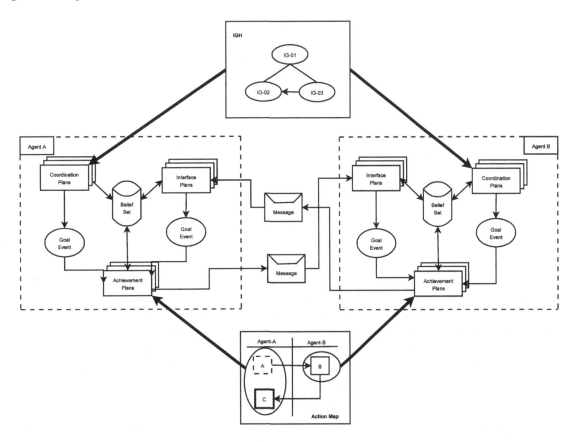

plans being triggered for *Process Bank Transaction* and *Organize Delivery*. The coordination plan for *Organize Delivery* will trigger the initial action of the relevant action map (*Check Book Availability*).

The third type of plans are interface plans, which are derived from the message descriptors and action maps. They are used to transform inter-agent messages into goals and events for intra-agent processing. Each incoming message is mapped to an internal event that triggers the appropriate plans. For example, when the *Delivery Manager* sends a request to the *Stock Manager* to check the availability of a book (refer to Figure 8), the *Stock Manager*'s interface plan converts the message into the internal event that will trigger the plan that corresponds to the appropriate action in the action map (*Check Stock*). The interface plans also check whether the agent has initialised the interaction, and if not, they trigger the creation of a hierarchy of coordination plans corresponding to the interaction goal hierarchy.

The following sections explain the representation of interaction goals, and the different plan types.

Interaction Goal Representation and Beliefs

As can be seen in Figure 10, agent beliefs connect the different plan types. Beliefs are used to pass information between plans so they can coordinate the agents through the interaction. The states of interaction goals are represented using a combination of three Boolean values per interaction goal: in, finished, and success. The in belief indicates that the interaction goal is currently active. The

Figure 11. Interaction goal states and valid transitions

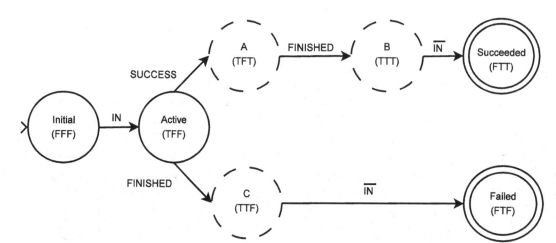

finished belief is used to indicate whether the interaction goal has been completed, whilst success (or succeeded) indicates whether the interaction goal has been successful.

The interaction goal states and valid transitions between them are shown in Figure 11. The dashed circles represent intermediate states that have no conceptual meaning, but are necessary to change state from *active* to either *succeeded* or *failed*. The Boolean string in parentheses show the values of the three beliefs in, finished, and success, respectively. Transitions between these states are triggered by the coordination and achievement plans (see algorithms 1-4).

Beliefs are also used to represent a number of other attributes in interactions. A summary of the agent's beliefs, along with examples, is shown in Table 2. The examples are presented as key:value pairs with default values for the given interaction selected.

For each interaction, each agent has a *role* belief which states the name of the agent's role in the interaction (e.g. the *Delivery Manager* role in the online book store interaction). The *role* beliefs are generally used to determine which roles need to take action in each interaction goal. The *initiator* role

Table 2. Belief structure and examples

Belief	Use	Example
role	Identifies the agent's role in the interaction.	role:deliveryManager
initiator	Identifies the interaction's initiator.	initiator:deliveryManager
Interaction Goal Initiators	A series of beliefs which identify the initiator of each IG (one per IG).	orderBookIGInitiator:salesAssistant processOrderIGInitiator:deliveryManager
Interaction Goal States	A series of beliefs used to represent the state of IGs, i.e. in, finished, and success. Used for Coordination-Achievement plan connections.	inOrderBookIG:false finishedOrderBookIG:false OrderBookIGSuccess:false
Interaction Goal Retries	A series of beliefs for retrying IGs. One for each IG that is allowed to be retried.	retryProcessBankTransaction:false
Interaction Specific Beliefs	Beliefs which are specific to the given interaction.	bookID:20 customerID:7

states which role initiated the interaction. This is needed for interaction goals in which the initiator is inherited.

The interaction goal initiator beliefs are a series of beliefs which identify an initiator for each interaction goal. The initiator role is responsible for taking the initial action for its designated interaction role, which will cause the other agents involved to take responsive actions and achieve the interaction goal.

The interaction goal retries are used to flag that their respective interaction goals are being retried. This is important as the agents will then try to achieve a different outcome than that achieved previously so that the interaction can proceed successfully. For more details on the action retry failure handling mechanism, see the section on achievement plans. The remainder of the beliefs are interaction specific, including beliefs that are based on data stores from the action maps.

Coordination Plans

Coordination plans, derived from interaction goals, are a common set of plans that guide the agents through their interactions. There are two variations of coordination plans, *compound* and *atomic*. Compound coordination plans are based on compound interaction goals, i.e. those that are composed of other interaction goals, such as *Order Book*, *Retrieve Details*, and *Process Order* (refer to Figure 4), whilst atomic coordination plans are derived from interaction goals that are not composed of other interaction goals (i.e. atomic interaction goal), such as *Retrieve Delivery Choice*, *Retrieve Credit Card Details*, *Process Bank Transaction*, and *Organize Delivery*. Compound coordination plans are involved with coordination between themselves and other coordination plans whilst atomic coordination plans deal with coordination between themselves and *achievement* plans.

In the implementation of a Hermes interaction, there is a coordination plan for each interaction goal. Algorithm 1 presents an example of a generic compound coordination plan. As this is a generic coordination plan, it is assumed that it is derived from an interaction goal named IG.

Algorithm 1. Generic (sequential) compound coordination plan for interaction goal IG

```
Require: in[IG] ==true
1.  terminate = false
2.
3.  while moreChildIGs() and not terminate
4.        // Get beliefs for next IG
5.        ChildIG = nextChildName()
6.
7.        // Coordination
8.        in[ChildIG] = true
9.        waitFor(finished[ChildIG] and not in[ChildIG])
10.       if not succeeded[childIG] then
11.          terminate = true
12.       end if
13. end while
14.
15. if all child IGs succeeded then
16.       succeeded[IG] = true
17. end if
18.
19. // Synchronization (with other Coordination plans)
20. finished[IG] = true
21. in[IG] = false
```

The following beliefs are initialized to `false` for each interaction goal IG when the agent is created: `in[IG]`, `finished[IG]` and `succeeded[IG]`. The trigger to execute a compound coordination plan is its `in` belief. In this case, it is when the `in` belief changes to true (as shown by the `Require` statement in Algorithm 1).

When a compound coordination plan is executed, its first step is to begin the achievement of its sub-coordination plans (i.e. child interaction goals) in the specified order[15]. Algorithm 1 shows an interaction in which all child interaction goals are to be achieved in sequence (denoted by the *while* loop). As such, the `IG` coordination plan begins by retrieving the name of the next child interaction goal to be achieved (line 5) The coordination plan then sets the `in` belief of the child interaction goal to `true` (line 8), which allows the child interaction goal's coordination plan to execute. The `IG` coordination plan then waits until the child interaction goal is achieved (line 9), and then attempts to achieve the following child interaction goal if the current one has been achieved successfully (lines 10-12).

When all its child interaction goals have been successfully achieved, the `IG` coordination plan sets its `succeeded` belief to `true` (lines 15-17). The last part of the compound coordination plan is to synchronize itself with the other coordination plans. That is, it sets its `in` and `finished` beliefs (in this case `in[IG]` and `finished[IG]`) to `false` and `true` respectively to signal its completion.

Algorithm 2 is an example of a generic atomic coordination plan. As with compound coordination plans, atomic coordination plans are triggered when their `in` beliefs change to `true` (refer to `Require` statement in Algorithm 2).

The first step of an atomic coordination plan is to execute the initial action (in the relevant action map) in an attempt to achieve itself. However, before that action is triggered, the atomic coordination plan ensures that it has not already been achieved (refer to line 1). This is important in situations where rollbacks are issued – there is no need to achieve a coordination plan that is already achieved. Furthermore, the atomic coordination plan ensures that only the initiator of this interaction goal begins the interaction (refer to line 2). If these conditions are met, the coordination plan triggers the initial action by dispatching the appropriate goal (line 3).

Once the goal has been dispatched, the atomic coordination plan must wait until the action (which is likely to trigger a series of other actions) completes. When the series of actions is completed, the `finished` belief of the current interaction goal will be set to `true`. Thus, as part of its synchronization with the achievement plans (implementations of the actions), the atomic coordination plan waits for its `finished` belief to be set to `true` (line 8). The last part of the atomic coordination plan is to set its `in` belief to `false`, signifying that it has been completed.

Algorithm 2. Generic atomic coordination plan for interaction goal IG

```
Require: in[IG] == true
1. if not succeeded[IG] then
2.       if role==initiator then
3.              dispatch(new triggerInitialActionGoal())
4.       end if
5. end if
6.
7. // Synchronisation (with Achievement plans)
8. waitfor(finished[IG])
9. in[IG] = false
```

Achievement Plans

Achievement plans, based on actions from the action maps, are used by the interacting agents as steps towards achieving an interaction goal. Therefore, achievement plans usually contain interaction-specific steps.

Algorithm 3 presents an example of a generic achievement plan. For an achievement plan to begin execution, it must be triggered by an appropriate goal event, as shown by the `Require` statement in Algorithm 3. Once triggered, the achievement plan must ensure that it is in the correct context, i.e. its interaction goal is active, before beginning to execute (refer to line 2). When the achievement plan is in the correct context, it executes interaction-specific code (lines 4 and 5).

If the achievement plan represents an action that achieves the interaction goal (i.e. a final action that terminates with success), then the interaction goal's `success` belief is set to `true` (lines 6-8). Furthermore, achievement plans representing final actions have a synchronization section which sets the `finished` belief of the interaction goal to `true`, signaling the completion of the interaction goal (lines 10-14).

The implementation of action failure handling mechanisms, *termination* and *action retry*, are simple and straightforward. When an action fails (i.e. an achievement plan fails), there are two options: terminate the interaction or attempt to recover by retrying the action with different parameters.

This first option, termination, is the simplest. In such a case, the programmer will need to add actions to request termination and to terminate the interaction.

For example, in Figure 8, the *Sales Assistant* will terminate the interaction if the customer is unable to provide a valid address or does not wish to purchase a suggested alternative book. To implement the termination, each role in the interaction is equipped with an action to request termination, i.e. *Request Termination*, and an action to actually terminate the interaction, i.e. *Terminate Interaction*. The termination is a chain-like sequence as follows. The *Sales Assistant* requests termination from the *Customer Relations*, which then requests termination from the *Delivery Manager*, which then requests termination from the *Stock Manager*. The *Stock Manager* then terminates its interaction and notifies the *Delivery Manager*, which in turn terminates its interaction and notifies the *Customer Relations*, which also terminates its interaction and notifies the *Sales Assistant*, which then terminates its interaction[16].

Algorithm 3. Generic achievement plan

```
Require: actionTriggerGoalEvent
1. // Synchronisation (with Coordination plan)
2. waitFor(in[IG])
3.
4. // AchieveIG (application specific)
5. ...
6. if action achieved IG  then
7.     succeeded[IG] = true // Action achieves IG
8. end if
9.
10. // Finish IG, only done if action is final
11. // Synchronisation (with Coordination plan)
12. if action is final then
13.     finished[IG] = true
14. end if
```

This sequence of actions can be quite easily added to the action map, however, to avoid unnecessarily cluttering the diagram, by convention, the *Terminate Interaction* action (in Figure 8) is understood to represent this sequence of actions. This is similar to the sequence used to specify rollback, as depicted in Figure 12.

Implementing the rollback failure handling mechanism, which addresses interaction goal failure, is more complicated than implementing terminations or action retries. Algorithm 4 is an example of a rollback achievement plan in which the *Sales Assistant* is rolling back from the *Organize Delivery* interaction goal to the *Process Bank Transaction* interaction goal as per the action map in Figure 8. The comments (in bold) present a general plan for rolling back with the code showing how the *Sales Assistant* rolls back in this particular example.

In general, a rollback is implemented by "saving" the interaction in a particular state and re-starting the entire interaction. The "saving" of the interaction is done by setting the interaction goal to which the agent wishes to roll back to be attempted next. This is done by setting its `in` belief to `true` and both its `finished` and `success` beliefs to `false`, which essentially flags the interaction goal as active, but not yet completed (lines 17-20 in Algorithm 4). Thus, it will be attempted next (unless there are other active but uncompleted interaction goals preceding it).

When the interaction is re-started, the agents will not re-attempt interaction goals that have already been successfully achieved. Thus, the agent will re-attempt the desired interaction goal next.

In Algorithm 4, the agent must firstly ensure that it is in the correct context (i.e. its current interaction goal is active) before it can carry out the rollback. In this case, the *Sales Assistant* must wait until the *Organize Delivery* interaction goal is active (lines 1 and 2). The agent then terminates the current interaction goal by setting its `in` and `success` beliefs to `false` and its `finished` belief to `true`.

Figure 12. Rollback sequence

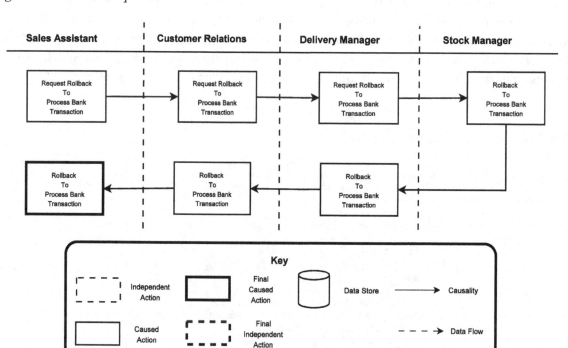

Algorithm 4. Sales Assistant rollback plan (from Organize Delivery to Process Bank Transaction)

```
Require: rollbackGoalEvent
1.  // Synchronise (with Coordination plan)
2.  waitFor(inOrganizeDelivery)
3.
4.  // 1. Terminate current IG unsuccessfully
5.  organizeDeliverySuccess = false
6.  finishedOrganizeDelivery = true
7.  inOrganizeDelivery = false
8.
9.  // 2. Wait for apex IG to terminate
10. waitFor(finishedOrderBook and not inOrderBook)
11.
12. // 3. Set appropriate beliefs to re-start interaction to begin at desired IG (shortcut)
13. // 3.1. Reset current IG beliefs
14. finishedOrganizeDelivery = false
15.
16. // 3.2. Set beliefs of IG to begin next interaction from (shortcut)
17. processBankTransactionSuccess = false
18. finishedProcessBankTransaction = false
19. inProcessBankTransaction = true
20.
21. // 3.3. Set beliefs for "retry" attempt
22. retryProcessBankTransaction = true
23.
24. // 4. Re-start interaction, set "in" belief of apex stage to "true"
25. inOrderBook = true
26.
27. // 5. Notify relevant agents
```

This will cause the interaction to fail, which the agent waits for (lines 9 and 10). After the interaction has failed, the agent sets the appropriate beliefs to re-start the interaction at the desired interaction goal (this is rollback-specific) and then re-starts the interaction.

In Algorithm 4 the *Sales Assistant* does not need to notify any agents (line 27) as it is the last agent to roll back (refer to Figure 12). However, in the case of all the remaining agents in the interaction in Figure 12, they would have to notify another agent that they have completed their rollback so that the next agent can then begin its rollback.

As with terminations, a similar sequence of actions is, by convention, understood by the `Rollback to Process Bank Transaction` action in Figure 8. That is, the *Sales Assistant* will request that the *Customer Relations* roll back to *Process Bank Transaction*, the *Customer Relations* will send a similar request to the next agent in the interaction, and so forth, until the last agent receives the request and rolls back. After rolling back, the last agent will notify the previous agent, which will then roll back and notify the previous agent, and so forth, until the *Sales Assistant* receives notification that all agents have rolled back. The *Sales Assistant* will then roll back. Refer to Figure 12 for a diagrammatical depiction of this sequence of actions.

CONCLUSION

We have presented Hermes, a goal-oriented methodology for designing and implementing flexible and robust intelligent agent interactions. The methodology includes design processes, design notations, design artifacts, and implementation guidelines which explain how the design artifacts can be mapped to any goal-plan agent platform.

As Hermes aims to be pragmatic, this has been assessed in an experimental evaluation (see (Cheong, 2008) for full details) in which 13 participants were given a common interaction scenario to design. The participants were firstly given a pre-evaluation questionnaire which assessed their skill and experience with agent interaction design. Based on the responses, the participants were equally, both in terms of numbers, and skill and experience level, divided into two groups. Both groups were given the same interaction scenario to design, however, one group was asked to use the Hermes methodology, whilst the other used the interaction design aspect of the Prometheus methodology. Each participant was provided with the appropriate training manual (Hermes or Prometheus). After completing their design interactions, participants were required to fill in a post-evaluation questionnaire which enquired about how they felt about their created design interactions, and how they felt about the processes they used to create them. In addition, the designs themselves were collected and analysed.

The participants' designed interactions were analysed with respect to four metrics: *Scenario Coverage*, *Flexibility*, *Robustness*, and *Design Time*. The first metric (*scenario coverage*) was used to assess how well the methodology guided the designer. Specifically, we considered whether any of the steps in the provided scenario were missed in the interaction, something that a good process should help the designer avoid. The next two metrics (*flexibility* and *robustness*) directly measured how successful the methodologies were at guiding developers towards producing flexible and robust interactions. The flexibility metric assessed the number of possible paths through the interaction (as a function of domain-specific interaction parameters, such as the number of possible meeting times). The robustness metric assessed the number of possible failures that were considered in the design. Finally, the design time metric simply measured how long it took to produce the design.

The results of the evaluation indicated that Hermes was successful:

- **Scenario coverage:** all of the designs produced with Hermes covered all 14 steps of the scenario whereas more than half of the designs produced by following Prometheus did not cover between 1 and 4 steps (difference being statistically significant[17] with p=0.04895).
- **Flexibility:** from each design we derived the number of paths through the interaction as a function of the number of alternative meeting times (m), the number of alternative rooms (r), and the number of alternative credit cards (c). Considering a range of reasonable values for these demonstrated significant differences (e.g. p=0.01632 for $m=c=r=3$) with the number of paths ranging from 4 to 2655 for Prometheus designs and from 164 to 405872 for Hermes (both with $m=c=r=3$).
- **Robustness:** we identified nine failures that could occur in the course of the interaction (but did not provide these to the designers). Of these nine, Prometheus designs identified 0-3 whereas Hermes designs identified 3-7, demonstrating better robustness in Hermes designs (p=0.001748).

However, one disadvantage of Hermes was that it took longer to follow the methodology (Prometheus designs ranged from 45 to 240 minutes, Hermes from 145 to 320, p=0.006993). An interesting observation, that was substantiated by the participants in their responses to the post-evaluation questionnaire, was that the way Hermes divides interactions, per interaction goals, was easier to follow than Prometheus' per agent division of the interaction. Otherwise, results from the post-evaluation questionnaire supported the evaluation results but were less conclusive, since they considered participants' opinions about the designs, as opposed to considering the designs themselves, and since they had a limited seven point (+3 to -3) response scale.

FUTURE RESEARCH

There are two tools to support the Hermes methodology. One is a simple design tool that allows designers to create interaction goal hierarchies and action maps, whilst the other is a code generation tool which accepts a syntactic description of a Hermes interaction and produces (partial) Jadex code. One area of future work is to improve tool support for Hermes, including:

- improvements in support for the processes and techniques, rather than just providing a 'sketch pad' for the Hermes notations;
- adding checking of designs for consistency; and
- integrating Hermes support into the Prometheus Design Tool (PDT).

As Hermes is purposely limited to the design of agent interactions, it has been integrated with Prometheus to enable designers to use goal-oriented interactions in agent system design (Cheong and Winikoff, 2006b). Apart from Prometheus, Hermes can also be integrated with other agent methodologies, however, this has not been done, and remains an area for future work.

Although Hermes was not explicitly created to design open systems interactions, this has been kept in mind during its development. As such, it should be possible to adapt Hermes to design interactions in open systems. This would require changing the implementation mapping to cater for non-BDI agents, but should not require significant changes to the design methodology. Additionally, Hermes can also be used to design interactions between and within teams, however, this work has not yet been researched.

Finally, there is scope for developing better techniques and notations for dealing with parallelism in interaction design.

REFERENCES

Bauer, B., Müller, J. P., & Odell, J. (2000). An extension of UML by protocols for multi-agent interaction. In *Proceedings of the Fourth International Conference on MultiAgent Systems*, (pp. 207-214).

Bauer, B., Müller, J. P., & Odell, J. (2001). Agent UML: A formalism for specifying multiagent software systems. In *First International Workshop on Agent-Oriented Software Engineering* (AOSE 2000), (pp. 91-103), Secaucus, NJ, USA: Springer-Verlag New York, Inc.

Benfield, S. S., Hendrickson, J., & Galanti, D. (2006). Making a strong business case for multiagent technology. In *Proceedings of the Fifth International Joint Conference on Autonomous Agents and Multiagent Systems (AAMAS '06)*, (pp. 10-15), Hakodate, Japan: ACM Press.

Bresciani, P., Giorgini, P., Giunchiglia, F., Mylopoulos, J., & Perini, A. (2004). Tropos: An agent-oriented software development methodology. *Journal of Autonomous Agents and Multi-Agent Systems*, *8*(3), 203-236.

Castelfranchi, C. (1995). Commitments: From individual intentions to groups and organizations. In Lesser, V. R. and Gasser, L., (eds.), *Proceedings of the First International Conference on Multiagent Systems*, (pp. 41-48), San Francisco, California, USA: The MIT Press.

Chaib-draa, B. (1995). Industrial applications of distributed AI. *Communications of the ACM, 38*(11), 49-53.

Cheong, C. (2008). Hermes: Goal-oriented interactions for intelligent agents. PhD thesis. School of Computer Science and Information Technology, RMIT University.

Cheong, C., & Winikoff, M. (2006a). Hermes: Designing goal-oriented agent interactions. In Bordini, R. H., Dastani, M., Dix, J., and El Fallah Seghrouchni, A., (eds.), *Programming Multi-Agent Systems (ProMAS 2005 post-proceedings),* volume 3862 of *Lecture Notes in Artificial Intelligence,* (pp. 168-183). Springer.

Cheong, C., & Winikoff, M. (2006b). Improving flexibility and robustness in agent interactions: Extending Prometheus with Hermes. In *Software Engineering for Multi-Agent Systems IV: Research Issues and Practical Applications (SELMAS 2005 post-proceedings),* volume 3914 of *Lecture Notes in Computer Science,* (pp. 189-206). Springer.

DeLoach, S. A. (2006). Engineering organization-based multiagent systems. In Garcia, A. F., Choren, R., de Lucena, C. J. P., Giorgini, P., Holvoet, T., and Romanovsky, A. B., editors, *Software Engineering for Multi-Agent Systems IV: Research Issues and Practical Applications (SELMAS 2005 post-proceedings),* volume 3914 of *Lecture Notes in Computer Science,* (pp. 109-125). Springer.

DeLoach, S. A., Wood, M. F., & Sparkman, C. H. (2001). Multiagent systems engineering. *The International Journal of Software Engineering and Knowledge Engineering, 11*(3), 231-258.

Dignum, V. (2004). *A model for organizational interaction: Based on agents, founded in logic.* PhD thesis, Utrecht University, The Netherlands.

Dignum, V., & Dignum, F. (2003). The knowledge market: Agent mediated knowledge sharing. In *Proceedings of the Third International/Central and Eastern European Conference on Multi-Agent Systems (CEEMAS 03),* (pp. 168-179).

Esteva, M., de la Cruz, D., & Sierra, C. (2002). Islander: An electronic institutions editor. In *Proceedings of the First International Joint Conference on Autonomous Agents and Multiagent Systems (AAMAS '02),* (pp. 1045-1052), Bologna, Italy: ACM Press.

Flores, R. A., & Kremer, R. C. (2004a). A pragmatic approach to build conversation protocols using social commitments. In *Proceedings of the Third International Joint Conference on Autonomous Agents and Multiagent Systems (AAMAS'04),* (pp. 1242-1243), New York, NY, USA: ACM Press.

Flores, R. A., & Kremer, R. C. (2004b). A principled modular approach to construct flexible conversation protocols. In Tawfik, A. and Goodwin, S., editors, *Advances in Artificial Intelligence,* (pp. 1-15). Springer-Verlag, LNCS 3060.

Fornara, N., & Colombetti, M. (2002). Operational specification of a commitment-based agent communication language. In *Proceedings of the First International Joint Conference on Autonomous Agents and Multiagent Systems (AAMAS '02),* (pp. 536-542), Bologna, Italy: ACM Press.

Fornara, N., & Colombetti, M. (2003). Defining interaction protocols using a commitment-based agent communication language. In *Proceedings of the Second International Joint Conference on Autonomous Agents and Multiagent Systems (AAMAS '03),* (pp. 520-527), Melbourne, Australia: ACM Press.

Huget, M.-P., & Odell, J. (2004). Representing agent interaction protocols with agent UML. In *Proceedings of the Fifth International Workshop on Agent Oriented Software Engineering (AOSE)*, (pp. 16-30), Springer-Verlag, LNCS 3382.

Huget, M.-P., Odell, J., Haugen, Ø., Nodine, M. M., Cranefield, S., Levy, R., & Padgham, L. (2003). FIPA Modeling: Interaction Diagrams. On *www.auml.org* under "Working Documents". Foundation For Intelligent Physical Agents (FIPA) Working Draft (version 2003-07-02).

Hutchison, J., & Winikoff, M. (2002). Flexibility and Robustness in Agent Interaction Protocols. In *Workshop on Challenges in Open Agent Systems* at the First International Joint Conference on Autonomous Agents and Multi-Agents Systems.

Jennings, N. R. (2001). An agent-based approach for building complex software systems. *Communications of the ACM, 44*(4), 35-41.

Jennings, N. R., Sycara, K. P., & Wooldridge, M. (1998). A roadmap of agent research and development. *Autonomous Agents and Multi-Agent Systems, 1*(1), 7-38.

Kumar, S., & Cohen, P. R. (2004). STAPLE: An agent programming language based on the joint intention theory. In *Proceedings of the Third International Joint Conference on Autonomous Agents and Multi-Agent Systems (AAMAS '04),* (pp. 1390-1391), New York, USA: ACM Press.

Kumar, S., Cohen, P. R., & Huber, M. J. (2002a). Direct execution of team specifications in STAPLE. In *Proceedings of the First International Joint Conference on Autonomous Agents and Multi-Agent Systems (AAMAS '02),* (pp. 567-568), Bologna, Italy: ACM Press.

Kumar, S., Huber, M. J., & Cohen, P. R. (2002b). Representing and executing protocols as joint actions. In *Proceedings of the First International Joint Conference on Autonomous Agents and Multi-Agent Systems (AAMAS '02),* (pp. 543-550), Bologna, Italy: ACM Press.

Munroe, S., Miller, T., Belecheanu, R. A., Pěchouček, M., McBurney, P., & Luck, M. (2006). Crossing the agent technology chasm: Lessons, experiences and challenges in commercial applications of agents. *Knowledge Engineering Review, 21*(4), 345-392.

Odell, J., Parunak, H. V. D., & Bauer, B. (2000). Extending UML for agents. In *Proceedings of the Agent-Oriented Information Systems* Workshop at the 17th National conference on Artificial Intelligence, pages 3-17, Austin, TX.

Padgham, L., & Winikoff, M. (2004). *Developing Intelligent Agent Systems: A Practical Guide.* John Wiley and Sons. ISBN 0-470-86120-7.

Reisig, W. (1985). *Petri Nets: An Introduction.* EATCS Monographs on Theoretical Computer Science. Springer-Verlag. ISBN 0-387-13723-8.

Singh, M. P. (1991). Social and psychological commitments in multiagent systems. In *AAAI Fall Symposium on Knowledge and Action at Social and Organizational Levels*, Monterey, California, USA.

Sycara, K. P. (1998). Multiagent systems. *AI Magazine, 19*(2), 79-92.

Vasconcelos, W., Sierra, C., & Esteva, M. (2002). An approach to rapid prototyping of large multi-agent systems. In *Proceedings of the 17th IEEE International Conference on Automated Software Engineering (ASE 2002),* (pp. 13-22).

Winikoff, M. (2006). Designing commitment-based agent interactions. In *Proceedings of the IEEE/WIC/ACM International Conference on Intelligent Agent Technology (IAT-06),* (pp. 363-370), Hong Kong.

Winikoff, M. (2007). Implementing commitment-based interactions. In *Proceedings of the Sixth International Joint Conference on Autonomous Agents and Multiagent Systems (AAMAS 2007),* (pp. 868-875), Honolulu, USA.

Wooldridge, M. (2002). *An Introduction to MultiAgent Systems.* John Wiley and Sons.

Yolum, P. (2005). Towards design tools for protocol development. In *Proceedings of the Fourth International Joint Conference on Autonomous Agents and Multiagent Systems (AAMAS '05),* (pp. 99-105), Utrecht, The Netherlands: ACM Press.

Yolum, P., & Singh, M. P. (2001). Commitment machines. In *Proceedings of the 8th International Workshop on Agent Theories, Architectures, and Languages (ATAL 2001),* Seattle, WA, USA. Pages 235-247 in post-proceedings published by Springer-Verlag (2002), LNCS 2333.

Yolum, P., & Singh, M. P. (2002). Flexible protocol specification and execution: Applying event calculus planning using commitments. In *Proceedings of the 1st Joint Conference on Autonomous Agents and MultiAgent Systems (AAMAS '02),* pp. 527-534, Bologna, Italy. ACM Press.

Yolum, P., & Singh, M. P. (2004). Reasoning about commitments in the event calculus: An approach for specifying and executing protocols. *Annals of Mathematics and Artificial Intelligence (AMAI), Special Issue on Computational Logic in Multi-Agent Systems, 42*(1-3), 227-253.

Zambonelli, F., Jennings, N. R., & Wooldridge, M. (2003). Developing Multiagent Systems: The Gaia Methodology. *ACM Transactions on Software Engineering Methodology, 12*(3), 317-370.

ENDNOTES

[1] Christopher Cheong carried out this research as part of his Ph.D. candidature in the School of Computer Science and Information Technology, RMIT University.

[2] Systems in which the components are explicitly designed to interoperate.

[3] Systems in which the components are not explicitly designed to interoperate but are able to do so by adhering to published standards.

[4] More precisely, to reach an interaction state where the product has been delivered.

[5] There are some similarities between the Hermes notations, especially action maps, and UML. Space precludes a detailed comparison, see (Cheong, 2008) for details.

[6] A *final* design artifact is defined as a non-intermediate artifact that is retained for design documentation purposes. In some steps of Hermes, *intermediate* artifacts are created to either provide a logical path which will guide the designer from one step to another or to allow the designer to check the created design. These artifacts are not intended to be retained as design documentation.

[7] This scenario is based on the book store design of (Padgham and Winikoff, 2004)

[8] These dependencies are different to causalities: they state that one interaction goal cannot begin until a preceding interaction goal has completed. A causality would state that a given interaction

goal causes another interaction goal to be achieved. This distinction is more apparent when the interaction goal hierarchy does not specify a sequence of interaction goals.

[9] In an earlier presentation we had four steps, here we have merged steps three and four together.

[10] To clarify the difference between causality and dependency, consider a situation in which there are three actions: *Action A*, *Action B*, and *Action C*. *Action A* causes *Action C* and *Action B* also causes *Action C* (i.e. A → C ← B). In this case, *Action C* is triggered when either *Action A or Action B* complete because causalities are used. However, if arrows are viewed as dependencies, then *Action C* can only occur after *both Action A* and *Action B* have completed (as *Action C* depends on both).

[11] Additional robustness comes from the rollback mechanism which is discussed later on.

[12] Unless one adds compensatory actions, in this case, to return the payment.

[13] In a typical system, payment is not normally charged before checking inventory stock, however, this system processes payment before checking inventory stock for expository purposes.

[14] JACK is a trademark of The Agent Oriented Software Group (www.agent-software.com)

[15] In this example we assume a sequential order. Space precludes a detailed discussion of parallelism, but see (Cheong, 2008) for details.

[16] In this example, the interaction is terminated sequentially. It is also possible to terminate the interaction in parallel.

[17] Statistical significance was tested using an exact Wilcoxon rank sum test.

Section II
Formal Approaches for Agent Organizations

Chapter VI
A Formal Framework for Organization Modeling and Analysis

Viara Popova
De Montfort University, UK

Alexei Sharpanskykh
Vrije Universiteit Amsterdam, The Netherlands

ABSTRACT

This chapter introduces a formal framework for modeling and analysis of organizations. It allows representing and reasoning about all important aspects of artificial and human organizations structured in a number of views, including performance-oriented, process-oriented, and power- and interaction-related aspects. The framework provides means to model formal (pre)defined organizational structures and dynamics, informal relations, and behavior of organizational actors. The meaning attached to the modeling concepts is specified based on the literature from Social Science. Unlike many existing organization modeling approaches, the proposed framework has formal foundations based on the order-sorted predicate logic which enables different types of analysis of organizational specifications of particular views and across views. The framework allows scalability of modeling and analysis of complex organizations, by considering them at different aggregation levels. Furthermore, the framework provides support for real-time management of organizational processes. The framework was applied in several case studies, one of which is discussed here.

INTRODUCTION

The modern world is unthinkable without organizations. The rapid scientific, societal and technological development of the last centuries, coupled with the changed environmental conditions gave rise to a great diversity of organizational forms and types of interaction between them. The structural and behavioral complexity of organizations is interdependent on the complexity of the environment, in which these organizations are situated. The complex, dynamically changing environment with insufficient resources often creates challenging obstacles for the satisfaction of the primary goals of any organization – to survive and prosper. To be successful, an organization should effectively and efficiently organize its internal structure and activities so that the fit with the environment is achieved. In reality these requirements are difficult to fulfill, since no universally applicable recipes exist that ensure the successfulness of an organization at all times and all cases. Therefore, most modern organizations suffer from various performance inefficiencies and inconsistencies that may have consequences for the organizational vitality. Often only a small number of these flaws can easily be identified, but can be revealed using more profound analysis methods.

Many of the techniques for analysis of organizational performance developed in organization theory are informal and imprecise, which undermines the feasibility and rigor of the analysis. For more precise evaluation of the organizational performance, for identification of performance bottlenecks and conflicts, detailed organizational analysis based on a formal organization model should be performed. Furthermore, a formal organization model constitutes a basis for many automated processes within enterprises (e.g., computer integrated manufacturing) and provides a foundation for inter-enterprise cooperation.

To enable formal analysis, this Chapter introduces a formal modeling framework that allows representing diverse aspects of organizational reality, within several perspectives, e.g. the process-related, performance-related and organization-related perspectives. Since individuals often exert significant influence on the organizational dynamics, also aspects related to human behavior are considered explicitly. The characteristics of the framework include:

- it allows the representation and analysis of organization models at different levels of abstraction in order to handle complexity and increase scalability;
- it enables formal verification and validation of models of different perspectives on organizations;
- it enables simulation for experimenting and testing hypotheses on the organizational behavior under different circumstances;
- it proposes computational analysis methods across multiple perspectives on organizations;
- it supports and controls the execution of organizational scenarios and the evaluation of organizational performance.

The framework proposes a wide spectrum of means for modeling and analysis of structures and dynamics of organizations of different types including mechanistic organizations that represent systems of hierarchically linked job positions with clear responsibilities and organic organizations characterized by highly dynamic, constantly changing, structure with non-linear behavior. Although the structure and behavioral rules for organic organizations can hardly be identified and formalized, by performing agent-based simulations with changing characteristics of proactive agents, useful insights into the functioning of such organizations can be gained. Furthermore, the framework supports reuse of parts of models.

The chapter is organized as follows. First the related literature is presented. Then the formal foundations of the framework are described. After that the case study used for illustration is introduced. An overview of the four modeling views is given. It is then discussed how the framework can be used in practice. Finally, the methods for organizational analysis are described. The Chapter ends with conclusions and future research directions.

RELATED LITERATURE

This Section provides a general overview of organization modeling and analysis approaches and techniques developed in three areas: organization theory, enterprise information systems and organization-oriented multi-agent systems.

Organization Theory

Organization theory distinguishes three aggregation levels, at which processes and structures of human organizations are studied: *micro, meso,* and *macro*. At the individual (*micro*) level the behavior of individuals and work groups is investigated. At the level of the whole organization (*meso* level) different aspects of the organizational structure and dynamics are considered. At the global (*macro*) level the interaction between the organization and its environment including other organizations, society, markets, is considered.

The specifications of organizations normally used in Organization Theory are represented by informal or semi-formal graphical descriptions that illustrate aspects of organizations at some aggregation level (Mintzberg, 1979) (e.g., decision making, authority relations). Often they are specified in an imprecise and ambiguous way, making it difficult to apply them in practice. One of the attempts to identify concrete, practically applicable recommendations for designing organizations is within contingency theory (Burton & Obel, 2004). The key thesis is that the structure and behavior of an organization should be defined based on particular environmental characteristics. To support this, the contingency theory identifies a number of generic principles for designing effective organizations which should be carefully adapted in the context of this particular organization. In the adaptation process inconsistencies and inefficiencies may be introduced that cannot be foreseen and identified by the contingency theory. To identify these inconsistencies and inefficiencies analysis techniques are required.

Another class of approaches for specifying quantitative organization models with precise semantics has been proposed in the System Dynamics Theory. Organizational descriptions specified in System Dynamics are based on numerical variables and equations that describe how these variables change over time. Such specifications can be computationally effective; however they lack ontological expressivity to conceptualize relations of different types of organizations. Furthermore, they abstract from single events, entities and actors and take an aggregate view on the organizational dynamics. Therefore, such approaches cannot be used for modeling organizations at the micro level.

The problem of the limited ontological expressivity of modeling has been addressed in the area of enterprise information systems, considered in the following Section.

Enterprise Information Systems

An enterprise information system (EIS) is any computing system automating the execution of process(es) of an enterprise. EISs are often built based on enterprise architectures. An *enterprise architecture* (EA) is an enterprise-wide, integrating framework used to represent and to manage enterprise processes, information systems and personnel, so that key goals of the enterprise are satisfied. Many different EAs have been developed CIMOSA (Bernus, Nemes & Schmidt, 1998), TOVE (Fox *et al*, 1997), ARIS (Bernus, Nemes & Schmidt, 1998). Based on common features of these architectures a generalized meta-framework GERAM (Generalized Enterprise Reference Architecture and Methodology) was developed (Bernus, Nemes & Schmidt, 1998). GERAM provides a template for the development and comparison of enterprise modeling frameworks. GERAM describes a number of dedicated views on enterprises. *The function view* concerns structural and behavioral aspects of the business processes of an enterprise. The following techniques are used: IDEF standards (Bernus, Nemes & Schmidt, 1998), statecharts, Petri-nets (Bernus, Nemes & Schmidt, 1998), semi-formal languages (BPML, etc.). *The information view* describes knowledge about objects as they are used and produced. The following data models are used: Entity-Relationship-diagrams, object-oriented representations, UML class diagrams. *The resource view* considers resources of an enterprise often modeled as separate entities in the existing frameworks with varying level of detail. *The organization view* defines responsibilities and authorities on processes, information and resources.

Although many architectures include a rich ontological basis for modeling different views, most of them provide limited support for automated analysis of models, addressed in the category *Enterprise Engineering Tools* of GERAM, primarily due to lack of formal foundations in these architectures.

Within several frameworks, analysis methods for particular views have been developed (e.g., process-oriented modeling techniques for the function view (van der Aalst *et al*, 2003), ABC-based techniques for the performance-oriented view (Tham, 1999)). Much less attention has been devoted to analysis performed across different views that allows investigating a combined influence of factors from different views on the organizational behavior. In (Dalal *et al*, 2004) an integrated framework for process and performance modeling is described that incorporates accounting/business parameters into a formal process modeling approach based on Petri-nets. However, key aspects as authority relations, goals, individual behavior are not considered. Another formal framework for business process modeling is described in (Koubarakis & Plexousakis, 2002) focusing on formal goal-oriented modeling using situation calculus. Modeling and analysis of processes and other organizational concepts are not properly addressed. A formal framework for verifying models specified in Unified Enterprise Modeling Language (UEML) is proposed in (Chapurlat, Kamsu-Foguem & Prunet, 2006). It identifies a general idea to use conceptual graphs for verifying enterprise models; however, neither technical nor experimental results are provided.

Usually EISs are based on predefined organizational specifications that guide and/or control processes performed by organizational actors. To enable modeling and analysis of behavior of organizational actors in different organizational and environmental settings, the agent paradigm is particularly useful.

Organization-Oriented Multi-Agent Systems

An agent is a piece of software with the ability to perceive its environment (virtual or physical), reason about its perception of this environment and act upon the environment. Interactions among agents often take place in the context of certain organizational formations (structures). Such structures may be intentionally designed to enforce rules on agent behavior or emerge from the non-random and repeated patterns of interactions among agents. The organizational structure provides means to coordinate the execution of tasks in a multi-agent system (MAS) and to ensure the achievement of organizational goals.

In (Horling & Lesser, 2005) several types of organizational structures are distinguished including hierarchies, holarchies, coalitions, teams, congregations, and federations, providing the agents with different degrees of autonomy. Usually the behavior of agents is restricted by a set of norms defined at different aggregation levels of the organizational structure. Currently many approaches for modeling normative MASs have been proposed in the literature. Often organizational structures are specified in terms of roles defined as abstract representations of sets of functionalities performed by an organization. Also, in the approach proposed in the paper diverse organizational structures are modeled as roles.

In Chapter III "Modelling Dimensions for Multi-Agent Systems Organizations" by Coutinho et al., eight dimensions for modeling of agent organizations are introduced: structures of roles and groups, dialogical interaction structures, goal/task decomposition structures, normative structures, environment, organizational evolution, organizational evaluation and ontologies. The modeling framework proposed in this Chapter considers explicitly all these dimensions, except for the organizational evolution. Nevertheless, this dimension can be also modeled by dynamics modeling means of the proposed framework.

The GAIA methodology (Zambonelli, Jennings & Wooldridge, 2003) addresses two development phases: analysis and design. At the analysis phase, roles and relations between them are identified. During design societies of agents are specified. GAIA does not capture the internal aspects of agents. The interaction of agents with the environment is not treated separately. In contrast, the approach proposed in this Chapter considers the internals of agents and interaction with the environment explicitly.

The original AGR organizational model (Ferber & Gutknecht, 1998) considers only structural aspects of organizations. Each organizational AGR model comprises a set of interrelated groups consisting of roles. AGR enforces no constraints on the internal architecture of agents. In Chapter IV "Towards an Integral Approach of Organizations in Multi-Agent Systems" by Ferber et al., an extension of the AGR model is proposed - the meta-model MASQ (Multi-Agent System based on Quadrants). This model is based on a 4-quadrant framework, where the system analysis and design is performed along two dimensions: an interior/exterior dimension and an individual/collective dimension. The framework proposed in this Chapter addresses all four quadrants, including mental states of agents and their externally observable behavior, physical world and its components, social norms and interaction conventions, shared knowledge. Furthermore, the framework of this Chapter provides a more refined view on each quadrant by distinguishing specific types of concepts, states, and relations, which will be introduced further in this Chapter.

MOISE (Hannoun *et al*, 2000) is an organizational model that provides descriptions along three levels: the individual level of agents; the aggregate level of large agent structures; the society level of global structuring and interconnection between agents and structures. In (Hubner, Sichman & Boissier, 2002) the methodology is extended with functional aspects (such as tasks, plans, and constraints on the behavior of a MAS). Our framework provides a more elaborated view on the functional aspects.

The TROPOS methodology (Bresciani, 2004) addresses three development phases of MASs: analysis, design and implementation. During analysis, a list of functional and non-functional requirements for the system is identified. During design, the structure and behavior of a system in terms of its subsystems related through data, control and other dependencies are defined. The implementation phase maps the models from the design phase into software by means of Jack Intelligent Agents. While TROPOS aims mostly at designing and implementing robust and orderly multi-agent systems, the framework proposed in this Chapter can be used for modeling and analysis of both artificial organizations of agents and human organizations. Thus, many aspects and relations inherent in human organizations are not used in TROPOS (e.g., power relations, workflow modeling).

The OperA framework (Dignum, 2003) focuses on social norms and explicitly defines control policies to establish and reinforce these norms. The framework comprises three components: the organizational model defining the structure of the society, consisting of roles and interactions; the social model assigning roles to agents; and the interaction model describing possible interactions between agents. Thus, the OperA framework addresses both organizational structure and dynamics. The internal representation of agents is not clearly defined in this framework.

FORMAL FOUNDATIONS OF THE PROPOSED FRAMEWORK

The proposed framework introduces four interrelated views: performance-oriented, process-oriented, organization-oriented, and agent-oriented. The first-order sorted predicate logic serves as a formal basis for defining dedicated modeling languages for each view. These languages provide high expressivity for conceptualizing a variety of concepts and relations using sorts, sorted constants, variables, functions and predicates. Furthermore, these languages allow expressing both quantitative and qualitative aspects of different views.

To express temporal relations in specifications of the views, the dedicated languages of the views are embedded into the Temporal Trace Language (TTL) (Sharpanskykh, 2008), a variant of the order-sorted predicate logic. In TTL the organizational dynamics are represented by a trace, i.e. a temporally ordered sequence of states. Each state is characterized by a unique time point and a set of state properties that hold. State properties are specified using the dedicated language(s) of the view(s). In TTL, formulae of the state language are used as objects. For enabling dynamic reasoning TTL includes special sorts: TIME (a set of linearly ordered time points), STATE (a set of all state names of an organization), TRACE (a set of all trace names), and STATPROP (a set of all state property names).

A state for an organization is described by a function symbol state of type TRACE×TIME→STATE.

The set of function symbols of TTL includes:

$\wedge, \vee, \rightarrow, \leftrightarrow$: STATPROP×STATPROP→STATPROP,
not: STATPROP→STATPROP,
$\forall, \exists$: SVARS×STATPROP→STATPROP,

which counterparts in the state language are Boolean propositional connectives and quantifiers. States are related to names of state properties via the formally defined satisfaction relation denoted by the infix predicate $\models$, state$(\gamma,t)\models p$, which denotes that the state property with a name p holds in trace γ at time point t. Both state(γ,t) and p are terms of TTL. In general, TTL terms are constructed by induction in a standard way from variables, constants and function symbols typed with all before mentioned TTL sorts. Transition relations between states are described by dynamic properties expressed by TTL-formulae. The set of atomic TTL-formulae is defined as:

(1) If v_1 is a term of sort STATE, and u_1 is a term of the sort STATPROP, then $v_1|=u_1$ is an atomic TTL formula.

(2) If τ_1, τ_2 are terms of any TTL sort, then $\tau_1=\tau_2$ is an atomic TTL formula.

(3) If t_1, t_2 are terms of sort TIME, then $t_1<t_2$ is an atomic TTL formula.

The set of well-formed TTL-formulae is defined inductively in a standard way using Boolean propositional connectives and quantifiers. TTL has semantics of the order-sorted predicate logic. A more detailed specification of the syntax and semantics of the TTL is given in (Sharpanskykh, 2008).

A set of structural and behavioral *constraints* imposed on organizational specifications can be identified. Formally, this set is represented by a *logical theory* consisting of formulae constructed in the standard predicate logic way from the terms of the dedicated language of the views (and of TTL if temporal relations are required). A specification is *correct* if the corresponding theory is satisfied by this specification, i.e., all sentences in theory are true in the logical structure(s) corresponding to the specification. The constraints are divided in two main groups: generic and domain-specific. *Generic constraints* define general restrictions for a view or the whole specification that need to be satisfied by the specification of every organization. Two types of generic constraints are considered. *Structural integrity and consistency constraints* are based on the rules of specification composition, e.g. constraints guaranteeing the internal consistency of a structure within a particular view. The *constraints imposed by the physical world* are not dictated by the framework but by the rules of the physical world which render certain situations impossible, e.g. an agent cannot be at two different physical locations at the same time. The set of generic constraints is predefined and can be reused for every specification.

Domain-specific constraints are dictated by the application domain and may be added or modified by the designer. They express facts and restrictions valid in the particular application domain but not necessarily in other domains. Domain-specific constraints can be *imposed by the organization* itself, *external parties,* e.g. the government, the society, other companies, as well as by *the physical world* of the specific application domain. Domain-specific constraints may or may not be directly reusable for other companies in the same or other domains. To support the process of designing such constraints, templates can be provided with parameters that can be customized by the designer.

INTRODUCTION TO THE CASE STUDY

The proposed framework was applied for modeling and analysis of an organization from the security domain within the project CIM (Cybernetic Incident Management, http://www.almende.com/cim/). This organization has many features of a mechanistic organization: in particular, hierarchically linked job positions with clear responsibilities that use standard well-understood technology. The formal documents of the organization provide diverse details about the structure and dynamics of the organization, which need to be formally represented in a feasible model of the organization. In particular, the following aspects should be considered: performance indicators (PIs) and goals; processes, resources and flows of processes; roles (positions) and different types of relations between them (e.g., interaction, power); characteristics and behavior of organizational agents allocated to roles (positions). Furthermore, relations between different aspects should be modeled as well (e.g., between tasks and goals; between roles and agents). The following Sections illustrate how the proposed framework can be used to create formal specifications for particular perspectives of the organization. These specifications can be further used to perform automated analysis.

The main purpose of the organization in focus is to deliver security services (surveillance, consultancy, training, etc.). The organization has a well-defined multi-level structure that comprises two divisions over several areas. The company employs approximately 230.000 persons with predefined job descriptions. The examples given in this Chapter are related to the planning of the assignment of security officers to customer locations. The planning process consists of forward (long-term) planning and short-term planning. Forward planning is the process of creation, analysis and optimization of forward plans for the allocation of security officers within the organization based on customer contracts. It is performed by a team of forward planners from the forward planning group under the supervision of the Manager Planning. The forward planning group is centralized for the organization as part of the department Operations Support and reports to the Operations Support Manager. During short-term planning, plans describing the allocation of security officers within certain area for a week are created and updated based on the forward plan and up-to-date information. Also as part of short-term planning, daily plans are created based on short-term plans and information coming from the security employees about their availability and other changes via data change forms. For each area, the short-term planning is performed by the area planning team led by its Team Leader. During short-term planning the planners can get supervision, advice or information from forward planners, depending on the specific circumstances. The planners also communicate with the area's Unit Manager who is in charge of the security employees within this area, takes care of collecting and processing the data change forms and supervises the daily plans execution.

In both types of planning, resources are used including the company's personnel database, customer contracts, data change forms, plans and other paper-based or electronic resources. Other activities of the planners include reporting to the management team, training for improving qualifications, evaluations, etc.

MODELING VIEWS

In this section, the views of the proposed framework are presented. Three of them, process-oriented, performance-oriented and organization-oriented, have prescriptive character and define the desired behavior of the organization. The fourth view, agent-oriented, describes and integrates agents into the framework.

The process-oriented view describes static hierarchies of organizational tasks and resources as well as flows of processes (workflows), and relations between these structures. *The performance-oriented view* defines the goals hierarchies of the organization, the relevant PIs and their relationships. Within *the organization-oriented view,* organizational roles, their interaction, authority, responsibility and power relations are defined. In *the agent-oriented view,* different types of agents with their capabilities are identified and principles for allocating agents to roles are formulated. The four views are connected via relations. Each view and the relations between views are discussed in the following subsections.

Process-Oriented View

The process-oriented view contains information about the organizational functions, how they are related, ordered and synchronized and the resources they use and produce. The main concepts are: task, process, workflow, resource type and resource which, together with the relations between them, are specified in the formal language L_{PR} (Sharpanskykh, 2008). A *task* represents a function performed in the organization and is characterized by *name, maximal_duration* and *minimal_duration*. Table 1 gives examples of tasks considered in the case study related to planning of the assignment of security officers to locations. The tasks were extracted from available company documents on procedures and job descriptions (as discussed later in this Chapter). Column 1 contains the identification numbers assigned to the tasks for convenient reference. Column 2 contains the names of the tasks reflecting their content. Columns 3 and 4 list the resources used and produced by the tasks.

Tasks can range from very general to very specific. General tasks can be decomposed into more specific ones using AND- and OR-relations forming hierarchies. Fig. 1 shows the refinement relations of task planning from the case study. The numbers correspond to column 1 of Table 1 and reflect the position of the task in the hierarchy. For example task process_new_data_forms (4.1) describes the processing (correcting and summarizing) of forms from the security officers containing information about changes in their availability. This is needed in the planning process to produce an up-to-date plan taking into account the availability of the security officers, therefore 4.1 is a subtask of the overall planning task 4.

Table 1. Tasks from the case study

Number	Name	Uses resource types	Produces res. types
4	planning		
4.1	process_new_data_change_forms	data change forms	analysis results of data change forms
4.2	create_and_inform_correct_and_optimized_shortterm_plan		
4.2.1	create_shortterm_plan		
4.2.1.1	shortterm_plan_creation_discussion	forward plan	information about a decision on assignment of a task of creating a short-term plan
4.2.1.2	estimate_human_capacity_per_location	forward plan, personnel data, customer order details, analysis results of daily change forms	data about available and required human capacity per location
4.2.1.3	assign_officers_to_tasks	forward plan, personnel data, the short-term planning procedure, data about available and required human capacity per location	information about the assignment of security officers
4.2.1.4	input_planning_data	planning software handbooks, the short-term planning procedure, information about the assignment of security officers	short-term plan for next month
4.2.2	check_and_improve_shortterm_plan	short-term plan for next month, the short-term planning procedure	correct short-term plan for next month
4.2.3	optimize_shortterm_plan	correct short-term plan for next month	correct optimized short-term plan for next month
4.2.4	inform_all_concerned_about_shortterm_plan	correct optimized short-term plan for next month	correct optimized short-term plan for next month
4.3	create_and_inform_daily_plan		

Figure 1. A part of the task hierarchy from the case study

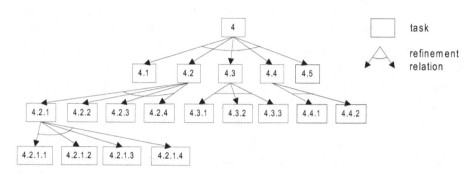

Each task can be instantiated in one or more processes in a workflow. A *workflow* is defined by a set of (partially) temporally ordered *processes*. Each process, except for the special ones with zero duration introduced below, is defined using a task as a template and all characteristics of the task are inherited by the process. Decisions are also treated as processes that are associated with decision variables taking as possible values the possible decision outcomes.

A workflow starts with the process BEGIN and ends with the process END; both have zero duration. The (partial) order of execution of processes in the workflow is defined by sequencing, branching, loop and synchronization relations. A *sequencing relation* starts_after expresses temporal-order precedence of processes. *Synchronization relations* define temporal relations between processes that are executed in parallel (starts_with, finishes_with, starts_during). *Branching relations* define and- and or-structures. An and(or)-structure with name *id*, starts with the zero-duration process begin_and(*id*) (begin_or(*id*)) and finishes by the zero-duration process end_and(*id*) (end_or(*id*)) represented graphically by rhombuses. Our treatment of and-structures is similar to the parallel split pattern combined with all types of the merge pattern from (Van der Aalst *et al.* 2003), represented here by an and-condition determining when the process following the and-structure may start. Our treatment of or-structures allows realizing both exclusive and multiple-choice patterns from (Van der Aalst *et al.* 2003). For every or-structure a condition is defined to determine which branches of the or-structure will start. *Loop relations* are defined over *loop*-structures with conditions that realize the cycle patterns from (Van der Aalst *et al.* 2003). A loop-structure *id*, starts with begin_loop(*id*) and finishes by end_loop(*id*). A Boolean condition and the maximal number of executions of every loop are specified.

The processes and the relations between them, expressed in L_{PR}, can be (partially) visualized as in Figures 2 and 3 at different levels of abstraction from very high-level (aggregated) to very detailed and specific level. Detailed levels of abstraction are achieved by refining processes into more specific ones using the refinement relations in the corresponding task hierarchies.

Within the case study, Fig. 2 presents the workflow that takes an aggregated view on the processes of daily planners performed during a contract period. Such processes as planning and check_plan_conformity can further be refined into more specific workflows using the identified hierarchy of tasks. Fig. 3(a) takes an aggregated view on the process planning, whereas Fig. 3(b) provides more specific details of this process by refining some of processes (i.e., provide_correct_data_change_forms_to_planners, update_and_inform_shortterm_plan and create_and_inform_daily_plan). The beginning of the workflow in Fig.

Figure 2. The workflow that takes an aggregated view on the activities of daily planners performed during a contract period

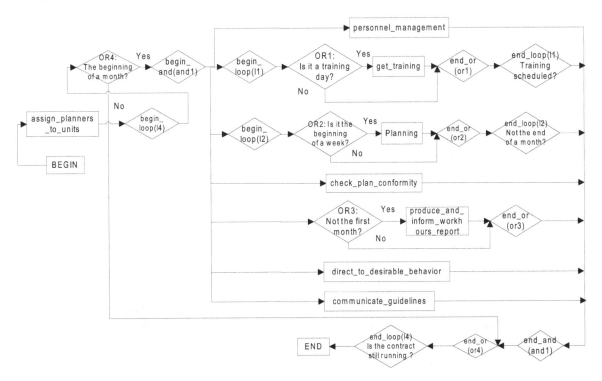

Figure 3. An aggregated view (a) and a detailed view (b) on the planning process

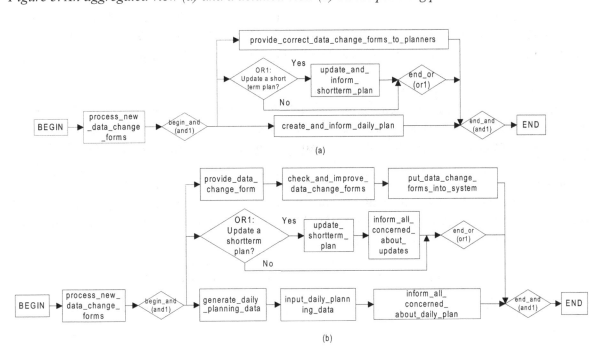

3(b) can be expressed in L_{PR} as follows:

starts_after(process_new_data_change_forms,BEGIN,0)
starts_after(begin_and(and1),process_new_data_change_forms,0)
starts_after(generate_daily_planning_data,begin_and(and1),0)
starts_after(begin_or(or1),begin_and(and1),0),...

Tasks use, consume or produce resources of different types. Resource types represent tools, supplies, components, data, etc. and are characterized by *name*, *category* (discrete, continuous), *measurement_unit*, *expiration_duration* (the length of the time interval when a resource type can be used). Resource types can sometimes be decomposed forming resource hierarchies, e.g. a database can consist of several data tables containing different information that can be used separately by different tasks, while other tasks might require the whole database. A resource type can have different function (purpose) from the resource types in its decomposition, e.g. a car has a different purpose from each of its components.

Resources are instances of resource types and inherit their characteristics, having, in addition, *name* and *amount.* Resources are used, consumed or produced by processes in the workflow. Multiple resources of the same resource type can be produced by different processes and are differentiated by their names.

Some resources can be shared, used simultaneously, by a set of processes (e.g., storage facilities, transportation vehicles). Sets of processes can be defined that are allowed to share specific resources. Our representation of shared resources differs from (Barkaoui & Petrucci, 1998) in several aspects: (1) the shared resource amount is used by processes simultaneously; (2) alternative sets of processes that are allowed to share a resource can be defined; (3) different amounts of a resource can be shared simultaneously; (4) specific conditions (requirements) for resource sharing can be defined. In the case study a short-term plan can be shared between the tasks inform_all_concerned_about_shortterm_plan and create_and_inform_daily_plan.

In the case study a number of resource types were identified, some listed in Table 1 in relation to the lowest-level tasks. Most of the identified resources are discrete (a forward plan, data change forms, customer order details). The resources used/consumed/produced by a higher-level task comprise the resources used/consumed/produced by the lower-level tasks in its refinement.

Sometimes it is important to monitor where the resources are at certain time points, for which the concept *location* is used e.g. representing the available storage facilities. Processes can add or remove resources of certain types from locations, which can be specified using predicates from the L_{PR} language (process_rem_resource_type_from, process_adds_resource_type_to: p:PROCESS $\times$ r:RESOURCE_TYPE $\times$ l: LOCATION).

The generic constraints for this view include structural constraints on the correctness of workflows, task and resource hierarchies and constraints from the physical world. For hierarchies, consistency should be maintained by making sure the set of inter-level constraints is satisfied. Consider two examples of such interlevel structural generic constraints:

GC_PO1: For every and-decomposition of a task, the minimal duration of the task is at least the maximal of all minimal durations of its subtasks.
  Formally, $\forall t$:TASK, t_1:TASK, L:TASK_LIST $\forall tp, \gamma$
  state$(\gamma, tp)|$=[is_decomposed_to(t,L) $\wedge$ is_in_task_list(t_1,L) $\rightarrow$ t.min_duration$\geq t_1$.min_duration]

GC_PO2: If a task uses certain resource type as input then there exists at least one subtask in at least one and-decomposition of this task that uses this resource type.

Formally, $\forall t$:TASK, rt:RESOURCE_TYPE, L:TASK_LIST, v:VALUE, $\forall tp,\gamma$

state$(\gamma,tp)|$=[task_uses$(t,rt,v) \wedge$ is_decomposed_to$(t,L) \rightarrow \exists t_1$:TASK, L_1:TASK_LIST, v_1:VALUE is_decomposed_to$(t,L_1) \wedge$ is_in_task_list$(t_1,L_1) \wedge$ task_uses$(t_1,rt,v_1)]$

Further, consider examples of physical world generic constraints:

GC_PO3: For every process that uses certain amount of a resource of some type as input, without consuming it, either at least that amount of resource of this type is available or can be shared with another process at every time point during the possible execution of the process.

GC_PO4: Non-sharable resources cannot be used by more than one process at the same time

Domain-specific constraints may or may not be directly reusable for the specification of other organizations in the same or other domains. Therefore to support the process of designing such constraints pre-specified templates expressed in L_{PR} can be used. Such templates, created by analysts skilled in logic for a particular organization, may be reused multiple times by different instantiations. A template is instantiated by assigning specific values to its parameters. Such reuse can reduce the effort for specifying domain-specific constraints for every organization. It also requires less expertise in logic than for the specification of a new constraint in formal language. An example of a template with its parameter in brackets is:

DC_PR1(rt:RESOURCE_TYPE): Resource of type rt is produced in the workflow.

Formally, $\exists p$:PROCESS, t:TASK, r:RESOURCE, v:VALUE $\forall tp,\gamma$ state$(\gamma,tp)|$=[process_output$(p,r) \wedge$ is_instance_of$(p,t) \wedge$ is_instance_of$(r,rt) \wedge$ task_produces$(t,rt,v)]$

For the case study this constraint may be instantiated e.g. into DC_PR1(daily_plan) meaning that a daily plan should be produced in the workflow.

Formally:

$\exists p$:PROCESS, t:TASK, r:RESOURCE, v:VALUE, $\forall tp,\gamma$ state$(\gamma,tp)|$=[process_output$(p,r) \wedge$ is_instance_of$(p,t) \wedge$ is_instance_of$(r,$daily_plan$) \wedge$ task_produces$(t,$daily_plan$,v)]$

It can also be instantiated for a short-term plan and for a forward plan as well as for other resources not directly related to planning.

Performance-Oriented View

Central notions in the performance-oriented view are goal and PI. Many organizations nowadays set goals to be achieved reflecting different aspects of the organizational performance. The goals are evaluated by monitoring and analyzing related PIs. Traditionally only numerical (often financial) PIs were considered such as costs, profits, number of clients, however today it is considered important to also monitor indicators such as customer satisfaction, employees' motivation which are qualitative and difficult to assess. Modeling of goals is supported to a various degree by a number of existing frameworks in enterprise modeling. However the concept of a PI has been underrepresented in the literature. Our approach differs in explicitly representing PIs, the link between a goal and the PI that measures its satisfaction and the relationships between PIs that can be used for reasoning at the design phase (discussed in the Section on methodological aspects). Here the concepts of the performance-oriented view are defined.

A PI is a quantitative or qualitative indicator that reflects the state or progress of the company, unit or individual. The characteristics of a PI include:

name;
definition;
type (continuous, discrete);
measurement *unit*;
time_frame (the length of the time interval for which it will be evaluated, e.g. per day, per month);
measurement *scale* (e.g. low-med-high);
min value;
max value;
source – the internal or external source used to extract the PI (company policies, mission statements, business plan, job descriptions, laws, domain knowledge, etc.);
owner (the performance of which role or agent it measures/describes);
threshold – the cut-off value separating changes in the value of the PI considered small and changes considered big, used to define the degree of causal influence between PIs (see below the discussion on relationships between PIs);
hardness – soft or hard, where soft means not directly measurable, qualitative (customer's satisfaction, company's reputation, employees' motivation), and hard means measurable, quantitative (number of customers, time to produce a plan).

For the part of the case study related to planning, using company documents, 33 PIs were identified, among which:

Name: PI5
Definition: average correctness of plans
Type: discrete
Time_frame: month
Scale: very_low-low-med-high-very_high
Source: mission statement, job descriptions
Owner: forward/short-term planning departments
Threshold: 2 units
Hardness: soft

Name: PI27
Definition: time to create new short-term plan
Type: continuous
Time_frame: month
Scale: REAL
Min_value: 0
Max_value: max_time_CST
Unit: hour

Source: job descriptions
Owner: short-term planning departments
Threshold: 24h
Hardness: hard

PIs can be related through various relationships. The following are considered in the framework: (strong) positive/negative causal influence of one PI on another, positive/negative correlation between PIs, aggregation (two PIs express the same measure at different aggregation levels). In deciding whether a causal influence is strong or not, the threshold characteristic of the PIs is used. If change above the threshold is observed then the relationship is considered strong. Relationships can be identified using e.g. company documents, domain knowledge, inference from known relations, statistical or data mining techniques, knowledge from other structures of the framework. Using these relations, a graph structure

Figure 4. The goal hierarchy for the case study

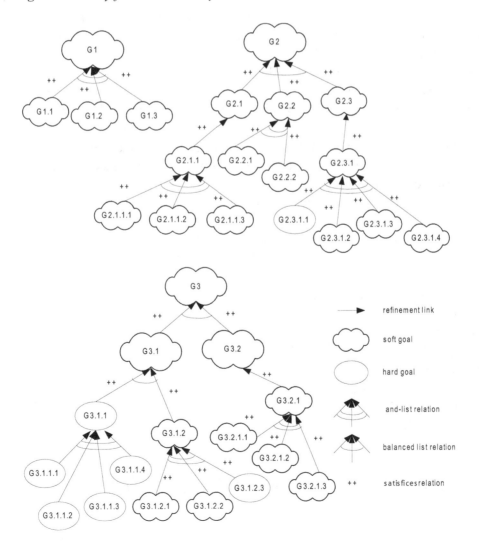

of PIs can be built. The PI structure for the case study discussed here is given in (Sharpanskykh, 2008) as well as more details on PIs and their relationships.

Based on PIs, PI expressions can be defined as mathematical statements over PIs that can be evaluated to a numerical, qualitative or Boolean value, e.g. PI5=high, PI5≥medium, PI27<8h but also PI5, PI27. PI expressions are used to define goal patterns. The *type* of a goal pattern indicates the way its property is checked: *achieved (ceased)* – true (false) for a specific time point; *maintained (avoided)* – true (false) for a given time interval; *optimized* – if the value of the PI expression has increased, decreased or approached a target value for a given interval. Some of the possible goal patterns that can be defined on the PIs and PI expressions given above are: "maintained PI5=high", "avoided PI27<8h", "increased PI5", etc.

Goals are objectives that describe a desired state or development and are defined by adding to goal patterns information on desirability and priority. The characteristics of goals include:

name;

definition;

priority;

evaluation_type – achievement goal (based on 'achieved' or 'ceased' goal pattern; should be evaluated for a time point) or development goal (based on 'maintained', 'avoided' or 'optimized' goal pattern; should be evaluated for a time interval);

horizon – for which time point/interval should the goal be satisfied;

ownership – organizational or individual;

perspective (for organizational goals) – which point of view the goal describes, of management, supplier, customer, or society;

hardness – hard (satisfaction can be established, the goal can be either satisfied or failed) or soft (satisfaction cannot be clearly established, instead degrees of *satisficing* are defined – the goal can be weakly or strongly satisficed or denied);

negotiability – is the goal negotiable when conflicts with other goals should be solved/avoided.

Examples of goals identified for the case study are:

Name: G3.2
Definition: It is required to maintain high efficiency of allocation of security officers
Priority: high
Horizon: long-term
Evaluation_type: development
Ownership: organizational
Perspective: management, customer
Hardness: soft
Negotiability: negotiable

Name: G3.1.1.1
Definition: It is required to achieve that the time to update a short-term plan given operational data is ≤48h
Priority: high

Figure 5. Interaction relations between the roles of the Safety_Organization considered at the first aggregation level

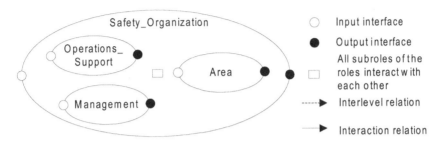

Figure 6. Interaction relations of Area (a) and Operation_Support (b) roles of the Safety_Organization considered at the second aggregation level and the Forward_Planning (c) and Team_Planning (d) roles of the Safety Organization considered at the third aggregation level

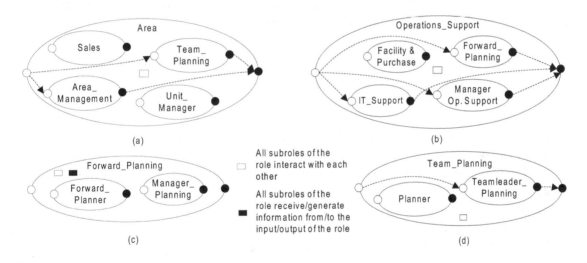

Horizon: short-term
Evaluation_type: achievement
Ownership: organizational
Perspective: management
Hardness: hard
Negotiability: negotiable

Goal can be refined into sub-goals forming hierarchies. Information about the satisfaction of lower-level goals can be propagated to determine the satisfaction of higher-level goals. A goal can be refined into one or more alternative lists of goals of AND-type or balanced-type (a more fine-tuned way of decomposition inspired by the weighted average function) (Sharpanskykh, 2008). For each type, specific propagation rules are defined to determine the satisfaction value (for hard goals) or the level of

Figure 7. The graphical representation of interaction relations between the roles Forward_Planner and Daily_Planner (the template) and their instances (the instantiated model)

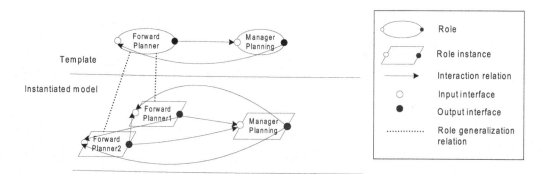

satisficing (for soft goals) of the higher-level goal. Fig. 4 shows the goals hierarchy for the forward and the short-term planning in our case study.

Using the concepts and relations of the performance-oriented view, constraints can be formulated. An example of a generic structural constraint is: "If two PIs are related by aggregation relation, they should have the same type and measurement unit". Formally:

$$\forall pi_1,pi_2{:}\text{PI}, \ \forall tp,\gamma \ \text{state}(\gamma,tp)|=[\text{aggregation\_of}(pi_1,pi_2) \rightarrow pi_1.\text{unit}=pi_2.\text{unit} \wedge pi_1.\text{type}=pi_2.\text{type}]$$

Organization-Oriented View

In the organization-oriented view organizations are modeled as composite roles that can be refined into composite or simple roles, representing as many aggregation levels as needed. The refined role structures correspond to different types of organization constructs (e.g., groups, units, departments). The view provides means to structure and organize roles by defining interaction and power relations on them. First, interaction relations are discussed.

Each role has an input and an output interface, for the interaction with other roles and the environment. Role interfaces are described in terms of interaction (input and output) ontologies: signatures specified in order-sorted logic. Generally speaking, an input ontology determines what information is allowed to be transferred to the input of a role (or the environment), and an output ontology predefines what information can be generated at the output of a role (or the environment). To specify a type of interaction (e.g., communication), the ontologies of both interacting roles (role-source of interaction r_1 and role-destination of interaction r_2) should include the predicate:

communicate_from_to(r_1:ROLE,r_2:ROLE,*s_act*:SPEECH_ACT,*message*:STRING),

where *s_act* is a speech act (e.g., inform, request, ask) and *message* is the content. Roles of the same aggregation level, allowed to interact, are connected by an interaction link indicating the direction of interaction. To represent information transition between roles of two adjacent aggregation levels (e.g., between a role representing a department and a role that belongs to this department), interlevel links are used. In Fig. 5-7 communication relations between the roles of the organization in focus are provided.

These relations correspond to the communication channels that exist (e.g., specified explicitly) in the organization and may be used in different organizational scenarios. In particular, Fig. 5 shows the interaction relations between the roles in the organization at the first aggregation level. Fig. 6 presents the relations within Area role (a) and within Operations_Support role (b) at the second aggregation level and the relations between the subroles of the roles Forward_Planning (c) and Team_Planning (d) at the third aggregation level. By using different levels of abstraction, scalability of graphical representation is achieved.

The representation of the environment may vary in organizational specifications. It can be defined by a set of objects with certain properties and states and by causal relations between objects. In other cases the dynamics of the environment is described by (high-level) processes and trends (e.g. changes of the market situation, natural environmental oscillations).

Interaction relations at the generalized level, represent templates that can be instantiated for a particular case. For example, the documents of the organization from the case study define standard patterns of interaction between the Forward_Planner and Manager_Planning roles that can be modeled at the generalized (template) level. However, for a more detailed analysis of the organizational dynamics, a more specific representation defining interaction relations between particular role instances of Forward_Planner role (e.g., from different planning teams) is needed (see Fig. 7).

The treatment of agent interaction in our framework differs from the agent interaction design approach described in Chapter V "Hermes: A Pragmatic Approach to Flexible and Robust Agent Interaction Design and Implementation" by Cheong and Winikoff. In this approach interaction goals are defined for agents that can be achieved by performing interaction acts. In our framework goals are related to interaction relations through processes that require this interaction.

Power relations on roles also constitute a part of the formal organizational structure. Roles may have different rights and responsibilities w.r.t. different aspects of task execution, such as execution, passive monitoring, consulting, making technological decisions (i.e., decisions on technical questions related to task content) and making managerial decisions (i.e., decisions on general issues related to the task). To specify responsibilities of roles the following relation is used: is_responsible_for: r:ROLE $\times$ *aspect*:ASPECT $\times$ a:TASK, task a is under responsibility of role r w.r.t. *aspect*. The responsibility relations for some tasks from Table 1 are as follows. For task process_new_data_change_forms the role Daily_Planner is responsible for task execution and the role Area_Manager is responsible for making technological and managerial decisions. For task create_and_inform_correct_and_optimized_shortterm_plan the role Forward_Planner is responsible for all aspects and role Teamleader_Planning is jointly responsible for execution. For task create_and_inform_daily_plan Teamleader_Planning is responsible for all aspects and Daily_Planner is jointly responsible for task execution.

The role granting responsibility for certain aspects of a task to another role should be (1) responsible for making managerial decisions w.r.t. this task; (2) superior of the role w.r.t. the task. Superior-subordinate relations w.r.t. organizational tasks are specified by: is_subordinate_of_for: r_1:ROLE $\times$ r_2:ROLE $\times$ a:TASK. In the case study a number of superior-subordinate relations were identified, including:

is_subordinate_of_for(Forward_Planner,Manager_Planning,create_and_inform_correct_longterm_plan), is_subordinate_of_for(Daily_Planner,Teamleader_Planning,create_and_inform_daily_plan).

Control over resources for roles is specified using the relation has_control_over: r_1:ROLE $\times$ *res*:RESOURCE.

Some of the generic constraints that define the consistency and integrity of any role interaction structure have been identified in this view:

GC_OO1: No role can be a subrole of itself at any aggregation level.
GC_OO2: Each subrole of a composite role *r* should interact with at least one other subrole of *r*.

Formally,

In the organizational structure Γ $\forall r_1$:ROLE, $\forall tp,\gamma$ state(γ,tp)|=[subrole_of_in(r_1,r,Γ) $\rightarrow$ $\exists r_2$:ROLE $\exists e$: INTERACTION_LINK subrole_of_in(r_2,r,Γ) $\wedge$ (connects_to(e,r_2,r_1,Γ) $\vee$ connects_to(e,r_1,r_2,Γ))]

Another set of generic consistency constraints is formulated over authority relations of the organization based on the literature from Social Science, among which:

GC_OO3: Only roles that have the responsibility to make managerial decision w.r.t. some process are allowed to authorize other roles for some aspect of this process

Formally,
$\forall r_1,r_2$:ROLE, $\forall a$:PROCESS, $\forall asp$:ASPECT, $\forall \gamma,tp$
state(γ,tp)|=[authorizes_for(r_1,r_2,asp,a) $\rightarrow$ is_responsible_for(r_1,manage_des,a)]

Some of the generic constraints ensure the consistency between the interaction and authority structures, e.g.:

GC_OO4: Roles related by a superior-subordinate relation should interact.

Formally,
$\forall r_1,r_2$:ROLE $\forall a_1$:PROCESS, $\forall tp,\gamma$ state(γ,tp)|=[is_subordinate_of_for(r_2,r_1,a_1) $\rightarrow$
$\exists e_1,e_2$:INTERACTION_LINK connects_to(e_1,r_2,r_1,Γ) $\wedge$ connects_to(e_2,r_1,r_2,Γ)]

GC_OO5: The role supervising the execution of a process should interact with the role performing the process.

Further, consider an example of a domain-specific constraint, particular instances of which are defined for the case study:

DC_OO1(r1:ROLE,r2:ROLE,information_type): Particular information should be transferred between specific roles.

In the case study a correct and optimized short-term plan should be provided to all concerned parties, among which is Unit_Manager. To represent such communication, an instantiated version of this constraint is used:

DC_OO1(Forward_Planner,Unit_Manager,correct_and_optimized_short_term_plan).

Agent-Oriented View

To create plausible organization models, in addition to formal (prescriptive, documented) aspects, also informal aspects of human behavior should be considered. Models of agents defined in the agent-oriented view are based on psychological and social theories (e.g., work motivation theories described in (Pinder, 1998)).

For each role a set of requirements on agent capabilities (i.e., knowledge and skills) and personal traits is defined. Requirements on knowledge define facts and procedures, confident understanding of which is required from an agent. Skills describe developed abilities of agents to use effectively and readily their knowledge for tasks performance. In the literature four relevant types of skills are distinguished: technical, interpersonal, problem-solving/decision-making and managerial skills. To enable testing (or estimation) of skills and knowledge, every particular skill and knowledge is associated with a PI (e.g., the skill 'typing' is associated with the PI "the number of characters per minute"). Personal traits are divided into five categories formulated in psychology (De Raad & Perugini, 2002): openness to experience, conscientiousness, extroversion, agreeableness, and neuroticism. Agent capabilities and traits can have different levels of importance. Whereas the required for a role capabilities and traits are compulsory for taking the role, desired capabilities and traits considered as an advantage.

Figure 8. Relations between the views of the framework

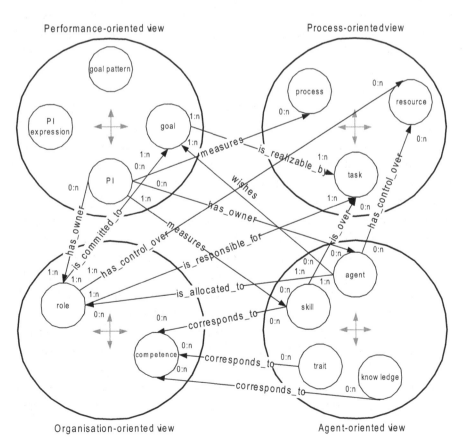

In the case study, the role Daily_Planner requires the agent to have knowledge and technical skills related to daily planning, as well as some interpersonal skills. The company also defined requirements on personal traits related to conscientiousness (self-discipline, responsibility, aim for achievement) and agreeableness (cooperative work style).

In general, the efficiency of allocation of an agent to a role is dependant on how well the agent's characteristics fit with the role requirements. However, modern organizations implement very diverse allocation principles (e.g., based on equality, seniority or stimulation of novices). Such principles can be formalized as allocation policies comprising TTL properties. In the case study the standard allocation policy was used: an agent is allocated to a role if s/he possesses the necessary capabilities and traits defined as the requirements for the role.

To model the dynamics of an agent in organizational context, the agent's intentional and motivational aspects are considered. In modern social science behavior of individuals is considered as goal-driven. It is recognized that high-level goals of individuals are dependant on their needs. Currently the following division of needs is identified in social science: *extrinsic needs* associated with biological comfort and material rewards; *social interaction needs* that refer to the desire for social approval, affiliation and companionship; *intrinsic needs* that concern the desires for self-development, self-actualization, and challenge.

In modern organizations when an individual is allocated to a role, the identification of his/her specific lower-level goals is performed in cooperation with a managerial representative of the organization. During this process, the high-level goals, based on the agent's needs are refined into more specific goals aligned with organizational goals using AND- and OR-relations. Often two types of such goals are distinguished: development (or learning) and performance goals. Development goals reflect wishes of agents to gain certain knowledge or some skills that are also useful for the organization. Performance goals usually concern the effectiveness and efficiency of the execution of the tasks already allocated to the agent. Both development and performance goals are formalized using the language of the performance-oriented view and may change over time.

The motivation of agents to perform certain tasks is important to ensure the satisfaction of both individual and organizational goals related (directly or indirectly) to these tasks. Therefore, the motivational aspect of the agent behavior should be explicitly represented in the models of agents. The highest motivation is demonstrated by an agent w.r.t. actions (e.g., the execution of organizational tasks) that (significantly) contribute to the satisfaction of his/her primary goals. For reasoning about agents' motivation and work behavior, Vroom's version of the expectancy theory (Pinder, 1998) is used which establishes causal dependencies between a number of individual, organizational and environmental parameters and the agent's motivation to perform certain actions (processes). The expectancy theory is one of the few organization theories that can be made operational and used for simulation.

The framework does not adhere to particular agent architecture (e.g., BDI, KARO). In the general case the dynamics of an agent can be specified by dynamic properties expressed in TTL. Furthermore, using TTL existing agent modeling architectures can be represented.

Unlike the other three views which are prescriptive, the agent-oriented view has descriptive character. Therefore no constraints specific to this view can be defined. However it is possible to define constraints involving the agent-oriented view and one or more other views. For example, a constraint between the agent-oriented, the process-oriented and the organization-oriented views can be the following: "Every recruited agent who has not performed a role in the organization in the past should attend a corporate induction event within 3 months of starting".

Relations Between the Views

The views of the framework are connected to each other via relations between their concepts. For example roles are committed to organizational goals and agents can be committed to individual or organizational goals. Goals must be realizable by tasks defined in the process-oriented view, which are represented (instantiated) by processes in the workflow. PIs measure aspects of the execution of processes (duration, output, precision, correctness, etc.) and can be owned by (reflect the performance of) roles and agents. Since roles in the organization-oriented view can be specified at different levels of aggregation, a PI can be owned by a single employee, a group or team or even the whole organization.

Roles are assigned responsibility for aspects of tasks execution such as technical or managerial decisions and execution. Agents described in the agent-oriented view can be assigned to roles for which different competences may be required. These competences can correspond to skills, traits and knowledge of agents. Skills are defined w.r.t. specific tasks and are measured by PIs. Also agents and roles may have control over resources.

The most essential relations and their cardinalities are depicted in Fig. 8 while the relations within the views are omitted.

Another way in which the views can be related is via constraints that can be expressed over concepts and relations from multiple views. Consider the following examples of generic constraints:

Over the process-oriented and organization-oriented views:

GC_MV1: At the beginning of each process for each of the basic aspects for this process (execution, tech_des, and manage_des) a responsible role should be assigned.

Over the performance-, process-oriented and organization-oriented views:

GC_MV2: If a role is committed to a goal, then this role should be responsible for some aspect(s) of a task(s) realizing this goal.

Figure 9. Dependencies between the structures of the four views

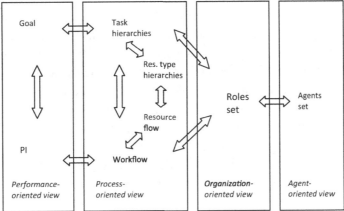

Formally,

$\forall r$:ROLE $\forall g$:GOAL $\forall tl$:TASK_LIST $\forall \gamma, tp$
state$(\gamma, tp)|=$[is_committed_to(r,g) $\wedge$ is_realizable_by(g,tl)
$\rightarrow \exists a$:TASK $\exists asp$:ASPECT is_in_task_list(tl,a) $\wedge$ is_responsible_for(r,asp,a)]

Consider a domain-specific constraint expressed over languages of multiple views:

DC_MV1(r:ROLE,dr:VALUE): The amount of working hours of each agent allocated to role r should not exceed dr

In this case study this constraint is instantiated into DC_MV2(Planner,8).

The relationships between the views also play a role in the process of organizational design with the framework. This is discussed in the next Section which is devoted to the methodology of using the framework.

METHODOLOGICAL ASPECTS

This Section describes how the framework can be used in practice, how the design process can be approached, structured and ordered, what issues need to be addressed, etc., depending on what information is available. First the general guidelines are discussed and then it is shown how they were used for the case study presented in this Chapter.

General Guidelines

The general approaches to organization design differ w.r.t. the presence and involvement of agents. The design can be performed without having in mind specific agents, the necessary agent profiles are composed at the later design stages based on the considered/designed tasks. Organizational design can also be performed w.r.t. a (partially) known set of agents who will take roles in the organization. Thus agents' skills and traits can be taken into account. Sometimes the agents are not only known but they have some degree of power to steer the design process.

The design process often starts with the identification of one or more high-level goals of an organization. These goals (initially still informally defined) should answer the question: why should the organization exist, what purpose will it serve? Such goals can be identified by the designer or emerge through communication and/or negotiation between the involved agents. In the second case the resulting organizational goals reflect to some extent the individual goals of the participating agents. In this way some possible conflicts between individual and organizational goals are prevented early. If conflicts appear, they can be addressed through negotiation and redesign at the later stages.

The higher-level goals are often more abstract. Through refinement, more specific, easier to evaluate, goals are formulated. Also, often the higher-level goals are long-term, strategic goals while their sub-goals are shorter-term tactical or operational goals. The leaves of the hierarchies should be goals formulated so that the corresponding PIs can clearly be associated with the processes in the workflow. In this way the satisfaction of every goal in the hierarchies can be evaluated.

Also at the earlier stage of the design process one or more general tasks are identified answering the question: what should the organization do? For identifying these tasks sometimes only the defined goals are considered. However when the involved agents are (partially) known, the definition of tasks can be based on the available skills and experience as well. These tasks are refined into task hierarchies. The used/produced resource types are identified which can also form hierarchies. Based on the tasks, processes are defined and organized into workflows possibly at different levels of abstraction. The level of elaboration of these structures can depend on the type of the organization. In mechanistic organizations the procedures are prescribed to a great degree of detail resulting in elaborate structures refined to simple tasks and processes. In organic organizations (e.g., adhocracies) the procedures are described at a higher-level of abstraction leaving the agents more freedom to choose how to perform them resulting in shallow task hierarchies and less elaborate workflows.

The design process can follow different paths through the views and concepts but several general guidelines can be formulated. When an informally defined goal is formalized and made more precise this should reflect on the PI structure, often meaning to define a new or revise an existing PI. A change in the goal hierarchy should also reflect on the task hierarchy by identifying new or existing tasks that can realize the new or revised goals. A change in the task hierarchy often brings changes to the current workflow design. Adding/revising processes in the workflow might give rise to new PIs to be monitored. When a PI is proposed it should be decided on its level of importance to understand if a new goal should be formulated based on it. The definition of roles is based on the currently defined tasks and processes. Fig. 9 shows the main dependencies between concepts and structures guiding the design process.

Power and authority relations between the defined roles are usually assigned at the later design stages. However different general schemes can be predefined and committed to at the earlier stages as well leaving the details for later. Such schemes reflect different types of organizations identified in organization theory such as: hierarchical, flat or team-based organizations which differ in the way the power is distributed, granted or accepted by roles (agents).

The choice of scheme should be driven by an analysis of the environment in which the organization should operate. For example a relatively stable environment tolerates a well-defined hierarchical structure which allows more efficiency. A changing environment can be addressed by a lighter, flexible and dynamic structure adaptable to changes. The environment in which the organization will operate should be considered at every design step and every view of the framework.

Sometimes instead of designing an organization from scratch, a specification of an existing one is created. Here a wide range of internal or external documents are used, e.g., company policies, job descriptions, mission statement, procedure descriptions, laws. However even the richest documentation leaves some information unspecified thus it is essential to involve domain experts and managers.

The Specification Process for the Case Study

The specification of the organization in the case study is designed based on existing job descriptions for the employees and documents describing the company mission, goals, structure and procedures. The process started with defining the involved roles, their decomposition and the general outline of the authority and power relations in the organization. For each role, its main tasks are defined in the job descriptions. These were used as basis for the construction of the task hierarchies. The predefined tasks were formalized and refined or aggregated where necessary introducing new tasks in the lower or higher levels of the hierarchies. Using the lowest-level tasks and the documentation on company procedures, the processes in the workflow and their relationships were defined. The company procedures on some aspects of the organization are relatively well documented such as the path of a customer contract, however, other are scarcely documented, e.g. training, evaluation and recruitment. There mostly the employees' job descriptions were used. Together with the tasks and processes, the relevant resource types and resources were identified which mostly describe forward, short-term and daily plans and various data coming from company's information systems, data change forms, various reports and summaries for the management team.

In parallel to the specification of the process-oriented view, the performance-oriented view was also specified. Here, the documents on company's mission and general goals were used as well as the job descriptions where some performance measures and goals for the individual roles are defined. Company's mission statement and goals were defined at a very high abstraction level using notions as customer satisfaction, employees' motivation, efficiency, effectiveness of operations. These were used to define the highest-level goals in the goals hierarchies. While the goals were refined, reformulated and formalized, the related PIs were identified. In contrast, the PIs and goals extracted from the job descriptions were very specific, however incomplete. They were used to define lower-level goals. Where necessary, intermediate goals were inserted to complete the goals structures. Other goals were based on statements from various company documents defining performance measures. First the PIs were defined, then the related goals. When the backbones of the process-oriented and the performance-oriented views became available, the process of relating them started by assigning goals and PIs to processes and tasks.

Finally, the specific authority and power relations were defined and formalized based on the roles and tasks hierarchies. Also the input and output ontologies for the roles were defined. The job descriptions provide well-defined requirements for agents performing the roles which were incorporated in the specification as capabilities required for roles.

Domain-specific constraints were extracted from all available documents at various steps of the process. Most of them were imposed by the organization to regulate its internal procedures and ensure high standard of service and communication with customers. Domain-specific constraints imposed by the physical world were mostly missing in the documentation as they were considered obvious. These were added based on domain knowledge.

ANALYSIS OF ORGANIZATIONAL STRUCTURES AND DYNAMICS

The formal foundations of the proposed framework enable three types of automated analysis (Sharpanskykh, 2008): consistency verification of specifications of every view (i.e., establishing the correctness w.r.t. a set of constraints), validation of correct specifications by simulation, analysis of actual executions of organizational scenarios based on specifications. In the following these analysis types are discussed briefly.

In the performance-oriented view a set of constraints and reasoning rules that ensure the consistency of PI and goal structures has been defined (Sharpanskykh, 2008). In the process-oriented view, structural consistency constraints are defined for the three types of structures: workflow, task and resource hierarchies. Verification of these constraints is supported by automatic tools. Workflow specifications can be analyzed at different abstraction levels. The organization-oriented view identifies sets of generic consistency constraints on interaction structures of roles and on formal authority relations. To check such constraints, both the interaction and authority structures are translated into the graph representation, in which each vertex corresponds to a role and each edge corresponds to an interaction/authority relation. Then, using algorithms from the graph theory the satisfaction of constraints can be established. The structures of the organization-oriented view can also be analyzed at different aggregation levels.

Based on correct specifications, simulation can be performed, in which different types of agents, defined using the concepts from the agent-oriented view, are allocated to the organizational roles. By considering different simulation scenarios of organizational behavior, the validation of organizational specifications can be performed using the dedicated tool.

To specify simulation models the temporal language LEADSTO (a sublanguage of the TTL) is used (Sharpanskykh, 2008) which enables modeling direct temporal dependencies between state properties. A specification of dynamic properties in LEADSTO format is executable and can often easily be depicted graphically. The simulation tool generates the simulation results in the form of a trace. Traces can be used for the validation of specifications by checking dynamic TTL properties in the environment TTL Checker (Sharpanskykh, 2008). Given a trace and a formalized property as input, the software will generate a result (positive or negative).

Correct organizational specifications can be used to guide and control the actual execution of processes. The execution data recorded by an EIS and structured in the form of a trace can be checked for conformity to a formal organization (the specification and the set of constraints). For this, the specification of the formal organization is translated into properties expressed in the execution language used for the formalization of the trace. These properties are checked on the trace using the TTL Checker software. Moreover, the designer may specify additional properties to be checked.

The traces may also be used to evaluate the PIs associated with the executed processes. These PIs are related to the leaves of the goals hierarchy, thus the satisfaction of these goals can be evaluated. The satisfaction values are propagated upwards to establish the satisfaction of higher-level goals determining the overall organizational performance.

CONCLUSION

This chapter describes a formal framework for modeling and analysis of organizations. The framework includes a rich ontological basis that comprises concepts and relations partitioned into four dedicated views: process-oriented, performance-oriented, organization-oriented and agent-oriented view. The framework can be used for representing different types of organizations ranging from mechanistic to organic.

The framework allows defining different types of constraints using the dedicated formal languages of the views. Moreover, it incorporates agent-based models of individuals based on social theories. In contrast to many existing architectures, the proposed framework allows performing different types of automated analysis of particular views and across views. Organizational specifications can be represented and analyzed at different levels of abstraction, which allows handling high complexity and increases scalability of modeling.

The framework allows reuse in several ways that accelerates and facilitates the modeling process. Libraries of commonly appearing parts of structures (goals and tasks hierarchies, PI-structures, work-flow graphs, etc.) can be reused for organizations in similar domains. The used tool allows defining parameterized templates (macros) for TTL formulae that can be instantiated in different ways which can also be used as support for designers not skilled in logics.

The views of the proposed framework are formalized based on intuitive, close to the natural, predicate languages, with concepts and relations that can be represented graphically. Currently, the graphical interface is provided for the performance-oriented view, other views are specified textually using dedicated tools. In the future, modeling related to other views will also be supported graphically which should increase the user-friendliness of the framework.

In the Chapter, the application of the proposed framework has been illustrated by a case study over an organization from the security domain. The proposed framework was also applied in the context of a case study from the area of logistics (http://www.almende.com/deal/). Currently, the framework is used for modeling and analysis of an air-traffic control organization.

FUTURE RESEARCH

Future work is planned to further facilitate the use of the framework in various organizational settings. One direction is to investigate how organizational change can be facilitated and modeled. Organizational change exerts great pressure and risk to an organization and its employees. Often the expected results are not reached, the budget and/or time constraints are exceeded, etc. Techniques to make the process more comprehensive and provide means for the analysis of the new, designed organization before the main investment is made can decrease the risk and provide better chance for success.

Furthermore, templates can be defined for different types of organizations that can be reused and become basis for new specifications. Specific aspects such as hierarchical, flat or team-based structure can be predefined to a certain extent giving the designer the opportunity to customize the template. Case studies to support the usability of the templates should be performed.

The presented framework is designed for modeling a single organization. Its environment can be modeled on a high level as environmental objects and characteristics that can change with time. Modern organizations often enter in cooperation with other organization such as customer or supplier organizations (supply chains) and certain degree of alignment is sometimes necessary. Techniques for modeling and analysis in such setting can be beneficial.

REFERENCES

Burton, R.M., & Obel, B. (2004). *Strategic Organizational Diagnosis and Design: Developing Theory for Application*. Dordrecht: Kluwer Academic Publishers.

Barkaoui, K., & Petrucci L. (1998). Structural analysis of workflow nets with shared resources. In W.M.P. van der Aalst, G. De Michelis, C.A. Ellis (Eds.), *Workflow Management: Net-based Concepts, Models, Techniques and Tools* (pp. 82–95). Lisbon: UNINOVA.

Bernus, P., Nemes, L., & Schmidt, G. (Eds.). (1998). *Handbook on Architectures of Information Systems* Heidelberg: Springer.

Bresciani, P., Giorgini, P., Giunchiglia, F., Mylopoulos, J., Perini, A. (2004). Tropos An Agent-Oriented Software Development Methodology. *Journal of Autonomous Agent and Multi-Agent Systems*, *8*(3), 203-236.

Chapurlat, V., Kamsu-Foguem, B., & Prunet, F. (2006). A formal verification framework and associated tools for enterprise modeling: Application to UEML. *Computers in industry, 57*, 153-166.

Dalal, N., Kamath, M., Kolarik, W., & Sivaraman, E. (2004). Toward an integrated framework for modeling enterprise processes. *Communications of the ACM, 47*(3), 83-87.

Dignum, V. (2003). *A model for organizational interaction: based on agents, founded in logic.* Ph.D. Dissertation, Utrecht University.

Ferber, J., & Gutknecht, O. (1998). A meta-model for the analysis and design of organizations in multi-agent systems. In Y. Demazeau (Ed.), *Proceedings of Third International Conference on Multi-Agent Systems* (pp. 128-135). IEEE Computer Society.

Fox, M., Barbuceanu, M., Gruninger, M., & Lin, J. (1997). An Organization Ontology for Enterprise Modelling. In M. Prietula, K. Carley, L. Gasser (Eds.), *Simulating Organizations: Computational Models of Institutions and Groups* (pp. 131-152). Menlo Park CA: AAAI/MIT Press.

Hannoun, M., Boissier, O., Sichman J.S., Sayettat, C. (2000). MOISE: An Organizational Model for Multi-agent Systems. In M.C. Monard, J.S. Sichman (Eds.), *Proceedings of the 7th Ibero-American Conference on AI: Advances in Artificial Intelligence, LNCS 1952* (pp. 156 – 165), Berlin: Springer.

Horling, B, & Lesser, V. (2005). A Survey of multi-agent organizational paradigms. *The Knowledge Engineering Review, 19*(4), 281-316.

Hubner, J.F., Sichman, J.S., & Boissier, O. (2002). MOISE+: Towards a structural, functional and deontic model for MAS organization. In C. Castelfranchi, L. Johnson (Eds), *Proceedings of the 1st International Joint Conference on Autonomous Agents and Multi-Agent Systems* (pp. 501-502), ACM.

Koubarakis, M., & Plexousakis, D. (2002). A formal framework for business process modeling and design. *Information Systems, 27*(5), 299–319.

Mintzberg, H. (1979). *The Structuring of Organizations.* Prentice Hall, Englewood Cliffs.

Pinder, C.C. (1998). *Work motivation in organizational behavior.* Upper Saddle River, NJ: Prentice-Hall.

De Raad, B., & Perugini, M. (2002). *Big Five Assessment.* Hogrefe & Huber.

Sharpanskykh, A. (2008). *On Computer-Aided Methods for Modeling and Analysis of Organizations.* Ph.D. Dissertation, VU University Amsterdam.

Tham, K.D. (1999). *Representation and Reasoning About Costs Using Enterprise Models and ABC*, PhD Dissertation, Enterprise Integration Laboratory, Department of Mechanical and Industrial Engineering, University of Toronto.

Van der Aalst, W., ter Hofstede, A., Kiepuszewski, B., & Barros, A.P. (2003). Workflow patterns. *Distributed and Parallel Databases, 14*(3), 5–51.

Zambonelli, F., Jennings, N.R., & Wooldridge, M. (2003). Developing multiagent systems: the Gaia Methodology. *ACM Transactions on Software Engineering and Methodology, 12*(3), 317-370.

ADDITIONAL READING

Allen, J.F. (1983). Maintaining knowledge about temporal intervals. *Communications of the ACM*, 26, 832–843.

Bacharach, S.B., & Lawler, E.J. (1980). *Power and politics in organizations*. Jossey-Bass, San Francisco.

Biddle, B. (1979). *Role Theory: Concepts and Research*. Krieger Publishing Co.

Blau, P.M., & Schoenherr, R.A. (1971). *The structure of organizations*. New York London: Basic Books Inc.

Bosse, T., Jonker, C.M., van der Meij, L., Sharpanskykh, A., & Treur, J. (2006). Specification and Verification of Dynamics in Cognitive Agent Models. In C. Butz, N.T. Nguyen, Y. Takama (Eds), *Proceedings of the 6th International Conference on Intelligent Agent Technology,* (pp. 247-254), IEEE Computer Society Press.

Carley, K.M. (1991). A Theory of Group Stability. *American sociological Review*, *56*, 331-354.

CIMOSA – Open System Architecture for CIM; ESPRIT Consortium AMICE (1993). Berlin: Springer-Verlag.

Donaldson, L. (2001). *The Contingency Theory of Organizations*. Sage, London.

Esteva, M., Rodriguez-Aguilar, J.A., Sierra, C., Garcia, P., Arcos, J.L. (2001). On the Formal Specification of Electronic Institutions. In F. Dignum, C. Sierra (Eds.), *Agent-mediated Electronic Commerce: the European AgentLink Perspective* LNAI 1991 (pp. 126-147), Springer.

Ferber, J., Michel, F., Baez-Barranco, J.-A. (2004). AGRE: Integrating Environments with Organizations. In *Proceedings of E4MAS, LNCS, vol. 3374/2005* (pp. 48-56), Springer.

Forrester, J.W. (1961). *Industrial dynamics*, Waltham, MA: Pegasus Communications.

Galbraith, J.R. (1978). *Organization design*. London Amsterdam Sydney: Addison-Wesley Publishing Company.

Giddens, A. (2006). *Sociology*, 5th edition. Polity, Cambridge.

Horenberg, J. (1994). *Organizational Behavior*. Hillsdale, NJ: Lawrence Erlbaum Associates.

Krauth, E., Moonen, H., Popova, V., & Schut, M. (2005). Performance Measurement and Control in Logistics Service Providing. In C.-S. Chen (Ed.), *Proceedings of ICEIS 2005* (pp. 239-247), INSTICC Press.

Lorsch, J.W., & Lawrence, P.R. (1970). *Organization design*. USA: Richard D. Irwin Inc.

Marlow, W.H. (1993). *Mathematics for Operations Research*. New York: Dover.

Maslow, A.H. (1970). *Motivation and Personality*, 2nd. ed. New York: Harper & Row.

Morgan, G. (1996). *Images of organizations*. SAGE Publications, Thousand Oaks London New Delhi.

Omicini, A. (2000). SODA: Societies and infrastructures in the analysis and design of agent-based systems. In M.J. Wooldridge, P. Ciancarini (Eds.), *Proceedings of Agent-Oriented Software Engineering Workshop* (pp. 185–193), Springer.

Pfeffer, J. (1982). *Organizations and organization theory.* Pitman Books Limited, Boston London Melbourne Toronto.

Rao, A.S. (1995). Decision procedures for propositional linear-time belief-desire-intention logics. In *Proceedings IJCAI-95 Workshop on Agent Theories, Architectures, and Languages*, 102-118.

Romme, A.G.L. (2003). Making a difference: Organization as design. *Organization Science, 14*, 558-573.

Sadler, P.J., Webb, T., & Lansley, P. (1974). *Management style and organisation structure in the smaller enterprise : a report on a research project conducted with the financial support of the Social science research council.* Ashridge: Ashridge Management Research Unit.

Scheer, A-W., & Nuettgens, M. (2000). ARIS Architecture and Reference Models for Business Process Management. In W.M.P. van der Aalst, J. Desel, A. Oberweis (Eds.), *Inter-operability of Workflow Applications: Local Criteria for Global Soundness, LNCS 1806* (pp. 366-389). Berlin: Springer.

Scott, W.G., Mitchell, T.R., & Birnbarum, P.H. (1981). *Organization theory: a structural and behavioural analysis*, USA, Illinois: Richard D. Irwin inc.

Scott, W.R. (2001). *Institutions and organizations.* SAGE Publications, Thousand Oaks.

Van der Aalst, W.M.P., & van Hee, K. (2002). *Workflow Management: Models, Methods, and Systems.* MIT Press.

Walter, B. (1968). *Modern systems research for the behavioral scientist*, Chicago: Aldine Publishing Co.

Warner, M., & Witzel, M. (2004). *Managing in Virtual Organizations.* Thomson Learning.

Yilmaz, L. (2006). Validation and Verification of Social Processes within Agent-Based Computational Organization Models. *Computational & Mathematical Organization Theory, 12*:4, 283-312.

Yu, E. (1997). Towards Modelling and Reasoning Support for Early-Phase Requirements Engineering. In Proceedings of the 3rd IEEE International Symposium on Requirements Engineering (pp. 226-235). IEEE Computer Society.

Yukl, G. (2006). *Leadership in organizations.* 6edn. Englewood Cliffs, NJ: Prentice-Hall.

KEY TERMS

Constraints: An expression over objects and/or processes that limits the organizational behavior.

Formal Organizational Analysis: Organizational analysis using formal methods.

Formal Organizational Modeling: Organizational modeling using formal methods.

Process-Oriented Modeling: Modeling of organizational flows of control, resources.

Chapter VII
Describing Agent Societies:
A Declarative Semantics

Maksim Tsvetovat
George Mason University, USA

ABSTRACT

Agent-based approaches provide an invaluable tool for building decentralized, distributed architectures and tying together sets of disparate software tools and architectures. However, while the agents themselves have been gaining complexity, and agent specification languages have been gaining expressive power, little thought has been given to the complexity of agent societies, and languages for describing such societies. In this chapter, I propose a declarative language designed specifically for describing in an expressive way a variety of social interactions. I attempt to avoid the fallacies of artificial restriction, and similarly confounding under-specification of the design domain, yet constructing a rigorous, machine-interpretable semantics. It is my hope that introduction of such semantic will lead to a constructive dialogue between communities of agent-based social modeling and agent-based software design, and lead to a greater integration of agent development toolkits and agent-based modeling toolkits.

MOTIVATION

Agent-based approaches provide an invaluable tool for building decentralized, distributed architectures and tying together sets of disparate software tools and architectures. However, while the agents themselves have been gaining complexity, and agent specification languages have been gaining expressive power, little thought has been given to the complexity of agent societies, and languages for describing such societies.

There are two fundamental approaches in design of multi-agent systems. In one approach, collaborative agents of heterogeneous functionalities coexist in a world where cooperation is expected, communication protocols are well-defined and interactions are largely scripted by the developers. In the second approach, large numbers of agents perform similar functions (e.g. price negotiations), abide by a small number of standard negotiation protocols (e.g. auctions) and interactions are strategic.

Both of these approaches are characteristic for engineered agent-based systems. By engineered systems I mean systems that are designed, as a whole, to perform a particular task or set of tasks, or to provide an infrastructure for human users of the system to perform their tasks. In engineered systems, efficiency and performance of the tasks are paramount, thus leading to simpler, well-defined interaction patterns. These patterns are generally a result of a distinct design effort, and represent an idealized view of how such interactions might happen. Within this scope of requirements, standard interaction protocols (e.g. FIPA(FIPA, 1997)), and agent communication languages of artificially limited expressive value (e.g. KQML(Finin, et al. 1994)) are appropriate and optimal for design and specification of the agent-based system.

Meanwhile, the social simulation and social network analysis communities have been facing a very different problem. In social simulation, the goal of the designers is to create a facsimile of a real-world social system (e.g. a terrorist network) as a means to study social phenomena in an in-silico experimental laboratory. In this pursuit, the most important notion is that of face validity, i.e. recognizability of interaction patterns and social structures within the context of the experimental subject. Thus, the notions of efficiency of agent interactions and their ability to complete tasks take a back seat to the notions of realistic representation.

Within the community of social modelers, different approaches to modeling interaction complexity exist. Some succumb to simplifying assumptions of grid-based "worlds", or interaction fields, borrowed from Artificial Life. Others model agent interaction as series of method calls within an object-oriented memory space. Finally, a small group of modelers has adopted the standards of engineered agent systems, and is engaging in design of complex artificial societies around tools that were designed for significantly less complexity of interactions.

Needless to say, all three approaches present their limitations. Grid-world interactions are spatially explicit and thus appropriate for models that take into account geographical features – but at the same time limit numbers and types of interactions possible within a neighborhood. Object-method calls are less limiting in terms of interaction types, but require separately developed design documentation (e.g. UML diagrams) to understand the social system without delving into the source code. KQML and FIPA-based tools present modelers with an opportunity to abstract away the physical interactions of agents and concentrate on modeling the underlying social system - and yet are too limited to allow for construction of highly complex relationships such as friendship, kinship, subordination and discipleship.

In this paper, I propose a declarative language designed specifically for describing in an expressive way a variety of social interactions. I attempt to avoid the fallacies of artificial restriction, and similarly confounding under-specification of the design domain, yet constructing a rigorous, machine-interpretable semantics.

It is my hope that introduction of such semantic will lead to a constructive dialogue between communities of agent-based social modeling and agent-based software design, and lead to a greater integration of agent development toolkits and agent-based modeling toolkits.

SOCIAL NETWORKS AND SOCIAL AGENTS

In this work, I draw heavily on the notions of social networks, and social network analysis. Social network analysis (SNA) can be described as an application graph-theoretical information representation and combinatorial algorithms to study of a gestalt of human systems.

The reason for creation of this bridge is simple - SNA was specifically designed for describing large, heterogeneous societies of human actors, and its concepts and findings should be just as applicable to design of agent societies.

Traditional social network analysis operates on a simple set of concepts: nodes of a social network are a homogenous set of people or groups of people and links between nodes represent connections or relationships between these people. Semantically, the existence of an edge signifies that a relationship of some sort exists between two constituent nodes:

$$G = \begin{cases} \{A, B, C, D\} \subseteq People \\ w_{1..n} = ConsistentWeightMetric \end{cases}$$

Thus, computing simple graph-theoretic measures upon the resultant graph produces interpretable results that allow detection of powerful or important nodes, communication gatekeepers, etc.

Krackhardt and Carley (Krackhardt and Carley, 1998) proposed an extension of the SNA semantics, concentrating knowledge about an organization or a group of agents in a format that could be analyzed using an expansion of standard network methods called the MetaMatrix. The MetaMatrix expanded the notion of a node in a network to include a large number of possible entities. In its original shape, the MetaMatrix encompassed nodes of types *Person, Knowledge,* and *Task* and introduced the concept of semantically loaded edges (i.e. *Task X* **requires** *Resource Y*).

Agent societies, as well as most human networks, however, cannot fit into a simplified mold of a valued graph. MetaMatrix semantics, while useful in simulating simple organizations(Tsvetovat, Reeves, 2007), is not sufficiently expressive with regard to the exact nature of interactions between agents. What we require for this task is a flexible, semantic way of describing both actors and social structures they are embedded in. These social structures may include cooperative relationships, competitive relations, delegation of tasks, supply of information and resources, and almost an infinite variety of other possible relationships. However, beyond an expressive language for describing such societies, we must be able to instantiate such a society given its description.

Figure 1. Vocabulary of the Relationship taxonomy

friendOf	acquaintanceOf	parentOf	siblingOf
childOf	grandchildOf	spouseOf	enemyOf
antagonistOf	ambivalentOf	lostContactWith	knowsOf
wouldLikeToKnow	knowsInPassing	knowsByReputation	closeFriendOf
hasMet	worksWith	colleagueOf	collaboratesWit
employerOf	employedBy	mentorOf	apprenticeTo
livesWith	neighborOf	grandparentOf	lifePartnerOf
engagedTo	ancestorOf	descendantOf	participantIn

NETWORKS AND LANGUAGES

Given an analogy of English grammar, a semantically loaded edge is a *verb* connecting two *nouns*:

Alice **likes** *Bob* very much.

Bob and *Carol* **study together**.

Carol **fights** with *Alice* in school.

The high-school love triangle described above could be a classic example of the way in which social network representation of relational knowledge fails to address the complexities of human relationships. Our language processing centers add layers of meaning to each noun and verb, and the shared experience of the humanity produces an understanding of what is actually happening – the same understanding inaccessible to machines until and unless the problem of natural language understanding is solved.

As examples of work in this direction, Carley(Carley, 1994) uses network analysis techniques to map the structure of relations between conceptual items used in science fiction narratives and maps these structural representations of meaning to compare cultural phenomena through times. Mohr(Mohr, 1998) elaborates a framework for uncovering semantic structures that emphasizes relations among lexical and semantic terms in a classification system and application of formal network analysis models or pattern matching techniques.

The implications of these lines of research is creation of a link between network analysis and "understanding of the relationship between culture and social structure built upon careful integration of micro and macro, and of cognitive and material perspectives"DiMaggio, 1998.

Our task, however, is considerably simpler. The systems we build, while of increasing complexity, do not need to capture the complexity of human nature or the shared linguistic concepts. They merely need to reflect a finite subset of semantic constructs relevant to building multi-agent systems, and allow for this subset to grow sustainably as new semantic constructs are added.

TAXONOMIES AND SOCIAL NETWORKS

Perhaps, a combination of linguistic constructs (i.e. nouns and verbs) and graph-theoretic analysis would present a sufficient boost to expressiveness of social network data, and allow its usage for instantiation of agent-based models? A number of approaches have been proposed to address this question.

For example, Relationship(Vitello and Davis, 2004) is an RDF(Brickley, et al, 2004) schema that defines a vocabulary for describing social interactions and relationships between people (see Figure 1). However, definition of a vocabulary falls short of rigorously specified social relationship semantics.

While a vocabulary set can be negotiated and agreed to by a community of researchers, it will remain incomplete as the richness of human relationships presents more nuances that is possible to express in a finite vocabulary. This may be acceptable for some artificial systems – which are finite by definition. However, if the vocabulary set lacks the capability of defining new relationships, it will artificially enforce limits on what kind of models can be built with it.

However, a more serious complication of a purely vocabulary-based specification of relationships is that a social network defined using this vocabulary is merely a labeled graph. While such graphs are

Box 1.

```
network := (relationship)*
 relationship := (relationshipVerb, fromNode, toNode)
 relationshipVerb isA ontologyVerb
 ontologyVerb := (verb, (attributeName, attributeValue)*)
 fromNode, toNode isA ontologyNoun
 ontologyNoun := (noun, (attributeName, attributeValue)*)
```

widely used to communicate relationship information to human users, it is not possible for computers to reason about such labelled graphs without an understanding of natural language. Thus, a further extension of language-based paradigm for expression of social structure data needs to be developed.

A Grammar for Expressing Relationships Between Entities

Use of a regular grammar provides us with a mechanism for expressing complex language-based concepts in a machine-understandable way. At first glance, such a regular grammar might be defined as show in Box 1.

Thus, a network is defined as a collection of relationships which consist of two nodes (represented by nouns) and a verb. The concept of isA specifies that an entity is an instance of another entity or class of entities already present in the ontology - thus allowing inheritance of properties from entity to entity.

Shapiro(Shapiro, 1982) has published a grammar-based means for interpretation of semantic networks. The methodology uses Augmented Transition Networks (ATNs) (Woods, 1970) to interpret a tree or a graph of the semantic network and transform it into natural language sentences.

The advantages of the grammar notation have been summarized as "(1) clearness and perspicuity, (2) generative powers, (3) efficiency of representation, (4) ability to capture representation regularities and generalizations, and (5) efficiency of operation"(Shapiro, 1982). ATN Grammars have been used as both parsing and generative tools for machine understanding in relational contexts(Woods, 1980).

$$Object \quad := \quad \begin{cases} ObjectID: \\ ParentID: \\ Attributes := ListOf\{attributeID, value\} \\ Methods := ListOf\{methodID, value\} \\ Rules := ListOf\{rule\} \end{cases} \tag{1}$$

Executable Verbs

As mentioned above, verbs inside interaction specifications not only describe the nature of the relationship between agents, but specify the kind of activity that the agents can engage in. In short, a verb is merely a proxy for an interaction protocol. In human systems these interaction protocols are implicit and are a part of one's upbringing (i.e. "This is how a well-behaved boy should talk to his elders"), or are explicitly provided through rules of interaction (e.g. rules of interaction on a stock trading floor). Agent societies tend towards the latter, with interaction rules frequently hard-coded into the agent itself.

Economou and Tsvetovat(Economou, et al, 2001) proposed that interaction protocols should be specified explicitly via a meta-protocol semantic structure shared by agents. In this structure, we expressed interaction protocols as a set of automata that allowed users to declaratively specify roles agents can take within a complex iterative interaction (e.g. an e-commerce negotiation). Instantiation of these declarative protocols was handled through a special interpreter built into the RETSINA agent platform - or through a compiler that generated Java code for compilation into other agent platforms.

Use of meta-semantics enabled us to engage in reasoning about interaction protocols as a part of agent design. For example, agent X could propose that another agent Y enters a commercial relationship with it. It would then supply Y with a declarative specification of its preferred interaction protocol. Agent Y could then analyze the protocol in terms of its requirements and commitments that he might have to enter. This analysis was done using graph-theoretic metrics on the protocol interaction graph.

In this paper, I build upon the idea of declarative interaction specification, and extend it to description of an entire agent society. This is done using a domain-specific language, called AgentScheme.

DESIGN OF AGENT NETWORK LANGUAGE

Agent Network Semantic Language—AgentScheme — is designed as an object-oriented extension of Scheme(Abelson, et al, 1985). The principles of object-orientation are derived from these specified by Atkinson(Atkinson, et al, 1989) and Cardelli(Cardelli, 1988).

An object is defined as follows:

*where **ObjectID** is a globally unique identifier, **ParentID** is an identifier of an object that the current object inherits attributes and rules from, Attributes is a list of attribute-value pairs, Methods is a list of method-procedure pairs, and Rules is a set of rules to be executed during object-resolution procedure.*

Objects are defined by using the *defobject* macro:

```
(defobject <object-id>//optional; defaults to a random unique id
  #:as #$ParentObject
  #:with-attr '((<name> <value>) (<name> <value>))
  #:with-methods '((<name> <procedure>) (<name> <value>))
```

All objects include a number of standard methods, including setting and retrieving values of properties, defining and executing object methods. More information on the design of AgentScheme object system can be found in (Tsvetovat, Carley, 2006).

Graph Representation

The object system of AgentScheme provides a foundation upon which a robust graph representation scheme is designed. A graph is traditionally defined as a set of nodes or vertices V connected by a set of edges E. AgentScheme adapts this definition to fit the constraints of the object system by creating two abstract objects - Node and Edge. Nodes and edges of each graph represented in AgentScheme are defined as child objects of these abstract objects.

Node and Edge objects are defined as:

$$Edge = \begin{cases} edgeID : uniqueID \\ from : N1 \Rightarrow Node \\ to : N2 \Rightarrow Node \\ protocol : State\ Machine\ specification \\ properties,\ methods\ and\ rules : inherited\ from\ Object \end{cases}$$

$$Node = \begin{cases} nodeID : uniqueID \\ edges : setOf(E \Rightarrow Edge) \\ properties,\ methods\ and\ rules : inherited\ from\ Object \end{cases}$$

Note that the definition of Node contains a list of edges emanating from it and the definition of Edge contains two objects of type Node. Such circular definition is permissible in AgentScheme due to delayed instantiation of properties (i.e., abstract object Edge will not be referenced until a concrete edge emanating from a concrete Node needs to be instantiated). However, it affords a remarkable convenience: in a graph traversal or calculation of graph-based metrics all required information for each node and edge is contained directly within the object and is accessible in constant time. Specification of protocols as I/O automata and reasoning about protocol state machines have been described in detail in (Economou, et al, 2001).

Of course, such savings of time come with a memory penalty, as each of the object references requires storage. The implementation of object references is quite memory-efficient and the penalty thus is fairly small. Moreover, such representation of graph elements does not require an external data structure other then what is provided by the object system - which counteracts or at least partially counteracts the memory penalty of maintaining circular data structures.

AgentScheme provides convenience macros *def*node and *def*edge to ease creation and derivation of graph nodes.

```
(defnode <nodeID> #:as <parent _ node>
 #:with-attr '(<list of attribute-value pairs>)
 #:with-edges '(
  (<edge-name> <edge-object>)
  ...list of edges...
 )
)

(defedge <edgeID> #:as <parent-edge>
 #:with-attr '(<list of attribute-value pairs>)
 #:from <source-node>
 #:to <target-node>
)
```

Subgraphs

At this point, the object system and graph representation of AgentScheme resembles a primordial soup. It is a giant collection of various objects, such as nodes and edges, loosely tied together by means of references between objects — but with no overarching structure. The only mechanisms for manipulating objects provided in the object system are these of robust retrieval of an object by its handle, and of object inheritance.

Such chaotic representation of knowledge is not extremely useful, as users need mechanisms to effectively prune datasets and control the focus of search or reasoning algorithms. However, installing a permanent overarching structure is too restrictive since it forces the objects into a configuration that may or may not be efficient for the problem at hand.

However, properties of AgentScheme objects can contain any data type supported by the language, including other objects. The implication of this is that one can trivially define compound objects that contain nodes and edges of a graph.

This yields to a ready definition of such important and useful notions such as subgraphs and regions of interest. These notions serve as a lens through which views of large datasets can be focused. Moreover, as objects can be members of multiple subgraphs, this allows for an unlimited number of views to be defined based on structure of the model and conditions presented by the data.

A subgraph is defined as

$$G_{sub} = v_{sub} \subseteq V, e_{sub} \subseteq E$$

where v_{sub} and e_{sub} are subsets of the vertex and edge sets, respectively. In AgentScheme, a subgraph is defined as a compound object whose properties contain all objects in G_{sub}.

If one wishes to manipulate multiple graphs at the same time within AgentScheme, he should define them using this method - as the format of a subgraph is the same as the format of the object-store and elements of a subgraph can be manipulated in the exact same manner as elements of the object-store. Moreover, the object-store itself can be thought of as a subgraph that encompasses every object defined in the system.

Box 2.

```
(defrule <rule name>
  (if [conditional expression or query]
      (then [a sequence of statements to be executed if condition is true])
      (else [a sequence of statements to be executed otherwise])
  )
)
-------
;; rules are specified at the time of object creation
(defobject obj1
 .....
 #:with-rules '((defrule rule_1 <rule specification>)
               (defrule rule_2 <rule specification>)))

;;rules are inherited from obj1
 (defobject obj2 #:as obj1
    .....
 )

;;rules are added to the object at runtime
 (addRule obj2 (defrule rule_3 <rule specification>))
```

Figure 2. Inference of inherited properties and transitive closure

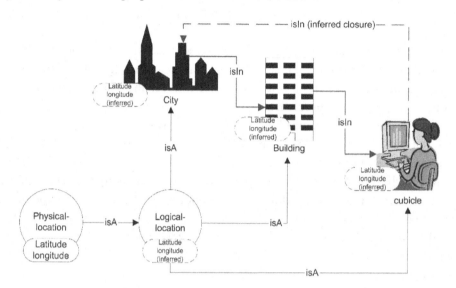

Box 3.

```
(defnode "location"
 #:with-attr '(("name" "") ("latitude" 0) ("longitude" 0))
 #:with-rules '(
  (defrule lat_range
   (if (and (< this.latitude -90) (> this.latitude 90)) (then (error))))
  (defrule lon_range
   (if (and (< this.longitude -180) (> this.longitude 180)) (then (error)))))
 )
```

INFERENCE IN SOCIAL NETWORKS

AgentScheme implements two types of inference on social network data. Object structure and system of property inheritance facilitate hierarchical inference, where properties of objects within the social network can be determined by inspecting their semantic predecessors within the object structure.

The second inference mechanism is that of graph-oriented rule resolution. In this mechanism, every object has a set of routines (rules) for checking its own self-consistency - i.e. the consistency of the internal state of the object with its external connections. The rules also provide for computing closures upon objects in the network (e.g. the transitive closure) and inferring existence of nodes and edges based on generalizable domain rules.

Rule Definition

A AgentScheme rule is specified using defrule macro. Rules can be placed into an object at the time of object creation through inheritance or at arbitrary times as specified by the user (Box 2).

Example

As a simple example, let me define a set of rules on domain of locations and places. The rules specify information about possible ranges of parameters, and a transitive closure of nested locations.

First, let us define the notion of location as a node with two attributes — latitude and longitude — and some constraints on the values of the attributes (Box 3):

-90≤latitude≤90
-180≤longitude≤180

This definition provides us an ability to define a multitude of physical locations which can be placed on a map. However, of more interest is the notion of a logical location. We can define a logical location with arbitrary granularity - it can be a table in a cafe, a street corner, a city, or the entire planet:

```
(defnode "logical-location" #:as #$location)
 (defedge "isIn" (from #$logical-location) (to #$logical-location)
   #:with-rules `(
     (defrule coords (and (setField from.latitude to.latitude)
                     (setField from.longitude to.longitude)))))$
```

The definition of *isIn* edge type allows for inference of a physical location (i.e. latitude and longitude) from a nesting series of logical locations. (see Figure 2)

However, nested location hierarchy exhibits one more property - transitivity. For example, if a table *isIn* a cafe *isIn* Pittsburgh it can be inferred that the table also *isIn* Pittsburgh, i.e., there is not only an edge from a node table to node cafe to node Pittsburgh but also an edge from node table to node Pittsburgh. Computing transitive closure can be done by defining *isIn* as a transitive edge:

```
(defedge "transitive-edge"
   #:with-rules `(
     (defrule transitive-closure
       (if (exists (this.to) (isParent? this.to.edge transitive-edge))
           (then (defedge #:as transitive-edge
                   (from this.from) (to this.to.edge)))))
)
```

The edge transitivity rule examines the edges connected to the target of the edge and if one of these edges is transitive (i.e. is a child object of a transitive edge) the transitive closure is computed by adding another edge. An edge can then be declared to be transitive by inheriting the rule from the transitive-edge object.

Figure 3.

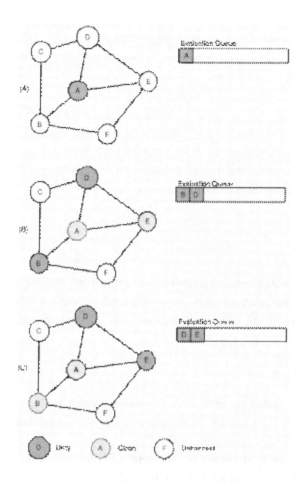

While a set of rules declaring transitive closure relations between locations is fairly simple, it illustrates the mechanism by which AgentScheme can infer values of attributes of nodes and edges, and create new entities based on sets of rules.

Rule Resolution Mechanism

The rule resolution mechanism in AgentScheme is decentralized and based on the idea of lazy evaluation – the notion that at every moment of time only objects that change need to be watched and re-evaluated by the rule resolver.

```
DO
  DEQUEUE object O from the evaluation queue
  RUN resolution rules of O and its parent objects
  IF an object other then O is altered, created or deleted by the rules
    THEN set the altered object's dirty bit to TRUE;
         add object to the evaluation queue
```

```
END IF
SET O's dirty bit to FALSE
UNTIL evaluation queue is empty
```

Every AgentScheme object is tagged with a dirty bit – a flag that signals whether an object's attributes have been changed recently or whether edges that connect the object to other objects have been added or dropped. If a change has been made, the object's dirty bit is set to true and the object is added to a queue of unresolved objects.

Note that a node that has been already resolved by the algorithm may be changed again by another node's rules and thus will be re-added to the evaluation queue. This produces the distinct possibility that this algorithm may not converge for all graphs but instead may produce an oscillating behaviour.

Oscillations are undesirable if the goal is to produce a stable state where every object has been resolved and marked as clean. However, if the intention is to model dynamic systems, oscillation is a valid behaviour and must be studied as such - instead of being considered a property of the evaluation algorithm.

The algorithm then should be modified to achieve a double goal: within each iteration of the algorithm, convergence should be achieved. In the same time, oscillations should be possible in space of multiple iterations. This dual goal can be achieved by maintaining a taboo-list of nodes that have been visited. If a node on the taboo list is referenced by another node, it does not get inserted into the evaluation queue but is still marked as dirty; it will be re-evaluated at the next iteration of the algorithm.

If the system is convergent, this algorithm will converge after a finite number of iterations. However, if the system is not convergent, breaking the process into a set of iterations allows the users to capture dynamic state of the system and trace it through the use of time series.

BUILDING A DYNAMIC AGENT SOCIETY

In this section, we use expressive power of our system to implement a simple agent society. In this model we explore self-organized criticality in an evolving social network, and look at the role of conflict in evolution of social networks. This model has been originally implemented in Java (using MASON toolkit) and presented by us at Agent 2007 conference(O'Grady, Roulau, Tsvetovat, 2007).

Our declarative re-implementation of the model presents a distinct advantage of explicitly specifying rules and semantics of agent interaction, and separating them from procedural implementation of the agents. Moreover, the declarative implementation is smaller by an order of magnitude ($\approx$200 lines of code in Scheme vs. $\approx$4000 lines of code in Java).

Model Specification

The complexity of human social structures often masks the simplicity involved in their development. Social networks are a product of dynamic processes and feedback. In other words, the ties that people make affect the topology of a network and the form of a network affects the ties that people make. Therefore, social network structure evolves in a path-dependent manner.

We have all witnessed social turmoil in our midst – or even have been involved in its very middle. A long-married couple decides on a divorce – and suddenly their friends are faced with difficult decisions. They may feel pressured to side with one partner or the other, potentially splitting long-standing friendships and dividing a formerly cohesive network into "his side" and "her side". As the wounds of the split-up heal, the space is opened up for creation of new friendships and romantic relationships, and the cycle starts again.

The example above illustrates several concepts. The first is the ability of change in network structure – particularly change of a destructive nature – to propagate through a network, potentially affecting a large number of people. Second, the network reacts to addition and deletion of edges in qualitatively different fashions, depending on its density, undergoing a phase transition(Newman, Barabasi and Watts, 2006). Finally, it has been observed(Kumar, 2006) that networks in the real world settle to a certain density, suggesting the presence of a dynamic equilibrium(Leskovec and Faloutsos, 2005). We hypothesize that conflicts play a regulatory role in social networks and help establish and maintain this dynamic equilibrium.

We implement a simple agent-based model to explore the complexities of network structures and the consequences of conflict upon these structures. We are interested in the micro-level mechanisms that produce the macro-level patterns observed in real-world networks. The agent-level rules are based on the structural balance theory Doreian, et al, 1996, derived from Heider's balance theory(Heider, 1979). Balance theory suggests that people, from the perspective of the individual, have a preference for bal-

Figure 4. Network growth (a) without and (b) with conflicts

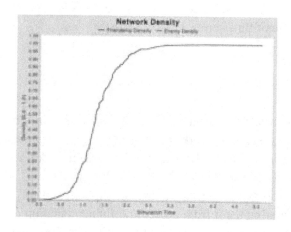 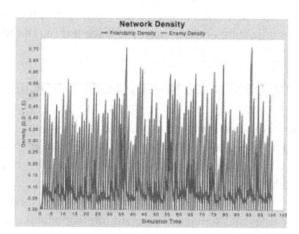

Figure 5. Propagation of conflicts in a dense network

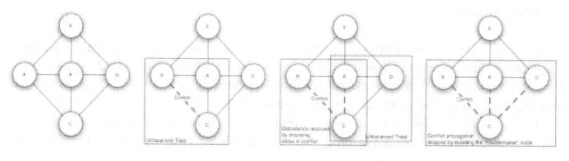

ance. Unbalanced structures occur when the primary individual perceives a dissonance between their affect and that of other objects. The agents address this dissonance through a change in affect and, thus, the network structure.

A simple triadic rule set can form the basis of a complex social network whose structure is dependent on the stability of the linkages: newly added actors or linkages act as generative processes (i.e. a couple's friends becoming friends) that percolate throughout the network. Similarly, conflict, which acts as a resistance process, may cause a relationship to reverse and can trigger a chain reaction, restructuring a network. Agents react to changes to their friendships and conflicts with a set of simple rules of triadic interaction:

Rule 1 A friend of my friend is my friend (Simmelian tie(Krackhardt, 1999))
Rule 2A An enemy of my friend is my enemy (social balance (Doreian, et al, 1996))
Rule 2B A friend of my enemy is my enemy
Rule 2C A enemy of my enemy is my friend

Rules 2A, 2B, and 2C actually represent the same balanced triad containing two conflict links and one friendship link – with the only difference being identity of the node invoking the rule.

Thus, we can simplify the agent behavior to the following statement:

Each node shall seek to be embedded in balanced triads
that are either fully connected Symmelian triads(Rule 1)
or conflict-balanced triads(Rule 2).

In the Java implementation, these rules only represent the start of implementation process, and required a month-long engineering effort to achieve the first proof of concept. In the declarative implementation, it suffices to define the agents and associated rules.

Declarative Implementation

Let us begin by declaring our agents and a basic edge semantics:

```
(defnode agent
 #:with-attr '((conflict-state 0) (degree 0))
)

(defedge friendOf
 #:from agent    //only agents can be connected as friends
 #:to agent
 #:with _ attr '((value 0))
)

(defedge enemyOf
 #:from agent    //only agents can be connected as enemies
 #:to agent
 #:with _ attr '((value 0))
)
```

This forms the basic structure and semantics of the model. Now we can generate a population of agents and some random connections between them (i.e. an Erdos random graph, in this case with a pre-set density of 5%):

```
(repeat (counter #:from 1 #:to 100 #:step 1)
 (defnode (genID counter)  #:as #$agent))

(map
 (lambda (a b) (
  (if (> (random) 0.95)
   (defedge (genID) #:as #$friendOf #:from a #:to b)))
 nodes nodes)
```

To implement rules regarding triadic structures, we will need to recognize triads based on whether they contain edges of type *friendOf, enemyOf* or contain a null edge NIL. Since recognition of triads is a very common task in social networks, we provide it in a built-in pattern-matching function:

(triadMatch root-node '(#$friendOf, #friendOf, NIL))

Let us now define the first rule. This rule applies directly to each node - thus it is defined through a local pattern.

[Rule 1] A friend of my friend is my friend

```
(defrule friendOfAFriend
 (let (triads (triadMatch #$this '(#$friendOf, #friendOf, NIL)))
 (if triads ;;if unbalanced triads are found
  (then ;;close any incomplete friend-of-a-friend triad
   (map
    (lambda (triad) (defedge #:as #$friendOf #:from #$this :#to (caddr tri-
ad)))
   triads)))))
```

[Rule 2A] An enemy of my friend is my enemy

```
(defrule enemyOfAFriend
 (let (triads (triadMatch #$this '(#$friendOf, #enemyOf, (or #$friendOf
NIL))))
 (if triads ;;if any unbalanced triads are found
  (then ;;create an enemyOf link to balance the triad
   (map
    (lambda (triad)
     (defedge #:as #$enemyOf #:from #$this :#to (caddr triad)))
   triads)))))
```

The remaining rules 2B and 2C are invariants of Rule 2A and are implemented by similarly matching a pattern of edges and creating or removing edges that do not fit the rule.

Finally, the rules are added to the Agent object we defined earlier, and we are ready to start the model.

We are using the KAWA Scheme interpreter built into MASON(Luke, et al, 2005) agent-based modeling toolkit. This allows us to use an existing agent-based system infrastructure, including high-quality data collection and plotting facilities, as well as network visualization using JUNG libraries.

Preliminary Results

To study the effect of conflict on the topology and density of networks, we propose a simple computational model: an agent-based version of a highly simplified social network. The model serves as an experimental environment using four 'social rules' previously described.

The base model consists of a static set of 100 agents, with Poisson scheduling. Initially, edges are added at random, thus generating an Erdös random graph(Erdos and Renyu, 1960), with density growing at a linear rate proportional to the probability of edge addition.

8.3.1 Phase Transition from Linear to Exponential Growth

At every activation, agents fire Rule 1 and attempt to close any of the open triads they are embedded in (i.e. "Friend of a friend is my Friend"). As density grows, an increasing number of friend-of-friend triads begin to connect into balanced triads and the growth of network density accelerates dramatically.

After network density passes a certain critical amount, the growth regime of the network shifts from linear to exponential, marking our first phase transition. In absence of conflict, our model produces a sigmoid curve of network density growth (fig. 4(a)). As network density approaches 1 (i.e. a fully connected graph), the growth slows due to lack of available open triads that can be closed.

8.3.2 Conflict Propagation

Conflict is introduced in the network at a constant probability, by changing a single friendship tie into an enemy tie. What happens then is illustrated on figure 5. In this simple example, a network consisting of 4 closed triads is struck by a conflict on a single edge. Triad A-B-C becomes unbalanced due to a conflict between B and C; thus A is forced to take sides in the conflict by choosing to remain friends with either B or C, at random. Adding conflict to the A-C edge forces another triad, A-C-D to become unbalanced, thus drawing agent D into the conflict. If agent D then chooses to isolate C from the rest of the network, the propagation of the conflict can be stopped. However, if instead it separates from A, this will cause the conflict to propagate further and destroy more links.

Having more ties increases an agents' probability of forming even more ties, but also increases the probability that a conflict between two agents spread throughout the network. Thus, percolation of both friendship and conflict is dependent upon the density and timing of agent connections.

As a result, network density begins to oscillate around a specific critical value, demonstrating self-organized criticality (Figure 4(b)).

DISCUSSION

AgentScheme has shown itself in practice as a highly expressive language for describing and reasoning about social networks and complex interaction patterns. Upon integration with the MASON agent-based modeling toolkit, we can combine advantages of compiled, procedural languages such as Java (speed, extensibility, portability to many operating systems) and flexibility and expressiveness of declarative programming. Such a tool should dramatically reduce development time needed to create complex agent-based social systems.

Meanwhile, an important question still remains to be addressed. Donald Knuth has once said "... anything we can think of can be automated. The things we do without thinking are much more difficult". In this specific case, the problem relates to the fact that much of what people know about the semantics of interpersonal interactions is in the realm of "common sense" — which is at best difficult to describe in formal terms, and at worst could be even difficult to describe in a human language, thus passing into the realm of poetry. A separate spur of this research thus attempts to address the difficulty of engineering semantic social networks through harvesting the "wisdom of crowds"(Tsvetovat, Reeves, 2007), providing us with more realistic representations of human interactions and interaction protocols.

REFERENCES

Abelson, H., Sussman, G. J., & JSussman, J. (1985). *Structure and Interpretation of Computer Programs.* Cambridge, MA and New York, NY: MIT Press and McGraw-Hill

Atkinson, M., Bancilhon, F., DeWitt, D., Dittrich, K., Maier, D., & Zdonik, S. (1989). The object-oriented database system manifesto. *In Proceedings of the First International Conference on Deductive and Object-Oriented Databases,* (pp. 223–240), Kyoto, Japan.

Woods, W. A. (1970). Transition network grammars for natural language analysis. *Communications of the ACM, 13*(10).

Cardelli, L. (1988). A semantics of multiple inheritance. *Information and Computation, 76,* 138–164.

Carley, K. M. (1994). Extracting culture through textual analysis. *Poetics, 22,* 291.

DiMaggio, P. (1998). Culture and cognition. *Annual Review of Sociology, 23,* 363.

Doreian, P., Kapuscinski, R., Krackhardt, D., & Szczypula, J. (1996). A brief history of balance through time. *Journal of Mathematical Sociology, 21*(1-2), 113–131.

Economou, G., Tsvetovat, M., Sycara, K., & Paolucci, M. (2001). Implicit commitments via protocol-level semantics. *In Workshop on Norms and Institutions in Agent Societies at Agents 2001,* Montreal, Canada.

Erdös and Rényi. (1960). On the evolution of random graphs. *Publication of Mathematics Institute of Hungian Academy of Sciences, 5,* 1761.

Brickley, D., Miller, E., Swick, R. (2004). *Rdf: Resource description framework.* http://www.w3.org/RDF/.

Finin, T., Fritzson, R., McKay, D., & McEntire, R. (1994). Kqml as an agent communication language. In N. Adam, B. Bhargava, and Y. Yesha, (eds.), *Proceedings of the 3rd International Conference on Information and Knowledge Management (CIKM'94),* (pp. 456–463), Gaithersburg, MD, USA: ACM Press.

Heider, F. (1979). *On Balance and Attribution. Perspectives on Social Networks.* New York: Academic Press.

Vitiello Jr., E., & Davis, I. (2004). *Relationship: A vocabulary for describing relationships between people.* http://purl.org/vocab/relationship.

Krackhardt, D. (1999). The ties that torture: Simmelian tie analysis in organizations. *Research in the Sociology of Organizations, 16,* 183–210.

Krackhardt, D., & Carley, K. M. (1998, June). A pcans model of structure in organizations. *Proceedings of the 1998 International Symposium on Command and Control Research and Technology,* (pp. 113–119).

Kumar, R., Novak, J., & Tomkins, A. (2006). Structure and evolution of online social networks. *In Proceedings of KDD-2006.*

Leskovec, J., & Faloutsos, J. K. C. (2005). Graphs over time: Densification laws, shrinking diameters, and possible explanations. *In 11th KDD,* (pp.177–187).

Luke, S. C., Liviu Panait, C. R., Sullivan, K., & Balan, K. B. (2005). Mason: A multi-agent simulation environment. *Simulation, 81*(7), 517–527.

Mohr, J. W. (1998). Measuring meaning structures. *Annual Review of Sociology, 24,* 345–370.

Newman, M., Barabási, A. L., & Watts, D. J. (2006). The Structure and Dynamics of Networks. Princeton, NJ Princeton University Press.

O'Grady, E., Roulau, M., & Tsvetovat, M. (2007). Network fracture: How conflict cascades regulate network density. *In Agent 2007,* Chicago, IL.

Shapiro, S. C. (1982). Generalized augmented transition network grapmmars for generation from semantic networks. *American Journal of Computational Linguistics, 8*(1), 12–25.

Specification-Part, F., & Management, N. (1997). *Foundation for intelligent physical 26 agents.*

Tsvetovat, M. (2005, June 15). Social Structure Simulation and Inference using Artificial Intelligence Techniques. PhD thesis, Carnegie Mellon University, Pittsburgh, PA.

Tsvetovat, M., & Carley, K. (2006, August). Simulating social systems requires multiple levels of complexity. *In Proceedings of World Congress on Social Simulation,* Kyoto, Japan.

Tsvetovat, M., & Reeves, D. M. (2007, July). Harnessing wisdom of crowds in semantic models of networks. *In 2007 UK Conference on Social Networks,* London, UK.

Woods, W. A. (1980). Cascaded ATN grammars. *American Journal of Computational Linguistics, 6*(1), 1–12.

Chapter VIII
Structural Aspects of Organizations

Davide Grossi
Utrecht University, The Netherlands

Frank Dignum
Utrecht University, The Netherlands

ABSTRACT

In this chapter we investigate how organizations can be represented as graphs endowed with formal semantics. We distinguish different dimensions of organizations. Each of these dimensions leads to a different structure in the organizational graph. By giving the graphs a formal semantics in Description Logic we show that it is possible to formalize the effect of the organization on the activities of the agents playing the roles of the organization. Such perspective, which combines quantitative (graph-theory) and qualitative (logic) methods is shown to provide a formal ground for the study and analysis of properties of organizations which are commonly addressed only informally.

"Als je voor elke positie de beste speler kiest, heb je nog geen sterk elftal maar een team dat als los zand uiteen valt."

"If you choose the best player for each position, you still don't get a strong team but a group which falls apart as loose sand."

J. Cruijff, Dutch football folklore

INTRODUCTION

In Multi-agent Systems (MAS) software agents enjoy some degree of autonomy (Wooldridge & Jennings, 1995), exactly like human agents in human societies. As a consequence, in MAS the same problem arises of guaranteeing the designed system to exhibit some desired global properties without hampering the agents' autonomy. The opportunity of a 'technology transfer' from the field of organizational and social theory to distributed Artificial Intelligence first (Fox, 1988), and then to MAS (V. Dignum 2003; Vázquez-Salceda, 2004) has often been advocated. In recent years, some research in MAS is even aiming at the explicit incorporation of entities such as organizations and institutions (normative systems) in computer systems, as testified by several contributions in the AAMAS conference series (Gini et al., 2002; Rosenschein et al., 2003; Jennings et al. 2004; F. Dignum et al., 2005; Weiss & Stone, 2006), the ALFEBIITE project (Pitt, 1999) and the COIN workshop series (Boissier et al., 2006; V. Dignum et al., 2007). Furthermore, several methodologies for MAS are based on organizational structures as their cornerstones such as, for instance, OperA (V. Dignum, 2003) and TROPOS (Bresciani et al., 2004), and GAIA (Zambonelli et al., 2003).

Notwithstanding this interest for organizations in MAS, little has been done to answer the key question "What is an organization?" or, less ambitiously, "How can an organization be formally represented?".

As a matter of fact, formal tools for the rigorous representation of organizational structure in MAS are not yet available and the study of organizational structure is still mainly informal. The literature on MAS—with very few exceptions such as in particular Hannoun et al. (2002) and Hübner et al. (2002)—addresses this type of structures only in an informal way by means of diagrams and charts like in Decker & Lesser (1995). In such informal studies, many issues remain hidden in the figures. We believe that, in order to successfully import the notion of organization for the design of MAS, "the space of organizational options must be mapped, and their relative benefits and costs understood" (Horling & Lesser, 2004), and to provide such a "map" a rigorous analysis of organizational structure plays a crucial role. If we want the notion of structure to be of any practical use for MAS, figures are plainly not enough, since they fail to address two fundamental aspects of organizational structures: 1) The formal (graph-theoretical) properties of the links between the roles in the structure; 2) The 'meaning' of those links, that is to say, the effects they have on the activities of the agents populating the organization. These considerations lead us to the research question of the present chapter: "How can we formally represent organizational structures and their effect on the activities of the agents?". More specifically, we will be addressing the following two issues:

1. What are the graph-theoretical properties of the links connecting the roles in the structure?
2. What is the 'meaning' of those links, that is to say, the effects they have on the activities of the agents operating the organization?

We will tackle these issues building on the results presented in Grossi et al. (2005), Grossi, Dignum et al. (2006), Grossi, Dignum, Dignum et al. (2007), Grossi, Dignum & Meyer (2007) and Grossi (2007). These results can be summed up into two key theses which constitute the content of the chapter. First, the structure of an organization is always multi-dimensional. That is to say, roles are connected by a number of different relations (who obeys whom? who communicates to whom? etc.), and not by just one relation as it is usually the case in network-based or chart-based representations of organizations.

Such structures therefore display several different types of connections which we represent and study as multigraphs, i.e., graphs containing links, or edges, of several different types. Second, the structure of an organization has a precise impact on the activities that the agents taking part in the organization can engage in. In other words, the graph-theoretical dimension of an organizational structure has a meaning in terms of the agent activities it makes possible. This "semantical" dimension of organizational structures will be studied by means of logic. The combined perspective will allow us to provide both quantitative methods based on graph-theory to compare different organizations from a structural point of view, and qualitative ones based on logic to address the types of interaction which different organizations make possible.

In Section 2 the basic intuitions and concepts grounding our analysis are introduced, which are imported from work on organization theory. Section 3 addresses the meaning of organizational structures in terms of the activities of the agents playing the roles in the structure. Labeled transition systems are used as the underlying mathematical tool. Roughly, we view the links in a structure as statements of global properties of transition systems. Such global properties concern the activities that can be executed by agents playing roles and the effects of those activities. This connects this semantic analysis of links with desirable graph-theoretical properties of organizational structures. If each link is related with specific activities, then certain configurations of links would make certain complex activities or interactions possible, whereas different configurations would make different activities and interaction patterns possible within the organization. Section 4 addresses this issue. We then turn to the issue of the adherence of organizational structures to desirable criteria such as, for instance, robustness and flexibility. A great deal of ongoing research in the field of organization-based MAS is devoted to compare and evaluate different types of organizations and their performances. Work on these issues varies from surveys comparing organizational paradigms (Horling & Lesser, 2004), to frameworks for representing and verifying organizational designs (Horling & Lesser, 2005), to studies concerning properties and performance of specific types of organizations (Scerri et al., 2004). Sections 5 and 6 are devoted to some graph-theoretical metrics for the quantitative analysis of organizational structures. Section 7 discusses some related work and future research lines. Conclusions follow in Section 8.

BACKGROUND

This section introduces the theoretical background of the chapter and the notion of organizational structure as multigraph.

Elements of a Theory of Organizational Structure in MAS

Work on organization in MAS[1] presents organizational structure as something mono-dimensional, though it often, but only implicitly, considers a multiplicity of structural aspects: "authority", "communication", "delegation", "responsibility", "control", "decision-making", "power", etc. It is our opinion that what was the case up to the sixties in the sociological literature about organizations, is now being the case in the literature about organizations in MAS. As explained in Harary et.al. (1965), "the word structure is found extensively in the literature of the social sciences. Social structure and such related concepts such as kinship structure, authority structure, communication structure, and sociometric structure are commonplace. [...] But despite the widespread use of structural concepts in the social sciences, it is fair to say that the formal analysis of structure has been relatively underdeveloped in these fields. The technical terminology employed in describing structures is meager; few concepts are defined rigorously. As a consequence, the social scientific description of structural properties tends to be couched in ambiguous terminology, and detailed studies of structure, as such, are rather rare".

Since then, sociology has developed a number of refined theories and mathematical tools to cope with the notion of organization. The present chapter exposes methods for developing similar tools which can be helpful in the design and analysis of MAS in terms of organizational notions, such as the notion of structure. To pursue this aim, the chapter relies on foundational work on social and organization theory like Selznick (1948), Morgenstern (1951) and Giddens (1984). According to these works, organizations do not exhibit one single structural dimension, but they are instead multi-structured objects. In particular, we view organizational structure as containing at least three relevant dimensions which we call: power, coordination and control.

What characterizes organizations is the possibility for the agents enacting the roles to delegate to other agents some of the tasks they are supposed to execute. Delegation consists in the possibility for an agent enacting a role to transfer a given task to a subordinated role. This transfer takes place in the form of a directed obligation (F. Dignum, 1999) from the agent enacting the first role to the agent enacting the subordinated one, the content of the obligation being the to-be-executed task. As a consequence of delegation, the addressee of the delegation becomes obliged to execute the task which belonged to the first agent. The possibility of delegating goals constitutes one of the essential aspects displaying what is usually called the "delegation" or "power" structure of an organization (Joerger & Johnson, 2001): who delegates to whom?

Since tasks are not always properly executed, organizations need to control their performance. If an agent fails in executing one of the stated or delegated tasks, some sort of supervising agent should take over the execution of that task. Potentially, the execution of any task can be object of control. With respect to control the relevant structural question is: who controls (supervises) whom?

The activity of an organization also relies on the *coordination* structure, which is a broadly investigated topic in MAS studies. Here, following Decker & Lesser (1995) and Grossi et al. (2004), we adopt a simple view on coordination, reducing it to the issue of the information with which agents enacting specific roles should be endowed in order to properly execute their tasks. Roles should have the information necessary for agents to appropriately enact them. Agents should know when to act, that is, they should be informed about the status of the activities of the organization upon which their activities depend, and what they are supposed to do. The point is that once a task is delegated and a correspondent obligation arises for a specific agent, a certain amount of information might be required for that agent to execute that task. Such information should therefore 'flow' within the organization to that agent. Because of this, an information mechanism which can keep track of this dynamics is crucial for the performance of an organization. To say it with Morgenstern, "The description of a delegation system [delegation structure] is incomplete unless the simultaneous signaling system [information structure] applied to it is also explicitly described" (Morgenstern, 1951, p.17). The coordination structure should guarantee that each agent is endowed with a representation of the actual state of the organization which is sufficient for it to properly enact its role. The question is then how the access and sharing of knowledge is structured within the organization: who informs whom?

To recapitulate, the *power structure* defines the task delegation patterns possible within the organization. The *coordination structure* concerns the flow of knowledge within the organization, and finally the *control structure* has to do with the task recovery functions of the organization. In other words, the existence of a power link between role r and role s implies that every delegation of tasks from agent i (enacting role r) to agent j (enacting role s) ends up in the creation of an obligation directed to agent s to execute the delegated task. If r and s are connected via a coordination link, then every information act from i to j ends up in creating the corresponding knowledge in agent j. Finally, a control link between r and s implies that agent i has to take over the tasks of agent j in case it fails to perform the requested tasks. As a result of this analysis, organizations will be represented as explicitly displaying a triple structure constrained on the basis of the interplay between the three notions of power, coordination, and control.

METHODOLOGICAL REMARKS

It is worth stressing two points before we move on to the next sections. First, even though our analysis will focus on the three aspects of delegation, supervision and information introduced in the previous section, we do not claim that they are the only ones playing a role in organizations, but only that they are among the most important and universal ones. Second, the terms we use to refer to the three structural dimensions related to delegation, supervision and information, that is, power, control, and coordination are used in a technical and very specific way. We do not claim to provide a full analysis of, e.g., the notion of power within organizations. Rather, in analyzing power ---for example--- we select a precise aspect of the notion which is amenable to formalization (i.e., delegation).

In other words, the chapter does not attempt to set forth a complete formal theory of organizations, which, given the complexity of the organization phenomenon, is hard, if not unfeasible. It is instead our aim to present a general method, grounded on formal tools such as logic and graph-theory, which can be systematically applied to the analysis and design of MAS in terms of organizational notions. It is our claim that the way we analyze the three dimensions of power, coordination and control, can also be followed for the analysis of other structural dimensions which can appear useful for specific application domains.

Finally, what the chapter presents does not presuppose a distinction between formal and informal social structures. The results presented can be applied any time an organizational structure (formal or informal) is considered to be in place. What falls outside the scope of our analysis are the dynamical aspects of structure, and the study of how organizational structures can be changed and evolve.

ORGANIZATIONAL STRUCTURE

A natural way of modeling the notion of organizational structure is via directed multigraphs (or, multidigraphs), which we represent here as systems of relations.

Definition 1. *(Organizational structure)*
An organizational structure Os is a tuple:

$$\langle Roles, R_{Pow}, R_{Coord}, R_{Contr} \rangle$$

where *Roles* is a non-empty finite set of roles, and $R_{Pow}, R_{Coord}, R_{Contr}$ are three irreflexive binary relations on *Roles* characterizing the Power, respectively, the Coordination and the Control structures.

For every R_k s.t. $k \in \{Pow, Coord, Contr\}$, we denote with $Roles_k$ the smallest subset of *Roles* such that, if $(x,y) \in R_k$ then $x,y \in Roles_k$. In other words, sets $Roles_k$ denote the set of roles involved in the structural dimension k. Each digraph $\langle Roles_k, R_k \rangle$ in *Os* will be referred to as the *structural dimension k of Os*.

We take the roles on which the organizational structure ranges (i.e., the elements of set *Roles*) to be enacted by one and only one agent. In practice, this boils down to a modeling issue: if two agents enacting the same role have to be connected by power, coordination or control links, then two different roles have to be specified which substitute the first one and which are played by only one agent. This finer level of granularity allows for a more refined snapshot of the structure of an organization. An analysis at a level where roles do not specify the relative positions of all agents with respect to all the structural dimensions would just fall short, missing many possibly relevant structural links. It follows from this distinction that a study of the organizational structure ranging on *role types* would abstract from those power, coordination, and control links that might be present between the *role tokens* specializing the same role type (e.g., the three attackers in a 4-3-3 strategy). Here we are interested in the analysis of structure at the level of the actual agents' positions within the organization, and thus at a finer level of granularity. The elements of the set *Roles* in a *Os* are then to be considered role tokens. In the rest of the paper, if not stated otherwise, we use the word role intending role token.

Enactment Configuration

Roles are positions in a structure, but they are positions which are occupied by agents. An enactment configuration for an organizational structure *Os* is a functional relation $EC \subseteq Roles \times Agents$ making explicit which agent out of a set *Agents* enacts which role: agent $i \in Agents$ enacts role $r \in Roles$ iff. *EC(r,i)* Relation *EC* is functional since, as stressed in the previous section, each role can be played by at most one agent[2]. A concrete organizational structure *COs* is a structure $\langle Os, Agents, EC \rangle$, i.e, an organizational structure plus a set of agents and an enactment configuration.

Structure with Formal Meaning

Definition 1 makes the structural aspect of an organization explicit, at least as far as the three dimensions of power, coordination and control are considered. Before studying organizational structures in graph-theoretical terms it is important to first face a second representational issue. Even after deciding to treat organizational structures as multi-graphs the problem remains of what each link in a structure actually means. This problem concern the formal semantics of structural links.

Roughly, the existence of a link of a certain type between two roles *r* and *s* indicates that a certain action can be performed by the agent playing *r* with respect to the agent playing *s* (i.e., that transitions of a specific type can be executed in the system), and that this action has some relevant consequences (i.e. a certain type of transition in the system always bears precise consequences). We develop this simple intuition showing how organizational structures can obtain a formal semantics in terms of labeled (or interpreted) transition systems (van Benthem et al., 1994).

With respect to this, it is worth noticing that the use of the word "semantics" in this Chapter is quite different from the use made in Chapter VII "Describing Agent Societies: A Declarative Semantics" by Tsvetovat. There, the term is used in a broader sense, while here semantics refers specifically to the mapping of organizational structures to labeled transition systems. This use of the term is in line with the standard conception of semantics in logic.

To pursue this aim, formal languages are needed which are able to express properties of transition systems which are relevant for our purposes. Such properties are eminently of two kinds:

1. *Executability*: in what type of states can a certain type of transition (i.e., agent's action) take place;
2. *Effect*: what are the effects of the execution of a certain type of transition (i.e., agent's action) in a certain type of state.

The formal expressions of such properties will then be used for giving meaning to each link in an organizational structure by viewing the links in the structure as concise ways to refer to sets of such transition systems properties. In other words, our key idea is that to draw a link in an organizational structure actually amounts to state a number of universal properties for the to-be-developed system. Such properties, which are properties of transition systems, represent in some way the "meaning" of the organizational links.

From the technical point, the formal languages we resort to are the ones of Description Logic, shortly DL, (Baader et al., 2002). The choice for these logical languages is motivated by their appealing complexity properties, and by the fact that they constitute a well-investigated and rich family of formalisms particularly tailored for talking about transition systems.

Description Logic, a Sketch

We use an expressive DL expanding the standard description logic language ALC with relational operators ($\circ, \neg, id$) to express complex transition types, and relational hierarchies (H) to express inclusion between transition types. Following a notational convention common within DL we denote this language with $ALCH^{(\circ, \neg, id)}$. We give a sketchy introduction to the syntax and semantics of this language and how it will be used for our purposes. For a more systematic introduction to DL we refer the reader to Baader et al. (2002).

Definition 2. *(Logical syntax of* $ALCH^{(\circ, \neg, id)}$*)*
Transition types and state type constructs are defined by the following BNF:

$$\alpha := a \mid \alpha \circ \alpha \mid \neg\alpha \mid id(\gamma)$$
$$\gamma := c \mid \bot \mid \neg\gamma \mid \gamma \sqcap \gamma \mid \forall\alpha.\gamma$$

where a and c are atomic transition types, respectively, atomic state types.

The intuitive reading of $\forall\alpha.\gamma$ is that "after all executions of transitions of type α, states of type γ are reached" (effect property), and $\neg\forall\alpha.\neg\gamma$ as "there exists an execution of α terminating in a γ state" (executability property). The operator $\circ$ denotes the concatenation of transition types. The operator *id* applies to a state description γ and yields a transition description, namely, the transition ending in states of type γ. It is the description logic variant of the test operator in Dynamic Logic (Kozen & Tiuryn, 1984). Notice that we use the same symbol $\neg$ for denoting the boolean operator of negation of both state and transition types.

The non-logical alphabets contain state types and transition types.

Definition 3. *(Non-logical alphabets)*

The non-logical alphabet is built from three sets: a finite set *Agents* of agents, a finite set *c_Form* of state type forms, and a finite set *a_Form* of transition type forms. Atomic state and transition types are built as follows:

$$c := c(i)$$
$$a := a(i,j)$$

where $i,j \in Agents$, $c \in c\_Form$ and $a \in a\_Form$.

Atomic state types c are indexed by an agent identifier i in order to express agent properties (e.g., *dutch(i)*), and atomic transition types a are indexed by a pair of agent identifiers *(i,j)* (e.g., *PAY(i,j)*) denoting the actor and the recipient of the transition. Obviously, other more complex forms of indexing are straightforwardly definable. By removing the agent identifiers from state types and transition types we obtain state type forms (e.g., *dutch*) and transition type forms (e.g., *PAY*).

A terminological box (henceforth TBox) $T = \langle \Gamma, A \rangle$ consists of a finite set Γ of state type inclusion assertions $\gamma_1 \sqsubseteq \gamma_2$), and of a finite set A of transition type inclusion assertions $(\alpha_1 \sqsubseteq \alpha_2)$.

As said before, the semantics of ALCH$^{(\circ, \neg, id)}$ is given in terms of interpreted transition systems (van Benthem et al., 1994). As usual, state types are interpreted as sets of states and transition types as sets of state pairs.

Definition 4. *(Semantics of* ALCH$^{(\circ, \neg, id)}$*)*

An interpreted transition system (or model) m for ALCH$^{(\circ, \neg, id)}$ is a structure $\langle S, I \rangle$ where S is a non-empty set of states and I is a function such that:

$$I(c) \subseteq S$$
$$I(a) \subseteq S \times S$$
$$I(\bot) = \varnothing$$
$$I(\neg\gamma) = S \backslash I(\gamma)$$
$$I(\gamma_1 \sqcap \gamma_2) = I(\gamma_1) \cap I(\gamma_2)$$
$$I(\forall\alpha.\gamma) = \{s \in S \mid \forall t,(s,t) \in I(\alpha) \Rightarrow t \in I(\gamma)\}$$
$$I(\neg\alpha) = S \times S \backslash I(\alpha)$$
$$I(\alpha_1 \circ \alpha_2) = \{(s,s'') \mid \exists s',(s,s') \in I(\alpha_1) \;\&\; (s',s'') \in I(\alpha_2)\}$$
$$I(id(\gamma)) = \{(s,s) \mid s \in I(\gamma)\}$$

Boolean operators on state types and $\exists$ are defined as usual. An interpreted transition system m is a model of a state type inclusion assertion $\gamma_1 \sqsubseteq \gamma_2$ if $I(\gamma_1) \subseteq I(\gamma_2)$. It is a model of a transition type inclusion assertion $\alpha_1 \sqsubseteq \alpha_2$ if $I(\alpha_1) \subseteq I(\alpha_2)$. An interpreted transition system m is a model of a TBox $T = \langle \Gamma, A \rangle$ if m is a model of each inclusion assertion in Γ and A.

Action Negation

In what follows we will need to represent also a form of negation of atomic transition types crudely corresponding to some notion of refraining from performing an action. It is well-known that this is a hard issue to solve in formalisms like the one just presented (see Broersen (2003)) and the readily available solution of using the negation $\neg$ of transition types is too strong, since such negation is interpreted as the complement w.r.t. the whole state space $S \times S$. We opt for a simple solution, which suits our needs without introducing heavy logical machinery that would not be used in our analysis. The non-logical alphabet of our language (see Definition) needs to be extended as follows: for every atomic transition type a, -a is also an atomic transition type. In addition, any occurrence of an atomic transition type -a in a TBox needs to be accompanied by the following role inclusion axiom: -$a \sqsubseteq \neg a^3$. More elegant but complex solutions to the problem can be found in Meyer (1988) and in the comprehensive survey Broersen (2003).

The formalism just presented will be used to tackle the issue of the semantics of structural links by translating a *COs* into a corresponding TBox. The idea is to express the intuitive understanding of the relations of power, coordination, and control which has been exposed in Section 2.1 by means of terminological axioms.

Enactment

First of all we consider the translation in logic of enactment links. An enactment configuration EC is translated by means of the state type forms $rea(i,r)$, where i is an element of *Agents* and r an element of *Roles*. Such state type forms denote that the agent i "enacts" role r (Dignum, 2003).

Definition 5. *(Meaning of enactment links)*

Let $Cos = \langle Roles, R_{Pow}, R_{Coord}, R_{Contr}, Agents, EC \rangle$. For all (r,i) if $EC(r,i)$ then $\mathbf{T}(Cos)$ contains the following axiom: $rea(r,i) \equiv \top$

Intuitively, an enactment configuration fixes which agents are playing which roles as a global property of the system.

It is worth noticing that the study of the semantics of organizational structures in terms of transition systems provides foundations for the development of programming languages for agent organizations (see, for example, Chapter XVI "A Programming Language for Normative Multi-Agent Systems" by Dastani et al.) as well as for MAS models (see, for example, Chapter IV "OMACS: A Framework for Adaptive, Complex Systems" by DeLoach). In fact, transition systems are the typical means for providing formal semantics for agent programming languages.

Institutional Links

This section is devoted to the semantic analysis of structural links related to the issuing of duties and obligations within the organization.

We say that role r has power over role s ($R_{Pow}(r,s)$ or $(r,s) \in R_{Pow}$) if and only if agents playing role r can always execute a delegation action towards agents playing role s and this action always results in a corresponding obligation for the recipient to execute the delegated action. The delegation action type is represented by the transition type forms $DEL(a)$, where a is the delegated transition type form.

The translation we are looking for should therefore translate power links as follows.

Definition 6. *(Meaning of power links)*

Let $Cos = \langle Roles, R_{Pow}, R_{Coord}, R_{Contr}, Agents, EC \rangle$. For all (r,s), if $R_{Pow}(r,s)$ then $\mathbf{T}(Cos)$ contains the following axioms for any transition type form a and agents $i,j \in Agents$:

$$rea(i,r) \sqcap rea(j,s) \sqcap \forall\text{-}a(i).viol(i) \sqsubseteq \exists DEL(a,i,j).\top \qquad (1)$$

$$rea(i,r) \sqcap rea(j,s) \sqcap \forall\text{-}a(i).viol(i) \sqsubseteq \exists DEL(a,i,j).(\forall\text{-}a(j)).viol(j) \qquad (2)$$

$$id(rea(i,r) \sqcap rea(j,s)) \circ DEL(a,i,j) \sqsubseteq a(i) \qquad (3)$$

Intuitively, the fact that r is linked to s by a power link means that agents enacting role r, if put under the obligation to perform a, can delegate action a to agents enacting role s (Formula 1), and they can do this successfully in the sense that they always create the corresponding obligation directed to the recipient of the delegation act (Formula 2). The last important aspect of the semantics of power links is that agents playing role r actually execute a *by* delegating its execution to agents playing role s. In other words, if an agent enacting role r delegates a it does not end up in a violation state.

It goes without saying that this interpretation of power is extremely restrictive[4]. The point we are making here is, again, of a methodological kind: structural links have a meaning, and this can be given in terms of transition systems as shown above for the notion of power adopted here. Other formal analyses of the vague notion of power are possible, and would naturally fit our formal framework if provided in terms of transition systems.

Along the same lines we can provide a translation of the links in the control structure.

Definition 7. *(Meaning of control links)*

Let $Cos = \langle Roles, R_{Pow}, R_{Coord}, R_{Contr}, Agents, EC \rangle$. For all (r,s), if $R_{Contr}(r,s)$ then $\mathbf{T}(Cos)$ contains the following axioms for any transition type form a and agents $i,j \in Agents$:

$$rea(i,r) \sqcap rea(j,s) \sqcap \forall\text{-}a(j).viol(j) \sqsubseteq \forall\text{-}a(j).(\forall\text{-}a(i).viol(i)) \qquad (4)$$

The fact that role r is linked to role s by a control link means that if agents playing role s ought to perform action a then agents playing role r ought to perform a in case the first agents fail to fulfill that obligation. Intuitively, a control link generates a sort of backup obligation addressed to the controllers. As such, control has to do with the normative dimension of the organization. The above considerations concerning the limitedness of the interpretation of power apply of course also to this notion of control.

To control means here to adjust deviant behaviour or to recover from failure. It concerns the generation of obligations triggered by the occurrence of violations. A different notion of control interpreted as some sort of sanctioning activity by an enforcer would exhibit in fact the same logical pattern:

$rea(i,r) \sqcap rea(j,s) \sqcap \forall\text{-}a(j).viol(j) \sqsubseteq \forall\text{-}a(j).(\forall\text{-}SANCTION(i,j).viol(i))$

for any transition type form *a* and agents *i,j∈Agents*. If *r* controls *s* then agents playing role *r* ought to sanction agents playing role *s* in case they violate some norm. Notice that Formulas 2 and 4 are effect laws, Formula 1 is an executability law and Formula 3 is a transition type inclusion statement.

However, structural links do not only have institutional meanings. The following section considers the semantic of structural links in terms of mentalistic notions, that is, in terms of the mental states of the agents involved in playing the roles of the link.

Mentalistic Links

We have seen in Section 2.1 that organizational structures have to do with the flow of information within an organization. In this view, an essential ingredient of coordination between two roles is that agents enacting the first role can communicate with agents playing the second role and can do that effectively, that is, actually modifying the epistemic state of the recipient. This perspective takes into the picture well-investigated mentalistic notions such as knowledge and belief.

In what follows, we will interpret the coordination links of an organizational structure by means of the notion of knowledge. Coordination links have to do with the flow of knowledge between the agents enacting the roles of the organization. There is a number of formalisms which investigate in depth the relation between knowledge and dynamics (for example, Meyer & van der Hoek (1995) and Baltag & Moss (2004)). For our purposes, it suffices here to show how we can represent knowledge in the framework of DL, thus avoiding to introduce further machinery. Again, the point we are stressing is that organizational structure can be given a semantics, in this case, of a mentalistic nature.

From a technical point of view, to represent knowledge in DL nothing else is needed than the introduction of special transition types *IND(i)*, for any agent *i*, representing a relation of indistinguishability, for agent *i*, between system states. It is then needed to state that these transition types denote reflexive, symmetric and transitive relations. Such expressivity is not common in DL. It is however enabled for instance in DL **SROIQ** (Horrocks et al., 2006) which allows for TBoxes containing role assertions of the type: *Sym(a), Trans(a), Refl(a)* where *a* is an atomic transition type. The semantics of such assertions is the obvious one.

Assuming such new expressivity for the underling DL language, it becomes then possible to represent the notion of knowledge, and to give a mentalistic semantics to coordination links. The information action type is represented by the transition type forms *INF(γ)*, where γ is a state type description belonging to a finite set of "communicable" state types[5].

Definition 8. *(Meaning of coordination links)*

Let $Cos = \langle Roles, R_{Pow}, R_{Coord}, R_{Contr}, Agents, EC \rangle$. For all *(r,s)*, if $R_{Coord}(r,s)$ then **T**(*Cos*) contains the following axioms for any transition type form *INF(γ)* and agents *i,j∈Agents*:

$$rea(i,r) \sqcap rea(j,s) \sqcap \forall IND(i).\gamma \sqsubseteq \exists INF(\gamma,i,j).\top \tag{5}$$

$$rea(i,r) \sqcap rea(j,s) \sqcap \forall IND(i).\gamma \sqsubseteq \forall INF(\gamma,i,j).(\forall IND(j).\gamma) \tag{6}$$

Intuitively, the fact that r is linked to s by a coordination link means that if agents enacting role r know that γ they can always inform agents enacting role s that γ (Formula 5), and they can do this successfully in the sense that they always create the corresponding knowledge in the recipient of the information act (Formula 6).

In fact, not only the coordination links, but also the power and control links have some mentalistic aspects. The functioning of these links relies on how much of the organization itself is known to the agents. In this respect, Definitions 6 and 7 should be restated by making the knowledge ingredient explicit:

Definition 9. *(Power and control based on knowledge)*

Let $Cos = \langle Roles, R_{Pow}, R_{Coord}, R_{Contr}, Agents, EC \rangle$. For all (r,s), if $R_{Pow}(r,s)$ then $\mathbf{T}(Cos)$ contains the following axioms for any transition type form a and agents $i,j \in AgentsZ$:

$$rea(i,r) \sqcap rea(j,s) \sqcap \forall IND(i).(\forall\text{-}a(i).viol(i)) \sqsubseteq \exists DEL(a,i,j).\top \tag{7}$$

$$rea(i,r) \sqcap rea(j,s) \sqcap \forall IND(i).(\forall\text{-}a(i).viol(i)) \sqsubseteq \forall DEL(a,i,j). \forall IND(i).(\forall\text{-}a(j)).viol(j)) \tag{8}$$

and if $R_{Contr}(r,s)$ then $\mathbf{T}(Cos)$ contains the following axioms for any transition type form a and agents $i,j \in Agents$:

$$rea(i,r) \sqcap rea(j,s) \sqcap \forall IND(i).(\forall\text{-}a(j).viol(j)) \sqsubseteq \forall\text{-}a(j). \forall IND(i).(\forall\text{-}a(i)).viol(i)) \tag{9}$$

This translation uses as pre- and postconditions of the agents' organizational activities the agents' knowledge about the relevant institutional states (e.g., directed obligations), rather than those states themselves. So, Formulas 7 and 8 concern the knowledge by the delegating agent that: 1) before delegating the task, it is under an obligation to perform it; 2) after delegating the task the recipient is under an obligation to perform it. Similarly, Formula 9 states in the antecedent that the controller knows the controlee is under an obligation, and in the consequent that the controller knows it is put under that obligation if the controlee fails.

LINKS, SEMANTICS, AND STRUCTURAL PROPERTIES

The formal semantics of structural links presented in the previous sections provides a formal ground for studying the interaction between the three dimensions of power, coordination and control. The present section shows how a formally specified semantics of structure can aid the understanding of structural properties concerning the interaction of the power, coordination and control dimensions.

Some Notation

Before getting started it is worth recollecting some standard graph theoretical notions which will be used in the rest of the chapter. An R_k-path (of length n) is a sequence $\langle x_1, \ldots, x_{n+1} \rangle$ of distinct elements of

Roles s.t. $\forall i\ 1\leq i\leq n\ (x_i,x_{i+1})\in R_k$. A R_k-semipath (of length n) is a sequence $\langle x_1,...,x_{n+1}\rangle$ of distinct elements of *Roles* s.t. $\forall i\ 1\leq i\leq n\ (x_i,x_{i+1})\in R_k$ or $(x_{i+1},x_i)\in R_k$. A *source* in *Roles*$_k$ is an element s s.t. $\forall d\in Roles_k$ with $d\neq s$ there exists a R_k-path from s to d. The *indegree* $id_k(d)$ of a point d in structure k is the number of elements d_l s.t. $(d_l,d)\in R_k$. The *outdegree* $od_k(d)$ of a point d in structure k is the number of elements d_l s.t. $(d,d_l)\in R_k$. We say a point d to be incident w.r.t. a k link if $1\leq id_k(d)$, and it is said to have emanating k links if $1\leq od_k(d)$.

Structural Interplay

We have seen that structure is necessary in order to reassign tasks via new obligations (delegation). Because of this dynamics organizations need to distribute relevant knowledge (information), and implement forms of performance assessment and recovery (monitoring). Somehow, the interplay between these structural dimensions lies in the delegation activity and is therefore based on the power relation. This is in accordance with many foundational investigations in the theory of organizations (Selznick, 1948; Morgenstern, 1951).

The observation above leads to the following two principles: the structure of the organization should see to it that each agent is always aware of its obligations (a sort of "ought implies know" principle); the structure of the organization should see to it that the tasks allocated to the agents are always executed (a "successful performance" principle).

Intuitively, the implementation of the "ought implies know" principle can be met by aligning the coordination structure with the power structure, so that every delegation action can be followed by a corresponding information action. The successful performance can never be guaranteed as the agents are autonomous and subject to failure. However, the control structure generates a new obligation for the controller each time the obligation has not been met by the controlled agent. In principle, also the controller can then violate this obligation leaving the goal unachieved. But, the more levels of controls are enacted, the stronger the principle can be thought of being implemented. This leads us to the following soundness criterion for organizational structures.

Definition 10. (Sound *Os*)

A sound organizational structure is a tuple: $\langle Roles, R_{Pow}, R_{Coord}, R_{Contr}\rangle$ where *Roles* is the finite set of roles, and $R_{Pow}, R_{Coord}, R_{Contr}$ are three irreflexive binary relations on *Roles* such that $\forall r,s\in Roles$:

$(r,s)\in R_{Pow}\Rightarrow$ there exists an R_{Coord}-path from r to s;

$(r,s)\in R_{Pow}\Rightarrow$ there exists a role $t\in Roles$ such that $R_{Contr}(t,s)$.

The occurrence of a power relation between role r and role s requires: the existence of a (finite) coordination path from r to s such that effective informative actions can transmit the relevant knowledge of agents enacting role r to agents enacting role s; and the existence of at least one element t (which might be r itself) which is in a control relation with s.

Why Structural Soundness?

By considering what the links are intended to mean, the question about how the different structural dimensions should interact can be given a more precise answer. We illustrate this point by means of a simple example.

Example 1. (Structural properties and the semantics of links) Consider the simple organizational structure depicted in Figure 1:

$$COs = \langle\{r,s,t\},\{(r,s)\},\{(r,s)\},\{(t,s)\},\{i,j,k\},\{(r,i),(s,j),(t,k)\}\rangle$$

Consider also the translation **T** constrained according to Definitions 7, 8 and 9. The following subsumptions are logically implied by **T**(Cos) for any a

$$rea(i,r) \sqcap rea(j,s) \sqcap rea(k,t) \equiv \top \tag{11}$$

$$DEL(a,i,j) \sqsubseteq a(i) \tag{12}$$

$$\forall IND(i).(\forall\text{-}a(i).viol(i)) \sqsubseteq \exists DEL(a,i,j).\top \tag{13}$$

$$\forall IND(i).(\forall\text{-}a(i).viol(i)) \sqsubseteq \exists INF(\forall\text{-}a(j).viol(j),i,j).\top \tag{14}$$

$$\forall IND(i).(\forall\text{-}a(i).viol(i)) \sqsubseteq \exists(DEL(a,i,j)\circ INF(\forall\text{-}a(j).viol(j),i,j).\top \tag{15}$$

$$\forall\text{-}a(j).viol(j) \sqsubseteq \forall\text{-}a(j).(IND(k).(\forall\text{-}a(k).viol(k))) \tag{16}$$

$$\forall IND(i).(\forall\text{-}a(j).viol(j)) \sqsubseteq \forall INF(\forall\text{-}a(j).viol(j),i,j).\forall IND(j).\forall a(j).viol(j)) \tag{17}$$

$$\forall IND(i).(\forall\text{-}a(i).viol(i)) \sqsubseteq \forall DEL(a,i,j).(\forall IND(i).(\forall\text{-}a(j).viol(j))) \tag{18}$$

Figure 1. Pictorial representation of Example 1

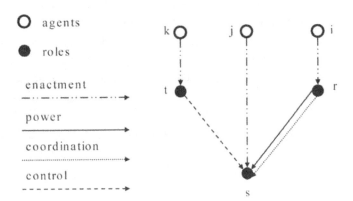

$$\forall \text{IND}(i).(\forall\text{-a}(i).viol(i)) \sqsubseteq \ \forall(\text{DEL}(a,i,j) \circ \text{INF}(\forall\text{-a}(j).viol(j)),i,j)).(\forall\text{IND}(j).(\forall\text{-a}(j).viol(j))) \qquad (19)$$

$$\forall \text{IND}(i).(\forall\text{-a}(i).viol(i)) \sqsubseteq \ \forall(\text{DEL}(a,i,j) \circ \text{INF}(\forall\text{-a}(j).viol(j)),i,j)).(\forall\text{IND}(j).(\forall\text{-a}(j).viol(j)) \qquad (20)$$
$$\sqcap \ \forall\text{-a}(j).(\forall\text{IND}(k).(\forall\text{-a}(k).viol(k)))$$

These subsumptions follow quite directly from Definitions 7, 8 and 9. Formula 11 states the enacting configuration in place in the system. Formulae 13-15 are all executability laws. The most interesting is Formula 15 which expresses that it is possible for agent i to first delegate a to agent j and then informing j that it has to perform a. This results from the organizational structure at issue, where the pair (r,s) belongs to both the power and the coordination structure.

Formula 16 expresses that all states in which agent j ought to perform a are states where if j does not perform a then it is the case that agent k knows it ought to perform a. It concerns the exercise of control by k on j. Formulas 17 and 18 deal with the effect of the information and delegation actions under this structural configuration. If i knows that j is obliged to perform a then by informing j about this, j also knows that it is obliged to perform a (Formula 17), and i always knows that j is obliged to perform a after it delegates a to j (Formula 18).

Finally, Formula 20 brings it all together stating that: if agent i ought to do a, then by i delegating a to j and then informing j that it ought to perform a, the system always reaches a state where j knows it ought to perform a and where if j does not comply with this obligation then agent k would know it ought to take over the execution of a.

The *COs* considered in Example 1 is a very simple instance of a sound organization. It is easy to see that soundness is what in fact guarantees that Formula 20 follows by applying the translation. The example considered is obviously a toy one, based on the simple semantics of the structural links presented above. However, it shows how they can provide a rigorous ground for the design of organizational structures themselves.

Once some properties are identified, the question arises how much a given organizational structure adheres to those properties. E.g. an organizational structure might not be sound, but only missing one coordination link. So, it is almost sound. In the next section we will take a closer look at some properties that can be partially fulfilled.

MEASURING ORGANIZATIONAL STRUCTURE

Section 4 has shown how the structure of organizations, as made formal in Definition 1, can be studied "semantically" by means of transition systems and Description Logic. The present section exploits Definition 1 to study organizational structures from the point of view of graph-theory. Upshot of the section is to develop a number of metrics which could sensibly measure the adherence of organizational structures to desirable structural properties (e.g. How connected is the structure? Is the structure flat or hierarchical? etc.). This adds quantitative methods of analysis to the qualitative ones described in Section 4.

The section is best read as a toolkit providing a number of quantitative tools for analyzing the structures of organizations. More concretely, it presents some equations measuring specific graph-theoretical aspects of structures[6]. First we will provide measures for structural properties concerning structural dimensions taken in isolation, and then structural properties concerning the interaction between different dimensions.

Completeness, Connectedness, Economy

Completeness and connectedness of an *Os* indicate how strongly roles are linked with one another within one of the structural dimensions k.

$$\text{Connectedness}_k(Os) = 1 - \frac{|\text{DISCON}_k|}{|Roles_k| * (|\text{Roles}_k| - 1)} \tag{21}$$

$$\text{Connectedness}_k(Os) = 1 - \frac{|\text{DISCON}_k|}{|Roles_k| * (|\text{Roles}_k| - 1)} \tag{22}$$

with $|R_k|>0$ and $DISCON_k$ the set of ordered pairs (x,y) of $Roles_k$ s.t. there is neither a R_k-semipath from x to y nor from y to x, i.e., the set of disconnected ordered pairs of the structural dimension $\langle Roles_k, R_k \rangle$. The condition $|R_k|>0$ states that the structural dimension k does indeed exist. If the structure does not exist it cannot be measured. As a consequence, $Completeness_k>0$. Stating that $Completeness(Os)=0$ thus means that $R_k=\varnothing$ and hence that no structure at all is given. In practice, Equation 21 measures the fraction of the actual links of the dimension $\langle Roles_k, R_k \rangle$ on all the available ones and Equation 22 measures how 'not disconnected' that dimension is. With respect to connectedness, an important notion is that of cutpoint or, in an organizational reading, *liason role* (Harary, 1959a), i.e., a role whose removal decreases the connectedness of the structure.

The *economy* of a given *Os* expresses a kind of balance between the two concerns of keeping the structure connected and of minimizing the number of links, i.e., minimizing completeness:

Figure 2. Example of organizational structure

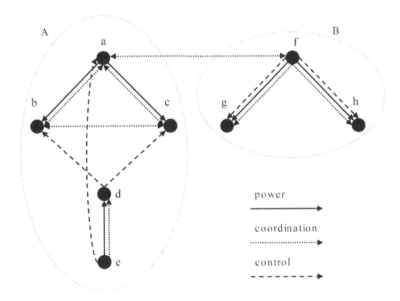

$$Economy_k(Os) = 1 - \frac{|R_k| - (|Roles_k| - 1)}{|Roles_k| * (|Roles_k| - 1) - (|Roles_k| - 1)} \tag{23}$$

With $|R_k| > 0$. The equation is based on the intuition according to which the most 'economical' digraph of n points consists of n-1 links, i.e., the minimum number of links which is still sufficient to keep the digraph connected. Indeed, the nominator of the fraction, consists of the number of links in the structural dimension k which are in excess or in defect w.r.t. the optimum of n-1 links. The denominator denotes the maximum number of links in excess in k. If $|R_k|=n$-1 then the value of $Economy_k(Os)$ is optimal, i.e., equal to 1. Notice that $Economy_k(Os)$=1 does not imply $Connectedness_k(Os)$=1, it only implies that there are enough links in R_k for it to be possibly connected. If the existence of symmetric links in R_k is assumed, then n-1 links are clearly not enough any more for guaranteeing connectedness. Notice also that $Economy_k(Os)$ can assume a value greater than 1, which indicates a sort of 'over-efficiency' of k. It is easy to see that, if $Economy_k(Os)$>1 then $Connectedness_k(Os)$<1.

Unilaterality, Univocity, Flatness

The properties of unilaterality and univocity express the tendency of an Os to display an orientation in its links (*unilaterality*), and the absence of redundant links ending up in the same role (*univocity*). Do the links of an Os always have a 'direction' or does the Os allow 'peer-to-peer' connections? And how many of those connections are such that no role has more than one incident link of the same structural dimension?

$$Unilaterality_k(Os) = 1 - \frac{|SIM_k|}{|R_k|} \tag{24}$$

$$Univocity_k(Os) = \frac{|IN_k|}{|Roles_k|} \tag{25}$$

$$Flatness_k(Os) = 1 - \frac{|CUT_k|}{|Roles_k|} \tag{26}$$

With $|R_k| > 0$ and SIM_k denotes the set of links (x,y) in R_k s.t. (x,y) is also in R_k i.e., $|SIM_k|$ is twice the number of symmetric links in k; IN_k denotes the set of roles x in $Roles_k$ s.t. $id_k(x)$=1 or $id_k(x)$=0, i.e., the set of roles which either have indegree equal to 1 in k or they are a source of k or of some subgraphs of k; and CUT_k denotes the set of roles x s.t. $od_k(x) \geq 1$ and $id_k(x) \geq 1$, that is to say, the set of roles which are at the same time addresser and addressee of k links. Intuitively, Equation 24 measures how much asymmetry is present in k, while Equation 25 measures how much a dimension k is univocal or "non ambiguous". The most univocal structures are assumed to be either the ones in which every point, except the source, has one and only one incident link (like in trees), or the ones in which exactly all points have only one incident link (like in cycles). Finally, Equation 26 measures the relative amount of points in dimension k which are not intermediate point in a k-path, in other words the amount of points the removal of which would not cut any k-path. Obviously, the lowest value of flatness is provided by cycles

Intuitively, unilaterality has to do with the level of subordination present in a structure. Consider the R_{Coord} dimension. The higher the number of unilaterality, the lower the amount of `peer-to-peer' information exchange within Os. Univocity has to do with the level of conflict and redundancies of a given structure. Consider the R_{Pow} dimension. The higher the level of univocity, the more unambiguous is the chain of commands, as well as the more fragile once a link is removed. Flatness has to do with the length of paths in a given structure. High flatness is of course typical in non-hierarchical organizations.

Detour, Overlap, Cover and Chain

The properties we address here describe how the different dimensions of an Os interact with one another[7].

The properties we call *detour* and *overlap* regard the degree to which a structural dimension j `follows' a structural dimension k. I.e. the degree to which j establishes corresponding paths for each link of k, so that the roles that are related by R_k links are also related by R_j-paths.

$$\text{Detour}_{jk}(Os) = \frac{|\text{PATH}_{jk}|}{|R_k|} \tag{27}$$

With $|R_k|>0$ and the set $PATH_{jk}$ is defined as the set of ordered pairs (x,y) s.t. $(x,y)\in R_k$ and there exists an R_j-path from x to y. Equation 27 measures the relative amount of R_j-paths between the elements of

Figure 3. Structural measures for Example 2

	Power	Coordination	Control
Completeness$_k$(Os)	5/56	11/56	5/56
Connectedness$_k$(Os)	1/4	31/56	26/56
Economy$_k$(Os)	51/49	45/49	51/49
Unilaterality$_k$(Os)	1	3/11	1
Univocity$_k$(Os)	1	5/8	1
Flatness$_k$(Os)	1	1/2	1
	Coord-Pow	Contr-Pow	Pow-Contr
Detour$_{jk}$(Os)	1	2/5	2/5
Overlap$_{jk}$(Os)	2	2/5	2/5
InCover$_{jk}$(Os)	1	4/5	4/5
OutCover$_{jk}$(Os)	1	2/3	2/3
Chain$_{jk}$(Os)	2/3	1/3	1/3
	Coord-Contr	Contr-Coord	Pow-Coord
Detour$_{jk}$(Os)	2/5	2/9	4/9
Overlap$_{jk}$(Os)	2/5	2/9	5/9
InCover$_{jk}$(Os)	1	5/6	5/6
OutCover$_{jk}$(Os)	2/3	2/5	3/5
Chain$_{jk}$(Os)	1/3	3/5	2/5

$Roles_k$ which have the same direction as the links in R_k. A special case of detour is the overlap. In fact, to measure how much does a dimension j overlap with a dimension k, it suffices to limit $PATH_{jk}$ to R_j-paths of length 1.   We define this as $LINK_{jk} \equiv R_k \cap R_j$. A set $LINK_{jk}$ consists of all the pairs (x,y) which are linked in R_k and in R_j.

$$\text{Overlap}_{jk}(Os) = \frac{|LINK_{jk}|}{|R_k|} \qquad (28)$$

With $|R_k|>0$. Intuitively, the more j-pairs correspond to k-pairs, the more j overlaps k in Os.

The property we call *in-cover* concerns the extent to which all the incident roles of k are also incident roles of a dimension j. We say that a dimension j *in-covers* a dimension k if all the roles which are addressees of a k link, are also addressees of a j link.

$$\text{InCover}_{jk}(Os) = \frac{|IN_j^+ \cap IN_k^+|}{|IN_k^+|} \qquad (29)$$

with $|R_k|>0$ and the set IN_i^+ is defined as the set of all elements x in $Roles_i$ such that $1 \le id_i(x)$. The equation describes how many of the incident roles of k are also incident roles in j.

Equation 29 can be easily modified in order to capture analogous properties which we call *out-cover* and *chain*. The first indicates the extent to which all the roles with emanating links in a dimension k are also roles with emanating links in a dimension j. The second one concerns the extent to which a dimension j is 'incident' to the emanating links in a dimension k, in the sense that the roles with incident links in j contain the roles with emanating links in k.

$$\text{OutCover}_{jk}(Os) = \frac{|OUT_j^+ \cap OUT_k^+|}{|OUT_k^+|} \qquad (30)$$

$$\text{Chain}_{jk}(Os) = \frac{|IN_j^+ \cap OUT_k^+|}{|OUT_k^+|} \qquad (31)$$

Table 1.

Completeness$_{\text{Coord}}$	1	Overlap$_{\text{Coord-Pow}}$	1
Connectedness$_{\text{Coord}}$	1	Chain$_{\text{Contr-Pow}}$	1
Univocity$_{\text{Pow}}$	0	Chain$_{\text{Contr-Coord}}$	1
Unilaterality$_{\text{Coord}}$	0	InCover$_{\text{Contr-Coord}}$	1
Univocity$_{\text{Contr}}$	0	OutCover$_{\text{Pow-Contr}}$	1
Flatness$_{\text{Contr}}$	0	OutCover$_{\text{Pow-Coord}}$	1

with $|R_k|>0$, IN_i^+ is as defined above and OUT_i^+ is the set of all elements x in $Roles_i$ such that $1 \leq od_i(x)$. Notice that the chain measure can be viewed as an inter-structural version of the flatness measure.

Notice, finally, that all structural measures defined above range between 0 and 1 except economy which can get values higher than 1, but is still optimal at 1 (higher values determine over-efficiency). So, for all properties it holds that the closer we get to 1 the more optimal it is.

Before ending the section, it is worth noticing how the qualitative methods exposed in Section 4 interact with the quantitative ones exposed here.

The usefulness of these measures for capturing aspects of the structural interplay can already be shown in relation with Definition 10. Via the equations above, it is possible to provide a quantification of the degree to which a given Os adheres to the soundness principle concerning the interplay of the three dimensions of power, coordination and control. If we have $Detour_{Coord-Power}(Os)=1$ and $InCover_{Contr-Pow}(Os)=1$ then, following Definition 10, Os is sound. Lower degrees of these measures would mean lower adherence to the soundness principle. Notice also that maximum soundness is trivially obtained via an overlap of both coordination and control structures on the power structure: that is, if $Overlap_{Coord-Pow}(Os)=1$ and $Overlap_{Contr-Pow}(Os)=1$, then Os is (maximally) sound. This is a typical example of interaction of qualitative and quantitative method in the study of structure.

An Example

In order to illustrate the measures introduced in the previous sections, an example is provided and discussed.

Example 2. (Organisational structure)

Consider the Os depicted in Figure 2. It is specified as follows:

$Roles = \{a,b,c,d,e,f,g,h\}$
$R_{Pow} = \{(a,b),(a,c),(e,d),(f,g),(f,h)\}$
$R_{Coord} = \{(a,b),(a,c),(b,a),(c,a),(b,c),(c,b),(e,d),(f,g),(f,h)\}$
$R_{Contr} = \{(d,b),(e,a),(d,c),(f,g),(f,h)\}$

We have that: $Roles_{Pow} = Roles_{Coord} = Roles_{Contr} = \{a, b, c, d, e, f, g, h\}$.

The Os in Example 2 specifies an organization where two substructures A and B are connected via a symmetric coordination link. Following the terminology of Horling & Lesser (2004), it represents a form of *federation*.

Table 2.

Completeness$_{Pow}$	0	Completeness$_{Coord}$	1
Connectedness$_{Pow}$	0	Connectedness$_{Coord}$	1
Chain$_{Contr-Pow}$	1	OutCover$_{Pow-Contr}$	1

Substructure B is a typical form of highly centralized hierarchy: all connections move from the source f to the subordinated roles g and h. Indeed, it exhibits the optimal level of *efficiency, unilaterality, univocity* and *flatness* (equal to 1) for all three structural dimensions. Completeness and connectedness are also the same for all three dimensions, respectively equal to 2/6 and to 1. Besides, there is a full reciprocal *overlap* (equal to 1) of all the three dimensions which, as shown in Section 5.3, implies the soundness of the structure.

Substructure A contains disconnected power hierarchies composed by roles a, b and c and roles d and e. In fact, we have that $Completeness_{Pow}(A)=3/20$ and $Connectedness_{Pow}(A)=7/10$. The coordination structure is more complete than the power one, $Completeness_{Coord}(A)=7/20$, due to the full connection holding between roles a, b and c. It is easily seen that Os is not maximally sound since $InCover_{Contr-Pow}(A)=2/3$. This is due to the fact that role d is not object of control although it is subordinated, in the power structure, to role e. In case e would delegate a task to d, a failure in accomplishing this task would not be recovered. This would definitely constitute a weak spot in an organization designed according to this structure. Interestingly, there is minimum overlap between R_{Contr} and R_{Pow}: $Overlap_{Contr-Pow}(A)=0$. This embodies a sort of complete "*separation of concerns*" between the power and the control dimensions. Controller roles are never in a power position with respect to the controlled roles. This is obviously a sensible design requirement for preventing connivances between controllers and roles in power positions. On the other hand, $OutCover_{Pow-Contr}(A)=1/2$ and $OutCover_{Poord-Contr}(A)=1/2$ show that there are controllers in A (one out of two) which have the possibility to delegate tasks and communicate with other roles (role e). Worth noticing is also the following: $Chain_{Contr-Pow}(A)=1/2$. I.e., half the roles in a power position are subjected to control. Interestingly, the only uncontrolled role in a power position is the controller role e itself, and in fact no control of the controller is implemented: $Flatness_{Contr}(A)=1$.

After joining the two substructures via a symmetric coordination link between roles a and f, the resulting structural measures of Os are as listed in Figure 3.

None of the three dimensions is connected, and coordination is the most connected among the three. This means that within each dimension, there exist unrelated clusters of roles. In particular, the roles in a controlling position within substructure A cannot communicate with the rest of the federation. It follows that all dimensions display high values of economy and even over-efficiency, like in the case of power and control. As to the degree of unilaterality and univocity, power and control enjoy a degree equal to 1, and they thus display typically hierarchical features. On the other hand, coordination is highly reciprocal except, as we have already noticed, within substructure B, and it maintains a high degree of univocity keeping therefore a low level of redundancies in coordination as well. As to the interplay between the different dimensions, Os inherits the flaw of substructure A which prevents it from enjoying the maximum degree of $InCover_{Contr-Pow}$, jeopardizing soundness. Coordination, instead, fully overlaps power guaranteeing the necessary flow of communication along the paths of delegation.

Table 3.

Connectedness$_{Pow}$	1	Unilaterality$_{Pow}$	1
Economy$_{Pow}$	1	Univocity$_{Pow}$	1
Economy$_{Coord}$	1	Economy$_{Contr}$	1
Overlap$_{Coord-Pow}$	1	Overlap$_{Contr-Pow}$	1
Overlap$_{Pow-Coord}$	1	Overlap$_{Pow-Contr}$	1

STRUCTURAL EVALUATION OF AGENT ORGANIZATIONS

Considerations about structure have always been relevant both in organizational sciences and MAS for explaining why, for instance, a network-based organization is more flexible than a hierarchy. In order to provide quantitative grounds for such judgments, in this section the metrics developed in Section 5 are connected to criteria which are commonly used to evaluate organizations.

We focus on three criteria: robustness, flexibility and efficiency. It should be immediately stressed that we do not claim such criteria to be analyzable only on the basis of structural considerations. We rather address what, just by looking at the structure of an organization, can be said about its robustness, flexibility and efficiency. The semantics of power, coordination, and control given in Section III guides the link between the graph-theoretical metrics and the criteria considered.

The content of this section can be considered complementary to what discussed in Chapter XVIII "A Framework for Dynamic Agent Organizations" by Fatima and Wooldridge where different aspects concerning the performance of organizations (e.g. resource allocation) are formally studied.

Robustness

Stimson (1996) states that "robustness is simply a measure of how stable the yield is in the face of anticipated risks. [...]. Adding robustness thus adds complexity". Robustness requires redundancies in the structural dimensions used for dividing tasks within organizations, i.e., the power and the coordination structures. Redundancy for a power structure means, therefore, low values of the $Univocity_{Pow}$ measure, and for a coordination structure also a low degree of the $Unilaterality_{Coord}$ in order to allow for symmetric coordination links. In particular, symmetric coordination links can substitute broken power links allowing for bilateral negotiations of tasks to replace direct delegation. Therefore, a high $Overlap_{Coord-Pow}$ would be a sign of robustness. In general the more complete and more connected ($Completeness_{Coord}$ and $Connectedness_{Coord}$) the coordination structure is the more robust is the organization.

For the same reasons, the control structure plays an important role for the robustness of an organization allowing for failure detection and reaction. This requires that each role in the power and coordination structures is controlled, suggesting a high degree of $Chain_{Contr-Pow}$ and $Chain_{Contr-Coord}$ and also of $InCover_{Contr-Coord}$, i.e., the control of roles to which coordination links are directed. It is also sensible to require controlling roles to be in power positions in order to possibly delegate the tasks they might have to take over from the controlled agents. This aspect can be fostered by high values of $OutCover_{Pow-Contr}$, which also call for high values of $OutCover_{Pow-Coord}$ in order for the delegation to be followed by appropriate information.

Furthermore, every role in the control structure should have a high in-degree (every role is monitored by many other roles), which corresponds to a low level of $Univocity_{Contr}$. By requiring $Flatness_{Contr}$ to be low we force long control paths and thus increase the level in which controllers are, in turn, controlled. The following tables recapitulate the considerations above.

Getting back to the organizational structure Os discussed in the example in Section 5.4, we see that it is not very robust. Nevertheless, it does score well in the robustness-related measures concerning the interaction between the three structures: $OutCover_{Pow-Contr}(Os)=2/3$, $OutCover_{Pow-Coord}(Os)= 3/5$, $Chain_{Contr-Coord}(Os)=3/5$ and $InCover_{Contr-Coord}(Os)=5/6$.

Flexibility

We start again with a quote from organizational theory: "Flexible organizations are able to adapt to changing circumstances" (Schoemaker, 2003). The redistribution of tasks within an organization is normally achieved via delegation through the power structure. However, an articulated power structure constrains the distribution of tasks to predisposed patterns. This suggests that, for enhancing flexibility at a structural level, low degrees of both $Completeness_{Pow}$ and $Connectedness_{Pow}$ are required.

The control structure can also make an organization more flexible by linking different parts of the power structure. Whenever an agent enacting a role in the power structure fails in executing a task, its controller can react and has the power to redistribute the task. Structurally, this corresponds to high values of $Chain_{Contr-Pow}$ and $OutCover_{Pow-Contr}$.

Network organizations and teams, where no power structure exists, are commonly indicated as the paradigmatic example of flexible organizations (Powell, 1990). Within these organizations a complete coordination structure is essential in order to facilitate communication between all roles such that the best agent to handle a new task can always be found. Completeness and connectedness ($Completeness_{Coord}$ and $Connectedness_{Coord}$) are therefore also linked to the enhancement of flexibility.

These considerations are recapitulated in Table 2.

With respect to the flexibility of the structure Os in Example 2, we see that it has a small power structure (connectedness and completeness are very low) and a reasonably connected coordination structure (= 31/56). These two aspects both enhance flexibility. This is indeed what we would expect from a "federation". It scores well also w.r.t. the $OutCover$ measure between power and control: $OutCover_{Pow-Contr}(Os)=2/3$.

Efficiency

According to Etzioni (1964), efficiency mostly refers to the amount of resources used by the organization to perform its tasks. However, organizational structure plays a role in this sense, since "links are not without cost in a social system" Krackhardt (1994).

The existence of a power structure in the form of a tree guarantees efficient distribution of tasks. Such a structure is obtained imposing value 1 for all the following measures: $Connectedness_{Pow}$, $Economy_{Pow}$, $Unilaterality_{Pow}$ and $Univocity_{Pow}$. As to coordination and control, economy ($Economy$) should also be required to be 1 for the simple reason that this would minimize the amount of links (without forcing a disconnection). In addition, the most efficient way in order to guarantee soundness (Definition 10) consists in mirroring the power dimension, therefore obtaining high levels for all measures of overlap, that is: $Overlap$ w.r.t. the related dimensions of $Coord-Pow$, $Contr-Pow$, as well as $Pow-Coord$ and $Pow-Contr$ (overlap needs to hold in both directions in order to force coincidence). It follows that a fully hierarchical organization (such as substructure B in Example 2) where all structures follow the same pattern forms the most efficient organization possible from a structural perspective.

Again, our considerations are recapitulated in Table 3.

The structure Os of the example in Section 5.4 incorporates a very efficient power structure. Unilaterality and univocity are optimal (equal to 1), as well as the overlap between coordination and power. On the other hand, the power structure covers only a small fraction of the whole organization ($Connectedness_{Pow}(Os)=1/4$). As a consequence, distribution of tasks via delegation can only partially take place.

Structural Evaluation and Semantics

This section has illustrated a key feature of the study of organizations in terms of their structures, which consists in the possibility of easily applying graph-theoretical considerations. In fact, the design of a concrete MAS might aim at incorporating an organizational structure enjoying a desirable degree of some structural properties according to the metrics presented in the previous section.

At the same time, by relating structural links to state and transition type subsumptions as proposed in Section 3, it becomes possible to check how adding or removing a link, and thus changing the value of some structural property of an *Os*, modifies the system specification in terms of the corresponding terminological axioms. This can easily be done by comparing the TBox **T**(*Os*) of the organization before the links are added or removed, with the TBox **T**(*Os'*) after the modification of the structure. The possibility of formally accounting for this sort of design feedback is a direct result of the attribution of meaning to structural links as well as the study of organizational structure in terms of multi graphs.

RELATED AND FUTURE WORK

The section discusses some related work and points to some relevant future research lines.

Organizational Structure and Responsibility

The concept of responsibility is central to a theory of collective agency and organizations. The possibility to delegate tasks to subordinated agents, or to successfully inform other agents about the actual state of the organization, or the possibility to put effective monitoring and recovery mechanisms in place are all aspects influencing the assessment of responsibilities within organizations. If an agent is appointed to perform a specific task, but it does not get the necessary knowledge for correctly performing it, can it be held responsible for a failure in the execution of the plan? And in what sense precisely is it responsible? Again, if an agent is appointed to a task but it delegates it to a subordinated agent, does the failure of the subordinated agent determine a form of responsibility for the first agent? And in what sense? Some of these questions are addressed in Grossi et al. (2004) and Grossi, Royakkers & Dignum (2006). In a nutshell, the less a group of agents is organized, the more blurred becomes the assessment of responsibilities within the group. We use the notions of power coordination and control structure, with their formal meaning in order to ground four different notions of responsibility within organized groups of agents, which can be used to capture notions of responsibility in terms of liability as well as in terms of causality.

Fine-Tuning Structure and its Meaning

The chapter has been built on both semantic aspects and graph-theoretical aspects of organizational structures. There is still much to pursue in both directions.

The obvious question to be addressed from the graph-theoretical point of view is whether organizations can be designed which are robust, flexible and efficient (optimal in all properties). From a structural point of view and as intuition suggests, it is easy to show that this is not possible. Consider, for instance, the coordination structure. Maximum robustness and flexibility both require $Economy_{Coord}$ equal to 0, while maximum efficiency requires $Economy_{Coord}$ equal to 1:

	Robustness	Flexibility	Efficiency
$Economy_{Coord}$	0	0	1

Intuitively, both robustness and flexibility increase the number of structural links and thus the costs of the organizational overhead, while efficiency reduces these overhead costs. Similar problems exist, for instance, for the power structure. The robustness criterion requires as many redundancies as possible, and therefore low levels of univocity, while flexibility demands the structure to be as small as possible and therefore with very low degrees of completeness.

Since it is not possible to maximize the adherence to all properties at the same time choices should be made between the concurrent criteria. Should for instance flexibility be privileged over efficiency? An extensive analysis of the interdependencies between equations - could provide useful insights on this type of issues.

From the point of view of the study of the meaning of structural links far deeper analysis than the one proposed in Section 3 can be provided. In particular, the links give rise to a context of communication that takes place along those links. See e.g. (Dignum & Dignum, 2007) for a first approach to this issue.

CONCLUSION

The chapter has put forth some proposals in order to lay the ground for a formal theory of organizations based on the notion of organizational structure. Following foundational work on organization theory and in particular Morgenstern (1951), we stressed that organizational structures consist of a number of different relations among roles, and they can be represented and analyzed as multidigraphs. Two lines have then been pursued.

The first line has shown how to interpret the links holding between different roles in a structure in terms of labeled transition systems (Section 3): the existence of a link always expresses something about the actions that the agent playing that role can perform, or ought to perform, and what are the consequences of those actions. Finally, it has been shown that by committing to a formal interpretation of the links of an organizational structure it becomes possible to analytically motivate the reasonableness of certain graph-theoretical properties of structure, e.g. soundness (Definition 10).

The second line has addressed the issue of the influence of organizational structures on the performance of organizations, aiming at providing quantitative methods for analyzing, comparing and evaluating different types of structures. First we provided a number of measures for quantifying the adherence of organizational structures to specific graph-theoretical features (Section 3). Second, these measures have been put in relation to the organizational criteria of robustness, efficiency and flexibility of an organization (Section 6).

We argue that these two lines are both necessary to analyze organizations and that these lines together form a sound basis for such analysis.

ACKNOWLEDGMENT

The authors would like to thank the co-authors of some of the works upon which this chapter has been built, namely, John-Jules Meyer, Virginia Dignum, Mehdi Dastani and Lamber Royakkers.

REFERENCES

Baader, F., Calvanese, D., McGuinness, D., Nardi, D., & Patel-Schneider, P. (2002). The description logic handbook. Cambridge: Cambridge University Press.

Baltag, A., & Moss, L. (2004). Logic for epistemic programs. Synthese, 139(2), 165–224. (Special issue on Logic, Rationality and Action)

Boissier, O., et al. (Eds.). (2006). Coordination, organizations, institutions, and norms in multi-agent systems. Proceedings of anirem 2005 and ooop 2005 (No.3913). Utrecht, The Netherlands: Springer. (Revised and selected papers)

Bresciani, P., Giorgini, P., Giunchiglia, F., Mylopoulos, J., & Perini, A. (2004). Tropos: An agent-oriented software development methodology. Journal of Autonomous Agents and Multi-Agent Systems, 8(3), 203–236.

Broek, E. L. van der, Jonker, C. M., Sharpanskykh, A., Treur, J., & Yolum, P. (2005, July). Formal modeling and analysis of organizations. In O. Boissier, V. Dignum, E. Matson, & J. Sichman (Eds.), Proceedings ofthe international workshop on organizations in multi-agent systems (ooop). Utrecht.

Broersen, J. (2003). Modal action logics for reasoning about reactive systems. Siks dissertation series no. 2003-2, Vrije Universiteit Amsterdam, Amsterdam, The Netherlands.

Castelfranchi, C. (2003). The micro-macro constitution of power. ProtoSociology,18, 208–268.

Decker, K., & Lesser, V. (1995). Designing a family of coordination algorithms. In V. Lesser (Ed.), Proceedings of icmas'95 (pp. 73–80). San Francisco, CA, USA: The MIT Press: Cambridge, MA, USA.

Dignum, F. (1999). Autonomous agents with norms. Artificial Intelligence and Law, 7, 69–79.

Dignum, F., Dignum, V., Koenig, S., Kraus, S., Singh, M. P., & Wooldridge, M. (Eds.). (2005, July, 25-29). The 4th international joint conference on autonomous agents and multiagent systems (aamas 2005). Utrecht, The Netherlands: ACM Press.

Dignum, V. (2003). A model for organizational interaction. SIKS Dissertation Series. Utrecht University, Utrecht, The Netherlands.

Dignum, V. Dignum, F. (2007). Coordinating tasks in agent organizations. or: Can we ask you to read this paper? In Dignum, V., et al. (Eds.). (2007). Coordination, organizations, institutions and norms in agent systems II, LNAI 4386. Springer.

Etzioni, A. (1964). Modern organizations. Prentice Hall.

Fox, M. S. (1988). An organizational view of distributed systems. Distributed Artificial Intelligence, 140–150.

Friedell, M. F. (1967). Organizations as semilattices. American Sociological Review, 32, 46–54.

Giddens, A. (1984). Social theory and modern sociology. Polity Press.

Gini, M., Ishida, T., Castelfranchi, C., & Johnson, W. L. (Eds.). (2002, July 15-19). The 1st international joint conference on autonomous agents & multiagent systems (aamas 2002). Bologna, Italy: ACM Press.

Grossi, D. (2007). Designing invisible handcuffs. formal investigations in institutions and organizations for multi-agent systems. PhD thesis, Utrecht University, SIKS.

Grossi, D., Dignum, F., Dastani, M., & Royakkers, L. (2005, July). Foundations of organizational structures in multiagent systems. In Proceedings of aamas'05, fourth international joint conference on autonomous agents and multiagent systems (pp. 690–697). ACM Press.

Grossi, D., Dignum, F., Dignum, V., Dastani, M., & Royakkers, L. (2006, May). Structural evaluation of agent organizations. In G. Weiss & P. Stone (Eds.), Proceedings of the 5th international joint conference on autonomous agents and multiagent systems (aamas 2006) (p. 1110 - 1112). Hakodate, Japan: ACM Press.

Grossi, D., Dignum, F., Dignum, V., Dastani, M., & Royakkers, L. (2007). Structural aspects of the evaluation of agent organizations. In V. Dignum et.al. (Eds.), Preproceedings coordination, organizations, institutions, and norms in multi-agents systems (coin 2006) (pp. 3–18). Springer.

Grossi, D., Dignum, F., & Meyer, J.-J.Ch. (2007, May). A formal road from institutional norms to organizational structures. In Proceedings of 6th international joint conference on autonomous agents and multiagent systems, aamas 2007. Honolulu, Hawai'i, US.

Grossi, D., Dignum, F., Royakkers, L., & Meyer, J.-J. C. (2004). Collective obligations and agents: Who gets the blame? In A. Lomuscio & D. Nute (Eds.), Proceedings of deon'04 (pp. 129–145).

Grossi, D., Royakkers, L., & Dignum, F. (2006). Organizational structure and responsibility: An analysis in a dynamic logic of organized collective agency. (To appear in the Journal of Artificial Intelligence and Law)

Hannoun, M., Boissier, O., Sichman, J. S., & Sayettat, C. (2000). MOISE: An organizational model for multi-agent systems. In IBERAMIA-SBIA (p. 156-165).

Harary, F. (1959a). Graph theoretic methods in the management sciences. Managemenet Science, 5(4), 387–403.

Harary, F. (1959b). Status and contrastatus. Sociometry, 22(1), 23–43.

Harary, F., Norman, R., & Cartwright, D. (1965). Structural models: An introduction to the theory of directed graphs. New York: JohnWiley & Sons.

Hohfeld, W. N. (1911). Some fundamental legal conceptions as applied in judicial reasoning. Yale Law Journal, 23(16), 16–59.

Horling, B., & Lesser, V. (2004). A Survey of Multi-Agent Organizational Paradigms (Computer Science Technical Report No. 04-45). University of Massachusetts.

Horling, B., & Lesser, V. (2005). Using ODML to model and design organizations for multi-agent systems. In O. Boissier, V. Dignum, E. Matson, & J. Sichman (Eds.), Proceedings ofthe international workshop on organizations in multi-agent systems (ooop). Utrecht, The Netherlands.

Horrocks, I., Kutz, O., & Sattler, U. (2006). The even more irresistible SROIQ. In P. Doherty, J. Mylopoulos, & C.Welty (Eds.), Proceedings of the 10th international conference on principles of knowledge representation and reasoning (kr 2006) (pp. 57–67). Menlo Park, California: AAAI Press.

Hübner, J. F., Sichman, J. S., & Boissier, O. (2002). Moise+: Towards a structural functional and deontic model for mas organization. In Proceedings of the first joint conference on autonomous agents and multi-agent systems (aamas'02). Bologna, Italy: ACM Press.

Ioerger, T., & Johnson, C. (2001). A formal model of responsibilities in agent-based teamwork. In Proceedings of the fifth international conference on autonomous agents, montreal, canada. ACM Press.

Jennings, N. R., Sierra, C., Sonnenberg, L., & Tambe, M. (Eds.). (2004, August 19-23). The 3rd international joint conference on autonomous agents and multiagent systems (aamas 2004). New York, NY, USA: IEEE Computer Society.

Jones, A. J. I., & Sergot, M. (1996). A formal characterization of institutionalised power. Journal of the IGPL, 3, 427–443.

Kamps, J., & Marx, M. (2002, June 9-12). Notions of indistinguishability for semantic web languages. In I. Horrocks & J. A. Hendler (Eds.), Proceedings of the semantic web - iswc 2002, first international semantic web conference (pp.30–38). Sardinia, Italy: Springer.

Kozen, D. D. Harel amd, & Tiuryn, J. (1984). Dynamic logic. In D. Gabbay & F. Guenthner (Eds.), Handbook of philosophical logic: Volume ii: Extensions of classical logic (p. 497-604). Dordrecht, The Netherlands: Reidel.

Krackhardt, D. (1994). Graph theoretical dimensions of informal organizations. In C. M. Carley & M. J. Prietula (Eds.), Computational organization theory (pp.89–110). Lawrence Erlbaum Associates.

Malone, T., & Smith, S. A. (1988). Modeling the performance of organizational structures. Operational Research, 36(3), 421–436.

Malone, T. W. (1987). Modeling coordination in organizations and markets. Manageement Sciences, 33(10), 1317–1332.

Meyer, J., & Hoek, W. van der. (1995). Epistemic logic for ai and computer science (Vol. 41). Cambridge University Press.

Meyer, J.-J.Ch. (1988). A di_erent approach to deontic logic: Deontic logic viewed as a variant of dynamic logic. Notre Dame Journal of Formal Logic, 29(1), 109–136.

Morgenstern, O. (1951). Prolegomena to a theory of organizations. Manuscript. Available from http://qss.stanford.edu/~godfrey/Morgenstern/prolegom.pdf

Pitt, J. (1999). ALFEBIITE project. European Project. Available from http://www.iis.ee.ic.ac.uk/~alfebiite/ab-overview-page.htm (IST 1999 10298) Powell, W. W. (1990). Neither market nor hierarchy: Network forms of organizations. Research in Organizational Behavior, 12, 295–336.

Rosenschein, G. S., Wooldridge, M., Sandholm, T., & Yokoo, M. (Eds.). (2003, July, 14-18). The 2nd international joint conference on autonomous agents & multiagent systems (aamas 2003). Melbourne, Victoria, Australia: ACM Press.

Ruiter, D. W. P. (1997). A basic classification of legal institutions. Ratio Juris, 10, 357–371.

Sartor, G. (2006). Fundamental legal concepts: A formal and teleological characterization. Artificial Intelligence and Law, 14, 101–142.

Scerri, P., Xu, Y., Liao, E., Lai, J., & Sycara, K. (2004, July). Scaling teamwork to very large teams. In Proceedings of the third international joint conference on autonomous agents and multiagent systems (aamas'04). New York, NY: ACM Press.

Schoemaker, M. (2003). Identity in flexible organizations: Experiences. In Dutch organizations creativity and innovation management (Vol. 12). Searle, J. (1969). Speech acts. an essay in the philosophy of language. Cambridge: Cambridge University Press.

Searle, J. (1995). The construction of social reality. Free Press.

Selznick, P. (1948). Foundations of the theory of organization. American Sociological Review, 13, 25–35.

So, Y., & Chon, K. (2005, July). A performance model for tree-structuresd multiagent organizations in faulty environments. In O. Boissier, V. Dignum, E. Matson, & J. Sichman (Eds.), Proceedings ofthe international workshop on organizations in multi-agent systems (ooop). Utrecht, The Netherlands.

Stimson, W. (1996). The robust organization: Transforming your company using adaptive design. Irwin Professional Publishing.

van Benthem, J., Eijck, J. van, & Stebletsova, V. (1994). Modal logic, transition systems and processes. Journal of Logic and Computation, 4(5), 811-855.

Vàzquez-Salceda, J. (2004). The role of norms and electronic institutions in multiagent systems. Birkh¨auser Verlag.

Weiss, G.,&Stone, P. (Eds.). (2006, May, 8-12). The 5th international joint conference on autonomous agents and multiagent systems (aamas 2006). Hakodate, Japan: ACM Press.

Wooldridge, M., & Jennings, N. R. (1995). Intelligent agents: Theory and practice. Knowledge Engineering Review, 10(2), 115–152.

Zambonelli, F., Jennings, N., &Wooldridge, M. (2003). Developing multiagent systems: the GAIA methodology. ACM Transactions on Software Engineering and Methodology, 12(3), 317–370

KEY TERMS

Control: It is the structural dimension concerning the supervision of tasks within the organization.

Coordination: It is the structural dimension concerning the flow of information within the organization.

Efficiency: It is the property of organizations concerning their ability to carry out their tasks with minimal amount of resources. The structural aspects of efficiency can be exactly quantified with graph-theoretical methods.

Enactment Link: It is a link connecting an agent to a role. An agent enacting a role is called role-enacting agent.

Flexibility: It is the property of organizations concerning their ability to adapt to different operative situations. The structural aspects of flexibility can be exactly quantified with graph-theoretical methods.

Institutional Link: It is a link in an organizational structure whose semantics is given in terms of normative notions such as obligation.

Mentalistic Link: It is a link in an organizational structure whose semantics is given in terms of epistemic/doxastic notions such as knowledge.

Power: It is the structural dimension concerning the delegation of tasks within the organization.

Robustness: It is the property of organizations concerning their stability in front of potential failures. The structural aspects of robustness can be exactly quantified with graph-theoretical methods.

ENDNOTES

[1]   See Horling & Lesser (2004) for a survey.

[2]   Alternatively, EC can be represented as a (partial) function.

[3]   Notice that these kind of axioms cannot be bridge axioms.

[4]   See Castelfranchi (2003) for a comprehensive overview of this issue.

[5]   The reason for this restriction is that we want to keep the alphabet of the language finite.

[6]   Equations 22, 23 and 24 below are an adaptation of equations presented in Krakhardt (1994). The rest is our original contribution.

[7]   In mathematical sociology the study of the interaction of a number of different social relations within a social structure has often be indicated as crucial:
      An actual group of people generally has more than one relation simultaneously operating. [...] The study of the influence of various relations on each other is in its infancy. However, this appears to be an extremely important field of endeavor (Harary, 1959a, p.402).
      Such issue has remained—to our knowledge—hardly investigated.

Chapter IX
A Logic for Agent Organizations

Virginia Dignum
Utrecht University, The Netherlands

Frank Dignum
Utrecht University, The Netherlands

ABSTRACT

Organization concepts and models are increasingly being adopted for the design and specification of multi-agent systems. Agent organizations can be seen as mechanisms of social order, created to achieve common goals for more or less autonomous agents. In order to develop a theory on the relationship between organizational structures, organizational actions, and actions of agents performing roles in the organization, we need a theoretical framework to describe and reason about organizations. The formal model presented in this chapter is sufficiently generic to enable the comparison of different existing organizational approaches to Multi-Agent Systems (MAS), while having enough descriptive power to describe realistic organizations.

INTRODUCTION

Organizing is important in distributed computational systems, just as it is important in human systems. Researchers, within both the computer science and the organization theory fields, agree that many concepts and ideas can be shared between the two disciplines to better understand human organizations and to design more efficient and flexible distributed systems (So and Durfee; 1998; Cohen, 1986; Fox, 1981). However, due to its nature, organizational theory research tends to be not very formal from a computational perspective, which makes it difficult when moving from its use as a concept or paradigm towards using social and organizational concepts for the formalization of social concepts in Multi-Agent Systems (MAS).

Given such different views, the difficulty of comparing, analyzing and choosing a given approach becomes clear. Even if our aim is not to solve this problem, in this chapter we present initial steps towards the specification of a formal model for the study of agent organizations. The motivations for this model are twofold. On the one hand, the need for a formal representation of organizations, with their environment, objectives and agents in a way that enables to analyze their partial contributions to the performance of the organization in a changing environment. On the other hand, such a model must be realistic enough to incorporate the more 'pragmatic' considerations faced by real organizations. Most existing formal models lack this realism, e.g. either by ignoring temporal issues, or by taking a very restrictive view on the controllability of agents, or by assuming complete control and knowledge within the system (cf. Wooldridge, van der Hoek, 2005; Santos et al, 1997). Formal models for organizations that are able to deal with realistic situations, must thus meet at least the following requirements (Dignum, Tick, 2007):

1. represent notions of ability and activity of agents, without requiring knowledge about the specific actions available to a specific agent
2. accept limitedness of agent capability
3. represent the ability and activity of a group of agents
4. deal with temporal issues, in special the fact that activity takes time
5. represent the concept of responsibility for the achievement of a given state of affairs
6. represent organizational (global) goals and its link to agents' activity, by relating activity and organizational structure

All of the above requirements are related to the more structural properties of an organization and will be met with the theory developed in this chapter. Furthermore, the following requirements are needed to enable complete representation and analysis of organization:

7. deal with resource limitedness and the dependency of activity on resources (e.g. costs)
8. represent organizational dynamics (evolution of organization over time, changes on agent population)
9. represent organizations in terms of organizational roles or positions
10. relate roles and agents (role enacting agents)
11. deal with normative issues (representation of boundaries for action and the violation thereof)

These requirements are related to the more operational aspects of an organization. E.g. the notion that agent activity has a cost (that is, choosing one or the other course of action is not only dependent on agent capabilities but also the costs of the action must compare positively to its benefits) is related to actual performance of an agent within the organizational structure (Dastani et al., 2003, Grossi et al, 2007a, Vazquez-Salceda et al., 2005). Due to space limitations we will not deal with these requirements in this chapter. Some related research on the analysis of organizational structures is presented in Chapter VIII, "Structural Aspects of Organization" by Grossi and F. Dignum.

This chapter is organized as follows. In section 2 we discuss related work and motivate the need for the formal language. In section 3 we define ability and activity of agents and groups. Section 4 presents the formal model for organization including structural and interaction properties. The use of our language for the modeling of organizations is exemplified in section 5. Finally, section 6 presents our conclusions and directions for future work.

RELATED WORK

Several approaches have already been presented to investigate the complexity of reasoning and analysis of multi-agent systems. In their own way, all approaches are concerned with some of the requirements above and can be basically divided into two categories: formal methods and engineering frameworks. Formal methods for MAS have a logical basis, typically based on dynamic, deontic and/or temporal logics (Wooldridge and van der Hoek, 2005; Santos et al, 1997; Governatori et al, 2002). However, the treatment of organizational concepts is basic and lacks realism. For instance, approaches based on ATL assume complete division of agent capabilities and total control over the domain, and the work presented in (Santos et al, 1997) lacks temporal issues. Furthermore, in most cases, an axiomatic formalization is provided but not a formal semantics. Engineering frameworks such as those presented in Chapters III, IV and V of this book, provide sound representation languages that include many realistic organizational concepts, However such approaches have often a limited formal semantic basis, which makes analysis and comparison difficult (Hübner et al, 2006; McCallum et al, 2006; van den Broek et al, 2006).

Organization Theory provides very useful concepts, and a pragmatic perspective, based on real world (human) organizations (Duncan, 1979; Mintzberg, 1993; Simon, 1991). However, results are often domain oriented and it is not clear how to translate them into formalisms for agent systems. It is often seen as a sound basis for conceptual design, proven in practice of human organizations for many years, but it must be formalized in order to make it usable for computational models of organizations. Computational organizational science is a new perspective that tries to combine the organization theory and engineering framework perspectives. It looks at groups, organizations and societies and aims to understand, predict and manage system level change (Carley, 2002). Several tools for the analysis and modeling of organizations have been proposed. Computational models, in particular those based on representation techniques and empirical simulation, have been widely used for several decades to analyze and solve organizational level problems. More recently, mathematical tools, including those of decision and game theory, probability and logic are becoming available to handle multiple agency approaches to organizations.

In practice, organizational level solutions are provided by mathematical a computational models based on probabilistic and decision theoretic approaches. A large body of work in this area is that of computational simulation, specifically agent-based social simulation (ABSS) (Davidsson, 2002). Computational simulations are based on formal models, in the sense that they provide a precise theoretical formulation of relationships between variables. Simulations provide a powerful way to analyze and construct realistic models of organizational systems and make possible to study problems that are not easily addressed by other scientific approaches (Harrison et al., 2007). Such formal models are however limited to the specific domain and difficult to validate. Techniques are thus needed that make possible the formal validation, comparison and extendibility of simulation models. As far as we are aware of, the language presented in this chapter, based on modal logic is a first attempt to provide such a meta-model for reasoning about computational models that has both a formal semantics as well as the capability to represent realistic concepts.

AGENTS AND GROUPS: CAPABILITY, ABILITY AND ACTIVITY

The notions of agent capability and action have been widely discussed in MAS. The intuition is that an agent possesses capabilities that make action possible. In the literature, there are many approaches to the formalization of these definitions[1]. Concerning the theory of action, two main perspectives can be distinguished. The first aims at the explicit representation of action by a specific agent, in terms of dynamic logic (Harel, 1984; Meyer, 2000), or situation calculus (MacCarthy, 1969); whereas the second is concerned with representing the fact that a certain result has been achieved, such as in the *stit* theories (Pörn, 1974) or in the notion of agency by Elgesem (1997). In both types of approaches, the notion of action is strongly linked to that of ability. However, there is no consensus on the meaning of capability which is taken to mean competence (the skill of making a certain proposition true), possibility (conditions are right for that activity), opportunity (both competence and possibility), or even permission (there are no prohibitions or constraints on the activity). As these distinctions are important for organizational theory, we aim to develop a theory in which all these concepts can be expressed properly.

Logic for Agent Organization

We present here a *logic for agent organization* (LAO), as an extension of the well-known branching time temporal logic CTL (Emerson, 1990). LAO includes the CTL modalities $\Diamond$ ('always in the future'), U ('until') and X ('in the next state') extended with modalities for agent ability, capability, attempt and activity introduced in the following subsections. For a set Φ of propositional variables, the language, L for LAO is the smallest superset of Φ such that:

- *true, false* $\in L$
- $p \in \Phi \Rightarrow p \in L$
- $\varphi, \psi \in L \Rightarrow \neg\varphi, (\varphi\vee\psi), X\varphi, \psi U\varphi, \Diamond\varphi \in L$

To give a precise definition of LAO, we start by introducing the semantic structures over which formulae of LAO are interpreted. A LAO model is a tuple $M = (\Phi, A, W, R, T, \pi)$, where:

- Φ is a finite, non-empty set of *propositional variables*,
- $A = \{a_1, ..., a_n\}$ is a finite, non-empty set of *agents*,
- W is a non empty set of states,
- R is a partial ordered set of (temporal) transitions between two elements of W, R: $W \times W$,
- T is the set of agent labels on elements of R, $T:R \rightarrow 2^A$,
- π is a valuation function which associates each $w \in W$ with the set of atomic propositions from Φ that are true in that world, $\pi : W \rightarrow 2^\Phi$

Each world, $w \in W$ describes the propositions of Φ that are true in that world, and, each proposition in Φ corresponds to a set of worlds where it is true. A transition between worlds represents an update of the truth value of (some) propositions in Φ. The semantics of LAO are based on those of CTL* (Emerson, 1990), which distinguishes between path and state formulae. A state formula is interpreted with respect to a state $w \in W$ and a path formula is interpreted with respect to a path through the branching time structure given by R. A path (or trace) in R is a (possibly infinite) sequence $(w_i, w_{i+1}, ...)$, where $w_i, w_{i+1} \in W$ and $\forall i:(s_i, s_{i+1}) \in R$. We use the convention that $r = (w_0, w_1, ...)$ denotes a path, and $t(i)$ denotes state i in path r. We write $M, w \models \varphi$ (resp. $M, r \models \varphi$) to denote that state formula φ (resp. path formula φ) is true in structure M at state w (resp. path r). The rules for the satisfaction relation $\models$ for state and path formulae in LAO are defined as:

- $M, w \models \top$
- $M, w \models p$ iff $p \in \pi(w)$, where $p \in \Phi$
- $M, w \models \neg\varphi$ iff not $M, w \models \varphi$
- $M, w \models \varphi \vee \psi$ iff $M, w \models \varphi$ or $M, w \models \psi$
- $M, w \models \Diamond\varphi$ iff $\forall r \in paths(W,R): r(0) = s$ then $M, r \models \varphi$
- $M, r \models p$ iff $M, r(0) \models p$
- $M, r \models \neg\varphi$ iff not $M, r \models \varphi$
- $M, r \models \varphi \vee \psi$ iff $M, r \models \varphi$ or $M, r \models \psi$
- $M, r \models \psi \, U \, \varphi$ iff $\exists \, i$ such that $M, r(i) \models \varphi$ and $\forall \, k \leq i$, $M, r(k) \models \psi$
- $M, r \models X\varphi$ iff $\forall \, r': (r,r') \in R$ then $M, r' \models \varphi$

This semantic definition above does not consider the agents in the system, and therefore does not make use of the semantic component T. Intuitively, the idea is that, in organizations, changes are for some part result of the intervention of (specific) agents. Formally, state transitions are labeled with the set of agents that influence the changes on that transition. That is, for a transition $r = (w,w') \in R$, $t(r)$ indicates the set of agents that indeed contribute to the changes indicated by that transition. Moreover, for each world $w \in W$ and each agent $a \in A$, we can indicate the set of transitions from w for which a has influence.

Definition 1 (Transition influence)

Given a world $w \in W$ and an agent $a \in A$, the transition influence of a in w, T_{aw}, is defined by: $T_{aw} = \{r \in R: r = (w,w')$ and $a \in t(r)\}$.

Agent action is based on the capabilities of the agent, but also on the moment circumstances in which the agent is. In the following, we will introduce extra modal operators to represent capability, ability, attempt and action of agents and groups.

Agent Capability, Ability and Activity

In this section, we draw from work in the area of the well known logical theory for agency and organized interaction introduced by Kanger-Lindahl-Pörn, more specifically from the work of (Santos et al., 1997) and (Governatori et al., 2002). In short, they assume that in organizations not all capabilities are always conductive of successful action - one can attempt to achieve something but without success. They've introduced three operators E, G and H. The first one, E, expresses direct and successful actions: a formula like $E_i\varphi$ means that the agent i *brings it about* that φ, that is, φ is a necessary result of an action by i. The second one, $G_i\varphi$, corresponds to indirect and successful actions, that is, $G_i\varphi$ means that i *ensures* that φ, that is, φ is a necessary result of an action of some agent following an action by i. Finally, their intended meaning of H is such that $H_i\varphi$ means that i *attempts* to make it the case that φ. The idea is that H is not necessarily successful.

In their work, an axiomatic definition of E, G and H is given. Our approach is to provide a semantic definition of the modal operators for capability, ability attempt and activity. Moreover, we agree with (Governatori et al., 2002) that the assumption taken in Santos et al., 1997) that indirect action always implies the impossibility for direct action is rather strong, and will not use it. We furthermore, base our definitions on temporal logic and not just in predicate logic in order to be able to express the notion that activity takes time.

Intuitively, in order to talk about agent activity, that is, that agent a 'causes' an expression φ to hold in some future state in a path from the current moment, we need to establish the control of the agent over the truth value of φ. For instance, it does not make sense to express $E_i sun\text{-}raises$ because whether the sun raises or not is not something that an agent can control. Control over a formula φ, or part of a state requires two things. On the one hand, the capability for φ (that is, the intrinsic skill to perform φ) and, on the other hand the ability for φ (that is, the extrinsic conditions to achieve φ). For example, I may have the capability of writing a letter, because I know how to write, but currently not have the ability, because I just happen not to have a pen with me (or a computer, or a pencil). In the following, we present the formal definition of capability and of ability that are necessary to later define agent activity and attempt. Inspired by the work of (Boutelier, 2004), and (Cholvy and Garion, 2001), we define the capabilities of an agent a as follows:

Definition 2 (Agent propositional capability)

Given a set of atomic propositions Φ and a set of agents A, for each agent $a \in A$ we partition Φ in two classes: the set of atomic propositions that agent a is capable of realizing, C_a, and the set of atomic propositions that a cannot realize, $\overline{C_a}$, where $\overline{C_a} = \Phi \setminus C_a$.

In order to be able to formally refer to the capability of an agent to realize any given expression of L, we need first to extend the above definition to describe the capability for composed propositions. Given a set C_a defining the propositional capability of a, we define Σ_a inductively as follows:

- $p \in C_a : p \in \Sigma_a$
- $p \in C_a : \neg p \in \Sigma_a$
- $\psi_1, \psi_2 \in C_a : \psi_1 \wedge \psi_2 \in \Sigma_a$

Agent capability $C_a \varphi$ can now be defined as:

Definition 3 (Agent capability)

Given a formula φ in L and an agent $a \in A$, agent a is capable of φ, represented by $C_a \varphi$ iff $\not\models \varphi$ and $\exists \psi \in \Sigma_a$, such that $\psi \to \varphi$.

Using this definition, it is trivial to prove that $\forall \psi \in \Sigma_a : C_a \psi$. Agent capability has the following properties:

- $\neg C_a \top$
- $C_a \varphi \wedge C_a \psi \to C_a (\varphi \wedge \psi)$

Note that $C_a \varphi \to C_a \neg \varphi$ does not hold as it can be seen by the following counterexample. Consider $\Phi = \{p,q\}$, $\varphi = (p \vee q)$ and $C_a p$. Then, $C_a (p \vee q)$, because $p \to p \vee q$. But $\neg C_a (\neg p \wedge \neg q)$, because $\neg (\neg p \to (\neg p \wedge \neg q))$. In the same way, it can be proven that $C_a \varphi \to \Diamond \varphi$ also does not hold.

Figure 1. Example of capability, ability and attempt

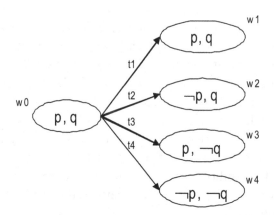

The definition of agent capability above enables the development of a very powerful framework for the specification of organizations as will be seen in the next sections. LAO provides an elegant and realistic approach to different domains. In particular, it enables multiple control over any formula, that several agents can independently control the same expression. This is a crucial and important difference with, e.g. ATL that restricts control over formulae to a single agent or coalition of agents (van der Hoek and Wooldridge, 2005). I.e. in ATL $\langle\!\langle\, C \,\rangle\!\rangle\, \varphi$ means that the coalition C can achieve φ no matter what agents outside C do. This is not the case in LAO.

Given a capability $C_a\varphi$, we can say that agent a controls φ, which means that a is able (possibly under certain conditions) to make φ hold. However, capabilities do not lead directly to ability. Intuitively, the ability of an agent to realize a state of affairs φ in a world w, depends not only on the capability of the agent but also on the status of that world. Therefore, we define the ability of a as follows:

Definition 4 (Agent ability)

Given a world $w \in W$ and an agent $a \in A$, the ability of a to realize φ, $G_a\varphi$, is defined by $w \models G_a\varphi$ iff $C_a\varphi$ and $\exists\, t \in T_{aw}: t = (w,w')$ and $w' \models \varphi$.

Agent ability refers to the potential of that agent to act in a world. However, intuitively, the expected result of agent action is that the desired state of affairs will hold in all worlds reachable from the current world. That is, that the agent will indeed influence the future worlds. Obviously, if the agent does not influence all futures from the current world, it cannot guarantee the overall success of its activity. We therefore define agent attempt, as follows:

Definition 5 (Agent attempt)

Given a world $w \in W$ and an agent $a \in A$, the attempt of a to realize φ, $H_a\varphi$, is defined by $w \models H_a\varphi$ iff $G_a\varphi$ and $\forall\, t \in T_{aw}: t = (w,w')$ and $w' \models \varphi$.

Attempt contains an element of uncertainty. Even if it is necessary that the agent has the capability to achieve a certain state of affairs, it can happen that, due to activity by other agents, with the same capability, the state of affairs will not hold in all worlds whose transitions are under the influence of the agent. That is, the definition of attempt yields that, in the case that there are other agents capable of realizing φ, those agents either have no influence over transitions in T_{aw} or also made an attempt to achieve φ. Formally:

- *If $w |= H_a\varphi$ then $\forall\, b \in A: b \neq a: (\neg C_b\varphi \vee H_b\varphi \vee (\forall\, t \in T_{aw}, t \notin T_{bw}))$*

As an example, consider the model $M = (\{p, q\}, \{a\}, \{w_0, ..., w_4\}, \{(w_0, w_1), ..., (w_0, w_4)\}, T, \pi)$, as depicted in Figure 1. M is further so that $C_a p$ and $(w_0, w_1) \in T_{aw0}$. In this model, it holds that:

- *$w_0 |= G_a p$ (because $C_a p$ and $w_1 |= p$);*
- *$w_0 |= H_a p$ iff $T_a w = \{(w_0, w_1), (w_0, w_3)\}$;*
- *not ($w_0 |= C_a(p \wedge q)$);*
- *not ($w_0 |= G_a(p \wedge q)$, because $\neg C_a(p \wedge q)$;*

The fact that an agent a has the capability to bring φ about does not mean that the agent will indeed ever do it. In fact, the agent also needs the ability (based on circumstantial conditions) for φ. On the other hand, the notion of attempt expresses the fact that an agent tries to achieve a certain state of affairs, but does not guarantee success. Obviously, agents must be able to *act* on the world and as such bring states of affairs to happen.

Because we abstract from the internal motivations of individual agents, we need ways to describe the result of agent action that are independent of particular actions available to the agent. The *stit* operator, $E_a\varphi$, introduced by (Pörn, 1974) allows referring to the externally `observable' consequences of an action instead of the action itself. *Stit* can be seen as an abstract representation of the family of actions that result in φ. In our approach we refine the definition of *stit* to include a temporal component that indicates the notion that action takes time.

Only when the agent influences all possible worlds out of the current one, we can say that the agent can see to it that a given state of affairs is achieved. In the special case in which all next possible states from a given state are influenced by an agent a, we say that a is **in-control** in w, represented by IC_a and defined formally as:

Definition 6 (Agent In-control)

Given a world $w \in W$ and an agent $a \in A$, a is in control in w, $IC_{a,,}$ iff $w |= IC_a$ iff $\forall\, w': (w,w') \in R \Rightarrow (w,w') \in T_{aw}$.

In the following we give our semantics of *stit*, in terms of agent attempt (definition 5) and in-control (definition 6)[2].

Definition 7 (Agent activity)

Given a world $w \in W$ and an agent $a \in A$, a sees to it that φ holds, $E_a\varphi$, is defined by $w |= E_a\varphi$ iff $H_a\varphi$ and IC_a.

$E_a\varphi$ represents the actual action of bringing φ about. From the semantics above: if a is able of φ and attempts to realize it in a world where it is in control, then $E_a\varphi$ 'causes' φ to be true in all next states from the current state. Furthermore, it is important to notice that we provide a temporal definition of $E_a\varphi$, that is, $\neg(E_a\varphi \to \varphi)$ but $(E_a\varphi \to X\varphi)$. This provides a more realistic notion of *stit* by incorporating the fact that action takes time and is not instantaneous, as we have discussed before (cf. Dignum et al., 2003) but is different from many other authors, e.g. (Santos et al., 1997).

The operator E has the following properties:

- $\neg E_a T$
- $E_a\varphi \to X\varphi$
- $E_a\varphi \to C_a\varphi$
- $E_a\varphi \to H_a\varphi$
- $E_a\varphi \to IC_a$
- $E_a\varphi \wedge E_a\psi \to E_a(\varphi \wedge \psi)$

Group Capability, Ability and Activity

By definition, agents are limited in their capabilities, that is, on what states of affairs they can bring about in the world. This implies that in MAS certain states of affairs can only be reached if two or more agents cooperate to bring that state about. One of the main ideas behind organizations is the notion that the combined action of two or more agents can result in an effect that none of the involved agents could bring about by themselves. In MAS there is very little research done on the notion of ability in a multi-agent context (Cholvy et al., 2005). In the following, we define the concept of combined capability, or *group capability*. As for single agents, we need to start by defining the capabilities of a group over atomic propositions. The idea behind this definition is that atomic propositions can be made 'small' enough to be controlled by a single agent. A group combines results from different agents into more complex actions.

Definition 8 (Group propositional capability)

Given a set of agents $Z=\{a_1,...,a_n\} \subseteq A$ and the sets C_{a_i} of atomic propositions controllable by each agent $a_i \in Z$, we define C_Z as the union of the controllable propositions by all agents in Z: $C_Z = \bigcup\limits_{i-1}^{n} C_{a_i}$

In the same way as for single agents, we define composed capability of a group Σ_Z as follows:

- $\forall \in C_Z, p \in \Sigma_Z$
- $\forall \in C_Z, \neg p \in \Sigma_Z$
- $\forall \psi_1, \psi_2 \in \Sigma_Z, \psi_1 \wedge \psi_2 \in \Sigma_Z$

Group capability $C_Z\varphi$ can now be defined as:

Definition 9 (Group capability)

Given a formula φ in L and a set of agents $Z \subseteq A$, Z is capable of φ, represented by $C_Z φ$ iff $\not\models φ$ and $\exists ψ \in Σ_Z$ such that $ψ → φ$.

The definitions of group ability, group attempt, group in-control, and group stit are similarly derived from the respective definitions for a single agent.

Definition 10 (Group ability)

Given a world $w \in W$ and a group $Z \subseteq A$, the ability of Z to realizeφ, $G_Z φ$, is defined by $w \models G_Z φ$ iff $C_Z φ$ and $\exists t \in T_{Zw}: t = (w,w')$ and $w' \models φ$.

Definition 11 (Group attempt)

Given a world $w \in W$ and a group $Z \subseteq A$, the attempt of Z to realizeφ, $H_Z φ$, is defined by $w \models H_Z φ$ iff $G_Z φ$ and $\forall t \in T_{Zw}: t = (w,w')$ and $w' \models φ$.

Definition 12 (Group in-control)

Given a world $w \in W$ and and a group $Z \subseteq A$, Z is in control in w, IC_Z, $w \models IC_Z$ iff $\forall w': (w,w') \in R \Rightarrow Z \subseteq t((w,w'))$.

Definition 13 (Group activity)

Given a world $w \in W$ and a group $Z \subseteq A$, Z sees to it that φ holds, $E_Z φ$, is defined by $w \models E_Z φ$ iff $H_Z φ$ and IC_Z.

Consider again the example in figure 1, in which agent *a* with $C_a p$ did not have the ability for $(p \wedge q)$. Now, suppose that there is an agent *b* such that, $C_b q$. In the same way as before also $\neg G_b(p \wedge q)$ holds. However, if we consider the group $Z = \{a, b\}$ we get $C_Z(p \wedge q)$, and thus $G_Z(p \wedge q)$, when $t_1 \in T_{Z_w}$. That is, together *a* and *b* are able of realizing $(p \wedge q)$. Group ability has the following properties (comparable to those of single agents):

- $\neg C_Z T$
- $C_Z φ \wedge C_Z ψ → C_Z (φ \wedge ψ)$
- $\forall a \in Z : C_a φ → C_Z φ$

Note that agent capability is a special case of group capability, when $Z = \{a\}$. This implies that all expressions controlled by one agent are also controlled by all groups in which that agent participates. This is different from the assumption made by e.g. (Wooldridge and van der Hoek, 2005) who use group control to refer to those formulas that are only controlled by the whole group, (and thus not controlled by any of its subgroups). In our model, this can be represented as a extra requirement on the definition 9 for group capability, as follows:

Proposition 1 (Joint capability)

A group $Z \subseteq A$ of agents is said to have joint capability for expression φ iff $C_Z \varphi$ and $\forall Z' \subseteq Z \, \neg C_{Z'} \varphi$.

Informally, whenever each of the agents in Z leaves, the group looses the capability for φ. Finally, group activity, $E_Z \varphi$, has the following properties:

- $E_Z \varphi \rightarrow C_Z \varphi$
- $E_Z \varphi \rightarrow X \varphi$
- $E_Z \varphi \wedge E_Z \psi \rightarrow E_Z (\varphi \wedge \psi)$
- $\neg E_Z T$

ORGANIZATIONS: STRUCTURE AND STRATEGY

The idea behind organization is that there are global objectives, not necessarily shared by any of the agents that can only be achieved through combined agent action. In order to achieve its goals, it is thus necessary that an organization employs the relevant agents, and assures that their interactions and responsibilities enable an efficient realization of the objectives.

In its most simple expression, and organization consists of a set of agents (together with their capabilities and abilities) and a set of objectives. In each moment, the state of the organization is given by a certain state of affairs that hold in that state. Formally, given a world $w \in W$, an *organization O* is defined by a set of agents, a set of objectives (missions or desires), and a set of (current) assets. Agents are the active entities that realize organizational activity[3]. Organizational objectives are the issues that the organization 'wishes' to be true in the world. Organizational assets are the issues that are true (and relevant to the organization) at a given moment, that is, the current state of the organization.

Worlds are represented as a set of propositions in Φ. Furthermore the agents that participate in the organization may leave or enter the organization, and the objectives of the organization may change. We therefore define an organizational instance to represent the organization in a given world $w \in W$ as $O^w = \{ A_O^w, D_O^w, S_O^w \}$.

The current state of the organization, S_O^w, corresponds to the set of formulas that are true in world w and relevant to O, and the objectives or desires of the organization, D_O^w, characterize the worlds (sets of formulas) that, at moment w, the organization wishes to reach[4]. Note that, organizational change means that the organization's composition (agents) and objectives may differ from world to world. Based on the definitions given in the previous sections, we are now in state to define organization capability (or scope of control). In fact, an organization is only as good as its agents. In this sense the scope of organizational control is defined by the union of the scopes of its agents' control together with the control of groups of its agents. Formally:

Definition 14 (Organization capability)

Given an organization O such that A_O is the set of agents in O, organizational capability C_O is defined as: $C_O = C_{A_O}$. That is, $C_O \varphi$ iff $\exists Z \subseteq A_O : C_Z \varphi$.

In practice, no organization will employ all agents in the world, nor control all possible states of affairs. One of the main reasons for creating organizations is efficiency, that is, to provide the means for coordination that enable the achievement of global goals in an efficient manner. Organization Theory has for many decades investigated the issue of organizational structure. Organizational structure has essentially two objectives (Duncan, 1979): Firstly, it facilitates the flow of information within the organization in order to reduce the uncertainty of decision making. Secondly, the structure of the organization should integrate organizational behavior across the parts of the organization so that it is coordinated. This raises two challenges: division of labor and coordination (Mintzberg, 1993). The design of organizational structure determines the allocation of resources and people to specified tasks or purposes, and the coordination of these resources to achieve organizational goals (Galbraith, 1977). Ideally, the organization is designed to fit its environment and to provide the information and coordination needed for its strategic objectives.

According to this definition of organization, even if the agents in the organization have group control over all organizational objectives, they still need to coordinate their activities in order to efficiently achieve those objectives. Furthermore, in most cases, the objectives of the organization are only known to a few of the agents in the organization, who may have no control over those objectives. It is therefore necessary to structure agents in a way that enables objectives to be passed to those agents that can effectively realize them. We need therefore to extend our organizational definition to include coordinating and task allocation concepts.

Organizational Structure

Often organizations use the notion of roles to distribute the responsibilities necessary for the functioning of the organization. *Role dependencies* indicate how the goals of different roles depend on each other, and how interaction is to be achieved. Depending on the specific implementation of the dependency relationship, this means that a role can demand the realization of a goal from another role, or request goals from another role. In organizational contexts this can also mean that the responsibility for some tasks lies with the role in the top of the hierarchy. As before, for simplicity sake, we will for the moment, abstract from the concept of role, and define dependencies between agents (seen as role enacting actors) as follows. A *structural dependency* relation between a set of agents $Z = \{a_1,..., a_n\}$, $\leq_Z : Z \times Z$ is a poset satisfying the following properties:

- $\forall a \in Z$: $a \leq_Z a$ *(reflexive)*
- $\forall a,b,c \in Z$: *if* $a \leq_Z b$ *and* $b \leq_Z c$ *then* $a \leq_Z c$ *(transitive)*

We are now able to extend the definition of organization to include the notion of dependency:

Definition 15 (Organization)

Given a model $M = (\Phi, A, W, R, T, \pi)$, a organization in a world $w \in W$ is defined by $O^w = \{ A_O^w, \leq_O^w, D_O^w, S_O^w \}$, where $A_O^w = \{a_1,..., a_n\}$, $(A_O^w, \leq_O^w)$ is a structural dependency relation in A_O^w, $D_O^w \subseteq \Phi$, and $S_O^w \subseteq L$.

Given an organizational structure, we can define dependency chains between two agents or between agents and groups as follows:

Definition 16 (Dependency chain)

Given a structured organization $O = \{A_O, \leq_O, D_O, S_O\}$, a dependency chain between two agents in A_O^w is defined as chain(a,b) iff

(1)   *$a = b$, or*
(2)   *$\exists\ c \in A_O$ such that $a \leq_O c$ and chain(c,b). Given a group $Z \subseteq A_O$, there is a chain(a,S) iff $\forall\ a' \in$: chain(a,a').*

Intuitively, the ordering relation in the set of agents stands for the interaction possibilities between agents. Organizational structures influence the way that agents in the organization can interact. The relation $a \leq_O b$ indicates that a is able to interact with b in order to request or demand some result from b. In this chapter, we will not further detail the types of interactions between agents (delegation, request, bid, ...) but assume that the relationship will achieve some result, through a more or less complex interaction process. More on this issue can be found in (Dignum and Dignum, 2007a).

Responsibility

To further refine the concept of organization, we need to be able to talk about the responsibilities[5] of agents in the organization. Responsibilities within an organization enable agents to make decisions about what each member of the organization is expected to do, and to anticipate the tasks of others (Grossi, 2007b). Informally, by responsibility we mean that an agent or group has to make sure that a certain state of affairs is achieved, $R_a\varphi$ either by realizing it itself or by delegating that result to someone else. In order to describe this notion of responsibility and delegation, we introduce a new operator, R_a, such that $R_a\varphi$ means that a is responsible for, or in charge of, achieving φ. Note that responsibility for a state of affairs does not guarantee successful achievement of that state of affairs. As such, we formally define responsibility in terms of attempt, as follows:

Definition 17 (Responsibility)

Given an organization $O = \{A_O, \leq_O, D_O, S_O\}$ and an agent $a \in A_O$, responsibility $R_a\varphi$ is such that: $R_a\varphi \equiv \Diamond(H_a\varphi \vee H_a R_b\varphi)$, for some $b \in A_O$.

The responsibility operator has the following properties:

- $\neg R_a T$
- $E_a\varphi \rightarrow R_a\varphi$
- $R_a\varphi \wedge R_a\psi \rightarrow R_a(\varphi \wedge \psi)$

Delegation of tasks is defined as the capability to make an agent, or group, responsible for that task. In an organization, delegation is associated with structural dependencies. That is, by nature their dependencies, some agents are in state of delegating their tasks to other agents, to make it the case that a result is achieved. Formally,

Definition 18 (Structured delegation)

Given an organization $O = \{A_O, \leq_O, D_O, S_O^w)$, delegation of φ between two agents a, b $\in A_O$ is defined as: if ($a \leq_O b$) then $C_a R_b \varphi$.

The responsibility of a group Z of agents, R_Z, is defined in a similar way. Given the notions of responsibility and structural dependency introduced above, we can define a *good organization*, as an organization $O = \{A_O, \leq_O, D_O, S_O^w)$ that satisfies the following requirement: $C_{A_O} \varphi \wedge R_a \varphi \rightarrow chain(a,Z) \wedge C_Z \varphi$, for $a \in A_O$ and $Z \subseteq A_O$. Good organizations satisfy the property $R_a \varphi \rightarrow \Diamond \varphi$, which informally says that if there is an agent responsible for a given state of affairs, then eventually that state will be reached.

In the following, we provide an example of structured organization. Consider the organization

$O = \{A, \leq, D, S^0)$, where:
$A = \{a,b,c,d\}$,
$\leq = \{(a \leq b),(a \leq c),(c \leq d)\}$,
$D = \{\rho\}$, where $\rho = ((p \wedge q) \vee (p \wedge r))$,
$S^0 = \{R_a \rho , C_b p, C_d q \; C_{\{a,c\}} r \}$

Note that the initial organizational state S^0 describes the capabilities of the agents in A and that agent a is responsible for the achievement of the organizational goal. This example also shows that organizations are dependent on the capabilities of their agents to achieve their objectives. In this case, without agent b, the organization can never achieve its goals. In the above organization, there are several ways for agent a to realize the organizational goal ρ, a possible strategy being:

s^1:	$E_a R_b p,\ E_a R_c q$
s^2:	$R_b p,\ R_c q$
s^3:	$R_b p,\ E_c R_d q$
s^4:	$R_b p,\ R_d q$
s^5:	$E_b p,\ E_d q$
s^6:	$p \wedge q$

Different properties can be defined for the responsibility operator, which identify different types of organizations. For example, a *well-defined organization* is an organization O such that: $\forall \varphi \in D_O, \exists Z \subseteq A_O: R_Z \varphi.$. That is, it is possible to find a group of agents within the organization that is responsible for each of the objectives of O.

Types of Organizations

Organizations come in many sorts and sizes. Notable is the work of (Mintzberg, 1993) on the classification of organizational structures. According to Mintzberg, environmental variety is determined by both environmental complexity and the pace of change. Inspired by and extending the work of

Mintzberg, researchers in Organization Theory have proposed a growing number of classifications for organizational structures, e.g. simple, bureaucracy, matrix, virtual enterprise, network, boundary-less organizations, conglomeration, alliance, etc. just to name a few forms. However, definitions and naming of organizational forms are often unclear and the classification of a specific organization into one of the proposed classes is not trivial, often resulting in hybrid forms. Based on the structure of control, (Burns and Stalker, 1961) distinguish two main types of organizational structures: hierarchies and networks. Using the formal definition of organization presented in the previous sections, we are able to specify the structural characteristics of these two types of organizations. In a hierarchy, organizational goals are known to the managers who delegate them to their subordinates who have the capabilities and resources to realize them. Formally,

Definition 19 (Hierarchy)

An organization $O = \{A_O, \leq_O, D_O, S_O^w)$ is said to be an hierarchy iff

- $M \subset A_O$, $M \neq \emptyset$, *such that* $\forall\, m \in M$, $\exists \varphi \in D_O$: $R_m \varphi$ *and* $\forall \varphi \in D_O$, $\exists m \in M\, R_m \varphi$
- $\forall a \in A_O$, $a \notin M$, $\exists m \in M$: *chain(m,a)*

That is, there is a group of managers M that together is responsible for all organizational goals and has a chain of command to all other agents in the organization. In a simple, flat, hierarchy, the manager group furthermore meets the following requirements:

$M = \{m\}$ *and* $\forall a \in A_O$, $m \leq_O a$.

In the same way, we formally define a network organization as:

Definition 20 (Network)

A organization $O = \{A_O, \leq_O, D_O, S_O^w)$ is said to be a network iff

- $\forall a \in A_O\, R_a \cup D_O \neq \emptyset$ *and* $\forall \varphi \in D_O$, $\exists\, a \in A_O$: $R_a \varphi$
- $\forall a \in A_O$, $\exists\, b \in A_O$: *chain(a,b)*

That is, every agent in the organization is responsible for some of the organizational goals, and has a delegation relationship to some other agent in the organization. A fully connected network also meets the following requirement: $\forall a, b \in A_O$: *chain(a,b)*. A **team** is a special case of network that meets the symmetry requirement *chain(a,b)* $\rightarrow$ *chain(b, a)*.

From the organization examples above, it can be seen that by using the formal definition of properties for organizations, different organization types can be specified and verified. Other organizational types can be defined by the specification of other properties.

CASE STUDY

We have applied the model presented in this chapter to formally describe several existing agent systems that simulate organizations and organizational adaptation. Those systems were taken from the literature and include such different domains as architectures for Command and Control (Kleinmann et al., 2005), RoboSoccer (Hübner et al., 2004), market regulation (Nissen, 2001) and sensor networks (Matson and DeLoach, 2004). LAO models simulate the existing scenarios and can be used to validate and compare approaches. The original works on those cases use different frameworks and were developed independently by other research groups. Due to space limitations, we will only discuss here one of the studied cases, namely the architecture for Command and Control presented in (Kleinmann et al., 2005).

Over the past several years, researchers within the A2C2 research program (Adaptive Architectures for Command and Control) have investigated the notion of organizational congruence (Kleinmann et al., 2005; Entin et al. 2003, Entin et al., 1999; Entin et al, 2004). In order to test their theories, in a laboratory experiment, a set of scenarios was developed to exploit the differences between organizational structures. Their idea was to design two different types of organizations and two different scenarios in order to test organizational congruence which distinguish between functional organizations and divisional / geographically-based organizations. Two types of scenarios were designed: one scenario would be congruent with divisional organizations but would be a "misfit", or incongruent to functional organizations. Conversely, the second scenario would be congruent with functional organizations but misfit to divisional organizations.

The study considers different types of agents. For simplicity, we assume 2 agents, a_1 and a_2, with search & rescue capabilities, and 2 agents, a_3 and a_4, with mine clearance capabilities. That is: C_{a_1} *search-rescue1*, C_{a_2} *search-rescue2*, C_{a_3} *mine-clear3*, and C_{a_4} *mine-clear4*. Furthermore, there are 4 agents with decision making responsibilities: the search & rescue commander *src*, the mine clearance commander *mcc*, and the commanders of the two bases *b1c* and *b2c*. Different organizations are achieved using different agent combinations:

- $O_1 : A_{O1} = \{src, a_1, a_2\}$ and $\leq_{O1} = \{(src \leq_1 a_1), (src \leq_1 a_2)\}$
- $O_2 : A_{O2} = \{mcc, a_3, a_4\}$ and $\leq_{O2} = \{(mcc \leq_2 a_3), (mcc \leq_2 a_4)\}$
- $O_3 : A_{O3} = \{b1c, a_1, a_3\}$ and $\leq_{O3} = \{(b1c \leq_3 a_1), (b1c \leq_3 a_3)\}$
- $O_4 : A_{O4} = \{b2c, a_2, a_4\}$ and $\leq_{O4} = \{(b2c \leq_4 a_2), (b2c \leq_4 a_4)\}$

According to the definitions used by A2C2 researchers, organizations O_1 and O_2 are functional organizations and O_3 and O_4 are divisional. The idea behind organizational congruence is that a certain organizational structure and population is in better state of achieving a desired state of affairs than others. So, divisional organizations will be better in achieving objectives that require different types of capabilities, while functional organizations are better when objectives require one specific type of capabilities.

A2C2 researchers designed different organizational scenarios to be congruent with one type of organization and incongruent with the other. A functional scenario is such that the mission, or objective, of the organization requires the use of all tools of one kind from different places, and a divisional scenario requires a combination of different tools in one place. Example of a functional scenario is search & rescue, or to clear mines in an area. Divisional scenarios require the combination of both types of operations. In our model, different scenarios are represented as desired states of affairs. For instance, the following scenarios can be considered:

- Functional Scenarios:
  - ○ D_1 = *search-rescue1* ∧ *search-rescue2*
  - ○ D_2 = *mine-clear3* ∧ *mine-clear4*
- Divisional Scenarios:
  - ○ D_3 = *search-rescue1* ∧ *mine-clear3*
  - ○ D_4 = *search-rescue2* ∧ *mine-clear4*

Given the organizations defined above, it is easy to see that, e.g., the divisional organization O_3 is congruent with a divisional scenario D_3, that is $C_{O3}D_3$, and the functional organization O_1 is congruent with D_1, that is $C_{O1}D_1$.

Furthermore, an organization is incongruent with a scenario if it cannot realize the objectives specified in that scenario. In the case that scenarios are incongruent with the organization, organizations will need to reorganize in order to fulfill that mission. For instance, organization O_3 is incongruent with D_1 = *search-rescue1* ∧ *search-rescue2* (i.e. ¬$C_{O3}D_1$). Specifically, O_3 cannot realize this objective because ¬C_{O3}*search-rescue2*. In order to be able to realize D_1, O_3 needs to enlist a_2. In reality, in the defense domain, commander *blc* can request a_2 from its superior *src*. Assuming that this succeeds the resulting organizations is as follows:

$$O_3' = (\{blc, a_1, a_3, a_2\}, \{(blc \leq a_1), (blc \leq a_3), blc \leq a_2)\}, D_1, S^0\}, \text{ where}$$

$S^0 = \{R_{blc}D_1, C_{a_1} \text{ } search\text{-}rescue1, C_{a_2} \text{ } search\text{-}rescue2, C_{a_3} \text{ } mine\text{-}clear3\}$, which is indeed congruent with the functional scenario D_1.

CONCLUSION

Organization concepts and models are increasingly being adopted for the design and specification of multi-agent systems. The motivations for this model are twofold. In the one hand, the need for a formal representation of organizations, with their environment, objectives and agents in a way that enables to analyze their partial contributions to the performance of the organization in a changing environment, and the comparison of different organizational designs. On the other hand, such a model must be realistic enough to incorporate the more 'pragmatic' considerations faced by real organizations. In this chapter we presented a first attempt at a formal model for organizational concepts, based on modal temporal logic. We have applied the proposed model to existing domain-specific systems proposed in recent literature.

The theoretical framework presented in this chapter, based on the notions of capability, *stit*, attempt and responsibility, can be extended to represent and analyze performance and dynamics of organizations.

Currently, we are extending LAO to include the formal specification of reorganization operators (Dignum and Dignum, 2007b, Dignum and Tick, 2007). The resulting extension to LAO enables represent and reason about changes in the organization, in a way that abstracts from the specifics of the reorganization process, that is, we refer to the resulting state of affairs without the need to specify the (communication) processes involved in achieving that state. In practice reorganization operations can be classified into three types: *staffing*, i.e. changes in the set of agents in the organization and their capabilities, *structuring*, i.e. changes in the organizational structure, and, *strategic*, i.e. changes in the objectives of the organization. A reorganization process takes into account the current performance and determines which characteristics of the organization should be modified in order to achieve a better performance. The general idea behind reorganization is that one should be able to evaluate the utility of the current state of affairs (that is, what happens if nothing changes), and the utility of future states of affairs that can be obtained by performing reorganization actions. The choice is then to choose the future with the highest utility.

In the future, we will extend the model to include deontic concepts and their relation to the operational concepts presented in this chapter. Also we will add the formal distinction between roles and agents. These elements are already described in other work, but need to be carefully merged with the current basic framework. Finally, we are engaged on developing a full axiomatization of LAO based on the modality properties described in this chapter, as well as on an implementation for simulating the reorganization process.

ACKNOWLEDGMENT

The research of the first author is funded by the Netherlands Organization for Scientific Research (NWO), through Veni-grant 639.021.509.

REFERENCES

Boutelier, C. (2004). Toward a logic for qualitative decision theory. In: Doyle, J., Sandewall, E., and Torasso, P., editors, *Principles of Knowledge Representation and Reasoning* (KR'94).

Burns, T., & Stalker, G. (1961). *The management of innovation.* Tavistock, London.

Carley, K. (2002). Computational organization science: A new frontier. *PNAS, 99*(3), 7257–7262.

Cholvy, L., & Garion, C. (2001). An attempt to adapt a logic of conditional preferences for reasoning with contrary to duties. *Fundamenta Informaticae, 47.*

Cholvy, L., Garion, C., & Saurel, C. (2005). Ability in a multi-agent context: A model in the situation calculus. In: *Proceedings of CLIMA VI.*

Cohen, M. (1986). Artificial intelligence and the dynamic performance of organization designs. In: March, J. and Weissinger-Baylon, R., editors, *Ambiguity and Command: Organizational Perspectives on Military Decision Making,* (pp. 53–71). Pitman.

Dastani, M., Dignum, V., & Dignum, F. (2003). Role assignment in open agent societies. In: *Proceedings of AAMAS03.* ACM Press.

Davidsson, P. (2002) Agent based social simulation: A computer science view. *Journal of Artificial Societies and Social Simulation, 5.*

Dignum, V., & Dignum, F. (2006). *Towards formal semantics for reorganization.* Technical Report UU-CS-2006-60, ICS - Utrecht University.

Dignum, V., & Dignum, F. (2007a). Coordinating tasks in agent organizations. Or: Can we ask you to read this paper? In: Pablo Noriega et al., editors, *Coordination, Organization, Institutions and Norms in MAS (COIN II)*, volume 4386 of LNAI, Springer.

Dignum, V., & Dignum, F. (2007b). Understanding organizational congruence: Formal model and simulation framework. In: *Proceedings of ADS-2007@SpringSim*, Spring Simulation Multi-conference, pages 178–184.

Dignum, V., Meyer, J., Dignum, F., & Weigand, H. (2003). Formal specification of interaction in agent societies. In: *Formal Approaches to Agent-Based Systems (FAABS)*, volume F2699 of LNAI. Springer.

Dignum, V. & Tick, C. (2007) Agent-based Analysis of Organizations: Formalization and Simulation. *Proceedings of IAT'07*, IEEE, (pp. 244-247).

Duncan, R. (1979). What is the right organizational structure: Decision tree analysis provides the answer. *Organizational Dynamics*, Winter: pp. 59–80.

Elgesem, D. (1997). The model logic of agency. *Nordic Journal of Philosophical Logic*, 2(2), 1–46.

Emerson, E. (1990). Temporal and modal logic. In: van Leeuwen, J., editor, *Handbook of Theoretical Computer Science*, B, 955–1072. MIT Press.

Entin, E. E., Diedrich, F. J., Kleinman, D. L., Kemple, W. G., Hocevar, S. G., Rubineau, B., and Serfaty, D. (2003). When do organizations need to change (part ii)? Incongruence in action. In: *Command and Control Research and Technology Symposium*.

Entin, E. E., & Serfaty, D. (1999). Adaptive team coordination. *Journal of Human Factors*, 41, 321–325.

Entin, E. E.,Weil, S. A., Kleinman, D. L., Hutchins, S. G., Hocevar, S. P., Kemple, W. G., & Serfaty, D. (2004). Inducing adaptation in organizations: Concept and experiment design. In: *Proceedings of the 2004 International Command and Control Research and Technology Symposium*.

Fox, M. (1981). An organizational view of distributed systems. *Transactions on Systems, Man, and Cybernetics*, 11(1), 70–80.

Galbraith, J. (1977). *Organization Design*. Addison-Wesley.

Governatori, G., Gelati, J., Rotolo, A., & Sartor, G. (2002). Actions, institutions, powers. preliminary notes. In: G. Lindeman et al., editor, *Proceedings of RASTA'02*, volume 318 of Mitteilung, pages 131–147. Fachbereich Informatik, Universitt Hamburg.

Grossi, D., Dignum, F., Dignum, V., Dastani, M., & Royakkers, L. (2007a). Structural aspects of the evaluation of agent organizations. In: Pablo Noriega et al., editors, *Coordination, Organization, Institutions and Norms in Agent Systems (COIN II)*, volume 4386 of LNAI. Springer.

Grossi, D., Royakkers, L., & Dignum, F. (2007b). Organizational structure and responsibility. an analysis in a dynamic logic of organized collective agency. *Journal of AI and Law*, to appear.

Harel, D. (1984). Dynamic logic. In: Gabbay, D. and Guenthner, F., editors, *Handbook of Philosophical Logic*, 2, 497–6049. D. Reidel Publishing Company.

Harrison, R., Lin, Z., Carroll, G., & Carley, K. (2007). Simulation modeling in organizational and management research. *Academy of Management Review*, to appear.

Hübner, J., Sichman, J., & Boissier, O. (2006). S-Moise+: A middleware for developing organized multi-agent systems. In: O. Boissier, et al., editors, *Coordination, Organization, Institutions and Norms in Agent Systems (COIN I)*, volume 3913 of LNAI, pages 64–78. Springer.

Hübner, J. F., Sichman, J. S., & Boissier, O. (2004). Using the Moise+ for a cooperative framework of MAS reorganization. In: *Advances in Artificial Intelligence (SBIA 2004)*, volume 3171 of Lecture Notes in Computer Science, pages 506–515. Springer.

Kleinman, D., Levchuk, G., Hutchins, S., & Kemple, W. (2005). *Scenario design for the empirical testing of organizational congruence*. Technical Report ADA440390, Naval Postgraduate School, Dept of Informational Science, Monterey, CA.

MacCarthy, J., & Hayes, P. (1969). Some philosophical problems from the standpoint of artificial intelligence. *Machine Intelligence*, *4*, 463–502.

Matson, E., & DeLoach, S. (2004). Enabling intra-robotic capabilities adaptation using an organization-based multi-agent system. In: *Proceedings of the 2004 IEEE International Conference on Robotics and Automation (ICRA 2004)*.

McCallum, M., Vasconcelos, W., & Norman, T. (2006). Verification and analysis of organizational change. In: O. Boissier, et al., editors, *Coordination, Organization, Institutions and Norms in Agent Systems (COIN I)*, volume 3913 of LNAI, pages 48–63. Springer.

Meyer, J. (2000). *Dynamic logic for reasoning about actions and agents*. Pages 281–311. Kluwer Academic Publishers.

Mintzberg, H. (1993). *Structures in Fives: Designing Effective Organizations*. Prentice Hall.

Nissen, M. (2001). Agent-based supply chain integration. *Information Technology and Management*, *2*(3), 289–312.

Pörn, I. (1974). Some basic concepts of action. In Stenlund, S., editor, *Logical Theory and Semantical Analysis*. Reidel.

Santos, F., Jones, A., & Carmo, J. (1997). Action concepts for describing organized interaction. In R.A. Sprague, J., editor, *Proceedings of HICCS*, volume V, pages 373–382. IEEE Computer Society Press.

Simon, H. (1991). Bounded rationality and organizational learning. *Organization Science*, *2*, *Special Issue: Organizational Learning: Papers in Honor of (and by) J. March* (1), 125–134.

So, Y., & Durfee, E. (1998). Designing organizations for computational agents. In Carley, K., Prietula, M. and Gasser, L., editors, *Simulating Organizations*, pages 47–64.

van den Broek, E., Jonker, C., Sharpanskykh, A., Treur, J., & Yolum, P. (2006). Formal modeling and analysis of organizations. In: O. Boissier, et al., editors, *Coordination, Organization, Institutions and Norms in Agent Systems (COIN I)*, volume 3913 of LNAI, pages 18–34. Springer.

van der Hoek, W., & Wooldridge, M. (2005). On the logic of cooperation and propositional control. *Artificial Intelligence*, 24(1-2):81–119.

Vazquez-Salceda, J., Dignum, V., & Dignum, F. (2005). Organizing multi-agent systems. *Journal of AAMAS*, *11*(3), 307–360. Springer.

KEY TERMS

(Agent or Group) Ability: Refers to the potential to realize a certain capability, that is, the extrinsic conditions for the realization of a certain state of affairs.

(Agent or Group) Capability: Describes the intrinsic skill of an agent or group of agents to realize a certain state of affairs.

Agent Organization: Comparable to human organizations, agent organizations are characterized by global goals and formalized social structures representing the stakeholder desired results. Can be seen as the structural setting in which agent interactions occur.

(Agent or Group) Responsibility: Describes the fact that an agent or group of agents is in charge of realizing a certain state of affairs, and can therefore be made accountable for it.

(Agent or Group) *Stit*: Meaning 'sees to it that' is the successful action of an agent or group of agents. A temporal stance on *stit* indicated that the result of activity is only valid in successor worlds.

Organizational Structure: Represents the relations between entities of an agent organization that are taken to be invariant through time. The main constructs found in it are roles, groups, and relationships between them.

Temporal Logic: System of rules and symbolism for representing, and reasoning about, propositions qualified in terms of time. It is often used to state requirements of hardware or software systems.

ENDNOTES

[1]   A concise overview can be found in (Cholvy et al., 2005).

[2]   This notion of stit provides a necessary interpretation of action, and as such is related to the dynamic operator [a]p, meaning that after performing action a it is necessarily the case that p.

[3]   Note that, for the purposes of this chapter, we see agents purely as actors in a organization, with no goals of themselves. We assume that, by acting according to their capabilities, agents work towards organizational objectives. That is, we abstract here from the motivation an individual agent may have to take up those organizational positions (Dastani et al, 2003).

[4]   From now on, whenever clear from the context, we'll drop the subscripts and superscripts.

[5]   In reality, responsibilities are associated with roles or positions in an organization. However, due to the simplification we make in this version of LAO, we do not - yet - distinguish between role and the role enacting agent.

Section III
Interactions in Organizations

Chapter X
Grounding Organizations in the Minds of the Agents

Cristiano Castelfranchi
ISTC-CNR, Italy

ABSTRACT

This chapter presents organizations as a macro-micro notion and device; they presuppose autonomous proactive entities (agents) playing the organizational roles. Agents may have their own powers, goals, relationships (of dependence, trust, etc.). This opens important issues to be discussed: Does cooperation require mentally shared plans? Which is the relationship between individual powers and role powers; personal dependencies and role dependencies; personal goals and assigned goals; personal beliefs and what we have to assume when playing our role; individual actions and organizational actions? What about possible conflicts, deviations, power abuse, given the agents' autonomy? MultiAgentSystems discipline should both aim at scientifically modeling human organizations, and at designing effective artificial organizations. Our claim is that for both those aims, one should model a high (risky) degree of flexibility, exploiting autonomy and pro-activity, intelligence and decentralized knowledge of role-players, allowing for functional violations of requests and even of rules.

INTRODUCTION

The main thesis of this chapter is that organization is a notion, a model, and a technical device that *presupposes* individual agents[1]; it is a way of exploiting and improving the co-powers[2] of agents, producing efficient cooperative results. Organizations have to be funded and grounded in the powers of the agents and in particular on and into their minds (knowledge, goals, reasoning, choice, etc.).

In fact, "Organization" is organization *of something*: precisely *of the activities of sub-units*, able to get and process information, to act in a coordinated manner, to co-operate, and to do this with some local – decentralized – autonomy, and adaptation to the context. In particular, 'organizations' are co-ordination structures for cooperation among several agents, in view of *iterated and typical problems* or problem-solving activities. Any 'organization' entails *some Multi-Agent (MA) plan*, and the agents have to work (case by case) within some common plan.

Some level of autonomy and of purposiveness of the component units is presupposed: the active entities able to play a role within the organization and its plans, must be able to perform actions in view of specific results, that is, to pursue and locally monitor goals (their 'tasks'), and must have some degree of 'autonomy' for adapting the action to its context and for solving problems.

'Autonomy' is a relational notion: X is autonomous *from* somebody else (Y) and *as for* something (O) (Castelfranchi, 1995a). Autonomous means that X doesn't depends on Y as for (having/realizing) O; does not need Y for this. X can have or realize O by itself. An active entity can be autonomous on various dimensions and for various "resources" or "activities": for example, for accessing information and data, for learning, for reasoning, for decision making, for abilities and skills, or for external material resources (money, a car, etc.). One might be autonomous as for a given O but not for another one. For example, X may be autonomous as for deciding but not as for the needed data, because she is blind; or, X may have the practical resources for doing action A, but not being able to do it, and she needs the help of Y for this.

"Agents" - as defined in MAS - are autonomous entities ("Autonomous Agents & MAS"): there is not a fully centralized processing; they have local independent information and results, and, sometimes, independent learning or reasoning; they have some pro-activity (Wooldridge and Jennings, 1995); they are regulated by internal representations (sometimes strictly 'purposive' ones, like in BDI Agents). The most qualifying and advanced form of autonomy obviously is autonomy in goals: when an agent has its own independent *motives*, and will pursue our objectives only if there is some reason and advantage for doing so.

In sum, for us, the "sociological" and "institutional" level of processing and activity must be funded on the basic notion of agents activity: action, decision, belief, plan, etc. and in particular on the *individual social* action. It is a typical mistake to try to found collective levels per se' or directly on individual agent theory ignoring sociality at the interpersonal level as the very basis of sociality at the collective level (Tuomela, 1995; Castelfranchi, 2003c). So, for example, there are typical and fundamental aspects to be modeled in organization, like 'dependence', or 'coordination', or 'delegation' and 'reliance', like 'goal-adoption' or help, that are already present at the interpersonal level and must be defined first of all at that level (see in this chapter Section on 'Socio-Cognitive Organization Pillars').

Given this premise and perspective several important issues should be taken into account in organization theory and design.

Is it better to organize an efficient coordination and cooperation of (at least partially) autonomous entities, or it would be better not having a real organization (in human-like sense), but just a well pre-programmed and orchestrated merely executive system.[3] Are true 'organizations' – presupposing autonomous members - just a human damnation, just due to human imperfection and limits; or there is some specific advantage in autonomous, intelligent, cooperative entities? Why building an 'organization' of 'Agents'? Why having problems with initiative and autonomy? Wouldn't be better many pre-organized perfect executors of their own tasks, understanding nothing, negotiating nothing, and changing nothing. Which are the advantages of autonomous entities playing roles, and which are the risks?

Since the agents have to play 'roles' within and for the organization and its activities, but they have their own individual 'mind', how is the dialectics, the complex relationship between the possible individual goals and preferences and the goals of the endowed role? In general, what does it means for an autonomous agent (with its own self-regulation. motives, information, ...) to endow and play a role?

Since any organization entails some MA plan, and the agents have to work (case by case) within some common plan, what about the relationship between that plan and the mind of the agents taking part in it? Should the plan be shared among the participants? What about the relationships between the agents 'collaborating' within the same plan? Are they aware of each other? Do they rely on the other, and do they explicitly 'adopt' the goal of the other relying on them?

Since agents have their own powers (skills, but possibly also resources like data), what are the relations between 'personal' powers and the powers required for playing the role? And – since the organization empowers its members and provides new resources or possibilities, is it possible the use of this for 'personal' advantages?

What are the relationships between the *interpersonal* relations of dependence, or coordination, or delegation, etc. (among the agents) and the organizational ones (among the 'roles')? Given our double-level approach (macro & micro) we have to discuss this.

Moreover, as we said, organizations presuppose autonomous active entities and are based on them, but are those 'members' really relevant or they become just replaceable, fungible instruments of the whole? Organizations can change their members, but on the other side autonomous agents (both human and artificial) could chose and change their organization (Grosz & Kraus, 1998).

We will put aside just two fundamental issues (very relevant ones, but less basic): (i) the necessary use of 'norms' (Conte et al., 1999; Dastani et al., 2002), the deontic nature of roles, actions, etc.; (ii) the 'institutional' character of actions and roles within the organization (Tummolini et al. 2006), the artificial powers given by the institution (Castelfranchi, 2003a). However, these issues are discussed and modeled in other chapters of this book, in particular in Section IV.

This analysis will be developed in a specific perspective and with an additional 'thesis': we will challenge any *anti-cognitive*, merely behavioral or rule-based approach to organization[4], and the idea that in ICT 'organization' be a new and *substitutive* 'metaphor', replacing the metaphor of Agents.

First of all, 'Agents' are not a "metaphor". On the one side, they are a way of thinking, a paradigm for conceiving and modeling complex dynamic problems due to distributed and local and autonomous computations and activities. On the other side, they are real causal entities driven by internal information processing; goal-oriented entities that can interfere with each other, compete for outcomes and resources, cooperate and achieve results far beyond their individual powers. That is, they are *real* 'agents' like the biological ones[5].

Second, (other thesis) 'organization' can be a useful new "metaphor" and model in AI and MAS, but is not a *'substitutive'* metaphor relative to 'Agents' and to their interaction (M-A systems); it is a complementary one. Agents cannot be 'substituted'. As explained, we have to ground the macro organizational (sociological, institutional) layers on the micro layer of individual agents' behaviors, controlled by their *internal* mechanisms of learning or of reasoning, and choosing.

INDIVIDUAL MINDS AND POWERS AND ORGANIZATIONAL ISSUES

A 'role' is something to be dressed, to be 'interpreted'; a mask, a character (Goffman, 1959). This means that the 'player' should assume the *goals* of the role: they must be represented in her/his mind and drive her/his behavior. The 'player' should assume the *powers* of the role, the dependence relations of the role; and also the *knowledge* and *information* of the role, and the way of thinking (for example the *preferences*) of the role; the *obligations* impinging on the role; something to be believed or at least 'assumed'; and even (if any) the *attitudes* and emotions appropriate to that role. Dressing a role means dressing a 'mind' regulating our behavior in that role; but this can create problems with the mind of an *autonomous* agent.

As we said, a crucial issue we will systematically analyze is the relationship between the *individual* mental attitudes (goals, plans, beliefs) and powers (abilities, resources, know how) and the *common* MA plans with its roles. This has many important facets. Let us deal with some of the questions already enounced.

In particular, in this section we will discuss the fact that agents playing the role do not necessarily have to understand the common plan, and to pursue the higher goals of the organization or of the plan their role and task is instrumental to (next sub-section); in the other sub-section we will make clear that agents have their own powers and that organization relies on this for their role-playing, and more in general we introduce the issue of the relation between the individual level, the actions, the goals, the beliefs of the individual, and those imposed by the role and supporting the role; for example: when the *action* of a member of the organization is an action "of" the organization? Or, are there possible conflicts between our personal *goals* and the goals we have to adopt and pursue while dressing our role? Or, there is something that as a role player we "have to *believe*" (or behaving *as if*) that we personally do not believe?

The Cooperative Plan is not Necessarily Shared or Understood by the Agents

Must the common plan (in which the agent co-operate) be 'shared'? Does the agent necessarily know the (part of the) plan he is 'delegating' to the other and factually is relying on?

A shared-plan approach to cooperation and organization is rather simplistic and naïf (Cohen-Levesque et a., 1990; Grosz & Kraus, 1998). A lot of cooperation works without any explicitly (mentally) represented shared plan among the participants. Not only – given the fact that a lot of cooperation is based on what we call 'open delegation' (see later), that is on the non-specification of the allocated task, but just on the assignment of a 'mission', of a goal to be realized in some way – the relying/delegating agent doesn't knows how the other will realize his share/part, his specific sub-plan. Also the involved delegated agents possibly understand, adopt, and cooperate to the higher goal of the plan (see Sections on "Socio-Cognitive Organization Pillars" and "Reconciling Organization and Autonomy"), but ignore the other parts of it. They have in mind a common goal, and they assume that the other has some share and plan, but they do not know that part of the 'common' plan.

Even when all parts of the plan are fully specified and must just be executed by the participants, not necessarily that plan is mentally shared by them. There may be just one boss building and having in mind all the detailed plan, and assigning sub-parts of it to various executors, that ignore each other and the whole plan, and even its sense and purpose. This is typical in industrial work, or in military plans.

'Organization' doesn't presupposes that the plan, the agents are cooperating within, be mentally shared by them. Quite the other way around: one of the advantages of organizations is precisely that a lot of roles in habitual plans or in possible generative plans are pre-defined and consolidated, and the performer of that part/role has not to know the whole plan or the specific higher goal, has not to negotiate about reciprocal roles, etc.

This is one of the reasons organizations are efficient and convenient (reduced cognitive costs, reduced negotiation costs, pre-established general agreement, etc.).

However, there are important principles to be stated:

(i) Necessarily the agent has some goal and plan in his mind (its role, mission, or task) and its contextual specification;

(ii) This mentally represented goal/plan at the individual (role player) level must (at least) be a sub-part of the multi-agent plan: a sub-goal instrumental to some higher goal of the general plan;

(iii) In explicit organizations – differently from emergent self-organizing systems – each part of the cooperative plan is or will be represented in at least one mind: the delegating mind or the delegated mind.

Moreover, to be true, even human organizations are not fully intelligently 'designed'; part of their structure and functioning is the result of an 'evolution', of a spontaneous emergent and self-organizing process which finds some dynamic equilibrium and functional stabilization; some division of labor, for example, or some practices or rules which have not been 'decided', but just automatically learned or 'accepted'. Sometimes those 'rules' are not aware, and remain just implicit. For sure merely emergent 'functions'- that are not cognitive 'goals' – are not shared in mental terms; they are only procedurally and implicitly shared among the participants in a given community of practice. In merely reactive or associative entities (like insects) the entire cooperation and organization is like this; it is not mentally understood (represented) and thus 'shared'. Some Agents' organization will be like this or a mixture of automatic/procedural and cognitive coordination structures.

The fact that *the individual not necessarily have to understand and agree with (adopt) the higher 'goals' of the organization and its functions*, and that the cooperation can be partially 'unaware' creates an important *dialectics* between individuals goals and organizational goals.

As we said, the goal of the agent while playing his role and in a given organizational plan must certainly implement the goal of the organization - for that plan or role - impinging on him, but not necessarily the agent understands, adopts, and deliberately cooperates with the higher goals his assigned role/plan is functional to. He might even disagree with those aims, if aware of them (consider, for example, military missions). Might thus the Agent unconsciously violate some moral or legal norm, or act against the interests of the delegating human on whose behalf it is assumed to work?

Moreover, are organizations 'instruments' of their individual agents, which use them for their own purposes? Or – vice versa - the individuals are fungible 'instruments' of the organization.

Organization looks as an *instrument* of its 'members' which need some coordination (for exploiting positive interferences and avoiding negative ones) (Castelfranchi, 1998) and some co-power (the power that individually they do not have, and is the result only of joint activities). However, given that individuals become relevant to the organization just for their knowledge, resources, skills, in a sense the organization gets 'autonomy' from its members: they are replaceable; what matters is not their 'individuality' but their role. Organization in its essence is an 'abstraction' from the specific individuals composing it; it just captures their 'functions'. The individuals become alienated *instruments* of their organizations.

As for artificial 'individuals', 'alienation' (perhaps) is not a problem, but there is a problem: should they be designed just in such a way, as merely functional and subordinated parts of their organization? Or they should be designed in a more autonomous and open way, able to *enter* in one organization or the other, to discover new solutions with their potential powers, and adaptively changing the organizations there are involved in?

Individual Goals and Powers and the Organizational Roles

Individual members of the organization (the role-players) *must* have their individual 'powers' and must have – if autonomous - their internally represented and driving 'goals' (goal-driven or purposive systems), and they might even have their 'private', 'personal' goals. Not only this is typical in human beings, but might hold also with artificial Agents, which either care of the personal goals of their 'user' or have their own personal 'motives'. This situation creates an important *dialectics* between individual powers and goals and organizational powers and goals.

Roles

First of all, 'role' is a relational notion; a predicate with different 'arguments'. It is the part (the actions to be done, task), of an agent, *in* a given *plan* or multi-agent event. 'Role' is the position, the share, and the contribution of that agent in that plan; complementary to the other 'roles' of the partners. In organizations there are 'roles' precisely because the organization is generating and implementing cooperative *plans*. In a sense an organization is a meta-plan: both, a plan for making specific and instantiated plans, and a generic, non-instantiated plan to be applied. So the roles in the organization are generalized roles to be instantiated case by case in specific plans. In an occasional robbery X can play *in that plan and event* the role of being on the lookout; if the group becomes a stable gang, X can have within the organization the nomic role of 'being on the lookout'; that means that when a specific robbery plan will be generated X will play that role in the instantiated plan. We will put aside this distinction between these two levels in the following discussion.

Powers

First of all, necessarily the agent assigned to a given role (in a specific plan or in an organization) should possess the powers for supporting and playing its role. Any role is played thanks to individual 'powers': practical skills to perform that action; cognitive abilities for recognizing stimuli and react timely and appropriately, or for deciding between alternatives, or for planning or adapting the task; knowledge (for example, a plan library) and collected data; sometimes some material external resource to be used; etc. Assigning a role must specify the needed personal powers (requirements). *The agent puts at the disposal and service of the organization its own powers and resources for the realization of the organizational goals.* There are organizations where this 'sacrifice' requires a counterpart, some compensation or exchange; and other organizations where this is not the case: the agent gets nothing in change.

Other powers are on the contrary provided by the organization itself: like materials, tools, etc.; like authorizations and permissions[6]; like artificial, institutional, role's powers: the power of 'arresting' for a policeman, the power of 'acquiting' for a judge, the power of 'signing' an official document for the president of an organization, and so on. As we said, we will not analyze here those powers (Castelfranchi, 2003a), but let us just make two important remarks.

First, notice that all of those special powers are superstructures of previous powers, are superimposed effects on preexisting individual actions: there is an individual action (performed thanks to individual powers) with its effects, for example 'say something' or 'blocking somebody' or 'writing', which are the *vehicle* of the institutional action with its conventional effects.

Second, the exercise of institutional powers requires that the role player and/or the act be 'marked' by some cue or symbol. In fact, to have the desired conventional effect the institutional agent and act must be recognized and acknowledged as such; since an institutional effect is due to the 'compliance' of the community (Tummolini. et al. 2006).

Personal Action or Role/Organizational Action?

This problem is even more general: Is the act, performed by X, a personal/private act? Or is an act performed in its role? If the agent is not only a role-player (has its own goals or doesn't play only within this organization) this is a serious problem that requires its own 'signaling' system.

Moreover: *when the action of an agent of the organization is an action **of** the organization?*

First of all: only when the agent acts in its 'role' and for its 'role'. But this is not enough. We should distinguish between the actions internal to the organization and for its working, and the external actions of the organization towards its clients or partners or competitors. Let's call only these: 'actions *of* the organization' as a global macro-agent. *Any organization's action actually is an action of some of its members*; is 'performed' by some of them. But not all the action of the members – although playing their roles – is an action of the organization. There are specific roles for the 'external' actions; specific powers and empowerment process; there are rules and norms establishing the action α of which member and in what conditions should 'count as' the action α' of the organization. For example, who, when and how has to 'sign' a contract in order the organization has signed a contract? Who and how has to deliver a given good or provide a service, in order the organization has delivered it? It depends on some specific 'rule' or 'convention' of that organization or of the broader community.

If X lacks some of the needed powers for the assigned role, the role will be ill-played, the performance will be inadequate. But there is also the case where the personal powers exceed the role requirements. This is quite a relevant case for a dynamic organization. Actually this creates the possibility for a better exploitation of the members, for new dependence relations and tasks. Also this creates the opportunity for 'informal' dependence structure and collaborations (see next Section). Also for this reason, the agents shouldn't be designed only for a restricted role within a unique and frozen organization.

Goals and Possible Conflicts

What is the relationship between the goals of the agent and the goals of his role (in a given plan or in general)?

As we said, the basic relation with an autonomous agent, is that the externally assigned goal, the organizational task must necessarily be 'adopted' by the agent, 'translated' into an internal goal of the agent, driving its planning activity and its action. The agent being self-regulated must put its skills and resources at the service of an 'internalized' goal acquired from outside (see Section on goal-adoption).

If the agent has its own goals (or the goals of its user, or of another organization it is involved in) *there might be 'conflicts' between the agent's goals and the assigned goal in a given plan or role.* Will the agent be able to violate? Will it actually violate deciding to 'prefer' its own goal and to harm the organization? Will the agent be a cheater (sparing resources) or a striker? The issue is not unrealistic or stupid, given that – as we saw – there might be 'moral' or 'legal' conflicts, or conflicts with the user's interests.

If the agents have personal goals (or more in general extra-organizational goals) given that within the organization they acquire new resources and they may have special role powers, are we protected against *abuse*? That is, a bad use: *the use of role resources and tools for personal purposes*; like the personal use of the telephone or of paper. In particular, are we protected from 'Power abuse', that is, *from the misuse of institutional powers for private interests*. In other terms, the agent uses its role powers for its personal goals. For example, the agent may have some authorization to get into reserved data, and it will use those protected data for other interests (spy and treason; stock-jobbing; etc.); or the agent may have the power of 'prohibiting' somebody else from doing something and it will do so just for personal competition with that guy/agent.

Beliefs/Acceptances

As role player one has frequently to believe something, or at least to 'assume', 'accept' something; that is to behave and reason *as if* one believes something. On the one side, one gets information and data, or has cognitive instruments that provides to him – as role player – certain beliefs that wouldn't be acquired as 'private', lay agent. On the other side – and more importantly – it might not matter what one personally believes; one must – given his position – assume that p, declare that p, and act as if p. A classical example is that of 'jury members' which have to decide who is the best, the winner painter in an exhibition. X's personal opinion is that W is really the best one, but the jury evaluation is that Z is the winner (although nobody considers him the best, but all the jury members placed him at their second best!). Finally, X is asked by journalist: "So, which is the best painter in your opinion; which do you believe to be the best?", and she has to answer: "Z is the best".

In other words, like for goals, *there can be conflicts between the personal beliefs of the agent and its role assumptions*: for example, a policeman can be persuaded of the innocence of a guy, but – given the current proofs – he has to assume that she is guilty and pursue her.

In sum, the role 'mind' and relational structure install themselves within the individual mind. Playing a role means endow a different mind, with all possible conflicts; and means to have additional means and powers, with all the possible uses.

ROLES' DEPENDENCE NETWORKS VS. INDIVIDUALS' DEPENDENCE NETWORKS

What are the relationships between personal dependence relationships among the role players, and the role dependence relationships within an organization?

Among individual agents (with their goals, skills, resources) acting in a 'common' environment (that is, with reciprocal 'interferences'), if they are not self-sufficient, there are objective *Dependency relationships* (Castelfranchi, 1998): X has for example a goal *Gx* but doesn't have the needed abilities or resources (for example, information) for achieving that goal; while another agent Y is able to realize *Gx* or has the needed resources; thus, as for realizing *Gx* X *depends on* (needs) Y, and on his service (to do the needed action or to provide the needed resource). Given that every agents has his/her own goals and powers, an objective *Dependency Network* emerges among them, determining whether in that word/context X's goal might be realized or not; how many possibilities/alternatives X has; how much X is dependent on Y (for how many goals, how important for X, with or without alternatives, etc. (Costa & Dimuro, 2007)). Of course, what mainly matters is whether X is aware of being dependent or not, and of which agent she needs. In such a case, she can establish exchanges or cooperation and compete with others. On the other side, if Y is aware of X's dependence on him, Y gets some 'power over' X, because he is in condition to frustrate or realize X's goal (*reward power*) (Castelfranchi, 2003a).

However, *when the agents endow some role they also find themselves in new Dependence Network.* Actually the same reasoning applies to Roles (that actually are some sort of depersonalized, abstract agents, like the characters in a drama), although less accidentally: usually in a designed way. Roles are conceived for realizing a given goal in some MA plan, where other agents are supposed to realize some complementary goals. The Roles presuppose specialized abilities and resources. Thus, *among a set of roles in a plan or in an organization (a generative system of plans) there exist a Dependence Network*: Role R1 needs and relies on action A of role R2, and vice versa (Sichman & Conte, 1996).

So, what are the relationships between personal dependence relationships among the role players, and the role dependence relationships within an organization?

The theory of this is the following one:

(i) Dependence relations in an organization are not free, *not freely emergent or established by the agents*; they are pre-established as dependencies among roles to be *instantiated* as dependences among the role-players. If it has been established that a nurse depends on a medical doctor (and on its authorization) as for giving a drug to a patient, or that a patient depends on the nurse of her department for obtaining some food, then a given nurse in a given day and department is dependent on the medical doctor for giving a drug to a specific patient; or a specific patient has to ask to the present nurse for obtaining some food. This mechanism of dependence-relations *derivation* from the role-dependence structure must be modeled.

(ii) On the other side, since role-playing – as we said - presupposes and exploits individual powers (capabilities), eventually when we – as role players – depend on role R, and thus on Y playing now that role, we finally depends on Y capabilities (at disposal of the role), and on her/his trustworthiness in really putting at disposal and using them for the role. She/he must be booth capable and loyal. *Officially R1 depends on R2, but actually R1 depends on the role-player of R2.* If actually the role-player of R2 doesn't have the required powers (or is not disposed to use them) R1 is powerless.

(iii) > *The goal we receive from the role makes us dependent on Y (we wouldn't depend on Y, personally).*

> The powers we receive from the organization, from our role, make the others dependent on us.

Thus, (normally) the objective dependence relations among roles, that must be instantiated among role-players, *create new dependence relations among people* (only potentially existing in advance, since usually the agent doesn't personally have the goal he gets from his role).

Analogously, the powers *given* by the organization, and not personally possessed by the role-player, exceed from the dependence network among the agents, and establish an additional network.

(iv) In sum, *the interpersonal dependence network and the role-derived dependence network among the agents should only marginally overlap.*

The role-derived dependence network goes beyond the previous interpersonal dependence network for two reasons: because the organization creates and gives to the agents both new goals and new powers.

However, another phenomenon should be enlightened.

(v) As we said, agents might have extra-role powers. That might allow *informal, unofficial 'dependency' relations and 'roles'* also within a formal organization. For example, in a given organization nobody is officially 'able to' take photos, or use statistics, or create a web-site; there is no such a role, or the guy assumed to be able and to have the duty of doing this is not really able; while, among the members of the organization another guy (Y) – which has not such a mansion at all – is actually able to do that, and the others knows this. Suppose that for a given task that service in needed and X asks Y to do that, without any obligation, and Y is willing to do so (for internal or social incentives). Y is not doing his 'job', is playing an informal role; but this can become a usual request, an unofficial but stable 'role'; giving rise to informal networks, communities of practices, which bypass or subvert the official organization. Here the new role-dependence is derived from the personal one.

Organizations (even artificial ones) should be able to discover, valorize, and exploit all potentialities of its members, at least occasionally, and even to evolve new roles from occasional practices. They must know the potential or evolving 'repertoire' of the recruited agents. The same agents can build new organizations among themselves.

SOCIO-COGNITIVE ORGANIZATION PILLARS: 'DELEGATION' AND 'ADOPTION' ATTITUDES

Organizations are strong and stable forms of cooperation; stable in the sense that they are non-occasional, they are destined to or made for several future cooperative plans exploiting the same (evolving) competencies, without the need of negotiating from the scratch that cooperation, based on general agreements and commitments to be instantiated and adapted to the new circumstances. Coordination and negotiation costs are reduced, specialization (the right agent at the right task + repeated experience) and division of labor increase productivity, and so on. Being a structure for MA plans and cooperation, its cognitive bases (needed 'mental mediators') are the same than in any basic form of cooperative coordination: *delegation* and *adoption*. Possibly in their explicit and strong forms, based on awareness, on *expectations*, on commitments, on obligations (and - in more 'institutional' forms - on true 'norms' (even legal ones), formal powers, etc.). Those basic attitudes among the cooperating agents (and roles) must be explicitly analyzed and formalized.

Let us here – while putting aside both the normative and the institutional issues – focus a bit on those basic socio-cognitive foundations, and on some important problem created by the agent autonomy and initiative, and how to deal with them.

What 'Goal-Adoption' is

Goal-Adoption is the most fundamental atom of 'sociality' in autonomous agents. Autonomous agents are self-regulated or governed; that is, they act (exploits their resources and powers) driven by internally represented goals, for achieving their purposes. They are 'purposive systems' in classical cybernetic sense. Otherwise they are not really 'autonomous' but stimulus (ambient) driven or hetero-directed by an external controller. They usually have also their own terminal goals, their motives and interests (this makes them 'autonomous' in a more radical and deep sense: motivation-autonomous). Now the 'prodigy' is that those self-regulated, goal-driven systems (don't be confused – as all economists do – with 'selfish'!) can *import goals* from other goal-driven, purposive systems, from outside, and put their 'body', skills, problem-solving capacity, and resources at disposal of the needs/desires of another agent. They spend their powers, and actively pursue the goal of another and for another. This is 'goal-adoption', and can be motivated by different reasons:

a)   it can (rarely) be 'altruistic', that is disinterested, non motivated by, non instrumental to higher personal (non-adoptive) calculated advantages (goals);

b)   it can be instrumental to personal/private returns, part of a selfish plan; like in commerce, where: "*It is not from the benevolence of the butcher, the brewer, or the baker that we expect our dinner, but from their regard to their own interest. We address ourselves, not to their humanity but to their self-love, and never talk to them of our own necessities but of their advantages.*" (A. Smith, *An Inquiry into the Nature and Causes of the Wealth of Nations,* 1776)

c)   it can be instrumental to a personal advantage, but shared with the other: for a common goal (strict 'cooperation').

One might consider (c) a sub-case of (b) (instrumental adoption) but actually the situation is significantly different. While in pure (b) a rational agent, if possible, should cheat and defeat the other, since is not interested at all in the goal-achievement of the other, and – if she has already obtained what she was expecting from the other – has no reason at all for doing as promised; in (c) defeating the other is self-defeating, since they need each other (depend on each other) for one and the same goal, and if X does not do her share she doesn't only defeat Y but also herself, since her goal will not be achieved.

There are various important forms of 'goal-adoption':

*   *Passive*: where X abstains from creating negative interferences and obstacles to Y; she just 'lets' the other (act and) achieve his goal; although she might prevent that.
*   *Active*: where X is actively performing a given action in the world in order to realize a goal of/for Y; either a terminal goal of him, or an instrumental goal in/for Y's plan: a step in his goal pursuit.

Another distinction is between:

*   *Spontaneous/Non-requested* goal-adoption: where there is no expectation and (implicit or explicit request) by Y; or
*   *Goal-Adhesion*: where X 'accepts' to help Y, since there is an (implicit or explicit) request (expectation, order, will, …) that she does something for Y.

X can be obliged or simply committed to 'help' Y, because for example she 'promised' to do so. The promise might have been spontaneous and non-due, but after the promise X gets some obligation to do that action (Castelfranchi, 1995b); so at the moment of the execution she also 'adhere' to the obligation impinging on her.

In sum, in explicit goal-adoption *X believes that Y has the goal Gy that p and comes to have (and possibly pursue) the goal that p just because she believes this.* Or better (since this definition could cover also some form of imitation), *the agent has the goal that the other agent achieves[7] /satisfies his goal.*

(GOAL *x* (OBTAIN *y g*))

where (OBTAIN *y g*) =def (GOAL *y g*) & (KNOW *y g*)[8]

Of course, what really matters is not just 'goal-adoption' (that is, the formulation of the other's goal in our mind as a goal of us) but that such a goal becomes an 'intention' of us, that we will prefer the goal for the other over other goals. In organization the incentives for such a 'preference' are material rewards, approval, internal rewards, the commitments and the expectations of the others, norms, possible sanctions, etc.

Delegation Ontology

There is no possible MA plan, no coordination with other autonomous agents, no cooperation, no organization, without the fact that *agent X has certain expectations (predictions + wishes) about Y's behavior, and relies, counts upon that behavior* in order to perform her action and achieve the goal. (To be true this even holds in individual plans, where X expects and counts on delegated natural processes and/or on future actions of her self).

The notion of 'delegation' deserves some clarification. There are three notions, partially embedded one in the other.

(i)   *Passive delegation*: where X is just counting on Y's action, exploiting it; but she didn't actively 'allocate' that action (share) to Y; she just mentally allocates that part of her plan to Y, relying on this. (We called this form also 'weak' delegation).

(ii)   *Active delegation*: where X actively assigns that part of the plan to Y (by authority or exchange or cooperative agreement or request for help, etc.). There are two forms:
   (iia) the 'Mild' one where X just actively induces, provokes the needed behavior of Y in order to exploit it, or counts upon Y's spontaneous adoption or help.
   (iib) 'Strong' delegation, where X counts on Y's adhesion to her explicit or implicit 'request': X counts on Y's adoption of her goal (for whatever reason) also due to the fact that Y knows that. 'Adhesion' is the adoption of X's goal that Y adopts her goal.

(iii)   *Institutional or Official delegation*: where X not only allocate a part of her plan to Y, but she also 'empowers' Y for doing this, and passes to him some resource, and (more important) some responsibility or duty which was of X or of the group or organization. Suppose that X has to do α and is accountable for this; she charges Y of α; Y answers to the 'client' or to X about α; and Y doing α 'counts as' X (or the organization) have done α (and this already is a form of institutional 'empowerment').

Notice that (iii) 'Institutional Delegation' contains (iib) 'Active Strong Delegation', which contains a basic nucleus of (i) 'Passive Delegation': the idea of 'relying on': Figure 1.

In sum, in explicit goal-delegation Y believes and has the goal (want, need, desire, wish) that X will do a given action (will realize goal Gy that p) and put this as part of his own plan. It is more than 'hope', it is a strong 'expectation' of Y on X's behavior, since Y *counts on* this for achieving his goals. Predictions are not enough for coordination and organization; they actually rely on full 'expectations'.

In MA plans, from spontaneous and occasional team-work to stable organizations, the role of these two complementary mental attitudes and 'moves' is usually overlooked and left implicit; this both in social and economic studies, in philosophy, in MAS (Tuomela, 1995; Castelfranchi, 2003c).

When X is performing her share within an organizational plan, she explicitly or implicitly is counting-on the work of other people/agents and is 'delegating' to them that work. When X is a member of an organization with a specified role for possible plans, her role is explicitly or implicitly counting-on the work of other roles and is 'delegating' to them that work.

Since there are *dependence relations* among 'roles' (not only among individuals) there necessarily are delegation-adoption relations among those roles. These are *instantiated* by the role-players while actuating the plan, and they can implicitly (unaware) or explicitly delegate-adopt to/from the other role-players.

Moreover, X is also aware of the existence of complementary roles and activities, that necessarily count on her activity and role; perhaps she doesn't know which are those activities or roles, and who are the involved agents; but she knows to be just a 'part' of a functional whole. While accepting her role or while doing her job and performing her action, she is explicitly or implicitly accepting the delegation and reliance of the other roles and role-players (the boss, the partners, etc.), and one of the reasons why she is doing as expected/requested is that this is expected and requested (delegated) by the organization, and by the partners she is cooperating with.

No organization would be possible without *delegation* of tasks (at least from the boss to the workers) and without *goal-adoption* by the delegated agent. In merely emergent, implicit forms of cooperation this is just implicit, but is there. For example, in the 'technical' or 'spontaneous' division of labor nobody has in mind and designs the emergent plan and organization (such that X will produce vegetables, Y will bring to the market meat, Z will produce crockery, …), but while going to the market X expects to find Y or Z (somebody) and that Y (somebody) brings meat and Z (somebody else) crockery, and X and Z do that also thanks to (as an effect of) X's expectations about their behaviors since they are reinforced by the rewards X will provide to this. Reciprocally, X will specialize in vegetables - abandoning other activities – just because she finds success in this (due to the other expectations), less concurrence, more demand, etc. She implicitly (rewards based reinforcement learning even with random attempts) or explicitly (understanding what the others believe and want) adopts the others' goals and delegates some goals to them.

Frequently, also the Commitment relations becomes merely 'impersonal' and implicit and instantiated within an organization and an organizational plan. Actually in an organization there is a social Commitment of each member with/to the organization (Castelfranchi, 1995b) about playing (when needed) a given role in a given plan. The 'promise', the 'pact', is with the organization (as abstract collective agent). However, this implicitly implies Social-Commitments to the other members of the organization. These are some sort of 'instantiations' of the generic and broad commitment to the organization ("to play my role" "to do my job"), but, since X has concretely to collaborate with Role 2 and with Y (playing such a role), that generic commitment is *instantiated* in the concrete commitment also to Y "to play my role, to do my job", on which he relies, and that he expects precisely on the basis of X's commitment to the organization and thus to its members.

RECONCILING ORGANIZATION AND AUTONOMY (AND INTELLIGENCE)

Combining now the autonomy of the agents and the basic moves of cooperation (adopting the goal of the other, and delegating an activity to the other) we get a very crucial (and nice) problem for both human and artificial organization. *How to deal with intelligent cooperative capacity and initiative of the agents?* As we said: Why building an 'organization' of 'Agents'? Why do not just building a well pre-programmed system of automata, of executive functions? Why having problems with initiative and autonomy? Wouldn't be better many pre-organized perfect executors of their own tasks, understanding nothing, negotiating nothing, and changing nothing?

The problem is that it is just impossible to predict all possible local and timely problems during the implementation and execution of future plans; the necessary local inputs and data, and the related opportunistic reactions and situated intelligent solutions. This is the advantage of (the need for) 'autonomous' agents acting 'on our behalf' but with their own acquired information and intelligence, able to follow rules and instructions, to realize a task but also to pursue a goal in a situated and adaptive way. Autonomous agents do learn or reason; they *adapt* their behavior to not fully predictable circumstances, to the context; they learn, evolve: either acquiring information or know how.

This advantage is usually greater than the risks and harms of autonomy. Also artificial agents should be autonomous and their stable forms of coordination and cooperation for complex and common purpose should be true 'organizations' with their 'roles' and 'mansions'.

Let us explain the basic important collaborative phenomena exploiting autonomy and initiative: Open-Delegation and Over-Adoption or hyper-collaboration, and their risks.

Open vs. Closed Delegation

'Open delegation' is when X gives Y a part in the plan without specifying the specific sub-plan, the action to be done, how to realize that part (Closed-delegation). She allocates to Y a 'goal' to be achieved, and lets Y free of finding the solution on the basis of his intelligence, competence, skills, decentralized information. Y is not a blind executors (like in tayloristic farms where workers were asked not to think!), it is a competent problem-solver: X has to trust not only Y's practical skills, but his cognitive skills (Locke, 1968).

Literal Adoption vs. Over- or Critical- Adoption

Literal Adoption is when Y just does as requested, nothing more or different. *Over-Adoption* or *Help* is when Y realizes that can do something more, useful to X, and spontaneously provides X more collaboration. Like for example in 'over-answering': when X asks Y "A ticket for Baltimore, please" and Y gives her the ticket but also says: "The train is late and it is not at the usual gate; they have changed today". Notice that: this is helpful only if Y has correctly understood X's intention (to take the train now).

Critical-Adoption is when Y – in order to realize X's goal and satisfy her needs – decides to do something different, to change the allocated plan. Either because X's request is wrong for her goals; or because it cannot be realized in those circumstances, or because Y is not able to do as requested but has a different solution. X asks Y an Aspirin and he gives her a fully equivalent drug.

When a truly cooperative agent will violate our request for helping us in a different way? In three basic cases:

- When he is not able or in condition to do as requested but can solve our problem in another way;
- When our request (and plan) is wrong; and he knows this and has the right solution;
- When our plan is not wrong (and he might do as requested) but there is a better solution.

This kind of intelligent and proactive 'cooperation' is necessary and typical in any human organization.

The risks of Open-Delegation are clear: Not necessarily Y has the competences, the local information, the intelligence for building the best situated plan, for solving the problem; not necessarily Y understands the full plan with its higher goals and constraints and designs its sub-plan respecting the general aims and rules.

The risks of Over-Adoption (doing more or differently than requested) are also clear: the minor one is doing redundant and useless things; but it is also possible that Y is completely mislead: he didn't understand the real higher goals of the request and his solution is completely wrong: you ask him for a match and he gently provides you a lighter, but the match actually wasn't for smoking but for your teeth.

Hyper-collaboration is very functional (compared with stupid and blind execution) but should it been explicitly negotiated, except in case of an immediate danger?

LEAVING ROOM TO 'FUNCTIONAL VIOLATIONS'

What are the functional limits that efficient organizations should impose to their agents' pro-activity, initiative, spontaneous help? Should organization allow hyper-collaboration? Should they allow violation of organizational rules and tasks not for personal advantages but for realizing the mission of the role? Our claim is "yes". Any human organization works thanks to this kind of 'flexibility'. If we do not allows this we cannot really exploit the intelligence, the initiative, the problem solving ability, the local and update information and feedback the agents can have.

Not only informal relationships can be vital for human cooperation (also mediated by computers), and for effective collaboration among artificial agents in MAS, but even tasks, rules, procedures, and norms, violations can be necessary.

In fact there is a very important phenomenon discovered in Work and Industrial Sociology and in Sociology of Organizations (what they call "the functional violation/disregard of norms"), which must be taken into account.

In our view this sociological phenomenon is just a special case of the general principle of Over- and Critical-Adoption and of its usefulness for a deep and effective help (cooperation) between agents. The worker/member is just over-critically-adopting the goals prescribed by the organization (tasks, rules, norms) taking into account the global plan, the current circumstances, the interest of the Organization, going beyond what has been literally prescribed or negotiated. As in the theory of Over- (Critical-) help, this decision does not depend on the agent's individual interests, preferences or advantages, but precisely on his willingness to collaborate and to adopt the interest of the helped agent.

In fact, "functional violation/disregard of norms" (FVN) is characterized in the following way in the sociological literature:

"The repeated and systematic violation of criteria, prescriptions and dispositions included in the normative apparatus that defines and regulates (through "norms", in a broad sense) a collective organized activity. This violation favors an acceptable level of functioning of the organization itself, while the literal and punctual application of the normative will produce levels of functioning either unacceptable or less efficacious" (Manciulli et al. 1986, p. XI).

As a quite revealing proof of the existence and efficacy of this behavior, sociologists cite strange "forms of sabotage consisting just in a rigorous application of rulements" (Mottez 1971) - what in Italy is called "white strike" and in France is called, very appropriately, "grève du zéle". As a classic of Industrial Sociology says:

" it is well known that the best way for sabotaging an organization is that of literally obeying all its rules and refusing to use our own judgment capacity. Beyond what is obtainable by commands, beyond what is controllable by supervision, beyond what is inducible by incentives or preventable by punishment, even in the execution of the more humble jobs there is a bit of discretion... This "discretion" can be used both to allow or to subvert the aims of the organization". (Bendix, 1959). (translated from Manciulli et al.)

It is important to underline that these violations are not selfish or rebellious acts, but are systematic and intended to favor the collective work. In fact, for "functional disregard" we mean *the deliberated violation of a norm/rule/prescription finalized to make the required/expected work (also) more functional to the organization's aims.*

For the theory of the 'functional violation', also the comprehension of the relationships between "formal" and "informal" level of organization, and the theory of "communities of practice" (Huberman and Hogg 1994; Lave 1991) and their effects are relevant: *informal organization is a necessary condition for the working of the formal one* (see also Chapter "Interactions Between Formal and Informal Organizational Networks" by Lamieri and Mangalagiu).

In our view, the understanding and the theory of this phenomenon are particularly important in AI and in general in Computer Science approaches to organization. In fact,

- if it is true that real organizations of any type cannot efficiently and adaptively work without regularly ignoring or violating some of their own rules, norms, procedures,
- if for being really collaborative and efficient a good worker/member has to frequently violate some of the rules that regulate his job and some of his official commitments to the organization,

one can predict *serious difficulties or damages in formalizing, applying, and supporting with information technology the formal and official procedures, rules and norms, and literal commitments within organizations.* The resulting system will be very rigid. Notice that several applications of AI to institutions and cooperative work are aimed precisely at such formalization. On the contrary, one should be able to *understand the logic and the function of that kind of "transgression"*, and to implement and support it. But to do this we need an explanation of that behavior and of its functionality, and we have to know when and why agents do resort to this behavior, and when and why it is useful or not.

In general, we believe that even with artificial organizations it might be better to focus not just on 'procedures' and 'rules' but on the 'results' (mission) and betting on Agents' empowerment, responsibility (Locke, 1968), autonomy, learning, and distributed control.

SOME CONCLUDING REMARKS

In sum, we have challenged any anti-cognitive, merely behavioral or rule-based approach to organization, by claiming that an organization presupposes a micro-layer of agents with some necessary level of autonomy and pro-activity. Those agents have some degree of internal regulation, of internal representation, and some goal-oriented activity. We have to ground the macro organizational (sociological, institutional) layers on the micro layer of individual agents' behaviors, controlled by their internal mechanisms of learning or reasoning and choosing.

Given this view, we have introduced the basic mental ingredients for taking part in cooperative activities and in organizational 'roles', and the serious issues that this opens.

We have argued about the unavoidable 'dialectics' that this will create between the individual mental attitudes and the role mind, and between the individual powers and dependencies and the role powers and dependencies.

Our claim is that MAS discipline should – on the one hand – aim at scientifically modeling human organizations; on the other hand, it should design artificial (agent-based) organizations for supporting human work or for coordinating and improving artificial agents' work. But in order to do this, for both those aims, we should *model a high (risky) degree of flexibility* as in human organizations, exploiting the strong *autonomy*, the decentralization and situatedness, the intelligence and knowledge of the role-players and their cooperative *pro-activity,* allowing for functional violations of requests and even of rules and norms.

As for the answers to one of our central questions (*Why building an 'organization' of 'Agents'? Why do not just building a well pre-programmed system of automata, of executive functions? Why having problems with initiative and autonomy? Wouldn't be better many pre-organized perfect executors of their own tasks, understanding nothing, negotiating nothing, and changing nothing. What are the advantages of autonomous entities playing roles, and which the risks?*), along this chapter several answers have been given: a MA plan cannot *a priori* be completely designed and specified. It must be instantiated and adapted locally, in the very moment of the execution of that specific part or task, on the basis of the local data, results, monitoring, and possibilities. It requires a decentralized perception, reaction, re-planning, adaptation, experience, etc. Moreover, to fully exploit the knowledge, skills, learning, intelligence, possible pro-activity, problem solving, and over-help of the agents, the organization must leave some degree of freedom, some autonomy to them. Of course, the broader their autonomy and initiative, and in particular their having 'personal' goals, the larger the risk of misunderstandings, violations, and power abuse.

The objective of the chapter was not to 'solve' (formalize, implement, experiment) any of these problems, but to signal them, to put some strategic challenge to the community. Also because, in our view, the basic notions for this approach (like the notion of personal powers, of co-powers, of role powers; or of 'reliance' and 'adoption'; or of 'over (critical) help; etc.) are rather clear, and can be formalized and implemented (and several people are working at their formalization with various approaches, like in the present book, or in NorMAS, ANIREM, MABSS, OOOP and many other WS communities).

REFERENCES

Castelfranchi, C. (1995a). Guaranties for Autonomy in Cognitive Agent Architecture. In M. Wooldridge and N. Jennings (Eds.) *Intelligent Agents.* Springer. LNAI 890, 56-70.

Castelfranchi, C. (1995b). Social Commitment: from individual intentions to groups and organizations. In *ICMAS'95 First International Conference on Multi-Agent Systems*, AAAI-MIT Press, 41-49 (Preliminary version in *AAAI Workshop on "AI and Theory of Group and Organization"*, Washington, D. C., May 1993).

Castelfranchi, C. (1998). Modelling Social Action for AI Agents. *Artificial Intelligence, 103,* 157-182.

Castelfranchi, C. (2003a). The Micro-Macro Constitution of Power, *ProtoSociology, An International Journal of Interdisciplinary Research* Double Vol. 18-19, (2003) *Understanding the Social II – Philosophy of Sociality,* Edited by Raimo Tuomela, Gerhard Preyer, and Georg Peter.

Castelfranchi, C. (2003b). Formalising the Informal? Dynamic social order,bottom-up social control, and spontaneous normative relations. *Journal of Applied Logic, 1(2003) 47-92.*

Castelfranchi, C. (2003c). Grounding We-intentions in Individual Social Attitudes. In Matti Sintonen & Petri Ylikoski & Kaarlo Miller (eds), *"Realism in Action - Essays in the Philosophy of Social Sciences".* Kluwer Publisher.

Castelfranchi C., & Falcone R. (1997). From Task Delegation to Role Delegation, in M. Lenzerini (Editor), *AI*IA97: Advances in Artificial Intelligence, Lecture Notes in Artificial Intelligence, 1321,* 278-289. Springer-Verlag.

Conte, R., Castelfranchi, C., & Dignum, F. (1999). Autonomous Norm Acceptance. In J. Mueller (ed) *Proceedings of the 5th International workshop on Agent Theories Architectures and Languages,* Paris, 4-7 July, 1999.

Costa, A. C., Dimuro, G., & Pereira (2007). Quantifying Degrees of Dependence in Social Dependence Relations. In: Luis Antunes; Keiki Takayama. (Org.). *The Seventh International Workshop on Multi-Agent Based Simulation* (LNAI 4442), *1,* 172-187. Berlin: Springer.

Dastani, M., Dignum, V., & Dignum, F. (2002). Organizations and Normative Agents. *In Proceedings of the First Eurasian Conference on Advances in Information and Communication Technology* (Eur-Asia-ICT 2002) Tehran, Iran, October 29-31.

Falcone, R., & Castelfranchi, C. (2000). Grounding Autonomy Adjustement on Delegation and Trust Theory, J*ournal of Experimental and Theoretical Artificial Intelligence, 12*(2), 149-152.

Goffman, E. (1959). *The Presentation of Self in Everyday Life.* University of Edinburgh Social Sciences Research Centre (II edition).

Grosz, B. J., & Kraus, S. (1998). The evolution of SharedPlans. In Rao, A., and Woolridge, M., (eds.), *Foundations and Theories of Rational Agency.*

Huberman, B. A., & Hogg, T. (1994). *Communities of practice. Performance and evolution.* Palo Alto, CA: Xerox Palo Alto Research Center.

Lave, J. (1991). Situated learning in communities of practices. In L. B. Resnik, J. M. Levine, & S. D. Teasley (Eds.), *Perspectives on Socially Shared Cognition* (pp. 63-82). Washington, DC.: APA.

Levesque, H., Cohen, P. & Nunes, J.. (1990). *On acting together.* In Proceedings *Eighth National Conference on AI,* pages 94--99. AAAI-Press and MIT Press, 1990.

Locke E. A. (1968). Towards a Theory of Task Motivation and Incentives. *Organ. Behav. Hum. Perform., 3,* 157-189.

Manciulli, M., Potesta', L., & Ruggeri, F. (1986). *Il dilemma organizzativo. L'inosservanza funzionale delle norme* (The Organizational Dilemma: The Functional Disregard of Norms) F. Angeli, Milano,

Mottez, B. (1971). *La sociologie industrielle.* CNRS, Paris.

Sichman, J. S., & Conte, R., (1998) On personal and role mental attitudes: A preliminary dependence-based analysis. In F. Oliveira, editor, *Advances in AI,* volume LNAI-1515, pages 1--10. Springer-Verlag, 1998.

Sichman, J. S., Conte, R., Castelfranchi, C., & Demazeau, Y. (1998). A Social Reasoning Mechanism Based On Dependence Networks. In M. Hunhs and M. Singh (Eds.) *Readings in Agents.* Morgan Kaufmann, S. Francisco, 416-21.

Tummolini, L., & Castelfranchi, C. (2006). Cognitive and Behavioral Mediation of Institutions: Towards an Account of Institutional Actions. In *Cognitive Systems Research.* 7(2006), 307-323.

Tuomela, R. (2000). *Cooperation: A philosophical study.* Dordrecht: Kluwer Academic.

Wooldridge, M., & Jennings, N. R. (1995) Intelligent Agents: Theory and Practice. *Knowledge Engineering Review, 10*(2).

KEY TERMS

Agent: Autonomous proactive (purposive) entities. "Agents" - as defined in MAS - are autonomous entities: there is not a fully centralized processing; they have local independent information and results, and, sometimes, independent learning or reasoning; they have some pro-activity (Wooldridge and Jennings, 1995); they are regulated by internal representations (sometimes strictly 'purposive' ones, like in BDI Agents); they have their own powers (skills, but possibly also resources like data). The most qualifying and advanced form of autonomy and of agency obviously is autonomy in goals: when an agent has its own independent *motives*, and will pursue our objectives only if there is some reason and advantage for doing so (self-motivated).

Autonomy: 'Autonomy' is a relational notion: X is autonomous *from* somebody else (Y) and *as for* something (O) (Castelfranchi, 1995a). Autonomous means that X doesn't depends on Y as for (having/realizing) O; does not need Y for this. X can have or realize O by itself. An active entity can be autonomous on various dimensions and for various "resources" or "activities": for example, for accessing information and data, for learning, for reasoning, for decision making, for abilities and skills, or for external material resources (money, a car, etc.). One might be autonomous as for a given O but not for another one. For example, X may be autonomous as for deciding but not as for the needed data, because she is blind; or, X may have the practical resources for doing action A, but not being able to do it, and she needs the help of Y for this.

Goal-Adoption: Goal-Adoption is when an autonomous agent X with her own goal comes to have a new goal (and possibly pursue it), since and until she believe that it is the goal of another agent Y, in order Y realizes his goal. Goal-Adoption can be there both for altruistic or for selfish reasons. A special kind of Goal-Adoption is *Goal-Adhesion*: where X 'accepts' to help Y, since there is an (implicit or explicit) request (expectation, order, will, ...) that she does something for Y.

Goal-Delegation: Agent X has certain expectations (predictions + wishes) about Y's behavior, and relies, counts upon that behavior in order to perform her action and achieve the goal; she is allocating a part of her plan to Y. X can just count on Y's action by exploiting Y's autonomous action; Y can be unaware. In stronger forms, X actively assigns that part of the plan to Y (by authority or exchange or cooperative agreement or request for help, etc.); Y accepts this. This notion of Delegation is more basic and broader than the 'institutional' notion (usually used in organizations), where X not only allocate a part of her plan to Y, but she also 'empowers' Y for doing this, and passes to him some resource, and (more important) some responsibility or duty which was of X or of the group or organization.

Organization: "Organization" is organization *of the activities of sub-units*, able to get and process information, to act in a coordinated manner, to co-operate, and to do this with some local – decentralized – autonomy, and adaptation to the context. In particular, 'organizations' are coordination structures for cooperation among several agents, in view of *iterated and typical problems* or problem-solving activities. Any 'organization' entails *some Multi-Agent (MA) plan*, and the agents have to work (case by case) within some common plan. One of the advantages of organizations is precisely that a lot of roles in habitual plans or in possible generative plans are pre-defined and consolidated, and the performer of that part/role has not to know the whole plan or the specific higher goal, has not to negotiate about reciprocal roles, etc. This is one of the reasons organizations are efficient and convenient (reduced cognitive costs, reduced negotiation costs, pre-established general agreement, etc.). In a sense an organization is a meta-plan: both, a plan for making specific and instantiated plans, and a generic, non-instantiated plan to be applied. So the roles in the organization are generalized roles to be instantiated case by case in specific plans.

Power: Internal and external resources, skills, capabilities, conditions, that make the agent 'able' and 'in condition' to do a given action and to realize a given goal. This is the "power of" doing an action, realizing a goal. There are various forms of social power; the most basic is the "Power over" the other: Y is dependent on X as for a given goal, thus X has Power over Y as for that goal.

Role: The role is what a member, an agent, is supposed (or better prescribed) to do within a multi-agent plan, and within an organization; the set of assigned goals, duties, powers, assumptions. His 'part', or 'share'; his 'mansion' and contribution to the global outcome. A role is something to be dressed, to be 'interpreted'; a mask, a character: the agent becomes a "role player".

ENDNOTES

[1]   One might claim that an organization can be constituted by several sub-organizations, not necessarily by individuals. This is true, but what matters is that: first, they would be non analyzed and treated as individual units; second, that finally one would arrive to an individual level of decomposition; third, what really matters is that organization is a *macro-level* of analysis presupposing a *micro-level* substratum of active (purposive) units; that is of 'Agents' (as argued in this chapter).

2   "Co-power" means that agent X and agent Y are not able or in condition to realize goal G independently from each other, by acting alone, while they are able to realize G by combining their individual powers (abilities, resources, knowledge, ..) and efforts. Sociality and cooperation can expand very much what the agents can achieve (Castelfranchi, 2003a).

3   Are Multi-*Agents* systems really useful, or the basic Distributed AI was/would be enough?

4   "Anti-cognitive" means that one attempts to model organization ignoring the mind of the role-playing agents, just in terms of behaviors and rules.

5   They can also act as 'agents' of somebody ('on behalf of') not only for their own purposes; but, in both cases, they maintain some autonomy, initiative (Wooldridge & Jennings, 1995; Castelfranchi, 1995) 'personal' knowledge or experience; they are not *hetero-directed*.

6   For 'permissions' and 'rights' as 'powers' and 'empowering' see Castelfranchi, 2003b.

7   In helping and goal adoption the awareness of Y is not necessary, and also Y's pursuit of his goal is not necessary. X's help might be spontaneous, unilateral, and total (doing everything necessary for realizing g for Y).

8   This definition too is not completely satisfactory. In fact, in the definition of OBTAIN, (GOAL y g) should be just presupposed: (GOAL x (OBTAIN y g)) shouldn't imply that (GOAL x (GOAL y g)).

Chapter XI
Modelling Interactions via Commitments and Expectations

Paolo Torroni
University of Bologna, Italy

Federico Chesani
University of Bologna, Italy

Pınar Yolum
Boğaziçi University, Turkey

Marco Gavanelli
University of Ferrara, Italy

Munindar P. Singh
North Carolina State University, USA

Evelina Lamma
University of Ferrara, Italy

Marco Alberti
University of Ferrara, Italy

Paola Mello
University of Bologna, Italy

ABSTRACT

Organizational models often rely on two assumptions: openness and heterogeneity. This is, for instance, the case with organizations consisting of individuals whose behaviour is unpredictable, whose internal structure is unknown, and who do not necessarily share common goals, desires, or intentions. This fact has motivated the adoption of social-based approaches to modelling interaction in organizational models. The idea of social semantics is to abstract away from the agent internals and provide a social meaning to agent message exchanges. In this chapter, we present and discuss two declarative, social semantic approaches for modelling interaction. The first one takes a state-oriented perspective, and models interaction in terms of commitments. The second one adopts a rule-oriented perspective, and models interaction in terms of logical formulae expressing expectations about agent interaction. We use a simple interaction protocol taken from the e-commerce domain to present the functioning and features of the commitment- and expectation-based approaches, and to discuss various forms of reasoning and verification that they accommodate, and how organizational modelling can benefit from them.

INTRODUCTION

Organizations can be seen as sets of entities regulated by mechanisms of social order and created by more or less autonomous actors to achieve common goals. If we consider open agent societies from an organizational point of view, we can identify a number of basic elements that design methodologies for agent societies should account for. These include formalisms for the description, construction and control of normative elements such as roles, norms and social goals, and mechanisms to formalize the expected outcomes of roles and to describe *interaction* in order to *verify* the overall behaviour of the society.

Interaction is one of the main elements of multi-agent organizational models, since it is the main—if not the only—way for agents to coordinate with one another (see the Chapter II "Modelling Dimensions for Agent Organizations" by Coutinho *et al.* for more information). In the literature, multi-agent communication has been the subject of a vast research activity addressing *semantic* and *engineering* aspects of multi-agent organizations. Two main approaches have emerged. In the early days of multi-agent research, a seemingly promising way to model agent interaction was largely inspired by Grice's and Searle's speech acts theory. This is now called the mentalistic approach since its focus is on the minds of the individuals participating in the interaction. Agent mental states would give motivation to message exchange, which in turn would affect the mental states of those participating in the exchange. This idea has been behind prominent Agent Communication Language (ACL) proposals such as KQML and FIPA-ACL. However, it became apparent that a semantics of agent communication based on mental states would necessarily impose significant restrictions on the architecture and operational behaviour of interacting parties, while making it difficult, at the same time, for an external observer to understand to what extent a message exchange would conform to such a semantics (Singh 1998).

Social approaches to agent communication seek to overcome these shortcomings and quickly gained large popularity. The idea of social semantics is to abstract away from the agent internals and provide a social meaning to agent message exchange. In other words, interaction is not motivated by the effect it may have on the mind of the agent, but instead on its visible effects on the agent's social environment. Besides paving the way to the development of a number of techniques aimed to make agent interaction verifiable by external observers, social semantics have proven to be a viable approach to accommodate truly open agent societies, since they do not pose restrictions of any sort on the nature and architecture of interacting parties. These are key factors that made social semantics much more widely adopted than mentalistic approaches, especially in the context of organizational models.

The second aspect we mentioned relates to multi-agent systems engineering and design. Again, social semantics of agent interaction has been successfully applied to Multi-Agent System (MAS) design, both with respect to methodologies and formal reasoning about models. Current Agent-Oriented Software Engineering methodologies—see for example Gaia (Zambonelli *et al.* 2003), MaSE (DeLoach *et al.* 2001), Prometheus (Padgham & Winikoff, 2004) and the Hermes methodology presented earlier on in this book (see Chapter V "Hermes: A Pragmatic Approach to Flexible and Robust Agent Interaction Design and Implementation," by Cheong and Winikoff)—include, at some design stage, modelling of actions, events, roles, normative relations and interaction protocols. It is possible to give a social semantics to these elements of a MAS by modelling them or their effect in terms of socially meaningful concepts. Modelling greatly benefits from the social semantics being declarative. A declarative, as opposed to procedural, semantics specifies what actions should be brought out in an interaction, rather than how they are brought out, and by doing so it helps to focus on the aims of the interactions and thus avoid designing unnecessarily over-constrained interaction patterns and modalities, as pointed out by Yolum & Singh (2002b).

Social semantics can be approached in two ways: by taking a state-oriented perspective, or a rule-oriented perspective. The main elements of these two approaches are, respectively, commitments and expectations. They both provide a formal, conceptually well-founded basis for modelling the interaction of agents while respecting their autonomy.

Commitments

The main motivation behind the commitment-based semantics of agent interaction, as opposed to, e.g., using AUML interaction protocol diagrams (Bauer *et al.* 2001), comes from the observation that to ensure flexibility in handling opportunities and exploiting opportunities, the agents should be able to deviate from rigid scripts. Representing the commitments that the agents have to one another and specifying constraints on their interactions in terms of commitments provides a principled basis for agent interactions. From a MAS modelling perspective, a role can be modelled by a set of commitments. For example, a seller in an online market may be understood as committing to its price quotes and a buyer may be understood as committing to paying for goods received. Commitments also serve as a natural tool to resolve design ambiguities. In general, the designers of the individual agents would be different from the designers of the roles in the multiagent system. For example, an online market would only specify the roles of buyer, seller, and broker and their associated commitments, but individual participants may, and would often prefer to, use differently implemented agents to play these roles. Finally, the formal semantics enables verification of conformance and reasoning about the MAS specifications to define core interaction patterns and build on them by reuse, refinement, and composition.

Central to the whole approach is the idea of manipulation of commitments, specifically, their creation, discharge, delegation, assignment, cancellation, and release. Commitments are stateful objects that change in time as events occur. Time and events are, therefore, essential elements of commitment conditions. The commitments present in the system and their state capture the state of the overall system, as obtained through the socially relevant actions performed thus far.

Commitments capture the social meaning of what agents have achieved so far, and can be used to judge their conformance and as a basis to reason about possible future evolutions of their interaction. An advantage of this approach is that the evolution of commitment state can be easily expressed using a finite state machine, which in turn has a direct implementation. Such an implementation can be used to create and manipulate commitments at run-time and directly verify whether the system is in a conformant state or not. Moreover, from the commitments, both designers and concerned agents can identify pending obligations and, in case of violation, the responsibilities of the debtors.

Commitments can be given various underlying semantics, depending on their intended use, such as on the modelling aspects that one wants to capture and on the types of verification that one wants to achieve. Some examples are temporal logics (linear or branching), nonmonotonic causal logic, and the event calculus, all of which have been applied to symbolically represent commitment machines.

Expectations

Social expectations have a similar motivation but a different purpose. Similar to commitments, the idea is to provide formal tools to specify and verify the good behaviour of an open MAS, based on the externally observable agent behaviour. Differently from commitments, expectations are not objects with a state, but abstract entities that model the possible events that would make the system evolve in conformance with a set of protocols. The main idea of expectation-based semantics is that in open and dynamic MAS, a large share of information is unknown: either because it is not specified or it is private knowledge, or—especially in the case of events—because it has not (yet) been observed by anyone or is still to occur. To capture the unknown, the reasoning conducted to manipulate expectations is intrinsically hypothetical, and the social semantics of expectations is based on abductive reasoning.

To model MAS interaction, expectation-based semantics specifies the links between the observed events and the possibly observable, yet unknown, events. It does so by setting constraints on the model, called social integrity constraints (SICs). (Integrity) constraints are ubiquitous in organizational modelling theory and they are at the core of other approaches presented in this book (see, for instance, the Chapter VI "A Formal Framework for Modeling and Analysis of Organizations" by Popova and Sharpanskykh). SICs are declarative representations of invariants, which can be used to specify the set of "good" execution traces, also called histories. Expectations are a general notion, to model events of any sort, and do not necessarily refer to specific roles. Events are expected to happen or not to happen, independently of the responsibility of the agents involved in the production or avoidance of such events. There are no explicit roles of debtors and creditors. However, it is possible to represent attributes of actions of any sort, such as the sender and recipient of a message, and finite domains and CLP constraints (Jaffar & Maher, 1994) over action elements, such as the content of messages. Time is also modelled as a variable with a finite domain. Using SICs, it is possible to represent typical patterns of interaction, such as alternatives, parallel execution, sequences, mutual exclusions, and deadlines. Finally, like in commitment-based approaches, the formal semantics enables verification of conformance and reasoning on the MAS specifications, to define core interaction patterns and build on them by reuse, refinement, and composition.

Indeed, one of the main features of the expectation-based semantics is the ability to reason at run-time on the evolution of a system in terms of happening events. Such a feature enables monitoring and run-time verification of the agent behaviour's conformance to protocols and can be used to indicate possible (future or past) sequences of events that would ensure overall conformance. Although expectations—differently from commitments—are not linked to the notion of responsibility, they do have a possible reading in relation with the deontic concepts of obligation, prohibition, fulfillment, and violation. As such, they are suited to model institutional facts: an essential element of organizations which will be discussed in detail in the following parts of this book (in particular, see Chapters XIV"Specifying Artificial Institutions in the Event Calculus," by Fornara and Colombetti, and XIX "Dynamic Specifications for Norm-Governed Computational Systems," by Artikis *et al.*).

The formal semantics of SICs is given in a computational logic framework called SCIFF. Such a semantics is based on abduction: expectations are modelled as abducibles and SICs are represented as integrity constraints. The SCIFF operational semantics is defined by an abductive proof procedure. Verification is performed by the proof procedure operating directly on the specification. At every point in time, expectations define the possible evolutions of the externally visible MAS behaviour that would ensure overall system conformance to protocols. Since there can be many ways to achieve a conformant behaviour, every event that adds to the previously observed ones does not in general produce a single set of expectations, but a number of alternative sets, and it can rule out other sets by identifying inconsistencies (e.g., events that are expected both to happen and not to happen).

Commitment-based and expectation-based semantics are complementary modelling paradigms, capturing two important perspectives on social interaction, and they can both be beneficial to the design, specification, and verification of agent organizations. The objective of this chapter is thus to provide an overview of the social semantics of agent interaction using commitments and expectations and to motivate its adoption in the context of organizational modelling.

In the next section, we provide some definitions and a brief literature review, to demonstrate the topicality of social semantics in a broad sense. Then we will elaborate more on the inspiring principles that motivate the adoption of social approaches in various areas, with an emphasis on methodological and verification issues that provide further motivation to the work presented here. In the following section, we will present the NetBill protocol: a running example to use throughout the chapter. We will then review two bodies of work, dealing with social semantics in two different ways: Yolum and Singh's commitment-based semantics and the SCIFF framework for expectation-based specification and verification of agent interaction. In the concluding sections, we discuss implementation and resources related to the presented approaches and conclude by briefly describing research directions, opportunities, and new trends, and the application of social semantics to new emerging areas such as the Semantic Web services and business process management.

BACKGROUND

Traditionally, finite state machines and Petri Nets have been the main formalisms for specifying network protocol. These formalisms are advantageous mainly because they are easy to be followed by the protocol participants. These formalisms are useful in enumerating the allowed sequences of messages, but do not capture the semantics of the messages that are exchanged. Hence, these formalisms leave no opportunity for the enacting agents to reason about the protocol. Obviously, this is not acceptable in open multiagent systems, where agents are autonomous and can and will decide how they will carry out their interactions. Thus, *declarative* approaches are needed to specify the meaning of messages and to provide agents means to reason about their messages.

Another important aspect of protocols is verification. Guerin & Pitt (2002) distinguish three possible types of verification, depending on the available information about the protocol players. A first type aims to *verify that an agent will always comply*. This type of verification can be performed at design time: given a representation of the agent, by means of some proof technique (such as *model checking*), it is possible to prove that the agent will always exhibit the desired behaviour. This kind of verification requires knowledge on the agent internals or specifications. A whole body of research is devoted to agent verification; a good introduction to it is given by Bordini *et al.* (2004).

More directly related to organizational modelling are the other two types of protocol verification: *verify compliance by observation* and *verify protocol properties*. The goal of the former is to check that the behaviour being observed is compliant with some specification. It does not require any knowledge about the internals, but only the observability of the agent behaviour. Since it is based on observations, this type of verification can be performed at run-time (or, if key events are logged, after execution). This type of verification is of the uttermost importance in real-life systems, whose heterogeneity and complexity are such that protocols must allow participants adequate freedom in order to enable an effective, open organization: too many strict rules could result in over-constrained protocols of little use.

The last type of verification instead can be performed at design time, and aims to prove that some property will hold for all the interactions that correctly follow the protocol. This type of verification is again crucial in organizations defining many complex protocols, where it would be difficult (if not impossible) to manually verify that a given protocol guarantees a given property. Protocol specification languages for agent organizations should offer (or at least support) tools for expressing formal properties, and verifying them.

The formalisms that we present in this chapter mainly accommodate compliance by observation and design-time verification of interaction properties. Later in this book, Viganò & Colombetti present alternative logic-based tools to verify organizations ruled by institutions, with an emphasis on reasoning on normative constructs (see Chapter XV "Verifying Organizations Regulated by Institutions" by Viganò and Colombetti).

Running Example: The NetBill Transaction Protocol

NetBill, proposed by Cox *et al.* (1995), is a security and transaction protocol optimized for the selling and delivery of low-priced information goods, like software programs, journal articles or multimedia files. The protocol rules transactions between two agents: a Merchant (*MR*), and a Customer (*CT*).

A NetBill server is used to deal with financial issues such as those related to credit card accounts of customer and merchant. In this example, we focus on the NetBill protocol version designed for non zero-priced goods, and do not consider the variants that deal with zero-priced goods. A typical protocol run is composed of three phases:

1. **Price Negotiation.** The customer requests a quote for some goods identified by a Product ID (PrID):

    priceRequest(PrID)

    and the merchant replies with the requested price (Quote):

    priceQuote(PrID, Quote)

2. **Goods Delivery.** The customer requests the goods:

    goodsRequest(PrID, Quote)

    and the merchant delivers it in an encrypted format:

    delivery(crypt(PrID, Key), Quote)

3. **Payment.** The Customer issues an Electronic Payment Order (EPO) to the merchant, for the amount agreed for the goods:

    payment(epo(Customer, crypt(PrID, Key), Quote))

    the merchant appends the decryption Key for the goods to the EPO, signs the pair and forwards it to the NetBill server:

    endorsedEPO(epo(Customer, crypt(PrID, Key), Quote), Key, MR)

    the NetBill server deals with the actual money transfer and returns the result to the merchant:

    signedResult(Customer, PrID, Price, Key)

    who will, in turn, send a receipt for the goods and the decryption key to the customer:

    receipt(PrID, Price, Key).

The Customer can withdraw from the transaction until she has issued the EPO message payment. The Merchant can withdraw from the transaction until she has issued the endorsedEPO message.

COMMITMENT-BASED SEMANTICS

Commitments are made from one agent to another agent to bring about a certain property (Castelfranchi, 1995; Singh, 1991; Singh, 1999). Commitments result from communicative actions. That is, agents create commitments and manipulate them through the protocol they follow. We can differentiate between two types of commitments: unconditional and conditional. An unconditional commitment is denoted as $C(x, y, p)$ and means that the debtor x commits to creditor y to bring about condition p (Singh, 1999). A conditional commitment is denoted as $CC(x, y, p, q)$ and means that if the condition p is satisfied, then x will be committed to bring about condition q. Conditional commitments are useful when a party wants to commit only if a certain condition holds or only if the other party is also willing to make a commitment.

Let us consider some example commitment from the NetBill protocol. The unconditional commitment,

C(merchant, customer, receipt(PrID, Price, K))

means that the merchant commits to sending the receipt for the given product. The conditional commitment,

CC(merchant, customer, payment(epo(customer, crypt(PrID, K), Quote)), receipt(PrID, Price, K))

specifies that the merchant commits to sending the receipt if the customer pays the money.

Singh (1999) defines six operations on commitments. In the following, x, y, z denote agents, and c, c' denote commitments.

1. create(x, c) establishes the commitment c. This operation can only be performed by the debtor of the commitment.
2. discharge(x, c) resolves the commitment c. The discharge operation can only be performed by the debtor of the commitment to mean that the commitment has successfully been carried out. Discharging a commitment terminates that commitment.
3. cancel(x, c) cancels the commitment c. The cancel operation is performed by the debtor of the commitment. Usually, the cancellation of a commitment is accompanied by the creation of another commitment to compensate for the cancellation.
4. release(y, c) releases the debtor from the commitment c. It can be performed by the creditor to mean that the debtor is no longer obliged to carry out his commitment.
5. assign(y, z, c) assigns a new agent as the creditor of the commitment. More specifically, the creditor of the commitment c may assign a new creditor z to enable it to benefit from the commitment. Operationally, commitment c is eliminated and a new commitment c' is created for which z is the creditor.
6. delegate(x, z, c) is performed by the debtor of commitment c to replace itself with another agent z so that z becomes responsible to carry out the commitment. Similar to the previous operation, commitment c is eliminated, and a new commitment c' is created in which z is the debtor.

The creation and manipulation of commitments is handled via the above operations. In addition to these operations, reasoning rules on commitments capture the operational semantics of our approach. Some of these operations require additional domain knowledge to reason about. For example, canceling a commitment may be constrained differently in each domain. Or, delegating a commitment to a third party may require agreements between agents. We abstract from these details to focus on the general approach. The reasoning rules we provide here only pertain to the create and discharge operations and the conditional commitments.

Discharge Axiom: A commitment is no longer in force if the condition committed to holds.

The following axiom captures how a conditional commitment is resolved based on the temporal ordering of the commitments it refers to.

Progress Axiom: When the conditional commitment CC(x, y, p, q) holds, if p becomes true, then the original commitment no longer relevant. Instead, a new commitment is created, to reflect that the debtor x is now committed to bring about q. Conversely, if q occurs when the conditional commitment CC(x, y, p, q) holds, the original commitment is terminated and no other commitment is created.

Modelling the NetBill Protocol

Rather than exploring the entire NetBill protocol, let us view a representative part of the protocol to explain how a commitment protocol is specified and executed. The two basic roles in the NetBill protocol are merchant (MR) and customer (CT). The commitments that exist in the NetBill protocol are inherently conditional. That is, both the customer and the merchant promise to bring about certain conditions if the other party also commits to bring about certain conditions.

The following abbreviations capture the conditional commitments that exist in the NetBill protocol.

- accept(i, m) abbreviates CC(CT, MR, goods(i), pay(m)), which means that the customer commits to paying amount m if he receives the goods i
- promiseGoods(i, m) abbreviates CC(MR, CT, accept(i, m),goods(i)), which means that the merchant commits to sending the goods if the customer promises to paying the agreed amount
- promiseReceipt(i, m) abbreviates CC(MR, CT, pay(m), receipt(i)), which means that the merchant commits to sending the receipt if the customer pays the agreed-upon amount
- offer(i, m) abbreviates (promiseGoods(i, m) ∧ promiseReceipt(i, m))

These commitments are created by exchange of messages. That is, each message corresponds to an operation on commitments. By exchanging messages, participants manipulate their commitments. The following lists the messages in the NetBill protocol and the commitments they create:

- priceQuote(PrID, Quote): promiseGoods(PrID, Quote), and promiseReceipt(PrID, Quote)
- goodsRequest(PrID, Quote): accept(PrID, Quote)
- delivery(crypt(PrID, Key), Quote): promiseReceipt(PrID, Quote)

In addition to creating the above commitments, the messages also bring about certain propositions. The following lists the messages and the propositions that they realize:

- delivery(crypt(PrID, Key), Quote): goods(crypt(PrID, Key))
- payment(epo(C, crypt(PrID, K), Quote)): pay(Quote)
- receipt(PrID, Price): receipt(PrID)

Executing the NetBill Protocol

Commitment protocol specification can either be used at run time to reason about the actions (Yolum & Singh, 2002b) or can be compiled into a finite state machine at compile time (Yolum & Singh, 2002a; Chopra & Singh, 2004). If it is used at run time, then agents working from the same commitment protocol specification can reason about the protocol logically and each can choose actions appropriate for its current situation. This is especially useful when exceptions arise since the agents can find alternatives to complete their interactions. A useful method for generating alternatives is planning. Since an agent knows its current state and its desired state, it can apply a planning algorithm to derive the actions that need to be executed to reach a goal state. This way, if the agent moves to an unexpected state (as a result of an exception), it can still construct plans to reach a final state. For example, assume that in the NetBill protocol, a customer wants to buy an item without learning the price first. Current NetBill specification requires the customer to ask the price first, hence will not allow this scenario. However, in the commitment-based specification, agents are not restricted to specific sequences of actions. Any agent can start the protocol, and at whatever state holds then. Hence, the customer can send the goodsRequest action above and thereby make a conditional commitment to pay if the merchant delivers the goods and promises the receipt. The merchant can then reason about the rest of the protocol to determine its actions, e.g., that if it wants to sell the item then it needs to send the goods, and so on.

However, if agents are not equipped with tools to reason about a commitment protocol specification, then the commitment protocols can be compiled into a finite state machine. Finite state machines are easy to execute. As a result of the compilation, agents only need to follow the transitions in the finite state machine.

Verifying Commitment Protocols

Verifying the compliance of protocols at run time means checking if agents follow the protocol by their actions. In terms of commitment protocols, an agent follows the protocol if it discharges its unconditional commitments. By observing the commitments operations, an agent can decide whether agents comply with a given commitment protocol. The observing agent can be a dedicated agent that keeps track of all the messages in the system. Conversely, each agent in the system may track the commitments in which it is involved and verify that the corresponding agents comply (Venkatraman & Singh, 1999). The main idea underlying this type of verification is to compose a trace of the current protocol execution and compare this to the protocol specification. One successful way of performing this comparison is with model checking at run time. By representing the protocol specification and the protocol execution in temporal logic, one can use existing model checking tools to find out if a particular execution is a legal outcome of the protocol.

Commitment-based semantics of protocols makes it possible to verify the properties at design time (Yolum, 2007). More specifically, given a commitment-based protocol, one can check important properties such as effectiveness, consistency, and robustness. The *effectiveness* of a commitment protocol captures if a given specification allows continual progress to reach a desired state. The *consistency* of a protocol shows whether the protocol can yield conflicting computations. Ideally, the participants of a protocol should not be able to execute actions that lead the protocol to enter an inconsistent state. By studying the effects of allowed commitment operations, one can infer whether the protocol is consistent. The *robustness* of a protocol shows how well the protocol tolerates exceptions. That is, if the protocol can be carried out in alternative ways, then the protocol will be more likely to succeed in completing the necessary transactions. One can study the robustness of protocols, by investigating how well it offers alternative execution paths.

All these aspects of commitment protocols can be studied by first representing a protocol in terms of a *commitment graph* in which the nodes represent possible commitments in the protocol and the edges represent the operations between the commitments. Using a commitment graph, one can check whether infinite loops can occur such that the effective progress of the protocol is endangered or existing operations are enough to ensure that the commitments created by the protocol can be discharged. Algorithms for detecting these properties have been implemented in a tool to study organizations (Shah Nawaz, 2007).

EXPECTATION-BASED SEMANTICS

Social expectations are a logic tool to give semantics to agent interactions. Intuitively, a set of expectations represents a possible evolution of the agent system towards a correct situation. In general, many possible evolutions of the MAS are coherent with its semantics, all of them being conformant. An expectation-based system should not commit to a predefined evolution, but provide a set of possible hypotheses on the future correct evolution of the system. For this reason, it is quite natural to give expectations a hypotheses-based semantics, such as an *abductive* semantics.

Abduction is one of the fundamental forms of inference identified by the philosopher Peirce (Hartshorne & Weiss, 1965), and is naturally embedded in logic programming as abductive logic programming (ALP) (Kakas *et al.* 1993). An abductive logic program includes a knowledge base *KB*, that is, a set of clauses that may contain predicates without definition, whose truth cannot be proven, but only *assumed*. Such predicates are called *abducibles* and are typically identified syntactically. The truth of a sentence, or a goal, *G* is decided as *G* being a logic consequence (indicated with the symbol $\models$, that stands for logic entailment) of the knowledge base and a set of assumptions:

$$KB \cup \Delta \models G$$

However, hypotheses cannot be assumed freely, because, depending on the application domain, some combinations of hypotheses should be forbidden, e.g., because they contradict each other. Thus, a set of *integrity constraints* typically restricts the combinations of predicates that can be abduced at the same time. Integrity constraints (IC) must all be entailed at all times by the union of the *KB* and the set of assumptions being devised:

$KB \cup \Delta \models IC$

The KB defines the structural description of the society. It includes for example the rules for joining and leaving the society, the definition and assignment of roles, and the organizational rules. Therefore, it has strong similarities with the organizational level identified by Dignum *et al.* (2002). The goal (*G*) can be considered as a "global goal" of the agent organization, external to the goal of each individual agent (Dignum & Dignum, 2007). In SCIFF, expectations are mapped on to abducible literals. Expectations can be positive, as in $\mathbf{E}(p,t)$, meaning that it is expected that an event *p* happens at some time *t*. They can also represent the need to avoid inconsistent behaviour, by stating that an action *p* should not be performed: $\mathbf{EN}(p,t)$ is a negative expectation saying that *p* should not happen at any time *t*.

In order for a MAS to comply with a specification, the events it produces must match the expectations. To this end, a literal $\mathbf{H}(p,t)$ is used to model an event *p* occurring at time *t*. To achieve a compliant history of events, if $\mathbf{E}(p,t)$ (resp. $\mathbf{EN}(p,t)$) is in the set of expectations, then $\mathbf{H}(p,t)$ should be (resp. not be) in the set of events.

Integrity constraints serve, as is usual in ALP, to avoid combinations of assumptions that do not make sense. But they also have two important purposes for modelling interaction: from a declarative perspective, they associate actual events and expectations; from an operational perspective, they introduce forward reasoning into the machinery of resolution-based logic programming. For example, the integrity constraint

$$\mathbf{H}(p,T) \rightarrow \mathbf{E}(r,T_1) \wedge T_1 \leq T+5$$
$$\vee \mathbf{EN}(s,T_2)$$

states that if an event *p* happens at some time *T*, then an event *r* is expected to happen within 5 time units, or else no event *s* should happen at any time. Operationally, specifications written in SCIFF are interpreted and executed in a corresponding proof-procedure, which monitors the evolution of happened events and processes them on-the-fly, providing as output sets of expectations. In the example above, upon the occurrence of event *p* at time 1 (i.e., $\mathbf{H}(p,1)$), the forward evaluation of the IC generates two alterative sets of expectations: $\{\mathbf{E}(r,T_1) \wedge T_1 < 6\}$ and $\{\mathbf{EN}(s,T_2)\}$. Such sets grow monotonically during the evolution of the interaction: as more events happen, they are recorded in a set called *history*, and are matched with the expected behaviour. In case of matching, the expectations are *fulfilled*, otherwise they are *violated*.

The SCIFF proof-procedure is an extension of the IFF proof-procedure defined by Fung & Kowalski (1997). It is based on a rewriting system, which applies a set of transitions to exhaustion, generating a derivation tree. In each node of the tree, the status records the important information, such as happened events, pending, fulfilled and violated expectations, and active CLP constraints. According to the declarative semantics, the MAS evolution is considered to be compliant to the specification if, and only if, there is at least one leaf node of the tree whose expectations are fulfilled.

Compared to other abductive languages, SCIFF shows unique features: use of variables in abducibles, ability to reason on evolving histories, expectations, concepts of fulfillment and violation, and a capability to reason about both existentially and universally quantified variables, also involving CLP constraints and quantifier restrictions (Bürckert, 1994). An in-depth description of language and proof-procedure is given by Alberti *et al.* (2008).

Box 1.

[SIC$_1$]	H(tell(MR, CT, priceQuote(PrID, Quote), ID), T)
	→ E(tell(CT, MR, priceRequest(PrID), ID), T2) ∧ T2 < T.
[SIC$_2$]	H(tell(CT, MR, goodsRequest(PrID, Quote), ID), T)
	→ E(tell(MR, CT, priceQuote(PrID, Quote), ID), Tpri) ∧ Tpri < T.
[SIC$_3$]	H(tell(MR, CT, delivery(crypt(PrID, K), Quote), ID), T)
	→ E(tell(CT, MR, goodsRequest(PrID, Quote), ID), Treq) ∧ Treq < T.
[SIC$_4$]	H(tell(CT, MR, payment(epo(CT, crypt(PrID, K), Quote)), ID), T)
	→ E(tell(MR, CT, delivery(crypt(PrID, K), Quote), ID), Tdel) ∧ Tdel < T.
[SIC$_5$]	H(tell(MR, netbill, endorsedEPO(epo(CT, crypt(PrID, K), Quote), K, MR), ID), T)
	→ E(tell(CT, MR, payment(epo(C, crypt(PrID, K), Quote)), ID), Tpay) ∧ Tpay < T.
[SIC$_6$]	H(tell(netbill, MR, signedResult(CT, PrID, Quote, K), ID), Tsign) ∧ MR ! = netbill
	→ E(tell(MR,netbill, endorsedEPO(epo(CT,crypt(PrID, K), Quote), K, M), ID),T) ∧ T < Tsign.
[SIC$_7$]	H(tell(MR, CT, receipt(PrID, Quote, K), ID), Ts)
	→ E(tell(netbill, MR, signedResult(CT, PrID, Quote, K), ID), Tsign) ∧ Tsign < Ts.
[SIC$_8$]	H(tell(CT, MR, payment(epo(CT, crypt(PrID, K), Quote)), ID), T)
	→ E(tell(MR, netbill, endorsedEPO(epo(CT, crypt(PrID, K), Quote), K, MR), ID), Tepo) ∧ T < Tepo ∧ MR ! = netbill.
[SIC$_9$]	H(tell(MR, netbill, endorsedEPO(epo(CT, crypt(PrID, K), Quote), K, MR), ID), T)
	→ E(tell(netbill, MR, signedResult(CT, PrID, Quote, K), ID), Tsign) ∧ T < Tsign.
[SIC$_{10}$]	H(tell(netbill, MR, signedResult(CT, PrID, Quote, K), ID), Tsign)
	→ E(tell(MR, CT, receipt(PrID, Quote, K), ID), Ts) ∧ Tsign < Ts.

Alongside SCIFF, a *generative* version of the proof-procedure, called g-SCIFF (Montali et al., 2008), can be used to perform an analysis of the formal properties of the protocols. It works by *generating* sets of compliant histories in a compact, intensional form. The set of generated histories can be then analysed and reasoned about formally.

Let us now show a possible SCIFF specification of the NetBill protocol and of one of its properties.

NetBill Protocol Specification in SCIFF

We can model the NetBill protocol using the SICs shown in Box 1. We assume that the network layer is reliable and that transmission time is negligible, so that the times of sending and receiving can be considered to be the same.

[SIC$_1$-SIC$_7$] are *backward* SICs, i.e., integrity constraints that state that if some set of events happens, then some other set of events is expected to have happened before. [SIC$_1$], for example, imposes that if MR has sent a priceQuote message to CT, stating that MR's quote for the goods identified by PrID is Quote, in the interaction identified by ID, then we expect that CT has sent to MR a priceRequest message for the same goods, in the course of the same interaction, at an earlier time.

[SIC_8-SIC_{10}] instead are *forward* SICs. [SIC_9] imposes that an endorsedEPO message from MR to the NetBill server be followed by a signedResult message, with the corresponding parameters. Note that we impose forward constraints only from the payment message onwards, because both parties (merchant and customer) can withdraw from the transaction during *Price Negotiation* and *Good Delivery*: hence the uttering of messages in the first part of the protocol does not lead to any expectation to utter further messages.

Forward and backward SICs have a different purpose. The former can be used to produce specifications in line with the philosophy of commitment-based semantics. They model a reactive behaviour and describe a step-by-step evolution of the interaction similarly to what we could do with a state machine. For example, the purpose of SIC_1 is to prevent unsolicited quotes (a priceQuote must always follow a priceRequest). If we deleted SIC_1 from the NetBill specification, we would enable unsolicited quotes. Conversely, if we replaced SIC_1 with the following forward SIC:

H(tell(CT, MR, priceRequest(PrID), ID), T)
$\rightarrow$ E(tell(MR, CT, priceQuote(PrID, Quote), ID), T2) $\wedge$ T < T2.

the semantics would be, instead, that a merchant must always respond to a priceRequest. Therefore, if we want to specify the protocol in such a way that agents can start at any time, skipping the previous steps, then forward SICs is what we want to use. Backward SICs instead can be used to give a protocol specification that more closely follows NetBill's original, rigid specification. Both types of SICs are well-suited to run-time verification. While each time there is a new communicative action forward SICs tell what should happen (or should be avoided) later, backward SICs instead tell what should have happened before for the system to be in a compliant state. Sometimes it is useful to have both SICs. This is the case, e.g., with SIC_5 and SIC_8. We can use SIC_5 for run-time verification and SIC_8 to specify the next message needed to keep the system compliant. Forward SICs can also be used to implement compliant agents, as it is shown by Alberti *et al.* (2006a).

Verifying Expectation-Based Protocols

Compliance to expectation-based protocols specified in the SCIFF language can be verified at run-time using the SCIFF proof-procedure. Design-time verification instead can be done using g-SCIFF.

A sample protocol property that can be verified using g-SCIFF is the following:

As long as the protocol is respected, the merchant receives the payment for some goods G if and only if the customer receives the goods G. (goods atomicity property, GAP)

To this end, we model payment by way of a signedResult message issued from the NetBill server, and goods receipt by way of two messages addressed to the customer, containing the encrypted goods (delivery message) and the encryption key (receipt message). Then, GAP can be expressed with a double implication:

H(tell(netbill, MR, signedResult(CT, PrID, Quote, K), ID), Tsign)
$\Leftrightarrow$ H(tell(MR, CT, delivery(crypt(PrID, K), Quote), ID), T)
$\wedge$ H(tell(MR, CT, receipt(PrID, Quote, K), ID), Ts)

and its validity can be automatically proven as shown by Chesani (2007). Design-time verification can address consistency to show that there exists at least one possible way to execute a protocol correctly. The existence of alternative protocol runs that bring the protocol to correct completion, which is related to the property of robustness mentioned earlier, is modelled via disjunctive SICs.

One of the advantages of the expectation-based approach is that there is a single language to specify protocols, verify their run-time execution and their properties at design-time. For run-time verification, SCIFF does not resort to model checkers, which can become quite costly in terms of memory use. Instead, SCIFF reasons on intensional state descriptions and it makes extensive use of a constraint solver. In this way, it is possible to model deadlines and, e.g., identify violations as soon as they expire without an expected event occurring.

SCIFF is embedded in the SOCS-SI interaction monitoring and verification system.[1] A protocol repository[2] contains a number of protocols modelled in SCIFF and some experimental results.

CONCLUSION

Mechanisms to describe and verify interaction are indispensable elements of engineering methodologies for agent societies. Commitment-based and expectation-based semantics are declarative approaches for specifying interaction protocols. Since both of these approaches are based on social semantics, they are verifiable without knowing the agents' internals.

Commitment protocols associate commitment operations with the messages of the agents so that by sending messages agents create or manipulate their commitments. Agents that follow these protocols can choose their actions by generating plans. This enables protocols to be executed flexibly. By maintaining the list of commitments in the system, an agent can verify whether others comply with the given protocol.

Expectation-based protocols use logic-based forward rules and a knowledge base to associate socially relevant events, such as agent messages, with expectations about what else should or should not happen. This enables protocols to be easily verified at run-time. It also enables reasoning with events together with other facts or hypotheses that can be made about the components and behaviour of an organization.

Expectations and commitments are important elements of organizational multi-agent systems. They exist outside of individual agents to specify and regulate the behaviour of an agent organization's members, and as such they could be used to express the organizational element inside a social artifact (Dignum & Dignum, 2007; Omicini *et al.* 2004).

The approaches presented in this chapter rely on the notions of openness and heterogeneity in MAS and are proposed to support organizational design and a positive integration of organizational and individual perspectives. Agents can reason upon the status of commitments and social expectations to plan and deliberate about future courses of actions. The fulfillment status of expectations and commitments can be verified to monitor the behaviour of a system and decide about reachability of goals in an organization-centric coordination perspective, while preserving the autonomy of the individuals.

While practical applications of agents to organizational modelling are being widely developed, work presented in this chapter answers to the need of formal theories to describe interaction. Interaction models often need to refer to other elements of the domain knowledge that are central in organizational models, such as roles and organizational facts. Formal theories should aim to bring together all these elements to accommodate design, monitoring, reasoning and verification. Previous work by Yolum & Singh (2002b) has shown how commitments can be embedded in a logical framework based on the event calculus. Expectations are an essential element of a general logical framework that integrates reactivity and rationality in the context of hypothetical reasoning and relying on the strengths of constraint-based reasoning. This poses the interesting question of how to gain the most benefit from the combination of commitments and expectations in an organizational modelling context, and paves the way to new interesting lines of research.

FUTURE RESEARCH DIRECTIONS

Commitments and expectations have different strengths and weaknesses with respect to expressive power and verification capability. Therefore, an interesting future direction would be a thorough study of their differences, to understand if and how these languages can be mapped to one other and how can be used together for protocol execution, monitoring, and verification.

A promising research direction being undertaken using both approaches is the application of such paradigms to the domain of Service Oriented Computing, especially in connection with advanced cross-enterprise service engagements. MAS and services have much in common (Singh & Huhns, 2005). Both aim to facilitate the integration of new applications, overcoming difficulties due to platform, language, and architecture heterogeneity and component autonomy. And when we think of services as real-life business services rather than merely as technical (web) services, the benefits of MAS organization modelling become more apparent. Services must both support individual perspectives, expressed in terms of policies, and overall notions of correctness and compliance, expressed via protocols. Viewed in this manner, the above discussions of commitments and expectations—although cast in the terms of protocols—apply to *service composition* in its broadest sense.

A real-life service engagement involves both commitments and expectations. The commitments encode the high-level contractual relationships among the participants and the expectations encode the rules of interaction as well as de facto modes of behaviour. Further, we can identify the protocols as patterns of interaction, which can be used to succinctly and reusably specify service engagements. In this manner, the design, modelling, verification, and enactment of organizations of business partners may readily be built on the approaches surveyed in this chapter. Take for example two possible candidate roles for a service engagement that we want to design. Are these two profiles interchangeable, with respect to the task at hand? Interoperability checking helps us define a set of possible alternatives that we can later evaluate based on extra-logical criteria in the economy of the organization. The adoption of a social approach for specifying and verifying interaction enables us to declaratively specify a minimal set of constraints that guarantee a fruitful collaboration, while respecting the autonomy of the individuals and avoiding harmful over-specification.

We and our colleagues have already begun work along this research path and have obtained several promising results. Recently, Singh and colleagues have applied the concept of commitment-based protocols to the service oriented architecture and business process management contexts, by addressing the problem of business process adaptability (Desai *et al.* 2006a) and of protocol composition (Desai *et al.* 2006b). Alberti *et al.* (2006b, 2007a) and Chesani *et al.* (2007) have applied social expectations to the specification of individual services and choreographies, to the formal study of the conformance of services to choreographies and of the interoperability of services. Further, expectations have been used to study goal reachability in the context of service contracting (Alberti *et al.* 2007b).

Another interesting issue concerns the declarative semantics of the approaches. Chopra & Singh (2004) and Xing *et al.* (2003) show how commitments can be mapped to various underlying logic-based formalisms. In these logics, the proof of properties for the specified system is usually done via model checking. Expectations, instead, adopt the abductive logic programming semantics. A future research direction is the investigation of how these different formalisms relate. In particular, in the context of organizational modelling and interaction verification, it is interesting to study the combination of model checking and proof-theoretic techniques to perform a variety of different verification tasks, such as conformance checking, static verification of properties, and interoperability between global and local models.

ACKNOWLEDGMENT

This work has been partially funded by the following projects: MIUR-PRIN 2005-011293,[3] MIUR-FIRB TOCAI.it,[4] TÜBİTAK-105E073.

REFERENCES

Alberti, M., Chesani, F., Gavanelli, M., Lamma, E., & Mello, P. (2006a). A verifiable logic-based agent architecture. In F. Esposito, Z. W. Ras, D. Malerba, G. Semeraro (Eds.), *Proceedings of the 16th International Symposium on Foundations of Intelligent Systems, LNAI 4203* (pp. 188–197). Berlin, Germany: Springer.

Alberti, M., Chesani, F., Gavanelli, M., Lamma, E., Mello, P., & Montali, M. (2006b). An abductive framework for a-priori verification of web services. In A. Bossi, M. J. Maher (Eds.), *Proceedings of the 8th ACM SIGPLAN Conference on Principles and Practice of Declarative Programming* (pp 39-50). New York, NY: ACM Press.

Alberti, M., Chesani, F., Gavanelli ,M., Lamma, E., Mello, P., Montali, M., & Torroni, P. (2007a). A rule-based approach for reasoning about collaboration between smart web services. In M. Marchiori, J. Z. Pan, C. de Sainte Marie (Eds.), *Proceedings of the 1st International Conference on Web Reasoning and Rule Systems, LNCS 4524* (pp. 279–288). Berlin, Germany: Springer.

Alberti, M., Chesani, F., Gavanelli, M., Lamma, E., Mello, P., Montali, M., & Torroni, P. (2007b). Web service contracting: Specification and reasoning with SCIFF. In E. Franconi, M. Kifer, W. May (Eds.), *Proceedings of the 4th European Semantic Web Conference, LNAI 4519* (pp. 68–83). Berlin, Germany: Springer.

Alberti, M., Chesani, F., Gavanelli, M., Lamma, E., Mello, P., & Torroni, P. (2008). Verifiable agent interaction in abductive logic programming: The SCIFF Framework. *ACM Transactions on Computational Logic, 9*(4), Article 29.

Bauer, B., Müller, J. P., & Odell, J. (2001). Agent UML: A formalism for specifying multiagent software systems. *International Journal of Software Engineering and Knowledge Engineering, 11*(3), 207–230.

Bordini, R. H., Fisher, M., Visser, W., & Wooldridge, M. (2004). Model checking rational agents. *IEEE Intelligent Systems 19*(5), 46–52

Bürckert, H. J. (1994). A resolution principle for constrained logics. *Artificial Intelligence, 66*, 235–271.

Castelfranchi, C. (1995) Commitments: From individual intentions to groups and organizations. In V. R. Lesser, L. Gasser (Eds.): *Proceedings of the First International Conference on Multiagent Systems* (pp. 41–48). Cambridge, MA: The MIT Press.

Chesani, F. (2007). *Specification, execution and verification of interaction protocols.* Unpublished doctoral dissertation, University of Bologna, Department of Computer Engineering (DEIS), Italy.

Chesani, F., Mello, P., Montali, M., & Storari, S. (2007). Agent societies and service choreographies: A declarative approach to specification and verification. In M. Baldoni, C. Baroglio, V. Mascardi (Eds.), *Agents, Web-Service, and Ontologies: Integrated Methodologies. Proceedings of the International Workshop MALLOW-AWESOME'007. Durham, September 6th-7th, 2007.* Retrieved May 26, 2008, from http://awesome007.disi.unige.it/proceedings.html

Chopra, A. K., & Singh, M. P. (2004). Nonmonotonic commitment machines. *Advances in Agent Communication, International Workshop on Agent Communication Languages, LNCS 2922* (pp. 183–200). Berlin, Germany: Springer.

Cox, B., Tygar, J. C., & Sirbu, M. (1995). NetBill security and transaction protocol. In D. E. Geer Jr (Ed.): *Proceedings of the First USENIX Workshop on Electronic Commerce.* Retrieved on May 26, 2008, from http://www.usenix.org/publications/library/proceedings/ec95/cox.html

DeLoach, S. A., Wood, M. F., & Sparkman, C. H. (2001). Multiagent systems engineering. *International Journal of Software Engineering and Knowledge Engineering, 11*(3), 231–258.

Desai, N., Chopra, A. K., & Singh, M. P. (2006a). Business process adaptations via protocols. In J. Zhao, M. Blake, P. Hung (Eds.), *Proceedings of the Third IEEE International Conference on Services Computing* (pp. 103–110). Washington, DC: IEEE Computer Society.

Desai N., Mallya, A. U. Chopra, A. K., & Singh, M. P. (2006b). OWL-P: A methodology for business process development. In M. Kolp, P. Bresciani, B. Henderson-Sellers, M. Winikoff (Eds.), *Agent-Oriented Information Systems III, 7th International Bi-Conference Workshop, LNCS 3529* (pp. 79–94). Berlin, Germany: Springer.

Dignum, V., & Dignum, F. (2007). Coordinating tasks in agent organization or: Can we ask you to read this paper? In P. Noriega, J. Vázquez-Salceda, G. Boella, O. Boissier, V. Dignum, N. Fornara, E. Matson (Eds.): *Coordination, Organisations, Institutions and Norms in Agent Systems II, LNCS 4386* (pp. 32–47). Berlin, Germany: Springer.

Dignum, V., Meyer, J.-J. Ch., Wiegand, H., & Dignum, F. (2002). An organisational-oriented model for agent societies. In: G. Lindemann, D. Moldt, M. Paolucci, B. Yu (Eds.), *Proceedings of the RASTA*

Workshop at AAMAS'02, Communications Vol. 318 (pp. 31–50). Hamburg University, Faculty of Informatics, Germany.

Fung, T. H., & Kowalski, R. A. (1997). The IFF proof-procedure for abductive logic programming. *Journal of Logic Programming, 33*(2), 151–165.

Guerin, F., & Pitt, J. (2002) Proving properties of open agent systems. In: C. Castelfranchi, W. Lewis Johnson (Eds.), *Proceedings of the First International Joint Conference on Autonomous Agents and Multi-Agent Systems* (pp. 557–558). New York, NY: ACM Press.

Hartshorne, C., & Weiss, P. (1965). *Collected papers of Charles Sanders Peirce, 1931–1958*. Cambridge, MA: Harvard University Press.

Jaffar, J., & Maher, M.J. (1994). Constraint logic programming: A survey. *Journal of Logic Programming, 19–20*, 503–582.

Kakas, A. C., Kowalski, R. A., & Toni, F. (1993). Abductive logic programming. *Journal of Logic and Computation, 2*(6), 719–770.

Montali, A., Alberti, M., Chesani, F., Gavanelli, M., Lamma, E., & Torroni, P. (2008). Verification from declarative specifications using Logic Programming. In M. Garcia de la Banda & E. Pontelli (Eds.), *Proceedings of the 24th International Conference on Logic Programming, LNCS*. Berlin, Germany: Springer.

Omicini, A., Ricci, A., Viroli, M., Castelfranchi, C., & Tummolini, L. (2004). Coordination artifacts: Environment-based coordination for intelligent agents. In: C. Castelfranchi, W. Lewis Johnson (Eds.), *Proceedings of the First International Joint Conference on Autonomous Agents and Multi-Agent Systems* (pp. 286–293). New York, NY: ACM Press.

Padgham, L., & Winikoff, M. (2004). *Developing intelligent systems: A practical guide*. Hoboken, NJ: John Wiley & Sons, Inc.

Shah Nawaz, S. (2007). *Commitment-based analysis of organizations: Dealing with inconsistencies*. Unpublished Master Thesis. Boğaziçi University, Department of Computer Engineering, Istanbul, Turkey.

Singh, M. P. (1991). Social and psychological commitments in multiagent systems. In *AAAI Fall Symposium on Knowledge and Action at Social and Organizational Levels* (pp. 104–106). Menlo Park, CA: AAAI Press.

Singh, M. P. (1998). Agent communication languages: Rethinking the principles. *IEEE Computer, 31*(12), 40–47.

Singh, M. P. (1999). An ontology for commitments in multiagent systems: Toward a unification of normative concepts. *Artificial Intelligence and Law, 7*, 97–113.

Singh, M. P., & Huhns., M. N. (2005). *Service-Oriented Computing*, Hoboken, NJ: John Wiley & Sons, Inc.

Venkatraman, M., & Singh, M. P. (1999). Verifying compliance with commitment protocols: Enabling open Web-based multiagent systems. *Autonomous Agents and Multi-Agent Systems, 2*(3), 217–236.

Xing J., & Singh, M. P. (2003). Engineering commitment-based multiagent systems: A temporal logic approach. In: J. S. Rosenschein, T. Sandholm, M. Wooldridge, M. Yokoo (Eds.), *Proceedings of the Second International Joint Conference on Autonomous Agents and Multi-Agent Systems* (pp. 891–898). New York, NY: ACM Press.

Yolum, P. (2007). Design time analysis of multiagent protocols. *Data and Knowledge Engineering, 63*, 137–154.

Yolum, P., & Singh, M. P. (2002a). Commitment machines. In J.-J. Ch. Meyer, M. Tambe (Eds.): *Proceedings of the 8th International Workshop on Agent Theories, Architectures, and Languages, LNAI 2333* (pp. 235–247). Berlin, Germany: Springer.

Yolum, P., & Singh, M.P. (2002b). Flexible protocol specification and execution: Applying event calculus planning using commitments. In: C. Castelfranchi, W. Lewis Johnson (Eds.), *Proceedings of the First International Joint Conference on Autonomous Agents and Multi-Agent Systems* (pp. 527–534). New York, NY: ACM Press.

Zambonelli, F., Jennings, N. R., & Wooldridge, M. (2003) Developing multiagent systems: The Gaia methodology. *ACM Transactions on Software Engineering and Methodology (TOSEM), 12*(3), 317–370.

ADDITIONAL READING

On Multi-Agent Organizational Paradigms

Horling, B., & Lesser, V. (2004). A survey of multi-agent organizational paradigms. *The Knowledge Engineering Review, 19*, 281–316.

On Agent-Oriented Software Engineering Methodologies

Zambonelli, F., & Omicini, A. (2004). Challenges and research directions in agent-oriented software engineering. *Autonomous Agents and Multi-Agent Sytems, 9*, 253–283.

Desai, N., Mallya, A.U., Chopra, A.K., & Singh, M.P. (2005). Interaction protocols as design abstractions for business processes. *IEEE Transactions on Software Engineering, 31(12)*, 1015–1027.

Bresciani, P., Giorgini, P., Giunchiglia, F., Mylopoulos, J., & Perini, A. (2004). Tropos: an agent-oriented software development methodology. *Autonomous Agents and Multi-Agent Systems, 8(3)*, 203–236.

Bergenti, F., Gleizes, M.-P., & Zambonelli, F. (Eds.). *Methodologies and software engineering for agent systems: The agent-oriented software engineering handbook*. Boston, MA: Kluwer Academic Publishers.

On Commitments

Desai, N., Chopra, A.K., & Singh, M.P. (2007). Representing and reasoning about commitments in business processes. In A. Howe and R. Holt (Eds.): *Proceedings of the 22nd AAAI Conference on Artificial Intelligence*, (pp. 1328–1333). Menlo Park, CA: AAAI Press.

Flores, R.A., Pasquier, P., & Chaib-draa, B. (2007). Conversational semantics sustained by commitments. *Autonomous Agents and Multi-Agent Systems* 14(2), 165–186.

Fornara, N. & Colombetti, M. (2002) Operational specification of a commitment-based agent communication language. In: C. Castelfranchi, W. Lewis Johnson (Eds.), *Proceedings of the First International Joint Conference on Autonomous Agents and Multi-Agent Systems* (pp. 535–542). New York, NY: ACM Press.

Singh, M.P. (2008) Semantical considerations on dialectical and practical commitments. In D. Fox, C. Gomes (Eds.): *Proceedings of the 23rd AAAI Conference on Artificial Intelligence*. Menlo Park, CA: AAAI Press.

Yolum, P., & Singh, M.P. (2007). Enacting protocols by commitment concession. In E. H. Durfee, M. Yokoo, M. N. Huhns, O. Shehory (Eds.): *Proceedings of the Sixth International Joint Conference on Autonomous Agents and MultiAgent Systems (AAMAS)*. (pp. 116–123). New York, NY: ACM Press.

Wan, F. & Singh, M.P. (2005). Formalizing and achieving multiparty agreements via commitments. In F. Dignum, V. Dignum, S. Koenig, S. Kraus, M. P. Singh, M. Wooldridge (Eds.): *Proceedings of the Fourth International Joint Conference on Autonomous Agents and MultiAgent Systems*. (pp. 770–777). New York, NY: ACM Press.

Winikoff, M. (2007). Implementing Commitment-Based Interaction. In E. H. Durfee, M. Yokoo, M. N. Huhns, O. Shehory (Eds.): *Proceedings of the Sixth International Joint Conference on Autonomous Agents and MultiAgent Systems (AAMAS)*. (pp. 868–875). New York, NY: ACM Press.

Winikoff, M., Liu, W., & Harland, J. (2005). Enhancing commitment machines. In J. A. Leite, A. Omicini, P. Torroni, P. Yolum (Eds.): *Proceedings of the Second International Workshop on Declarative Agent Languages and Technologies, LNAI 3476* (pp. 198–220). Berlin, Germany: Springer.

On Computational Logic-Based Agents

Fisher, M., Bordini, R.H., Hirsch, B., & Torroni, P. (2007). Computational logics and agents: A road map of current technologies and future trends. *Computational Intelligence, 23(1)*, 61–91.

Mascardi, V., Martelli, M., & Sterling, L. S. (2004). Logic based specification languages for

intelligent software agents. *Theory and Practice of Logic Programming, 4(4)*, 429–494.

Torroni, P. (2004). Computational logic in multi-agent systems: Recent advances and future directions. *Annals of Mathematics and Artificial Intelligence, 42(1–3)*, 293–305.

On the Logics Mentioned in the Chapter

Abductive Logic Programming

Kakas, A.C., Kowalski, R.A., & Toni, F. (1998). The role of abduction in logic programming. In D.M. Gabbay, C.J. Hogger and J.A. Robinson (Eds.): *Handbook of logic in artificial intelligence and logic programming, vol. 5* (pp. 235–324). Oxford, UK: Oxford University Press.

Constraint Logic Programming

Marriott, K., & Stuckey, P.J. (1998). *Programming with constraints: An introduction.* Cambridge, MA: The MIT Press.

Event Calculus

Kowalski, R., & Sergot, M. J. (1986). A logic-based calculus of events. *New Generation Computing, 4(1)*, 67–95.

Model Checking

Clarke, E.M., Grumberg, O., & Peled, D.A. (2000). *Model checking.* Cambridge, MA: The MIT Press.

Temporal Logic

Emerson, E.A. (1990). Temporal and modal logic. In J. van Leeuwen (Ed.): *Handbook of theoretical computer science, Part B* (pp. 995–1072). Amsterdam, The Netherlands: North-Holland.

Nonmonotonic Causal Theories

Giunchiglia, E., Lee, J., Lifschitz, V., McCain, N., & Turner, H. (2004). Nonmonotonic causal theories. *Artificial Intelligence, 153(1–2)*, 49–104.

On Tools and Applications

Desai, N., Chopra, A.K., Arrott, M., Specht, B., & Singh, M.P. (2007). Engineering foreign exchange processes via commitment protocols. In L.-J. Zhang, W. van der Aalst, P. C. K. Hung (Eds.): *Proceedings of the Fourth IEEE International Conference on Services Computing* (pp. 514–521). Washington, DC: IEEE Computer Society.

KEY TERMS

Commitment: In simple terms, a directed obligation from one agent to another to bring about a particular condition. A commitment is open to manipulation from its participants.

Declarative Semantics: Association of meaning that specifies what rather than how. Communication with declarative semantics specifies what actions should be brought out in an interaction, rather than how they are brought out.

Expectation: An abstract entity that captures the possible events that would make a multiagent system conform to its requirements.

Execution Flexibility: Providing agents options in carrying out their interactions. Protocols that support execution flexibility allow agents to handle exceptions and take advantage of opportunities at run time.

Interaction Protocol: A set of rules that regulate the interactions between agents that work together.

Verification of Agent Compliance: Checking if agents that participate in a protocol follow the protocol rules.

Verification of Protocol Rules: Checking if protocol rules enable agents to carry out the protocol as desired. If protocol rules are specified incorrectly, possibly leading to deadlocks or livelocks, their verification should signal this.

ENDNOTES

[1]   http://lia.deis.unibo.it/research/socs_si/
[2]   http://lia.deis.unibo.it/research/socs_si/protocols.html
[3]   Specification and verification of agent interaction protocols. Project Home Page: http://www.ricercaitaliana.it/prin/dettaglio_prin_en-2005011293.htm
[4]   Knowledge-oriented technologies for enterprise aggregation in Internet. Project Home Page: http://www.dis.uniroma1.it/~tocai/

Chapter XII
Communications for Agent–Based Human Team Support

Gita Sukthankar
University of Central Florida, USA

Katia Sycara
Carnegie Mellon University, USA

Joseph A. Giampapa
Carnegie Mellon University, USA

Christopher Burnett
University of Aberdeen, Scotland

ABSTRACT

This chapter discusses the problem of agent aiding of ad-hoc, decentralized human teams so as to improve team performance on time-stressed group tasks. To see how human teams rise to the challenge, we analyze the communication patterns of teams performing a collaborative search task that recreates some of the cognitive difficulties faced by teams during search and rescue operations. Our experiments show that the communication patterns of successful decentralized ad-hoc teams performing a version of the task that requires tight coordination differ both from the teams that are less successful at task completion and from teams performing a loosely coupled version of the same task. We conclude by discussing: (1) what lessons can be derived, from observing humans, to facilitate the development of agents to support ad-hoc, decentralized teams, and (2) where can intelligent agents be inserted into human teams to improve the humans' performance.

INTRODUCTION

Teams are a form of organizational structure where the decision-making is a bundle of interdependent activities that involve gathering, interpreting and exchanging information; creating and identifying alternative courses of action; choosing among alternatives by integrating the often different perspectives of team members; implementing a choice and monitoring its consequences. It is well recognized that proficient teams achieve goals and accomplish tasks that otherwise would not be achievable by groups of uncoordinated individuals. While previous work in teamwork theory (Salas and Fiore, 2004) has focused on describing ways in which humans coordinate their activities, there has been little previous work on which of those specific activities, information flows and team performance can be enhanced by being aided by software agents. This chapter reports work on, (a) characteristics and challenges of human teamwork, related to decentralization and self-organization in time-stressed situations, (b) study of human teamwork performance that incorporate these challenges in order to establish a baseline, and (c) identification of fruitful ways for agents to aid human teams with these characteristics.

In this chapter, we focus on examining the coordination and self-organization problems faced by decentralized ad hoc human teams. Ad hoc teams are groups that are brought together for the duration of a task and who lack prior experience training together as a team. An ad hoc team can be as simple as a group playing a pick-up soccer game in the park or as complicated as a multinational peacekeeping forces working alongside personnel that lack previous operational experience working together. Much of the previous work on human teamwork for time-stressed situations, most of it in commercial aviation and the military, has focused on (a) teams where the team members already have an assigned role (e.g. a pilot, co-pilot and navigator in cockpit teams), (b) where the team already has a given authority structure, and (c) where the team members were collocated. Recent interest in supporting emergency response teams, military interest in operations other than war, and coalition operations, motivates the need for teams that engage in time-stressed tasks, are distributed in space and time, and are ad hoc in their organization.

Some important issues arise in ad hoc teams: when faced with a new task, how do team members that come together as a team for the first time create roles and allocate them to team members, when no organizational structure is exogenously provided? To design and build software agents that can assist ad hoc and self-organizing human teams tackling unfamiliar tasks, we need to address this question. If the supporting agents are insensitive to shifts in the team's organization, they cannot effectively monitor the team's activities. (Please see Chapter XIX, "Dynamic Specifications for Norm Governed System" by Artikis et al., for more discussion on the problem of run-time organizational shifts).

Although our research is focused towards the ultimate goal of developing agent assistants for human teams, we believe that this work is also relevant to researchers studying purely agent-based teamwork, especially as agents become increasingly sophisticated and capable of human-like teamwork.

Work in the team literature (Fiore et al. 2003) has found that establishing effective communication patterns are the key to creating effective ad hoc agent systems and human teams; this is especially true for distributed ad hoc teams in which communication is cited as a key problem area (Pascual et al., 1999). Our research is an initial step towards the problem of identifying communication patterns of teamwork of ad hoc and distributed teams in time-critical situations so that suitable agent aiding strategies could be developed. The identification of the patterns is through communication logs collected from human teams. The results of prior research on team communication have typically been used for developing guidelines for team training. In contrast, we are interested in using team communication results for monitoring team performance by software agents that would be used for team aiding. The focus of our initial human team experimentation is to (a) establish a baseline of human-only teamwork for a given task domain and (b) ascertain the relative importance of different information flows for the team task in order to derive "insertion points" for agent assistance of human teams. These insertion points are not merely limited to coordination and information flows, but include teamwork self-organization, maintenance and task completion.

BACKGROUND

Research in human team performance suggests that experienced teams develop a shared understanding or *shared mental model* to coordinate behaviors by anticipating each other's needs and adapting to task demands (Fiore and Schooler, 2004). Furthermore, for such teams, both tacit and explicit coordination strategies are important in facilitating teamwork processes. Explicit coordination occurs through external verbal and non-verbal communications, whereas tacit coordination is thought to occur through the meta-cognitive activities of team members who have shared mental models of what should be done, when, and by whom (Entin and Serfaty, 1999; Fiore et al., 2001; Hoeft et al., 2006). A team's shared mental model thus allows the team members to coordinate their behavior and better communicate depending on situational demands. Initial theorizing on training shared mental models suggests that for teams to successfully co-ordinate their actions, they must possess commonly held knowledge structures, such as knowledge of teammates' roles and responsibilities along with team tasks and procedures. Due to lack of previous co-training, ad hoc teams face the additional challenge of having to establish shared mental models as they perform the task; not only does this potentially increase the communication demands of ad hoc teams but forming incompatible mental models can hinder progress towards team goals (Cannon-Bowers et al., 1993).

Having agents aid human teams similarly requires the establishment of shared cognition, common ground between humans and agents. Creating this shared cognition between human and agent teammates is the biggest challenge facing developers of mixed-initiative human/agent organizations. The limiting factor in most human-agent interactions is the human's ability and willingness to spend time communicating with agents in a manner that both humans and agents understand (Sycara and Lewis, 2004). Horvitz (1999) formulates this problem of mixed-initiative interaction as a process of managing uncertainties: (1) managing uncertainties that agents may have about the human's goals and focus of attention, and (2) uncertainty that humans have about agent plans and status. Creating agent understanding of human intent and making agents' results intelligible to a human are problems that must be addressed by any mixed-initiative system, whether the agents reduce uncertainty through communication, inference, or a mixture of the two.

Agent Roles in Human Teams

Sycara and Lewis (2004) identify three primary roles played by agents interacting with human teams.

- **Agents support individual team members in completion of their own tasks.** These agents often function as personal assistant agents and are assigned to specific team members (Chalupsky et al., 2001). (Please see Chapter XXI, "Software Personal Agents for Human Organizations" by Okamoto et al., for more information about personal assistance agents.) Task-specific agents utilized by multiple team members (e.g., (Chen and Sycara, 1998)) also belong in this category.

- **Agents support the team as a whole.** Rather than focusing on task-completion activities, the agents directly facilitate teamwork by aiding communication and coordination among humans and agents, as well as focus of attention. The experimental results summarized in (Sycara and Lewis, 2004) indicate that this can be a very effective aiding strategy for agents in hybrid teams.
- **Agents assume the role of an equal team member.** These agents are expected to function as "virtual humans" within the organization, capable of the same reasoning and tasks as their human teammates (Traum et al., 2003). This is the hardest role for a software agent to assume, since it is difficult to create a software agent that is as effective as a human at both task performance and teamwork skills.

There are additional research challenges, specific to the team role assumed by the agent. Agents that support individual human team members face the following challenges: (1) modeling user preferences; (2) determining optimal transfer-of-control policies (Scerri et al., 2003); (3) considering the status of user's attention in timing services (Horvitz, 1999). Agents aiding teams (Lenox et al., 1997, 1998, 2000; Lenox, 2000), face a different set of problems: (1) identifying information that needs to be passed to other team members before being asked; (2) automatically prioritizing tasks for the human team members; (3) maintaining shared task information in a way that is useful for the human users. Agents assuming the role of equal team members (Traum et al., 2003; Fan et al., 2005, 2006) must additionally be able to: (1) competently execute their role in the team; (2) critique team errors; (3) independently suggest alternate courses of action. Perhaps because of these challenges, there are very few prior results on human-agent team aiding and teamwork. Examples of tasks that were investigated include target identification (Lenox et al., 1997, 1998), achievement of a military rendezvous plan (Lenox et al., 2000; Lenox, 2000) and delivery of supplies to troops (Fan et al., 2005, 2006). All of this prior work has uniformly found that human-agent teams exhibited superior performance over human-only teams not only in achievement of task objectives but also in performance stability. This finding was typically attributed to the fact that the agents in these works were successful in reducing the cognitive load of the human subjects by performing part of the task.

Team Coordination

Decentralized teams that are connected by some sort of network, called network-centric teams, face exacerbated challenges in teamwork, especially for time critical tasks. Coordination is challenging in network-centric environments because entities are often geographically dispersed and may be unfamiliar with other entities as well as the specific task or mission. This situation leads to what has been called "team opacity" (Fiore et al., 2003) and has been frequently associated with differences in process behaviors, poorer shared understanding, and lean communication, relative to co-located teams (Cooke et al., 2007). In fact, teams often adapt to these situations through spontaneous self-organization of their coordination structure (Cooke and Gorman, 2007).

It is important to note that we do not consider coordination in information theoretic terms (Shannon and Weaver, 1949) in which information is encoded, decoded and passively moved among different team members with some degree of uncertainty based on channel capacity. Rather, coordination involves active communication or mediation among team members in a social network (Friedkin, 1998).

Consequently, our coordination metrics do not measure amount of information passed or uncertainty, but instead extend social network theory or coordination theory by quantifying the effectiveness of coordination patterns.

Team coordination in network-centric teams may be predictive of the performance of the team, and to some degree, the social system in which the team is embedded. However, team coordination is not identical to team performance. Sometimes poor coordination can result in fortuitously positive outcomes and even the best coordination can sometimes fail to prevent a negative outcome.

Based on prior research, coordination improves with team experience and training, but decays over long retention intervals (Cooke and Gorman, 2007). The development of coordination skill is a large part of the development of collective competence of the social group. Coordination, therefore, is a team skill that can be trained. It is also a skill that can be quantified and modeled. The measurement and modeling of the development of coordination in network-centric teams is challenging due to the nonlinearities associated with interactions in complex distributed systems (Cooke et al., 2007), due for example to positive feedback loops among different team members.

AIDING HUMAN TEAMS

One of the goals of agent technology is to create agents that can perform part of the tasks that face the humans so as to improve team performance. Galbraith observed that "the more uncertainty in a task, the more information processing necessary to achieve a given level of performance" (Galbraith, 1977). Hence, having the agents assist either in information processing or decreasing uncertainty should improve the team's performance. Based on experiments of student project teams, Kraut suggests that a human team's resultant state of coordination, defined as the degree to which interdependencies are managed well, is an important predictor of team performance (Kraut et al., 2005). This state of coordination can be created by mechanisms such as communication, shared cognition, and team history. If agents can improve the state of coordination between team members or reduce the cost of achieving a good state of coordination, the team performance should improve.

Ad hoc teams face unique set of barriers to effective team performance, especially if they are also distributed. Pascual et al. (1999) surveyed forty military personnel with extensive experience working in both ad hoc and distributed teams. Communications, achieving situational awareness, engaging in standard teamwork behaviors, and demonstrating leadership were listed as major problems by the majority oft he subjects. Leaders of ad hoc organizations face difficulties in task allocation, anticipating team members' actions, and anticipating team problems. Ad hoc team members commonly experienced communication problems (1) in knowing when to communicate updates to their team members (2) in knowing whom to ask for information (3) in providing and accepting feedback.

Agent Support Systems

The utility of agent support systems has been demonstrated in a number of operational domains. Fan et al. (2005, 2006) have evaluated the use of cognitive agents within a collaborative Recognition-Primed Decision model (RPD) for supporting human teams performing military decision tasks. In one task (Fan et al., 2005), the human teams had to maximize the amount of supplies delivered to the troops by successfully protecting an airport. The agents were able to participate in human teams and increase the amount of supplies delivered when the humans were under time stress. In a second task, Command and Control teams had to react to incoming threats menacing a metropolis from crowds, insurgents, and improvised explosive devices. The task is difficult because it is 1) real-time and 2) involves context switching. The human-agent C2 teams performed much better than the human-only teams at the same level of task complexity; moreover the human-agent team performances are significantly more stable than the human-only performances.

Prior research for agent aiding in human teams (Lenox et al., 1997, 1998, 2000; Lenox, 2000) has involved two different types of cognitive tasks. In the MokSAF experiments (Lenox et al., 2000; Lenox, 2000), the team mission involves three commanders that, starting from different geographical points, must rendezvous at a particular point and time with a particular force configuration. The planning task is deliberative, iterative and flexible. The commanders must coordinate the number and types of vehicles they plan to move from the individual start points to the rendezvous point. The mission briefing supplied to the commanders provides them with a list of vehicles that should arrive at the rendezvous point. In addition, the commanders are instructed to avoid generating routes that lie on the same path as any other commander, and that they should coordinate their routes through the communication center to avoid this. Each commander selects units for his/her platoon from a list of available units. Commanders have 15 minutes to determine the composition of their platoon, and plan a route from a starting point to the rendezvous point for that platoon. Once a commander is satisfied with the individual plan, s/he can share it with the other commanders and resolve any conflicts. Conflicts can arise due to shared routes, shared resources, or the inability of a commander to reach the rendezvous point at the specified time. The experiments were performed to investigate a number of hypotheses. Can agent-based assistance assist in the completion of team tasks? If assistance is provided in achieving the individual goal, then does this improve the achievement of the team goal? Does agent-based aiding become more effective as the complexity of the intangible aspects of a planning problem increase? Experimental results showed that the agent aiding provided better decision support both for individual route planning and team-based planning as compared to the baseline (unaided) condition (Lenox et al., 2000; Lenox, 2000).

Work by (Lenox et al., 1997, 1998) examined agent aiding in another domain, a target identification task where a moderate fidelity simulation (TANDEM) was used. The TANDEM simulation was developed under the TADMUS (tactical decision making under stress) program of the US Office of Naval Research and simulates cognitive characteristics of tasks performed in the command information center (CIC) of an Aegis missile cruiser. The cognitive aspects of the Aegis command and control tasks which are captured include time stress, memory loading, data aggregation for decision making and the need to rely on and cooperate with other team members (team mode) to successfully perform the task. Instead of interpreting displayed radar signals to acquire diagnostic information about targets, TANDEM participants access this information manually from menus. In the TANDEM task subjects must communicate to exchange parameter values in order to identify and take action on a large number of targets (high workload) and are awarded points for correctly identifying the targets (type, intent, and threat), and taking the correct action (clear or shoot). Extensive experimentation with different types of agent aiding on a large number of human teams (60 teams of three subjects each) concluded that (a) agent aiding significantly increased human team performance, and (b) agent aiding of the team as a whole improved performance more than aiding individual team members.

These evaluations of human-agent teams are encouraging because they demonstrate that agents can produce a measurable difference in human team performance.

Search and Rescue Domain

To create a baseline of decentralized ad hoc team performance in a time-stressed domain, we monitored teams of human subjects performing a collaborative search task in simulation. Search and rescue is a challenging, team task with a potentially high payoff since inadequate team performance can result in fatalities. The collaborative search task that we designed for our experiments, the team scavenger hunt, recreates some of the challenges faced by expert human teams during search and rescue operations. To implement the task, we reconfigured a scenario in the multi-player game and battlefield simulator, Operation Flashpoint (OFP version 1.96) (Flashpoint, 2001), by customizing the pre-game briefing, map, object triggers, and scoring mechanism.

In the team scavenger hunt, human subjects have to read a map, navigate a 3D simulated environment and recover a collection of objects (bottles) within a bounded amount of time. We modeled a bottle search task since, unlike modeling rescuing of victims, it was possible to insert static objects in the game (bottles) and log the interactions of the human subjects. The bottle search task has many common elements with the search and rescue of victims task. The task is designed to evaluate the team's ability to develop and execute a search plan under time-stress. As an experimental task, the team scavenger hunt offers several advantages: (1) it can be learned and executed within a short period of time by novice subjects; (2) it can be simulated within a variety of test beds; (3) it offers a simple team performance metric: number of objects collected.

We first provide a *task analysis* of how civilian human teams perform wilderness search and rescue operations summarized from (Goodrich et al., 2007; Setnicka, 1980). We assume that many aspects of the task analysis are also applicable to different types of search and rescue teams, such as military teams or emergency response teams. A goal-directed task analysis of wilderness search and rescue operations identified the following list of operational goals and sub-goals (Goodrich et al., 2007). The italicized task elements are also applicable to our simulated collaborative search task.

1. Stage preparation
    (a) Reporting party call
    (b) Activation call
    (c) Assemble (prepare for search)
2. Acquire missing person description
    (a) Gather missing person information
    (b) Determine missing person's intent
3. *Develop search plan*
    (a) Create a perimeter
    (b) *Assign priority to clues*
    (c) *Update map information*
    (d) *Create a priority pattern*
    (e) *Organize resources for search execution*
    (f) *Communicate search plan*
4. *Execute search plan*
    (a) *Follow plan*
    (b) *Find signs (or absence of)*

(c) Keep searchers safe

(d) *Communicate acquired information*

5. Recover victims

(a) First aid for victims

(b) Rescue, extract, or recover the missing person

6. *Debrief search team*

(a) *Determine what happened*

(b) *Evaluate how the team can improve*

Wilderness search and rescue operations pose the following challenges to expert human teams (Goodrich et al. 2007): (1) information overload of the incident commander while assimilating information collected by the field teams; (2) the creation of accidental holes in the search pattern due to poor execution of the search plan by the field teams; (3) poor priority assignments in the search plan due to false clues and hunches. In the next section, we describe our experimental version of the collaborative search task, the team scavenger hunt, which tests the ability of human subjects to collaborate to develop and execute a team search plan in a simulated environment.

Experimental Testbed

The experiments focused on the activity of three human players acting through virtual characters in the Operation Flashpoint (OFP version 1.96) simulated physical environment to find and crush liquor bottles in twenty minute test periods in different experimental conditions.

In OFP, terrain around and including the village of *Flers* on the island of *Normandie* was chosen as the focal point for the one practice and three experimental scenarios. The area is a tract of land that is 512 meters long in a north–south direction (N/S), and 768 meters long in an east–west direction (E/W); in all, 393,216 square meters. On the 2-dimensional (2D) Operation Flashpoint map, this area corresponds to 4 map squares N/S, 6 map squares E/W, where each map square corresponds to 128 meters by 128 meters. Exploratory benchmarks determined that, depending on search technique and ability, it could take a single OFP civilian virtual character from sixty to ninety minutes to explore all 24-map squares of this scenario. In twenty minutes, a civilian character can thoroughly explore roughly ten map squares of the surrounding countryside. The village of Flers occupies four map squares; part of the village is organized in a radial street plan and another part has a N/S, E/W grid of streets and buildings. Given the area and layout, we have observed that it requires from ten to twenty minutes for the virtual civilian character to search the area.

Experimental Task

In this section, we analyze the baseline performance and the communication patterns of human ad hoc teams performing the collaborative search task.

Seventeen teams of three paid subjects, each, were recruited to participate in the pilot study. Human subjects self-assessed and reported their abilities to play first person video games in terms of the following classification: novice, medium expertise, or expert. Combined expertise of the teams varied from "two novices and a medium expert" to a team of "three experts." (See Figure 2.) Note that expertise in playing video games does not imply expertise in search and rescue.

Each team member played the game through an assigned and dedicated laptop. The seating of the three-team members was such that they could not look at each other's screen. The human subjects were forbidden to share computer screens, note sheets or other such aids — they could only describe their locations, intentions and actions in the game by using verbal communications and the 2D OFP map of Flers. All verbal communications were recorded using TeamSpeak (TeamSpeak, 2001).

Time was taken during a practice session to instruct the players on the key and mouse commands for the game. Players were instructed on how to move their characters, find and crush bottles, query bottle counts, and how to use additional aids that are available to their avatars. After sighting a bottle, a player must move their avatar to within a couple of meters of it in order to crush it and get credit for the crush. When they are close enough to crush the bottle, the command to crush that type of bottle, e.g. **Crush Martini Bottle**, will appear in the player's command menu at the bottom right corner of their screen. Feedback to the player is given in multiple ways: (1) the sound of a vehicle crashing into a wall, (2) puffs of oily black smoke emanating from the morphing bottle, (3) the morphing of the bottle into a crumpled form. If the player queries their bottle count, they will see that it has increased by one.

Once a player has crushed a bottle, the command to crush it is removed from their menu, never to appear again for that bottle, even if they happen upon its crushed remains at a later time. If a player encounters the remains of a bottle that was crushed by a teammate, they can choose to invoke the command to crush it in order to avoid false detection of that crushed bottle at a later time. No penalty was assessed for attempting to crush an already crushed bottle.

The five ways of detecting a bottle are:

1. *Visual detection*, in which the human player "sees" a bottle via the unmagnified vision of their avatar;
2. *Magnified visual detection*, in which the human player slightly magnifies (roughly, 3X) their avatar's field of vision;
3. *Visual detection via binoculars*, in which the avatar uses binoculars for a narrower but more distant field of view;
4. *Non-visual proximity sensing*, in which the player is notified of a bottle's presence whenever their avatar comes within "sensing range" of the bottle. A bottle is sensed based on the expertise of the OFP avatar and if the player is proximate to it. This game effect is useful if the bottle is on the other side of a hedge or if the player accidentally passes the bottle. It does not work if the bottle is in a terrain depression, or more than a few meters away from the player. The notification consists of the player's command menu appearing in the bottom right corner of their screen, with the added command, "Crush X Bottle", where X indicates the type of bottle.
5. *Tool tip sensing* of the bottles from the 2D map view of the world. OFP avatars can navigate the environment in a 2-dimensional map view. When in 2D map view, the player's avatar is represented as two concentric red circles with a radial line indicating the avatar's bearing. If the human user moves the mouse cursor over the area of the map in the vicinity of the avatar, they can detect any objects that they could normally see in the visual detect mode. When an object is detected, a "tool tip" label appears next to it, indicating the object's type.

We evaluated the three experimental conditions:

- # **Bottles Known**, in which the subjects knew how many total bottles they were trying to recover; the performance measure was a team score, where each found bottle counted for one point.
- # **Bottles Unknown**, in which the subjects did not know how many bottles were hidden in the search area; the performance measure was a team score, where each found bottle counted for one point.
- **Bottle Portfolio** condition, where subjects were given a bonus of 100 points, if s/he had collected a "portfolio" of 7 bottles, each of a different kind. The different available types of bottles were told to the subjects by the experimenter: a portfolio was comprised of a set of Martini, Barbera, Jack Daniels, Seagram's, Napoleon, Baileys, and Whisky bottles. The bottle type was visible on the interface, when a subject was close enough to see the bottle. Subjects could also determine the bottle type through their command interface (e.g., "Crush Barbera"), and through the tool tips feature of the 2-D map view. Duplicate bottles counted simply one point.

Figure 1. The coding scheme that was used to label team communications

High-Level Categories	Utterance ID	Description	
Information Sharing: (1)_Info about tasks, logistics (2)_Info about location & movement of self & others	1	Requesting or Communicating Team Members' Location	
	2	Any Reference to Terrain or Map Features	
	3	Question / Indication of Bottle Locations	
	4	Personal Tips	
	20	Situation Assessment of Equipment	
	26	Question about Means of Doing Something	
Self-Organization: (1)_Information About Organizational Structure (2)_Establishing Authority Structure	5	Communication for Role Allocation	Team Planning Before Execution
	6	Communication for Division of Execution Space	
	7	Communication for Role Allocation	Team Planning During Execution
	8	Communication for Division of Execution Space	
	32	Discussion of Capability	
Problem Solving: (1)_Setting goals (2)_Forming hypotheses, predictions (3)_Making plans	12	Hypothesis about Bottle Locations	
	18	Plan or Activity Critiquing / Plan Suggestions	
	23	Considering / Evaluating Alternatives	
	24	Suggesting Individual or Team Strategies	
Meta-Cognition: (1)_Monitoring team progress (2)_Assessing team performance (3)_Reporting on own progress, past actions	9	Bottle Count	
	10	Object Count	
	11	Coverage Progress	
	29	Reporting Status / Activity	
	31	Request for Status Check	
	33	Monitoring Remaining Time in Session	
Team Coordination: (1)_Coordinating with others on on-going task (2)_Directing actions of others (3)_Stating one's intentions (4)_Backup Behaviors	15	Communicating Intent with Respect to Action	
	16	Communicating Intent with Respect to Changing Location	
	21	Commands	
	28	Permission / Request for Agreement to Do Something	
	30	Offer of Help	
	34	Request for Help	
Non-task Related:	13	System Problems: Keyboard Lockups, Game Window Loses Focus, etc.	
	14	Personal Discussion	
Interpersonal Affect:	19	Social Encouragement	
	22	Justifying Behavior, Action, or Plan	
Closed Loop Communications: (1)_Acknowledgment (2)_Disagreement (3)_Elaborations	17	Acknowledgment / Agreement / Answers to Questions	
	27	Disagreement	
	25	Clarification Question	

The three experimental conditions were *counterbalanced*, namely the conditions were executed in varying order among the teams to mitigate order effects. The subjects had 20 minutes to perform the task in each experimental condition.

We created these different experimental conditions in order to observe the communication patterns, their similarities and differences in the different conditions, in particular in the non-portfolio vs. the portfolio conditions. We hypothesized that there would be significant differences since the portfolio condition engenders additional dependencies among the tasks of team members; hence it would require tighter coordination. We also wanted to see whether there were any differences in the high performing teams vs. the low performing teams in the portfolio vs. non-portfolio conditions. Although there is consensus among teamwork researchers that communication patterns alone cannot predict performance, we remain interested in the potential for agent intervention to improve performance by improving communication for low performing teams. Further, we are interested in identifying communications and communication patterns that could be used by agents to understand team goals, individual roles, personal difficulties, strategies and progress to the team goal, so as to provide better assistance. Moreover, we hypothesized that there would be differences in the self-organization of the teams in the portfolio vs. the non-portfolio conditions, again due to the need for tighter coordination in the portfolio condition.

To analyze the coordination demands of the collaborative search task, we recorded all audio communications between team members. The audio files were manually transcribed to produce the logs of utterances that were segmented into conversational moves (Hirokawa, 1983). According to this scheme, a conversational move unit is an uninterrupted utterance of a team member that has a discrete problem solving function. Figure 1 shows the main categories and subcategories of the codes we used plus examples for each. The codes represent task related problems solving and coordination categories that are consistent with current teamwork literature (Fischer et al., 2007). In addition to the communication categories used by other researchers, we included categories of utterances relevant to team self-organization. These aspects were not needed in prior work where, unlike for ad hoc teams, team structure and role allocation were already in place.

Figure 2. The performance of the teams in all three test conditions

Team		# Bottles Recovered / Total # Bottles in Scenario			Portfolio Score	
Number	Subject Expertise	# Bottles Known	# Bottles Unknown	Portfolio Condition	Raw	%age
1	novice, medium, expert	84.62%	78.57%	64.29%	204 / 307 =	66.45%
2	novice, expert, expert	73.33%	54.76%	28.57%	8 / 307 =	2.61%
3	novice, novice, expert	60.53%	66.67%	42.86%	12 / 307 =	3.91%
4	novice, novice, medium	77.27%	35.71%	39.29%	11 / 307 =	3.58%
5	medium, expert, expert	86.36%	73.81%	78.57%	208 / 307 =	67.75%
6	novice, medium, medium	59.52%	52.38%	46.43%	12 / 307 =	3.91%
7	expert, expert, expert	81.82%	76.19%	60.71%	17 / 307 =	5.54%
8	medium, expert, expert	94.00%	80.95%	57.14%	109 / 307 =	35.50%
9	medium, medium, expert	76.60%	80.95%	71.43%	113 / 307 =	36.81%
10	expert, expert, expert	97.78%	64.29%	50.00%	107 / 307 =	34.85%
11	medium, expert, expert	80.85%	90.48%	42.86%	105 / 307 =	34.20%
12	novice, novice, expert	82.93%	83.33%	57.14%	109 / 307 =	35.50%
13	medium, expert, expert	88.24%	69.05%	53.57%	201 / 307 =	65.47%
14	medium, expert, expert	67.44%	73.81%	42.86%	12 / 307 =	3.91%
15	expert, expert, expert	95.35%	90.48%	71.43%	113 / 307 =	36.81%
16	medium, medium, medium	84.62%	76.19%	28.57%	8 / 307 =	2.61%
17	novice, medium, medium	74.42%	71.43%	42.86%	12 / 307 =	3.91%
mean	—	80.33 ± 11.07%	71.71 ± 14.03%	51.68±14.51%	26.08±24.32%	

RESULTS

Data were collected in a three condition repeated measures experimental design and were analyzed using the SPSS software.

Team Performance

Figure 2 reports the performance of all the teams in our initial set of experiments, measured by percentage of bottles crushed by each team. We had each subject self assess their expertise at computer games; this information is reported in the second column. The subjects participated in an initial practice session during which they were learning the user interface (results not shown). We evaluated the performance of the teams on three search tasks presented in counterbalanced order: (1) a session in which the subjects knew the total number of bottles hidden on the map (labeled in the table as # **Bottles Known**), (2) a session in which the subjects did not know how many bottles they were trying to recover (# **Bottles Unknown**), and (3) a session where the subjects were supposed to construct portfolios. For that condition, there were 28 hidden bottles, of which there were 7 unique types, thus enabling the formation of 4 portfolios in the ideal case.

A repeated measures ANOVA shows that team performance in the **#Bottles Unknown** condition was poorer than in the **#Bottles Known** condition ($F_{1,15} = 6.659$, p=.02) indicating that knowing the goal (total number of bottles to be found) improved performance. This effect is likely based on the commonly observed distinction between self-terminating and non-terminating searches. Where the bottle count is known the task can be stopped when all bottles have been found. Conversely, if bottles remain to be found, the subjects are aware of this and can intensify their search. Subjects in the # **Bottles Unknown** condition have no such standard and as a consequence they have greater difficulty in regulating their search behavior. Of more interest to us is the difference in coordination demand between the two conditions. In the # **Bottles Unknown** condition, a good team strategy would require team members to search different areas but otherwise allow them to act independently. Taking advantage of the additional

Figure 3. Bottles found in the three conditions

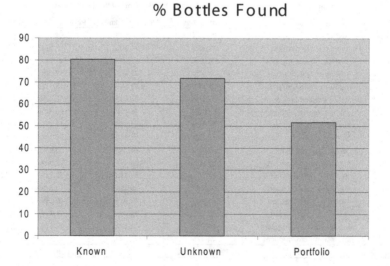

Table 1. Differences in communications across conditions

Communication code	$F_{2,14}$	Sig	Unknown vs. known	Unknown vs. Portfolio	Known vs. Portfolio
(3) reference bottle locations	19.258	p=.0001	N.S.	p=.001	p=.0001
(8) division of search space	6.437	p=.004	N.S.	p=.007	N.S.
(12) hypotheses, bottle locations	4.109	p=.026	N.S.	N.S.	p=.05
(15) action intent	15.021	p=.0001	N.S.	p=.003	p=.0001
(21) commands	7.979	p=.002	N.S.	p=.043	p=.004
(22) justification for action/plan	3.516	p=.042	N.S.	N.S.	N.S.
(25) clarification of question	12.988	p=.001	N.S.	p=.001	p=.014
(29) reporting status	6.202	p=.005	N.S.	p=.01	N.S.
(30) offer of help	10.464	p=.0001	N.S.	p=.001	p=.041
(32) discuss capability	3.630	p=.038	N.S.	p=.05	N.S.
(34) request help	33.549	p=.0001	N.S.	p=.0001	p=.0001

information in the # **Bottles Known** condition, however, requires exchange of bottle counts and other coordinating communications. If we see better performance in the # **Bottles Known** condition, and that superiority depends upon communication and coordination, then we should observe differences in communications patterns as well. The third, **Portfolio** condition, places greatly increased coordination demands on the team. In this condition, the reward associated with collecting individual bottles is dwarfed by the potential portfolio construction reward. Assembling a portfolio, however, may require players to pass up duplicate bottles, locate and report bottles needed for another's portfolio, and other more complex interdependent behavior. We should therefore expect to see substantial differences in communication patterns between the Portfolio and the other two conditions. Because collecting bottles is secondary to assembling portfolios for this group we should also expect lower bottle scores. Figure 3 shows the mean percent bottles found for each of these groups. Differences in performance were found between the three conditions ($F_{2,14}= 36.617$, p<.0001) with paired comparisons showing teams in the portfolio condition to find fewer (p < .0001) bottles than in either of the other conditions.

Differences in communications patterns across the three conditions were found for eleven of the thirty-four coded categories using a repeated measures ANOVA with paired comparisons.

As Table 1 shows all significant differences in communications were found between the Portfolio and the two bottle search conditions (N.S means non-significant). The differences involving communications such as bottle locations and hypotheses about locations, intended actions and their justifications, and communications characterizing teamwork such as offering and requesting help are of the sort that might be expected to distinguish the relatively independent bottle collection tasks from the high coordination demand required for assembling portfolios.

Analysis of Team Communication

To assess the communication demands of the collaborative search task, we compiled frequency counts of the different types of team communication.

Five of the 34 utterance categories: (2) reference to terrain or map features, (12) hypotheses about bottle locations, (14) unrelated personal discussion, (15) communication of intended action, and (23) evaluating alternatives were found to be related to team performance in the non portfolio conditions through a series of step-wise regressions. Teams in the # **Bottles Unknown** condition that exerted the least coordination demand produced the simplest model containing only two independent variables, (14) and (15). The frequency of unrelated discussions, $\beta=.433$, $t_{14}=2.205$, $p=.045$, and communicated intent, $\beta=-.433$, $t_{14}=-2.305$, $p=.037$, significantly predicted the bottles found with a regression explaining about half of the variance, $R^2=.504$, $F_{2,14}=7.116$, $p=.007$, in the number of bottles. Our finding that extraneous communication helped and conveying intent hurt in this condition reinforces our contention that the # **Bottles Unknown** task requires independent search by teammates. Communications such as (15) that encourage unnecessary coordination hurt performance while those that supplant potentially disrupting alternative communications (14) actually helped.

The # **Bottles Known** condition, that stands to benefit from coordination, yields more complex communication patterns. Unlike the # **Bottles Unknown** regression, (15) communication of intent, now contributes positively, $\beta=.323$, $t_{12}=2.68$, $p=.02$, to predicting bottles found. Related communications (23) involving sharing hypotheses also contributes positively, $\beta=.502$, $t_{12}=4.162$, $p=.001$, as does (14) unrelated discussion, $\beta=.323$, $t_{12}=2.68$, $p=.02$, that we have argued may benefit performance by supplanting inappropriate task related communications. Communication code (2) reference to terrain or maps, enters the model negatively, $\beta=-.392$, $t_{12}=-3.32$, $p=.006$. We speculate that this may be due to the fact that players that talked a lot about terrain features may have been disoriented and lost; such players retrieved few bottles. This four variable regression significantly predicted the bottles found and explained almost all of the variance, $R^2=.842$, $F_{4,12}=16.003$, $p=.0001$, in the number of bottles.

Teams in the **Portfolio** condition had a substantially different task since their scores were dominated by the portfolio bonus. Nevertheless, we examined the relation between their communication patterns and *number of bottles found* before looking at the more salient relation between communications and *scores*. (where the score includes the bonus for constructing portfolios). Our **Portfolio** data were fit by a five variable regression on bottles found. (29) reports of status, $\beta=.687$, $t_{11}=6.17$, $p=.0001$, (17) acknowledgment/agreement, $\beta=.504$, $t_{11}=4.777$, $p=.001$, and (34) request for help, $\beta=.265$, $t_{11}=2.522$, $p=.028$, were all positively related to bottles found. (1) communicating location, $\beta=-.518$, $t_{11}=-4.851$, $p=.001$, and (31) request for status, $\beta=-.353$, $t_{11}=-3.353$, $p=.006$, were negatively related. As for the earlier conditions we presume that communications (1) and (31) place cooperative demands on team members that detract from the independent task of accumulating bottles. This five variable regression significantly predicted the bottles found and explained almost all of the variance, $R^2=.916$, $F_{5,11}=24.029$, $p=.0001$, in the number of bottles.

Regression on score, the more salient performance measure in the **Portfolio** condition, revealed a different set of predictors. Data were fit by a four variable regression on team score with all variables providing positive contributions. Communication types (10), Object account, $\beta=.85$, $t_{12}=6.827$, $p=.0001$, (19) social encouragement, $\beta=.450$, $t_{12}=3.615$, $p=.003$, (11) reported coverage, $\beta=.315$, $t_{12}=2.708$, $p=.018$, and (15) communication of intent, $\beta=.278$, $t_{12}=2.293$, $p=.041$ contribute positively to the model. This four variable regression significantly predicted team scores and explained a substantial amount of the variance, $R^2=.906$, $F_{4,12}=29.075$, $p=.0001$, in scores. These differences in predictors for bottle count and scores suggest that different team processes may be involved. To explore the possibility that teams were using different processes to attain these goals we examined the correlation between number of bottles found and team scores. The positive correlation between bottles found and score, $r_{15}=.73$, $p < .001$ suggests that teams with good searchers were better at both finding more bottles and assembling portfolios. This debunks the notion that the negative relation observed between (1) communicating

Figure 4.

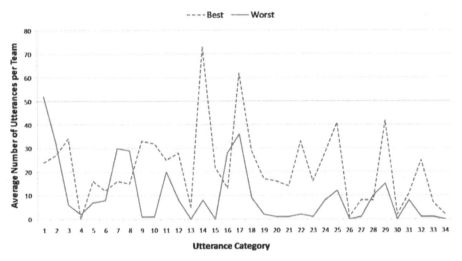

Comparison of the Best Performing Team with the Worst Performing Team in the Non-Portfolio Condition

Figure 5.

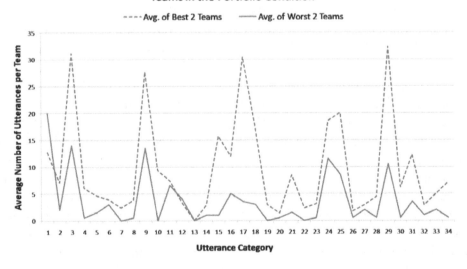

Comparison of 2 Best Performing Teams with the 2 Worst Performing Teams in the Portfolio Condition

location and (31) request for status in the regression on bottles found resulted from allowing team members to search independently accumulating more bottles by freeing them from coordination demands. A more likely explanation is that agents that talk a lot about position may have been lost and thus do not retrieve many bottles.

To further explore communication patterns in teams we report the results of the highest and lowest performing teams in the non-portfolio condition, **#Bottles Known** (called in the graphs the "Non-Portfolio Condition") and in the **Portfolio** condition. We do not report the communications pattern of the **#Bottles Unknown** condition since, as Table 1 shows, the differences in the communication among the two non-portfolio conditions were not significant. Moreover, we report here the highest and lowest performing team so that their differences may give us some clue as to the types of agent assistance that would be beneficial (See Discussion section.)

From the graphs of Figures 4 and 5 we make a variety of observations. First, we robustly find that the lower performing teams in both portfolio and non-portfolio conditions communicate less in all communication categories. This is consistent with social theories of teamwork, where communication is considered one of the most important teamwork dimensions. In addition we see that, consistent with theories of teamwork (Salas and Fiore, 2004) the communication frequency peaks of high performing teams in both conditions were for teamwork behaviors such as inventory monitoring (code 9), object counts (code 10), offering suggestions (code18), describing intentions (code 15), acknowledgments (code 17), and monitoring the passing of time (code 33). We also note some differences. In the non-portfolio condition, offering help (code 30) is not utilized much due possibly to the more loosely coupled nature of the task, whereas in the portfolio condition, there is a frequency peak there.

Team Self-Organization

In our experiments, we were particularly interested in observing differences in self-organization between (a) roughly equally performing teams (high/low) in the non-portfolio vs. portfolio condition, and (b) of high performing vs. low performing teams in the portfolio condition. We were also interested in observing any adaptations of the organizational structure during task execution.

To examine this question we first looked at the relationship between expertise with video games within teams and team performance. To consider the possible organizational dynamics we looked at the min, max, and average experience of groups to examine how team composition had affected performance. The rationale of this comparison is that team performance may be dominated by deficiencies of the weakest member (min), strengths of the most experienced member (max), or reflect their independent performance (avg). Our data show clear variation across the three conditions. In the # **Bottles Unknown** condition which promotes independent search all three estimates of team experience were correlated with bottles found: min(experience), $r_{15}=.44$, p < .05, max(experience), $r_{15}=.52$, p < .05, and avg(experience), $r_{15}=.50$, p < .05. In the # **Bottles Known** condition which relies more directly on coordination min(experience), $r_{15}=.63$, p < .01 and avg(experience), $r_{15}=.59$, p < .05 were significantly correlated but max(experience) was not. This pattern is reversed for the **Portfolio** condition in which max(experience), $r_{15}=.49$, p < .05 and avg(experience) $r_{15}=.44$, p < .05 were significantly correlated but min(experience) was not. These patterns suggest that substantially different forms of organization were most successful under the different conditions. In the # **Bottles Unknown** condition the independence of team members searches was reflected through correlations with all three measures. In the # **Bottles Known** condition which required team members to track one another's finds but without more elaborate coordination the lack of skill of the weakest member proved predictive of team performance. Finally, in the more complex **Portfolio** condition that required some structure of authority the skill of the most skilled team member proved to be a determining factor in team performance.

In further analyses we looked for differences across two organizational structures: (a) an authority structure and (b) a functional structure. In terms of authority structure, one of the striking observations is that none of the teams elected a leader, although in a few teams a team member volunteered to, for

Figure 6. Transcript of communication between subjects at the beginning of the search. This group of utterances was categorized as an example of team planning before execution. The "64" refers to a row on the map. There are significant pauses between the utterances; during one such pause, one of the subjects changes their mind and decides to cover a different area.

A - Ann, B - Jon, C – Tom
A	Okay do we want someone to stay in the courtyard and do those bottles?
B	I'll do that and then head east
C	I'll do the same area that I did before.
B	I'll clear the courtyard and then clear the road to the south.
A	I'll work on the northern part and 64.
C	I think I'm going to stay closer to the town and circle around.

example, keep track of time or do some other team supporting behavior. In terms of functional structure, the nature of the search task encourages functional division of the search space (e.g. search the village, search the northern part of the countryside), and allocation of roles according to that spatial division. Figure 6 presents a transcript pertaining to the planning for spatial role allocation in one of the teams. It is a typical example of team planning communication at the beginning of a search session. The three subjects quickly develop a search strategy in which each subject assumes responsibility for covering a certain region. Another way that roles could be allocated would be in terms of ascertaining capabilities of the different team members (e.g. fast runners, adept at using the binoculars). A third way of role allocation would be in terms of whether a team member would be a bottle "marker" or a bottle "picker."

We observe from Figures 6 and 7 that in both non-portfolio and portfolio conditions the frequency of utterances pertaining to self-organization, namely utterances for role allocation (code 5), and division of execution space (code 6) during the planning phase is lower for the low performing teams than for the high performing teams.

In the non-portfolio condition, most of the team planning discussions was related to the division of the execution space: how to allocate the efforts of the team members to cover the entire map within the 20-minute test period. Although some teams agreed on a division of labor at the beginning of the task period, many teams modified their search strategies during execution based on their perceived task progress with respect to area coverage or their assessment of which areas contained a higher bottle density.

Besides the role allocation based on spatial dimensions, in the portfolio condition, we observe additional organizational structure and role specialization. An examination of the transcript of the highest performing team in the portfolio condition shows that the team had a sophisticated plan for role allocation. Below, we present a summary of the utterances of the highest performing team in the portfolio condition that suggest individual specialty roles:

1. Elect a player to be the first to achieve a portfolio. (role = 1st to achieve a portfolio)
2. After the first player achieves a portfolio, a second teammate should be chosen to form a portfolio. (role = 2nd to achieve a portfolio)
3. All teammates mark bottles to help the portfolio achiever make a portfolio. (role = bottle marker)

4. In the second half of the game, revert to self-interested roles ("Crush indiscriminately.") (role = self-interested search and retrieval)

5. Divide the space (intention of covering west, middle, east). (role = forage specific geographic area)

6. Decide whether a teammate should be responsible for keeping track of teammates' inventories in addition to their own inventory. (role = inventory keeper for situation awareness)

The low frequency of utterances concerning role allocation (Figures 6 and 7) of the worst performing teams shows that they do not spend enough time to plan about role allocation. We also observed that in the non-portfolio condition, the worse performing team have a higher frequency of utterances about role allocation *during execution*, meaning that they probably are trying to adapt for the lack of planning. In the portfolio condition, there is no appreciable difference between the role allocation utterances of the best and worst performing teams during execution.

Another interesting observation is that in both the non-portfolio and portfolio conditions, the worst performing teams have much lower frequency of utterances than the best performing concerning discov-

Figure 7. Excerpt of Team 3 transcript for the Portfolio condition. This is an example of a player experiencing a localization failure. Player B is confused about his/her absolute position on the map; Player C is attempting to help B localize. The first column gives timestamps.

MMSS		A - Ann, B - Jon, C - Tom
1357	C	I think I'm half way to clearing my area. I see Ann
1409	B	you see me? I don't see you
1417	C	you are way over by the edge
1425	B	so now I'm lost again
1434	B	I'm south and wanted to go more east

Figure 8. Excerpt of Team 1 transcript for the Portfolio condition. Player C is confused about the correct path to take to a marked bottle. Player C is leading A to the bottle location, costing the team valuable search time.

	A - Ann, B - Jon, C – Tom
A	I am but I don't see it, like I just went past that area
C	Um, where are you? Yeah you're in the wrong place, come back south
A	come back south... oh yes I did overshoot it again, where is that triangular thing
C	Can you see me, in the 3d mode?
A	ummm, no
C	Ok you see me?
A	Yes I see you, ok we're doing that, the lead
C	I think
A	Ok I think I saw something, nope that was something else
C	Just follow me
A	Yeah
C	Right in here, see it? RIght by the fire
A	Ah, no I totally missed this area thanks

ery of capabilities (code 32), for example good runner, good user of binoculars etc. Clearly, discovering the capabilities of different teammates is a precursor to good role allocation. Moreover, discovering of teammates' capabilities is a very crucial need in ad hoc teams that have not trained together.

DISCUSSION

There are too many possible agent support activities that could be implemented and are potentially relevant to the collaborative search task to exhaustively test all possibilities. Here we concentrate on the ones that could be inferred from our experiments. The four basic categories of possible interventions include: 1) agents that help the humans with basic task skills like navigation or providing user interface assistance; 2) agents that monitor task progress such as timekeeping or coverage monitoring; 3) agents that check whether all team members are fulfilling agreements on plan and roles related to the team search pattern; 4) agents that help humans with their teamwork skills such as regulating communications with teammates or alerting players to possible assistance opportunities. Looking at the analysis of communication gives us some valuable clues regarding the merits of these possible assistance strategies.

Navigation Failure

Two types of utterances (1: player location) and (2: terrain features) were negatively correlated with performance across multiple conditions and were symptomatic of players experiencing navigation or movement failures. Seeing groups of contiguous utterances of (1) (player location) often indicated that the subjects were having trouble localizing and were straying into each other's territory. In the transcript in Figure 7, player B is clearly off course and has strayed into player C's territory. In the Transcript

Figure 9. Excerpt from the Team 10 transcript for the Portfolio condition (executed 2nd). The team members devise a test to determine who has the best sensing capability, and then discuss a strategy that uses that capability and a possible assist role based on that strategy. There is a high communication frequency. Team plan and role formulations are often fragmentary and interspersed with actions and observations that are unrelated to the plan formulation.

MMSS	A - Ann, B - Jon, C - Tom	
0000	A	Who has the sensing thing? It's beginning.
0003	A	Like run off, don't get them all first
0007	B	Leave them there?
0008	A	Then go to the next grid over, see who can see them then we'll know
0015	A	Alright so let's say right at the beginning we all run off to what was it, F-63?
0023	B	Well that little courtyard is where they all are
0024	A	Maybe if we run to the edge right between F and G
0033	A	Then we can see who can see, then we go from there
0040	A	What do we want to do from there?
0043	C	Once we know who it is, the person who can't see well should stay close and get the easy stuff
0050	A	Maybe they should go with the sensing person
0055	C	How much time are we really saving by having someone work with them?
0101	C	Do you (inaudible) stick together so they can just use their eyeballs together?
0110	C	Well I don't have the good sensing and I can still see about half a square
0116	A	So that other part's open but you can't see anything because of the elevation.
0119	A	I'm going, started heading towards the west

of Figure 8, we see that player C helps guide the disoriented player A to the bottles. The failure of one team member to localize penalizes team performance in multiple ways: (a) distracting the lost player from the primary task of searching for bottles; (b) reducing the total coverage of the team when the lost player fails to cover his/her planned area; (c) costing other players search time as they attempt to assist the lost player. Utterances of type (2) were used by players to discuss terrain features when they were (a) impeded by obstacles such as hedges; (b) crossing the line of flags that marked the boundary.

Capability-Based Role Allocation

One of the highest performing teams, Team 10, spent a significant amount of time assessing their character's physical capabilities and allocating roles based on their assessment. Figures 9 and 10 are excerpts from voice log transcripts that were recorded during Team 10's experimental session. Team 10 was unique in a variety of ways:

1.   It was the best performing team in the **#Bottles Known** condition.
2.   The team members experimented with the capabilities of their virtual characters, such as the use of binoculars, the relative speeds of their respective characters, and the sensing capabilities of the characters in each scenario.
3.   The team members experimented with the contexts in which the capabilities could be best used to their advantage, such as in which parts of the terrain binoculars provided the best advantage.

Figure 10. Excerpt from the Team 10 transcript for the Known condition (executed 3rd). The team members evaluate and critique their past performance, as well as revise their team strategy and respective roles. They decide to drop the specific test for determining a character's sensing capabilities, and agree that the best performer should provide a supportive role after finishing his section of eight 2-D map squares. This team improved its performance in successive sessions, and demonstrated the best performance of all teams in this condition.

MMSS		A - Ann, B - Jon, C - Tom
0341	B	Well, OK, strategy, what do you want to do?
0347	C	To me, it doesn't seem like there hasn't been very good coverage from far away.
0350	C	Do you want to break into groups? We just keep running over each other. Should we break into sections?
0356	C	Like we did last time
0400	C	Well we ended up in the same square, at one point.
0401	C	But that's because we never really throw ourselves down and stuck to it. Do you want to do what we talked about in the first place, and just eight, eight, eight? The person who does something well, should quickly, should just trust the map ...
0414	B	Clear, at one point.
0416	C	And then come back and help the others. Don't take the easy ones in the middle and just get out there.
0421	B	Yeah, yeah, yeah, definitely. You just get out there.
0423	C	If you find one, take it. It only takes two seconds to click. Don't, don't wait, don't waste, don't take the chance.
0426	A	Well, this is not one where we have to limit ourselves.
0431	B	No, we just take as many as we can.
0436	C	After the first few seconds, it's pretty obvious if you're the guy or not, so I don't think we need to take the time for that test.
0442	B	Yeah.
0443	C	You know what I mean? At least in the past it's been pretty obvious.

4. The team experimented with team strategies and roles in which capabilities could be leveraged to their performance advantage. For example, in the practice session, the team experimented with the strategy of having a person run from hilltop to hilltop and scan for bottles with their binoculars and depending on their findings, thus direct the search efforts of their teammates.
5. Team 10 displayed a tendency to investigate role specializations where the more capable players provided more support to the team and less capable players performed easier tasks, such as clearing areas where it was easier to find bottles.

The text in Figure 9 provides an example of the team dynamic just before the start of the session. In the previous session, they discovered that each character has a different sensing distance, and they spent some time trying to understand which character could sense the farthest. At the start of this session, player "Ann" suggests that everyone leave the bottles uncrushed in the courtyard where they start, and to run out of the courtyard. If they monitor their character's progress in the 2-D map, at a certain point they will not sense the bottles that they left behind in the courtyard; hence their "sensing distance", expressed in terms of 2-D map squares. Utterances 0003 – 0019 are where Ann explains this testing technique. Later utterances (not shown) represent a discussion about how the team should organize once they determine which character has the best sensing ability.

In the excerpted transcript shown in Figure 10, Team 10 plans their strategy just before beginning the Known condition. Player "Tom" complains (utterance 0347) about the lack of adequate coverage of the extreme areas of the terrain surrounding the village. He re-proposes dividing up the search space (utt. 0350), like last time (utt. 0356), but quickly follows with criticisms about how the team poorly executed their plan, previously. Namely, everyone should concentrate on executing the search in their area of terrain (utt. 0401) without deviating from their sector, and to not just search in the village where bottles are easier to find (utt. 0416). Tom also does not think it is necessary to spend time on testing a character's sensing ability (utt. 0436 and 0443), claiming that it is "pretty obvious if you're the guy or not," and suggests that the role for that person should be to clear their area as quickly as possible using the 2-D map (utt. 0401), and at completion, help the other teammates (utt. 0416).

Figure 11. Excerpt from the Team 16 transcript for the Portfolio condition (executed 1ˢᵗ). There is a disagreement between players Jon and Tom about whether to split up or stay together.

MMSS	A - Jon, B - Ann, C - Tom	
0345		[GAME START]
0350	C	Alright so I say we go around the buildings and crush as many bottles as we can
0358	A	Yeah and try to maximize the time, I was going to say we should probably split up, each of us take two vertical columns
0410	C	But it will be harder to look for the bottles
0412	B	Oh the bottles aren't displayed on the map anymore
0415		(Personal Discussion)
0509	C	Yeah so we should all run together
0515	A	OK, I think maybe we would cover more ground if we split up
0526	A	I'm going, started heading towards the west
0531	C	Ok, let's go to the west first

Conflict Management

Although most of the teams were able to decide on a course of action without disagreement, some of the teams had problems agreeing on a search plan. Figure 11 is an excerpt from the transcribed voice log of Team 16's Portfolio condition, which they executed first of the three conditions. This transcription is remarkable in the way that it illustrates an incompatibility of mental models of the teammates. Player Ann suggests that the team should split up, each member responsible for searching the terrain that corresponds to two adjacent columns on the 2-D terrain map (utterance 0358). Player Tom, on the other hand, believes that it would be easier to find bottles if the players searched the same space, together. Ann offered the reason that splitting up would enable the team to cover more ground (utt. 0515). The two players do not resolve their differences, and for the first couple of minutes, Ann would propose an area of terrain for her to search, and Tom would commit to searching the same terrain. After the players each find bottles, and a couple of minutes have passed, Tom finally announces that he will search in the opposite direction opposite to Ann. Precious time was lost, not all terrain was covered, and indeed, Team 16 tied as one of the worst performing teams in the Portfolio condition. (See Figure 2.) In a post-experiment interview with the human subject who played Ann, he confessed that he lost confidence in his ability to propose further strategies or roles to Tom, fearing that they would not be well received. Indeed, Ann and Tom did not begin to discuss the strategy for forming a portfolio of different bottle types until less than half the time remained in the session. Player "Jon," meanwhile, did not participate in the planning or strategizing, and crushed four of the eight bottles that the team collectively found.

Modeling Team Intention

Developers of agent support systems for ad-hoc human teams face substantial challenges, as illustrated by the transcripts above. The main challenge remains: how can team-supporting agents acquire a model of what the human team members intend to do and thereby be enabled to monitor their task execution and coordination as a team? This is related to the problem of agents translating organizational norms into specific reasoning rules, described in Chapter XIII, "Autonomous Agents Adopting Organizational Roles" by van der Vecht et al.

First, there is information in human team communications that agents can use to understand human intentions, strategies, plans and roles. Although the human communications may be noisy and fragmented, and may not contain explicit relevance to strategy, plan or role as the above transcripts attest to, statistical language understanding techniques could be utilized by the agents to make correct inferences. Second, a significant portion of the vocabulary used to express such team-oriented communications is provided by the context of the execution environment. Therefore, it would alleviate the problem that agents have to infer what the humans are doing, if the agent has knowledge of the execution environment. Additionally, we observed that there is frequently a disconnect between what humans say and what they do. A proclamation that *a person will do X* can be interpreted as an *announcement of intention* as well as an *announcement of commitment*. This gives rise to a requirement that agents be multi-modal, namely they integrate information about the proclaimed intention along with environmental information, such as actual team member location and activity.

Creating a single agent that would have a high level of awareness of the mission and environmental context is very challenging, if not impossible. Our strategy would be to have different agents aiding different aspects of the task so that the agent's scope of representation and inference would be limited, thus facilitating agent implementation. In addition, the above observations motivate considerations of an agent interface design that does not rely exclusively on voice recognition and natural language understanding techniques, but which also incorporates multi-modal and on-demand human input features.

Agent Assistance Strategies

The data analysis, transcripts, observations of human subject behavior, and anecdotal post-experiment interviews with subjects provide suggestions and insights into specific intervention actions that an agent might execute to assist a human team. Here we discuss three general types of intervention actions: 1) aiding individual task work skills 2) regulating team communication 3) assisting with team planning.

Many of the subjects experienced problems with the navigation aspect of the task. A posttest questionnaire revealed that novice subjects were frequently disoriented in the environment, even when switching from 2-D map to virtual reality. When human subjects became lost or disoriented, they spent more time discussing terrain features, their locations, where they wanted to go, and how to get there, than actually dedicated to their task of finding bottles. This is illustrated by transcripts 9 and 10 and also by the regression analysis results where utterance on player location (1) and terrain features (2) was negatively correlated with performance. Agents could aid disoriented team members in a variety of ways: (a) displaying guide arrows to prevent players from wandering in loops; (b) providing directions to players trying to reach a specific point on the map; (c) reporting individual deviations from the teams' stated search plan. Moreover, automatic detection by the agent of these problems could be done through interpretation of utterances that refer to location.

More generally, agents can support human teams in the realm of task execution coaching. The type of coaching could range from reminding teammates to "stick with the plan" or ``their roles," "stay on pace," and to offer tips on improving search strategy, technique, and reminders when subjects overlook features and critical notices.

Meta-level team communication and planning is another area amenable to agent assistance. Although Team 16 eventually converged on a team strategy for the Portfolio condition, they did so when it was too late to have a positive impact on their performance. One of the ways an agent could support decentralized ad hoc teams is to support the team process, such as stimulating conversations about techniques, evaluations of team and individual progress, and requiring teammates to provide rationale for certain suggestions and decisions.

Regulating communication has been demonstrated to be useful in other agent support systems in which agents were used as mechanism for reducing the information overload created by indiscriminate player broadcasts (Fan and Yen, 2007). Indiscriminate communication of intent (15) and unnecessary requests for status (31) are negatively correlated with performance in some of the conditions, although communication of intent can be positively correlated with performance (e.g., the **Bottles Known** condition). The problem is communicating the right information to the right person in a timely fashion. Information routing is a task that agents are well suited for. There are many possibilities for agent aiding in this area, ranging from the simplest ones of having the agent forward status messages to the relevant player or having the agent use activity recognition to infer player goal intention directly from their movement. Interestingly, social type communications (e.g., unrelated discussion and social encouragement) were positively correlated with higher performance in some of the conditions and seemed to occur with players who felt relaxed enough with the interface and the cognitive demands of the task to chat with the other players. The key point is the reduction of cognitive overload, rather than indiscriminate elimination of all communications.

Based on this analysis, adding navigational aids and reducing information overload are likely to be productive and easily implemental agent support strategies for assisting players in our simulated collaborative search task.

We believe that these principles can also be extended to assist team members in real search and rescue operations. For instance, unnecessary radio chatter could be a significant problem for real search and rescue operations since broadcast style communications will reach dozens of people and yet most of the information communicated is likely to be relevant to only a small number of searchers. Becoming disoriented is even more hazardous in real world search domains and can happen even to survival experts. Although the details of the user interface will be different in the real world (e.g., interacting with the user through handhelds or headsets), the basic principles of assistance remain the same.

CONCLUSION

Decentralized ad hoc teams face difficult teamwork challenges, in particular, concerning communication and self-organization. This set of experiments was designed to (1) create a baseline of decentralized, ad hoc team performance in time stressed situations and (2) determine where agent aiding is likely to have the greatest impact.

When faced with the unfamiliar task of portfolio collection, human teams responded by developing various organization and communication strategies. The encoding of the utterances and their analysis allowed us to conclude that agent aiding for situation awareness and self-organization would help low performing teams increase their performance.

FUTURE RESEARCH DIRECTIONS

Our research study was an initial attempt to characterize the communication patterns of ad hoc teams operating in a particular domain. As we move towards a theory of agent-support for ad hoc teams, there are still many unanswered research questions and experiments that remain to be performed. One of the important areas of research could be to study the effect of organizational structure for these very dynamic and time stressed tasks. How do teams with different organizational structures perform on the same task? How do task-domain and organizational-structure interact to affect team performance? Is self-organization viable for highly complex team tasks?

Another interesting open research area is to study the effects of agent-support strategies: how do ad hoc teams respond to proven agent-support strategies (e.g., task monitoring) that have been used successfully with non ad hoc teams? Can agent-support be used to compensate for a lack of organizational structure in highly complex team tasks?

A third research area is identifying linguistic markers so that agents could best infer the intent of the teammates, with respect to the various subtasks and organizational roles of team members. Some research questions include: do teams communicate as they self-organize? Can we identify linguistic markers that are highly correlated with shifts in organizational structure?

We believe that ad hoc teams will become increasingly common in the future as organizations strive to become agile, adaptive, and responsive to rapidly changing global demands. Identifying answers to these questions will substantially benefit the future developers of agent-support systems.

ACKNOWLEDGMENT

Research was sponsored by the U.S. Army Research Laboratory and the U.K. Ministry of Defence and was accomplished under Agreement Number W911NF-06-3-0001. The views and conclusions contained in this document are those of the author(s) and should not be interpreted as representing the official policies, either expressed or implied, of the U.S. Army Research Laboratory, the U.S. Government, the U.K. Ministry of Defence or the U.K. Government. The U.S. and U.K. Governments are authorized to reproduce and distribute reprints for Government purposes notwithstanding any copyright notation hereon.

We would like to thank Michael Lewis for his invaluable help with the experimental design and analysis.

We would like to thank Lori R. Price for her assistance with editing and formatting this chapter.

REFERENCES

Cannon-Bowers, J., Salas, E., & Converse, S. (1993). Shared mental models in expert team decision making. In Castellan, J., (eds), *Individual and group decision making*. Lawrence Erlbaum Associates.

Chalupsky, H. et al. (2001). Electric Elves: Applying agent technology to support human organizations. In *Proceedings of the Innovative Applications of Artificial Intelligence Conference*.

Chen, L., & Sycara, K. (1998). Webmate: A personal agent for browsing and searching. In *Proceedings of the Second International Conference on Autonomous Agents*.

Cooke, N., & Gorman, J. (2007). Assessment of team cognition. In Karwowski, P., (ed), *International Encyclopedia of Ergonomics and Human Factors*. Taylor and Francis Ltd.

Cooke, N., Gorman, J., Pedersen, M., & Bell, B. (2007). Distributed mission environments: Effects of geographic distribution on team cognition, process, and performance. In Fiore, S. and Salas, E., (eds.), *Toward a science of distributed learning and training*. American Psychological Association.

Entin, E., & Serfaty, D. (1999). Adaptive team coordination. *Human Factors, 41*.

Fan, X., Sun, B., Sun, S., McNeese, M., & Yen, J. (2006). RPD-Enabled agents teaming with humans for multi-context decision making. In *Proceedings of International Conference on Autonomous Agents and Multiagent Systems (AAMAS)*.

Fan, X., Sun, S., McNeese, M., & Yen, J. (2005). Extending the recognition-primed decision model to support human-agent collaboration. In *Proceedings of International Conference on Autonomous Agents and Multiagent Systems (AAMAS)*.

Fan, X., & Yen, J. (2007). Realistic cognitive load modeling for enhancing shared mental models in human-agent collaboration. In *Proceedings of the Sixth International Joint Conference on Autonomous Agents and Multi-Agent Systems (AAMAS-07)*.

Fiore, S., Salas, E., & Cannon-Bowers, J. (2001). Group dynamics and shared mental model development. In London, M., (ed.), *How people evaluate others in organizations: Person perception and interpersonal judgment in industrial/organizational psychology*. Lawrence Erlbaum Associates.

Fiore, S., Salas, E., Cuevas, H., & Bowers, C. (2003). Distributed coordination space: towards a theory of distributed team performance. *Theoretical Issues in Ergonomic Science, 4*.

Fiore, S., & Schooler, J. (2004). Process mapping and shared cognition: Teamwork and the development of shared problem models. In Salas, E. and Fiore, S., (eds.), *Team Cognition: Understanding the Factors that Drive Process and Performance*. American Psychological Association.

Fischer, U., McDonnel, L., & Orasanu, J. (2007). Linguistic correlates of team performance: Toward a tool for monitoring team functioning during space missions. *Aviation, Space, and Environmental Medicine, 78*(5), B87 – B95. Section II.

Flashpoint (2001). Operation flashpoint: Cold war crisis. http://en.wikipedia.org/wiki/Operation_Flashpoint. Accessed May 2007.

Friedkin, N. (1998). *A structural theory of social influence*. Cambridge University Press.

Galbraith, J. (1977). *Organization Design*. Addison–Wesley Publication Company.

Giampapa, J., & Sycara, K. (2001). Conversational case-based planning for agent team coordination. In *Case-Based Reasoning Research and Development: Proceedings of the Fourth International Conference on Case-Based Reasoning*, ICCBR 2001, volume 2080, pages 189–203.

Giampapa, J. Esch, S., John, B., Singh, R., & Sycara, K. (2003). Evaluation criteria for the MORSE simulation environment. Technical Report CMU-RI-TR-03-38, Robotics Institute, Carnegie Mellon University, Pittsburgh, PA.

Goodrich, M., Quigley, M., Humphrey, C., Adams, J., Gerhardt, D., Cooper, J., Buss, B., & Morse, B. (2007). *Mini-UAVs for visual search in wilderness search: Tasks, autonomy, and interfaces*. Technical Report BYUHCMI 2007-1, Brigham Young University.

Hirokawa, R. Y. (1983). Group communication and problem-solving effectiveness: an investigation of group phases. *Human Communication Research, 9*, 291–305.

Hoeft, R., Kochan, J., & Jentsch, F. (2006). Automated team members in the cockpit: Myth or reality. In Schulz, A. and Parker, L., (eds.), *Series: Advances in Human Performance and Cognitive Engineering Research*. Elsevier Science.

Horvitz, E. (1999). Principles of mixed-initiative user interfaces. In *Proceedings of SIGCHI*.

Kraut, B., Fussell, S., Lerch, F., & Espinosa, A. (2005). Coordination in teams: Evidence from a simulated management game. *Journal of Organizational Behavior*.

Lenox, T. (2000). *Supporting teamwork using software agents in human-agent teams*. PhD thesis, Westminster College.

Lenox, T., Hahn, S., Lewis, M., Payne, T., & Sycara, K. 2000). Agent-based aiding for individual and team planning tasks. In *Proceedings of IEA 2000/HFES 2000 Congress*.

Lenox, T., Lewis, M., Roth, E., Shern, R., Roberts, L., Rafalski, T., & Jacobson, J. (1998). Support of teamwork in human-agent teams. In *Proceedings of IEEE International Conference on Systems, Man, and Cybernetics*.

Lenox, T., Roberts, L., & Lewis, M. (1997). Human-agent interaction in a target identification task. In *Proceedings of IEEE International Conference on Systems, Man, and Cybernetics*.

Pascual, R. G., Mills, M. C., & Blendell, C. (1999). Supporting distributed and ad-hoc team interaction. In *People in Control: An International Conference on Human Interfaces in Control Rooms, Cockpits and Command Centres*, number 463 in Conference Publication, pages 64 – 71. IEE.

Salas, E. and Fiore, S., (eds.) (2004). *Team Cognition: Understanding the Factors that Drive Process and Performance*. American Psychological Association.

Scerri, P., Pynadath, D., Johnson, L., Rosenbloom, P., Schurr, N., & Tambe, M. (2003). A prototype infrastructure for distributed robot-agent-person teams. In *Proceedings of International Conference on Autonomous Agents and Multiagent Systems (AAMAS)*.

Setnicka, T. (1980). *Wilderness Search and Rescue*. Appalachian Mountain Club.

Shannon, C., & Weaver, W. (1949). *The mathematical theory of communication*. University of Illinois Press.

Sycara, K., & Lewis, M. (2004). Integrating agents into human teams. In Salas, Fiore, S., & Fiore, E. (eds.), *Team Cognition: Understanding the Factors that Drive Process and Performance*. American Psychological Association.

TeamSpeak (2001). Teamspeak communication system. http://www.goteamspeak.com. Accessed May 2007.

Traum, D., Rickel, J., Gratch, J., & Marsella, S. (2003). Negotiation over tasks in hybrid human-agent teams for simulation-based training. In *Proceedings of International Conference on Autonomous Agents and Multiagent Systems (AAMAS)*.

RECOMMENDED READING LIST

Burstein, M., & Diller, D. (2004). A framework for dynamic information flow in mixed-initiative human/agent organizations. *Applied Intelligence, 20*(3).

Cannon-Bowers, J., Salas, E., & Converse, S. (1993). Shared mental models in expert team decision making. In Castellan, J., (ed.), *Individual and group decision making*. Lawrence Erlbaum Associates.

Cannon-Bowers, J., & Salas, E., (ed.) (1998), *Making Decisions Under Stress: Implications for Individual and Team Training*. American Psychological Association.

Fan, X., Yen, J., & Volz, R. (2005b). A theoretical framework on proactive information exchange in agent teamwork. *Artificial Intelligence, 169*, 23–97.

Grosz, B., & Kraus, S. (1996). Collaborative plans for complex group action. *Artificial Intelligence, 86.*

Horvitz, E. (1999). Principles of mixed-initiative user interfaces. In *Proceedings of SIGCHI.*

Lenox, T., Hahn, S., Lewis, M., Payne, T., & Sycara, K. (2000). Task characteristics and intelligent aiding. In *Proceedings of International Conference on Systems, Man, and Cybernetics.*

Levesque, H., & Cohen, P. (1990). On acting together. In *Proceedings of National Conference on Artificial Intelligence (AAAI).*

Lewis, M. (1998). Designing for Human-Agent Interaction. *AI Magazine, 19*(2).

Orasanu, J. (1990). Shared mental models and crew performance. In *Proceedings of the 34th Annual Meeting of the Human Factors Society.*

Orasanu, J., & Salas, E. (1993). Team decision making in complex environments. In Klein, G., Orasanu, J., Calederwood, R., and Zsanbok, C., editors, *Decision making in action: Models and methods.* Ablex.

Salas, E., Bowers, C., & Edens, E. (2001). *Improving teamwork in organizations:Applications of resource management training.* Lawrence Erlbaum Associates.

Salas, E., & Fiore, S., (ed.) (2004). *Team Cognition: Understanding the Factors that Drive Process and Performance.* American Psychological Association.

Sierhuis, M., Bradshaw, J., Acquisti, A., van Hoof, R., Jeffers, R., & Uszok, A. (2003). Human-agent teamwork and adjustable autonomy in practice. In *Proceedings of 7th International Symposium on Artificial Intelligence (I-SAIRAS).*

Sycara, K., & Lewis, M. (2004). Integrating agents into human teams. In Salas, E. and Fiore, S., (ed.), *Team Cognition: Understanding the Factors that Drive Process and Performance.* American Psychological Association.

Sycara, K., Paolucci, M., Giampapa, J., & van Velsen, M. (2003). The RETSINA multiagent infrastructure. *Autonomous Agents and Multi-agent Systems, 7*(1).

Tambe, M. (1997). Towards flexible teamwork. *Journal of AI Research, 7.*

Warner, N., Letsky, M., & Cowen, M. (2005). Cognitive model of team collaboration: macrocognitive focus. In *Human Factors and Ergonomics Society (HFES) 49th Annual Meeting.*

Warner, N., & Wroblewski, E. (2004). The cognitive processes used in team collaboration during asynchronous, distributed decision making. In *Command and Control Research and Technology Symposium.*

Yen, J., Fan, X., Sun, S., Hanratty, T., & Dumer, J. (2004a). Agents with shared mental models for enhancing team decision-making. *Decision Support Systems.*

KEY TERMS

Ad Hoc Teams: A group of people that are brought together to achieve common goals for the duration of the task but who lack the experience of training together as a team.

Agent: An agent is a system that maintains a computational model of goal-directed and adaptive behavior. For the purposes of this chapter, we use agent to specifically refer to software systems.

Agent Support Systems: An agent-based software system that renders assistance to a human or group of humans that are trying to collaboratively accomplish a particular task. In this chapter, we focus on agent support systems that assist with team tasks rather than individual tasks.

Communication: The process of transferring information between humans or agents. In these experiments, communication between team members was measured by counting conversational moves, an uninterrupted utterance of a team member that has a discrete problem solving function.

Search and Rescue: An operation mounted by emergency services to find a lost person or recover victims from a disaster. Response teams usually have a doctrine or set of guidelines that they follow when constructing a search plan and allocating searchers to regions.

Shared Mental Models: A set of beliefs that a group of people holds in common about how the world works. The process of working together and training together creates shared mental models in human teams and is an important aspect of team cognition.

Teamwork: The state that occurs when groups of humans (or agents) commit to a shared set of goals and roles. Agents can achieve an understanding of teamwork through various formalisms that allow them to reason about establishing commitment through communication.

Chapter XIII
Autonomous Agents Adopting Organizational Rules

Bob van der Vecht
Utrecht University, The Netherlands
TNO Defense, Security and Safety, The Netherlands

Frank Dignum
Utrecht University, The Netherlands

John-Jules Ch. Meyer
Utrecht University, The Netherlands

ABSTRACT

This chapter discusses how autonomous agents can adopt organizational rules into their reasoning process. Agents in an organization need to coordinate their actions in order to reach the organizational goals. Organizational models specify the desired behaviour in terms of roles, relations, norms, and interactions. We have developed a method to translate norms into event-processing rules of the agents. We propose a modular reasoning model that includes the organizational rules explicitly. Since the agents are autonomous, they will have their own reasoning rules next to the organizational rules. The modular approach allows for meta-reasoning about these rules. We show that this stimulates bottom-up dynamics in the organization.

INTRODUCTION

Organizations benefit from autonomous decisions by their participants. This is visible in human organizations. Not only the formal organizational structure but also the informal circuit of communication and interaction between actors determines the success of an organization. In human organizations a participant's contribution is evaluated based on the organizational requirements as well as the extra achievements. Someone who takes initiative and builds up a personal network is often higher valued than someone who sticks to the official rules and does not do anything extra. The capability to act and make decisions in unexpected situations is usually perceived as a positive characteristic of human actors.

How does the observation that organizations benefit from participants' initiatives translate to multi-agent coordination that are based on organizational theory? Every organization is created for a specific objective. The organizational model describes the desired global behaviour using abstract concepts such as roles, relations and norms. Its specification is meant to guarantee certain requirements, for example, about the information flow. However, since the agent is assumed to be an autonomous entity, decision making is a local process of the agent. Therefore, it is important to maintain agent autonomy within the multi-agent coordination model. The organizational rules should guide the choices of the agent, but the organization cannot control the agent's decision-making process.

In this research, we investigate how to make agents aware of organizational rules. At the same time we allow them to take initiatives besides the formal structure. We propose a modular approach with which agents can adopt organizational rules into their reasoning model. The reasoning model separates the organizational rules from the actual decision-making process. This way, the agent's decision-making process can be defined separately from the coordination mechanism.

At the same time, the modular approach allows for meta-reasoning about different behavioural rules, which makes the agent independent from the organizational structure. The agent is not limited in its decision-making. It knows how to follow the organizational norms and it is able to take other initiatives. Therefore, the model guarantees agent autonomy.

The chapter is structured as follows. First we discuss related work on agent organizations. We motivate our choice to use the OperA model to describe organizations and we give an example of the use of OperA. Next, we describe a reasoning model with which an agent can adopt organizational constraints to its decision making and we show how the organizational rules are adopted by the agent. Then we discuss how the agent and the organization come together. We investigate bottom-up dynamics in organizations using the autonomy of agents and we give examples. Finally, we conclude the chapter.

BACKGROUND: AGENTS AND ORGANIZATIONS

In our research we use human organizations as inspiration. From this point of view, we consider an organization as a description of roles, relations and interactions to achieve certain coordination. We assume that the agents fulfilling organizational roles are autonomous entities; they have control over their internal state and their behaviour (Jennings, 2000). This implies that the organizational model specifies behavioural guidelines for the agents to assure desired features such as task coordination or information flow. The agents should follow those guidelines, but they are not forced to do so by definition. Researchers in multi-agent systems have introduced the organizational metaphor to achieve coordination between autonomous agents. Organizational models specify coordination mechanisms between agents in abstract concepts, such as roles, relations and norms.

In this section we discuss related work on organizational models. We describe how different approaches allow agents to take up organizational tasks and we describe the consequences for the agents' autonomy.

Models for Agent Organizations

Several organizational descriptions have been proposed. Please see Chapter II "Modelling Dimensions for Multi-Agent Systems Organizations" by Coutinho et al. for an extensive comparison of several approaches. Here, we briefly discuss the features of some organizational descriptions.

One of the first was the Agent Group Role (AGR) model (Ferber & Gutknecht, 1998), which introduced the concepts of roles, groups and interaction between roles. The model focuses on defining the structural aspects of the organization. The interaction between agents is defined within the role description. The AGR model does not consider abstract behaviour rules, such as norms. An extension to the AGR model is described in Chapter III of this book, "Towards an Integral Approach of Organizations in Multi-Agent Systems" by Ferber et al. The model present a methodology for the design of other system aspects as well, including the agents and the environment of a multi-agent system.

The OperA model (Dignum, 2004) proposes a more expressive way for defining organizations by introducing an organizational model, a social model and an interaction model. This approach explicitly distinguishes between the organizational model and the agents that act in it. Agents become aware of the organizational rules via contracts that specify these rules.

Another approach is Moise+ (Hübner et al., 2002), which also separates the organizational model from the agent model. The organization is defined in terms of a structural, a functional and a deontic model. The structural model describes the roles, groups and relation between them. The functional model contains a task diagram for the common goal. The deontic model connects the other two models in a normative way. In order to operationalize the organization, a middleware has been developed that checks whether actions of agents are allowed or not according to the governing organizational rules.

Other organizational models, such as (Matson & DeLoach, 2005) and OCMAS described in Chapter IV "Organizational Model for Adaptive Complex Systems" by DeLoach, are based on formal semantics and transition rules. The possible states of the organization are described by state transitions. The state description captures the whole system; they include the organizational structure as well as the internal knowledge of the agents. The model has been developed to enable reorganization at runtime.

Electronic institutions as described in (Esteva et al., 2001) and (García-Camino et al., 2007) are norm-based coordination models for open multi-agent systems. The norms are specified in a multi-agent middleware, to regulate agents' actions. The institution actively interacts with the agents.

Agent Autonomy

Organizational models pose expectations on the agents' behaviour. Our assumption is that agents are autonomous entities, which implies that they have control over their internal state and over their behaviour (Jennings, 2000). Therefore, it is not straightforward to operationalize organizations. How do we ensure that the agent is aware of the organizational rules, without interfering with the agent's decision-making process? The different approaches for coordination have different consequences for the autonomy of the agents that participate in the system.

The AGR model (Ferber & Gutknecht, 1998) includes the individual agent behaviour in the specification of the roles. Also, all interaction is predefined and presented at low level. The agents in the AGR model are autonomous; they are outside of the organization. However, the organizational rules specify the desired behaviour in detail. If the agent follows the rules, the detailed level leaves the agents no choice in how they actually pursue the goals that belong to their role.

The middleware of Moise+ (Hübner et al., 2002) checks whether choices of agents are compatible with the organizational specification. The agents make decision locally, but the middleware can overrule the decisions of the agents. The organization becomes an active entity that has the possibility to interfere in the agents decisions. Therefore, the agents are not fully autonomous in executing their choices. The same holds for the electronic institutions (Esteva et al., 2001) (García-Camino et al., 2007).

OperA (Dignum, 2004) specifies contracts that describe the behavioural guidelines of a specific role. The internals of the agents are fully separated from the organizational specification. The only requirement is that the agents need to be able to understand the contracts. The agents are still fully autonomous in making decisions.

Organizational models based on formal transitions (Matson & DeLoach, 2005) include internal knowledge of the agents within the specification. The agents are restricted by the organizational specification. As in our case agents are supposed to have control over their internal state, this is not appropriate for our aims.

The OperA approach is compatible with our notion of autonomous agents. Furthermore, it has expressive semantics to define organizations. Therefore, we have chosen to use OperA for the organizational specification. In order to use OperA, we still need a mechanism to describe the adoption of organizational contracts into an agent's reasoning model. In Sect. 4 we show how autonomous agents can adopt organizational rules. In the following section we will give an example of an organization specified in the OperA model.

The OperA Model

OperA (Dignum, 2004) provides a formalized specification language for agent organizations. OperA describes an operational organization in three parts:

- The organizational model: roles, relations, interactions
- The social model: population of organization, linking agents to roles
- The interaction model: describes interactions given organizational model and agents

The organizational model contains the description of the roles, relations and interactions in the organization. It is constructed based on functional requirements of the organization. The social model and the interaction model are the link between the organizational description and the executing agents. Here the organizational rules are translated to contracts for the agents fulfilling the roles. OperA includes a formal language to describe those contracts.

In an operational organization the social model and the interaction model can be dynamic, because of agents entering or leaving the organization. The organizational model is in principal static as long as no structural changes are carried through. The administrative tasks to keep track of the different organizational models are specified in organizational roles.

Agents enacting roles in an organization are expected to have some minimal knowledge about the concepts that are used to set up social contracts. The contracts are described in deontic expressions. The agents need to know the deontic concepts *permission*, *obligation* and *prohibition*. Furthermore, the description includes relations between roles. The agent needs to know the meaning of such a relation. For example, a *hierarchical* relation between role $r1$ and $r2$ implies that a request from $r1$ is interpreted as an obligation by $r2$. OperA presents a formal description of the relevant concepts.

EXAMPLE OF AN ORGANIZATIONAL DESCRIPTION

In this section we present an example of an organizational model in OperA. We use a fire brigade to illustrate how an organization is specified and how the behaviour rules for the agents are constructed.

The fire brigade operates in a world where fires appear that need to be extinguished. In the organization we define two roles; *coordinator* and *firefighter*. The coordinator makes a global plan and tells the firefighters which fire they should extinguish. The coordinator has a global view of the world. The firefighters perform the actual tasks in the environment; they move to a fire location and extinguish the fires. They have only local views.

There is a hierarchical relation between the two roles, the coordinator is the superior of the firefighters and can send orders to the firefighters, which fire they have to extinguish. We want to show different forms of coordination within this organization. In our implementation, we achieve this by changing the autonomy level of the decision-making process of the firefighters.

A generic methodology to analyze a given domain and determine the type and structure of an application domain resulting in an OperA agent organization model is described in (Dignum et al., 2004). The methodology provides generic facilitation and interaction frameworks for agent societies that implement the functionality derived from the coordination model applicable to the problem domain. Standard organization types such as market, hierarchy and network, can be used as starting point for development and can be extended where needed and determine the basic norms and facilitation roles necessary for the society. A brief summary of the methodology is given in Table 1.

We focus on the organizational model of our firefighter organization. Below we define the coordination level, environment level and behaviour level.

Coordination Level

At the coordination level, the coordination type of the society is determined based on the characteristics of the problem domain. There are several possibilities, for example a hierarchical model, a market based model or a network model. A hierarchical model is the most common structure in crisis management organizations such as our group of firefighters. The following characteristics are typical for a hierarchical organization:

Table 1. Methodology for designing agent organizations

	Step	Description	Result
OM	Coordination Level	Identifies organization's main characteristics; purpose, relations, norms	Stakeholders, facilitation roles, coordination requirements
	Environment Level	Analysis of expected external behaviour of system	Operational roles, use cases, normative requirements
	Behaviour Level	Design of internal behaviour of system	Role structure, interaction structure, norms, roles, scripts
SM	Population Level	Design of enactment negotiation protocols	Agent admission scripts, role enactment contracts
IM	Interaction Level	Design of interaction negotiation protocols	Scene script protocols, interaction contracts

- The leading goals for agents are global, organizational goals
- Relations between agents are fixed
- Communication is specified by design

We have chosen for a hierarchical organization, since this is the most common structure in crisis management organizations such as our group of firefighters. Based on the choice for a hierarchical model we define the environment level and behaviour level.

Environmental Level

In the environment level, interaction between the organization and the environment is analyzed. Ontologies are needed to define organizational concepts and to define communication. Furthermore, the functional requirements of the organization are specified. This includes the global organizational purpose and the local objectives of the roles. We define coordination rules in terms of norms.

Organizational Function

The purpose of our firefighter organization is to detect fires in the environment and extinguish them as soon as possible.

Ontologies

Besides OperA concepts to specify the organizational model, we need a communication language between the agents. We will use four performatives for the communication between the agents: *Request*, *Accept*, *Reject* and *Inform*.

Secondly we need domain-level ontology to describe all objects in the environment, and the actions that the agents can communicate and reason about. Our domain ontology consists of one object, *Fire*, and one action, *Extinguish* and three states that describe the status of an agent with respect to its tasks: *Busy, Done, Free.* Furthermore the agents can send messages.

Table 2. Role table of the firefighter organization

Role	Relation to Society	Role Objectives	Role Dependencies
Applicant	Potential member	Join organization	Root
Root	From hierarchy model	Assign coordinator role to applicant	Applicant
Coordinator	From hierarchy model	Monitor fires	
		Assign firefighter role	Applicant
		Monitor status of firefighters	Firefighter
		Assign fires to firefighters	Firefighters
Firefighter	Realization of extinguishing fires	Extinguish fires	
		Inform about status	Coordinator

Table 3. The norms of the firefighter organization

Norm	
Situation	Handling extinguish-request
Responsibilities	Initiator: coordinator Action: firefighter
Triggers	Pre: coordinator sends extinguish-request Post: coordinator is informed about accept
Norm specification	**Whenever** extinguish-request from coordinator **then** firefighter **is** obliged **to do** accept-request

Norm	
Situation	Announce status
Responsibilities	Initiator: firefighter Action: firefighter
Triggers	Pre: status change Post: inform coordinator about status
Norm specification	**Whenever** status-change **then** firefighter **is** obliged **to do** inform-coordinator-about-status

Roles

We do not consider external stakeholders of our organization. We will describe the roles in our organization. The roles are based on a functional analysis of the task of the organizational purpose. The roles are described in Table 3.2.

A hierarchical organization needs a *root* role to take care of delegation of roles. The root role will give the role definitions to the agent highest in hierarchy and provide it with a social contract to specify the required behaviour. In our case, the highest role is the *coordinator* role.

The coordinator role has as objective to hire firefighters. It will assign the firefighter rule to applicant agents. Furthermore it has the objectives to monitor the fires in the world, to monitor the firefighters, and to assign fires to firefighters. For the last two objectives the coordinator is dependent on the firefighters.

We specify the firefighter role with the objectives to extinguish fires, to inform the coordinator about its status.

Dependencies between the roles appear from the description of the role objectives. We have defined the coordinator as the highest role in the organization. Therefore it has a hierarchical relation with the firefighter role, where the coordinator is the superior of the firefighters.

Norms

We specify the norms that hold between the coordinator and the firefighter roles in Table 3. In the first norm we describe how a firefighter agent handles requests to extinguish fires. The firefighter is obliged to accept the request from the coordinator. This norm follows directly from the hierarchical relation between the two roles.

We define a second norm telling that the firefighter should keep the coordinator informed about its status. The information is needed by the coordinator in order to do its tasks properly. This norm guarantees the required information sharing within our organization.

Behaviour Level

Here, we describe the social model and the interaction model as defined in OperA. Typically, a hierarchical organization has a relatively detailed social model and interaction model. This implies that the norms in the social model and the communication protocols in the interaction model do not leave much space for individual contracts with the agents. We assume that the behaviour rules as described in this level of the development of the organization match with the contracts with the agents.

Social Model

In the social model we define the social contract for the agents that fulfil the roles. We describe the dependencies between the agents in more detail. The coordinator role just specifies the role objectives, with no further obligations. For the firefighter role we have defined some additional norms:

1.   Whenever extinguish-request from coordinator then firefighter is obliged to do accept-request.
2.   Whenever status-change then firefighter is obliged to do inform-coordinator-about-status.

As we explained, the first norm follows directly from the hierarchical relation between the two roles. Therefore, the social contracts for firefighter agents should only capture the second norm.

Interaction Model

The interaction model describes interaction contracts. An interaction contract between two agents describes a protocol that is followed by the agents during interaction scenes. (Dignum et al., 2003) presents a formal language to specify the interaction between agents in behaviour rules.

Table 4. The interaction contracts of the firefighter organization

Interaction Contract	
Parties	Coordinator C, Firefighter F
Scene	Extinguish request
Clauses	**If** received(F, C, extinguish-request(fire)) **then obliged** F **to** answer(F, C, accept-refuse)

Interaction Contract	
Parties	Coordinator C, Firefighter F
Scene	Inform about status
Clauses	**If** received(C, F, status-report) **then** nothing

The agents have interaction contracts for all interaction scenes. In our example, there should be interaction scenes and contracts between applicant and root and between applicant and coordinator roles. However, they are only relevant to set up the organization. We will focus on the interaction contracts between the coordinator and firefighter roles here, as this interaction will occur during the execution.

Interaction contracts are agreed upon by agents playing the roles and encountering interaction scenes. We propose possible interaction contracts between agents playing firefighter and coordinator, Table 4.

The first contract specifies the interaction between the firefighter and coordinator for the situation where the coordinator sends a request to the firefighter to extinguish a certain fire. The contract specifies that the firefighter is obliged to answer whether it accepts or rejects the request. The second contract specifies the interaction for the scenes in which the firefighter informs the coordinator about its status. The agents agreed that the coordinator does not need to respond.

The interaction contracts from Table 4 pose another behaviour rule on the firefighter agent:

3.   Whenever extinguish-request from coordinator then firefighter is obliged to do answer-accept/refuse.

Towards an Operational Organization

We have specified the organizational model in terms of roles, relations and interaction and we have defined contracts for agents that want to participate in the organization. Although agents are autonomous entities, we expect them to follow the organizational rules. When an agent joins an organization, it should adopt a contract that contains these rules.

We do not want to specify the internals of an agent when we specify the organization. We have developed a reasoning model that represents the organizational rules separately from the agent's decision-making rules. Therefore, the adoption of contracts can be done dynamically. In the next section we describe the agent's reasoning process in further detail.

AUTONOMOUS AGENTS IN ORGANIZATIONS

The assumption that agents are autonomous entities is important in agent organizations. The organization specifies coordination at a high level. The agents should be aware of the organizational rules, but they still make their own decisions.

In Sect. 2, we have discussed other research concerning coordination of autonomous agents. The AGR model (Ferber & Gutknecht, 1998) gives a low level and detailed description of the desired behaviour. The organizational middleware of Moise+ (Hübner et al., 2002) makes that the organization itself becomes an active entity, whereas we let the organization exist only in the agents. The organizational models based on formal transition rules (Matson & DeLoach, 2005) do not meet our requirement that the agent's internals have to be defined separately from the organization. We have adopted the OperA approach that describes the coordination via contracts for the agents joining the organization.

We believe that a modular approach in the agent's reasoning model is a promising way to adopt organizational rules into the decision-making process. By separating the organizational rules from the decision-making process of the agent we can guarantee the autonomy of the agent. Furthermore, the adoption of contracts can be done dynamically and the contracts can be changed at runtime.

Figure 1. Two phases in the agent's reasoning model

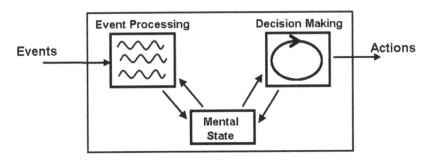

In this section we show how autonomous agents can adopt organizational rules into their reasoning model. We explain briefly the reasoning model as described in (van der Vecht et al., 2007).

Autonomous Decision Making

Being autonomous means that agents have control over their internal state and over their behaviour. The first implies that an agent determines its beliefs by itself. The second implies that decision-making on action is a local process.

Coordination implies that agents influence each other in order to coordinate their behaviour. Therefore, an agent *allows* influence on its mental state. For example, if an agent accepts a request to do a certain task from another agent, it adds the task to its goal base. We argue that an autonomous agent controls how other agents influence its internal state.

Our approach to operationalize autonomy is to give the agent a choice in processing external events. The agent makes its own decisions, and it decides how other agents can influence its decision-making process. We introduce a component in the agent's reasoning model to deal with external events. We show how organizational rules can be specified in this reasoning component.

Event Processing in the Agent Reasoning-Model

Here we explain briefly the reasoning model we described in (van der Vecht et al., 2007) and we show how it can be used to adopt organizational rules into the reasoning process. In the agent's reasoning-process we distinguish a phase for event processing and a phase for decision making as shown in Figure 1. The event-processing phase gives the agent control over how it is being influenced by external events. The decide phase focuses on the decision of action.

In the event-processing phase the agent prepares the decision-making phase. External influences are processed here. External influence can be an agent's observations or messages from other agents. We have chosen to implement the event-processing phase with reasoning rules of the format same format as reasoning rules in BDI implementations such as 3APL (Dastani et al., 2003b) and AgentSpeak(L) (Rao, 1996):

```
<HEAD> <- <GUARD> | <BODY>
```

The head of a rule is the event that triggers the rule. The guard should match the beliefs of the agent. The body of the rule expresses the influence of the event on the agent's reasoning process. For example, the following message describes that a request of a superior is to be accepted:

```
message(SENDER, request, TASK) <- superior(SENDER) | AddGoal(TASK)
```

The message is the trigger of the rule and the guard verifies with the agent's belief base whether the sender is a superior of the agent. If so, the request is accepted by adding the task to the agent's goals.

From Organizational Rules to Event-Processing Rules

We use the rules for event processing to specify how an agent's internal state is influenced by external events. The organizational specification describes behaviour rules that are meant to guide the agent's decision-making process. We propose to translate the organizational rules from the organizational description to event-processing rules for agent decision-making.

We have to define the set of required elements to translate organizational rules to event-processing rules. Analysis of the OperA model shows that norms are based on triggers. The triggers, which can be messages or observations, are external events, and therefore can be used as head of the event-processing rules. In the following, we propose to use a general message format consisting of a sender, a performative and the actual content. Observations must have the same format as agent beliefs.

The guards of the event-processing rules are restrictions based on internal beliefs of the agent. A guard can contain any set of beliefs. The example event-processing rule of the previous paragraph shows an example.

The body contains the effect of the external event on the internal state of the agent. This is of course dependent on how the internals of an agent are represented. If we consider BDI-agents, for example, the effect of external events then is described in terms of belief changes and goal changes of the agent.

Effects on the Mental State

Even when we consider BDI-agents, there are several ways to translate the organizational rules into internal state changes. One possibility is to transfer everything into beliefs that containing the result of the norm; *obliged(action))*, *permitted(action))*, etc. If this option is chosen, the assumption is that the decision-making process knows how to deal with those beliefs in such a way that the norms are fulfilled.

Table 5. An ontology of event-processing rules that describe organizational rules

Rule element	Description	Possible values
Head	External event that triggers the rule	- message(Sender, Performative, Content) - observation(Content)
Guard	Situational constraints	Any belief set of the agent
Body	Effect on agent's mental state	- AddGoal(Goal) - AddBelief(Belief) - IgnoreEvent()

Another option is to translate the obligations directly to goals, and permissions and prohibitions into beliefs. The result of a event-processing rule would be internal actions to add goals or beliefs: *AddGoal(Action), AddBelief(prohibited(Action))* or *AddBelief(permitted(Action))*. Then, an obligation leads automatically to a goal, and the fulfilling is in the hands of the deliberation cycle of the agent, where goals are selected. Prohibition and permissions are added to the belief base in order to make better decisions on action, without forcing anything.

It is possible to choose to remove mental elements. For example a prohibition may lead to remove the goal if it existed in the goal base. Drawback is that the goal cannot automatically be recovered if the situation allows it later on again.

In a more sophisticated set-up the decision-making procedures allow for different options concerning the effect on the mental state. For example the BDOING framework (Dignum et al., 2002) specifies an agent that derives its goals based on several aspects: norms, obligations, desires. In this framework, an obligation does not automatically lead to a goal, but can be stored as an (organizational) obligation.

If the agent has the capability to derive the deontic concepts based on derivation rules, one can add more specific constraints as well to the agent's belief base. For example, time constraints or contextual constraints can be added that describe the validity of an obligation, permission or prohibition over time.

The internal structure of the decision-making process determines the possible effects on the agent's mental state. This shows the generality of our approach. The consequence is, however, that we cannot present the one way of translating organizational rules that would work for all agent types.

For the remainder of this chapter, we propose to translate permissions and prohibitions with the *AddBelief* predicate to describe that the task is permitted or prohibited. Obligation will be added to the goal base directly using *AddGoal*.

Specification of Event-Processing Rules

We describe behavioural rules as event-processing rules that result in a change of the agent's mental state. Now we give an example of how to translate organizational rules into event-processing rules. In Table 5, we show possible values of the elements that we use to construct those rules. We assume that we can translate all organizational rules into event-processing rules by using those elements.

Prior Organizational Knowledge

In Sect. 2.3 we explained that some minimal prior knowledge is required. An agent taking up a role in the organization should know the meaning of deontic concepts and of relational terms. The meaning of the deontic concepts *obligation*, *permission* and *prohibition* are part of the ontology for event-processing rules. We translate an obligation for the agent using the *AddGoal* predicate. This predicate adds the task directly to the goal base of the agent.

The agent should know the meaning of relational concepts, such as the hierarchical relation that we use in our example organization. The meaning of a hierarchical relation between an agent and its superior can be described by the following behaviour rule: *Whenever an agent receives a request from a superior then the agent is obliged to accept the request.*

When we translate this behavioural rule to an event-processing rule using the above described elements we get:

```
message(SENDER, request, TASK) <- superior(SENDER)
        | AddGoal(TASK)
```
(r1)

We gave this rule as example of an event-processing rule in Sect. 4.2. The above rule is considered to be general knowledge of the agent. The rule does not belong to a specific organization or a specific role.

Adopting Organizational Rules

Taking up a role in an organization means that an agent is expected to act following the constraints described in the role specification. In this section we show how organizational rules can be translated to event-processing rules for the agents. In the previous section we have shown how the required organizational prior knowledge is captured by the language specification and by some event-processing rules.

We continue with specific organizational rules using the example of the fire brigade. The firefighter organization shows three behavioural rules that a firefighter agent has to follow in that role. The rules are described by the norms in the social contracts and in the interaction contracts. The behavioural rules as described in Sect. 3.3 are:

1. Whenever extinguish-request from coordinator then firefighter is obliged to do accept-request.
2. Whenever status-change then firefighter is obliged to do inform-coordinator-about-status.
3. Whenever extinguish-request from coordinator then firefighter is obliged to do answer-accept/refuse.

The first rule directly follows from the semantic meaning of the hierarchical relation between coordinator and firefighter. Therefore it is not part of the social contract. The other two rules are organization-specific and need to be described explicitly. As discussed in Sect. 4.3 the rules are triggered by events. They hold when certain conditions are true, and they result in expected reaction of the agents. We can translate those rules directly to reasoning rules for event processing using the language elements presented in 4.3.

```
observe( status-change ) <- TRUE
        | AddGoal( send(coordinator, inform, new-status) )
```
(r2)

Table 6. The event-processing rule of a firefighter agent

Rule Id	Origin	Rule
r1	General interaction rule	message(SENDER, request, TASK) :- superior(SENDER) | AddGoal(TASK)
r2	Firefighter organization	observe(status-change) :- TRUE | addGoal(send(coordinator, inform, new-status))
r3	Firefighter organization	message(coordinator, request, extinguish(F)) :- TRUE | addGoal(send-answer(C, request, extinguish(F)))
r4	Personal rule	message(SENDER, request, TASK) :- busy() | IgnoreEvent()

```
message( coordinator, request, extinguish(F) ) <- TRUE
            | AddGoal( send-answer(C, request, extinguish(F)) )        (r3)
```

Organizational rules are part of the social contracts and interaction contracts that the agent agrees upon when its joins an organization. They can directly be transferred to event-processing rules. These reasoning rules capture all behavioural rules that belong to the role which the agent has taken up. We show that adopting those reasoning rules is a way to make the agent aware of the organizational constraints.

The agent adds those reasoning rules to the event-processing phase that we have defined previously. This phase determines the degree of external influence an agent allows into its reasoning. The agent limits the autonomy level of the decision-making phase with the organizational constraints. Next we show that the agent can reason about those rules, and therefore it actively controls how it is being influenced.

THE AGENT

Earlier in this chapter we have described the firefighter organization and the organizational contracts that hold for the agents performing the firefighter role. Now we will give an overview that shows how all parts come together and we show that the autonomy of the agents is guaranteed.

The Event-Processing Rules

An agent adopting the firefighter role adopts three objectives: *extinguish fires*, *inform about status*, and *announce assistance*. This can be read from Table 2. If no further coordination is specified, the agent can pursue those objectives however it wants. In its decision-making process, the agent chooses the actions that lead to the objectives. But the agent has to deal with organizational rules.

In the reasoning model, we have added the event-processing phase that precedes the decision-making phase. We define event-processing rules that specify the effects of events on the agent's mental state, given certain conditions. Personal preferences of the agent can be described, for example that the agent ignores incoming requests when it is busy with other tasks. Also, general interaction rules are specified, for example, a rule that captures the meaning of a hierarchical relation.

If an agents adopts joins an organization, it adopts knowledge about relations between roles. The general interaction rules together with the knowledge about role relations provide coordination. Furthermore, the agent adopts organizational norms by translating them to event processing-rules. Via this mechanism the agent allows the norms to restrict or guide its decision-making process. In Table 6 we have listed the reasoning rules from the example organization and we have added a personal preference rule *r4*.

Modularity

In our reasoning model we have separated the event-processing rules from the actual decision-making process. This modularity has the advantage that it can reason about those rules. The agent knows the origin of the event-processing rules. Because the agent can make this distinction, it has the possibility to prioritize the event-processing rules and therewith it deliberately chooses to follow specific norms.

When organizational rules are embedded in the actual decision-making process, the agent will follow the norms implicitly. It might not be aware anymore of which norms it follows and it might not be aware of which norm belongs to which organization or role.

Another advantage of the modularity is that it becomes easy to add or change the event-processing rules, and thus change organizational norms. This process would be more complicated when the organizational rules are mixed in the decision-making rules.

Guarantee of Autonomy

The agent adds the event-processing rules derived from the organizational contracts to own event-processing rules. We assume that, when an autonomous agent agrees with a contract, it deliberately chooses to do so. We further assume that the rules for event-processing are possible and correct representations of organizational norms, so if the agent follows the event-processing rules it automatically follows the organizational norms.

The modularity in our approach allows for more complex reasoning about the event-processing rules. We claim that this guarantees autonomy of the agent; it knows how to follow the organizational rules, but it still has the possibility reason about them and take the chance to violate organizational norms. In the next section we give examples of meta-reasoning.

DYNAMICS IN AGENT ORGANIZATIONS

All static coordination mechanisms have their advantages and drawbacks. In a dynamic situation it is not possible to choose one coordination type that will always lead to the best performance. The main reason is that unexpected situations can occur that were not known at design time and that may not fare well with the selected coordination mechanism.

We have described a mechanism based on organizational concepts that specifies the coordination rules at an abstract level. At the same time, it preserves the actors' autonomy. However, the specified interaction rules in organizational models are static. When we follow the adoption of organizational rules from the previous sections, there are two ways to achieve dynamics in an organizational model:

- **Top-down:** a new organizational model is defined, and the agents change their contracts with the organization. As a consequence they adopt different reasoning rules for influence control, which will change the coordination.
- **Bottom-up:** the agents change the priority of reasoning rules for influence control by themselves if they notice that the organizational model fails. They adjust their autonomy to repair the organizational failure.

The top-down dynamics can be achieved by carrying out structural changes. Specific roles are required to start reorganizations. Bottom-up dynamics originate in autonomous choices of the agents. Our interest is in the bottom-up dynamics of the organization.

Van der Vecht et al. (2007) showed dynamic coordination by allowing the agents choose their autonomy level. The agents acted following organizational rules, but also decided not to follow the rules in specific situations. Organizations in complex environments can benefit from *adjustable autonomy* of agents. In this section we argue how meta-reasoning about event-processing rules can achieve bottom-up dynamics in the organization.

Furthermore, an organization can benefit from the pro-activeness of agents and from the 'informal' actions and communication. Every organization is created for an objective. Its specification is meant to guarantee certain requirements, for example, about the information flow. The agents are often able to do many things outside of organizational specifications without violating any organizational rule.

Both issues, meta-reasoning and informal processes, are directly related to the autonomy of the agents. We will discuss them in more detail and show the dynamics in organizations using example scenarios.

Meta-Reasoning about Event-Processing Rules

An autonomous agent controls its internal state. Therefore, it should have control over external influences. The modular feature of our approach allows so. The event-processing rules are derived from a contract with an organization. They can be role-specific. At the same time an agent can have event-processing rules from other roles, or from itself.

We can tag the event-processing rules with their origin. For example, rule r1 from Sect. 4.6 captures the meaning of a hierarchical relation, and as such it is part of the agent's knowledge. It is not organization or role-specific. Rules r2 and r3 from Sect. 4.7 are adopted via a contract with the firefighter organization. The agent can distinguish between different rules based on their origin. It knows that if it gives full priority to the organizational rules, it follows the organizational norms. It still has the possibility to prefer its own event-processing rules; however, this may lead to violation of organizational norms.

In (van der Vecht et al., 2007) situations are described where organizations benefit from violation of norms. An agent's local observations can conflict with organizational rules. For example, if a firefighter feels that he is in danger he could ignore a request from the coordinator and give priority to his own goals in order to stay safe. He deliberately gives priority to his own goals, and therewith risks violating the organizational norm.

The ability to distinguish between the reasoning rules can be used for prioritization of the rules. This can be done by applying machine-learning techniques. A learning agent can learn the situations in which specific rules should have priority, such as the *danger*-example.

Another option is to prioritize based on heuristics. Prioritization is studied in argumentation logics (Brewka, 1994). Argumentation as been applied reason about interaction between agents (Kakas et al., 2005). Our rule-based approach of event-processing fits very well with this type of meta-reasoning. We describe an example in the next paragraph.

Violations

The agent can use meta-reasoning via prioritization to handle norm violations. Imagine that the agent has the limitation that he can only extinguish one fire at the same time. It receives a request to extinguish fire *F1* and it adopts the task. While it is busy extinguishing the fire, it receives a request to extinguish fire *F2*. Immediately accepting the second request would lead to a violation of the first, since *F1* has not been extinguished yet. The agent knows that the violation of the first request stems from rule *r1* that gives meaning to the hierarchical relation.

The agent might as well have some personal preference to finish tasks before taking up new ones:

```
message(SENDER, request, TASK) <- busy() | IgnoreEvent()          (r4)
```

However, this rule would lead to a violation of the request to extinguish *F2*. Both rules *r1* and *r4* are applicable.

Several prioritization rules can be thought of to handle those violations. One can judge the requests and choose the violation that is least bad. For example, "fire *F1* is more serious that fire *F2*, and therefore I violate the second request, so I apply rule *r4*". Or one can judge the rules that give rise to the violations. For example, "General interaction rules are more important than personal preferences, therefore I apply rule *r1* and I will violate the request to extinguish *F1*".

Attitudes

Situation-based prioritization is a type of meta-reasoning. Given that an agent can reason about norms, it can use meta-reasoning to take different attitudes with respect to the organization. In the example described above, the agent has to choose between two violations. One of the solutions proposed, gives priority to a specific type of event-processing rule. This represents the attitude of an agent with respect to the organization. In the example, the agent gives priority to the organization.

Sichman & Conte (1998) and Dastani et al. (2003a) describe several possible attitudes. For example, an agent can adopt the organizational goals and drop its private goals, or it can still prefer its own goals above the organizational ones. The agents' attitudes have an effect on the performance of the organization. McCallum et al. (2008) describes organizational change in terms of influences between the roles. The model we presented in this chapter allows the actual implementation of agent types with different attitudes.

Informal Processes

Meta-reasoning about event-processing rules guarantees agent autonomy and allows for norm violation. In the introduction we argued that participant's initiatives are another benefit for the organization that follows directly from agent autonomy.

An organization is always specified for a certain purpose, possibly conflicting with the agents' individual purposes. Furthermore, the organizational rules guarantee required features, such as information flow, in order to optimize its performance. However, the agents are free to do what they want besides the organizational guidelines.

For example, interaction protocols are defined to guarantee a certain distribution of information, but the agents can chat with each other and exchange knowledge without violating the norms. In that case, the information distribution is larger than required by the norms only, which could make the organization more robust.

These informal processes are especially interesting when unexpected events occur that affect the organizational coordination mechanism. A scenario in the firefighter organization can demonstrate the benefits of informal communication between firefighters clearly. In our example, the organizational rules specify the communication between the coordinator and the firefighters. Nothing is said about mutual communication between the firefighters. This implies that it is not forbidden to communicate. Therefore, we consider communication between the firefighters as informal communication. If two firefighters share their knowledge about a fire while extinguishing it, the extinguishing process might go faster. As a consequence, the organization performs better due to the informal communication.

Unexpected events that undermine the coordination can be overcome by informal processes. If, for example, the communication between some of the firefighters and the coordinator falls out, the organizational specification fails. The information flow as defined by the interaction protocols does not lead to the optimal knowledge for the coordinator; he misses the status of some of the firefighters. The informal communication between firefighters can be used by an individual firefighter to restore the information flow. If one firefighter tells another firefighter about its status, and this firefighter communicates it to the coordinator, the information flow in the organization is restored.

CONCLUSION

Agents in an organization need to coordinate their actions in order to reach the organizational goals. Organizational models specify the desired behaviour in terms of roles, relations, norms and interactions. However, the actors in an organization are autonomous entities that control their internal state and their behaviour. In this research we have shown how organizational rules can be adopted by autonomous agents. We have developed a way to translate norms into reasoning rules for event-processing. The reasoning rule contains a trigger, situational constraints and an effect on the agent's mental state that are derived from the norm specification.

We have proposed a modular reasoning model to make organizational rules explicit. Since the agents are autonomous entities they will have their own reasoning rules next to the organizational rules. The modular approach makes that the agents can distinguish between different event-processing rules and that they are aware of the organizational rules. This allows for meta-reasoning about event processing, and gives the agent control over its internal state. It guarantees the autonomy of the agent and at the same time makes group coordination possible.

FUTURE RESEARCH DIRECTIONS

An important aspect of our method is the translation from the norms to reasoning rules of the agent. We have used a simple example of a firefighter organization to illustrate our ideas. More complex organizations might introduce complex behavioural rules and we have to evaluate whether we can express them in our language for event-processing rules. Furthermore, we argued that the possible effects on an agent's mental state are dependent on its decision-making process. This has implications for the translation as well.

We have presented some advantages of using modularity in the reasoning model. In our approach, the agent can do meta-reasoning reason about the event-processing rules, and thus about norms. We have used *prioritization* of event-processing rules as example of meta-reasoning. As future work we want to investigate different methods of meta-reasoning, such as argumentation-based techniques.

ACKNOWLEDGMENT

The research reported here is part of the Interactive Collaborative Information Systems (ICIS) project, supported by the Dutch Ministry of Economic Affairs, grant nr: BSIK03024.

REFERENCES

Brewka, G. (1994). Reasoning about priorities in default logic. In *Proceedings of the twelfth national conference on Artificial intelligence, 2*, 940– 945. Menlo Park, CA, USA: American Association for Artificial Intelligence.

Dastani, M., Dignum, V., & Dignum, F. (2003a). Role assignment in open agent societies. In *Proceedings of the International Conference on Autonomous Agents and Multi-Agent Systems 2003* (pp. 489 – 496). ACM Press.

Dastani, M., van Riemsdijk, B., Dignum, F., & Meyer, J.-J. C. (2003b). A programming language for cognitive agents: Goal directed 3apl. In *Programming Multi-Agent Systems 2003 (PROMAS 2003)* (pp. 111–130).

Dignum, F., Kinny, D., & Sonenberg, L. (2002). From desires, obligations and norms to goals. *Cognitive Science Quarterly, 2*(3-4), 407–430.

Dignum, V. (2004). *A Model for Organizational Interaction: based on Agents, founded in Logic.* Utrecht University.

Dignum, V., Dignum, F., & Meyer, J.-J. Ch. (2004). An agent-mediated approach to the support of knowledge sharing in organizations. *Knowledge Engineering Review, 19*(2), 147–174.

Dignum, V., Meyer, J.-J. Ch., Dignum, F., & Weigand, H. (2003). Formal specification of interaction in agent societies. In Hinchey, M., Rash, J., Truszkowski, W., Rouff, C., & Gordon-Spears, D., (Eds.), *Formal Approaches to Agent-Based Systems (FAABS'02), volume 2699 of LNAI* (pp. 37–52). Springer.

Esteva, M., Padget, J., & Sierra, C. (2001). Formalizing a language for institutions and norms. In J.-J. Ch. Meyer, & M. Tambe, (Eds.), *Intelligent Agents VIII, volume 2333 of LNAI* (pp. 348–366). Springer.

Ferber, J., & Gutknecht, O. (1998). A meta-model for the analysis and design of organizations in multi-agent systems. In *ICMAS '98: Proceedings of the 3rd International Conference on Multi Agent Systems*, (pp. 128), Washington, DC, USA. IEEE Computer Society.

García-Camino, A., Rodríguez-Aguilar, J. A., & Vasconcelos, W. W. (2007). A distributed architecture for norm management in multi-agent systems. In *Coordination, Organization, Institutions and Norms in Agent Systems III, volume 4870 of Lecture Notes in Computer Science* (pp. 275–286). Springer.

Hübner, J. F., Sichman, J. S., & Boissier, O. (2002). A model for the structural, functional, and deontic specification of organizations in multi-agent systems. In *Advances in Artificial Intelligence, volume 2507 of LNCS* (pp. 439–448). Springer.

Jennings, N. R. (2000). On agent-based software engineering. *Artificial Intelligence, 117*(2), 277–296.

Kakas, A., Maudet, N., & Moraitis, P. (2005). Modular representation of agent interaction rules through argumentation. *Autonomous Agents and Multi-Agent Systems, 11*(2), 189–206.

Matson, E., & DeLoach, S. (2005). Formal transition in agent organizations. In *IEEE International Conference on Knowledge Intensive Multiagent Systems (KIMAS '05)* (pp. 235–240).

McCallum, M., Vasconcelos, W. W., & Norman, T. J. (2008). Organisational change through influence. *Journal of Autonomous Agents and Multi-Agent Systems*.

Rao, A. S. (1996). Agentspeak(l): Bdi agents speak out in a logical computable language. In W. V. de Velde, & J. Perram, (Eds.), *Proceedings of the Seventh Workshop on Modelling Autonomous Agents in a Multi-Agent World, volume 1038 of LNAI* (pp. 42–55). Springer.

Sichman, J., & Conte, R. (1998). On personal and role mental attitude: A preliminary dependency-based analysis. In *Advances in Artificial Intelligence, LNAI 1515* (pp. 1–10). Springer.

Van der Vecht, B., Dignum, F., Meyer, J. J. C., & Neef, M. (2007). A dynamic coordination mechanism using adjustable autonomy. In *Coordination, Organization, Institutions and Norms in Agent Systems III, volume 4870 of Lecture Notes in Computer Science* (pp. 83–96). Springer.

KEY TERMS

Adjustable Autonomy: *Adjustable autonomy* means that an agent varies the degree of autonomy of its decision-making process. The degree of autonomy depends on how much the decision-making process is influenced by others. Agents can show adjustable autonomy by dynamically dealing with external influences.

Agent: An agent is autonomous entity that actively pursues its goals and is able to interact with others.

Autonomy: *Autonomy* in the context of agents means that the agent has control over its internal state and over its behaviour. The first implies that the agent controls how external events influence its internal state. The second implies that the agent has a local decision-making process to decide on actions.

Meta-Reasoning: Meta-reasoning is reasoning about the reasoning process itself. In this chapter, prioritization of reasoning rules is used as an example of meta-reasoning.

Organizational Model: An organizational model describes the objectives and the structure of an organization in terms of roles, norms, relations between roles and interactions between roles. The description does not include descriptions of participants that with fulfil the roles.

Organizational Rules: Organizational rules specify the desired behaviour of the actors in the organization. They are part of the organizational model.

Reasoning Rules: Reasoning rules specify steps in the decision-making process of the agent. There can be several types of reasoning rules with different purposes, for example, goal planning, event processing, or plan revision.

Section IV
Norms and Institutions

Chapter XIV
Specifying Artificial Institutions in the Event Calculus

Nicoletta Fornara
Università della Svizzera italiana, Switzerland

Marco Colombetti
Università della Svizzera italiana, Switzerland
Politecnico di Milano, Italy

ABSTRACT

The specification of open interaction systems is widely recognized to be a crucial issue, which involves the problem of finding a standard way of specifying: a communication language for the interacting agents, the entities that constitute the context of the interaction, and rules that regulate interactions. An approach to solve these problems consists in modelling open interaction systems as a set of artificial institutions. In this chapter we address this issue by formally defining, in the Event Calculus, a repertoire of abstract concepts (like commitment, institutional power, role, and norm) that can be used to specify every artificial institution. We then show how, starting from the formal definition of these concepts and of application-dependent concepts, it is possible to obtain a formal specification of a system. By using a suitable tool, it is then possible to simulate and monitor the system's evolution through automatic deduction.

INTRODUCTION

The specification of *open interaction systems*, which can be *dynamically* entered and left by *heterogeneous*, *autonomous*, and *self-interested* agents, is widely recognized to be a crucial issue in the development of distributed applications on the Internet. The interacting agents may be heterogeneous because they may be developed by different designers; as a consequence, no assumptions can be made on their internal architecture and it is impossible to access their internal states. Agents may be self-interested because they act on behalf of different human counterparts that, in general, do not share a common goal. Finally, agents are autonomous because they are not centrally controlled, but act on the basis of private strategies.

The specification of such systems involves two main problems: the first is the definition of a standard way of specifying a communication language for the interacting agents and of the context of the interaction; the second, which derives from the assumption of the agents autonomy, is finding a way to regulate interactions so that agents may have reliable expectations on the future development of the system. A possible approach to solve those problems consists in modelling the interaction systems as a set of *artificial institutions*. By this term we mean the digital counterpart or extension of a human institution, like for example the institution of language, the institution of property, or the institution of auctions.

In our view the definition of a specific artificial institution (Fornara et al., 2008) consists of: (i) a component, called meta-model, which includes the definition of basic entities common to the specification of every institution, like the concepts of commitment, institutional power, role, and norm, and the actions necessary for exchanging messages; (ii) a component specific to the institution in question, which includes the specification of the powers and norms that apply to the agents playing roles in the institution, and the definition of the concepts pertaining to the domain of the interaction (for example the actions of paying or delivering a product, bidding in an auction, etc.). The aim of this chapter is to give a formal definition of the domain-independent component and to illustrate the domain-dependent component through a meaningful example.

In the literature on multi-agent systems, various concepts that have some similarities or analogies with our idea of an artificial institution have been proposed. In the Nineteen-eighties, Carl Hewitt introduced the concept of open systems (Hewitt, 1986); in (Artikis et al., 2002) Artikis and colleagues give a detailed definition of the term open societies and use the term institution as a synonym, without distinguishing, as we do, an open system from an artificial institution; Noriega, Sierra and colleagues use the term electronic institution (Noriega, 1997, Esteva et al., 2001) to indicate *"the rules of the game-a set of conventions that articulate agents' interactions"*. According to Arcos and colleagues (2005) *"The essential roles (electronic institutions) play are both descriptive and prescriptive: the institution makes the conventions explicit to participants, and it warrants their compliance."* (p. 193); therefore electronic institutions are very similar to our artificial institutions, even if usually they do not allow for the violation of rules and thus do not address the management of sanctions. In (Vázquez-Salceda et al., 2005) Vázquez-Salceda and colleagues concentrate their attention on the organizational perspective of an open system. There are moreover works that are mainly focused on the normative component of a system, usually called Normative Framework (López y López et al., 2005) or Normative System (Boella et al., 2007). In this chapter we formalize OCeAN (Ontology, CommitmEnts, Authorizations, Norms) (Fornara et al., 2007, Fornara et al., 2008), a meta-model for the specification of artificial institutions, using a variant of the Event Calculus, the Discrete Event Calculus (DEC) introduced by Mueller (Mueller, 2006). Based on many-sorted first order logic, DEC is suited for reasoning about action and change: by means of axioms it is possible to describe how certain properties of a domain change according to the occurrence of events or actions at different time points. The DEC formalization of *OCeAN* consists of a set of events, fluents, and axioms that describe the entities, and their evolution in time, that can be used in the specification of a wide range of artificial institutions. The specification of an interaction system is therefore given by the conjunction of those axioms with some domain-dependent definition of fluents, events, and axioms, plus the definition of the initial state of the system.

A fundamental advantage of using the Event Calculus for the specification of systems is that, exploiting suitable tools, it is possible to perform different types of reasoning, and in particular: *prediction*, where given an initial situation and a sequence of events the resulting situation is deduced; *planning*, where the sequence of actions that bring from an initial situation to a goal situation is discovered; and *postdiction*, where given a final state and a sequence of events one seeks an initial state. In this work we will mainly concentrate on *deduction*, that is: given a description of a system based on the fundamental concepts of our meta-model, an *initial situation*, and an *event narrative* (i.e., a sequence of events that happens in the system), we are interested in tracking the evolution of the state of the system for simulation and monitoring purposes. To this aim to test our example we use the Discrete Event Calculus Reasoner 1.0[1] (Mueller, 2006, Chapter 13), a tool that relies on various satisfiability solvers and provers to perform reasoning.

The main contribution of this chapter with respect to our previous works (Fornara & Colombetti, 2004) (Fornara et al., 2007), (Fornara et al., 2008), (Fornara & Colombetti, 2007) is the formal definition of the *OCeAN* meta-model using the Discrete Event Calculus. The adoption a formal language for the specification of our meta-model lead us to revise and spell out in details certain concepts. In particular we have studied how to define powers at design time in terms of the roles played by the agents, and to dynamically let agents assign and remove powers during run-time. We have also refined our notion of role considering the possibility to define roles related to different institutional entities and the need to assign and dismiss roles during the dynamic evolution of the system. Finally we have revised mechanisms for the enforcement of norms through a detailed management of sanctions.

This chapter is organized as follows. In the next section we compare our approach with other existing proposals. In the following section we present our meta-model of artificial institutions. Then we give an example of the formalization of a system and describe the simulation of its temporal evolution. Finally we draw some conclusions and discuss some possible directions for future research.

BACKGROUND

In the literature there are some contributions using the Event Calculus for the formalization of various concepts that are relevant for agent interactions in open systems. Yolum and Singh (2004) concentrate their attention on the formal specification of social commitment for the flexible specification of protocols (see also Chapter XI "Modeling Interactions via Commitments and Expectations" by Torroni et al.). They reason about a given specification using Shanahan's abductive Event Calculus planner (Shanahan, 2000). Their notion of commitment is quite similar to ours, even if their specification of the content (or condition) of commitments is context-dependent, and they do not have a notion of temporal proposition to express the interval of time when an action has to be (or not to be) performed.

Artikis et al. in (Artikis et al., 2002) study the specification and animation of *open computational systems* using the Event Calculus. The software platform presented for automated animation of the global state of the system is very interesting. Their fundamental concepts (like power, normative position, and role) are close to the ones introduced in our work; the main difference is that in their work these concepts and the corresponding axioms are limited to the example proposed (the formalization of the Contract Net Protocol (Smith, 1980)), whereas in our work we present a set of concepts, and the axioms that characterize them, with the aim of defining an application-independent meta-model for the definition of open interaction systems.

In (Farrell et al., 2005) Farrell and colleagues use an XML version of the Event Calculus called *ecXML* to specify *contracts*, for example a mail service agreement between a Service Provider and a Service Customer. This work highlights the importance of simulating and monitoring the evolution of contracts by means of a Java implementation of a reasoner. However, our use of the Discrete Event Calculus has the advantage of allowing for a richer variety of types of reasoning (e.g., planning), thanks to the existence of tools like the Discrete Event Calculus Reasoner 1.0. Moreover, like in the previous case our model is more general, and would treat contracts as a special type of artificial institutions.

Another interesting declarative approach to the definition of an Agent Communication Language, called *SC-IFF* (see Chapter XI "Modeling Interactions via Commitments and Expectations by Torroni et al. for more information), is based on the Social Integrity Constraints language. It is based on the notion of *expectation* (considered similar to a commitment) and on the idea of defining the semantics of communicative acts by specifying the future desirable communicative acts that have to be performed, within a certain instant of time, after the performance of a given communicative act; this without an explicit representation of the context of the interaction that in our model is obtained with the definition of various types of fluents, making the content of the acts simpler. The verification of one specification is possible thanks to a proof-procedure based on Abductive Logic Programming.

In the literature there are significant contributions on the specification of open multiagent systems adopting the institutional or organizational paradigm. The main difference between our approach and other proposals (Artikis et al., 2002), (Vázquez-Salceda et al., 2005), (Arcos et al., 2005), (López y López et al., 2005), (García-Camino et al., 2005), (Cliffe et al., 2006), (Cardoso & Oliveira, 2007) (see also the Chapter II "Modelling Dimensions for Agent Organizations" by Coutinho et al. and Chapter XV "Verifying Organizations Regulated by Institutions" by Viganò and Colombetti) is its completeness: we define a set of concepts and an Agent Communication Language (ACL) (inclusive of declarations) that if adopted as a standard would make it possible for an agent to interact with different systems without being redesigned. The semantics of communicative acts and of norms are both based on a notion of *social commitment* that is objective and external - two fundamental characteristics in systems where the internal architecture of the interacting agents is unknown and no assumption can be made on their collaborative or competitive behavior. The systematic use of commitment has also the advantage of reducing the number of different constructs on which agents have to reason when planning their actions.

Among the previously mentioned articles the one which is closely related to our work is (Vázquez-Salceda et al., 2005) where the *OMNI* framework for modelling agent organizations is presented. Given that they adopt an organizational perspective their model allows to specify the global goals of the system independently from the participating agents, similarly to our proposal they tackle the problem of specifying norms, whereas a crucial distinction that is not highlighted is the one between the power and the permission to perform an action, a crucial distinction when the semantics of declarations is defined.

THE OCEAN META-MODEL

In our previous works (Fornara & Colombetti, 2004), (Fornara et al., 2007), (Fornara et al., 2008), (Fornara & Colombetti, 2007) we have presented and thoroughly discussed the *OCeAN* meta-model of artificial institutions that can be used to specify at a high level open interaction systems, where heterogeneous and autonomous agents may interact. In our view the fundamental components that characterize artificial institutions are: a *core ontology* for the definition of a set of concepts, actions/events, and *institutional actions*, used in the interaction; the *counts-as* relation and the notion of *power*, that are necessary for the concrete performance of institutional actions; and the *norm* construct, used to impose obligations and prohibitions to perform certain actions on agents interacting with the system, that are crucial for the specification of flexible interaction protocols, like for example the ones used in electronic auctions (Viganò et al., 2006). In particular powers and norms are expressed at design time in terms of the roles played by the agents. Such concepts, and in particular the fundamental notion of *commitment*, are used to specify an Agent Communication Language (ACL). Moreover to represent the *content* and the *condition* of commitments and norms, and their relation with time, we will introduce the notions of a *temporal proposition* and of an *evaluated temporal proposition*. Summarizing, in this chapter we introduce: the sorts *agent, action, and institutional action (iaction)*, which are fundamental for our meta-model; the following fluents for describing basic concepts:

- Temporal Proposition (TP) and Evaluated Temporal Proposition (ETP);
- Commitment and Precommitment;
- Power and Context;
- RoleOf and HasRole;
- Norm;

and the events/actions that impact on such fluents, described by means of axioms. We will also introduce an action for exchanging messages and define a set of axioms that specify an Agent Communication Language (ACL).

Specification of an Interaction System

In our view an open dynamic interaction system is a system that agents may use to interact with each other by means of a set of communicative acts. Those interactions may be in particular regulated by a set of norms that prescribe a flexible interaction protocol. The specification of an open dynamic interaction system (as showed also in the example) consists of: (i) the set of fluents, events/actions and axioms that compose the *OCeAN* meta-model that will be presented in this section; (ii) those fluents, events/actions and axioms necessary for the specification of a category of artificial institutions (e.g., for the specification of the institution of auctions we have to introduce a fluent for representing auctions and axioms to create suitable powers and norms); (iii) those fluents, events/actions and axioms specific to a certain subtype of the category of institutions of interest (e.g., the English or the Dutch Auctions (Fornara et al., 2007, Viganò et al., 2006); (iv) when it is the case, the definition of artificial multi-institutions (Cliffe et al., 2007) that *use* other artificial institutions (the analysis of the definition of an institution using other institutions in important, but is beyond the scope of this chapter); (v) finally those fluents, events/actions and axioms specific to a concrete system (like those necessary to represent the products on sale and to specify the initial state of the system). To simulate the evolution of the system it is also necessary to define the history of the events that happen in the system at every instant of time.

The Formalism

The Event Calculus

The formalism that we use to define the main concepts of an artificial institution is a version of the Event Calculus: the Discrete Event Calculus (DEC). The Event Calculus (Kowalski & Sergot, 1986, Miller & Shanahan, 2002, Mueller, 2006, Shanahan, 1997, Shanahan, 1999) is a formalism for reasoning about action and change that has been introduced by Kowalski and Sergot in 1986 and since then has evolved considerably (Mueller, 2007). In this work we use a version of the Event Calculus, the Discrete Event Calculus (DEC), introduced by Mueller (Mueller, 2006) to improve the efficiency of automated reasoning by limiting time to the integers. DEC is adopted in the Discrete Event Calculus Reasoner 1.0, a tool that we used to test the axioms of our model of artificial institutions and to run a simulation of the specification of a system, as discussed in the example.

Conventions

The Event Calculus is based on many-sorted first order logic (Mueller, 2006). To make formulas more readable, we adopted a number of notational conventions.

Throughout the chapter predicate symbols, function symbols and nonnumeric constants start with an uppercase letter, and variables start with lowercase letters. Variables that are not explicitly quantified are assumed to be universally quantified. The notation $\psi \equiv_{def} \varphi$ defines ψ as an abbreviation of φ. We adopt the unique name axioms (Mueller, 2006, p. 31), whose meaning is that different constants refer to different objects. If a sort is a subsort of another sort we separate the child sort from the parent sort with a colon; for example, *agent:object* means that *agent* is subsort of the sort *object*. In general, the sort of a variable is determined by removing the final digits from the variable; for example, the variable *agent1* has sort *agent*. When an axiom contains only one variable of a given sort, the name of the variable coincides with the name of the sort (i.e., the variable *agent* has sort *agent*). Sometimes, to have a more perspicuous variable name we do not follow this convention; in such cases the sort of the variable is specified in the text before the axiom using colon as separator, for example *debtor:agent*.

The sort of function symbols, including fluents, and of their arguments is specified through prototypes: the prototype $s_0 f(s_1,...,s_n)$, where $s_0, s_1,..., s_n$ are sorts, means that function symbol f is to be applied to n terms of sorts $s_1,..., s_n$, and that the resulting term is of sort s_0.

The Discrete Event Calculus

The predicates of the Event Calculus are used "for saying what happens when, for describing the initial situation, for describing the effects of actions, and for saying what fluents hold at what times" (Shanahan, 1999). The Event Calculus introduces the basic sorts *event*, *fluent*, and *timepoint* with variables e, f, and t. The predicates of the Event Calculus that will be used in this chapter are:

- *Happens(e, t)*: event e happens at timepoint t. In the Event Calculus the performance of an action is regarded as an event. We assume that two events of the same type never happen at the same time instant; therefore an event type plus an instant of time univocally identify an event token.

- *HoldsAt(f, t)*: the fact described by fluent *f* holds at timepoint *t*.
- *Initiates(e, f, t)*: event *e* initiates fluent *f* at *t*. Its intuitive meaning is that if event/action *e* occurs at *t* then *f* will holds after *t*. Note that at a different time instant the occurrence of the same event may not start the fluent *f*.
- *Terminates(e, f, t)*: event *e* terminates fluent *f* at timepoint *t*. If *e* occurs at time *t* then *f* will no longer hold after *t*.

The *ReleasedAt(f, t)* predicate, used in the following DEC axioms, means that fluent *f* is released from the commonsense law of inertia at time point *t*. The axioms of the Discrete Event Calculus (DEC) that are crucial for the comprehension of this chapter are as follows (for a complete list see (Mueller, 2006, p. 27)).

DEC5

$$(HoldsAt(f,t) \land \neg ReleasedAt(f, t+1) \land \neg \exists e \, (Happens(e,t) \land Terminates(e,f,t))) \rightarrow HoldsAt(f,t+1)$$

DEC6

$$(\neg HoldsAt(f,t) \land \neg ReleasedAt(f, t+1) \land \neg \exists e \, (Happens(e,t) \land Terminates(e,f,t))) \rightarrow \neg HoldsAt(f,t+1)$$

DEC9

$$(Happens(e,t) \land Initiates(e,f,t)) \rightarrow HoldsAt(f,t+1)$$

DEC10

$$(Happens(e,t) \land Terminates(e,f,t)) \rightarrow \neg HoldsAt(f,t+1)$$

Fundamental Sorts

To the basic sorts of the Event Calculus we add the following sorts: *agent*, to represent the agents that interact with the system; *action:event*, a subsort of *event*, to represent those events that are brought about by agents, for example we may need to introduce the action for delivering a product:

action Deliver(agent,agent,product);

iaction:event, a subsort of *event*, to represent *institutional actions*, that is, actions that change institutional attributes, which exist only thanks to common agreement. Note that agents cannot perform institutional actions by exploiting causal links occurring in the natural world, as would be done to open a door; rather, as we shall see later institutional actions have to be performed by means of suitable *declarations*. We also introduce the fluent

fluent Done(agent; action),

to represent that an action has been performed by an *agent*. In the chapter we will sometime use the variable *actor:agent* to represent the agent that performs the action. For every type of action it is then necessary to introduce an axiom to initiate the relevant *Done* fluent when such an action takes place, for example:

Dn

Initiates(Deliver(actor,agent,product), Done(actor,Deliver(actor,agent,product)),t)

Temporal Propositions

Temporal propositions are propositions that become true or false over a predefined time interval, according to rules that will be specified below. The fluents used to represent temporal propositions exploit the following sorts (the axioms reported in brackets specify that the variables belonging to the corresponding sorts may assume a limited set of values):

sort mode $[\forall x{:}mode\ (x = Forall \vee\ x = Exist)]$
sort ptime:integer $[\forall x{:}ptime\ (x \geq 1)]$

We then introduce the sort *tp:fluent* of temporal propositions as a subsort of the sort *fluent*, and define the following function symbol used to represent temporal propositions:

tp TP(fluent,ptime,ptime,mode)

In the axioms we shall use variable *prop:fluent* (abbreviation of *proposition*) having sort *fluent* as the first argument of temporal propositions, and variables $t_{start}{:}ptime$ and $t_{end}{:}ptime$ of sort *ptime* to define a specific time interval. The fourth argument, of sort *mode*, is used to distinguish the case where it is required that the TP fluent holds at every instant between t_{start} and t_{end} (*Forall*) from the case where it is required that the TP fluent holds at least at one instant between t_{start} and t_{end} (*Exist*). For example, a temporal proposition with mode *Forall* can be used to state that the price of a certain product is x euro for the current month, and a temporal proposition with mode *Exist* can be used to state that an agent will pay a certain amount of money to another agent in the current week.

Every time an agent uses a temporal proposition (for example in the exchange of a message) it has to initiate its fluent by means of the *AttCreateTP(fluent,ptime,ptime,mode)* (attempt to create a temporal proposition) action in order to be able to trace the evolution of the state of temporal propositions and therefore monitoring commitments fulfillment or violation. The *AttCreateTP()* action, if certain conditions are satisfied, initiates a new temporal proposition:

TP1 $(t_{start} \leq t_{end}) \wedge \neg HoldsAt(TP(prop, t_{start}, t_{end}, mode),t) \rightarrow$
$\qquad Initiates(AttCreateTP(prop, t_{start}, t_{end}, mode), TP(prop, t_{start}, t_{end}, mode),t)$

Evaluated Temporal Propositions

Intuitively, at any given instant a temporal proposition may be *True*, *False* or undefined (*Undef*) as depicted in Figure 1. For example, the temporal proposition it will rain today may be undefined at 4 pm; it may become true, say, at 6 pm, if it starts raining; or it may become false at midnight, if it has not rained for the whole day.

We introduce a new fluent, ETP, to represent an evaluated temporal proposition, that is, a temporal proposition with an attached truth value:

Figure 1. The life-cycle of evaluated temporal proposition

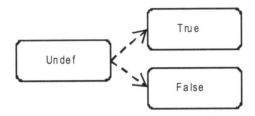

sort value [$\forall x{:}value\ (x{=}Undef \lor x{=}True \lor x{=}False)$]
fluent ETP(tp, value)

As depicted in Figure 1 a temporal proposition with mode *Exist* usually (different cases are treated in the following) is initialized to *Undef*, it becomes *True* if an event that initializes its *prop* happens between t_{start}-1 and t_{end}-1 (extremes included) (it means that *prop* starts to hold between t_{start} and t_{end}), otherwise at t_{end} it becomes *False*. Differently a temporal proposition with mode *Forall* usually is initialized to *Undef*, it becomes *False* if at t_{start} its *prop* does not hold or if an event that terminates its *prop* happens between t_{start} and t_{end}-1 (extremes included) otherwise at t_{end} it becomes *True*.

The action *AttCreateTP()* that initiates a temporal proposition also initiates an evaluated temporal proposition ETP with the correct truth-value. If a new temporal proposition is created at a time *t* that precedes t_{start}-1, indifferently from its *mode*, an *Undef* ETP has to be created:

ETP0 $t{<}(t_{start}{-}1) \land (t_{start} \leq t_{end}) \land \neg HoldsAt(TP(prop,t_{start},t_{end},mode),\ t) \rightarrow$
$\qquad Initiates(AttCreateTP(prop,t_{start},t_{end},mode),\ ETP(TP(prop,t_{start},t_{end},mode),Undef),t)$

The axioms to treat cases where the temporal proposition is created at a time that follows t_{end} and where it is created at a time that is inside the interval of time defined by t_{start}-1 and t_{end} can be found in (Fornara & Colombetti, 2008).

The following axioms are used to change the truth-value of an existing *Undef* evaluated temporal proposition with *mode Exist* on the basis of the temporal evolution of its *prop*. The axioms for the temporal evolution of evaluated temporal propositions with *mode Forall* can be written in a similar way. If an event *e* that initiates the *prop* happens within the interval of time defined by t_{start}-1 and t_{end}-1 (inclusive), the same event *e* also initiates an evaluated temporal proposition whose *value* is *True*:

ETPE1 *HoldsAt(ETP(TP(prop,t_{start},t_{end},Exist),Undef),t) $\land$ Initiates(e,prop,t) $\land$ (t_{start}-1$\leq$ t $<$$t_{end}$) $\rightarrow$*
$\qquad$ *Initiates(e, ETP(TP(prop,t_{start},t_{end},Exist),True),t)*

If t_{end} is reached without the temporal proposition becoming *True*, passing time t_{end} initiates the evaluated temporal proposition with *value* equal to *False*. To represent the event that a certain instant of time is elapsed, we introduce a new event *Elapse(time)* that we assume to happen every time a certain instant of time is reached as described by the following axiom:

A1 *Happens(Elapse(t),t)*

ETPE2 $HoldsAt(ETP(TP(prop,t_{start},t_{end},Exist),Undef),t) \rightarrow$
    $Initiates(Elapse(t_{end}), ETP(TP(prop,t_{start},t_{end}, Exist),False),t)$

Axioms of the form of ETPE1, where the *Initiates()* predicate is in the antecedent of an axiom, are useful to resolve the *ramification problem*, that is the situations where one event has some indirect effects, for example in this case event *e* has the effect to initiate *prop* and also the effect to transform the related *ETP* from *Undef* to *True*. As discussed in (Mueller, 2006, p. 110) unfortunately it is impossible to compute circumscription of this type of axioms. Therefore in the actual specification of a system, if we have a finite set of axioms that state that $E_1,...,E_n$ initiate *Prop1*, we will have to transform ETPE1 in *n* different axioms obtained by removing *Initiates()* from the antecedent and using E_1, or E_2, or E_n in the *Initiates()* of the consequent. This operation has to be done for every axioms that has $Initiates(e,p,t)$ in the antecedent.

Every time that a *True* or *False* evaluated temporal proposition is initiated by the event *e*, the corresponding *Undef* proposition is terminated by the same event, indifferently from its mode:

ETP1 $Initiates(e,ETP(tp,True),t) \rightarrow Terminates(e,ETP(tp,Undef),t)$

ETP2 $Initiates(e,ETP(tp,False),t) \rightarrow Terminates(e,ETP(tp,Undef),t)$

Finally, we introduce with the following axiom the identically *True* evaluated temporal proposition, that initially holds and is never terminated. Its proposition is represented by introducing the constant *PTrue* that has sort *fluent*.

$HoldsAt(ETP(TP(PTrue,1,1,Exist),True),0)$

Commitment and Precommitment

Commitment, precommitment, and conditional commitment will be used later to express the semantics of a library of communicative acts, to express active norms and to monitor the fulfillment or violation of obligations and prohibitions of the various agents at run-time.

Commitment

The fluent used to represent commitments, whose life-cycle is depicted in Figure 2, is as follows:

fluent Comm(state, agent, agent, tp, tp, source, id).

In the axioms we shall use the more perspicuous variables name *debtor:agent* and *creditor:agent* as the second and third argument, and *content:tp* and *condition:tp* as the fourth and fifth argument. The sort used to represent the *state* of a commitment is:

sort state [∀x:state (x = Active ∨ x = Cond ∨ x = Pending ∨ x = Cancelled ∨ x = Fulfilled ∨ x = V iolated)].

Figure 2. The life-cycle of precommitment and commitment

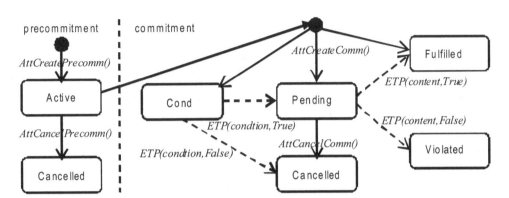

The sort used to represent the *source* of a commitment used to distinguish a commitment created by a communicative act from a commitment created by the activation or violation of a norm is:

sort source [∀*x:source* (*x = CA* ∨ *x = Norm* ∨ *x = Sanction*)].

Finally the sort used to represent the *id* of the norm that created the commitment or the time instant when the communicative act that generated the commitment has been performed:

sort id:integer [∀*x:id* (*x* ≥ 1)]

Differently from other approaches (Yolum & Singh, 2004), we introduce one fluent to represent both conditional and unconditional commitment, so that we do not need to define different axioms and different communicative acts to create two types of commitment and to update their states. Another advantage is that information about the condition can be kept during the life-cycle of the commitment: in fact, all information about the condition is lost if the conditional commitment is transformed into an unconditional commitment (like in (Yolum & Singh, 2004)) when the condition starts to hold.

Before creating a commitment a certain set of conditions have to be verified (for example the time interval of the *condition* must precede the time interval of the *content*) and on the basis of the truth-value of the temporal propositions used as *content* and as *condition* a different commitment has to be created. Therefore, to improve the modularity of the system we introduce the institutional action *AttCreateComm(agent,agent,tp,tp,source,id)* (attempt to create a commitment), whose effect, when successful, is to create a commitment as stated in the axioms reported below.

As regard as the *content* and the *condition* of a commitment, it is possible to have different situations when a new commitment is created: the truthvalue of the *condition* and of the *content* are *Undef*, or the truth-value of the *condition* is *True* (or initiated to *True* contemporary to the commitment creation) and the truth-value of the *content* is *Undef* or *True* (or initiated to *True* contemporary to the commitment creation). Here we will report only the axiom to treat the first situation, for a complete list of axioms to treat the other situations see (Fornara & Colombetti, 2008). Abbreviations:

d=debtor, c=creditor, s=source,

content $\equiv_{def}$ TP(prop1,t1$_{start}$,t1$_{end}$,model)

condition $\equiv_{def}$ TP(prop2,t2$_{start}$,t2$_{end}$,mode2)

C01 *t2$_{end}$ < t1$_{start}$ $\land$ ¬HoldsAt(Comm(state, d, c, content, condition, s, id), t) $\land$*
    HoldsAt(ETP(content,Undef), t) $\land$ HoldsAt(ETP(condition,Undef), t) $\land$ ¬∃e (Happens(e, t)
    $\land$ Initiates(e, ETP(condition, True), t)) $\rightarrow$ Initiates(AttCreateComm(d, c, content, condition, s,
    id), Comm(Cond, d, c, content, condition, s, id), t)

In the life-cycle of a commitment (Figure 2), dotted lines represent state changes due to events happening in the system that modify the truth-value of the *content* or of the *condition* of the commitment, as described in the following axioms. A *Cond* commitment becomes *Pending* when the evaluated temporal proposition of its *condition* with *value True* starts to hold; if the evaluated temporal proposition of the *condition* with *value False* starts to hold, the *Cond* commitment becomes *Cancelled*:

C1 *HoldsAt(Comm(Cond, d, c, content, condition, s, id), t) $\land$ Initiates(e, ETP(condition, True), t) $\rightarrow$*
    Initiates(e,Comm(Pending, d, c, content, condition, s, id), t)

C2 *HoldsAt(Comm(Cond, d, c, content, condition, s, id), t) $\land$ Initiates(e, ETP(condition, False), t) $\rightarrow$*
    Initiates(e,Comm(Cancelled, d, c, content, condition, s, id), t)

A *Pending* commitment becomes *Fulfilled* when the evaluated temporal proposition of its *content* with truth-value *True* starts to hold:

C3 *HoldsAt(Comm(Pending, d, c, content, condition, s, id), t) $\land$ Initiates(e, ETP(content, True), t) $\rightarrow$*
    Initiates(e,Comm(Fulfilled, d, c, content, condition, s, id), t)

A *Pending* commitment becomes *Violated* when the evaluated temporal proposition of its *content* with truth-value *False* starts to hold:

C4 *HoldsAt(Comm(Pending, d, c, content, condition, s, id), t) $\land$ Initiates(e, ETP(content, False), t) $\rightarrow$*
    Initiates(e,Comm(Violated, d, c, content, condition, s, id), t)

To terminate a commitment whose state has been replaced by another one, we introduce a predicate *Replace(state1,state2)*, that is true if *state1* can be reached from *state2*. In particular the following predicates are true:

Replace(Pending,Cond)   *Replace(Cancelled,Cond)*

Replace(Cancelled, Pending)   *Replace(Fulfilled, Pending)*

Replace(Violated, Pending)

We then define:

C5 *Initiates(e, Comm(state1,d,c,content,condition,s,id), t) ∧ HoldsAt(Comm(state2,d,c,content,condition, s,id), t) ∧ Replace(state1,state2) →Terminates(e,Comm(state2, d, c, content, condition, s, id), t)*

Another institutional action that manipulates commitments is *AttCancelComm(agent,agent,tp,tp)* (attempt to cancel a commitment), that transforms a *Cond* or *Pending* commitment into a *Cancelled* one and its effect is defined by the following axiom:

C6 ∃ *state (state=Cond ∨ state=Pending) ∧ HoldsAt(Comm(state, d,c,content,condition,s,id), t)* → *Initiates(AttCancelComm(d,c,content,condition), Comm(Cancelled, d, c, content, condition, s, id), t)*

Precommitment

The commitment defined so far can be used to express the meaning of various speech acts like *assertions* and *promises*. However, it is not possible to express the meaning of directive speech acts, like *requests*. When an agent requests another agent to do something, it is trying to induce the other agent to make a commitment, and the other agent can commit itself by just *accepting* the request. We represent this situation by means of *precommitment*, a type of commitment that may also play a crucial role in the phase of negotiation of a new commitment when more than two agents are involved. A precommitment is similar to a commitment, but has one more attribute: the time that may elapse between the creation of the precommitment and action of accepting or refusing it, which is represented in the axioms by means of the variable t_{out}:*ptime*. The following fluent, whose life-cycle is depicted in Figure 2, is used to represent precommitments:

fluent Precomm(state, agent, agent, tp, tp, ptime, source, id)

To create a precommitment the *AttCreatePrecomm(agent,agent,tp,tp,ptime,source,id)* institutional action has to be performed. Its effects are described by the following axiom (where *content* and *condition* are defined in the previous section):

P1 *¬HoldsAt(Precomm(state, d, c, content, condition, t_{out}, s, id), t) ∧ t < t_{out} ∧ t2$_{end}$ < t1$_{start}$ →*
Initiates(AttCreatePrecomm(d, c, content, condition, t_{out}, s, id),
Precomm(Active, d, c, content, condition, t_{out}, s, id), t)

The action *AttAcceptPrecomm(agent,agent,tp,tp)* of accepting an existing *Active* precommitment implies the creation of a new commitment:

P2 *Happens(AttAcceptPrecomm(d, c, content, condition), t)∧∃t$_{out}$(HoldsAt(Precomm(Active, d, c, content, condition, t_{out}, s, id), t) ∧ t < t_{out}) →Happens(AttCreateComm(d, c, content, condition, s, id), t)*

If a precommitment is accepted it is terminated:

P3 *HoldsAt(Precomm(Active, d, c, content, condition, t_{out}, s, id), t) ∧ t < t_{out} →*
Terminates(AttAcceptPrecomm(d, c, content, condition), Precomm(Active, d, c, content, condition, t_{out}, s, id), t)

We need moreover to define the *AttCancelPrecomm(agent,agent,tp,tp)* action that the *debtor* of a precommitment can perform to refuse a precommitment, transforming it into a *Cancelled* one and terminating the *Active* one:

P4 *HoldsAt(Precomm(Active, d, c, content, condition, t_{out}, s, id), t)* $\land t < t_{out} \rightarrow$
Initiates(AttCancelPrecomm(d, c, content, condition), Precomm(Cancelled, d, c, content, condition, t_{out}, s, id), t)

P5 *HoldsAt(Precomm(Active, d, c, content, condition, t_{out}, s, id), t)* $\land t < t_{out} \rightarrow$
Terminates(AttCancelPrecomm(d, c, content, condition), Precomm(Active, d, c, content, condition, t_{out}, s, id), t)

Similarly if t_{out} is elapsed without the precommitment being accepted (i.e., it is still *Active*) it has to be transformed into a *Cancelled* one and the *Active* one has to be terminated:

P6 *HoldsAt(Precomm(Active, d, c, content, condition, t_{out}, s, id), t)* $\rightarrow$
Initiates(Elapse(t_{out}), Precomm(Cancelled, d, c, content, condition, t_{out}, s, id), t)

P7 *HoldsAt(Precomm(Active, d, c, content, condition, t_{out}, s, id), t)* $\rightarrow$
Terminates(Elapse(t_{out}), Precomm(Active, d, c, content, condition, t_{out}, s, id), t)

Agent Communication Language

In this section we define a library of agent speech acts. Following Bach and Harnish (1979), we distinguish between two types of speech acts: *communicative acts*, similar to those defined by FIPA ACL communicative acts library (FIPA, 2002), and *declarative acts* or *declarations*. Speech acts of the first type (like promising, informing, and requesting), are important because reflect the everyday use of language. Declarative communicative acts, usually neglected by other approaches (FIPA, 2002, Finin et al., 1997), are also important because by means of them it is possible to perform institutional actions, like opening an auction or giving the power to perform certain actions to an agent. We define the following sort that is used to specify the type of the message exchanged between two agents:

sort type [$\forall x:type$ (*x = Promise* $\lor$ *x = Inform* $\lor$ *x = Request* $\lor$ *x = Agree* $\lor$ *x = Refuse* $\lor$ *x = Cancel* $\lor$ *x = Declare*)]

Communicative Acts

In our model we define the following base-level actions to represent the exchange of a certain message, where the second type of message exchange is necessary for the performance of requests with a specified deadline for acceptance or refusal:

ExchMsg(type, agent, agent, tp, tp)
ExchMsg1(type, agent, agent, tp, tp, ptime)

In the axioms we will use the more perspicuous variables name *sender:agent* and *receiver:agent* as second and third argument of a message. The performance of a *Promise* communicative act implies the attempt to create a commitment, provided that the *content* is referred to the future (i.e., t_{1start} is greater than the time *t* of the performance of the act), and represents the performance of an action by the *sender* of the message (*content* and *condition* are the two temporal propositions previously defined):

Axiom Promise *Happens(ExchMsg(Promise, sender, receiver, content, condition), t) $\wedge$ ($t1_{start}$ > t) $\wedge$ prop1 = Done(sender, action) $\rightarrow$Happens(AttCreateComm(sender, receiver, content, condition, CA, t), t)*

The performance of an *Inform* communicative act implies the attempt to create a commitment:

Axiom Inform *Happens(ExchMsg(Inform, sender, receiver, content, condition), t) $\rightarrow$*
    Happens(AttCreateComm(sender, receiver, content, condition, CA, t), t)

It is worth to observe that an act of informing can be about something happened in the past or something that will happen in the future. An *Inform* act about the performance of a future action will have the same consequences as a promise. To distinguish between promising to perform an action and informing that an action will be performed, it would be necessary to take into consideration aspects, like the agents interests, that concern the internal architecture of the interacting agents; this is beyond the scope of this chapter and would reduce the possibility of applying our model to arbitrary open systems. The performance of a *Request* communicative act implies the attempt to create a precommitment (with the *receiver* of the message as *debtor* of the upcoming commitment), provided that the *content* is referred to the future and is about the performance of an action by the *receiver* of the message:

Axiom Request *Happens(ExchMsg1(Request, sender, receiver, content, condition, t_{out}), t) $\wedge$ ($t1_{start}$ > t) $\wedge$ prop1 = Done(receiver, action) $\rightarrow$ Happens(AttCreatePrecomm(receiver, sender, content, condition, t_{out}, CA, t), t)*

The meaning of an *Agree* communicative act is expressed by means of the *AttAcceptPrecomm()* action that, if the accepted precommitment exists, transforms it into a commitment:

Axiom Agree *Happens(ExchMsg(Agree, sender, receiver, content, condition), t) $\rightarrow$*
    Happens(AttAcceptPrecomm(sender, receiver, content, condition), t)

The meaning of a *Refuse* communicative act is expressed by means of the *AttCancelPrecomm()* action that transforms the precommitment, if it exists, into a *Cancelled* one:

Axiom Refuse *Happens(ExchMsg(Refuse, sender, receiver, content, condition), t) $\rightarrow$*
    Happens(AttCancelPrecomm(sender, receiver, content, condition), t)

The meaning of a *Cancel* communicative act is expressed by means of the *AttCancelComm()* action that transforms a *Cond* or *Pending* commitment, having as *creditor* the *sender* of the message, into a *Cancelled* one:

Axiom Cancel *Happens(ExchMsg(Cancel, sender, receiver, content, condition), t)* →
Happens(AttCancelComm(receiver, sender, content, condition), t)

Declarations

Declarations are a very special type of speech act that, if certain contextual conditions hold, change the institutional state of the system, that is, the part of the system that exists only thanks to the common agreement of the interacting agents (or of their designers). We view an artificial interaction system as a technological instrument that enriches and creates new types of interaction among human beings. Such a system has to represent: (i) *physical objects* that exist in human reality, like a book that has to be sold in an auction; (ii) *institutional entities* of human reality, like the amount of money that has to be paid to buy a book; (iii) *institutional entities* created and managed within the artificial system to implement communicative interactions among agents, like for instance the concept of commitment, the notion of auction, or the notion of price. These institutional entities may be modified by declarations. For instance, the declaration that an electronic auction is open, made by an agent that has the power to do it, makes it actually open.

To deal with institutional entities we introduce *institutional actions*, which are a special type of actions (Colombetti & Verdicchio, 2002) and are crucial for the formalization of declarations. Given that the performance of institutional actions have to be *public* (that, is made known to the relevant agents), we assume that to perform an institutional action an agent has to perform a declaration by sending a particular type of message. Following Searle's approach to the construction of social reality (Searle, 1995), we assume that the *"counts-as"* relation binds the performance of a base-level action, like sending a message, to the performance of an institutional action, if certain contextual conditions are satisfied. We deal with such contextual conditions in the next subsection.

Contextual Conditions and Power

The most important condition that has to be satisfied for a declaration to count as the declared institutional action is that the *sender* of the message has the *power* to perform the institutional action. We therefore provide a specific treatment for this aspect of the context. Assuming that suitable institutional actions have been defined (with sort *iaction*, a subsort of *event*), to express the fact that an *agent* has the power to perform an institutional action we introduce the fluent:

fluent Power(agent, iaction)

For example, we may want to specify that agent *Bob* has the power to perform the institutional action *AttCreateComm()* with itself as the *creditor*, agent *Mark* as the *debtor* (*Bob* may be *Mark*'s boss), and as *content* a temporal proposition representing that some photocopies are made from instant 2 to instant 5 (without any further *condition*):

HoldsAt(Power(Bob, AttCreateComm(Mark,Bob, TP(Done(Mark, Photocopy), 2, 5,Exist), TP(PTrue, 1, 1,Exist))), 0)

To specify all other relevant aspects of the context of a declaration we introduce another fluent, *Context(iaction)*, that holds if certain contextual conditions are satisfied. Such a fluent may initially hold or may be initiated by a suitable axiom. For example, we may want to represent that an auction (represented with the fluent *Auction(state,id, t_{init})*) may be opened by the institutional action *OpenAuction(id)* only if a certain instant of time t_{init} has elapsed:

Initiates(Elapse(t_{init}),Context(OpenAuction(id)), t)

Before introducing an axiom to define the effects of a declaration we first introduce a new base-level action for exchanging a message of type declare:

ExchMsgD(Declare, agent, agent, iaction)

The communicative act of declaring a certain institutional action counts as the performance of the declared institutional action if certain conditions hold, and if the *sender* of the message has the power to perform the declared institutional action, as described by the following axiom:

Axiom Decl *Happens(ExchMsgD(Declare, sender, agent, iaction), t) $\wedge$ HoldsAt(Power(sender,iaction),t) $\wedge$ HoldsAt(Context(iaction),t) $\rightarrow$ Happens(iaction,t)*

Empower and Disempower

Given that the power is a fluent, it would be natural to introduce a new institutional action that can be used during the run time of a system to *empower* and another to *disempower* a given agent to perform a given institutional action. They are institutional actions because they change an institutional fluent, the power, that exists thanks to the common agreement of the interacting agents. Moreover given that they are institutional actions, their effects will take place only if the actor has the power to perform them. The *Empower()* and *Disempower()* institutional actions are defined as follows (where the first agent (for which we will use the variable *actor:agent*, is the one that gives/removes the power to/from the second agent):

iaction Empower(agent, agent, iaction)
iaction Disempower(agent, agent, iaction)

The effect of performing an *Empower()* institutional action is given by the following axiom:

Axiom Power1 *Initiates(Empower(actor, agent, iaction), Power(agent, iaction), t)*

The effect of performing a *Disempower()* action is to terminate a given power:

Axiom Power2 *HoldsAt(Power(agent, iaction), t) $\rightarrow$ Terminates(Disempower(actor, agent, iaction), Power(agent, iaction), t)*

To avoid infinite chains of empowerments, it is necessary to state what powers initially hold when the system start to run, that is, what powers hold at time 0. For example, agent *Bob* may initially have the power to perform an *AttCreateComm*() action with every possible agent as *creditor* and every possible *content* and *condition* as described by the following axiom:

HoldsAt(Power(Bob, AttCreateComm(Bob, creditor, content, condition)), 0)

This approach has the limitation that usually it is impossible to know at design time the name of the actual agents. As we will see in next section, this problem may be overcome by introducing the notion of *role*. The same power can also be created at time *t* by an agent *Ag*1 (if it has the right power) by declaring the following action:

Empower(Ag1,Bob, AttCreateComm(Bob, creditor, content, condition))

Role

The set of powers and norms (introduced later) that hold in an interaction system at a certain instant of time may be created (like the other fluents introduced so far) by the interacting agents using the proper institutional action (actually in this work we will not define the institutional action for creating norms at run-time) or may be devised by the (human) designers of the system at design time. Given that at design time it is impossible to know the concrete agents that will be actually involved at run time in an interaction we need to introduce the notion of *role* and to introduce some mechanisms to define powers and norms in term of roles. Moreover we need to make it possible during the run time phase to deduce powers and norms that apply to a given agents on the basis of the roles that it plays.

As regard as the notion of role, in an artificial system we could have for example the role of *auctioneer* or *participant* of a certain run of an auction, *boss* or *employee* of a certain company for example an Auction House, *debtor* or *creditor* of a certain commitment, *student* or *professor* of a certain university etc. Coherently with those examples in our view a role may be viewed as a label that can be used in place of the identifier of a specific agent in the design of a certain institution, and it may be related to: a specific institution/organization or institutional agent (like a university), to an institutional activity (like a run of an auction), or to an institutional relation (like a commitment), that is, a role relates an agent with an institutional "*entity*". In literature it is possible to find different other definitions of the notion of role, for an overview of those approaches see (Masolo et al., 2004).

It is important to notice that during run-time some roles must necessarily be played by certain agents. For example it makes no sense having a commitment without an agent playing the role of *debtor* and another one playing the role of *creditor* ; similarly it makes no sense having a run of an auction without an agent playing the role of *auctioneer* and at least other two other agents as *participants*.

We assume that every institutional entity is explicitly represented in our model, and we introduce the sort *ientity:fluent* as a subsort of the sort *fluent* to represents them. For example we have already introduced the fluent to represent commitments, we may define the following fluent to represent a run of an auction (where the sort *astate* (auction state) may assume the values: *Registration, Open,Closed,* and we will use the variable t_{init}:*ptime* as third argument):

ientity Auction(id, astate, ptime)

or a fluent to represent an organization:

ientity Organization(*id*)

To express the fact that an agent plays a given role within a certain institutional entity, we introduce the following fluent:

fluent HasRole(*agent, role, ientity*)

where the *sort role* is used to represent names of possible roles like *Debtor*, *Creditor*, etc. For example if the following fluent holds at time *t*:

HoldsAt(*HasRole*(*Bob,Employer,Organization*(01)), *t*)

it means that agent *Bob* play the role of *Employer* in the organization with identifier 01 a time *t*. Moreover, to express that a certain role is meaningful only in relation to a certain institutional entity we introduce the following fluent:

fluent RoleOf(*role, ientity*)

For example, to state that the role *Auctioneer* is meaningful in the context of the run of an auction the following fluent has to be initiated:

RoleOf(*Auctioneer, Auction*(*id, astate, t_{init}*))

It is important to remark that every time that a new institutional entity is initiated it is also necessary to initiate the set of roles that it defines (that is a set of *RoleOf*() fluents) and, if it is the case, the correct *HasRole*() fluents. For example when a new commitment fluent is initiated, it is also necessary to initiates the *RoleOf*() fluent that defines the role of *Debtor* and *Creditor* and to initiate new *HasRole*() fluents to state that the first agent that appear in the new commitment plays the role of *Debtor* and the second one plays the role of *Creditor*. Therefore the following axioms have to be introduced (where $e_c =_{def} AttCreateComm$(*agent*1, *agent*2, *content, condition, s, id*):

Initiates(e_c,*RoleOf*(*Creditor,Comm*(*agent*1,*agent*2,*content,condition,s,id*)),*t*)
Initiates(e_c,*RoleOf*(*Debtor,Comm*(*agent*1,*agent*2,*content,condition,s,id*)),*t*)
Initiates(e_c,*HasRole*(*agent*1,*Debtor,Comm*(*agent*1,*agent*2,*content,condition,s,id*)),*t*)
Initiates(e_c,*HasRole*(*agent*2,*Creditor,Comm*(*agent*1,*agent*2,*content,condition,s,id*)),*t*)

In other situations, like for example for the roles defined by a run of an *Auction*, it is not be necessary to assign all the roles to specific agents when the institutional entity is created, but it has to be possible to assign the role of *Auctioneer* and *Participant* to various agents subsequently. In order to be able to perform such an institutional action we introduce the *AssignRole(agent,agent,role,ientity)* action that when performed assign the new role to the involved agent, as described by the following axiom:

Axiom Role1 *HoldsAt(RoleOf(role,ientity),t)* →
    Initiates(AssignRole(actor,agent,role,ientity),HasRole(agent,role,ientity),t)

and another action *DismissRole(agent,agent,role,ientity)* to remove an agent from a given role:

Axiom Role2 *HoldsAt(HasRole(agent,role,ientity),t)* →
    Terminates(DismissRole(actor,agent,role,ientity),HasRole(agent,role,ientity),t)

Given that *AssignRole()* and *DismissRole()* are two institutional actions, their *actor* needs to have the right powers to successfully perform them. As performing such actions through declarations is the only way to assign or dismiss roles, we have the problem of initially assigning a role to each agent. To solve this problem we introduce a special agent, the *interaction-system* (*IntSystem*), and assume that it has the power to assign every role and every power to other agents and that the *Context()* to perform those actions initially holds.

Conditional Power

Previously we introduced the notion of power; here we introduce the general notion of conditional power and a crucial type of conditional power, conditioned by the roles that agents play in the system. In the design of an artificial institution it may be useful to specify conditional powers, that is, powers that starts to hold if certain conditions start to hold or if certain events happen in the system. For example agent *Bob* may acquire the power to create commitments for himself when he becomes of age. To initiate a power when a given event E_i happens in the system, we have to add an axiom like the following one to our specification:

Happens(E_p t) → *Happens(Empower(IntSystem, Agent, Iaction), t)*

Obviously such power may be terminated by another event E_t as stated by the following axiom:

Happens(E_p t) → *Happens(Disempower(IntSystem, Agent, Iaction), t)*

In general if *n* events, with *n* > 1, must happen for a power to be created, and we do not know their temporal order, we need to write *n* axioms to initiate the right power. For example the following two axioms are needed when two events must happen:

Happens(E_1, t_1) ∧ t_1 <= t ∧ Happens(E_2, t) → *Happens(Empower(IntSystem, Agent, Iaction), t)*

Happens(E_2, t_1) ∧ t_1 <= t ∧ Happens(E_1, t) → *Happens(Empower(IntSystem, Agent, Iaction), t)*

Power Expressed by Means of Roles

An important type of conditional power is the power conditioned by the fact that the involved agents play certain roles. In the design phase of a system, to express that a power is initiated when certain agents start to play some role it is necessary to introduce axioms similar to the ones presented in the previous section. For example the following axiom expresses the fact that the agent playing the role of *Boss* of an organization has the power to create commitments for the agents playing the role of *Employee* in the same organization (in this axiom, an agent becomes the *Boss* first, and then another agent becomes the *Employee*; an axiom treating the opposite order of events has also to be introduced):

Happens(AssignRole(IntSystem,agent1,Boss,Organization(1)),t_1) $\wedge$ t_1<=t $\wedge$
Happens(AssignRole(IntSystem,agent2,Employee,Organization(1)),t) $\rightarrow$
Happens(Empower(IntSystem,agent1,AttCreateComm(agent2,agent1,content, condition)),t)

Similarly it is necessary to add the following axiom to dismiss the power when an agent dismisses the relevant role:

HoldsAt(Power(agent1,AttCreateComm(agent2,agent1,content,condition)),t) $\wedge$
(Happens(DismissRole(IntSystem,agent1,Boss,Organization(1)),t) $\vee$ *Happens(DismissRole(IntSystem, agent2,Employee,Organization*(1)),t)) $\rightarrow$
Happens(DisempowerRole(agent1,AttCreateComm(agent2,agent1,content, condition)),t)

Commitment and Precommitment Powers

Institutional actions like *AttCreateComm()*, *AttCancelComm()* can be performed by exchanging a message of a particular type (for example a promise) or can be declared. In the latter case, for the declaration to be successful the sender of the message must have the power to declare those actions. Therefore we have to introduce some axioms to initiate reasonable powers. First of all, every agent has the power to perform an *AttCreateComm()* institutional action with itself as the debtor (first argument) and any other agent as the creditor (second argument) of the future commitment:

Axiom CommPower1 *agent1 $\neq$ agent2 $\rightarrow$ Happens(Empower(IntSystem,agent1,*
*AttCreateComm(agent1,agent2,content,condition,s,id)),*0)

The agent that becomes the creditor of a commitment will have the power to cancel it:

Axiom CommPower2 *Happens(AttCreateComm(agent1,agent2,content,condition,s,id),t) $\rightarrow$*
Happens(Empower(InsSystem,agent2, AttCancelComm(agent1,agent2,content,condition)),t)

Moreover, the agent that becomes the debtor of a precommitment will have the power to accept or refuse it:

Axiom PrecommPower1 *Happens(AttCreatePrecomm(agent1,agent2,content,condition,t_{out}),t) $\rightarrow$*
Happens(Empower(IntSystem,agent1,AttAcceptPrecomm(agent1,agent2,content, condition),t)

Axiom PrecommPower2 *Happens(AttCreatePrecomm(agent1,agent2,content,condition,t_{out}),t) $\rightarrow$*
Happens(Empower(IntSystem,agent1,AttCancelPrecomm(agent1,agent2,content, condition),t)

Norms

A norm is used to impose a certain behavior on certain agents in the system identified by means of the norm's *debtor*. The norm *content* is a temporal proposition that describes the actions that the debtor have to perform (if the norm expresses an *obligation*) or not to perform (if the norm expresses a *prohibition*) within a specified interval of time. In our model if for a given agent an action is not obliged nor prohibited it is permitted, obviously if it is an institutional action the agent need also to have the power to perform it in order that its effects take place (in particular the value of the attribute t_{start} of the *content* is always equal to the time of occurrence of the event that activates the norm). The obligation or prohibition could be conditioned to the truth of another temporal proposition indicated in the *condition* attribute of the norm.

An agent can reason whether to fulfill or not to fulfill a norm on the basis of the sanctions (as discussed later) and of whom is the *creditor* of the norm, as proposed also in (Kagal & Finin, 2005, López y López et al., 2005). For example, an agent with the role of auctioneer may decide to violate a norm imposed by the auction house if it is in conflict with another norm that regulates trade transactions in a certain country. Moreover the creditor of a norm is crucial because, given that it becomes the creditor of the commitments generated by the norm, it is the only agent authorized to cancel such commitment.

To enforce norms it is necessary to specify *sanctions*. Regarding this aspect there are numerous reasons to develop systems where agents may violate the rules, first of all as discussed in (Fornara & Colombetti, 2007), the obligation to perform an action in principle cannot be regimented[2], secondly systems that are able to manage violations (sometimes also due to software error) are more robust, finally it is important to remark that given that it is impossible to predict at design phase all the interesting and fruitful behaviors that may emerge in an interaction, to reach an optimal solution for all participants (Zambonelli et al., 2003), it may be profitable to allow agents to violate their obligations and prohibitions. We speak about sanctions to stress the need to punish violations, but the mechanisms for the management of *rewards* can be easily introduced in a similar way. As discussed in (Fornara & Colombetti, 2007) and differently from other approaches (López y López et al., 2005), (Vázquez-Salceda et al., 2005), (Grossi et al., 2007) that do not investigate in detail this aspect, we think that a complete model of sanctions have to distinguish between two different type of actions: the action that the violator of a norm has to perform to extinguish its violation and the action that the agent in charge of norm enforcement may perform to deter agents from violating the norm. Therefore a norm has to specify: (i) what we call the *active sanction* (*a-sanction*) that is the action that the violator should perform within a certain interval of time to extinguish its violation and that can be represented in our model through a temporal proposition; (ii) what we call the *passive sanction* (*p-sanction*) that is the new power that the agent entitled to enforce the norm acquire in case of violation of the norm. Regarding this second type of action, it is important to underline that in case of violation the agent entitled to enforce the norm gets a new power whereas another norm (that in (López y López et al., 2005) is called *enforcement norm*) may oblige the enforcer agent to punish the violation.

A norm becomes active every time that its *activation event estart* happens. For example a norm may be used to represent a contract that obliges an organization to pay the salary to its employees every time that the end of the month is reached, or a set of norms may be used to formalize a protocol, for example an auction protocol, and oblige the auctioneer to declare the new ask price every time that a new valid bid is received, or to declare the winner when a certain need to monitor its evolution in time and to react to its *violation* with suitable *sanctions*. Given that in our meta-model we have already defined a construct, the social commitment, which can be used to perform that task, we define a set of axioms that transform a norm into a commitment when its activation event happens. This makes it possible to resolve another interesting problem: the problem to detect and manage the violation or fulfillment of more than one activation of the same norm. We introduce the following fluent to represent norms:

fluent Norm(id, agent, agent, tp, tp, event, tp, fluent)

In the axioms on norms we shall use variables *debtor:agent* and *creditor:agent* as the second and third argument of a norm, variables *content:tp* and *condition:tp* as the fourth and fifth argument, variable e_{start}*:event* to refer to the activation event, the variable *a-sanction:tp* for the active sanction, and variable *p-sanction:fluent* for the passibe sanction. We need therefore to define an axiom to manage the creation of a commitment every time that a norm becomes active (abbreviations: *d=debtor, c=creditor*):

Axiom ActivateNorm *HoldsAt(Norm(id,d,c,content,condition,e_{start},a-sanction,p-sanction),t)* $\wedge$ *Happens(e_{start},t)* $\rightarrow$ *Happens(AttCreateComm(d,c,content,condition,Norm,id),t)*

If event *e* initiates the commitment related to a norm to *Violated*, that event *e* initiates also the power, described in the *passive-sanction*, for certain agent to perform the actions that have been devised to deter the agent from misbehaving, as described by the following axiom:

Axiom PassiveSanction *HoldsAt(Norm(id,d,c,content,condition,e_{start},a-sanction,p-sanction),t)* $\wedge$ *Initiates(e,Comm(Violated,d,c,content,condition,Norm,id),t)* $\rightarrow$ *Initiates(e,p-sanction,t)*

If event *e* initiates the commitment related to a norm to *Violated* that event *e* initiates also the commitment to perform the action described by the temporal proposition in the *active-sanction* attribute:

Axiom ActiveSanction *HoldsAt(Norm(id,d,c,content,condition,e_{start},a-sanction,p-sanction),t)* $\wedge$ *Initiates(e,Comm(Violated,d,c,content,condition,Norm,id),t)* $\wedge$ *Happens(e,t)* $\rightarrow$ *Happens(AttCreateComm(d,c,a-sanction,TP(PTrue(),1,1,Exist),Sanction,id),t)*

Where the label "*Sanction*" as *source* attribute of the commitment means that the commitment has been generated as sanction of the norm with identifier *id* and the violation of this type of commitment will initiates neither another commitment nor a new power.

Norms Expressed in Terms of Roles

Norms with specific agent as debtor and creditor have to holds in the initial state of the system, if fact for this work we will not introduce actions for creating norms at run-time. Given that in the design phase of a system it is impossible to know the name of the agents that will actually interact with the system, it is crucial to express norms in terms of the roles played by the agent in the interaction system. This can be obtained by means of suitable axioms (like the ones that we introduced to express power in terms of roles) that initiate a certain norm when an agent enter a given role. Given that the agents involved in a norm are the *debtor* and the *creditor* it may be necessary to define two axioms for the conditional initiation of a norm when those agents start to play a certain role. For example the norm that obliges the agent that play the role of *Boss* of an organization to pay x euro to the agents playing the role of *Employee* when the end of the month is reached can be expressed using the following axiom:

$E_1 =_{def} AssignRole(agent_x, agent1, Boss, Organization(1))$
$E_2 =_{def} AssignRole(agent_x, agent2, Employee, Organization(1))$
$TP1 =_{def} TP(Done(agent1, Pay(agent1, agent2, x)), t, t + 2, Exist)$
$TP2 =_{def} TP(PTrue(), 1, 1, Exist)$
$TP3 =_{def} TP(Done(agent1, Pay(agent1, agent2, x*1.1)), t + 3, t + 5, Exist))$

$Happens(E1, t_1) \wedge t_1 <= t \rightarrow$
$Initiates(E2, Norm(agent1, agent2, TP1, TP2, Elapse(31), TP3,$
$Power(InstAgent, ChangeReputation(agent1, 2))), t)$

where we assume that *ChangeReputation(agent,integer)* is an institutional action adding a given value to the reputation of an agent. The other axiom can be obtained exchanging $E1$ with $E2$. It is also necessary to write two axioms to terminate the norm when an agent dismisses the role of *Boss* or of *Employee*.

EXAMPLE

The Discrete Event Calculus Reasoner 1.0[3] as previously discussed is a tool that can be used to perform deduction, abduction and model finding starting from a domain description. Using such a tool and its deduction capabilities we verified that given a specification of an interaction system (consisting of the Discrete Event Calculus axioms, the OCeAN axioms introduced so far, and domain specific axioms), an initial situation, and a narrative of known event occurrences (that is a set of axioms that specify what happen in the system and when) there is only one model that satisfies them and represents how the system state will evolve.

The Discrete Event Calculus Reasoner 1.0 relies on various satisfiability (SAT) solver transforming formulas of first-order logic into formulas of the propositional calculus and by restricting the problem to a finite universe. Entailment in the propositional calculus is decidable but it is *NP-complete*. In practice (even if sometimes it is necessary to write more specific axioms) the specification of our examples (with over 10,000 variables) can be solved quite efficiently. In particular the axioms of our model can be quite forwardly transformed in a specification processable by the tool and introducing some adaptations due to certain tool limitations. In this section we will present an example that partially shows the dynamic evolution of a system designed for the execution of electronic auctions[4]. A detailed example of the usage of ACL axioms can be found in (Fornara & Colombetti, 2008).

Here we partially describe and test a system for the execution of electronic auctions, and simulate the evolution of its state for one possible event narrative. To exhaustively test the correctness of a given specification we would have to simulate the evolution of a system for every possible narrative and verify its correctness. As previously discussed the specification of this system consists of: (i) the set of fluents, events/actions and axioms that compose the *OCeAN* meta-model; (ii) the fluents, events/actions and axioms necessary for the specification of the institution of auctions (we introduce the fluent for representing auctions and the axioms Auc1, Auc2, AucPower1, and AucNorm1 to create powers and norms); (iii) the fluents, events/actions and axioms specific to a certain type of auction like for example the English

Auction; (iv) and finally the fluents, events/actions and axioms specific to a concrete system, like the fluent used to represent a product and the actions of paying or delivering it.

The *ientity* for representing auctions has been introduced as *Auction(id,astate,t$_{init}$)*. The effect of the *OpenAuction(id)* institutional action is defined introducing the following axioms:

Axiom Auc1 *HoldsAt(Auction(aid,Reg,t$_{init}$),t) → Initiates(OpenAuction(id),Auction(aid,Open,t$_{init}$),t)*

Axiom Auc2 *HoldsAt(Auction(aid,Reg,t$_{init}$),t) → Terminates(OpenAuction(id),Auction(aid,Reg,t$_{init}$),t)*

The initial state of the system is given by the following fluents that hold at time 0. The first represents the auction with *id* 01 and *t$_{init}$* 4, the other two represent the fact that the auction entity defines the roles of *Auctioneer* and *Participant*, and the last one represents the context for performing the specified *OpenAuction()* institutional action:

Auction(01,Reg,4)
RoleOf(Auctioneer,Auction(01,Reg,4))
RoleOf(Participant,Auction(01,Reg,4))
Context(OpenAuction(01,Reg,4))

The following axiom initiates the power, for the agent playing the role of *Auctioneer*, to declare open the auction for which it is playing that role, if at least two agents are already playing the role of *Participant*:

Axiom AucPower1 $\exists$ *t$_{init}$ Happens(AssignRole(agent1,agent3,Participant,Auction(aid,Reg,t$_{init}$)),t$_1$)* $\wedge$
t$_1$≤ t $\wedge$ *Happens(AssignRole(agent1,agent4,Participant,Auction(aid,Reg,t$_{init}$)),t$_2$)* $\wedge$ *t$_2$≤ t* $\wedge$
Happens(AssignRole(agent1,agent2,Auctioneer,Auction(aid,Reg,t$_{init}$)),t) →
Happens(Empower(agent1,agent2,OpenAuction(aid)),t)

Given the following definitions of temporal propositions:

TP1 =$_{def}$ TP(Done(OpenAuction(01)), t$_{init}$, t$_{init}$ + 1,Exist)
TP2 =$_{def}$ TP(PTrue(), 1, 1,Exist))
TP3 =$_{def}$ TP(Done(Pay(Bob, AuctionHouse, 1)), t$_{init}$ + 2, t$_{init}$ + 3,Exist)

the following axioms initiates the norm that creates the obligation for the agent playing the role of *Auctioneer* to declare open the auction when *t$_{init}$-1* is elapsed:

Axiom AucNorm1 *Initiates(AssignRole(agent,agent1,Auctioneer,Auction(aid,Reg,t$_{init}$)),*
Norm(id,agent1,AuctionHouse,TP1,TP2,Elapse(t$_{init}$-1),TP3,Power(AuctionHouse,DecTrust(agent1))), t)

The description of the system is available in the file "Auction.e". Given the following history of events:

Happens(AttCreateTP(TP1), 0).
Happens(ExchMsgD(Declare,IntSystem,Bob,AssignRole(IntSystem,Bob,Auctioneer,Auction(01,Reg,4))),1).
Happens(ExchMsgD(Declare,IntSystem,Carl,AssignRole(IntSystem,Carl,Participant,Auction(01,Reg,4))),1).
Happens(ExchMsgD(Declare,IntSystem,Luke,AssignRole(IntSystem,Luke,Participant,Auction(01,Reg,4))),1).
Happens(ExchMsgD(Declare,Bob,Carl,OpenAuction(01)),4).

the output produced, that is, a simulation of the evolution of the state of the system is as follows. Fluents that become true are indicated with a plus sign ("+") and fluents that become false are indicated with a minus sign ("-"):

0
Happens(Elapse(0), 0).
Happens(AttCreateTP(TP1), 0).
1
Happens(Elapse(1), 1).
Happens(ExchMsgD(Declare, IntSystem, Bob,
AssignRole(IntSystem, Bob, Auctioneer, Auction(01, Reg, 4))), 1).
Happens(ExchMsgD(Declare,IntSystem,Carl,AssignRole(IntSystem,Carl,Participant,Auction(01,Reg,4))),1).
Happens(ExchMsgD(Declare,IntSystem,Luke,AssignRole(IntSystem,Luke,Participant,Auction(01,Reg,4))),1).
Happens(AssignRole(IntSystem, Bob, Auctioneer, Auction(01, Reg, 4)), 1).
Happens(AssignRole(IntSystem, Carl, Participant, Auction(01, Reg, 4)), 1).
Happens(AssignRole(IntSystem, Luke, Participant, Auction(01, Reg, 4)), 1).
Happens(Empower(IntSystem, Bob, OpenAuction(01)), 1).
+ETP(TP1, Undef).
+ETP(TP3, Undef).
+TP1().
+TP3().

Thanks to Axiom Decl the declared institutional actions happen (given that their contexts and the right powers hold). Moreover thanks to Axiom AucPower1 a certain *Empower()* institutional action happens. Axioms TP1 and ETP0 initiates the temporal propositions and the evaluated temporal propositions.

2
Happens(Elapse(2), 2).
+HasRole(Bob, Auctioneer, Auction(01, Reg, 4)).
+HasRole(Carl, Participant, Auction(01, Reg, 4)).
+HasRole(Luke, Participant, Auction(01, Reg, 4)).
+Power(Bob, OpenAuction(01)).
+Norm(N1, Bob, AuctionHouse, TP1, TP2, Elapse(3), TP3,Power(AuctionHouse, DecTrust(Bob))).

Thanks to Axiom Role1 the effects of the *AssignRole()* action takes place and the agents start to hold the role of *Auctioneer* or of *Participant*. Thanks to Axiom Power1 the power for agent *Bob* to open the auction where it play the role of *Auctioneer* starts to hold. Thanks to Axiom AucNorm1 the norm that obliges the agent playing the role of *Auctioneer* for a certain auction to declare open such an auction is created.

3
Happens(Elapse(3), 3).
Happens(AttCreateComm(Bob, IntSystem, TP1, TP2, SNorm, N1), 3).

Thanks to Axiom ActivateNorm when the *estart* event of a norm happens the norm becomes active and the *AttCreateComm()* action to create the related commitment happens.

4
Happens(Elapse(4), 4).
Happens(ExchMsgD(Declare, Bob, Carl, OpenAuction(01)), 4).
Happens(OpenAuction(01), 4).
+Comm(Pending, Bob, AuctionHouse, TP1, TP2, SNorm, N1).

Given that the right context and the power hold thanks to Axiom Decl the declared *OpenAuction()* action happens and thanks to axiom C03 (see (Fornara & Colombetti, 2008)) a *Pending* commitment is initiated.

5
-Auction(01, Reg, 4).
+Auction(01, Open, 4).
-ETP(TP1, Undef).
+ETP(TP1, True).
-Comm(Pending, Bob, AuctionHouse, TP1, TP2, SNorm, N1).
+Comm(Fulfilled, Bob, AuctionHouse, TP1, TP2, SNorm, N1).

Thanks to axioms Auc1 and Auc2 an *Open* auction is initiated and the obligation to open the auction between time 4 and time 5 generated by norm *N1*, which is represented by means of the commitment, is *Fulfilled* (axiom ETPE1 and C3).

CONCLUSION AND FUTURE RESEARCH DIRECTIONS

Using the Event Calculus, we have presented a formal specification of the *OCeAN* meta-model for open artificial institutions. With respect to other formalisms with well-understood formal semantics, the main advantage of the Event Calculus is that it allows for the execution of the formal specification of a system to test its correctness, while retaining the expressiveness of first order logic.

Our formal definition of *OCeAN* allows one to define and test the specification of an open interaction system, conceived as a set of artificial institutions. Given that all components of *OCeAN* are explicitly defined in logic, in principle it is possible to design agents that can interact with different OCeAN-based interaction systems without being reprogrammed. Other possible applications of our meta-model are the specification and monitoring of contracts by means of commitments, and the flexible specification of protocols using norms and the library of communicative acts.

Indeed, *OCeAN* is still incomplete under a number of respects. For example, it will be important to understand how a new institution may be defined using, or inheriting concepts from, other institutions. It is also important to understand whether and how the meta-model has to be enriched to be used for different types of applications, like for example for *Virtual Enterprises* (Cardoso & Oliveira, 2004), for the flexible specification of system for knowledge sharing (Dignum et al., 2004), or for collaborative environments. Moreover, it will be necessary to analyse and formally specify different types of institutional powers: for example, it may be useful to distinguish between the power to perform an action as many time as needed from the power to perform it only once, and to analyse the type of power required by passive sanctions.

In particular we plan to continue our research with a focus on mixing human and artificial agents in hybrid multiagent systems within a given organizational structure, as an environment for complex collective activities. The practical design and implementation of such systems involves the study of two interconnected problems. The first is to develop a framework that allows one to design software agents able to interact with different open systems (for example different running auctions) without being re-programmed; this requires that software agents are able to access a formal description of the interaction system, including the context of the interaction and the norms regulating the system, and to reason at runtime on how to reach their goals. The second problem is how to use and extend artificial institutions to represent the human organizational structures within which interactions take place, assuming that the software agents participating in the interaction have sufficient reasoning capabilities.

ACKNOWLEDGMENT

Supported by the Hasler Foundation, Project 2204, "Artificial institutions: Specification of open distributed interaction systems"

REFERENCES

Arcos, J. L., Esteva, M., Noriega, P., Rodríguez-Aguilar, J. A., & Sierra, C. (2005). Engineering open evironments with electronic institutions. *Engineering applications of artificial intelligence, 18*(2), 191 –204.

Artikis, A., Sergot, M., & Pitt, J. (2002). Animated Specifications of Computational Societies. In C. Castelfranchi and W. L. Johnson, editor, *AAMAS 2002*, pages 535–542. ACM Press.

Bach, K., & Harnish, R. M. (1979). *Linguistic Communication and Speech Acts*. MIT Press, Cambridge, MA.

Boella, G., van der Torre, L. W. N., & Verhagen, H., (eds.) (2007). *Normative Multi-agent Systems, 18-23 March 2007*, volume 07122 of *Dagstuhl Seminar Proceedings*. Internationales Begegnungs- und Forschungszentrum für Informatik (IBFI), Schloss Dagstuhl, Germany.

Cardoso, H. L., & Oliveira, E. (2007). Institutional reality and norms: Specifying and monitoring agent organizations. *International Journal of Cooperative Information Systems, 16*(1), 67–95.

Cardoso, H. L., & Oliveira, E. C. (2004). Virtual enterprise normative framework within electronic institutions. In *ESAW 2004*, 14–32.

Cliffe, O., Vos, M. D., & Padget, J. A. (2006). Answer set programming for representing and reasoning about virtual institutions. In Inoue, K., Satoh, K., and Toni, F., (eds.), *CLIMA VII, Hakodate, Japan, May 2006*, volume 4371/2007 of *LNCS*, pages 60–79. Springer Berlin.

Cliffe, O., Vos, M. D., & Padget, J. (2007). Specifying and reasoning about multiple institutions. In Noriega, P., Vázquez-Salceda, J., Boella, G., Boissier, O., Dignum, V., Fornara, N., and Matson, E., editors, *COIN II*, volume 4386/2007 of *LNCS*, pages 67–85. Springer Berlin.

Colombetti, M. & Verdicchio, M. (2002). An analysis of agent speech acts as institutional actions. In Castelfranchi, C. and Johnson, W. L., editors, *AAMAS 2002*, pages 1157–1166.

Dignum, V., Dignum, F., & Meyer, J.-J. (2004). An agent-mediated approach to the support of knowledge sharing in organizations. *Knowl. Eng. Rev.*, *19*(2), 147–174.

Esteva, M., Rodríguez-Aguilar, J. A., Sierra, C., García, P., & Arcos, J. L. (2001). On the formal specification of electronic institutions. In Dignum, F. and Sierra, C., editors, *Agent Mediated Electronic Commerce, The European AgentLink Perspective*, volume 1991 of *LNAI*, pages 126–147. Springer.

Farrell, A. D. H., Sergot, M. J., Sallé, M., & Bartolini, C. (2005). Using the event calculus for tracking the normative state of contracts. *International Journal of Cooperative Information Systems (IJCIS)*, *14*(2-3), 99–129.

Finin, T., Labrou, Y., & Mayfield, J. (1997). KQML as an agent communication language. In Bradshaw, J. M., editor, *Software Agents*, chapter 14, pages 291–316. AAAI Press / The MIT Press.

FIPA (2002). Foundation for Intelligent Physical Agents (FIPA) Communicative Act Library Specification. http://www.fipa.org.

Fornara, N. & Colombetti, M. (2004). A commitment-based approach to agent communication. *Applied Artificial Intelligence an International Journal*, *18*(9-10), 853–866.

Fornara, N. & Colombetti, M. (2007). Specifying and enforcing norms in artificial institutions. In Boella, G., van der Torre, L., and Verhagen, H., editors, *Normative Multi-agent Systems*, number 07122 in Dagstuhl Seminar Proceedings. Internationales Begegnungs- und Forschungszentrum fuer Informatik (IBFI), Schloss Dagstuhl, Germany.

Fornara, N., & Colombetti, M. (2008). Formal specification of artificial institutions using the event calculus. Technical Report 5, Università della Svizzera italiana.

Fornara, N., Viganò, F., & Colombetti, M. (2007). Agent communication and artificial institutions. *Autonomous Agents and Multi-Agent Systems*, *14*(2), 121–142.

Fornara, N., Viganò, F., Verdicchio, M., & Colombetti, M. (2008). Artificial institutions: A model of institutional reality for open multiagent systems. *Artificial Intelligence and Law*, *16*(1), 89–105.

García-Camino, A., Noriega, P., & Rodríguez-Aguilar, J. A. (2005). Implementing norms in electronic institutions. In *AAMAS'05*, pages 667–673, New York, NY, USA. ACM Press.

Grossi, D., Aldewereld, H., & Dignum, F. (2007). Ubi lex, ibi poena: Designing norm enforcement in e-institutions. In Noriega, P., Vázquez-Salceda, J., Boella, G., Boissier, O., Dignum, V., Fornara, N., and Matson, E., editors, *COIN II*, volume 4386 of *LNCS*, pages 101–114. Springer Berlin.

Hart, H. L. A. (1961). *The Concept of Law*. Clarendon Press, Oxford.

Hewitt, C. (1986). Offices are open systems. *ACM Trans. Inf. Syst.*, *4*(3), 271–287.

Kagal, L., & Finin, T. (2005). Modeling Conversation Policies using Permissions and Obligations. In van Eijk, R., Huget, M., and Dignum, F., editors, *Developments in Agent Communication*, volume 3396 of *LNCS*, pages 123–133. Springer.

Kowalski, R. A., & Sergot, M. J. (1986). A logicbased calculus of events. *New Generation Computing*, *4*(1), 67–95.

López y López, F., Luck, M., & d'Inverno, M. (2005). A Normative Framework for Agent-Based Systems. In *Proceedings of the First International Symposium on Normative Multi-Agent Systems, Hatfield*.

Masolo, C., Vieu, L., Bottazzi, E., Catenacci, C., Ferrario, R., Gangemi, A., & Guarino, N. (2004). Social roles and their descriptions. In Dubois, D., Welty, C., and Williams, M., editors, *Proceedings of the Ninth International Conference on the Principles of Knowledge Representation and Reasoning (KR2004), Whistler, Canada, June 2-5 2004*, pages 267–277.

Miller, R., & Shanahan, M. (2002). Some alternative formulations of the event calculus. In Kakas, A. C. and Sadri, F., editors, *Computational Logic: Logic Programming and Beyond: Essay in Honour of Robert A. Kowalski, Part II*, volume LNCS 2408, pages 452–490. Springer, Berlin.

Mueller, E. T. (2006). *Commonsense Reasoning*. Morgan Kaufmann, San Francisco.

Mueller, E. T. (2007). Event calculus. In van Hermelen, F., Lifschitz, V., and Porter, B., (eds.), *Handbook of Knowledge Representation*. Elsevier, Amsterdam.

Noriega, P. (1997). *Agent mediated auctions: The Fishmarket Metaphor*. PhD thesis, Universitat Autnoma de Barcelona.

Searle, J. R. (1995). *The construction of social reality*. Free Press, New York.

Shanahan, M. (1997). *Solving the Frame Problem*. MIT Press, Cambridge, MA.

Shanahan, M. (1999). The Event Calculus Explained. In Wooldridge, M. J. & Veloso, M. M., editors, *Artificial Intelligence Today: Recent Trends and Developments*, volume LNCS 1600, pages 409–430. Springer, Berlin.

Shanahan, M. (2000). An abductive event calculus planner. *Journal of Logic Programming*, *44*(1-3), 207–240.

Smith, R. G. (1980). The contract net protocol: High-level communication and control in a distributed problem solver. *IEEE Transactions on Computers*, *C-29*(12), 1104–1113.

Vázquez-Salceda, J., Dignum, V., & Dignum, F. (2005). Organizing multiagent systems. *Autonomous Agents and Multi-Agent Systems*, *11*(3), 307–360.

Viganò, F., Fornara, N., & Colombetti, M. (2006). An Event Driven Approach to Norms in Artificial Institutions. In Boissier, O., Padget, J., Dignum, V., Lindemann, G., Matson, E., Ossowski, S., Simao Sichman, J., and Vázquez-Salceda, J., (eds.), *COIN I*, volume LNAI 3913, pages 142–154. Springer Berlin.

Yolum, P., & Singh, M. (2004). Reasoning about commitment in the event calculus: An approach for specifying and executing protocols. *Annals of Mathematics and Artificial Intelligence*, *42*, 227–253.

Zambonelli, F., Jennings, N. R., & Wooldridge, M. (2003). Developing multiagent systems: The Gaia methodology. *ACM Transactions on Software Engineering and Methodology (TOSEM)*, *12*(3), 317–370.

ADDITIONAL READING

d'Inverno, M., & Luck, M. (2001). *Understanding agent systems*. Springer-Verlag, New York, USA.

Ferber, J. (1999). *Multi-Agent Systems: An Introduction to Distributed Artificial Intelligence*. Addison-Wesley Longman Publishing Co., Inc., Boston, MA, USA.

Searle, J. R. (1969). *Speech Acts: An Essay in the Philosophy of Language*. Cambridge University Press, Cambridge, United Kingdom.

Weiß, G., (ed.) (1999). *Multiagent Systems: A Modern Approach to Distributed Artificial Intelligence.*. Cambridge, MA, USA: MIT Press.

Woolridge, M. (2001). *Introduction to Multiagent Systems*. New York, USA: John Wiley & Sons, Inc.

KEY TERMS

Agent Communication Language: A language to be used by software agents for their communicative exchanges. Most proposals are inspired by Speech Act Theory; the best known are KQML (Knowledge Query and Manipulation Language) and FIPA-ACL.

Artificial Institution: The digital counterpart or extension of a human institution, like for example the institution of language, or the institution of auctions. The definition of a specific artificial institution consists of the definition of basic entities common to the specification of every institution, like the concepts of commitment, institutional power, role, and norm, and of a component specific to the institution in question, which includes the specification of the powers and norms that apply to the agents playing roles in the institution, and the definition of the concepts pertaining to the domain of the interaction.

Institutional Power: The status that enables certain agent, particularly when act in specific roles, to create or modify institutional facts (i.e., facts that exist hold to the collective agreement of the interacting agents or of their designers).

Norm: A formal specification of a deontic relation that aims at regulating the interactions among software agents and creating expectations on the future development of the system.

Open Interaction System: A software system that can be dynamically entered and left by heterogeneous, autonomous, and self-interested agents.

Role: A conceptual device that allows one to abstract from individual agents when they interact within an institutional framework. For example, we may have the roles of *auctioneer* and *participant* in an auction, *boss* or *employee* in a company, *debtor* and *creditor* of a commitment, etc. Coherently with these examples, a role may be viewed as a label that can be used in place of the identifier of a specific agent in the design of an institution. Roles connect agents to institutional entities like: a specific institutional agent or organization (e.g., an auction house or a university), an institutional activity (e.g., a run of an auction), or an institutional relationship (e.g., a commitment or a state of ownership).

Social Commitment: A commitment is a construct that binds a debtor with respect to a creditor to the performance of an action or to the fact that a state of affair holds. Commitment are used in this chapter to express the semantics of a library of communicative acts, to represent active norms, and to monitor the fulfillment or violation of obligations and prohibitions of the various agents at run-time.

ENDNOTES

[1]   http://decreasoner.sourceforge.net/

[2]   With regimentation (Hart, 1961) we mean the introduction of control mechanisms that does not allow agents to violate obligations or prohibitions.

[3]   http://decreasoner.sourceforge.net/

[4]   Files containing system specification for the Discrete Event Calculus Reasoner 1.0 that uses the axioms presented in this work and different simulations output obtained running those systems with different history of events are available at http://www.people.lu.unisi.ch/fornaran/code/Examples.html. Those simulations have been executed using Gygwin running on Windows XP on a desktop CORE2 DUO 1.8 GHz RAM 2 Gbyte

Chapter XV
Verifying Organizations Regulated by Institutions

Francesco Viganò
Università della Svizzera italiana, Switzerland

Marco Colombetti
Università della Svizzera italiana, Switzerland
Politecnico di Milano, Italy

ABSTRACT

Institutions have been proposed to explicitly represent norms in open multi-agent systems, where agents may not follow them and which therefore require mechanisms to detect violations. In doing so, they increase the efficiency of electronic transactions carried out by agents, but raise the problem of ensuring that such institutions are not characterized by contradictory norms, and provide agents with all the needed powers to fulfill their objectives. In this chapter we present a framework to verify organizations regulated by institutions, which is characterized by a precise formalization of institutional concepts, a language to describe institutions, and a tool to model check them. Finally, to evaluate and exemplify our approach, we model and verify the Chaired Meeting Institution, showing that the verification of institutional rules constitutes a necessary step to define sound institutions.

INTRODUCTION

To automate tasks whose performance is regulated by *norms*, like the allocation of human organs (Vázquez-Salceda, Dignum, & Dignum., 2005) or the bargain of goods in competitive markets (Noriega, 1997), *electronic institutions* have been proposed as a mechanism to represent norms in agent organizations (Noriega, 1997) where agents are developed by different entities and their internal states are not accessible. The term "electronic institution" is often used to refer to either the *rules* that regulate open multiagent systems, the *organization* that enforces them (Esteva, Rodríguez-Aguilar, Sierra, García,

& Arcos, 2001), the *software implementation* of institutional rules (Esteva, Rodríguez-Aguilar, Rosell, & Arcos, 2004), or a specific *formalism* to describe them (Esteva, Rodríguez-Aguilar, Sierra, & Vasconcelos, 2004). For the sake of clarity, in this chapter we will adopt the term "institution" to refer to a set of rules and concepts regulating agent interactions and which may be enforced by an organization (an electronic institution according to Esteva et al. (2001)). This use of the terms "institution" and "organization" is inspired by (Searle, 1995), where an institution is any collectively accepted system of rules which creates institutional facts, and by (North, 1990), where institutions are the rules of a society regulating interactions and activities of organizations.

In contrast with (Moses & Tennenholtz, 1995), where norms (also named *social laws*) are assumed to be respected by agents because they are designed by a single organization, in open systems it is unrealistic to expect that autonomous agents will always comply with norms. In particular, like other social concepts (e.g., *expectations* (Alberti, Gavanelli, Lamma, Chesani, Mello, & Torroni, 2006) or *commitments* (Yolum & Singh, 2004) (Fornara, Viganò, & Colombetti, 2007)), norms describe interactions in terms of public observable entities which reflect how an agent should behave. For this reason, most efforts have been devoted to the development of *normative languages* amenable to automatic monitoring (e.g., (García-Camino, Noriega, & Rodríguez-Aguilar, 2005)) and *tools* to either avoid violations (Hübner, Simão Sichman, & Boissier, 2005) or detect and sanction them at runtime (e.g., (Esteva, Rodríguez-Aguilar, Rosell, & Arcos, 2004)). Doing so increases the efficiency of transactions carried out by agents (Noriega, 1997), but raises the problem of ensuring that such systems of rules are not characterized by contradictory norms, and allow agents to fulfill the objectives of the organization that has developed the system. This is especially important when norms of institutions are complex and cannot be reduced to a simple protocol that agents should follow, making it prohibitive to foresee all possible evolutions admitted by them.

Unfortunately, most approaches do not provide tools to automatically verify what properties are guaranteed when norms are followed or violated. As a consequence, designers can specify a set of norms which can be enforced at runtime, but they cannot check if such norms are consistent, undesirable behaviors are actually forbidden, and interactions terminate with positive outcomes when norms are correctly followed. For instance, in (Viganò & Colombetti, 2007) we showed that the rules of the Dutch Auction Institution discussed in (García-Camino, Rodríguez-Aguilar, Sierra, & Vasconcelos, 2006) admit infinite bidding rounds. The lack of tools for the verification of norms defined by institutions may be problematic, since institutions have been put forward to provide safe and reliable environments for agents (Esteva, Rodríguez-Aguilar, Sierra, García, & Arcos, 2001).

Automated formal verification should be considered as an important step for the development of organizations regulated by institutions, because it can increase their reliability by ensuring that they satisfy certain properties. The development of formal frameworks to model and automatically verify organizations is therefore essential, but only few attempts have been proposed in the literature to introduce automated formal methods to verify them (e.g. (Huget, Esteva, Phelps, Sierra, & Wooldridge, 2002)). In our opinion, *model checking* (Clarke, Grumberg, & Peled, 1999) can play an important role to evaluate the consistency of the rules governing an agent organization, to ensure its compliance with the rules defined by a human institution, and to compare design alternatives arising from different interpretations of such rules.

The remainder of this chapter is organized as follows. In the next section we provide an overview of the main approaches proposed in the literature to *model* and *verify* systems regulated by norms. In particular, we will focus our attention on the most recent contributions in the context of multiagent systems, showing the main advantages and current limitations of such proposals. Then we start the presentation of our approach by introducing the syntax and semantics of a temporal extension of first order logic, which is used throughout the chapter to formalize institutional concepts and to express properties of institutions. In the following section we present the syntax and semantics of a language, named FIEVeL (*F*unctions for *I*nstitutionalized *E*nvironments *V*erification *L*anguage), which allows to model institutions in terms of the concepts formalized in the previous section. After having presented our conceptual framework, we exemplify our approach by introducing a formalization of the *Chaired Meeting Institution* inspired by the one proposed in (Jonker, Schut, Treur, & Yolum, 2005), and which is verified in the following section, where we depict a tool developed to apply model-checking techniques to verify organizations ruled by institutions. Finally, we draw some conclusions and present some directions for future works.

BACKGROUND

Organizational concepts like norms, roles, etc. have been proposed to *model* and *regulate* interactions in open multiagent systems where autonomous agents can decide to deviate from their expected behavior. Several frameworks have been developed to enforce rules defined by institutions at runtime, but only little attention has been devoted to the verification of such rules. In this section we will present an overview of the main proposals to model and verify norms, comparing in particular the expressiveness of the proposed *normative languages*.

Esteva et al. (2001) presented a graphical notation to model institutions as labeled transition systems, where two types of norms are distinguished: (i) *performative structures*, which represent permitted communicative acts and are modeled as finite state machines, and (ii) *normative rules*, which represent obligations activated by the performance of certain acts and are expressed through conditional rules. One of the main advantages of this language resides in the fact that designers have at their disposal a tool for editing institutions (Esteva, de la Cruz, & Sierra, 2002) and another tool to enact and automatically monitor agent interactions (Esteva, Rodríguez-Aguilar, Rosell, & Arcos, 2004). To verify such systems, in (Huget, Esteva, Phelps, Sierra, & Wooldridge, 2002) and (Cliffe & Padget, 2002) the authors described two syntactic translations of institutions into languages amenable to model checking. For instance, in (Huget, Esteva, Phelps, Sierra, & Wooldridge, 2002) an institution is translated into a MABLE agent (Wooldridge, Huget, Fisher, & Parsons, 2006), but, since the meaning of labels is not clear from the notation only (Vasconcelos, 2003), both approaches allow designers to define and verify only properties regarding the syntactic structure of an institution. Moreover, the translation presented in (Huget, Esteva, Phelps, Sierra, & Wooldridge, 2002) treats the performative structure (which represents permissions) as defining obligations that are always fulfilled by agents. As a consequence, the model checker may answer that a certain property holds when it is not the case and vice versa.

To increase the expressiveness of normative constructs described in (Esteva, Rodríguez-Aguilar, Sierra, García, & Arcos, 2001), García-Camino et al. (2005) extended the normative language proposed in (Vázquez-Salceda, Aldewereld, & Dignum, 2005) and provided an implementation to detect violations within the AMELI framework (Esteva, Rodríguez-Aguilar, Rosell, & Arcos, 2004). On the on hand, the normative language proposed in (García-Camino, Noriega, & Rodríguez-Aguilar, 2005) provides high level constructs to represent certain recurrent patterns of conditional norms, on the other hand temporal operators cannot be nested. For this reason, in (García-Camino, Rodríguez-Aguilar, Sierra,

& Vasconcelos, 2006) the authors defined a machine language to model norms, which is characterized by a greater expressiveness and flexibility.

The definition of normative languages suitable for the synthesis of runtime monitors of agent interactions has received a considerable attention in the context of institutions. Fornara et al. (2007) proposed a framework to model norms and constitutive rules defined by institutions where commitments are used to model both the semantics of communicative acts and norms, providing a unified model for reasoning about effects of agent communication and norms. In particular, in (Fornara, Viganò, & Colombetti, 2007) norms have been described as rules fired by events and which create commitments for agents when certain conditions are met. The notation proposed in (Fornara, Viganò, & Colombetti, 2007) is based on an intuitive semantics of institutional concepts, which does not suffice for the development of a framework to verify agent behavior.

In Yolum and Singh (2004) communicative acts of agents create commitments whose temporal evolution is modeled through axioms of the Event Calculus (Kowalski & Sergot, 1986), which is exploited to reason about runs compatible with commitments. As in (Carabelea & Boissier, 2006), the content of commitments is expressed through a fixed structure characterized by an activating condition and the action that the debtor ought to perform once the condition is satisfied. Indeed, as observed in (Cranefield, 2006), more complex situations arise in practical applications and more expressive languages should be provided to designers to model what agents are expected to do. In particular, Cranefield (2006) extended the work on commitments carried out by Verdicchio and Colombetti (2006) and proposed a framework to monitor agent commitments whose content is expressed using the $hyMTL^{\pm}$ logic, a temporal logic characterized by past and future operators defined over time intervals. To our best knowledge, the author has not developed a framework to verify whether commitments are inconsistent and it is possible to satisfy them.

In (Artikis, Kamara, Pitt, & Sergot, 2004) and (Pitt, Kamara, Sergot, & Artikis, 2005) systems regulated by norms (named normative systems) are described by using a formalism inspired by the Event Calculus. As a consequence, designers have at their disposal flexible and expressive constructs to describe norms, but the soundness of norms can be guaranteed only by a series of systematic runs of the system (Pitt, Kamara, Sergot, & Artikis, 2005). The absence of a precise formalization of institutional concepts, which for instance provides an axiom to state that every institutional action must be empowered in order to be successfully executed, obliges the authors to specify this fact for every single action and for every role. Despite the terminology used in this chapter being quite similar the one adopted by Artikis et al. (2004), in (Artikis, Kamara, Pitt, & Sergot, 2004) *physical actions* can be performed only if agents play a specific role, suggesting that such actions are actually institutional. Since the Event Calculus provides only for simulating system descriptions, to investigate properties of such systems in (Artikis, Sergot, & Pitt, 2003) and (Sergot & Craven, 2006) the C+ language (Giunchiglia, Lee, Lifschitz, McCain, & Turner, 2004) has been proposed to model and verify normative systems. In particular, Sergot and Craven (2006) extended C+ with a deontic component capable of classifying states as *green* (compliant) or *red* (a violation has occurred) with respect to the valuation of certain fluents, such that a state may be considered green with respect to certain norms and red with respect to others. Such classification is performed only by considering the current value of fluents, without considering the temporal evolution of the system. To model more complex situations, designers must record the history of the system with *ad hoc* fluent.

In (Cliffe, De Vos, & Padget, 2007) the authors proposed to model institutions through InstAL (*Inst*itution *A*ction *L*anguage), a language whose constructs resemble the ones of the Event Calculus.

The main advantage of InstAL is that answer set programming techniques can be exploited to verify properties of institutions, although only finite time intervals can be considered during the computation of sets compatible with institutional rules. In (Cliffe, De Vos, & Padget, 2007) obligations are modeled in terms of three events, describing what event fulfils or violates them, and what event is generated when a violation is detected. Conditional norms cannot be directly modeled and must be encoded by describing how the occurrence of certain events activates or deactivates obligations. Moreover, according to (Cliffe, De Vos, & Padget, 2007), the semantics of InstAL considers that all acts that are not permitted are prohibited and a permission to perform an act is explicitly modeled as a fluent which may hold even when it is impossible to execute it.

Alberti et al. (2006) proposed to model agent interactions in terms of two concepts, *events* produced by agents and *expectations* over future events. When agents interact, a logic-based tool keeps trace of generated events and checks whether expectations arising from such interactions are satisfied. It seems to us that the notion of expectation is useful to monitor whether a society as a whole is compliant with a specification, but by itself does not allow agents to reason about their expected behaviors. For instance, in the formalization of the English auction presented in (Alberti, Gavanelli, Lamma, Chesani, Mello, & Torroni, 2006), after an agent has bid, the monitoring system expects that either another agent offers a higher price, or the auctioneer declares the winner. Indeed, the former expectation does not mean that participants are obliged to bid, while the latter represents the fact that an auctioneer is obliged to declare that the highest bidder is the winner: therefore, it may be difficult for agents to understand when an expectation actually represents an obligation and which agent has to fulfill it.

In (Jonker, Sharpanskykh, Treur, & Yolum, 2007) the authors described a framework to model and analyze organizations. As in (Jonker, Schut, Treur, & Yolum, 2005), Jonker et al. (2007) model organizations as set of roles characterized by precise interfaces, whose inputs and outputs are formally specified by Temporal Trace Language (TTL) axioms. The adoption of a formal language to model organizations provides the possibility of generating models satisfying TTL axioms and to verify their properties, although such tasks are carried out by assuming that agents always satisfy their specifications. Indeed, as in (Finger, Fisher, & Owens, 1993), in closed systems all agents might be assumed to be reliable, although as observed in (Artikis, Kamara, Pitt, & Sergot, 2004) even the environment may cause the violation of norms. Instead, such assumption seems quite counterintuitive at the time of modeling open systems, like commercial relations existing among organizations as in (Jonker, Sharpanskykh, Treur, & Yolum, 2007). Actually, in (Jonker, Schut, Treur, & Yolum, 2005) a treatment of violations of axioms is presented (which are regarded as exceptions to general interaction rules), although the authors implicitly assume that a rule cannot be indefinitely violated by agents.

Indeed, reasoning about what properties are satisfied by organizations when agents follow their norms is important to evaluate their *functionality* (e.g., they allow agents to fulfill their objectives without violating their obligations and prohibitions), but properties holding when agents are not compliant should also be investigated. To do so, Raimondi and Lomuscio (2007) proposed a tool to model check multiagent systems modeled as *deontic interpreted systems* (Lomuscio & Sergot, 2002) and a specification language characterized by a modal operator which considers only computations compliant with an interaction protocol. The tool described in (Raimondi & Lomuscio, 2007) is very efficient, but its input language does not offer high level constructs to describe under what conditions a violation occurs, whereas it requires designers to explicitly list the set of states that each agent may reach, and to classify them as *red* (an agent violates the protocol) or *green*. This fact is exploited by the tool to efficiently encode the corresponding transition system, but it may become a cumbersome activity when norms are complex. Moreover, although red states are such only because they violate a protocol (Raimondi & Lomuscio, 2007), such classification is not inferred from the protocol but must be manually provided independently of it: therefore designers may introduce discrepancies among the protocol and the classification of states.

In (Agotnes, van der Hoek, Rodríguez-Aguilar, Sierra, & Wooldridge, 2007) the authors proposed *Normative Temporal Logic* (NTL), that is, a generalization of CTL (Emerson & Halpern, 1986) to reason about normative systems. In particular, *NTL* allows designers to investigate time aspects and the role played by each norm to guarantee a certain property. With this respect, out approach is very similar with the one presented in (Agotnes, van der Hoek, Rodríguez-Aguilar, Sierra, & Wooldridge, 2007). The main difference resides in how norms are represented, since while in (Agotnes, van der Hoek, Rodríguez-Aguilar, Sierra, & Wooldridge, 2007) norms are described by manually listing what transitions of the model are considered to be compliant with them, in our approach norms are represented at a high level and the burden of classifying states and transitions is carried out by an automatic translation.

INSTITUTIONAL CONCEPTS

While in (Pitt, Kamara, Sergot, & Artikis, 2005) (Cliffe, De Vos, & Padget, 2007) (Fornara, Viganò, & Colombetti, 2007) institutional states are described and are assumed to exist independently of agent deontic relations (institutionalized powers, obligations, etc.), following Searle (Searle, 1995) we think that, with the exception of those related with the creation of meaning, institutional facts cannot be described or exist without deontic relations. In fact, when an agent modifies or creates a new institutional fact, it is actually modifying some powers, obligations, or prohibitions for another agent or for itself. For instance, when the auctioneer declares a new current price, participants are empowered only to make higher bids.

Institutional facts are built thanks to the ability of agents to collectively impose new statuses, named *status functions,* that is "a *status* to which a *function* is assigned" (Searle, 1995, p. 40). When a new status function is imposed on an agent by a community of agents, it performs certain functions independently of its physical features. Furthermore, status functions become manifest only when they are necessary to perform actions (Searle, 1995): therefore, when agents impose a new status function, they are actually creating new possibilities of action for agents themselves. A typical example of status function is the concept of *owner*, since an agent owns an object not thanks to its own physical features, but only because a community of agents so recognizes. Other examples of status functions are the notion of *president* or *employee*, which have been usually regarded as *roles*. Indeed the concept of status function shares several features with the concept of role (refer to (Boella & van der Torre, 2005) for an overview), but we perceive it to be broader, since its definition does not presuppose a structured preexisting organization. Moreover, the term status function better represents the fact that we are concerned with statuses whose existence depends on those agents that recognize them as existing and which are assigned to agents to create new institutionalized powers or to regulate their use.

Starting from this theory, we model all institutional facts in terms of status functions imposed on agents, which are named *agent status functions*. In particular, we describe agent status functions in terms of deontic relations, which represent what actions are empowered, obliged, forbidden, or permitted for an agent. In doing so, institutional events can be characterized in terms of what status functions are imposed or revoked, which helps to clarify how each institutional event changes agent deontic relations.

We express the semantics of status functions and related institutional concepts in terms of an ordered many-sorted first-order temporal logic (OMSFOTL), that is, is a many-sorted first-order logic (Manzano, 1993) enriched with temporal operators and hierarchies of sorts. The signature of an OMSFOTL logic consists of a finite nonempty set of *sort symbols* Σ, a *hierarchy of sorts* $\leq_\Sigma$ (where $\sigma_1 \leq_\Sigma \sigma_2$ means that sort σ_1 is a *subsort* of sort σ_2), finite sets of *constants* ($\mathcal{C}$), *function symbols* ($\mathcal{F}$), and *predicate symbols* ($\mathcal{P}$), and a denumerable set of *variables* ($\mathcal{V}$). Moreover, an OMSFOTL signature defines function ξ which assigns a sort to every variable and every constant, and a signature (i.e. a sequence of sorts) to every function and predicate symbol. Given sorts Σ, the set $\mathcal{T}_\sigma$ of *terms of sorts* σ is the smallest set such that:

- $v \in \mathcal{T}_\sigma$ if $v \in \mathcal{V}$ and $\xi(v) \leq_\Sigma \sigma$;
- $c \in \mathcal{T}_\sigma$ if $c \in \mathcal{C}$ and $\xi(c) \leq_\Sigma \sigma$;
- $f(t_1, t_2, \cdots, t_n) \in \mathcal{T}_\sigma$ if $f \in \mathcal{F}$, $\xi(t_i) \leq_\Sigma [\xi(f)]_i$ for $1 \leq i \leq n$ and $[\xi(f)]_o \leq_\Sigma \sigma$

where $[\xi(q)]_i$ refers to the i-th sort of the signature of a predicate or function symbol q. The set $\mathcal{T}$ of *terms* is the union of the sets $\mathcal{T}_\sigma$ for all $\sigma \in \Sigma$ and the set $\mathcal{A}$ of *atomic formulae* is the smallest set such that:

- $(t_1 = t_2) \in \mathcal{A}$ if there exists sort σ such that $\xi(t_1) \leq_\Sigma \sigma$ and $\xi(t_2) \leq_\Sigma \sigma$;
- $p(t_1, t_2, \cdots, t_n) \in \mathcal{A}$ if $p \in \mathcal{P}$ and $\xi(t_i) \leq_\Sigma [\xi(p)]_i$ for $1 \leq i \leq n$.

The set of *formulae* is defined according to the following grammar:

$$\varphi ::= \alpha \mid \neg\varphi \mid \varphi \wedge \varphi \mid \forall x \varphi \mid X\varphi \mid \varphi U \varphi \mid E\varphi$$

where α is an atomic formula.

The semantics of OMSFOTL is given with respect to a Kripke structure $M = \langle S, R, S_0, \{D_\sigma\}_{\sigma \in \Sigma}, I \rangle$, where S is a set of *states*, S_0 is a set of *initial states*, R is a *total relation* on S, D_σ is the *domain* of sort σ, and I is an *interpretation function* that maps for each state $s \in S$:

- every constant c of sort σ onto an element $I(c,s) \in D_\sigma$ and $I(c, s_1) = I(c, s_2)$ for each $s_1, s_2 \in S$;
- every function symbol f of signature $\langle \sigma, \sigma_1, ..., \sigma_n \rangle$ onto a function $I(f, s): D_{\sigma_1} \times \cdots \times D_{\sigma_n} \to D_\sigma$;
- every predicate symbol p of signature $\langle \sigma_1, ..., \sigma_n \rangle$ onto a function $I(p, s): D_{\sigma_1} \times \cdots \times D_{\sigma_n} \to \{0,1\}$;

An *assignment* of values to variables is a function val that assigns an element $val(x)$ to every variable. Assignment val' is an x-*variant* of assignment val (in symbols $val' \approx_x val$) if $val'(x) = val(x)$ for every variable distinct from x. Given model M, an assignment val, and a state $s \in S$, the denotation $den(t, s)$ of a term t at state s is defined as follows:

- $den(v, s) = val(v)$ for every variable v ;
- $den(c, s) = I(c, s)$ for every constant c ;
- $den(f(t_1, ..., t_n), s) = I(f, s)(den(t_1, s), ..., den(t_n, s))$ for every functional term $f(t_1, ..., t_n)$.

Following (Emerson & Halpern, 1986), we define the semantics of formulae containing temporal operators with respect to infinite sequences of states $s_0, s_1, s_2, \cdots$. In the sequel we use π_k to denote the k -th state of path π and π^k for the suffix of path π starting at state π_k . Given a model M , assignment val and a formula φ , we say that φ is *true* in a model M under valuation val and over a path π in M $(M, val, \pi \vDash \varphi)$ when:

- $M, val, \pi \vDash (t_1 = t_2)$ iff $den(t_1, \pi_0) = den(t_2, \pi_0)$;
- $M, val, \pi \vDash p(t_1, \dots, t_n)$ iff $I(p, \pi_0)(den(t_1, \pi_0), \dots, den(t_n, \pi_0)) = 1$;
- $M, val, \pi \vDash \neg\varphi$ iff $M, val, \pi \nvDash \varphi$;
- $M, val, \pi \vDash \varphi \wedge \psi$ iff $M, val, \pi \vDash \varphi$ and $M, val, \pi \vDash \psi$;
- $M, val, \pi \vDash \forall x\varphi$ iff $M, val', \pi \vDash \varphi$ for every $val' \approx_x val$;
- $M, val, \pi \vDash X\varphi$ iff $M, val, \pi^1 \vDash \varphi$;
- $M, val, \pi \vDash \varphi U\psi$ iff there exists an $i \geq 0$ such that $M, val, \pi^i \vDash \psi$ and for all $i > j \geq 0$ $M, \pi^j \vDash \varphi$;
- $M, val, \pi \vDash E\varphi$ iff there exists path π' such that $\pi_0 = \pi'_0$ and $M, val, \pi' \vDash \varphi$.

Expressions *true, false*, $(\varphi \vee \varphi)$, $(\varphi \rightarrow \varphi)$, $(\varphi \leftrightarrow \varphi)$, and $(\exists x\varphi)$ are defined in terms of $\neg$, $\wedge$, and $\forall$ in the conventional manner, and temporal operators F , G , R , and the path quantifier A are introduced as abbreviations as usual (Clarke, Grumberg, & Peled, 1999) to state that eventually φ holds ($F\varphi \equiv trueU\varphi$), φ is satisfied by all states of a path ($G\varphi \equiv \neg F\neg\varphi$), φ releases ψ ($\varphi R\psi \equiv \neg(\neg\varphi U\neg\psi)$), and that all paths satisfy φ ($A\varphi \equiv (E(\varphi$).

An OMSFOTL logic has the same expressive power of a temporal first-order logic (Abadi, 1989) and, assuming that each sort σ is associated to a finite domain, it is equivalent to CTL^* (Emerson & Halpern, 1986), since its models can be encoded with a finite number of atomic propositions. Despite that, we adopt OMSFOTL for two main reasons: (i) it represents an abbreviated form for long and complex formulae and (ii) institutions describe rules that typically are independent of the cardinality of domains and which can be naturally expressed by allowing quantification over sorts. In particular, we use OMSFOTL to provide a precise formalization of institutional concepts and to define the semantics of FIEVeL, not to prove properties of models. Instead, as we shall explain in the following sections, properties of our models are verified by applying model checking techniques developed for propositional logic (Clarke, Grumberg, & Peled, 1999). With this respect, the adoption of OMSFOTL allows us to automatically generate different models, to check what properties are verified by them and, since also properties are expressed through OMSFOTL formulae, to verify the very same property over different models.

In the remainder of this section we explain what sorts, functions, and predicates are introduced to represent institutional concepts. For instance, the notion of agent status function induces sort σ_{sf} and the function $subject$ ($\xi(subject) = \langle\sigma_{aid}, \sigma_{sf}\rangle$), which denotes the agent (σ_{aid}) the status function has been assigned to. A status function may be currently $assigned$ or *revoked* ($\xi(assigned) = \langle\sigma_{sf}\rangle$), reflecting the fact that an agent acquires or loses certain deontic relations. Status functions are *modified* ($\xi(modified) = \langle\sigma_{sf}\rangle$) when certain institutional events happen, otherwise they continue to be assigned (unassigned) to the same agent:

$$AG\forall f\big(\neg Xmodified(f) \rightarrow (assigned(f) \leftrightarrow Xassigned(f))\big) \qquad \text{(A. 1)}$$

$$AG\forall f\big(\neg Xmodified(f) \rightarrow \exists a(subject(f) = a \leftrightarrow Xsubject(f) = a)\big) \qquad (A.\,2)$$

where $\xi(f) = \sigma_{sf}$.

In our framework, status functions are regarded as possibly empty aggregates of deontic relations that can be expressed in terms of two main concepts, *institutionalized powers* (Jones & Sergot, 1996) and *norms*. As we will see, we represent powers as necessary conditions for the performance of institutional actions, while norms are regarded as temporal formulae which classify states. In particular, we assume that the compliance of agents with norms is detected with a strategy similar to the one presented in (Cranefield, 2006): as a consequence, each norm induces a set of monitors, whose states represent a set of (negated) atomic formulae that should be satisfied by the current state and a set of temporal formulae that should be satisfied by future states. As in (Cranefield, 2006), monitors decide whether an OMSFOTL formula is satisfied only by considering a *finite trace*: therefore, they assume that a formula is *true*, if any path characterized by such prefix satisfies the formula, *false* if there is no path that may satisfy it, or *undefined* if there are paths that satisfy or violate it.

It is worth observing that if norms are monitored by automata considering only finite traces, eventualities (e.g., $F\varphi$ or $\theta U\varphi$) are regarded with a semantics which is slightly different than the one presented above. The main difference resides in the fact that the satisfaction of temporal operator U requires that formula φ eventually holds. Instead, our monitors may infinitely wait for the occurrence of φ . This fact may be problematic, since, for instance, an unsatisfiable formula like $(F\varphi \wedge G\neg\varphi)$ is indefinitely monitored without detecting that it is equivalent to *false*. Other approaches like (Finger, Fisher, & Owens, 1993) and (Jonker, Schut, Treur, & Yolum, 2005) solved this problem by imposing a policy to agents which obliges them to satisfy a formula as soon as possible, such that a contradiction is detected if the satisfaction of a formula is indefinitely postponed. It seems to us that such solution can be hardly applied to model an *open* multiagent system, since it would be equivalent to represent a system where agents are no longer autonomous (they cannot violate norms). Similarly, the representation of norms as Büchi automata (Clarke, Grumberg, & Peled, 1999), as traditionally done in model checking to represent LTL formulae (Daniele, Giunchiglia, & Vardi, 1999), would be equivalent to introduce assumptions on the behavior of agents, which in general may not reflect how agents really behave. For this reason, despite the mentioned problems, we think that our approach better reflects what may happen in an open system.

To model norms, we introduce sort σ_o , whose individuals represent a set of *monitors* of temporal formulae, and which is characterized by the predicate $violated$ $(\xi(violated) = \{\sigma_o\})$. Moreover, given sort σ_{state}, which introduces constants $initial$, $violation$, and $inactive$ $(\xi(inactive) = \{\sigma_{state}\})$, sort σ_o also defines the function $state$ $(\xi(state) = \{\sigma_{state}, \sigma_o\})$, which keeps trace of the temporal evolution of a monitor. Agents are subject to norms when certain status functions are imposed on them: as a consequence, when a violation occurs the $subject$ of the status is considered to be the *violator*. To model the interdependency among monitors and status functions, we introduce function $ofStatus$ $(\xi(ofStatus) = \{\sigma_{sf}, \sigma_o\})$, which denotes the status function a monitor is associated to. A monitor of a norm ω characterized by a temporal formula φ_ω starts to check whether φ_ω is satisfied when the associated status function is assigned to an agent (state $initial$):

$$AG\forall o\forall f\big((ofStatus(o) = f \wedge assigned(f) \wedge modified(f)) \rightarrow state(o) = initial\big) \qquad (A.\,3)$$

where $\xi(o) = \sigma_o$ and $\xi(f) = \sigma_{sf}$. Since then, if formula φ_ω is satisfied, then the norm is considered to be fulfilled and the monitoring process is interrupted (state *inactive*). Instead, if formula φ_ω cannot be satisfied by any possible evolution of the institution, a violation is detected (state *violation*). Otherwise, the monitoring process of formula φ_ω is continued. Moreover, monitors are considered to be *inactive* also when a status function is not assigned:

$$AG\forall o\forall f\left((ofStatus(o) = f \wedge \neg assigned(f)) \rightarrow state(o) = inactive\right) \tag{A.4}$$

Finally, we impose that a monitor detects a violation (predicate *violated* is *true*) if and only if state *violation* is reached:

$$AG\forall o(violated(o) \leftrightarrow state(o) = violation) \tag{A.5}$$

An institution and its physical environment evolve because events (σ_{ev}) occur or agents perform actions ($\sigma_{act} \leq_\Sigma \sigma_{ev}$). In open environments, agents are characterized by heterogeneous architectures: as a consequence, we regard agents as generators of events labeled with the identifier of the agent that has performed it (the *actor*). Each event type e induces a sort σ_e, three predicates, $happens_e$, $prec_e$, and eff_e, which express if an event of type e happens, and what conditions must be satisfied before and after its occurrence. Following (Searle, 1995), we classify events into two different sorts: *base-level events* (σ_{be}), like *time* events and *exchange-message* events, and *institutional events* (σ_{ie}), like the 18th birthday and the act of transferring the ownership. Base-level events reflect changes that are produced in the physical world or that are relative to lower level institutions. We do not name these kinds of events "physical" because, strictly speaking, most events are somehow dependent on language and therefore institutional (Searle, 1995). Despite that, in most cases the deontic relations we want to model are not affected by the institutional nature of those events, and therefore we can ignore it. Instead, institutional events modify institutional reality by imposing or revoking status functions and occur only because a community of agents recognizes their effects. As a consequence, they cannot be directly produced by the environment or by an agent. Following (Searle, 1995) the occurrence of an institutional event is subordinated to the occurrence of another event conventionally associated to it. More precisely, an institutional event *ie* that is not an action occurs if and only if its preconditions are satisfied and an event conventionally related to it happens:

$$AG\forall \bar{x}\left(\left(prec_{ie}(\bar{x}) \wedge \bigvee_{e \in \sigma_{ev}} Xconv_{e-ie}(\bar{x})\right) \leftrightarrow Xhappens_{ie}(\bar{x})\right) \tag{A.6}$$

where predicate $conv_{e-ie}$ represents the existence of a convention among event e and institutional event ie, and $\bar{x}$ is a set of variables determined by the signature of predicate $happens_{ie}$. Instead, in the case of institutional actions ($\sigma_{ia} \leq_\Sigma \sigma_{ie}$) a further condition must be satisfied, namely, the actor must be empowered to perform the institutional action ia:

$$\tag{A.7}$$

$$AG\forall \bar{x}\left(\left(prec_{ia}(\bar{x}) \wedge \bigvee_{\sigma_f \leq_\Sigma \sigma_{sf}} \exists s\left(subject(s) = actor \wedge empowered_{ia-\sigma_f}(s, \bar{x}) \wedge assigned(s)\right) \wedge \bigvee_{a \in \sigma_{act}} Xconv_{a-ia}(\bar{x})\right) \leftrightarrow Xhappens_{ia}(\bar{x})\right)$$

where $\bar{x}$ contains variable $actor$ referring to the actor of action ia and predicate $empowered_{ia-\sigma_f}$ reflects the fact that status functions s of sort σ_f may be conditionally empowered to perform institutional action ia. Finally, all types of events are characterized by the following axiom:

$$AG\forall\bar{x}\big(Xhappens_e(\bar{x}) \rightarrow eff_e(\bar{x})\big) \tag{A. 8}$$

which states that if an event occurs, its effects take place.

MODELING INSTITUTIONS WITH FIEVeL

In this section, we shall present FIEVeL (*F*unctions for *I*nstitutionalized *E*nvironments *V*erification *L*anguage), a language to model institutions in terms of the concepts introduced in the previous section, and whose semantics is given by explaining what OMSFOTL symbols and axioms are induced by each construct. For the sake of brevity, we limit our presentation to the constructs that are necessary to understand the example reported in this chapter, omitting, for instance, the treatment of sanctions. As we can observe in Figure 1, a FIEVeL model is composed by three main sections, namely *basic-sort definition*, *base-event definition*, and *institution definition*.

Basic Sorts

To model agent identifiers, FIEVeL assumes the existence of a basic sort, σ_{aid}. Analogously, designers can introduce new basic sorts to abstract certain features of an interaction domain (e.g., values that agents can offer, questions that they may ask, etc.). Basic sorts are declared according to the following grammar:

```
basic-sort  ::= symbol ("=" "{" element (","element)* "}")?;
```

Each basic-sort clause induces a sort σ_{symbol} and optionally enumerates the elements belonging to it, such that each element clause introduces a constant symbol $element$ of sort σ_{symbol} and an individual in its domain D_{symbol}.

Base-Level Events

In this chapter we will focus on a single type of event, namely *messages*, which are assumed to be sent by an agent (the *actor*) over a reliable communication channel. FIEVeL models messages as constituted by a *message type* and a (possibly empty) set of *arguments* as follows:

```
message     ::= "message" msg-type "(" signature? ")";
signature   ::= (argument ("," argument)*);
argument    ::= name ":" sort;
```

where msg-type is a symbol. Each message clause induces a sort $\sigma_{msg-type}$ ($\sigma_{msg-type} \leq_{\Sigma} \sigma_{be}$) and three predicates, $happens_{msg-type}$, $prec_{msg-type}$, and $eff_{msg-type}$, whose signature is determined by the `signature` clause. In particular, all messages are characterized by an additional argument of sort σ_{aid} representing the *sender* of the message, and we assume that predicates $prec_{msg-type}$ and $eff_{msg-type}$ are always evaluated to *true*, i.e. messages can always be sent and they do not affect the environment.

Institutions

Institutions define three main concepts: (i), *status functions*, which describe powers and norms assigned to agents; (ii), *institutional events*, i.e. events that change statuses modifying agent deontic relations; and (iii), *conventions*, which describe what events may count-as certain institutional events. For this reason, a FIEVeL institution is modeled according to the following grammar:

```
institution ::= "institution" symbol "{" status⁺ inst-events conventions "}";
```

such that each status function is characterized by a set of attributes, powers, and norms as follows:

```
status    ::= "status-function" status-id "(" (function ("," function)*)? ")"
"{"

             key? powers? norms? "}";
function ::= name ":" sort;
key       ::= "key" symbol ("," symbol)*;
```

where `status-id`, `name`, and `sort` are symbols. Each `status` clause induces a subsort of sort σ_{sf} ($\sigma_{status-id} \leq_{\Sigma} \sigma_{sf}$) and a set of functions, where each function f_{name} of sort σ_{sort} has signature $\xi(f_{name}) = \langle \sigma_{sort}, \sigma_{status-id} \rangle$. By default, FIEVeL assumes that each sort $\sigma_{status-id}$ is characterized by a single individual, unless designers have defined a `key` clause. A key is constituted by a set of functions, whose values, like the *primary key* in relational databases, uniquely indentify individuals of sort $\sigma_{status-id}$:

$$AG\forall s_1 \forall s_2 \left(\left(\bigwedge_{f \in Key(\sigma_{status-id})} f(s_1) = f(s_2) \right) \to s_1 = s_2 \right) \tag{A.9}$$

where $\xi(s_1) = \xi(s_2) = \sigma_{status-id}$. Moreover, the set of key functions are assumed to be constant, while all other functions may change when a status is modified by an institutional event. Otherwise they refer to the same individual as required by the axiom

$$AG\forall s \left(\neg Xmodified(s) \to \bigwedge_{function \in NotKey(\sigma_{status-id})} \exists x (function(s) = x \leftrightarrow Xfunction(s) = x) \right) \tag{A.10}$$

where $\xi(s) = \sigma_{status-id}$ and $\xi(x) = \xi(function)$ for each function not belonging to the key. A status function $\sigma_{status-id}$ may be also characterized by a (possibly empty) set of institutionalized powers, which are modeled as follows:

```
power ::= ia "<-" expression ";";
```

where `ia` is a symbol referring to an institutional action and `expression` is an OMSFOTL formula such that: (i) it does not contain temporal operators; (ii) it may contain unbounded occurrences of a variable f of sort $\sigma_{status-id}$; and (iii) unbounded occurrences of variables $\bar{x}$ referring to arguments declared by institutional action ia (see below) may occur. Each `power` clause induces a predicate $empowered_{\sigma_{status-id}-ia}$ defined as follows:

$$\textbf{AG}\forall f\forall \bar{x}\left(empowered_{\sigma_{status-id}-ia}(f,\bar{x}) \leftrightarrow \textbf{expression}\right) \tag{A. 11}$$

where $\xi(f) = \sigma_{status-id}$ and sorts of variables $\bar{x}$ are determined by institutional action ia. Instead, if a status $\sigma_{status-id}$ does not explicitly defines a power for an institutional action ia, then predicate $empowered_{\sigma_{status-id}-ia}$ is assumed to be equivalent to $false$, that is, the status does not empower the agent to execute an action of type ia.

Similarly to powers, norms are associated to status functions according to the following syntax:

```
norm ::= norm-id ":" expression ";";
```

where `norm-id` is a symbol, and `expression` is an OMSFOTL formula where temporal operators and unbounded occurrences of a variable f of sort $\sigma_{status-id}$ may appear. Each `norm` clause induces a sort $\sigma_{norm-id}$ subsort of sort σ_o ($\sigma_{norm-id} \leq_\Sigma \sigma_o$) such that for each individual i of sort $\sigma_{status-id}$ there exists an individual $m_{norm-id,i}$ of sort $\sigma_{norm-id}$.

Given a norm ω characterized by formula φ_ω and associated to an individual i, let $\varphi_{\omega,i}$ be the corresponding formula obtained by substituting unbounded occurrences of variable f with i. Let $N_{\varphi_{\omega,i}} = \langle Q, I, \delta, q_0, F \rangle$ be a *deterministic finite automaton* which recognizes prefixes compatible with formula $\varphi_{\omega,i}$, where Q is a finite set of *states*, I is a set of *formulae*, $\delta: Q \times I \to Q$ is a *transition function*, $q_0 \in Q$ is an *initial state*, and F is a set of *final states*. Automaton $N_{\varphi_{\omega,i}}$ induces a set of axioms constraining how a monitor $m_{\omega,i}$ evolves when certain states of affairs are reached and the associated status function i is assigned and not modified, such that given any two states $q_1, q_2 \in Q$ and a formula φ_k, if $(q_1, \varphi_k, q_2) \in \delta$ then the Axiom Schema is induced

$$\textbf{AG}\left(\left(state(m_{\omega,i}) = q_1 \wedge X(\varphi_k \wedge \neg modified(i) \wedge assigned(i))\right) \to Xstate(m_{\omega,i}) = q_2\right) \tag{A.12}$$

where $m_{\omega,i}$ is a monitor of sort σ_ω. Moreover, states Q affect sort σ_{state} such that each state $q \in Q$ of automaton $N_{\varphi_{\omega,i}}$ is conveniently mapped over individuals of sort σ_{state}. To reduce the number of reachable states of the system, we impose further restrictions on the behavior of each automaton $N_{\varphi_{\omega,i}}$ (here represented as axioms), such that: (i), if a monitor has reached the *inactive* state, then it does not change until the associated status is modified:

$$\textbf{AG}\left(\left(state(m_{\omega,i}) = inactive \wedge X(\neg modified(i) \wedge assigned(i))\right) \to Xstate(m_{\omega,i}) = inactive\right) \tag{A.13}$$

and (ii), after a violation is detected, a monitor goes to state *inactive*:

$$\textbf{AG}\left(\left(state(m_{\omega,i}) = violation \wedge X(\neg modified(i) \wedge assigned(i))\right) \to Xstate(m_{\omega,i}) = inactive\right) \tag{A.14}$$

which means that once a violation is detected, monitor $m_{\omega,i}$ stops its activity until status i is assigned by the occurrence of an institutional event. Intuitively, FIEVeL allows designers to model obligations and prohibitions of agents, while it does not define any construct to explicitly represent that an agent is permitted to perform an action as, for instance, in (Pitt, Kamara, Sergot, & Artikis, 2005) or (Vázquez-Salceda, Aldewereld, & Dignum, 2005). Instead, we consider that a certain state of affairs φ is permitted if it can be reached without violating any norm.

As discussed in the previous section, institutional events modify deontic relations of agents by imposing or revoking status functions. To describe the signature of institutional events, their preconditions, and their effects, FIEVeL provides the following syntax:

```
inst-event     ::= type id "(" signature? ")" precondition "eff" post (","
post)*;
type           ::= "institutional-event" | "institutional-action";
precondition ::= "pre" expression ";"
post           ::= (selection "-X->")? effects;
selection      ::= var+ "(" expression ")";
effects        ::= var modify "[" (term "=" term (","  term "=" term)* )? "]";
modify         ::= "assign" | "revoke";
```

where `id` is a symbol and `post` is constituted by (i) an (optional) *selection expression* and (ii) an expression describing what statuses are assigned or revoked when the institutional event happens. As we will see, effects hold when an event occurs, while the selection expression is evaluated in the previous state: for this reason, we separate the selection expression from the effects through symbol -X->. Each `inst-event` clause induces a sort σ_{id} either subsort of σ_{ie} (`institutional-event`) or σ_{ia} (`institutional-action`), and three predicates $happens_{id}$, $prec_{id}$, and eff_{id}, whose signature is determined by the `signature` clause. As messages, also institutional actions are characterized by an additional argument, which represents the *actor* of the action. As we have seen, given an institutional event or an institutional action, Axioms (A. 6) and (A. 7) regulate when predicate $happens_{id}$ evaluates to *true*, while predicate $prec_{id}$ is constrained by clause `precondition` as follows:

$$AG\forall\bar{x}(\ prec_{id}(\bar{x}) \leftrightarrow \textbf{expression}) \tag{A. 15}$$

where $\bar{x}$ represents variables determined by the `signature` clause and `expression` is an OMS-FOTL formula which does not contain temporal operators. Institutional events differ from base-level events because their occurrence modifies powers and norms of agents, which means that they modify status functions imposed on them. The effects of an institutional event are described by the following axiom:

$$AG\forall\bar{x}\left(\ eff_{id}(\bar{x}) \leftrightarrow \bigwedge_{i=1}^{Post(id)} post_{id-i}(\bar{x})\right) \tag{A. 16}$$

such that each `post` clause introduces the definition:

$$AG\forall\bar{x}\left(\ (post_{id-i}(\bar{x})\right.$$

$$\left.\leftrightarrow\forall\bar{s}_i\left(\ \text{expression}\rightarrow\exists t_i X\left(\ [\neg]assigned(t_i)\wedge modified(t_i)\wedge\bigwedge_{l=1}^{L} term_{l,1}=term_{l,2}\right)\right)\right)$$

(A.17)

where $\bar{s}_i$ is a set of variables defined by the selection expression and t_i represents status functions that will be assigned or revoked. Notice that if a `post` clause does not define any *selection expression*, `selection` is assumed to be equivalent to *true* .

Axioms (A. 5), (A. 7), (A. 8), and (A. 16) highlight the main difference between the absence of permission, due to the existence of a prohibition, and the absence of institutionalized power: if an agent is prohibited to perform institutional action ia but performs it anyway, the effects of the action take place and the obligation not to perform the action is violated; on the contrary, if the agent is not empowered, institutional action ia cannot happen and its effects will not take place. As observed in (Viganò, Fornara, & Colombetti, 2006), within a single institution it is always possible to regulate the performance of an institutional action either by revoking powers or by creating prohibitions. Instead, a base-level action can only be regulated by defining prohibitions to not execute it, unless we can modify the environment in such a way that it becomes impossible to perform it. Moreover, Axioms (A. 16) and (A. 17) allow us to define under what conditions a status function is *modified*. In particular, a status f is *affected* by an institutional event e if it satisfies the selection expression and all assignments of a post expression as required by the axiom

$$AG\forall f\forall\bar{x}\left(\ Xaffected_e(f,\bar{x})\leftrightarrow\bigvee_{i=1}^{Post(e)}\forall\bar{s}_i\left(\ \mathbf{expression}_i\wedge\exists t_i\left(t_i=f\wedge X\bigwedge_{l=1}^{L}term_{i_{l,1}}=term_{i_{l,2}}\right)\right)\right)$$ (A.18)

where $\xi(f)=\sigma_{sf}$, variables $\bar{x}$ are induced by the signature of institutional event e , and variables $\bar{s}_i$ and t_i are determined by the i -th post expression. As a consequence, a status function f is modified if and only if an institutional event e occurs and affects it:

$$AG\forall f\left(\ modified(f)\leftrightarrow\left(\bigvee_{e\in\sigma_{ie}}\exists\bar{x}_e X(happens_e(\bar{x}_e)\wedge affected_e(f,\bar{x}_e))\right)\right)$$ (A.19)

In our framework, conventions are regarded as relations existing among types of events, such that the occurrence of an event of type x may count-as the occurrence of an institutional event of type y. In FIEVeL such relation is specified according to the following grammar:

```
convention   ::= event-x "[" expression "]" "=c=>" event-y "[" conv-vars "]";
conv-vars    ::= (symbol "=c=>" symbol)*;
```

where both `event-x` and `event-y` are defined as symbols. Each `convention` clause induces a new predicate $conv_{ev_x-ev_y}$, whose signature is equal to the signature of the institutional event ev_y

Figure 1. Fragments of the Chaired Meeting Institution coded in FIEVeL

```
1   basic-sorts
2     item;
3     question;
4     pstate={yes,not};
5     ...
6   base-events
7     message endMsg(r:aid);
8     message askMsg(q:question,r:aid);
9     ...
10  institution meeting {
11    status-function chair(){
12      powers openMeeting <- true;
13    }// chair
14    status-function inmeeeting(){
15      powers closeMeeting <- ¬∃c(assigned(c));
16             openItem <- ¬∃c(assigned(c));
17    }//inmeeting
18    status-function participant(speaker:pstate){
19      key subject;
20    }//participant
21    status-function current(it: σitem){
22      powers ask <- ∃p(assigned(p)∧subject(p)=ag);
23             end <- ∃p(assigned(p)∧subject(p)=ag∧speaker(p)=yes);
24             closeItem <- ¬∃p(assigned(p)∧speaker(p)=yes);
25    }// current
26    institutional-events
27      institutional-action ask(q:question,r:aid)
28        pre ¬∃p(assigned(p)∧speaker(p)=yes);
29        eff p assign [subject(p)=ag,speaker(p)=yes];
30      institutional-action end(r:aid)
31        pre true;
32        eff p assign [subject(p)=ag,speaker(p)=not];
33    ...
34    conventions
35      askMsg[true]=c=>ask[r=c=>r q=c=>q];
36      endMsg[true]=c=>end[r=c=>r];
37    ...
38  }
```

where $\xi(c) = \sigma_{current}$ and $\xi(p) = \sigma_{participant}$.

$(\xi\left(conv_{ev_x-ev_y}\right) = \xi\left(happens_{ev_y}\right))$ and which is satisfied when an event of type ev_x occurs and when expression is satisfied, as required by the axiom

$$AG\, \forall \bar{y}\left(Xconv_{ev_x-ev_y}(\bar{y}) \leftrightarrow \exists \bar{x}\left(\bigwedge_{y \in \bar{y}} y = x_i \wedge \textbf{expression} \wedge X\, happens_{ev_x}(\bar{x}) \right) \right) \qquad (A.20)$$

where $\bar{y}$ represents a set of variables whose names and sorts are determined by event ev_y, $\bar{x}$ stands for a set of variables determined by event ev_x, and variables $\bar{y}$ are compared with variables $\bar{x}$ according to the relations defined by the conv-vars clause. While in (Fornara, Viganò, & Colombetti, 2007) only the act of exchanging messages play the role of conventional event *x*, FIEVeL considers that any base-level event or institutional event can be used as a conventional event. For instance, in an auction a round of offers may be closed by the expiration of a deadline, and the declaration of the winner (an institutional act) may count-as the act of closing an auction.

THE CHAIRED MEETING INSTITUTION

To exemplify the syntax and semantics of FIEVeL, in this section we formalize the rules regulating a *chaired meeting*, that is, a meeting during which *participants* talk only when they are explicitly permitted by a *chair*. Our formalization is inspired by the one presented in (Jonker, Schut, Treur, & Yolum, 2005), although in this chapter we will focus only on aspects regulating how participants are requested to intervene into the discussion, which also means that they are permitted to talk. For this reason, we assume that a meeting is characterized by a fixed *agenda* (i.e., a set of *items* that should be debated), and agents cannot propose to consider new items. In the remainder of this section, we first present the constitutive rules of the Chaired Meeting Institution and subsequently we introduce norms regulating agent actions.

Figure 1 reports our formalization of the Chaired Meeting Institution, where status functions, institutional actions, and conventions necessary to carry out a meeting have been defined. First of all, lines 2-3 define sorts σ_{item} and $\sigma_{question}$, which respectively represent the set of items that will be discussed and questions that can be asked during the meeting. Moreover, line 4 introduces sort σ_{pstate} to represent whether a participant is the designated speaker. To model what events are relevant for the enactment of a meeting, we introduce several message types, which induce certain predicates as explained above. For instance, message *endMsg* induces predicate $happens_{endMsg}$ of signature $\xi(happens_{endMsg}) = \langle \sigma_{aid}, \sigma_{aid} \rangle$, representing the fact that an agent sends a message of type *endMsg* to another agent.

A meeting is opened by the *chair*, which is always empowered to do so (line 12). When a meeting is opened, the status function *inmeeting* is assigned to the chair such that, if no item is currently debated, it can start the discussion regarding a specific topic or close the meeting. During the discussion of an item, the chair manages the meeting thanks to the powers provided by status function *current*, characterized by the function *it* denoting the current item ($\xi(it) = \langle \sigma_{item}, \sigma_{current} \rangle$). In particular, status function *current* empowers the chair to ask questions to participants, to assign or revoke the status of being the designated speaker, and finally to declare closed the ongoing debate (lines 22-24).

Moreover, the Chaired Meeting Institution defines a set of institutional actions and a set of conventions for executing them. For instance, to assign the status of being the designated speaker to a participant, the chair is empowered to perform institutional action *ask*, which is conventionally performed by exchanging a message of type *askMsg* (see line 35). Analogously, the chair can revoke the status of being the current speaker by executing institutional action *end*. By combining powers, conventions, preconditions, and effects of institutional actions, we obtain the following axioms, stating that an agent successfully performs institutional action *ask* only if (i) status function *current* is assigned to it, (ii) it sends a message of type *askMsg* to a participant, and (iii) no agent is the designated speaker

$$AG \forall a \forall r \forall q \left(X happens_{ask}(a, r, q) \right.$$
$$\leftrightarrow \left(X happens_{askMsg}(a, r, q) \right. \tag{A.21}$$
$$\wedge \exists c \left(assigned(c) \wedge subject(c) \right.$$
$$\left. = a \wedge \exists p (assigned(p) \wedge subject(p) = r) \wedge \neg \exists p (assigned(p) \wedge speaker(p) = yes) \right) \Big) \Big)$$

which is obtained by combining (and simplifying) Axioms (A. 7), (A. 15), and (A. 20), and where $\xi(a) = \xi(r) = \sigma_{aid}, \xi(q) = \sigma_{question}, \xi(c) = \sigma_{current}$, and $\xi(p) = \sigma_{participant}$. Similarly, from

Axioms (A. 8), (A. 16), and (A. 17) we obtain that the institutional effects of act *ask*, which assigns the status of being the speaker to a participant, are expressed by the formula

$$\textbf{AG}\forall a \forall r \forall q (\textbf{X} happens_{ask}(a, r, q) \rightarrow \exists p \textbf{X}(subject(p) = r \rightarrow (speaker(p) = yes \wedge assigned(p) \wedge modified(p))))$$

(A.22)

where $\xi(a) = \xi(r) = \sigma_{aid}$, $\xi(q) = \sigma_{question}$, $\xi(c) = \sigma_{current}$, and $\xi(p) = \sigma_{participant}$.

For the sake of presentation, in Figure 1 we have reported only constitutive rules of the Chaired Meeting Institution, which define possible actions that agents can carry out, but do not ensure that empowered agents will necessarily perform them. To represent norms associated to statuses, in this section we will adopt the notation $O(n, c, \varphi)$, which stands for the FIEVeL constructs to represent that a norm n is associated to status c such that φ holds. Moreover, for the sake of convenience, we introduce the temporal operator $\textbf{B}(\varphi, t)$, which is satisfied if formula φ holds before t time events occur and is recursively defined as follows:

- $\textbf{B}(\varphi, t) \equiv \neg happens_{time}(\ ) \textbf{U} \varphi$ if $t = 0$;
- $\textbf{B}(\varphi, t) \equiv (\neg happens_{time}() \vee \textbf{XB}(\varphi, t - 1)) \textbf{U} \varphi$ if $t > 0$.

To regulate the execution of empowered and possible actions defined by the Chaired Meeting Institution, we introduce the following norms:

- the chair starts the meeting before t_{start} time instants:

$$O(c_1, chair, \textbf{B}(happens_{open}(subject(f)), t_{start}))$$

- the chair does not open a meeting twice:

$$O\left(c_2, chair, \textbf{G}\left(happens_{open}(subject(f)) \rightarrow \neg \textbf{XF}happens_{open}(subject(f))\right)\right)$$

- if no item is currently debated, the chair starts a discussion or closes the meeting in t_{no} time instants:

$$O\left(i_1, inmeeting, \neg \exists c \, assigned(c)\right.$$
$$\left. \rightarrow \textbf{B}(\exists i \, happens_{start}(subject(f), i) \vee happens_{close}(subject(f)), t_{no})\right)$$

where $\xi(c) = \sigma_{current}$ and $\xi(i) = \sigma_{item}$;

- a chair does not close a meeting before all items have been discussed

$$O\left(c_3, chair, \forall i \left(\neg happens_{close}(subject(f)) \textbf{U} happens_{terminate}(subject(f), i)\right)\right)$$

- the chair terminates a discussion at most after $t_{terminate}$ instants since status *current* has been assigned

$$O(cu_1, \textbf{current}, \textbf{B}(happens_{terminate}(subject(f), it(f)), t_{terminate}))$$

- the chair does not start a discussion regarding the same item twice

$$O\left(c_4, chair, \textbf{G}\forall i(happens_{terminate}(subject(f), i) \rightarrow \neg \textbf{F}happens_{start}(subject(f), i))\right)$$

- if the chair asks a question, either it receives an answer or it asks the same question to another agent before t_{answer} instants

$$\mathcal{O}\left(c_5, \text{chair}, G\forall a\forall q\left(happens_{ask}(subject(f), a, q)\right.\right.$$

$$\left.\left. \rightarrow B\left(happens_{talk}(a) \vee \exists r\left(\neg r = a \wedge happens_{ask}(subject(f), r, q)\right), t_{answer}\right)\right)\right)$$

where $\xi(a) = \xi(r) = \sigma_{aid}$, $\xi(q) = \sigma_{question}$, and $\xi(c) = \sigma_{current}$;

- a participant ought not to talk when it is not the current speaker:

$$\mathcal{O}\left(p_1, \text{participant}, G\left(speaker(f) = not \rightarrow \neg happens_{talk}(a)\right)\right)$$

MODEL CHECKING AGENT ORGANIZATIONS

Model checking is an automated technique to verify whether a system satisfies a temporal property (Clarke, Grumberg, & Peled, 1999). To do so, systems are represented as finite state machines and efficient labeling algorithms are applied to check whether their temporal evolutions satisfy certain desirable properties. One of the main limitations of model checking resides in the size of models that can be verified, since the composition of several finite state machines tend to generate systems characterized by a huge number of states. To solve this problem, *symbolic techniques* (McMillan, 1993) have been put forward to efficiently represent and manipulate states as Ordered Binary Decision Diagrams (OBDDs) (Bryant, 1986), a canonical representation of Boolean functions such that equivalent Boolean functions (e.g., propositional formulae) are represented by the same OBDD.

In this section we present a *symbolic model checker* based on the CUDD library (Somenzi, 2005), a library to manipulate OBDDs, and which has been specifically developed to simulate and verify properties of organizations regulated by institutions modeled with FIEVeL. As we have shown, FIEVeL allows designers to describe constitutive and regulative rules of institutions, which correspond to a set of symbols and a set of OMSFOTL axioms Φ. Since model checking techniques have been developed to check systems characterized by finite sets of states, we apply them to verify whether organizations including a limited number of agents, objects, etc. satisfy certain properties. In this respect, one of the main advantages of using OMSFOTL resides in the fact that different models can be automatically synthesized and verified by describing what individuals characterize *basic domains*, while all remaining domains are inferred without human intervention.

A description of an organization is provided according to the following syntax:

```
model-def ::= "model-definition" "basic-sorts" domain+ "initial-state" assign-
ment+;
domain    ::= symbol "=" "{" symbol ("," symbol)* "}" ";";
assignment::= var "assign" "(" term "=" term ("," term "=" term)* ")" ";"
```

where each domain clause refers to an existing basic sort σ and introduces a set of constants of sort σ which are mapped over different individuals of domain D_σ. Moreover, each assignment clause defines a formula φ_{ass_i} as follows:

$$\varphi_{ass_i} \equiv \exists x \left(\bigwedge_j \left(term_{1,j} = term_{2,j}\right) \wedge assigned(x) \wedge modified(x) \right) \qquad \text{(A. 23)}$$

where x is a variable of a sort representing status functions, and assignments are used to identify what individual is *assigned* and *modified* at the initial state.

In principle, a FIEVeL institution and a description of an initial state of an organization correspond to a Kripke structure $M(\bar{v}) = \langle S(\bar{v}), R(\bar{v}, \bar{v}'), S_0(\bar{v}) \rangle$, where $S(\bar{v})$ is a set of states (assuming that each state corresponds to a valuation of atomic propositions $\bar{v}$), $S_0(\bar{v})$ is a set of initial states, and $R(\bar{v}, \bar{v}')$ is a total relation on $S(\bar{v})$ where $\bar{v}'$ is a second set of propositions used to represent states reachable from states encoded by variables $\bar{v}$. Unfortunately, the direct generation of the corresponding OBDDs is computationally expensive, due to the number of variables required to encode the organization and the complexity of the obtained OBDDs. To solve this problem we attempted to use a SAT solver to enumerate all possible states and transitions of the organization compatible with the rules of the institution. Despite the significant improvement in the time and memory required to build the Kripke structure, norms provoked a considerable increase of the number of states and transitions encountered by the SAT solver. For this reason, to obtain a symbolic representation of both constitutive rules and norms, we separate their treatment and their encoding into OBDDs. In doing so, we efficiently encode constitutive rules and exploit them to reduce the complexity of constructing automata corresponding to monitors of norms.

Given a FIEVeL institution and an initial state of an organization, to obtain an equivalent propositional model our tool translates the institution into a set of axioms Φ, computes the set of individuals composing each domain D_σ for each sort σ, and defines a formula φ_0 that should be satisfied by the initial state. To encode constitutive rules, we introduce a set of atomic propositions $\bar{k}$ determined by defining a function μ which maps OMSFOTL symbols into a set of atomic propositions. Given a sort σ, let σ_s be the supersort of σ such that there does not exists another sort σ_2 such $\sigma_s \leq_\Sigma \sigma_2$, and let N_{σ_s} be the cardinality of domain D_{σ_s}. Mapping μ determines set $\bar{k}$ as follows:

- each function f of sort σ induces a set of propositions $\bar{k}_{f(x_1, x_2, \ldots, x_n)}$ of cardinality $\log_2 N_{\sigma_s}$ such that $\mu[f(x_1, x_2, \ldots, x_n)] = \bar{k}_{f(x_1, x_2, \ldots, x_n)}$ for each valuation of variables $\bar{x}$;
- each predicate p induces a proposition $k_{p(x_1, x_2, \ldots, x_n)}$ such that $\mu[p(x_1, x_2, \ldots, x_n)] = k_{p(x_1, x_2, \ldots, x_n)}$ for each valuation of variables $\bar{x}$;
- constant symbols do not introduce any additional proposition: instead, each constant c is mapped onto a sequence of truth values which correspond to the binary representation of the individual referenced by it ($\mu[c] = binary(c)$).

It can be shown that if domains and symbols defined by an institution are finite, the size of set $\bar{k}$ induced by mapping μ is finite.

Assuming that there exists a constant symbol for each individual of every domain and, for simplicity, that only variables and constants can appear as arguments of functions and predicates, we define a translation of OMSFOTL formulae into propositional formulae as follows:

$$\tau[t_1 = t_2] = \bigwedge_{i=0}^{\log_2 N_\sigma} (\mu[t_1]_i \leftrightarrow \mu[t_2]_i)$$

Table 1.Assignments admitted by organizations regulated by the Chaired Meeting Institution

|aid|	|item|	$|\overline{k}|$	|sol|	time (sec)	$|\overline{w}|$	$\mid R(\overline{w},\overline{w}')\mid$	$\mid S(\overline{w})\mid$
3	1	30	21	0.009	5	99	22
3	2	32	31	0.011	6	206	43
4	1	34	31	0.010	5	181	32
4	2	35	64	0.016	7	372	63

where σ is the common supersort of terms t_1 and t_2, and $\mu[t]_i$ refers to the i -th proposition (or equivalently the i -th truth value) corresponding to the encoding of term t ;

- $\tau[p(x_1, x_2, \dots, x_n)] = \mu[p(x_1, x_2, \dots, x_n)]$;

- $\tau[\exists x\varphi] = \bigvee_{c \in C_{\xi(x)}} \varphi_c$ where c ranges over constants of sort $\xi(x)$ and φ_c is the result of replacing every unbounded occurrence of variable x in φ with an occurrence of c ;

- $\tau[\neg\varphi] = \neg\tau[\varphi]$;

- $\tau[\varphi \wedge \psi] = \tau[\varphi] \wedge \tau[\psi]$;

- $\tau[X\varphi] = \tau[\varphi]'$, that is, we apply translation τ and then variables $\overline{k}$ are substituted with variables $\overline{k}'$;

- $\tau[AG\varphi] = \tau[\varphi] \wedge \tau[X\varphi]$ if φ does not contain the *next* temporal operator (X), otherwise $\tau[AG\varphi] = \tau[\varphi]$.

As mentioned above, although the OBDD corresponding to $R(\overline{k}, \overline{k}')$ can be directly obtained by applying τ to axioms Φ ($R(\overline{k}, \overline{k}') = \bigwedge_{\varphi \in \Phi} \tau[\varphi]$), in practice its generation tends to be extremely slow. To overcome such problem, we apply the algorithm described in (Sheridan, 2004) to convert propositional formula $\tau[\bigwedge_{\varphi \in \Phi} \varphi]$ into conjunctive normal form (CNF), whose satisfying assignments are searched by invoking Minisat (Eén & Sörensson, 2004), an efficient SAT solver. In this case, $R(\overline{k}, \overline{k}')$ is defined as the OBDD corresponding to the disjunction of all $r_i(\overline{k}, \overline{k}')$ solutions found by the solver ($R(\overline{k}, \overline{k}') = \bigvee_{0 \le i \le n} r_i(\overline{k}, \overline{k}')$).

Table 1 reports how the cardinality of sorts σ_{aid} and σ_{item} affects the number of propositional variables $\overline{k}$, the number of solutions, and the time spent by the SAT solver to find them. Such results have been obtained under Linux on a laptop equipped with a pentium 1.66 GHz and 1 GB of RAM. Observing Table 1, we can notice that the number of solutions n found by the SAT solver is considerably smaller than the number of states that can be encoded by variables $\overline{k}$. We also observe that if a state $s(\overline{k})$ is *reachable*, then there exists a solution $r_i(\overline{k}, \overline{k}')$ such that the valuation of variables $\overline{k}'$ is equal to the valuation of variables $\overline{k}$ corresponding to state $s(\overline{k})$. As a consequence, n represents an upper bound of the number of reachable states. This fact suggests that once we know the total number of assignments satisfying the CNF formula induced by axioms Φ, we can build a Kripke structure $M(\overline{w}) = \langle S(\overline{w}), R(\overline{w}, \overline{w}'), S_0(\overline{w})\rangle$, equivalent to $M(\overline{k})$, but defined over a set of variables determined by the logarithm in base 2 of n increased by 1, since it may be the case that some transitions depart from the initial state but none of them reach it. In doing so, the time required to build the symbolic representation of the organization and the time required to verify its properties can be considerably reduced, since the number of symbolic variables negatively affects the time required to manipulate OBDDs (Bryant, 1986).

Table 1 allows us to compare the number of symbolic variables $\overline{w}$ with the number of atomic propositions $\overline{k}$, showing that variables $\overline{w}$ encode more efficiently the set of reachable states. It is worth observing that, in general, the number of solutions enumerated by the SAT solver (increased by one) constitutes only an upper bound to the number of reachable states of the Kripke structure. As a consequence, the number of states that can be encoded with variables $\overline{w}$ may be considerably larger with respect to the actual size of reachable states $S(\overline{w})$. Unfortunately, the exact number of reachable states cannot be determined only by considering the set of assignments encountered by the SAT solver and requires the construction of the Kripke structure $M(\overline{k})$, which, due to the number of variables $\overline{k}$, tends to be computationally expensive. Moreover, observing Table 1, we notice that the actual number of transitions of the Kripke structure $M(\overline{w})$ is typically greater than the number of solutions found by the SAT solver. This is achieved by abstracting certain variables (e.g., variables corresponding to events) and contributes to reducing the search space of the SAT solver.

As explained in the previous sections, a norm ω associated to a status function σ_f and characterized by a temporal formula φ_ω, induces a set of monitors σ_ω such that each individual $m_{\omega,i}$ represents the monitor of the compliance of the i-th individual of sort σ_f with norm ω. Each monitor $m_{\omega,i}$ undergoes a life cycle, represented by function $state$, which depends on (i), the temporal evolution of the status function to which it is associated (as described by Axioms (A. 4), (A. 3), and (A. 3)) and (ii) the temporal evolution of the institution or the environment due to the temporal formula φ_ω (as required by Axiom (A. 14)) where unbounded occurrences of variable f are substituted with constant i. In particular, to determine how the institution and the environment affect a monitor of a norm, we exploit the algorithm proposed in (Daniele, Giunchiglia, & Vardi, 1999) improved by considering information provided by the Kripke structure $M(\overline{w})$ to simplify the auomaton (e.g., transitions of the automaton are compatible with relation $R(\overline{w}, \overline{w}')$) and to define under what conditions a formula is *syntactically implied* by a set of formulae. Moreover, to obtain a minimal automaton, we use a function of the AMoRE library (Matz, Miller, Potthoff, & Thoma) which produces a minimal *deterministic finite state machine* $D_{\varphi_{\omega,i}}$ which can be symbolically represented by introducing two sets of propositional variables $\overline{m}_{\omega,i}$ and $\overline{m}'_{\omega,i}$ for each monitor $m_{\omega,i}$, and by applying encoding μ and translation τ such that: (i) $\mu\left(state(m_{\omega,i})\right) = \overline{m}_{\omega,i}$ and (ii) obtained formulae are encoded as OBDDs. With doing so, each monitor $m_{\omega,i}$ induces a Kripke structure $M(\overline{m}_{\omega,i})$ and the symbolic representation $M(\overline{v})$ of an

Table 2. Size of the Kripke $M(\overline{v})$ and time required to verify property (P. 1)

|aid|	|item|	$\mid R(\overline{v}, \overline{v}')\mid$	$\mid S(\overline{v})\mid$	MC (sec)
3	1	34049	6825	0.036
3	2	141170	27383	0.148
4	1	305662	48033	0.288
4	2	1267427	194157	0.502

organization regulated by constitutive and regulative rules defined by a FIEVeL institution is obtained as the combination of the Kripke structures $M(\bar{k})$ and all structures $M(\bar{m}_{\omega,i})$.

Table 2 reports the size of the transition relation $R(\bar{v}, \bar{v}')$ and the number of reachable states $S(\bar{v})$ obtained by assuming $t_{start} = t_{no} = t_{answer} = 1$ and $t_{terminate} = 3$. Comparing Table 1 and Table 2 we observe that the number of states and transitions of the Kripke structures has considerably increased, but OBDDs allow us to efficiently manipulate and verify them. It is worth remarking that the definition of norms does not affect the number of assignments found by the solver, since their temporal evolution is not explicitly represented by axioms Φ considered by the SAT solver. This fact is particularly important, since other approaches based on SAT techniques (e.g. (Sergot & Craven, 2006)) directly encode information regarding norms into the CNF, which in principle may cause an explosion of the number of assignments found by the SAT solver. Moreover, Table 2 clearly shows that when there are many norms characterized by complex temporal relations, the set of states of a system considerably increases. In such systems, the explicit enumeration and classification of all possible reachable states (as in (Raimondi & Lomuscio, 2007)) becomes unfeasible, and therefore designers should be provided with constructs to model norms at a higher level.

Once we have built the Kripke structure $M(\bar{v})$, we translate each property $\psi \in \Psi$ into CTL^* exploiting a translation ϑ which preserves unchanged atomic formulae, Boolean and temporal operators, and removes quantifiers as done by translation τ. Then, if $\vartheta[\psi]$ is such that temporal operators are always preceded by path quantifiers we verify whether $M(\bar{v}) \vDash \vartheta[\psi]$ by applying symbolic algorithms described in (Clarke, Grumberg, & Peled, 1999), otherwise given that $\vartheta[\psi] = A\rho$ and ρ does not contain path quantifiers, we check whether $\mathcal{M}(\bar{v}) \vDash \rho$ following the approach described in (Clarke, Grumberg, & Hamaguchi, 1997). Table 2 shows time required to verify whether organizations regulated by the Chaired Meeting Institution are characterized by a consistent set of norms, that is, there exists a legal outward transition for every state. Consistency checking is formalized by the following property:

$$AG(EX \, \forall o \neg violated(o)) \qquad \qquad (P. 1)$$

where $\xi(o) = \sigma_o$. Property (P. 1) is satisfied by no organization, since when none of the participants answers, the chair always violates a norm as described by the following property

$$A((G\forall a \, \neg happens_{talk}(a) \wedge F\exists a\exists r\exists q happens_{ask}(a,r,q)) \rightarrow F\exists o \, violated(o)) \qquad (P. 2)$$

where $\xi(a) = \xi(r) = \sigma_{aid}$, $\xi(q) = \sigma_{question}$, and $\xi(o) = \sigma_o$. Property (P. 2) is satisfied by all verified organizations and we can investigate whether norms cu_1 and c_5 cause the inconsistency

$$A((G\forall a \, \neg happens_{talk}(a) \wedge F\exists a\exists r\exists q happens_{ask}(a,r,q)) \rightarrow F(\exists o_1 \, violated(o) \vee \exists o_2 \, violated(o)))$$
$$(P. 3)$$

where $\xi(o_1) = \sigma_{cu_1}$ and $\xi(o_2) = \sigma_{c_5}$. Also property (P. 3) holds in all organizations, which confirms that norms cu_1 and c_5 are inconsistent. It is interesting observing that norm c_5, has been introduced in the Chaired Meeting Institution to model the exception handling of *Role Interaction property RI1* defined in (Jonker, Schut, Treur, & Yolum, 2005). According to (Jonker, Schut, Treur, & Yolum, 2005), property $RI1$ requires agents asked by the chair to eventually answer, and its exception handling obliges the chair to eventually ask the same question to another agent if after 5 seconds no answer has been received. Indeed, if we assume that normally agents will eventually answer to questions (as done in (Jonker, Schut, Treur, & Yolum, 2005)), rule $RI1$ and its exception handling correctly model how a meeting is carried out, since if an agent does not answer, the chair can rely on the fact that other agents will fulfill rule $RI1$. On the contrary, when participants are not willing to answer, the chair always violates the exception handling of $RI1$, not because it has abstained from performing obliged actions or has performed a prohibited action, but because other agents do not fulfill their role interaction properties as soon as possible as assumed in (Jonker, Schut, Treur, & Yolum, 2005) following (Finger, Fisher, & Owens, 1993). This fact is detected within our approach even specifying a weaker norm, which permits the chair to ask the same question before t_{answer} instants have elapsed. In contrast, the execution semantics exploited in (Jonker, Schut, Treur, & Yolum, 2005) rules out paths where agents do not answer, introducing a further requirement which is not explicitly present in the logical specification.

CONCLUSION

In this chapter we have presented an approach to model check agent organizations regulated by institutions which is characterized by a precise formalization of institutional concepts and a language, named FIEVeL, to model constitutive and regulative rules. Moreover, we have presented a tool which automatically translates institutions into Kripke structures and checks their properties by applying symbolic algorithms. As observed in the previous section, in this chapter we have not proposed new algorithms to verify institutions, but a formal approach to represent institutional concepts that can be used to model and verify them. In particular, we provide high level constructs to describe norms that allow our tool to automatically classify states and transitions of organizations, while other approaches based on symbolic techniques, like (Agotnes, van der Hoek, Rodríguez-Aguilar, Sierra, & Wooldridge, 2007) and (Raimondi & Lomuscio, 2007), require designers to manually classify them.

Since we use standard symbolic algorithms to model check institutions, in principle it would be possible to verify FIEVeL institutions with other symbolic model checkers like NuSMV (Cimatti, et al., 2002) or MOCHA (Alur, Henzinger, Mang, Qadeer, Rajamani, & Tasiran, 1998). To do so, an organization should be represented as a propositional model optimized as discussed above and its symbolic representation should be encoded with the input language accepted by each model checker. It is worth remarking that before generating such propositional models, it is necessary to reduce the number of propositional variables required to represent organizations and to use the symbolic representation of an organization to lower the number of states necessary to represent automata induced by monitors of norms.

Moreover, we have exemplified our framework by modeling the Chaired Meeting Institution, showing the importance of checking organizations by considering how norms are monitored at runtime. In doing so, we do not introduce hypothesis that are not satisfied in open systems and we are capable of detecting whether the normative system is consistent (i.e., there exists a legal outward transition for every state). While in (Agotnes, van der Hoek, Rodríguez-Aguilar, Sierra, & Wooldridge, 2007) or (Raimondi & Lomuscio, 2007) the authors assume that the considered normative system is always consistent, in our approach the absence of contradictory norms represents a desirable property that a rational institution ought to satisfy and that can be verified by our model checker. In particular, in our approach conflicting norms induce a Kripke structure which is still serial (each state has at least a successor), but there are states which are followed only by states which violate norms. Moreover, one of the main advantages of our approach resides in the fact that, as exemplified by property (P. 3), it is possible to reason about the violation of certain subsets of norms and to investigate whether a property holds in an institution when such norms are not violated. This fact is particularly important, because it may be the case that norms are correctly defined, but desirable properties do not hold simply because agents are autonomous and we cannot assume that they will always comply with norms. Finally, the Chaired Meeting Institutions shows that the adoption of a high level language allows designers to model and verify complex systems of rules, despite the expressiveness of the language may hide that such systems correspond to Kripke structures characterized by huge number of states and transitions even when we consider a small number of agents.

FUTURE RESEARCH DIRECTIONS

At the moment, FIEVeL allows one to model and verify organizations regulated by a single institution. So far, with the exception of the works presented in (Viganò, Fornara, & Colombetti, 2006) and (Cliffe, De Vos, & Padget, 2007), the research on multiple interdependent institutions has received little attention. Viganò et al. (2006) presented a set of relations that can be defined among institutions, but the model is based on an intuitive semantics and only a few of the possible relations have been considered. Instead, Cliffe et al. (2007) presented a language to model interdependencies among institutions only in terms of the *conventional generation of events*. Their treatment of such relation is based on the hypothesis that an institution may be empowered to generate institutional events in another institution, while we deem that powers can be conferred only to agents through status functions and not to institutions themselves.

Despite FIEVeL has been conceived as a language amenable to model checking, its semantics provides for the development of an automatic translation of constitutive rules into Prolog. Moreover, we think that techniques developed to monitor the fulfillment of commitments (Cranefield, 2006) can be easily adapted to represent the compliance of agents with norms. As a consequence, FIEVeL would provide a unified approach to support the development process of institutions and organizations, allowing designers to *model* institutions, to *verify* their property, and finally to *enforce norms* at runtime in agent organizations regulated by them.

In this chapter we have focused on modelling and verifying interaction rules, reducing agents as labels characterizing events. Indeed, frameworks to support the design and verification of agents that act in institutionalized environments are required. In (Vasconcelos, Sierra, Esteva, Sabater, & Wooldridge, 2004) a methodology to synthesize agents that follow the rules of an electronic institution (Esteva, Rodríguez-Aguilar, Sierra, García, & Arcos, 2001) is presented. One of the main advantages of the approach described in (Vasconcelos, Sierra, Esteva, Sabater, & Wooldridge, 2004) resides in the fact that the development of agents can be supported by tools. Unfortunately, as in (Huget, Esteva, Phelps, Sierra, & Wooldridge, 2002) only norms regarding the protocol are considered and only techniques to execute agents are provided.

ACKNOWLEDGMENT

This research has been supported by the Hasler Foundation project 2255, "Model Checking and Monitoring Norms defined by Interdependent Institutions". The authors would like to acknowledge Federico Heras Viaga for making available a modified version of Minisat computing all assignments admitted by a CNF. Moreover, the authors would also like to thank Alessio Lomuscio and Franco Raimondi for their comments on an initial implementation of the symbolic model checker described in this chapter.

REFERENCES

Abadi, M. (1989). The Power of Temporal Proofs. *Theoretical Computer Science*, 35-83.

Agotnes, T., van der Hoek, W., Rodríguez-Aguilar, J., Sierra, C., & Wooldridge, M. (2007). On the Logic of Normative Systems. *Proceedings of the 20th International Joint Conference on Artificial Intelligence*, (pp. 1175-1180).

Alberti, M., Gavanelli, M., Lamma, E., Chesani, F., Mello, P., & Torroni, P. (2006). Compliance Verification of Agent Interaction: a Logic-based Software. *Applied Artificial Intelligence, 20*(2-4), 133-157.

Alur, R., Henzinger, T. A., Mang, F. Y., Qadeer, S., Rajamani, S. K., & Tasiran, S. (1998). MOCHA: Modularity in Model Checking. *Proceedings of the 10th International Conference on Computer Aided Verification* (pp. 521-525). Springer.

Artikis, A., Kamara, L., Pitt, J., & Sergot, M. (2004). A Protocol for Resource Sharing in Norm-Governed Ad Hoc Networks. In *Declarative Agent Languages and Technologies II* (Vol. 3476 of LNCS, pp. 221-238). Springer.

Artikis, A., Sergot, M., & Pitt, J. (2003). Specifying Electronic Societies with the Causal Calculator. *Agent-Oriented Software Engineering III. 2585 of LNCS*, pp. 1-15. Springer.

Boella, G., & van der Torre, L. (2005). The Ontological Properties of Social Roles: Definitional Dependence, Powers and Roles Playing Roles. *Proceedings of the Workshop on Legal Ontologies and Artificial Intelligence Techniques.*

Bryant, R. E. (1986). Graph-based Algorithms for Boolean Function Manipulation. *IEEE Transactions on Computers, 35*(8), 677-691.

Carabelea, C., & Boissier, O. (2006). Coordinating Agents in Organizations Using Social Commitments. *Electronic Notes in Theoretical Computer Science, 150*(3), 73-91.

Cimatti, A., Clarke, E., Giunchiglia, E., Giunchiglia, F., Pistore, M., Roveri, M., et al. (2002). NuSMV Version 2: An OpenSource Tool for Symbolic Model Checking. *Proceedings of the International Conference on Computer-Aided Verification. 2404 of LNCS*. Springer.

Clarke, E. M., Grumberg, O., & Peled, D. (1999). *Model Checking.* MIT Press.

Clarke, E., Grumberg, O., & Hamaguchi, K. (1997). Another Look at LTL Model Checking. *Formal Methods in System Design, 10*(1), 47-71.

Cliffe, O., & Padget, J. (2002). A Framework For Checking Interactions Within Agent Institutions. *Proceedings of the Workshop on Model Checking and Artificial Intelligence I.*

Cliffe, O., De Vos, M., & Padget, J. (2007). Specifying and Reasoning about Multiple Institutions. In *Coordination, Organizations, Institutions, and Norms in Agent Systems* (Vol. 4386 of LNCS, pp. 67-85). Springer.

Cranefield, S. (2006). A Rule Language for Modelling and Monitoring Social Expectations in Multi-agent Systems. In *Coordination, Organization, Institutions and Norms in Agent Systems I* (Vol. 3913 of LNAI, pp. 246-258). Springer.

Daniele, M., Giunchiglia, F., & Vardi, M. (1999). Improved Automata Generation for Linear Temporal Logic. *Proceedings of the 11th International Conference on Computer Aided Verification* (pp. 249-260). Springer.

Eén, N., & Sörensson, N. (2004). An Extensible SAT-solver. *Proceedings of the 6th Conference on Theory and Applications of Satisfiability Testing* (pp. 502-518). Springer.

Emerson, E., & Halpern, J. (1986). "Sometimes" and "not never" revisited: On branching versus linear time temporal logic. *Journal of the ACM, 33*(1), 151-178.

Esteva, M., de la Cruz, D., & Sierra, C. (2002). ISLANDER: an electronic institutions editor. *Proceedings of the 1st Conference on Autonomous Agents and Multiagent Systems*, (pp. 1045-1052).

Esteva, M., Rodríguez-Aguilar, J., Rosell, B., & Arcos, J. (2004). AMELI: An Agent-based Middleware for Electronic Institutions. *Proceedings of the 3rd Conference on Autonomous Agents and Multi-Agent Systems* (pp. 236-243). ACM Press.

Esteva, M., Rodríguez-Aguilar, J., Sierra, C., & Vasconcelos, W. (2004). Verifying Norm Consistency in Electronic Institutions. *Proceedings of the Workshop on Agent Organizations: Theory and Practice*, (pp. 8-15).

Esteva, M., Rodríguez-Aguilar, J., Sierra, C., García, P., & Arcos, J. (2001). On the Formal Specification of Electronic Institutions. In *Agent Mediated Electronic Commerce, The European AgentLink Perspective* (Vol. 1991 of LNAI, pp. 126-147). Springer.

Finger, M., Fisher, M., & Owens, R. (1993). METATEM at Work: Modelling Reactive Systems Using Executable Temporal Logic. *Proceedings of the 6th International Conference on Industrial and Engineering Applications of Artificial Intelligence and Expert Systems*, (pp. 209-218).

Fornara, N., Viganò, F., & Colombetti, M. (2007). Agent Communication and Artificial Institutions. *Autonomous Agents and Multi-Agent Systems, 14*(2), 121-142.

García-Camino, A., Noriega, P., & Rodríguez-Aguilar, J. (2005). Implementing Norms in Electronic Institutions. *Proceedings of the 4th Conference on Autonomous Agents and MultiAgent Systems*, (pp. 667-673).

García-Camino, A., Rodríguez-Aguilar, J., Sierra, C., & Vasconcelos, W. (2006). A Rule-based Approach to Norm-Oriented Programming of Electronic Institutions. *ACM SIGecom Exchanges, 5*(5), 33-40.

Giunchiglia, E., Lee, J., Lifschitz, V., McCain, N., & Turner, H. (2004). Nonmonotonic Causal Theories. *Artificial Intelligence, 153*(1-2), 49-104.

Hübner, J., Simão Sichman, J., & Boissier, O. (2005). S-MOISE+: A Middleware for Developing Organised Multi-agent Systems. In *Coordination, Organizations, Institutions, and Norms in Multi-Agent Systems I* (Vol. 3913 of LNCS, pp. 64-78). Springer.

Huget, M., Esteva, M., Phelps, S., Sierra, C., & Wooldridge, M. (2002). Model Checking Electronic Institutions. *Proceedings of the Workshop on Model Checking and Artificial Intelligence I.*

Jones, A., & Sergot, M. (1996). A formal characterisation of institutionalised power. *Journal of the IGPL , 4*(3), 429-445.

Jonker, C., Schut, M., Treur, J., & Yolum, P. (2005). Formal Analysis of Meeting Protocols. In *Multi-Agent and Multi-Agent-Based Simulation* (Vol. 3415 of LNCS, pp. 114-129). Springer.

Jonker, C., Sharpanskykh, A., Treur, J., & Yolum, P. (2007). A framework for formal modeling and analysis of organizations. *Applied Intelligence, 27*(1), 49-66.

Kowalski, R., & Sergot, M. (1986). A Logic-based Calculus of Events. *New Generation Computing, 4*, 67-95.

Lomuscio, A., & Sergot, M. (2002). A formulation of violation, error recovery, and enforcement in the bit transmission problem. *Journal of Applied Logic, 1*(2), 93-116.

Manzano, M. (1993). Introduction to many-sorted logic. In *Many-sorted logic and its applications* (pp. 3-86). John Wiley & Sons.

Matz, O., Miller, A., Potthoff, A., & Thoma, W. (n.d.). *AMoRE - Automata, Monoids, and Regular Expressions.* Retrieved 1 15, 2008, from http://amore.sourceforge.net/

McMillan, K. (1993). *Symbolic Model Checkin: An Approach to the State Explosion Problem.* Kluwer Academic.

Moses, Y., & Tennenholtz, M. (1995). Artificial Social Systems. *Computers and AI, 14*(5), 533-562.

Noriega, P. (1997). *Agent mediated auctions: The Fishmarket Metaphor.* Ph. D. thesis, Universitat Autònoma de Barcelona.

North, D. (1990). *Institutions, Institutional Change and Economics Performance.* Cambridge University Press.

Pitt, J., Kamara, L., Sergot, M., & Artikis, A. (2005). Formalization of a voting protocol for virtual organizations. *Proceedings of the 4th Conference on Autonomous agents and Multi-Agent Systems* (pp. 373-380). ACM Press.

Raimondi, F., & Lomuscio, A. (2007). Automatic verification of multi-agent systems by model checking via ordered binary decision diagrams. *Journal of Applied Logic, 5*(2), 235-251.

Searle, J. (1995). *The construction of social reality.* Free Press.

Sergot, M., & Craven, R. (2006). The Deontic Component of Action Language nC+. In *Proceedings of the 8th Workshop on Deontic Logic in Computer Science* (Vol. 4048 of LNCS, pp. 222-237). Springer.

Sheridan, D. (2004). The Optimality of a Fast CNF Conversion and its Use with SAT. *In Proceedings of the 7th Conference on Theory and Applications of Satisfiability Testing.*

Somenzi, F. (2005). *CUDD: CU Decision Diagram Package.* Retrieved 1 15, 2008, from http://vlsi.colorado.edu/~fabio/CUDD/

Vasconcelos, W. (2003). Logic-Based Electronic Institutions. In *Proceedings of the Workshop on Declarative Agent Languages and Technologies* (Vol. 2990 of LNCS, pp. 221-242). Springer.

Vasconcelos, W., Sierra, C., Esteva, M., Sabater, J., & Wooldridge, M. (2004). Rapid Prototyping of Large Multi-Agent Systems Through Logic Programming. *Annals of Mathematics and Artificial Intelligence, 41*(2-4), 135-169.

Vázquez-Salceda, J., Aldewereld, H., & Dignum, F. (2005). Norms in Multiagent Systems: from Theory to Practice. *International Journal of Computer Systems Science & Engineering, 20* (4), 225-236.

Vázquez-Salceda, J., Dignum, V., & Dignum., F. (2005). Organizing Multiagent Systems. *Autonomous Agents and Multi-Agent Systems, 11*(3), 307-360.

Verdicchio, M., & Colombetti, M. (2006). From Message Exchanges to Communicative Acts to Commitments. *Electronic Notes in Theoretical Computer Science, 157*(4), 75-94.

Viganò, F., & Colombetti, M. (2007). Symbolic Model Checking of Institutions. *Proceedings of the 9th International Conference on Electronic Commerce* (pp. 35-44). ACM Press.

Viganò, F., Fornara, N., & Colombetti, M. (2006). An Event Driven Approach to Norms in Artificial Institutions. In *Coordination, Organization, Institutions, and Norms in Multi-Agent Systems* (Vol. 3913 of LNAI, pp. 142-154). Springer.

Wooldridge, M., Huget, M., Fisher, M., & Parsons, S. (2006). Model Checking for Multiagent Systems: the Mable Language and its Applications. *International Journal on Artificial Intelligence Tools, 15*(2), 195-226.

Yolum, P., & Singh, M. (2004). Reasoning about Commitments in the Event Calculus: An Approach for Specifying and Executing Protocols. *Annals of Mathematics and Artificial Intelligence, 42*(1-3), 227-253.

ADDITIONAL READING

Dastani, M., Dignum, V., & Dignum, F. (2003). Role-assignment in open agent societies. *Proceedings of the 2nd Conference on Autonomous Agents and Multi-Agent Systems* (pp. 489-496). ACM Press.

Farrell, A., Sergot, M., Sallé, M., & Bartolini, C. (2005). Using the Event Calculus for Tracking the Normative State of Contracts. *Journal of Cooperative Information Systems, 14*(2-3), 99-129.

Fasli, M. (2002). On Commitments, Roles, and Obligations. *In Proceedings of the 2nd Workshop of Central and Eastern Europe on Multi-Agent Systems. 2296 of LNCS*, pp. 93-102. Springer.

Ferber, J., & Gutknecht, O. (1998). A Meta-Model for the Analysis and Design of Organizations in Multi-Agent Systems. *Proceedings of the 3rd Conference on Multi Agent Systems* (pp. 128-135). IEEE Computer Society.

Geilen, M. (2004). On the Construction of Monitors for Temporal Logic Properties. *Electronic Notes in Theoretical Computer Science, 55*, 1-19.

Grossi, D., Meyer, J.-J. C., & Dignum, F. (2005). Modal Logic Investigations in the Semantics of Counts-as. *Proceedings of the 10th Conference on Artificial Intelligence and Law,* (pp. 1-9).

Hart, H. (1961). *The Concept of Law* (2nd ed.). Oxford University Press.

Huth, M., & Ryan, M. (2004). *Logic in Computer Science. Modelling and Reasoning about Systems* (2nd ed.). Cambridge University Press.

López y López, F., & Luck, M. (2003). Modelling Norms for Autonomous Agents. *Proceedings of the 4th Mexican International Conference on Computer Science,* (pp. 238-245).

Masolo, C., Vieu, L., Bottazzi, E., Catenacci, C., Ferrario, R., Gangemi, A., et al. (2004). Social Roles and their Descriptions. *Proceedings of the 9th International Conference on the Principles of Knowledge Representation and Reasoning,* (pp. 267-277).

Mazzarese, T. (2000). Permesso forte e permesso debole: note a margine. *Analisi e diritto* .

Meyer, J.-J., & Wieringa, R. (1993). *Deontic Logic in Computer Science.* John Wiley & Sons.

Searle, J. (2005). What is an institution? *Journal of Institutional Economics, 1*(1), 1-22.

Vardi, M., & Wolper, P. (1994). Reasoning about infinite computations. *Information and Computation, 115*(1), 1-37.

Wooldridge, M. (2001). *Introduction to Multiagent Systems.* John Wiley & Sons.

Zambonelli, F., Jennings, N. R., & Wooldridge, M. (2003). Developing multiagent systems: the Gaia methodology. *ACM Transactions on Software Engineering and Methodology , 12*(3), 317-370.

KEY TERMS

Model Checking: A set of automatic techniques to automatically verify logical properties of systems, which are typically represented as Kripke structures.

Ordered Binary Decision Diagrams (OBDDs): A canonical representation for Boolean functions where variables always appear in the same order. OBDDs offer a compact way to represent Boolean functions and to determine if they are equivalent. Unfortunately, the size of OBDDs depends on the variable ordering, and checking that an order is optimal is NP-complete.

Status Function: A "collectively recognized *status* to which a *function* is assigned" (Searle, 1995, p. 41). Status functions represent a particular case of *agentive functions*, that is, functions ascribed by agents in relation with their personal interests.

Symbolic Model Checking: A set of techniques which exploit OBDDs to represent both systems and their properties.

Chapter XVI
A Programming Language for Normative Multi-Agent Systems

Mehdi Dastani
Utrecht University, The Netherlands

Nick A.M. Tinnemeier
Utrecht University, The Netherlands

John-Jules Ch. Meyer
Utrecht University, The Netherlands

ABSTRACT

Multi-agent systems are viewed as consisting of individual agents whose behaviors are regulated by an organizational artifact. This chapter presents a programming language that aims at facilitating the implementation of norm-based organizational artifacts. The programming language is presented in two steps. We first present a programming language that is designed to support the implementation of non-normative organizational artifacts. These artifacts are specified in terms of non-normative concepts such as the identity of participating agents, the identity of the constituting environments in which individual agents can perform actions, and the agents' access relation to the environments. The programming language is then modified and extended to support the implementation of norm-based artifacts. Such artifacts are specified in terms of norms being enforced by monitoring, regimenting, and sanctioning mechanisms. The syntax and operational semantics of the programming language are discussed and explained by means of a conference management system example.

INTRODUCTION

In this chapter, multi-agent systems are considered as consisting of individual agents that are autonomous and heterogeneous. The first assumption implies that each individual agent pursues its own design objectives and the second one implies that the internal states and operations of individual agents may not be known to external entities (Zambonelli, Jennings, & Wooldridge, 2003; Esteva, Rodríguez-Aguilar, Rosell, & Arcos, 2004). In order to achieve the overall goal of such multi-agent systems, the observable/external behavior of individual agents and their interactions should be regulated.

There are two main approaches to regulate the external behavior of individual agents. The first approach is based on coordination artifacts that are specified in terms of low-level coordination concepts such as synchronization of processes (Ricci, Viroli, & Omicini, 2007). The second approach is motivated by organizational models, normative systems, and electronic institutions (Searle, 1995; Jones & Sergot, 1993; Esteva et al., 2004; Grossi, 2007). In this approach, norms are used to regulate the behavior of individual agents.

Using a social and normative perspective is conceived as a way to make the development and maintenance of multi-agent systems easier to manage. A plethora of social concepts (e.g., roles, social structures, organizations, institutions, norms) has been introduced in multi-agent system methodologies, such as Gaia (Zambonelli et al., 2003), models such as OperA (Dignum, 2004), Moise+ (Hübner, Sichman, & Boissier, 2002), and electronic institutions and frameworks such as AMELI (Esteva et al., 2004) and S-Moise+ (Hübner et al., 2002). See also Chapters VI, VIII and XIV for other models that specify multi-agent systems in terms of social and organizational concepts.

Norms in multi-agent systems can be used to specify the standards of behavior that agents ought to follow in order for the overall objectives of the system to be met. However, to develop a multi-agent system does not boil down to state a number of standards of behavior in the form of a set of norms, but rather to organize the system in such a way that those standards of behavior are actually followed by the agents. This can be achieved by regimentation or enforcement mechanisms (Jones & Sergot, 1993).

When regimenting norms all agents' external actions leading to a violation of those norms are made impossible. Via regimentation (e.g., gates) the system prevents an agent from performing a forbidden action (e.g., entering an underground train platform without a ticket). However, regimentation drastically decreases the agent's autonomy. Instead, enforcement is based on the idea of responding after a violation of the norms has occurred. Such a response, which includes sanctions, aims to return the system to an acceptable state. Crucial for enforcement is that the actions that violate norms are observable by the system (e.g., fines can be issued only if the system can detect travelers entering the underground system without a ticket).

The main contribution of this chapter is to present and discuss a simplified version of a programming language that is designed to implement norm-based artifacts that can be used to regulate the behaviors of individual agents constituting a multi-agent system. Such artifacts are assumed to be used by individual agents to perform their external actions in the shared environment(s) and to pass messages to each other. In the next section, we present the syntax and semantics of a programming language that can be used to specify a (non-normative) multi-agent system. This programming language is then modified and extended to allow the implementation of norm-based artifacts. The modified programming language provides constructs to represent norms and mechanisms to enforce them. Then, an example is given to illustrate the use of the programming language. The chapter will be closed by discussing some norm-based approaches to multi-agent systems available at the moment in the literature, among which, ISLANDER/AMELI (Esteva et al., 2004) and S-MOISE+ (Hübner et al., 2002). The chapter will be concluded by some remarks and suggestions for future research directions.

PROGRAMMING MULTI-AGENT SYSTEMS

This section presents the syntax and semantics of a programming language that is designed to implement non-normative multi-agent systems that consist of a number of agents and a number of external environments (e.g., different databases, services, or other computer systems). Individual agents are assumed to be implemented in a programming language, not necessarily known to the multi-agent system programmer, though the programmer is assumed to have a reference to (or the identifier of) the (executable) program of each individual agent. Moreover, it is assumed that individual agents can perform their external actions directly in the (external) environments and that the environments determine the effects of those actions. A (non-normative) program that implements a multi-agent system only determines which and how many individual agents should be created to participate in the multi-agent system, and in which environments each agent can perform actions. Such a program can be considered as the implementation of an artifact that regulates the interaction between agents and their environments (Ricci et al., 2007). The syntax of this programming language is presented in Figure 1 using the EBNF notation. In the following, we use < ident > to denote a string and <int> to denote an integer.

According to this syntax, a multi-agent system program, MAS _ Prog, consists of a non-empty list of clauses, each of which specifies one or more agents with certain access relation to external environments. In each clause, <agentName> is a unique name to be assigned to the individual agent that should be created, <agentProg> is the reference to the (executable) agent program that implements the agent, <nr> is the number of such agents to be created (if the number is greater than one, then the agent names will be indexed by a number), and <environments> is the list of the names of the environments that the agents can access and in which it can perform actions. It should be stressed that the presented programming language does not specify how individual agents are programmed; it only requires a reference to their (ecutable) programs. The following is an example of a non-normative multi-agent system program that implements a conference management system.

```
pc _ chair     : pc _ prog    2     @reviewers _ db, reviews _ db, papers _ db,
                                     authors _ db
reviewer       : rev _ prog   30    @reviews _ db, papers _ db
author         : aut _ prog   50    @authors _ db, papers _ db
```

Figure 1. The EBNF syntax of multi-agent programs

```
MAS _ Prog      = (<agentName> ":" <agentProg> [<nr>] [<environments>])*;
<agentName>     = <ident> ;
<agentProg>     = <ident> ;
<nr>            = <int> ;
<environments>  = "@"<ident>*;
```

This program implements a multi-agent system consisting of two program chairs, with the names `pc _ chair₁` and `pc _ chair₂`, thirty reviewers with the names $reviewer_1$,..., $reviewer_{30}$, and fifty authors with the names $author_1$,..., $author_{50}$. In this example, the references to the executable programs that implement a program chair, a reviewer, and an author are assumed to be `pc _ prog, rev _ prog` and `aut _ prog`, respectively. For a realistic conference management system the executable programs for program chairs, reviewers, and authors could be interfaces that allow human users to access certain databases and perform certain actions in those databases. Note the agents' access relation to the environments `reviewers _ db`, `reviews _ db`, `papers _ db`, and `authors _ db`. According to this program, an author cannot access the database that contains the reviews and a reviewer cannot access the database that contains the authors' information.

One way to define the semantics of this simple programming language is by means of operational semantics. Using operational semantics, one needs to define the configuration (i.e., state) of multi-agent systems and the transitions that such configurations can undergo through transition rules. The configuration of a multi-agents system can be defined in terms of the configuration of individual agents and the state of their shared external environments. The state of the shared environment is a set of facts that hold in that environment.

Definition 1. (Multi-agent system configuration) *Let P be the set of first-order ground atoms denoting facts. Let A_i be the configuration of individual agent* i *and* Σ *be the set of external shared environments, where each environment* $\sigma \in \Sigma$ *is a consistent set of literals built from set P. The configuration of a multi-agent system is defined as* $\langle A_1,..., A_n ; \Sigma \rangle$.

The configuration of multi-agent systems can change for various reasons, e.g., because individual agents perform actions (either internal actions, communication actions, or external actions) or because of the internal dynamics of the external environments (the state of a clock changes independently of an individual agent's action). In operational semantics, transition rules specify under which conditions and in which way configurations can change, i.e., they specify which transitions between configurations are allowed and when they can be derived. In this chapter, we only consider the transition rules that specify the transitions of multi-agent system configurations. Since we do not make any assumption about the internals of individual agents, we can neither define an individual agent configuration nor specify under which conditions and in which ways an individual agent configuration can change. Therefore, we cannot present transition rules to specify transitions between individual agents' configurations. In order to present the transition rules for multi-agent systems, we only assume that individual agents can make a transition by performing either an internal (non-observable) or an external (observable) action including communication actions that are considered as external actions. Similarly, we do not make any assumption about the internals of environments such that we cannot present transition rules to specify the transitions between the states of the environments. We only assume that the environment can make a transition either to accommodate the effect of an agent's action or because of its internal dynamics.

Definition 2. (Transitions of individual agents and environments) *Let A_i and A_i' be configurations of individual agent i, $\sigma, \sigma' \in \Sigma$ be two states of an environment, $\alpha(i, t_1...,t_k)$ be an (observable) external action performed by agent i with ground terms $t_1,...,t_k$ denoting some domain elements, and $msg(i,j,\phi)$ be a message sent by agent i to agent j with formula ϕ representing the content of the message. Then, the following transitions capture the execution of an agent's external action (1), the realization of the* *effects of an agent's external action in an environment (2), sending a message by an agent (3), receiving a message by an agent (4), the execution of an agent's internal action (5), and the change of an environment due to its internal dynamics (6).*

1. $A_i \xrightarrow{\alpha(i,t_1,...,t_k)!} A_i'$: *agent i performs external action α*
2. $\sigma \xrightarrow{\alpha(i,t_1,...,t_k)?} \sigma'$: *environment σ accommodates the effect of action α*
3. $A_i \xrightarrow{msg(i,j,\varphi)!} A_i'$: *agent i sends message msg with content ϕ to agent j*
4. $A_j \xrightarrow{msg(i,j,\varphi)?} A_j'$: *agent j receives message msg with content ϕ from agent i*
5. $A_i \longrightarrow A_i'$: *agent i performs an internal action*
6. $\sigma \longrightarrow \sigma'$: *environment σ changes due to its internal dynamics*

The first transition indicates that an individual agent configuration A_i changes to A_i' when it executes an external action. The execution of the external action by an individual agent broadcasts an event that carries the information about the performed action. The event is assumed to contain the action name, the agent's name that performs the action, the name of the environment in which the action should be performed, and the values of the action's parameters. The broadcast of the event in the transition is captured by the label that consists of the external action name followed by an exclamation mark (i.e., $\alpha(i, t_1,...,t_k)!$). This event, which is available at the multi-agent system level, will be passed to the external environment to realize its effect.

The second transition captures the realization of the effect of an agent's external action in an environment. In fact, the environment undergoes a state transition to accommodate the effect of the external action when it receives an event carrying the information about the performed external action. This is done by labeling the transition with the external action name and the corresponding parameters followed by a question mark (i.e., $\alpha(i, t_1,...,t_k)?$).

The third transition indicates that an individual agent configuration A_i changes to A_i' when it sends a message to another individual agent j. Besides changing the agent's configuration, the execution of a send action broadcasts an event that contains the message information. This is done by labeling the transition with the sent message followed by an exclamation mark (i.e., $msg(i,j,\varphi)!$). Note that the send action is considered as an observable action as it broadcasts an event which is available at the multi-agent level.

The fourth transition indicates that an individual agent configuration A_j changes to A_j' when it receives a message from another individual agent i. This is done by labeling the transition with the received message followed by a question mark (i.e., $msg(i,j,\varphi)?$).

The fifth transition indicates that an individual agent configuration A_i changes to A_i' when it executes an (arbitrary) internal action. In fact, this transition allows individual agent configurations to change without broadcasting any event. The transition of an agent configuration without any observable event is considered as an internal transition.

Finally, the sixth transition indicates that the state of the environment can change due to its internal dynamics. Note that the state transition of an environment can be derived by means of two transition rules: one that realizes the effect of an external action and one that captures the internal dynamics of the environment.

In the following, we present the transition rules for deriving multi-agent system transitions. Such transition rules specify under which conditions and in which way a multi-agent system configuration can change. The conditions used in the multi-agent system transition rules can be either conditions on the multi-agent system configuration, the possibility of individual agent transitions, or the possibility of state transition of the environments. It is important to note that the multi-agent system transition rules, which specify possible multi-agent system transitions, determine the space of possible executions of a multi-agent system. As noted, a multi-agent system transition can take place because individual agents perform actions (internal, external, or communication actions) or because of the internal dynamics of the environment. In order to coordinate the execution of an agent's external action and its corresponding effect on an environment, we need to synchronize the transition of the individual agent configuration, caused by executing the external action, and the transition of the environment, caused by the corresponding effect of the external action. Such synchronization ensures that the effect of the external action cannot interfere with the effects of other external actions of the same or other agents performed in the same environment. Also, the corresponding send and receive actions of two agents should be synchronized in order to ensure that the sent messages are indeed received.

Definition 3. (Multi-agent system transition rules) *Let* $\langle A_1,...,A_i,...,A_n;\Sigma \rangle$ *be a multi-agent system configuration,* $\alpha(i, t_1,...,t_k)$ *be an external action,* $msg(i,j,\phi)$ *be a message, and* θ *be a substitution assigning values to variables. The transition rules for deriving multi-agent system transitions are defined as follows:*

$$\frac{A_i \xrightarrow{\alpha(i,t_1,...,t_k)!} A_i' \quad \sigma \xrightarrow{A(I,x_1,...,x_k)?\,\theta} \sigma' \quad \theta = \{A/\alpha,\, I/i,\, x_1/t_1,...,x_k/t_k\} \quad \sigma \in \Sigma}{\langle A_1,...,A_i,...,A_n;\Sigma \rangle \longrightarrow \langle A_1,...,A_i',...,A_n;(\Sigma \setminus \{\sigma\}) \cup \{\sigma'\} \rangle}$$

$$\frac{A_i \xrightarrow{msg(i,j,\phi)!} A_i' \quad A_j \xrightarrow{msg(I,j,x)?\,\theta} A_j' \quad \theta = \{I/i,\, x/\phi\}}{\langle A_1,...,A_i,...,A_j,...,A_n;\Sigma \rangle \longrightarrow \langle A_1,...,A_i',...,A_j',...,A_n;\Sigma \rangle}$$

$$\frac{A_i \longrightarrow A_i'}{\langle A_1,...,A_i,...,A_n;\Sigma \rangle \longrightarrow \langle A_1,...,A_i',...,A_n;\Sigma \rangle}$$

$$\frac{\sigma \longrightarrow \sigma' \quad \sigma \in \Sigma}{\langle A_1,...,A_n;\Sigma \rangle \longrightarrow \langle A_1,...,A_n;\ (\Sigma \setminus \{\sigma\}) \cup \{\sigma'\} \rangle}$$

The first transition rule indicates that if an individual agent can execute an external action and the corresponding environment can realize the effect of the action simultaneously, then the multi-agent system can make a transition through which the agent and the environment are changed. In this transition rule, the expression $A(I,x_1,...,x_k)?$ (with variables A, I, and $x_1,...,x_k$) indicates that the environment σ expects to receive an action with a name A performed by an agent I and some domain information $x_1,...,x_k$. In fact, we assume that an environment can receive actions at any moment in time. The reception of action α performed by agent i with domain information $t_1,...,t_k$, which is denoted by expression $\alpha(i, t_1,...,t_k)!$ in the same transition rule, provides a (ground) substitution θ that binds variables A, I, and $x_1,...,x_k$.

The second transition rule captures the exchange of messages between agents. In particular, it states that if an agent can send a message to a second agent and the second agent is able to receive the message, then the agents can exchange the messages simultaneously. In this transition rule, the expression $msg(I,j,x)?$ (with variables I and x) indicate that the agent j is able to receive a message from an agent

I with some content x. Note that when a message is received (denoted by msg(i,j,φ)?) a substitution is provided to bind these variables.

The third transition rule indicates that if an agent can perform an internal action, then the multi-agent system can make a transition through which only that agent configuration is changed. Finally, the fourth transition rule captures the internal dynamics of the environments by allowing the environments to change independent of the agents.

PROGRAMMING MULTI-AGENT SYSTEMS WITH NORMS

In this section, we modify and extend the programming language that is presented in the previous section in order to facilitate the implementation of normative multi-agent systems. In fact, the modified and extended programming language is designed to implement norm-based artifacts that can be used to regulate the behavior of individual agents. It is important to note that such norm-based artifacts model multi-agent system organizations. For simplicity and without losing generality, we assume only one external environment. Again, individual agents are assumed to be implemented in a programming language, not necessarily known to the multi-agent system programmer, and the programmer is assumed to have a reference to the (executable) program of each individual agent. Most noticeably it is not assumed that the agents are able to reason about the norms of the system since we do not make any assumptions about the internals of individual agents.

However, unlike in the previous section, we assume that the effect of an individual agent's action in the environment is determined by the multi-agent system organization, and not by the environment itself. In fact, the environment is assumed to be a part of the organization and controlled by it. The proposed multi-agent system programming language should therefore provide programming constructs that allow programmers to specify the initial state of the environment and implement the effects of possible agents' actions in it. In addition, we propose programming constructs to implement norms, and mechanisms to monitor and enforce norms. A multi-agent program is thus considered as the implementation of a norm-based artifact which in turn models a multi-agent system organization. Such a program observes the actions performed by the agents, determines their effects in the environment (which is shared by all individual agents), determines the violations caused by performing the actions, and possibly, imposes sanctions.

The initial state of an environment can be implemented by means of a set of facts. In order to implement the effects of the external actions of individual agents in the environment, we propose a programming construct by means of which it can be indicated that a set of facts should hold in the environment after an external action is performed by an agent. As external actions can have different effects when they are executed in different states of the environment, we add a set of facts that function as the pre-condition of those effects. In this way, different effects of one and the same external action can be implemented by assigning different pairs of facts, which function as pre- and post-conditions, to the action.

We consider norms as being represented by counts-as rules (Searle, 1995), which ascribe "institutional facts" (e.g. "a violation has occurred") to "brute facts" (e.g. "the size of the paper is greater than 15 pages"). In our framework, brute facts constitute the factual state of the multi-agent organization, which is represented by the environment (initially set by the programmer), while institutional facts constitute the normative state of the multi-agent organization. The institutional facts are used with the explicit aim of triggering the system's reactions (e.g., sanctions). As showed in (Grossi, 2007) counts-as rules enjoy a rather classical logical behavior. In our framework, the counts-as rules are implemented as simple rules that relate brute and institutional facts. It is important to note that the application of counts-as rules corresponds to the triggering of a monitoring mechanism since it signals which changes have been taken place and what are the normative consequences of the changes.

Sanctions can also be implemented as rules, but follow the opposite direction of counts-as rules. A sanction rule determines what brute facts will be brought about by the system as a consequence of institutional facts. Typically, such brute facts are sanctions, such as fines. Notice that in human systems sanctions are usually brought about by specific agents (e.g. police agents). This is not the case in our computational setting, where sanctions necessarily follow the occurrence of a violation if the relevant sanction rule is into place (comparable to automatic traffic control and issuing tickets). It is important to stress, however, that this is not an intrinsic limitation of the system which, by the way, does not aim at mimicking human institutions but rather providing the specification of computational systems.

Syntax

In order to represent brute and institutional facts in our normative multi-agent system programming language, we introduce two disjoint sets of first-order atoms to denote these facts. The syntax of the modified and extended normative multi-agent system programming language is presented in Figure 2 using the EBNF notation. In the following, we use <b-atom> and <i-atom> to be first-order atoms taken from two different disjoint sets of first-order atoms. Moreover, we use <ident> to denote a string and <int> to denote an integer.

A normative multi-agent system program, N-MAS _ Prog, starts with a non-empty list of clauses, each of which specifies one or more agents. The list of agent specifications is preceded by the keyword

Figure 2. The EBNF syntax of normative multi-agent programs

```
N-MAS _ Prog            =   "Agents: "          (<agentName> <agentProg> [<nr>])⁺ ;
                            "Facts: "                       <bruteFacts>;
                            "Effects: "                     <effects>;
                            "Counts-as rules: "             <counts-as>;
                            "Sanction rules: "              <sanctions>;
<bruteFacts>            =   <b-literals>;
<effects>              =   ("{"<b-literals>"}" <actionName> "{"<b-literals>"}")⁺;
<counts-as>            =   ( <b-literals> "⇒" <i-literals> )⁺;
<sanctions>            =   ( <i-literals> "⇒" <b-literals> )⁺;
<agentName>           =   <ident> ;
<agentProg>           =   <ident> ;
<nr>                  =   <int> ;
<actionName>          =   <ident> ;
<b-literals>          =   <b-literal> {"," <b-literal>} ;
<i-literals>          =   <i-literal> {"," <i-literal>} ;
<literals>            =   <literal> {"," <literal>} ;
<literal>             =   <b-literal> | <i-literal> ;
<b-literal>           =   <b-atom> | "not" <b-atom> ;
<i-literal>           =   <i-atom> | "not" <i-atom> ;
```

'**Agents:**'. Unlike in the non-normative multi-agent system programming language, we do not specify the agents' access relation to environments in these clauses because we assume that the access relations can and should be specified by means of norms and sanctions. In each clause, <agentName> is a unique name to be assigned to the individual agent that should be created, <agentProg> is the reference to (or the identifier of) the (executable) agent program that implements the agent, and <nr> is the number of such agents to be created (if the number is greater than one, then the agent names will be indexed by a number). After the specification of individual agents, the initial state of the environment is specified as a set of first order literals denoting brute facts. The set of literals is preceded by the keyword '**Facts:**'. The effects of an external action of an individual agent are specified by triples consisting of the action name, together with two sets of literals denoting brute facts. The first set specifies the states of the environment in which the action can be performed, and the second set specifies the effect of the action that should be accommodated in the environment. The list of the effects of agents' external actions is preceded by the keyword '**Effects:**'. A counts-as rule is implemented by means of two sets of literals. The literals that constitute the antecedent of the rule can denote either brute or institutional facts, while the consequent of the rules are literals that denote only institutional facts. This allows rules to indicate that certain brute or institutional fact counts as other institutional fact. For example, selling drugs is a violation (institutional fact), but this violation together with the (brute) fact that the income tax of selling drugs is not paid is considered as another violation (institutional fact). The list of counts-as rules is preceded by the keyword '**Counts-as rules:**'. Finally, the list of sanctions rules can be specified in a normative multi-agent program. The antecedent of a sanction rule consists of literals denoting institutional facts while the consequent of a sanction rule consists of literals denoting brute facts. The list of sanction rules are preceded by the keyword '**Sanction rules:**'. The following is an example of a normative multi-agent system program that implements a small part of a conference management system.

```
Agents:
    pc_chair       pc_prog    2
    author         aut_prog   50
Facts:
    phase(closed).
    pc(pc_chair1).
    pc(pc_chair2).
    authors([author1,…,author50]).
    received([]).
Effects:
    { pc(A), phase(closed) }
      open(A)
    { -phase(closed), phase(submission) }

    { phase(submission), received(Rs), authors(As), member(A,AS) }
      upload(A,Id)
    { not received(Rs), received([(A,Id)|Rs])}
Counts-as rules:
    received(As) and member((A,Id),As) and pages(Id) > 15    =>    viol_size(A)
Sanction rules:
    Viol_size(A)     =>     fined(A,25)
```

This program creates two program-chair agents and fifty authors. The brute facts, which specify the initial state of the environment, indicate that the conference management system is in the closed phase, the names of the pc chairs are `pc_chair1` and `pc_chair2`, the authors' names are `author1,...,author50`, and the list of submitted papers is empty. In this part of the conference management system, we have included only two effects. The first one indicates that the conference management system can (only) be opened if the opening action is performed by a program chair and the conference management system is in the closed phase. The effect that should be accommodated is that the system is not in the closed phase anymore, but in the submission phase. The second effect indicates that uploading a paper by an author in the submission phase updates the list of the received papers with a pair representing the author name and the paper's identifier. The only counts-as rule that we have included in this example specifies that a submitted paper with a size greater than 15 pages creates a size violation. Finally, the sanction rule included in this example specifies that a size violation imposes a sanction, which is in this case issuing a fine of 25 euro for the author of the paper.

Operational Semantics

The state of a normative multi-agent system consists of the state of the external environment, the normative state of the organization, and the states of individual agents.

Definition 4. (Normative multi-agent system configuration) *Let P_b and P_n be two disjoint sets of first-order literals denoting atomic brute and institutional facts (including $viol_\perp$), respectively. Let A_i be the configuration of individual agent i. The configuration of a normative multi-agent system is defined as $\langle \mathbf{A}, \sigma_b, \sigma_n \rangle$ where $\mathbf{A} = \{A_{1,...,} A_n\}$, σ_b is a consistent set of ground literals from P_b denoting the brute state of the multi-agent system, and σ_n is a consistent set of ground literals from P_n denoting the normative state of the multi-agent system.*

Before presenting the transition rules for specifying possible transitions between normative multi-agent system configurations, we need to define the ground closure of a set of literals (e.g., literals representing the environment) under a set of rules (e.g., counts-as or sanction rules) and the update of a set of ground literals (representing the environment) with another set of ground literals based on the specification of an action's effect. Let $l = \Phi(\bar{x}) \Rightarrow \Psi(\bar{y})$ be a rule, where Φ and Ψ are two sets of first-order literals in which sets of variables $\bar{x}$ and $\bar{y}$ occur. We assume that $\bar{y} \subseteq \bar{x}$ and that all variables are universally quantified in the widest scope. In the following, $cond_l$ and $cons_l$ are used to indicate the condition Φ and consequent Ψ of the rule l, respectively. Given a set R of rules and a set X of ground literals, we define the set of applicable rules in X as:

$$\text{Appl}^R(X) = \{ \ (\Phi(\bar{x}) \Rightarrow \Psi(\bar{y}))\theta \mid \Phi(\bar{x}) \Rightarrow \Psi(\bar{y}) \in R \ \& \ X \models \Phi\theta \ \& \ \theta \text{ is a substitution} \}$$

The ground closure of X under R, denoted as $\text{Cl}^R(X)$, is inductively defined as follows:

$$\mathbf{B} : \text{Cl}_0^R(X) = X \cup \left(\bigcup_{l \in \text{Appl}^R(X)} \text{cons}_l \right)$$

$$\mathbf{S} : \text{Cl}_{n+1}^R(X) = \text{Cl}_n^R(X) \cup \left(\bigcup_{l \in \text{Appl}^R(\text{Cl}_n^R(X))} \text{cons}_l \right)$$

We should emphasize that the counts-as rules obey some constraints. We consider only sets of counts-as rules such that 1) they are finite; 2) they are such that each condition has exactly one associated consequence (i.e., all the consequences of a given condition are packed in one single set cons); and 3) they are such that for counts-as rule k, l, if $\text{cond}_k \cup \text{cond}_l$ is inconsistent (i.e., contains p and $-p$), then $\text{cons}_k \cup \text{cons}_l$ is also inconsistent. That is to say, rules trigger inconsistent conclusions only in different states. Because of these properties (i.e., finiteness, consequence uniqueness and consistency) of counts-as rules R one and only one finite number $m+1$ can always be found such that $\text{Cl}_{m+1}^R(X) = \text{Cl}_m^R(X)$ and $\text{Cl}_m^R(X) \neq \text{Cl}_{m-1}^R(X)$. Let such $m+1$ define the ground closure X under R, i.e., $\text{Cl}^R(X) = \text{Cl}_{m+1}^R(X)$.

In order to update the environment of a normative multi-agent system with the effects of an action performed by an agent, we use the specification of the action effect as implemented in the normative multi-agent system program, unify this specification with the performed action to bind the variables used in the specification, and add/remove the resulted ground literals of the post-condition of the action specification to/from the environment. In the following, we assume a function *unify* that returns the most general unifier of two first-order expressions.

Definition 5. (Updating environment with action effects) *Let $\overline{x}$, $\overline{y}$, and $\overline{z}$ be sets of variables whose intersections may not be empty, $\phi(\overline{y}) \; \alpha(\overline{x}) \; \psi(\overline{z})$ be the specification of the effect of action α, and $\alpha(\overline{t})$ be the actual action performed by an agent, where $\overline{t}$ consists of ground terms. Let σ be a ground set of literals, $unify(\alpha(\overline{x}), \alpha(\overline{t})) = \theta_1$, and $\sigma \models \phi(\overline{y}) \theta_1 \theta_2$ for some ground substitution θ_2. Then, the update operation $update(\sigma, \alpha(\overline{t}))$ is defined as follows:*

$$update(\sigma, \alpha(\overline{t})) = (\sigma \setminus \{\phi \mid \phi \in \psi(\overline{z}) \theta_1 \theta_2 \; \& \; NegLit(\phi)\}) \cup \{\phi \mid \phi \in \psi(\overline{z}) \theta_1 \theta_2 \; \& \; PosLit(\phi)\}$$

In this definition, the variables occurring in the post-condition of the action specification are first bound and the resulted ground literals are then used to update the environment. Note that negative literals from the post-condition (i.e., $NegLit(\phi)$) are removed from the environment and positive literals (i.e., $PosLit(\phi)$) are added to it.

Like for non-normative multi-agent systems, we do not make any assumptions about the internals of individual agents. Therefore, for the operational semantics of normative multi-agent systems we assume the same set of transitions (for individual agent configurations as well as for the environment states) as specified in Definition 2. Given these transitions, we can define a new transition rule to derive transitions between normative multi-agent system configurations. Because our focus here is to introduce a monitoring and sanctioning system based on agents' external actions, the transition rules for the communication actions, the internal agents' actions, and the internal dynamics of the environment remain the same as for non-normative multi-agent systems. Of course, one can easily introduce norms and sanctions for communication actions as well. However, this issue is outside the scope of this chapter.

Definition 6. (Normative multi-agent system transition rule) *Let $\langle A, \sigma_b, \sigma_n \rangle$ be a configuration of a normative multi-agent system. Let R_c be the set of counts-as rules, R_s be the set of sanction rules, and $\phi(\overline{y}) \; \alpha(\overline{x}) \; \psi(\overline{z})$ be the specification of the effect of action α. The transition rule for the derivation of normative multi-agent system transitions is defined as follows:*

$$A_i \in A \qquad A_i \xrightarrow{\alpha(i,t_1,...,t_k)!} A_i' \qquad (\sigma_b' = update \; \sigma_b, \alpha(t_1,...,t_k))$$

$$\dfrac{\sigma_n' = Cl^{R_c}(\sigma_b') \; \backslash \; \sigma_b' \qquad \sigma_n' | \neq viol_\perp \qquad S = Cl^{R_s}(\sigma_n')\backslash\sigma_n' \qquad \sigma_b' \cup S| \neq \perp}{\langle A,\sigma_b, \sigma_n \rangle \longrightarrow \langle A',\sigma_b' \cup S, \sigma_n' \rangle}$$

where $\mathbf{A}' = (\mathbf{A} \setminus \{A_i\}) \cup \{A_i'\}$ *and* $viol_\perp$ *is the designated literal for regimentation.*

This transition rule captures the effects of performing an external action by an individual agent on both external environments and the normative state of the multi-agent system. First, the effect of $\alpha(t_1,...,t_k)$ on the environment σ_b is computed. Then, the updated environment is used to determine the new normative state of the system by applying all counts-as rules to the new state of the environment. Sanctions are then computed by applying all sanction rules to the new normative state of the system and added to the environment. Note that the external action of an agent can be executed only if it does not result in a state containing $viol_\perp$. This captures exactly the regimentation of norms. Hence, once assumed that the initial normative state does not include $viol_\perp$, it is easy to see that the system will never be in a $viol_\perp$-state. Note also that the environment, which is updated with both action effects and sanctions, remains consistent through transitions. This is guaranteed by the definition of the update operation (def. 5) as well as the last condition in the transition rule. This condition ensures that the update of the environment with sanctions does not entail inconsistency. Finally, it should be emphasized that the above transition rule is based on an agent's external (observable) action and that in our framework the internal (non-observable) actions of agents can neither be regimented nor sanctioned.

AN EXAMPLE

To illustrate how normative multi-agent systems can be implemented in the programming language proposed in this chapter, we use an example regarding a simplified version of a conference management system. Like any other conference management system (abbreviated as CMS from now on), this system is designed to support the program chair, the authors and the reviewers with their activities. These activities

Figure 3. Different phases of a conference management system

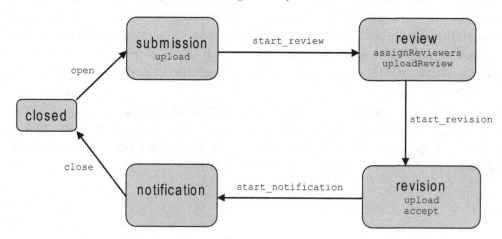

include the uploading of papers by the authors, the assignment of reviewers to the received papers by the program chair and the sending of reviews by the reviewers. A CMS typically goes through different phases. These phases are depicted as rounded rectangles in the diagram illustrated in Figure 3.

The arrows indicate the transitions between the different phases, and the labels correspond to the actions that can be executed by the program chair to shift from phase to phase. The specific actions that can be executed by the agents in a phase are listed inside the rectangles corresponding to a phase. In the submission phase authors upload their papers. As soon as the review phase is started, the program chair assigns reviewers to the received papers. These reviewers then start to review the papers and upload their reviews. In the revision phase authors have the possibility to upload their revised papers. The reviews are of course also sent to the authors by the program chair. This aspect of the system is not modeled here. At the end of the revision phase the program chair decides which papers are accepted. Finally, the authors are notified in the notification phase. This aspect of the system is also not modeled here.

The code of this normative multi-agent system program is depicted in Figure 4. The environment consists of several databases that store information about authors, received papers and the assignment of reviewers to papers. In this normative multi-agent system program these databases are represented by Prolog-like lists. In particular, the list of received([(a,id),...]) contains information about authors identified by a and their papers identified by id. Similarly, the list reviewers([(a,id),...]) contains pairs associating reviewers with papers. The lists received, revised and accepted are respectively used to keep track of the received, revised and accepted papers. The tuple (a,id,r) in the list reviews indicates that review r for paper id was sent by reviewer a. The different phases of the submission system are identified by predicates with the name of the particular phase. The Facts, which implement brute facts, determine the initial state of the environment. Initially, the system is closed, and all previously mentioned lists are empty, since no papers have been uploaded yet.

The Effects specify how the environment changes due to the execution of agents' actions. Each effect is of the form {precondition} action {postcondition}. The first effect, for instance, specifies that uploading a paper with Id by agent A in the submission phase results in the addition of this paper to the list of received papers (by addition of Id to the list of received papers). The author should be registered to the system as author of that particular paper (A should be in the list of authors). If the same action is performed in the revision phase, the paper is not added to the list of received papers, but to the list of revised papers. This is modeled by the second effect. Note that the pre-condition of this effect states that a paper can only be uploaded during the revision phase if it has been accepted already, expressed by member((A,Id),Acs). It is assumed that it is possible to determine whether an author-paper tuple (A,Id) is a member of the list of authors Acs. The third effect specifies the act of assigning reviewers to papers by agent A. Its pre-condition states that only the program chair (expressed as pc(A)) can perform this action. Moreover, note that the program chair provides the full list of pairs associating reviewers with papers. The fourth effect specifies the act of uploading a review by a reviewer. The fifth effect specifies the act of sending the list of accepted papers by the program chair. Note that the pre-condition states that the program chair can only accept papers that are actually revised, i.e., subset(As,Rs). The final effects pertain to the shifting from phase to phase. These actions can only be performed by the program chair.

The Counts-as rules determine the normative effects for a given state of the environment. The first rule, for example, states that papers should not exceed 15 pages. More particular, if agent A is the author of paper Id and the size of this paper (determined by pages(Id)) is more than 15 pages, this counts-as a violation caused by agent A. This violation is represented by the predicate viol _ size,

Figure 4. The normative multi-agent program implementing conference management system

```
Agents:
   pc _ chair         pc _ prog   2
   author             aut _ prog  50

Facts:
   Phase(closed).
   pc(pc _ chair1).
   pc(pc _ chair2).
   authors([author1,…,author50]).
   reviewers([]).
   received([]).
   revised([]).
   reviews([]).
   accepted([]).

Effects:
   {phase(submission), received(Rs), authors(As), member(A,As) }
           upload(A,Id)
   {not received(Rs), received([(A,Id)|Rs]) }

   {phase(revision), accepted(Acs), member((A,Id),Acs), revised(Rs) }
           upload(A,Id)
   {not revised(Rs), revised([(A,Id)|Rs]) }

   {phase(review), pc(A), reviewers(OldPRs) }
           assignReviewers(A,PRs)
   {not reviewers(OldPRs), reviewers(PRs) }

   {phase(review), reviewers(PRs), member((A,Id),PRs), reviews(Rs) }
           uploadReview(A,Id,R)
   {not reviews(Rs), reviews([(A,Id,R)|Rs]) }

   {phase(revision), pc(A), received(Rs), subset(As,Rs), accepted(OldAs) }
           accept(A,As)
   {not accepted(OldAs), accepted(As) }

   {pc(A), phase(closed)}
              open(A)
   {-phase(closed), phase(submission)}

   {pc(A), phase(submission)}
           start _ review(A)
   {-phase(submission), phase(review)}

   {pc(A), phase(review)}
           start _ revision(A)
   {-phase(review), phase(revision)}

   {pc(A), phase(revision)}
           start _ notification(A)
   {-phase(revision), phase(notification)}
```

continued on following page

Figure 4. continued

```
    {pc(A), phase(notification) }
              close(A)
    {-phase(notification), phase(closed)}

Counts-as rules:
    received(As) and member((A,Id),As) and pages(Id) > 15   =>   viol_size(A)

    authors(As) and reviewers(Rs) and member((A,Id),As) and member((A,Id),Rs) =>
    viol⊥

    Phase(notification) and accepted(Acs) and member(Id,Acs) and revised(Rs) and
    not member(Id,Rs)  =>  viol_revision(Id)

    Phase(revision) and reviewers(RPs) and member((A,Id),RPs) and reviews(Rs) and
    not member((A,Id,R),Rs)  =>  viol_review(A)

Sanction rules:
    viol_size(A)        => fined(A,25)
    viol_revision(Id)   => rejected(Id)
    viol_review(A)      => blacklist(A)
```

with arguments A (denoting the agent causing the violation). This information is used in determining the sanctions. The second rule states that reviewers cannot review their own paper, i.e., being the author and reviewer of the same paper with Id counts as a violation. Because it is absolutely undesirable for a reviewer to review its own paper, this rule is marked by the special proposition $viol_\perp$. The operational semantics of the language takes then care that the designated literal $viol_\perp$ can never hold during any run of the system (see Definition 6) by blocking actions that would lead to such a state. In this particular example it thus means that whenever the program chair tries to assign a reviewer to its own paper this action blocks. The third rule states that accepted papers should be revised during the revision phase. More precisely, if the notification phase is reached and the paper is a member of the accepted papers, but not a member of the revised papers, then this counts as a violation. The last rule states that reviewers should send their reviews on time, that is, before the start of the revision phase. Note that due to the construction of the pre-condition of the action uploadReview it is not possible to upload a review in a phase other than the review phase.

The Sanction rules determine the punishments that are imposed as consequences of violations. The sanction of having uploaded a paper of more than 15 pages is a fine of 25 euros for the author A of that paper, denoted by fined(A,25). This fine is then issued by the environment by, for example, charging the creditcard of the author. The sanction of not having revised a paper during the revision phase is that this paper is rejected. It should be noted that the paper is not removed from the list of accepted papers; rejected(Id) merely states that the paper becomes eligible for removal. It is the responsibility of the program chair to actually remove the paper from the list of accepted papers. This aspect is not modeled in this example. Finally, reviewers that did not upload in their reviews on time are punished by being put on a blacklist.

RELATED WORK

To date, several frameworks for constructing multi-agent systems by means of social concepts have been proposed, e.g., S-MOISE+ (Hübner et al, 2005), AMELI (Esteva et al., 2004), MadKit (Gutknecht et al., 2001) and KARMA (Pynadath et al., 2003). In this section we relate these approaches to our approach of a normative agent programming language.

S-MOISE+ is an organizational middleware that follows the MOISE+ model (Hübner et al., 2002). This middleware acts as an interface between the agents and the system as specified by a MOISE+ specification. In MOISE+ a multi-agent system is specified as an organization, distinguishing three main aspects. Firstly, the structural aspect describes the social structure of the organization independently from the agents that will participate in it. The structure is described in terms of concepts such as groups, roles and links between the roles. Roles are used (as usual) as placeholders for agents that will interact in the organization, that is to say, to abstract from the agents that will eventually act in the organization. At the structural level it is specified, for instance, who communicates to whom, which roles cannot be played by the same agent and how many agents can enact a certain role. The middleware ensures that the organizational structure is respected as agents take up and act in their roles. Secondly, the functional aspect is concerned with the functioning of the organization. It provides the agents with information about how global goals (collective goals (Castelfranchi, 1998), for instance, scoring a soccer goal by a team of players) can be achieved, and how agents should work together in reaching these goals. In particular, it specifies social schemes, a kind of global plans that are stored in the organization, describing which sub-goals should be achieved and in which order to reach the global goal. Coherent sets of sub-goals of a scheme, i.e. goals that belong together and form a single task, are grouped together by the so-called missions. Finally, the deontic aspect of MOISE+ specifies the roles' permissions and obligations in the organization, or rather, to which missions an agent playing a certain role is permitted/obligated to commit. The middleware informs agents when goals belonging to their missions should be pursued and prevents them from committing to missions they do not have permission to.

S-MOISE+ combines structural, functional and normative (deontic) aspects of an organization, whereas our approach focuses only on the normative aspect of multi-agent system organizations (see Chapter II "Modeling Dimensions for Agent Organizations" by Coutinho et al. for a more extensive classification of organizational dimensions). The normative aspect of S-MOISE+, however, lacks a monitoring mechanism to detect whether the agents actually fulfill the goals belonging to their obligated missions; it is the agent's own responsibility to inform the middleware about achieved goals. S-MOISE+ is thus somewhat constrained to agents that are benevolent with respect to the organizational goals. We relax this constraint by implementing a monitoring mechanism to detect violations of the norms, and a sanctioning mechanism to impose sanctions accordingly. Moreover, the norms of our framework can be used to normatively assess the state of the system and are not limited to the expression of missions that an agent is permitted/obliged to commit to.

In (Kitio et al., 2007) an extension of S-MOISE+ has been proposed that mainly involves an architectural change of the S-MOISE+ middleware. Instead of viewing an organization as a middleware, an organization is now viewed as a set of organizational agents (agents that are designed as part of the organization) and artifacts that external agents can use to inspect and interact with. These organizational artifacts embody the functioning of the organization, and the organizational agents are responsible for creating and managing them. External agents can both interact with the artifacts and the organizational agents. The novelty is that in this new architecture the organizational agents make decisions about the organization instead of the organizational middleware making these decisions. Such decisions range from selecting which particular social scheme can be used best in reaching a global goal to altering the organizational structure. The assumption is that it is easier to design organizational agents to undertake these tasks than changing the middleware. This allows for a more flexible implementation of organizations and facilitates reorganization at runtime. Its underlying model is, however, still based on the MOISE+ model. Therefore, the previous observation that S-MOISE+ lacks a monitoring and sanctioning mechanism still holds. Although it should be noted that (Kitio et al., 2007) suggests that the artifacts can be designed to allow for violations of the deontic specifications, such that the organizational agents can observe these violations and take actions accordingly. This proposal is comparable to our approach of a monitor and sanctioning mechanism, with the difference that in our case these functions are fulfilled by the organization and not by an agent. It is, however, not explained how to implement an organizational agent equipped with this task.

Similar to our approach, in KARMA and MadKit a multi-agent system is implemented by means of social concepts such as roles, groups and global goals. KARMA, following the STEAM model, enables teamwork among (heterogeneous) agents by the coordination of global plans specifying how global collective goals should be achieved (cf. social schemes of MOISE+). It is primarily aimed at the functioning of the organization, whereas our approach focuses on the normative aspect. MadKit, following the AGR (Agent Group Role) model (see also Chapter III "Towards an Integral Approach of Organizations in Multi-Agent Systems" by Ferber et al.), also lacks an explicit normative dimension, but is rather concerned with the organizational structure that is specified in terms of roles and groups (cf. structural dimension of MOISE+). In conclusion, KARMA and MadKit focus on different social aspects that are complementary to the normative dimension of our solution.

Another approach of multi-agent system development that is concerned with the normative aspect is AMELI, a platform for executing electronic institutions (Esteva et al. 2001), the computational counterpart of human institutions. These institutions are specified with the graphical tool ISLANDER (Esteva et al., 2002). In ISLANDER/AMELI an institution is viewed as a dialogic system in which the only interactions that take place in the system are speech acts performed by the agents. Which speech acts the agents can perform and which roles the agents can take up in the organization is defined by the dialogic framework. The interactions amongst agents take place in so-called scenes, group meetings in which agents exchange messages to achieve certain tasks. Associated to these scenes are communication protocols specifying the permitted dialogs. These protocols thus specify which speech acts can be performed by the agents interacting in the scene. How agents can legally move from scene to scene is specified by the performative structure. Such a performative structure is a network capturing the transitions that agents can make between different scenes. Finally, certain circumstances in one scene (e.g., winning an auction) might lead to obligations in other scenes (e.g., an obligation to pay). Such obligations that are outside the scope of scenes are expressed as global norms that hold in the entire institution. These norms specify which obligations hold when certain speech acts have (not) been uttered in particular scenes. Just like the norms expressed by the protocols and the performative structure, these obligations can only refer to speech acts that should be uttered.

The dialogic framework of ISLANDER/AMELI is comparable to our specification of actions; both specify which actions the agents can perform in the system. However, our specification is about the effect in the environment, whereas the dialogic framework of ISLANDER/AMELI defines all the elements needed for interaction between agents. Regarding the normative aspect, the norms of ISLANDER/AMELI are very concrete norms in the form of ``ought-to-do's'' on speech acts, while in our approach we are primarily concerned with more abstract, declarative norms ('ought-to-be', cf. d'Altan et al. 1996; Dignum, 2002; Aldewereld, 2007) expressing a particular state of the environment. Another difference is that in ISLANDER/AMELI it is possible to distinguish between norms (protocols) that are local to scenes and norms that are global, while in our approach norms are always global to the system. Furthermore, agents cannot deviate from the behavior specified by the protocols and the performative structure, and norms can never be violated; agents must typically have fulfilled all obligations before they can proceed to other scenes. The AMELI middleware rules out all actions that do not conform to the specification. In ISLANDER/AMELI the behavior of agents is thus regulated via full regimentation, thereby restricting their autonomy. This is an aspect which our approach intends to relax by implementing monitoring and sanctioning mechanisms.

In (Aldewereld, 2007) a proposal has been sketched that involves extending ISLANDER/AMELI such that it allows the norms to be violated. This is achieved through the addition of integrity constraints, rules with an antecedent specifying the state of the institution in which a norm has been violated and a consequent specifying the accompanying sanctions and repairs. Similar to the norms of ISLANDER/ AMELI, the antecedent marking the states that count as violations refer to speech acts uttered by agents in particular scenes. The sanctions and repairs are also specified in terms of speech acts that should be uttered by so-called enforcers. An enforcer is an internal agent belonging to the AMELI platform that uses the integrity constraints to detect violations and is designed to impose the corresponding repairs and sanctions.

The integrity constraints of the approach mentioned above are comparable to the counts-as rules and sanctioning rules of our approach. They both indicate when an undesirable state is reached and define the accompanying sanctions and repairs to be imposed by the platform. However, as this proposal is based on ISLANDER/AMELI, it inherits their limitations. The integrity constraints are based on speech acts in contrast to our norms that refer to the state of the environment. Moreover, it is not clear how a sanction such as fining an agent should be imposed using only speech acts. Finally, the model proposed by Aldewereld does not provide concrete programming constructs with operational semantics that can be used to implement normative systems.

CONCLUSION AND FUTURE WORK

In this chapter, we first presented a programming language for implementing multi-agent systems without norms. Using this programming language, we explained that multi-agent systems can be implemented in terms of individual agents that can participate in the multi-agent system, the environments in which individual agents can perform actions, and the access relation that determines which agents can access which environment. We then modified and extended the presented programming language and did propose a new programming language for implementing normative multi-agent systems. Using this new programming language one can implement normative multi-agent systems in which the behavior of individual agents are regulated by means of monitoring and sanctioning mechanisms. These mechanisms are specified in terms of social concepts such as norms (represented as counts-as rules) and sanctions (represented as sanctioning rules). In particular, we explained that the effects of individual agents' external actions are first accommodated in the multi-agent system environment. These effects may then trigger some specific norms, based on which sanctions can be decided and imposed. The sanctions are considered as modifications in the multi-agent system environment. The programming language is endowed with formal operational semantics therefore formally grounding the use of certain social notions —eminently the notion of norm, regimentation and enforcement— as explicit programming constructs. Finally, in order to illustrate the use of the proposed programming language for implementing normative multi-agent systems, we presented a normative multi-agent system program that implements some parts of a conference management system. A short review of existing related works is provided and their relations to our proposal are briefly discussed.

We have already implemented an interpreter for the programming language for non-normative multi-agent systems. (see http://www.cs.uu.nl/2apl/). Currently, we are working to build an interpreter for the modified programming language. This interpreter will be used to execute normative multi-agent system programs. Also, we are currently working to devise a logic and its corresponding semi-automatic proof checker that can be used for verifying properties of programs that are implemented in the proposed programming language for normative multi-agent systems. It may be clear that the proposed programming language lacks explicit constructs to implement other social and organizational concepts such as roles, groups, and relations defined on them. Future work aims at extending the programming language with constructs to support the implementation of a broader set of social concepts and structures, and more complex forms of enforcement (e.g., policing agents) and norm types (e.g., norms with deadlines). Another important aspect that should be studied in future work is related to the dynamics of organization. For our programming framework this means how the specification of an organizational artifact can change at run-time. Please see Chapters XVIII "A Framework for Dynamic Agent Organiations" by Fatima and Wooldridge and XIX "Dynamic Specifications for Norm-Governed Systems" by Artikis et al. for a discussion on this issue.

ACKNOWLEDGMENT

Thanks to Davide Grossi for the fruitful discussions we had on the subject of this paper.

REFERENCES

Aldewereld, H. (2007). *Autonomy vs. Conformity - An Institutional Perspective on Norms and Protocols*. PhD Dissertation. Utrecht University, SIKS dissertation series 2007-10.

Castelfranchi, C. (1998). Modelling social action for ai agents. *Artificial Intelligence, 103*(1-2), 157–182.

d'Altan, P., Meyer, J. J.Ch., & Wieringa, R. J. (1996). An Integrated Framework for Ought-to-Be and Ought-to-Do Constraints, *Artificial Intelligence and Law 4*, 77-111.

Dignum, F. (2002). Abstract norms and electronic institutions. In *Proceedings of Regulated Agent-Based Social Systems: Theories and Applications (RASTA'02)*, 93–104.

Dignum, V. (2004). *A model for organizational interaction*. PhD Dissertation. Utrecht University, SIKS dissertation series 2004-1.

Esteva, M.; Rodríguez-Aguilar, J., Sierra, C., Garcia, P., & Arcos, J. (2001). On the formal specifications of electronic institutions. In *Agent Mediated Electronic Commerce, The European AgentLink Perspective.*, 126–147. London, UK: Springer-Verlag.

Esteva, M., Rodríguez-Aguilar, J., Rosell, B., & Arcos, J. (2004). Ameli: An agent-based middleware for electronic institutions. In *Proceedings of the third international joint conference on Autonomous Agents and Multiagent Systems (AAMAS'04).* New York, USA.

Esteva, M., de la Cruz, D., & Sierra, C. (2002). Islander: An electronic institutions editor. In *Proceedings of the first international joint conference on Autonomous agents and Multiagent Systems (AAMAS'02)*, 1045–1052. New York, USA.

Grossi, D. (2007). *Designing invisible handcuffs*. PhD Dissertation, Utrecht University, SIKS dissertation series 2007-16.

Gutknecht, O., & Ferber, J. (2001). The madkit agent platform architecture. In *Revised Papers from the InternationalWorkshop on Infrastructure for Multi-Agent Systems*, 48–55. London, UK: Springer-Verlag.

Hübner, J. F., Sichman, J. S., & Boissier, O. (2002). Moise+: Towards a structural functional and deontic model for mas organization. In *the proceedings of the first international joint conference on Autonomous agents and Multiagent Systems (AAMAS'02)*. New York, USA.

Hübner, J. F., Sichman, J. S., & Boissier, O. (2005). S-moise+: A middleware for developing organised multiagent systems. In Boissier, O., Padget, J. A., Dignum, V., Lindemann, G., Matson, E. T., Ossowski, S., Sichman, J. S., & Vzquez-Salceda, J., (eds.), In *proceedings of the workshop Coordination, Organization, Institutions and Norms in Agent Systems*, volume 3913, Lecture Notes in Computer Science, 64–78. Springer.

Jones, A. J. I., & Sergot, M. (1993). On the characterization of law and computer systems. In Meyer, J.J.Ch., and Wieringa, R.J., (eds.), *Deontic logic in computer science: Normative System Specification. John Wiley & Sons.*

Kitio, R., Boissier, O., Hbner, J. F., & Ricci, A. (2007). Organisational artifacts and agents for open multi-agent organisations: Giving the power back to the agents. In *proceedings of the workshop Coordination, Organizations, Institutions, and Norms in Agent Systems III, 4870*, 171–186. Springer.

Pynadath, D. V., and Tambe, M. (2003). An automated teamwork infrastructure for heterogeneous software agents and humans. In the *International Journal of Autonomous Agents and Multi-Agent Systems, 7*(1-2), 71–100.

Ricci, A., Viroli, M., & Omicini, A. (2007). Give agents their artifacts: The A&A approach for engineering working environments in MAS. In *Proceedings of the sixth international joint conference on Autonomous Agents and Multiagent Systems (AAMAS'07).* Honolulu, Hawai'i, USA.

Searle, J. (1995). *The construction of social reality.* ISBN 0684831791, Free Press.

Zambonelli, F., Jennings, N., & Wooldridge, M. (2003). Developing multi-agent systems: The GAIA methodology. *ACM Transactions on Software Engineering and Methodology 12*(3), 317–370.

KEY TERMS

Enforcement Mechanism: A (computational) mechanism that can enforce norms by changing the state of a multi-agent system. Such a mechanism is an integral part of multi-agent system organizations.

Multi-Agent Programming Language: A programming language that provides constructs to implement various multi-agent system concepts such as roles, communication, environment, resources, services, access relation, norms and sanctions.

Multi-Agent System Organization: The organizational part of a multi-agent system. This part of a multi-agent system consists of entities that aim at coordinating the behavior of individual agents.

Norm-Based Artifact: An organizational artifact that is designed and implemented in terms of normative concepts.

Normative Multi-Agent System: A multi-agent system in which the behavior of individual agents are coordinated by means of norms.

Organizational Artifact: A (computational) entity that is designed and implemented to coordinate the behavior of individual agents. An organizational artifact is the implementation of a multi-agent system organization.

Regimentation: A (computational) mechanism by means of which the system is prevented to be in a violated state.

Section V
Organizational Dynamics

Chapter XVII
A Minimal Dynamical
MAS Organization Model

Antônio Carlos da Rocha Costa
Universidade Católica de Pelotas, Brazil

Graçaliz Pereira Dimuro
Universidade Católica de Pelotas, Brazil

ABSTRACT

This chapter presents the Population-Organization model, a formal tool for studying the organization of open multi-agent systems and its functional and structural dynamics. The model is minimal in two senses: it comprises a minimal set of extensional concepts able of adequately accounting for the notion of dynamic organization; and, it is a core organization model upon which a certain kind of dynamical rules can be defined, to account for the action of intensional organizational elements like prestige, power, morality, and so forth. The chapter gives a detailed presentation of the core model, in a version adapted for describing organizations where interactions have a periodic character. We also illustrate how the model supports intensional organizational processes, by introducing a sample set of moral rules for agents playing roles in informal organizations.

INTRODUCTION

This chapter focuses on the presentation of the Population-Organization (PopOrg) model, a formal model for the functional and structural dynamics of open multiagent systems (MAS). The PopOrg model was introduced in (Demazeau & Costa, 1996), and revised in (Costa & Dimuro, 2008) to incorporate the notion that organizational interactions are exchange processes.

The PopOrg model is based on several principles:

- that a MAS is best described by separately specifying its organization structure and its population structure;
- that the core part of an organization structure is its set of organizational roles, together with the set of organizational links that relate those roles;
- that the core part of a population structure is its set of agents, together with the set of social exchanges that relate those agents;
- that the population structure makes the organization structure work by implementing the organizational roles and links;
- that the organization structure constrains the set of possible behaviors and interactions that the agents may have in the system;
- that social links between agents are exchange processes, where agents exchange services and objects among each other;
- that organizational links are exchange processes, where roles exchange services and objects among each other;
- that the model should be minimal, in the sense that it should have the least set of concepts enabling an adequate description of the system, but that it should be adaptable and extensible, to contemplate special features needed in particular modelling applications;
- that the model should be extensional, in the sense that it should contemplate essentially the objective aspects of the dynamics of multiagent systems (actions performed, objects exchanged, structural changes, etc.), and that any subjective, intensional aspect (prestige, power, morality, etc.) should be added a posteriori, through specially defined intension-driven organizational rules;
- that the forms of the intension-driven organizational rules should not constrain the definition of the model's minimal core.

The chapter has two main goals. The first one is to extend the PopOrg model to make it contemplate the periodicity inherent in most of the organizational behaviors and interactions that happen in MAS. Such periodicity is an enabling condition for an agent's proper assessment of the quality of its insertion in the system, which is an indispensable capability for any autonomous agent when the system is open and structurally dynamic, that is, when the agent can freely decide on entering or leaving the system, and on conserving or changing the way it is inserted in it.

The second purpose of this chapter is to illustrate the way in which the model's extensional approach allows for the description of how intensional organizational processes operate as causal elements that may impact the extensional structure of the system. In particular, the chapter illustrates how the operational notion of morality for MAS, introduced in (Costa & Dimuro, 2007), can be supported by the model as a set of intension-driven organizational rules.

The chapter is organized as follows. Next section introduces the background of the chapter. Then, we present the latest version of the PopOrg model, the one adapted to deal with organizations where organizational interactions have a periodic character. In the sequence, we illustrate how the intensional issue of morality in multiagent systems can be tackled with the help of intension-driven organizational rules. We conclude the chapter by pointing to future research directions.

CONCEPTUAL BACKGROUND AND RELATED WORKS

Previous Works on Modeling the Dynamics of Multiagent Organizations

The study of the organizational aspects of MAS, and their functional dynamics, is with the area since its beginnings (Reddy et al., 1976), but started to receive spread attention only in the late 1980's and early 1990's (Gasser et al.,1987; Pattison et al., 1987; Boissier & Demazeau, 1996; Tambe, 1996; Ferber & Gutknecht, 1998; Ferber et al., 2003; Hannoun et al., 1998; Noriega et al., 1998; Zambonelli et al., 2001; Gasser, 2001) stimulated by some previous seminal works (e.g., (Fox, 1979)).

With the advancement of the study, several notions of MAS organization arose, most of them based on the idea that an organization is a mechanism to impose constraints on the possible behaviors of a system's agents, in order to induce the agents to behave in ways that contribute to the achievement of the system's goals.

The notion of an organizational role that an agent may play in a system occupies a central position in the organization structure of a multiagent system. The so-called role model of the organization structure (Zambonelli, et al., 2001) (that is, the set of the system's organizational roles, together with the way such roles are linked to each other) serves as the main organizational mechanism, through which those behavioral constraints are imposed on the agents. In particular, intensive efforts have recently been developed to capture through normative systems (i.e., sets of social norms expressing behavioral and interactional permissions and obligations) the essential aspects of such role models (see, e.g., Dastani et al., 2002; Boella et al., 2006).

The investigation of structural dynamics of MAS organizations also has a long tradition, going back to at least (Corkill, 1983), where the notion of structural dynamics of the organization concerned the particular issue of the temporal evolution of the agent coordination mechanism, in accordance with the evolution of the demands of the system's task. So, the understanding that there is a need to modify and adapt the organization of the system in a dynamic way (that is, during the systems functioning), in response to varying demands of the environment, has always been there in the area. However, only in the 1990's the study of the structural dynamics of organizations started to receive attention as a concern in itself (Gasser & Ishida, 1991), spreading effectively mainly in the late 1990's and early 2000's.

Those works, however, usually concentrated on techniques and strategies for reorganization, few works being concerned at the time with general models of structural dynamics, in the sense of the PopOrg model (Demazeau & Costa, 1996; Costa et al., 1994, Bordini et al., 1995). In particular, the study of methods for the reorganization of a MAS has received increased attention recently. In the reorganization models that were so devised, various alternative methods for MAS reorganization were introduced, such as role reallocation (e.g., (Matson, 2005; Hoogendoorn & Treur, 2006)), task and resources reallocation (e.g., (Fatima & Uma, 1998; So & Durfee, 1993))[1], modifications in hierarchical relationships between roles (e.g., (Zheng-guang et al., 2006)), composition and decomposition of groups of agents (e.g., (Corkill, 1983)), reallocation of obligations (e.g., (McCallum et al., 2006)), etc. Also, full algorithms for reorganization of MAS were introduced, as the ones studied in, e.g., (Kashyap, 2006; Picard, et al., 2006; Zhong & DeLoach, 2006).

On the other hand, various ways in which organizational roles may be related to each other, in connection to intensional organizational elements such as reputation, power, etc., were also explored in the literature, allowing for the definition of various types of organization structures, as analyzed, e.g., in (Grossi et al., 2005).

The inclusion of all those specialized kinds of organization structures and reorganization mechanisms in a single model leads to models that are not minimal in the sense proposed in the PopOrg model (see, e.g., the organizational model in (Hübner, 2006)). A survey and comparison of the most important of such larger organization models is presented in (Coutinho et al., 2007).

We have chosen to refrain from adopting such all-encompassing tendency in our work, and looked for a modular approach supported by a minimal model, so that the model can be adapted to fit particular demands of its applications. For instance, in this chapter we introduce periodicity in interactions (see the next section).[2]

On the other hand, we had a further goal, in the definition of the PopOrg model. The main reason for the need of a structural dynamism in a MAS organization, and the corresponding changes in the organization structure, has traditionally been considered to be the demands of the environment and the requirements of adaptability that they imply (see, e.g., (Gasser & Ishida, 1991)).

However, in the PopOrg model we also aimed at formally bringing to the forefront the internal causes of the dynamism of the organization structures, on equal footing with the external causes. That is, we aimed at the formal expression of both the pressures of the environments for changes in the systems, as well as the subjective reasons of the agents for such changes (in a way similar to what, in another context, was termed the distinction between internal and external forces operating on the systems organization (Matson, 2005)). However, in this chapter we deal only with internal causes.

The mechanism added to the basic PopOrg to allow for the expression of the agents' subjective reasons for systems changes was an exchange value-based mechanism, on the basis of which the agents could assess their interactions and decide on their continuation or interruption. This is used here to show how the model can support the addition of dynamical rules describing the effect of intensional organizational processes, as previously sketched in (Costa & Dimuro, 2008) and in (Costa & Dimuro, 2007).

The current version of the PopOrg model is our present answer to the challenge of finding a right balance between completeness, modularity and conceptual economy in the formalization of the functional and structural dynamics of multiagent organizations.

The Evolution of the PopOrg Model

The Population-Organization model was introduced in (Demazeau & Costa, 1996), as a minimal dynamical MAS organization model, allowing for the modeling of the functional and structural dynamics of systems composed of small groups of agents. It does not aim the modeling of systems with large agent populations, where the individuality of the agents is obscured by the effects of their massive behaviors.

PopOrg adopts an interactionist point of view in what concerns the basic structure of an organization, taking the notion of interaction to mean exchange of services or objects between agents (Piaget, 1995; Homans, 1961; Blau, 2005; Emerson, 1976).

The PopOrg model clearly separates the organization and the population structures of a MAS, considering that the organization structure of a system is implemented by the system's population of agents through two main mechanisms: the playing of organizational roles by agents, and the realization of organizational links between roles by social interactions that are established between the agents that play those roles.[3]

Organizational roles were conceived, since the beginning, as sets of behaviors that the agents playing the roles may have to perform in the organization. That is, organizational roles are seen as behavioral specifications for the execution of functions in organizations. On the other hand, no specific semantics was initially assigned to the organizational links, which were treated in a rather abstract way. However, the model was updated in (Costa & Dimuro, 2008), so that organizational links were construed as exchange processes realized between roles, those processes being loosely characterized as temporally ordered sets of actions. Interactions between agents in the population structure were also construed in (Costa & Dimuro, 2008) as exchange processes between agents.

The modeling of the structural dynamics of MAS is neatly formulated in the model. Its central components are, on the one hand, the operations of creation and elimination of organizational elements like roles and links, and on the other hand, the entering and leaving of the systems by the agents, and the creation and elimination of interactions between them.

Recently, the issue of the intensional, subjective factors that may influence the evolution of the dynamical structure of a multiagent system began to be tackled. As proposed by (Piaget, 1995), many subjective issues concerning the way an individual is inserted in a society can be reduced to the problem of the assessment of the quality of the interactions that such insertion allows him to have. In particular, they can be reduced to the problem of the equilibrium and stability of such interactions. So, to set the stage for the treatment of such intensional issues, the system of exchange values defined in (Piaget, 1995) was introduced into the PopOrg model (Costa & Dimuro, 2008), to allow the agents to assess the quality of the exchanges they are having. This exchange value-based approach to social interactions is briefly explained in next section.

The PopOrg Model and its Notion of Interaction

The exchange value-based approach to social interactions proposed in (Piaget, 1995) (cf. also (Homans, 1961; Blau, 2005; Emerson, 1976)) considers that every social interaction is an exchange of services between the agents involved in it. Exchange values are the values with which agents evaluate the social exchanges they have with each other. A service is any action or behavior that an agent may perform, which influences positively (respectively, negatively) the behavior of another agent, favoring (respectively, disfavoring) the effort of the latter to achieve a goal. The evaluation of a service involves not only affective and emotional reactions, but also comparisons to social standards.

Typical evaluations are expressed using qualitative values (such as, e.g., good, very good, regular, insufficient, excellent, bad, very bad, etc.), which should thus be expressed in a qualitative way (Dimuro et al., 2005; Dimuro & Costa, 2006b). So, they are neatly of a subjective, qualitative, intensional character. With those evaluations, a qualitative economy of exchange values arises in the society. Such qualitative economy requires various rules for its regulation. Most of those rules are either of a moral or of a juridical character (Piaget, 1995).

Exchange behaviors between two agents α and β can be defined as sequences of exchange steps performed between them. Following (Piaget, 1995), the two kinds of exchange steps are called $I_{\alpha\beta}$ and $II_{\alpha\beta}$. In steps of the kind $I_{\alpha\beta}$, the agent α takes the initiative to perform a service for agent β, with *investment* (also called cost) $r_{I_{\alpha\beta}}$. Subsequently, β receives the service, and gets a *satisfaction* (also called benefit) of qualitative value $s_{I_{\beta\alpha}}$. If β was to pay back α a return service immediately, like in a barter, he would probably try to "calibrate" his service so that it would have an investment r equal to $s_{I_{\beta\alpha}}$, so that α would get a return satisfaction with value s equal to $r_{I_{\alpha\beta}}$ if the exchange was to be fair (i.e., if the agents were prone to be fair).

The definition of exchange steps assumes, however, that the return service may not be performed immediately, so that a kind of bookkeeping may be necessary, in order for the involved values not to be forgotten. That is the purpose of the two other values involved in the exchange step: $t_{I_{\beta\alpha}}$ is the debt that β assumes with α for having received the service and not having paid it back yet; $v_{I_{\alpha\beta}}$ is credit that α gets on β for having performed the service and not having being paid yet. A fair exchange step (Piaget (1995) calls it an equilibrated exchange step) is one where all the involved values are qualitatively equal:

$$r_{I_{\alpha\beta}} = s_{I_{\beta\alpha}} = t_{I_{\beta\alpha}} = v_{I_{\alpha\beta}}.$$

To take account of the differences between qualitative exchange values, such values are assumed to be comparable with respect to their relative qualitative magnitudes. That is, if EV is the set of qualitative exchange values, it is assumed that values in EV can be compared by an order relation $\leq$, so that $(EV, \leq)$ is a (partially) ordered scale of exchange values, assumed in this work to be common to all agents in the society.[4] Thus, e.g., if it happened that $r_{I_{\alpha\beta}} \geq s_{I_{\beta\alpha}}$, then agent α made an investment, during his service, that was greater than the satisfaction that agent β got from it.

An exchange step of kind $II_{\alpha\beta}$ is performed in a different way. In it, agent α charges agent β for a credit with qualitative value $v_{II_{\alpha\beta}}$, which he has on β. Subsequently, β acknowledges a debt with value $t_{II_{\beta\alpha}}$ with α, and performs a return service with value $r_{II_{\beta\alpha}}$. In consequence, α gets a return satisfaction with value $s_{II_{\alpha\beta}}$. Fairness for $II_{\alpha\beta}$ steps is defined similarly as for $I_{\alpha\beta}$.

It is assumed that exchange values can be qualitatively added and subtracted from each other, so that balances of temporal sequences of exchange steps can be calculated. An exchange process between any two agents α and β may then be defined as any sequence of exchanges stages of kinds I and/or II.

Besides the above two conditions, one further condition is required in order that a sequence of exchange steps be fair: $\sum v_{II_{\alpha\beta}} \approx \sum v_{I_{\alpha\beta}}$ (that is, at the end of the sequence, α should have charged a sum total of credits which is exactly the sum total of credits he has acquired on β, no more, no less).

The values $r_{I_{\alpha\beta}}, r_{II_{\alpha\beta}}, s_{I_{\alpha\beta}}, s_{II_{\alpha\beta}}$ are called material values, generated by the evaluation of immediate exchanges, that is, they refer to the assessment of actual services. The values $t_{I_{\alpha\beta}}, t_{II_{\alpha\beta}}, v_{I_{\alpha\beta}}, v_{II_{\alpha\beta}}$ are said to be the virtual (or, potential) values, concerning deferred exchanges, thus representing values which are expected to be realized in the future, and so referring to services that have yet to be performed.

In summary, Piaget (1995) introduces a qualitative algebra with which one can model and analyze social exchanges between agents, determining in a qualitative way the degree of fairness of those exchanges.

Consider a linear discrete time structure $T = 0, 1, \ldots$, and denote by $r_{I_{\alpha\beta}}^{\tau,e}$ the investment done by the agent α when performing a service for the agent β in an exchange stage of type $I_{\alpha\beta}$, at time $\tau \in T$, in an exchange process e, and similarly for the other exchange values in this exchange stage[5]. Consider a notation for the values in exchange stages of type $II_{\alpha\beta}$, $I_{\beta\alpha}$ and $II_{\beta\alpha}$ similar to that for $I_{\alpha\beta}$. The balance of exchange values that any two agents α and β have accumulated, at some time $\tau \in T$, along the exchanges they have performed through an exchange process e that started at time 0, is defined by

$$bal(\alpha, \beta, e, t) = (\mathbf{R}_{I_{\alpha\beta}}^{t,e} + \mathbf{R}_{II_{\alpha\beta}}^{t,e}, \mathbf{S}_{I_{\alpha\beta}}^{t,e} + \mathbf{S}_{II_{\alpha\beta}}^{t,e}, \mathbf{T}_{I_{\alpha\beta}}^{t,e} + \mathbf{T}_{II_{\alpha\beta}}^{t,e}, \mathbf{V}_{I_{\alpha\beta}}^{t,e} + \mathbf{V}_{II_{\alpha\beta}}^{t,e};$$
$$\mathbf{R}_{I_{\beta\alpha}}^{t,e} + \mathbf{R}_{II_{\beta\alpha}}^{t,e}, \mathbf{S}_{I_{\beta\alpha}}^{t,e} + \mathbf{S}_{II_{\beta\alpha}}^{t,e}, \mathbf{T}_{I_{\beta\alpha}}^{t,e} + \mathbf{T}_{II_{\beta\alpha}}^{t,e}, \mathbf{V}_{I_{\beta\alpha}}^{t,e} + \mathbf{V}_{II_{\beta\alpha}}^{t,e}), \tag{1}$$

where $\mathbf{R}_{I_{\alpha\beta}}^{t,e}, \mathbf{R}_{II_{\alpha\beta}}^{t,e}, \cdots \mathbf{V}_{I_{\beta\alpha}}^{t,e}, \mathbf{V}_{II_{\beta\alpha}}^{t,e}$ are the sums of the investment, satisfaction, debt and credit values acquired by α and β in the time interval $[0,t]$ in stages of types $I_{\alpha\beta}$, $II_{\alpha\beta}$, $I_{\beta\alpha}$ and $II_{\beta\alpha}$ of the exchange process e, given by[6]

$$\mathbf{R}_{I_{\alpha\beta}}^{t,e} = \sum_{0 \le \tau \le t} r_{I_{\alpha\beta}}^{\tau,e}, \mathbf{R}_{II_{\alpha\beta}}^{t,e} = \sum_{0 \le \tau \le t} r_{II_{\alpha\beta}}^{\tau,e}, \mathbf{S}_{I_{\alpha\beta}}^{t,e} = \sum_{0 \le \tau \le t} s_{I_{\alpha\beta}}^{\tau,e}, \cdots, \mathbf{T}_{II_{\beta\alpha}}^{t,e} = \sum_{0 \le \tau \le t} t_{II_{\beta\alpha}}^{\tau,e}, \mathbf{V}_{I_{\beta\alpha}}^{t,e} = \sum_{0 \le \tau \le t} v_{I_{\beta\alpha}}^{\tau,e}, \mathbf{V}_{II_{\beta\alpha}}^{t,e} = \sum_{0 \le \tau \le t} v_{II_{\beta\alpha}}^{\tau,e}. \quad (2)$$

Clearly, the balance *bal* can be extended to any set of exchange processes E, obtaining the function $Bal(\alpha, \beta, E, t)$ that gives the balance of exchange values that agents α and β have accumulated, at time t, while performing the set of exchange processes E.

An exchange process is equilibrated at time t if and only if the balance of the exchanges satisfies the three equilibrium conditions

$$\mathcal{C}_{\alpha\beta}^{t}: \quad \left(\mathbf{R}_{I_{\alpha\beta}}^{t} + \mathbf{R}_{II_{\alpha\beta}}^{t} = \mathbf{S}_{I_{\beta\alpha}}^{t} + \mathbf{S}_{II_{\beta\alpha}}^{t}\right) \wedge \left(\mathbf{S}_{I_{\beta\alpha}}^{t} + \mathbf{S}_{II_{\beta\alpha}}^{t} = \mathbf{T}_{I_{\beta\alpha}}^{t} + \mathbf{T}_{II_{\beta\alpha}}^{t}\right) \wedge \left(\mathbf{T}_{I_{\beta\alpha}}^{t} + \mathbf{T}_{II_{\beta\alpha}}^{t} = \mathbf{V}_{I_{\alpha\beta}}^{t} + \mathbf{V}_{II_{\alpha\beta}}^{t}\right)$$

$$\mathcal{C}_{\beta\alpha}^{t}: \quad \left(\mathbf{R}_{I_{\beta\alpha}}^{t} + \mathbf{R}_{II_{\beta\alpha}}^{t} = \mathbf{S}_{I_{\alpha\beta}}^{t} + \mathbf{S}_{II_{\alpha\beta}}^{t}\right) \wedge \left(\mathbf{S}_{I_{\alpha\beta}}^{t} + \mathbf{S}_{II_{\alpha\beta}}^{t} = \mathbf{T}_{I_{\alpha\beta}}^{t} + \mathbf{T}_{II_{\alpha\beta}}^{t}\right) \wedge \left(\mathbf{T}_{I_{\alpha\beta}}^{t} + \mathbf{T}_{II_{\alpha\beta}}^{t} = \mathbf{V}_{I_{\beta\alpha}}^{t} + \mathbf{V}_{II_{\beta\alpha}}^{t}\right) \quad (3)$$

$$\mathcal{C}_{\alpha\beta}\mathcal{C}_{\beta\alpha}^{t}: \quad \left(\mathbf{V}_{I_{\alpha\beta}}^{t} + \mathbf{V}_{II_{\alpha\beta}}^{t} = 0\right) \wedge \left(\mathbf{V}_{I_{\beta\alpha}}^{t} + \mathbf{V}_{II_{\beta\alpha}}^{t} = 0\right)$$

The conditions guarantee that, if the relationship is equilibrated at time t, all investment made in services was fully credited to the agent that performed them and every credit charged was fully paid (conditions $\mathcal{C}_{\alpha\beta}^{t}$ and $\mathcal{C}_{\beta\alpha}^{t}$), and agents that charged other agents charged just the correct values that were owed ($\mathcal{C}_{\alpha\beta}\mathcal{C}_{\beta\alpha}^{t}$).

This system of exchange values has been used previously in our analysis of the equilibrium of social exchanges in multiagent systems (Dimuro et al., 2005; Dimuro & Costa, 2006a; Dimuro & Costa, 2006b; Dimuro et al., 2006c; Dimuro et al., 2007; Costa & Dimuro, 2007; Costa & Dimuro, 2008).

Other uses of exchange value-based mechanisms have already been presented in the MAS literature, such as supporting the task of partner selection (Rodrigues & Luck, 2006; Rodrigues & Luck, 2007), and supporting the incorporation of sociability as a means to improve coordination mechanisms (Grimaldo et al., 2008).

THE POPORG MODEL WITH PERIODIC SOCIAL EXCHANGES

In this section, we present the details of the PopOrg model, in a version where all organizational and social exchanges are assumed to have a periodic character, allowing for a more realistic modeling of situations in which exchange value-based assessment of organization structures may happen.

Periodic Agent Behaviors and Exchange Processes

Consider a non-empty set of agents **Ag** and let **Act** be a non-empty set of actions (communication actions and actions on concrete objects of the environment) that may be performed by the agents in **Ag**. Let $T = 0, 1, \cdots$ be a linear discrete time structure.

An agent behavior is modeled as a function $bh : T \to \wp(\mathbf{Act})$ that specifies, for each $t \in T$, a subset of actions that an agent can perform at time t, so that an agent behavior determines a sequence of sets of actions available for the agent to perform. We denote by $\mathbf{Bh}$ the set of all agent behaviors.[7]

In some cases, it is possible to observe that a sequence of actions performed by an agent, within some of its behaviors, occurs repeatedly from time to time, configuring a periodic agent behavior:

Definition 1. An agent behavior $bh : T \to \wp(\mathbf{Act})$ is said to be λ-periodic (or a behavior with period λ), for $\lambda \in \mathbb{N}$ and $\lambda \geq 1$, if and only if each two consecutive right-open time intervals $T_k = [t_{k\lambda}; t_{(k+1)\lambda})$, $T_{k+1} = [t_{(k+1)\lambda}; t_{(k+2)\lambda}) \subseteq T$, with $k = 0, 1, \cdots$, have a common sub-period between them, that is, there are sub-intervals $\Pi_k = [t_i, t_{i+\delta}) \subseteq T_k$, $\Pi_{k+1} = [t_j, t_{j+\delta}) \subseteq T_{k+1}$, with $\delta \geq 1$, such that $bh(t_{i+l}) = bh(t_{j+l}) \neq \varnothing$, for $l = 0, 1, \ldots, \delta - 1$. An agent behavior is strongly λ-periodic if it holds that $\delta = \lambda$, so that $\Pi_k = T_k$, and the time intervals T_k are said to be periods with length λ.

The sequence of sets of actions that repeat themselves at each sub-period δ is called the periodic task performed by the agent (see Example 1).

An exchange process between any two agents is modeled as a function $e : T \to \wp(\mathbf{Act}) \times \wp(\mathbf{Act})$ that specifies, for each time $t \in T$, a pair of subset of actions, determining a sequence of exchanges available for any two agents to perform, and which they perform by executing together or interleaving appropriately their corresponding actions. The set of all exchange processes is denoted by $\mathbf{Ep}$.

Analogously to Definition 1, it is possible to define periodic exchange processes.

The Time-Variant PopOrg Model

A time-variant Population-Organization structure, $POPORG = (POP, ORG, IMP)$, is a pair of structures, namely, the population structure POP and the organization structure ORG, together with an implementation relation IMP.

The Time-Variant Population Structure

The population of a multiagent system consists of the set of agents that inhabit it, at each time $t \in T$. The population structure of a multiagent system is its population set together with the set of behaviors that the agents are able to perform, and the set of exchange processes that they can establish between them (for simplicity, we consider only pairwise exchanges), at each time $t \in T$.

Definition 2. A time-variant population structure is a tuple $POP = (AG, ACT, BH, EP_{Ag}, Bc, Ec)$, where, for all time $t \in T$:

- $AG^t \in \wp(\mathbf{Ag})$ is the system's population, at time $t \in T$;
- $ACT^t \in \wp(\mathbf{Act})$ is the set of all possible agent actions, at time $t \in T$;
- $BH^t \in \wp(\mathbf{Bh})$, where $BH^t \subseteq [T \to \wp(ACT^t)]$, is the set of all possible agent behaviors, at time $t \in T$;
- $EP_{Ag}^t \in \wp(\mathbf{Ep})$, where $EP_{Ag}^t \subseteq [T \to \wp(ACT^t) \times \wp(ACT^t)]$, is the set of all possible exchange processes between agents, at time $t \in T$;
- $Bc^t : AG^t \to \wp(BH^t)$ is the behavior capability function of the agents, at time $t \in T$;

- $Ec^t : AG^t \times AG^t \to \wp(EP^t_{Ag})$ is the exchange capability function of the agents, at time $t \in T$.
- $\forall a_1, a_2 \in AG^t \; \forall e \in Ec^t(a_1, a_2) \; \forall t' \in T:$

$$Proj_1(e(t')) \subseteq \bigcup\{b(t') \mid b \in Bc^t(a_1)\} \quad \wedge \quad Proj_2(e(t')) \subseteq \bigcup\{b(t') \mid b \in Bc^t(a_2)\} \tag{4}$$

The population state at time t of a time-variant population structure, denoted by $POP^t = (AG^t, ACT^t, BH^t, EP^t_{Ag}, Bc^t, Ec^t)$, fixes the population of the system, the set of possible agent behaviors and the set of possible exchange processes between pairs of agents at time t, but not the behaviors and exchange processes actually performed, which will be chosen at that time from among those possibilities according to the particular internal states of the agents, and the states of the (social and physical) environment. Note, however, that the intensional, subjective reasons for such choices are not modeled in the extensional PopOrg model.

The set of all states of population structures is denoted by **Pop**.

If all the components of a population structure remain fixed in time, that is, for all $t \in T$, $AG^t = Ag$, $ACT^t = Act$, $BH^t = Bh$, $EP^t_{Ag} = Ep$, $Bc^t = bc$ and $Ec^t = ec$, then $Pop = (Ag, Act, Bh, Ep, bc, ec)$ is called a time-invariant population structure, so that a time-invariant population structure is a constant time-variant population structure.

An exchange process in a particular state of population structure $POP^t = (AG^t, ACT^t, BH^t, EP^t_{Ag}, Bc^t, Ec^t)$ gives rise to exchange behaviors, that is, behaviors that the agents perform during the exchange processes. Such exchange behaviors may or may not be explicitly defined in BH^t:

Definition 3. Let $e \in Ec^t(a_1, a_2)$ be an exchange process between two agents $a_1, a_2 \in AG^t$ in a particular state POP^t. The behavior $b^e_{a_1}$ defined by $b^e_{a_1}(t') = Proj_1(e(t'))$, with $t' \in T$, is called the exchange behavior of a_1 determined by e, in POP^t. If $b^e_{a_1} \notin Bc^t(a_1)$, then $b^e_{a_1}$ is said to be an implicit behavior of a_1. Analogously, we define $b^e_{a_2}$, the (possibly implicit) exchange behavior of a_2 determined by e, in POP^t.

It should be clear that a λ-periodic exchange process established between two agents requires that each of the agents presents at least one (possibly implicit) λ-periodic exchange behavior. On the other hand, one sees that the exchange behavior determined by a λ-periodic exchange process is also λ-periodic:

Proposition 1. Let $e \in Ec^t(a_1, a_2)$ be a λ-periodic exchange process between agents $a_1, a_2 \in AG^t$ in a particular state POP^t. The exchange behaviors $b^e_{a_1}$ and $b^e_{a_2}$, respectively determined on a_1 and a_2 by e in POP^t, are λ-periodic.

Proof: Consider a particular population state POP^t. Since e is λ-periodic, then, analogously to Definition 1, for each two consecutive time intervals $T_k = [t_{k\lambda}; t_{(k+1)\lambda}), T_{k+1} = [t_{(k+1)\lambda}; t_{(k+2)\lambda}) \subseteq T$, with $k = 0, 1, \ldots$, there are sub-intervals $\Pi_k = [t_i; t_{i+\delta}) \subseteq T_k$ and $\Pi_{k+1} = [t_j; t_{j+\delta}) \subseteq T_{k+1}$, with $\delta \geq 1$, such that $e(t_{i+l}) = e(t_{j+l})$, for $l = 0, 1, \ldots, \delta - 1$, and so that $Proj_1(e(t_{i+l})) = Proj_1(e(t_{j+l}))$. By Definition 2, one has that $Proj_1(e(t_{i+l})) \subseteq \bigcup\{b(t_{i+l}) \mid b \in Bc^t(a_1)\}$ and $Proj_1(e(t_{j+l})) \subseteq \bigcup\{b(t_{j+l}) \mid b \in Bc^t(a_1)\}$. So there is an enumeration of behaviors $\{b^w_{a_1}\}_{w=1,\ldots,h} \subseteq Bc^t(a_1)$, such that, for each pair of consecutive time intervals $T_k, T_{k+1} \subseteq T$, it holds that $Proj_1(e(t_{i+l})) = \bigcup^h_{w=1} b^w_{a_1}(t_{i+l})$ and also $Proj_1(e(t_{j+l})) = \bigcup^h_{w=1} b^w_{a_1}(t_{j+l})$. Thus, we have $\bigcup^h_{w=1} b^w_{a_1}(t_{i+l}) = \bigcup^h_{w=1} b^w_{a_1}(t_{j+l})$, for $l = 0, 1, \ldots, \delta - 1$, and the exchange behavior $b_{a_1}^e(t) = \bigcup_{w=1}^h b_{a_1}^w(t)$, determined by the exchange process e on a_1 in POP^t (see Definition 3), is λ-periodic. The proof for $b_{a_2}^e$ is similar. $\lozenge$

Example 1. Consider a particular population state POP^t, with the population at time t composed by three agents a, a' and a'', that is, $AG^t = \{a, a', a''\}$. Consider that the set of agent actions available at time t is $ACT^t = \{\gamma_1, \gamma_2, \gamma_3, \gamma_4, \gamma_1', \gamma_2', \gamma_3', \gamma_4', \gamma_1'', \gamma_2'', \gamma_3'', \gamma_4''\}$, and let $BH^t = \{bh_1, bh_2, bh', bh''\}$ be the set of agent behaviors existing at time t, with the behavior capability function defined as:

$$Bc^t = \{a \mapsto \{bh_1, bh_2\}, a' \mapsto \{bh'\}, a'' \mapsto \{bh''\}\},$$

where:

- bh_1 and bh_2 are non-periodic agent behaviors defined as:

$$bh_1 = \{0 \mapsto \{\gamma_1, \gamma_3\}, \ 1 \mapsto \{\gamma_1\}, \ 2 \mapsto \varnothing, \ 3 \mapsto \{\gamma_4\}, \ 4 \mapsto \varnothing, \ 5 \mapsto \{\gamma_1, \gamma_2\}, \ 6 \mapsto \{\gamma_2\}, \ 7 \mapsto \varnothing\}$$

$$bh_2 = \{0 \mapsto \{\gamma_3\}, 1 \mapsto \{\gamma_2, \gamma_4\}, 2 \mapsto \varnothing, 3 \mapsto \{\gamma_2, \gamma_3\}, 4 \mapsto \{\gamma_2\}, 5 \mapsto \{\gamma_1, \gamma_2\}, 6 \mapsto \{\gamma_2\}, 7 \mapsto \{\gamma_1\}\}$$

- bh' and bh'' are periodic agent behaviors defined as:

$$bh' = \{0 \mapsto \{\gamma_1'\}, \ 1 \mapsto \{\gamma_2'\}, \ 2 \mapsto \{\gamma_3'\}, \ 3 \mapsto \varnothing,$$
$$4 \mapsto \varnothing, \ 5 \mapsto \{\gamma_1'\}, \ 6 \mapsto \{\gamma_2'\}, \ 7 \mapsto \varnothing\}, \text{ with period } \lambda = 4$$

$$bh'' = \{0 \mapsto \{\gamma_2'', \gamma_3''\}, \ 1 \mapsto \{\gamma_3'', \gamma_4''\}, \ 2 \mapsto \{\gamma_2''\}, \quad 3 \mapsto \{\gamma_1''\},$$
$$4 \mapsto \varnothing, \quad 5 \mapsto \{\gamma_2'', \gamma_3''\}, \ 6 \mapsto \{\gamma_3'', \gamma_4''\}, \ 7 \mapsto \{\gamma_2''\}\}, \text{ with period } \lambda = 4$$

Let $EP_{Ag}^t = \{ep_{a,a'}, ep_{a'',a'}\}$ be the set of exchanges processes between agents, existing at time t, with the exchange capability function defined as:

$$Ec^t = \{(a, a') \mapsto \{ep_{a,a'}\}, (a'', a') \mapsto \{ep_{a'',a'}\}\},$$

where the periodic exchange processes are defined as

$$ep_{a,a'} = \{0 \mapsto (\{\gamma_1\}, \{\gamma_1'\}), \ 1 \mapsto (\{\gamma_2\}, \{\gamma_2'\}), \ 2 \mapsto (\varnothing, \{\gamma_3'\}), \quad 3 \mapsto (\{\gamma_4\}, \varnothing),$$
$$4 \mapsto (\varnothing, \varnothing), \quad 5 \mapsto (\{\gamma_1\}, \{\gamma_1'\}), \ 6 \mapsto (\{\gamma_2\}, \{\gamma_2'\}), \ 7 \mapsto (\varnothing, \varnothing) \quad \}, \text{ with period } \lambda = 4$$

$$ep_{a'',a'} = \{0 \mapsto (\{\gamma_2'', \gamma_3''\}, \{\gamma_1'\}), \ 1 \mapsto (\{\gamma_3''\}, \{\gamma_2'\}), \quad 2 \mapsto (\{\gamma_2''\}, \{\gamma_3'\}), \ 3 \mapsto (\{\gamma_1''\}, \varnothing),$$
$$4 \mapsto (\varnothing, \varnothing), \quad 5 \mapsto (\{\gamma_2'', \gamma_3''\}, \{\gamma_1'\}), \ 6 \mapsto (\{\gamma_3''\}, \{\gamma_2'\}), \ 7 \mapsto (\{\gamma_2''\}, \varnothing)\}, \text{ with period } \lambda = 4$$

Note that bh' and bh'' represent finite periodic behaviors, with sub-periods $\delta = 2$ and $\delta = 3$, respectively, and the corresponding periodic tasks are $\{t_i \mapsto \{\gamma_1'\}, \ t_{i+1} \mapsto \{\gamma_2'\}\}$ and $\{t_i \mapsto \{\gamma_2'', \gamma_3''\}, \{t_{i+1} \mapsto \gamma_3'', \gamma_4''\}, \{t_{i+2} \mapsto \gamma_2''\}\}$.

Observe that the following exchange behaviors happen

$$b_a^{ep} = Proj_1(ep) = \{0 \mapsto \{\gamma_1\}, \quad 1 \mapsto \{\gamma_2\}, \quad 2 \mapsto \varnothing, \quad 3 \mapsto \{\gamma_4\},$$
$$4 \mapsto \varnothing, \quad 5 \mapsto \{\gamma_1\}, \quad 6 \mapsto \{\gamma_2\}, \quad 7 \mapsto \varnothing \ \}, \text{ with period } \lambda = 4$$

$$b_{a'}^{ep} = Proj_2(ep) = \{0 \mapsto \{\gamma_1'\}, \quad 1 \mapsto \{\gamma_2'\}, \quad 2 \mapsto \{\gamma_3'\}, \quad 3 \mapsto \varnothing,$$
$$4 \mapsto \varnothing, \quad 5 \mapsto \{\gamma_1'\}, \quad 6 \mapsto \{\gamma_2'\}, \quad 7 \mapsto \varnothing\}, \text{ with period } \lambda = 4$$

where it is possible to observe the projection functions of Eq. (4). The behaviors b_a^{ep} and $b_{a'}^{ep}$ are the periodic exchange behaviors that the agents a and a' present during the periodic exchange process ep. Since $b_a^{ep} \notin Bc^t(a)$, such exchange behavior is an implicit behavior of a, induced on it by ep. Note that $b_{a'}^{ep} \in Bc^t(a')$, so $b_{a'}^{ep}$ is an explicit behavior of a'. Observe that b_a^{ep} is periodic although bh_1 and bh_2 are not.

The Time-Variant Organization Structure

To introduce organization structures with periodic interactions between roles, let a role r be defined as a non-empty subset of behaviors in **Bh**, that is, $r \in \wp(\mathbf{Bh})$ and $r \neq \varnothing$. Denote by **Ro** the set of all roles.

Definition 4. A periodic link l between a pair of roles $r_1, r_r \in \mathbf{Ro}$ is defined as a tuple $l = (r_1, r_2, e)$, specifying the periodic exchange process $e \in \mathbf{Ep}$ that the linked roles r_1 and r_2 may have to perform. The set of periodic links is denote by **Li**.[8]

An organization structure is composed by a set of roles and a set of periodic links that may be established between roles, which must be in the link capability of the any two roles involved in a exchange process.

Definition 5. A time-variant organization structure with periodic links is a tuple $ORG = (RO, LI, Lc)$, where for all time $t \in T$:

- $RO^t \in \wp(\mathbf{Ro})$ is the set of possible roles at time t;
- $LI^t \in \wp(\mathbf{Li})$ is the set of possible periodic links at time t;
- $Lc^t : RO^t \times RO^t \to \wp(Li^t)$ is the link capability function at time t;
- $\forall l = (r_1, r_2, e) \in LI^t : l \in Lc^t(r_1, r_2)$, that is, every link has to be in the link capability of the two roles that it links at time t;

- $\forall r_1, r_2 \in RO^t \ \forall e \in \mathbf{Ep} \ \forall t \in T : (r_1, r_2, e) \in LI^t \Rightarrow$

$$\forall t' \in T : Prj_1(e(t')) \subseteq \bigcup \{b(t') \mid b \in r_1\} \quad \wedge \quad Prj_2(e(t')) \subseteq \bigcup \{b(t') \mid b \in r_2\} \tag{5}$$

For each time $t \in T$, the organization state $ORG^t = (RO^t, LI^t, Lc^t)$ fixes the sets of possible roles RO^t, periodic links LI^t and link capability function Lc^t that the system has at that time. It fixes also the set of exchange processes between roles in execution at time t, namely, $EP_{Ro}^t = \{e \mid l = (r_1, r_2, e) \in LI^t\}$, and it happens that $LI^t \subseteq RO^t \times RO^t \times Ep_{Ro}^t$. However, the role behaviors and organizational exchange processes in links that are actually performed at time t, are intensionally chosen by the agents from those possibilities, i.e., they are not determined by the structural state of the organization, which just fixes the set of possibilities.

The set of all organization states is denoted by **Org**.

If all the components of an organization structure remains fixed in time, that is, for all time $t \in T$, $RO^t = Ro$, $LI^t = Li$, $Lc^t = lc$, then $Org = (Ro, Li, lc)$ is called a time-invariant organization structure, so a time-invariant organization structure is a constant time-variant organization structure.

Given an organization link $l = (r_1, r_2, e) \in LI^t$ in a particular organization state ORG^t, it is possible to determine, in an analogous way of Definition 3, the exchange behaviors determined by the exchange process e on each role, which may or may not be implicit role behaviors, that is, role behaviors that are not explicitly defined in the roles that it links.

Definition 6. Let $l = (r_1, r_2, e) \in LI^t$ be a λ-periodic link, where e is a λ-periodic exchange process between the roles $r_1, r_2 \in RO^t$ in a particular state ORG^t. The exchange behavior $b_{r_1}^e$ defined by $b_{r_1}^e(t') = Proj_1(e(t'))$, with $t' \in T$, is the behavior of the role r_1 determined by e in ORG^t. If $b_{r_1}^e \notin r_1$, then $b_{r_1}^e$ is said to be an implicit behavior of the role r_1 in e, in ORG^t. Analogously, we define $b_{r_2}^e$, the (possibly implicit) exchange behavior of the role r_2 in e, in ORG^t.

Periodic links are established by roles that have at least one (possibly implicit) periodic behavior:

Proposition 2. Let $l = (r_1, r_2, e) \in LI^t$ be a λ-periodic link in a particular state ORG^t, where $e \in EP_{Ro}^t$ is a λ-periodic exchange process between the roles $r_1, r_2 \in RO^t$. Then, in ORG^t, there exist (possibly implicit) exchange behaviors $b_{r_1}^e$ and $b_{r_2}^e$ of the roles r_1 and r_2, respectively, that are λ-periodic.

Proof: By an argument similar to that used in the proof of Proposition 1, the exchange behaviors $b_{r_1}^e$ and $b_{r_2}^e$ in the λ-periodic exchange process e are also λ-periodic. $\lozenge$

The Time-Variant Implementation Relation

We introduce, now, the implementation relation that determines (i) the ways in which the roles are assigned to agents, and (ii) the ways in which links are supported by the exchanges processes:

Definition 7. A time-variant implementation relation for $ORG = (RO, LI, Lc)$ over $POP = (AG, ACT, BH, EP, Bc, Ec)$ is a time-indexed set of states of implementation relations IMP, with $IMP^t \subseteq (RO^t \times AG^t) \cup (LI^t \times EP_{Ag}^t)$, where at each time $t \in T$:

- $RO^t \times AG^t$ is the set of all possible role implementations, that is, the set of all possible ways of assigning roles to agents at time t, so that if $(r, a) \in IMP^t$, then the role r is implemented by agent a at time t (possibly in a shared, non-exclusive way);

- $LI^t \times EP_{Ag}^t$ is the set of all possible link implementations, that is, the set of possible ways of implementing periodic organizational links, so that if $(l, e) \in IMP^t$, then the link l is said to be implemented (in a possibly shared, non-exclusive way) by the exchange process e, at time t.

The set of all states of implementation relations is denoted by **imp**.

A proper implementation relation is one that respects organizational roles and organizational links by correctly translating them in terms of agents, behaviors and exchange processes.

In the following, let $IMP^t \subseteq (RO^t \times AG^t) \cup (LI^t \times EP_{Ag}^t)$ be an implementation relation at time t.

Definition 8. A role $r \in RO^t$ is said to be properly implemented at time $t \in T$, whenever there is a subset of agents $A \subseteq AG^t$ such that the following conditions hold:

- $\forall a \in A : (r,a) \in IMP^t$, that is, all agents in A help to implement r at time t;
- $\forall t' \in T : \bigcup\{b_r(t') \mid b_r \in r\} \subseteq \bigcup\{b_a(t') \mid b_a \in Bc^t(a), a \in A\}$, that is, the set of behaviors required by the role r may be performed by the agents of A (in a possibly shared, non-exclusive way).

An immediate consequence of Definition 8 is that:

Proposition 3. Let $r \in RO^t$ be a role properly implemented by a subset of agents $A \subseteq AG^t$ at time $t \in T$. If there is a λ-periodic role behavior $b_R \in r$, then there is a λ-periodic exchange behavior $b_A : T \to \wp(\mathbf{Act})$ such that $b_A(t') \subseteq \bigcup\{b(t') \mid b \in Bc^t(a), a \in A\}$, for all $t' \in T$.

Proof: It is immediate. Define $b_A = b_R$. Then, either $b_A \in Bc^t(a)$ for some $a \in A$, or else $b_A \notin BH^t$. In the latter case, b_A is said to be an implicit behavior jointly performed by the subset of agents A. $\Diamond$

Definition 9. A periodic link $l = (r_1, r_2, e) \in LI^t$ is properly implemented at time $t \in T$ whenever there is a subset $E \subseteq \bigcup\{Ec^t(a_1, a_2) \mid (r_1, a_1), (r_2, a_2) \in IMP^t\}$ of the set of exchange processes determined by the exchange capability of the agents that implement the roles r_1 and r_2, such that the following conditions hold:

- $\forall e' \in E : (l, e') \in IMP^t$, that is, every exchange process in E helps to implement l;
- $\forall t' \in T : e(t') \subseteq \bigcup\{e'(t') \mid e' \in E\}$, that is, the exchange process required by l may be performed by the ones in E (in a possibly shared, non-exclusive way).

Proposition 4. Let $l = (r_1, r_2, e) \in LI^t$ be a periodic link properly implemented by a set $E \subseteq Ec^t(a_1, a_2)$ of exchange processes between agents $a_1, a_2 \in AG^t$. Then:

(i) The organizational link l determines between $a_1, a_2 \in AG^t$ a λ-periodic exchange process $ep : T \to \wp(\mathbf{Act}) \times \wp(\mathbf{Act})$ such that $ep(t') \subseteq \bigcup\{e'(t') \mid e' \in E\}$, for all $t' \in T$ (ep is an implicit exchange process if $ep \notin Ec^t(a_1, a_2)$ for any $a_1, a_2 \in AG^t$);

(ii) The exchange behaviors $b_{a_1}^{ep}$ and $b_{a_2}^{ep}$, respectively determined by the exchange process ep on the agents $a_1, a_2 \in AG^t$ (see Definition 3), are also λ-periodic.

Proof. The proof of (i) is immediate, defining $ep = e$, since e is λ-periodic (Definition 5). The proof of (ii) follows from Proposition 1. $\Diamond$

Definition 10. IMP^t is a proper implementation relation at time $t \in T$ if and only if:

(i) each role $r \in RO^t$ is properly implemented by a subset of agents $A_r \subseteq AG^t$; and

(ii) each periodic link $l = (r_1, r_2, e) \in LI^t$ is properly implemented by a subset $E \subseteq \bigcup \{ Ec^t(a_1, a_2) \mid (r_1, a_1), (r_2, a_2) \in IMP^t \}$ of the exchange processes determined by the exchange capabilities of the agents that properly implement the roles r_1 and r_2.

The Time-Variant Population-Organization Structure

Definition 11. A time-variant population-organization structure is a structure $POPORG = (POP, ORG, IMP)$, where, at each time $t \in T$, the state of POPORG is given by $POPORG^t = (POP^t, ORG^t, IMP^t)$, with $POP^t = (AG^t, ACT^t, BH^t, EP_{Ag}^t, Bc^t, Ec^t)$ and $ORG^t = (RO^t, LI^t, Lc^t)$, so that $IMP^t \subseteq (RO^t \times AG^t) \cup (LI^t \times EP_{Ag}^t)$. The set of all states of population-organization structures is denoted by **PopOrg**.

Note that the definition of time-variant population-organization structure does not guarantee that the relation *IMP* is proper at each time. That is, we assume that time-variant population-organization structures may pass through structural states where the population improperly implements the organization.

$POPORG = (POP, ORG, IMP)$ is properly implemented if and only if *IMP* is a proper implementation relation. If the components of *POPORG* remain fixed, that is, for all time $t \in T$, $POP^t = Pop$, $ORG^t = Org$ and $IMP^t = Imp$, then $PopOrg = (Pop, Org, Imp)$ is a time-invariant population-organization structure.

Example 2. Consider a particular *POPORG* system in a structural state $POPORG^t = (POP^t, ORG^t, IMP^t)$, depicted in Figure 1, where POP^t is the population state at time t of the population structure given in Example 1. Consider also that the organization state at time t is $ORG^t = (RO^t, LI^t, Lc^t)$, and let $RO^t = \{r, r'\}$ be the set of existing roles at time t, where the roles r and r' are defined by $r = \{b_1, b_2\}$ and $r' = \{b'\}$, respectively, with the periodic role behaviors defined as

Figure 1. A structural state of a POPORG system

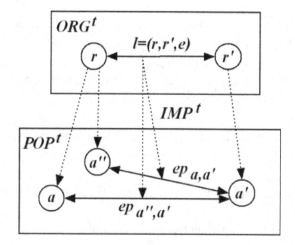

$$b_1 = \{0 \mapsto \{\gamma_1\}, \quad 1 \mapsto \{\gamma_3'', \gamma_4''\}, \quad 2 \mapsto \{\gamma_2''\}, \quad 3 \mapsto \varnothing,$$
$$4 \mapsto \varnothing, \quad 5 \mapsto \{\gamma_1\}, \quad 6 \mapsto \{\gamma_3'', \gamma_4''\}, \quad 7 \mapsto \{\gamma_2''\}\}, \text{ with period } \lambda=4$$

$$b_2 = \{0 \mapsto \{\gamma_2'', \gamma_3''\}, 1 \mapsto \{\gamma_2\}, \quad 2 \mapsto \{\gamma_2''\}, 3 \mapsto \{\gamma_1''\},$$
$$4 \mapsto \varnothing, \quad 5 \mapsto \{\gamma_2'', \gamma_3''\}, 6 \mapsto \{\gamma_2\}, 7 \mapsto \{\gamma_2''\}\}, \text{ with period } \lambda=4$$

$$b' = \{0 \mapsto \{\gamma_1'\}, \quad 1 \mapsto \{\gamma_2'\}, \quad 2 \mapsto \varnothing, \quad 3 \mapsto \varnothing,$$
$$4 \mapsto \varnothing, \quad 5 \mapsto \{\gamma_1'\}, \quad 6 \mapsto \{\gamma_2'\}, \quad 7 \mapsto \varnothing\}, \text{ with period } \lambda=4$$

Let $LI^t = \{l\}$ be the set of periodic links existing at time t, where the link $l = (r, r', e)$ between the roles r and r' is specified by the periodic exchange process

$$e = \{0 \mapsto (\{\gamma_1\}, \{\gamma_1'\}), \quad 1 \mapsto (\{\gamma_3''\}, \{\gamma_2'\}), \quad 2 \mapsto (\varnothing, \varnothing), \quad 3 \mapsto (\{\gamma_1''\}, \varnothing),$$
$$4 \mapsto (\varnothing, \varnothing), \quad 5 \mapsto (\{\gamma_1\}, \{\gamma_1'\}), \quad 6 \mapsto (\{\gamma_3''\}, \{\gamma_2'\}), \quad 7 \mapsto (\{\gamma_2''\}, \varnothing)\}, \text{ with period } \lambda=4$$

Consider also that the link capability function is given by $Lc^t = \{(r, r') \mapsto l\}$. Then, the implementation relation defined as $IMP^t = \{(r, a), (r, a''), (r', a')\} \cup \{(l, ep_{a,a'}), (l, ep_{a'',a'})\}$ is a proper implementation relation of $POPORG^t = (POP^t, ORG^t, IMP^t)$ on POP^t. Note that if the exchange stage $1 \mapsto (\{\gamma_3'', \gamma_4''\}, \{\gamma'\})$ were to happen in the exchange process e of the link l, instead of the exchange stage $1 \mapsto (\{\gamma_3''\}, \{\gamma_2'\})$, then the IMP^t relation would not be proper, because $\{\gamma_3'', \gamma_4''\} \nsubseteq Proj_1(ep_{a,a'}) \cup Proj_1(ep_{a'',a'})$, where the projection functions are those used in equation (5).

MAS with Dynamic PopOrg Structure

The structural dynamics of a MAS (Demazeau & Costa, 1996) is the dynamics that deals with the way the structure of the system varies in time, thus, it is the dynamics of the system's population and organization structures. Let $\mathbf{PopOrg} = \mathbf{Pop} \times \mathbf{Org} \times \mathbf{imp}$ be the universe of all possible states of population-organization structures, that is, the universe of all triples of population states, organization states and states of implementation relations.

Definition 12. A MAS with dynamic structure is a tuple $MAS = (\mathbf{PopOrg}, D)$ where, for each time $t \in T$, $D^t \subseteq \mathbf{PopOrg} \times \mathbf{PopOrg}$ is the system's overall structural dynamics, such that for any structural state $PopOrg \in \mathbf{PopOrg}$, at time $t \in T$, there is a set of possible next structural states, denoted by $D^t(PopOrg^t) \subseteq \mathbf{PopOrg}$.

The Basic Temporal Evolution of MAS with Dynamic Structure

For any MAS with dynamic structure, given an initial population-organization structural state $PopOrg \in \mathbf{PopOrg}$, the temporal evolution of the system is given by a time-variant population-organization structure $POPORG$, where

(i) $POPORG^0 = PopOrg$, that is, the initial structural state at time 0 is $PopOrg$, and

(ii) $POPORG^{t+1} \in D^t(POPORG^t)$, for any time $t \in T$.

The choice of the next structural state $POPORG^{t+1}$ that will be assumed by the MAS at time $t+1$ is made, at time $t \in T$, on the basis of various intensional, subjective factors extant in the system, like, e.g., preferences of agents, social norms, political powers, etc.

In some cases, it may happen that the system's overall structural dynamics may be separated into three coordinated sub-structural dynamics $D^t = D_P^t \times D_O^t \times D_I^t$: the population dynamics $D_P^t \subseteq \mathbf{Pop} \times \mathbf{Pop}$, the organizational dynamics $D_O^t \subseteq \mathbf{Org} \times \mathbf{Org}$, and the implementation dynamics $D_I^t \subseteq \mathbf{imp} \times \mathbf{imp}$. In such cases, the coordination between the system's overall dynamics and the three sub-structural dynamics may be given compositionally by

$$(POP^{t+1}, ORG^{t+1}, IMP^{t+1}) \in D^t((POP^t, ORG^t, IMP^t))$$
$$\Rightarrow POP^{t+1} \in D_P^t(POP^t) \quad \wedge \quad ORG^{t+1} \in D_O^t(ORG^t) \quad \wedge \quad IMP^{t+1} \in D_I^t(IMP^t) \tag{6}$$

In equation (6), it is clear that a particular transition from a structural state $POPORG^t$ to a next structural state $POPORG^{t+1}$ may be caused by changes in the population, in the organization, in the implementation relation, or by any combination of such changes.

It may be the case that POP^{t+1} presents either a different set of agents AG^{t+1} or a different set of actions ACT^{t+1}, probably inducing different sets of agent behaviors BH^{t+1} and exchange processes EP^{t+1}, as well as different behavioral capability and exchange capability functions Bc^{t+1} and Ec^{t+1}. In other cases, the changes may appear directly in the set of agent behaviors BH^{t+1}, by introducing completely different new behaviors, or by just modifying some of the periods of the previously available behaviors, which may probably cause changes in the set of exchange process EP^{t+1} or in the periods of some of such processes. Inversely, direct changes in the set of exchange processes EP^{t+1} may require corresponding changes in the set of agent behaviors BH^{t+1}.

A similar analysis can be done considering the unrestricted changes that may occur in the organization structure or in the implementation relation, relatively to a particular transition from a structural state $POPORG^t$ to a next structural state $POPORG^{t+1}$.

MAS with Periodic Structural Dynamics

Observe that in certain systems the changes in their population-organization structures happen only in a periodic way:

Definition 13. A structural dynamics $D : T \to \mathbf{PopOrg} \times \mathbf{PopOrg}$ is said to have periodic occurrences of changes, with maximum delay $\lambda \in \mathbb{N}$, $\lambda \geq 1$, if, for any sequence of time intervals $T_k = [t_{k1}; t_{(k+1)1}) \subseteq T$, $k \in \mathbb{N}$, for each time interval T_k, there is at least one time $t' \in T_k$ such that for all time $t \in T_k$:

$$POPORG^{t+1} = POPORG^t \quad \text{if} \quad t \neq t';$$
$$POPORG^{t+1} \neq POPORG^t \quad \text{if} \quad t = t'. \tag{7}$$

AN EXCHANGE VALUE-BASED MORAL SYSTEM FOR THE POPORG MODEL

Building on the PopOrg model with periodic exchanges, and on the exchange value-based mechanism for the assessment of social relationships, it is possible to conceive an operational notion of morality for MAS.

Morality in Human Society and Organizations

Morality as a research area (see, e.g., (Furrow, 2005)) is concerned with the relationships that people establish between them, the value that people assign those relationships, and the rules of behavior for the conservation and improvement of valued relationships. The common name morality, on the other hand, is taken as a synonym for moral system, as already used above in the chapter, and better explained presently.

The three central ideas for any attempt of transposing morality to the domain of artificial agents, are:

(i)   **Moral system:** a moral system is a system of rules and values that help the agents to keep sound the social relationships they establish between them. Moral rules determine criteria for judging if behaviors are acceptable in social relationships;

(ii)   **Moral judgements:** moral judgements are the expression of the results of the moral assessments of social behaviors that were performed in given social situations. Moral judgements are expressed in terms of praise or blame for the behaviors that are judged.

(iii) **Moral reactions:** the reactions that some agents may have to certain behaviors of given agents, as determined by moral judgements of those behaviors. Moral reactions may be directed to the agents responsible for those behaviors, and also to other agents. Moral reactions, expressed in correspondence to moral judgements of praise or blame for the performed behaviors, operate respectively as rewards or sanctions to the agents that performed those behaviors.

An Informal Account of Exchange Value-Based Moral Systems

By the agents' continuously assigning exchange values to the services exchanged, and by their continued accounting of such values, an economy of exchange values emerges in the society, tightly connected to the functional dynamics of the system (e.g., to the variations in the efficiency, readiness or quality with which the agents perform their services) and to the structural dynamics of the system (when the system's structure is allowed to be time-variant).

In (Piaget, 1995) such economy of exchange values is proposed as the basis for an operatory explanation of morality, under the assumption that the aim of a morality is the conservation of the extant social relationships that are positively valued by the agents. We note that such view is completely coincident with the approach proposed by the theory of social dependence (Castelfranchi et al., 1992a), on the basis of which one can assume that agents should be lead to care about others because of the objective dependence that they have between each other, due to the agents' usual lack of capability to fully achieve their goals solely by themselves.

Thus, we are led to conclude that a circle of ideas exists, linking the various approaches sketched above, so that an attempt can be made to establish a particular notion of morality for multiagent systems, namely: (1) the basic fact of the objective social dependences (Castelfranchi et al., 1992a) leads agents to look for other agents, in order to exchange services that will help each other to achieve both the goals required by the roles that they perform in the system and the individual goals that the agents have by themselves; (2) such exchange of services constitutes the operational basis for the social relationships that the agents establish with one another (Piaget, 1995), supporting the organizational links between their respective roles, as defined in the PopOrg model; (3) morality concerns essentially the caring about social relationships and the aim of conserving them when they are, possibly in different ways, beneficial to the agents involved in them (Furrow, 2005); (4) the assessment and valuation of a social relationship existing between two agents can be neatly performed on the basis of the exchange values that emerge from the exchange of services promoted by such relationship; (5) so, morality may possibly be expressed in terms of rules that help agents to decide about the correctness or wrongness of each other actions, basing their decisions on the achievement or not of equilibrated balances of exchange values, and taking as one of the basic moral values the conservation of social relationships; (6) moreover, moral reactions to such moral judgements may lead social relations be continued or discontinued, in accordance with the positive or negative results of those judgements, thus functionally and structurally affecting the organization of the system.

The operational exchange value-based moral systems that may arise from such circle is thus a set of values and rules that enable agents to: (1) qualitatively evaluate the services they exchange between each other; (2) commit to debts and credits acquired from services performed earlier; (3) reason with the moral rules that aim the conservation of social relationships that are beneficial to the agents involved in them; (4) take moral judgements (praises and blames) into consideration in their social reasoning, that is, when they are deciding how to behave with respect to other agents in the society; (5) act on each other by expressing rewards (punishments) for actions that fit (do not fit) the moral rules adopted in the society, according to the judgements realized.

The Exchange Value-Based Moral System and its Support in the PopOrg Model

For simplicity, we consider here only a case where the organization structure is time-variant, the population structure is time-invariant, and each organizational role is implemented by just one agent.

Let $Pop = (Ag, Act, Bh, Ep, bc, ec)$ be a time-invariant population structure and $ORG = (RO, LI, Lc)$ a time-variant organization structure implemented by Pop, and let IMP be the time-variant implementation relation. They constitute a time-variant population-organization structure $PopORG = (Pop, ORG, IMP)$, which is assumed here to vary just in the set of organizational links, and in their implementations.

Among others, there may happen two kinds of changes in the set of links LI^t, at time $t+1 \in T$: (1) either a new link l is created, so that $LI^{t+1} = LI^t \cup \{l\}$; or (2) a link l is removed from LI^t, so that $LI^{t+1} = LI^t - \{l\}$. The problem we face here is that of the formalization of the conditions under which, at a time $t+1 \in T$, a link l is added to (or removed from) the set of links LI^t, due to the moral judgements that the agents may make about each other behaviors during organizational exchanges.[9]

Let the balance of exchange values of any subset $E = \{e_1, \cdots, e_n\} \in \wp(Ep)$ of exchange processes that agents $a_1, a_2 \in Ag$ have accumulated, at time $t \in T$, be given by the function $Bal : Ag \times Ag \times \wp(Ep) \times T \to EV^8$, defined by

$$Bal(\alpha, \beta, E, t) = (\mathbf{R}_{I_{\alpha\beta}}^{t,E} + \mathbf{R}_{II_{\alpha\beta}}^{t,E}, \mathbf{S}_{I_{\alpha\beta}}^{t,E} + \mathbf{S}_{II_{\alpha\beta}}^{t,E}, \mathbf{T}_{I_{\alpha\beta}}^{t,E} + \mathbf{T}_{II_{\alpha\beta}}^{t,E}, \mathbf{V}_{I_{\alpha\beta}}^{t,E} + \mathbf{V}_{II_{\alpha\beta}}^{t,E};$$

$$\mathbf{R}_{I_{\beta\alpha}}^{t,E} + \mathbf{R}_{II_{\beta\alpha}}^{t,E}, \mathbf{S}_{I_{\beta\alpha}}^{t,E} + \mathbf{S}_{II_{\beta\alpha}}^{t,E}, \mathbf{T}_{I_{\beta\alpha}}^{t,E} + \mathbf{T}_{II_{\beta\alpha}}^{t,E}, \mathbf{V}_{I_{\beta\alpha}}^{t,E} + \mathbf{V}_{II_{\beta\alpha}}^{t,E}), \tag{8}$$

where

$$\mathbf{R}_{I_{\alpha\beta}}^{t,E} = \sum_{0 \le \tau \le t} r_{I_{\alpha\beta}}^{\tau,E}, \cdots, \mathbf{V}_{II_{\beta\alpha}}^{t,E} = \sum_{0 \le \tau \le t} v_{II_{\beta\alpha}}^{\tau,E} \tag{9}$$

are the sums of the investment, satisfaction, debt and credit values acquired by $a_1, a_2 \in Ag$ in the time interval $[0, t]$ in stages of types $I_{\alpha\beta}$, $II_{\alpha\beta}$, $I_{\beta\alpha}$ and $II_{\beta\alpha}$ of the exchange processes $e_1, \cdots, e_n \in E$.

Let the exchange processes of $E = \{e_1, \cdots, e_n\}$ be periodic exchanges with periods $\lambda_1, \cdots \lambda_n$, respectively. Let λ be the greatest of such periods. Let k ($k > 1$) be the least number of consecutive λ-periods of exchanges that the agents have to perform in order to be able to reliably assess the exchanges. Then, after the occurrence of k consecutive λ-periods, each agent $a_1, a_2 \in Ag$ is able to judge, at any time $t \geq k\lambda$, if the balance $Bal(a_1, a_2, E, k\lambda)$ is beneficial, fair, or harmful for himself.

For that, since the most basic exchange value-based moral rule concerns the equilibrium of the material exchanges, we introduce the notion of qualitative amount of material profit, given by the strictly ordered set $AMP = (\{neg, null, pos\}, <)$, where $neg < null < pos$. Then, the qualitative material profit of agent a_1 in its periodic exchange process e with agent a_2 is given by the function $MP_{a_1:a_2,e} : T \rightarrow AMP$, defined as:

$$MP_{a_1:a_2,e}(t) = \begin{cases} pos & \text{if} \quad \mathbf{S}_{I_{a_1 a_2}}^{t,e} + \mathbf{S}_{II_{a_1 a_2}}^{t,e} > \mathbf{R}_{I_{a_1 a_2}}^{t,e} + \mathbf{R}_{II_{a_1 a_2}}^{t,e}, \\ null & \text{if} \quad \mathbf{S}_{I_{a_1 a_2}}^{t,e} + \mathbf{S}_{II_{a_1 a_2}}^{t,e} = \mathbf{R}_{I_{a_1 a_2}}^{t,e} + \mathbf{R}_{II_{a_1 a_2}}^{t,e}, \\ neg & \text{if} \quad \mathbf{S}_{I_{a_1 a_2}}^{t,e} + \mathbf{S}_{II_{a_1 a_2}}^{t,e} < \mathbf{R}_{I_{a_1 a_2}}^{t,e} + \mathbf{R}_{II_{a_1 a_2}}^{t,e}, \end{cases} \tag{10}$$

where $\mathbf{R}$ and $\mathbf{S}$ are, respectively, the accumulated satisfaction and investment values at time t, in stages of type $I_{a_1 a_2}$ and $II_{a_1 a_2}$ of the exchange process e, as defined in equation (2). The qualitative material profit function $MP_{a_1 a_2, e} : T \rightarrow P$ can be naturally extended to consider a set E of exchange processes, namely to $MP_{a_1 a_2, E} : T \rightarrow P$, using the sum of satisfaction and investment values defined in equation (9). We can leave both e and E implicit, when it causes no confusion.

Let's now turn to the operational morality that builds on the conditions for equilibrated social exchanges, given in the second section of this chapter. The moral rule defining the equilibrium of material profits is given informally by:

$ME_{(a_2:r_2, a_1:r_1, l)}$:
If agents a_1 and a_2, playing roles r_1 and r_2, respectively, have been interacting according to a certain periodic link l, and it happens that agent a_2 got greater material profit from the interaction than agent a_1 got from it, then it is expected that at some time in the future agent a_2 performs a service for agent a_1, in return for the greater profit received, and such that the final profit received by a_1 from the return service equals the final profit received by a_2.

An action of performing a return service is thus a moral action, according to this moral system, if it respects such rule: if it keeps the material profit of each agent equal to the profit of the other.

Formally, the moral rule $ME_{(a_2:r_2, a_1:r_1, l)}$ introduced above may be crudely expressed, in a tentative way, using first order predicate calculus,

$ME_{(a_2:r_2, a_1:r_1, l)}$:

$$l = (r_1, r_2, e) \Rightarrow \tag{11}$$

$$\forall t \in T : (MP_{a_2:a_1}(t) > MP_{a_1:a_2}(t)) \Rightarrow (prfm(a_2, \sigma, a_1, t+1) \ \wedge \ (MP_{a_2:a_1}(t+1) = MP_{a_1:a_2}(t+1))),$$

where $prfm(a_2, \sigma, a_1, t+1)$ indicates that at time $t+1$ agent a_2 performs a service σ for a_1, with the meaning that if at any time $t \in T$ it happens that a_2 has profited more than a_1 from the periodic interaction, then at the next time $t+1$ it should perform a service for a_1 in order to equilibrate their respective profits.[10]

With respect to the basic exchange value-based moral rule $ME_{(a_2:r_2,a_1:r_1,l)}$, two possible moral reactions will be specified, as an example. Let us define first, however, the form of moral judgements that support such moral reactions. The moral judgement by an agent a of the behavior of agent a_2 in situations where a_2 is supposed to re-install the equilibrium in its relationship with agent a_1, can be given a formal definition as follows.

Let $RMJ = \{blame, praise\}$ be the set of possible results of moral judgements. Then, the moral judgement by an agent a, at time τ, on the basis of the moral rule $ME_{(a_2:r_2,a_1:r_1,l)}$, of the behavior of agent a_2 toward agent a_1, concerning their periodic exchanges during a time interval $[t, t']$, with $t' \leq \tau$, is given by the function $MJ_{ME_{(a_2:r_2,a_1:r_1,l)}} : Ag \times T \times \wp(T) \to RMJ$, defined as

$$MJ_{ME_{(a_2:r_2,a_1:r_1,l)}}(a,\tau,[t,t']) = \begin{cases} praise & \text{if } a \text{ judges, at time } \tau, \text{ that moral rule} \\ & ME_{(a_2:r_2,a_1:r_1,l)} \text{ was respected in the interval } [t,t']; \\ blame & \text{otherwise,} \end{cases} \quad (12)$$

which we also denote by the expressions $a \mapsto^\tau ME_{(a_2:r_2,a_1:r_1,l)}{}^{[t,t']} = praise$ and $a \mapsto^\tau ME_{(a_2:r_2,a_1:r_1,l)}{}^{[t,t']} = blame$, respectively. Note that a moral judgement like $MJ_{ME_{(a_2:r_2,a_1:r_1,l)}}$ can be made by any agent in the system which is able of moral reasoning, that is, able to take moral rules into account in its social reasoning.

Now, with respect to the sanctions and rewards, simple moral reactions can be informally specified thus:

$ScntRwrd_{ME}(a_1,a_2,l,[t,t'])$:
Agent a_1 continues to interact with agent a_2 according to the organizational link l as long as agent a_2 respects the moral rule ME during the time interval $[t,t']$, and a_1 sanctions a_2 with the ceasing of the interaction if the moral rule is disrespected during that interval.

This can be formally expressed in a preliminary way as follows, with the help of the formal rules $Rwrd_{ME}(a_1,a_2,l,[t,t'])$ and $Snct_{ME}(a_1,a_2,l,[t,t'])$, defined below.

Consider a given time $t \in T$ and a structural state $PopORG^{t'} = (Pop, ORG^{t'}, IMP^{t'})$, for some $t' = t + k\lambda$, where $k \in \mathbb{N}$ is the least number of exchange periods λ that agents $a_1, a_2 \in Ag$ need to evaluate their interaction. Let $a_1, a_2 \in Ag$ be interacting in $PopORG$, and respectively playing roles r_1 and r_2, from time t to time t'. That is, $(r_1, a_1), (r_2, a_2) \in IMP^\tau$, for all $\tau \in [t,t']$. For all $\tau \in [t,t']$, let IMP^τ and LI^τ be fixed, with $l = (r_1, r_2, e) \in LI^\tau$ being a periodic organizational link between roles r_1 and r_2. If it was the case that l was properly implemented by a subset $E \subseteq ec(a_1,a_2)$ of exchange process during the time interval $[t,t']$, then, by Proposition 4(i), l determines, between $a_1, a_2 \in Ag$, a (possibly implicit) λ-periodic exchange process ep such that $ep(t') \subseteq \bigcup\{e'(t') \mid e' \in E\}$, for all $t' \in T$, and $ep = e$. Assume that E effectively exists, and that $E = \{e_1, \cdots, e_n\}$, where the respective periods are $\lambda_1, \cdots, \lambda_n$, with $\lambda_i \leq \lambda$ for $i = 1, \cdots, n$.

Considering that the moral judgement of the behavior of agent a_2 toward agent a_1, concerning their periodic exchanges during the time interval $[t,t']$, is done by the agent a_1 itself, at time t', the reward and sanction rules that formalize the procedure of moral reaction $ScntRwrd_{ME}(a_1,a_2,l,[t,t'])$ may be written as

$$\frac{a_1 \mapsto^{t'} ME_{(a_2:r_2,a_1:r_1,l)}^{[t,t']} = praise}{LI^{t'+1} = LI^{t'} \quad \wedge \quad IMP^{t'+1} = IMP^t} Rwrd_{ME}(a_1,a_2,l,[t,t']) \tag{13}$$

$$\frac{a_1 \mapsto^{t'} ME_{(a_2:r_2,a_1:r_1,l)}^{[t,t']} = blame}{LI^{t'+1} = LI^{t'} - l \quad \wedge \quad IMP^{t'+1} = IMP^t - \{(l,e') \mid e' \in E\}} Snct_{ME}(a_1,a_2,l,[t,t']) \tag{14}$$

the rule (13) meaning that agent a_1 preserves the link l as a consequence of the effort of agent a_2 toward mainting the equilibrium of the interaction, and the rule (14) meaning that agent a_1 cancels the link l as a consequence of the attitude of agent a_2 of refusing to effort to keep the interaction in equilibrium.

Note that the rules causally relate subjective operations (moral assessments of attitudes) to objective effects (maintenance and elimination of organizational links), thus reflecting the assumption of the PopOrg model that the intensional and the extensional aspects of a MAS can be causally related to each other.

CONCLUSION AND FUTURE RESEARCH DIRECTIONS

This chapter presented the current version of the PopOrg model and used it to illustrate a central assumption of the conceptual framework underlying the model, namely, that the PopOrg model allows a suitable support for intensional organizational processes, connecting the subjective aspects of the social actions of agents with their objective effects on the organization structure and functioning of the system. To illustrate such feature of the PopOrg model, we first defined an operational, exchange value-based notion of morality for MAS and the moral judgements and their associated reward and sanction procedures, and then showed how such moral system could be formalized using the organizational and populational elements of the model. However, we have not given a complete operational moral system for MAS. Such work should be seen as complementary to the one presented here, and so a work to be done in the near future.

Also, we have not fully explored the implications of the distinction between intensionality and extensionality assumed by the PopOrg model. In particular, we have not exposed and analysed a full system model based on such distinction, where the PopOrg model would enter as the extensional part of the full model, the intensional part being modeled in a way of its own. Such work would be in line with the proposal that norms are two-fold objects (Conte & Castelfranchi, 2006), with a social and a mental aspect, and that they operate by following a mental path in the individual agents, involving goals, commitments, etc. Since norms are but one particular kind of intensional objects, a more general notion of mental path, applicable to other kinds of intensional organizational objects that also have that two-fold character (e.g., organizational values, goals, etc.), would be of central importance to the clarification of the way the PopOrg model could be coupled to a model able to support intensional organizational processes (see also Chapter X "Grounding Organizations into the Minds of the Agents" by Castelfranchi, for the need of accounting for intensional issues, in an adequate account of organizations).

ACKNOWLEDGMENT

This chapter benefited from previous discussions with H. Coelho, C. Castelfranchi, R. Bordini and J. Hübner. We thank them for their suggestions and criticisms. We also thank the referees for their valuable comments. This work was partially supported by FAPERGS and CNPq.

REFERENCES

Blau, P. (2005). *Exchange & power in social life*. New Brunswick: Transaction Publishers.

Boella, G., van der Torre, L., & Verhagen, H. (2006). Introduction to normative multiagent systems. *Computational & Mathematical Organization Theory, 12*(2-3), 71-79.

Boissier, O., & Demazeau, Y. (1996). ASIC: An architecture for social and individual control and its application to computer vision. In *Distributed software agents and applications, LNCS n. 1069* (pp. 135-149). Berlin: Springer.

Bordini, R. H., Costa, A. C. R., Hübner, J. F., & Viccari, R. M. (1995). Language support for agent migration. In *1st International Conference on Multi-Agent Systems, ICMAS* (p. 441). San Francisco.

Castelfranchi, C., Miceli, M., & Cesta, A. (1992a). Dependence relations among autonomous agents. In E. Werner, & Y. Demazeau (Eds.), *Decentralized A.I.-3* (pp. 215-227). Amsterdam: Elsevier.

Conte, R., & Castelfranchi, C. (2006). The mental path of norms. *Ratio Juris, 19*(4), 501-17.

Corkill, D. D. (1983). *A framework for organizational self-design in distributed problem solving networks*. Ph. D. Thesis, University of Massachusetts.

Costa, A. C. R., & Dimuro, G. P. (2007). A basis for an exchange value-based operational notion of morality for multiagent systems. In J. Neves, M. Santos & J. Machado (Eds.), *Progress in artificial inteligence, 13th Portuguese Conference on Artificial Intelligence, EPIA 2007, LNAI n. 4874* (pp. 580-592). Berlin: Springer.

Costa, A. C. R., & Dimuro, G. P. (2008). Semantic concepts for a formal structural dynamics of situated multiagent systems. In J. Sichman, J. Padget, S. Ossowski, & P. Noriega (Eds.), *Coordination, organizations, institutions, and norms in agent systems III, LNAI n. 4870* (pp. 139-154). Berlin: Springer.

Costa, A. C. R. , Hübner, J. F., & Bordini, R. H. (1994). On entering an open society. In *11th Brazilian Artificial Intelligence Symposium, SBIA* (pp. 535-546). Fortaleza: UFC.

Coutinho, L. R., Sichman, J. S., & Boissier, O. (2007). Modeling dimensions for multi-agent systems organization. In *1st. International Workshop on Agent Organizations: Models and Simulations (AOMS'07)*. Hyderabad, India.

Dastani, M. M., Dignum, M. V., & Dignum, F. P. M. (2002). Organizations and normative agents. In *1ˢᵗ. Eurasian Conference on Advances in Information and Communication Technology (EurAsia ICT 2002)* (pp. 982-989). Berlin: Springer.

Demazeau, Y., & Costa, A. C. R. (1996). Populations and organizations in open multi-agent systems. In *1st National Symposium on Parallel and Distributed AI, PDAI'96*. Hyderabad, India.

Dimuro, G. P., Costa, A. C. R., & Palazzo, L. M. (2005). Systems of exchange values as tools for multi-agent organizations. *Journal of the Brazilian Computer Society, 11*(1), 31–50. (Special Issue on Agents' Organizations).

Dimuro, G. P., & Costa, A. C. R. (2006a). Interval-based Markov Decision Processes for regulating interactions between two agents in multi-agent systems. In J. Dongarra, K. Madsen, & J. Wasniewski (Eds.), *Applied parallel computing: Revised selected papers of the 7th International Conference, PARA 2004, Lyngby, 2004, LNCS n.3732* (pp. 102-111). Berlin: Springer.

Dimuro, G. P., & Costa, A. C. R. (2006b). Exchange values and self-regulation of exchanges in multi-agent systems: the provisory, centralized model. In S. Brueckner, G. Serugendo, D. Hales, & F. Zambonelli (Eds.), *Engineering self-organising systems: Revised selected papers of the third international workshop, ESOA 2005, Utrecht, 2005, LNAI n. 3910* (pp. 75-89). Berlin: Springer.

Dimuro, G. P., Costa, A. C. R., L. V. Gonçalves, L. V., & Hübner, A. (2006c). Regulating social exchanges between personality-based non-transparent agents. In A. Gelbukh, & C. A. Reyes-Garcia (Eds.), *MICAI 2006: Advances in artificial intelligence, LNAI n. 4293* (pp. 1105-1115). Berlin: Springer.

Dimuro, G. P., Costa, A. C. R., L. V. Gonçalves, L. V., & Hübner, A. (2007). Centralized regulation of social exchanges between personality-based agents. In P. Noriega, J. Vázquez-Salceda, G. Boella, O. Boissier, V. Dignum, N. Formara, & E. Matson (Eds.), *Coordination, organizations, institutions and norms in MAS II, LNAI n. 4386* (pp. 16–23). Berlin: Springer.

Emerson, R. (1976). Social Exchange Theory. In A. Inkeles, J. Colemen, & N. Smelser (Eds.), *Annual Review of Sociolog*. Palo Alto: Annual Reviews.

Fatima, S. S., & Uma, G. (1998). An adaptive organizational policy for multi-agent systems. In Y. Demazeau (Ed.), *Third International Conference on Multiagent Systems, ICMAS 1998, Paris* (pp. 120-127). Los Alamitos: IEEE Computer Society.

Ferber, J., & Gutknecht, O. (1998). Aalaadin: A meta-model for the analysis and design of organizations in multi-agent systems. In Y. Demazeau (Ed.), *Intermational. Conference on Multi-Agent Systems, ICMAS 98* (pp. 128-135). Paris: IEEE Press.

Ferber, J., Gutknecht, O., & Michel, F. (2003). From agents to organizations: An organizational view of multi-agent systems. In P. Giorgini, J. P. Müller, & J. Odell (Eds.), *Agent-oriented software engineering IV, 4th international workshop, AOSE 2003, Melbourne, Australia, July 15, 2003, Revised Papers, LNCS n. 2953* (pp. 214-230). Berlin: Springer.

Fox, M. S. (1979). *Organization structuring: Designing large complex software* (Tech. Rep. CMU-CS-79-155). Pittsburgh: Carnegie-Mellon University.

Furrow, D. (2005). *Ethics*. London: Continuum.

Gasser, L. (2001). Organizations in multi-agent systems. In *10th European Workshop on Modeling Autonomous Agents in a Multi-Agent World, MAAMAW-2001. Annecy.* (available at http://www.isrl. uiuc.edu/~gasser/papers/)

Gasser, L., Braganza, C., & Herman, N. (1987). MACE: A flexible testbed for distributed AI research. In M. N. Huhns (Ed.), *Distributed artificial intelligence* (pp. 119-152). London: Pitman Publishers.

Gasser, L., & Ishida, T. (1991). A dynamic organizational architecture for adaptive problem solving. In T. L. Dean, & K. McKeown (Eds.), *9th National Conference on Artificial Intelligence, AAAI 1991* (pp. 185-190). Cambridge: MIT Press.

Giddens, A. (1984). *The constitution of society: Outline of the theory of structuration.* Cambridge: Polity Press.

Grimaldo, F., Lozano, M., & Barber, F. (2008). Coordination and sociability for intelligent virtual agents. In J. Sichman, J. Padget, S. Ossowski, & P. Noriega (Eds.), *Coordination, Organizations, Institutions, and Norms in Agent Systems III., LNAI n. 4870.* Berlin: Springer.

Grossi, D., Dignum, F., Dastani, M., & Royakkers, L. M. M. (2005). Foundations of organizational structures in multiagent systems. In F. Dignum, V. Dignum, S. Koenig, S. Kraus, M. P. Singh, & M. Wooldridge (Eds.), *4rd International Joint Conference on Autonomous Agents and Multiagent Systems, AAMAS 2005, 2005, Utrecht* (pp. 690-697). New York: ACM Press.

Hannoun, M., Boissier, O., Sayettat, C., & Sichman, J. (1998). Towards a model of multi-agent systems' organization. In *CMOT'98 - International Workshop on Computational and Mathematical Organization Theory.* (pp. 31-32). Montreal.

Hübner, J. F., Boissier, O., & Sichman, J. S. (2006). Programming MAS reorganisation with MOISE+. In J. Meyer, et al. (Eds), *Foundations and practice of programming multi-Agent systems, Dagstuhl Seminars n. 06261.* Dagstuhl: IFBI.

Homans, G. (1961). *Social behavior: Its elementary forms.* New York: Harcourt, Brace & World.

Hoogendoorn, M., & Treur, J. (2006). An adaptive multi-agent organization model based on dynamic role allocation. In *IEEE/WIC/ACM Intelligent Agent Technology, IAT'06* (pp. 474-481). Washington: IEEE Computer Society.

Ishida, N., Kaneko, M., & Allada, R. (1999). Biological clocks. *Proceedings of the National Academy of Sciences, 96,* 8819–8820.

Kashyap, S. (2006). *Reorganization in multiagent organizations.* Master Dissertation, Kansas State Univeristy.

Matson, E. T. (2005). Abstraction of transition properties in multiagent organizations. In A. Skowron, J. P. A. Barthès, L. Jain, R. Sun, P. Morizet-Mahoudeaux, J. Liu, & N. Zhong, (Eds.), *IEEE/WIC/ACM International Conference on Intelligent Agent Technology, Compiegne, France, 2005* (pp. 169-172). Los Alamitos: IEEE Computer Society.

McCallum, M., Vasconcelos, W. W., & Norman, T. J. (2006). Verification and analysis of organisational change. In O. Boissier, J. Padget, V. Dignum, G. Lindemann, E. Matson, S. Ossowski, J. S. Sichman &

J. Vázquez-Salceda (Eds.), *Coordination, organizations, institutions, and norms in multi-agent systems, LNAI n. 3913* (pp. 48-63). Berlin: Springer.

Noriega, P.; Sierra, C., & Rodríguez, J. (1998). The fishmarket project. Reflections on agent-mediated institutions for trustworthy E-Commerce. In *Workshop on Agent-mediated Electronic Commerce, AmEC-98, International Conference on Electronic Commerce, ICEC-98,, April*. Seoul, Korea.

Pattison, H., Corkill, D., & Lesser, V. (1987). Instantiating descriptions of organizational structures. In M. Huhns (Ed.), *Distributed artificial intelligence,1,* 59-96. London: Pitman Publishers.

Piaget, J. (1963). *The origins of intelligence in children*. New York: W.W. Norton & Company.

Piaget, J. (1995). *Sociological studies*. London: Routlege.

Picard, G., Mellouli, S., & Gleizes, M. P. (2006). Techniques for multi-agent system reorganization. In O. Dikenelli, M. P. Gleizes, & A. Ricci (Eds.), *Engineering societies in the agents world VI, LNCS n. 3963* (pp. 142-152). Berlin: Springer.

Reddy, D. R., Erman, L. D., Fenneli, R. D., & Neely, R. B. (1976). The Hearsay Speech Understanding System: An Example of the Recognition Process. *IEEE Transactions. on Computers, 25*(4), 422-431.

Rodrigues, M. R., & Luck, M. (2006). Analysing partner selection through exchange values. In L. Antunes & J. Sichman (Eds.), *VI Workshop on Agent Based Simulations, LNAI n. 3891* (pp. 24–40). Berlin: Springer.

Rodrigues, M. R., & Luck, M. (2007). Cooperative interactions: an exchange values model. In P. Noriega, J. Vázquez-Salceda, G. Boella, O. Boissier, V. Dignum, N. Fornara, & E. Matson (Eds.), *Coordination, organizations, institutions and norms in agent systems II, LNAI n. 4386* (pp. 63-70). Berlin: Springer.

So, Y., & Durfee, E. (1993). An organizational self-design model for organizational change. In *Working notes of the AAAI-93 Workshop on Artificial Intelligence and Theories of Groups and Organizations: Conceptual and Empirical Research, July 1993* (pp. 8-15). Washington D.C.

Tambe, M. (1996). Teamwork in real-world, dynamic environments. In *Proceedings of the Second International Conference on Multi-Agent Systems (ICMAS-96)*. Menlo Park: AAAI Press.

Zheng-guang, W., Xiao-hui, L., & Qin-ping, Z. (2006). Adaptive mechanisms of organizational structures in multi-agent systems. In *Agent computing and multi-agent systems, LNCS n. 4088* (pp. 471-477). Berlin: Springer.

Zambonelli, F., Jennings, N., & and Wooldridge, M. (2001). Organizational abstractions for the analysis and design of multi-agent systems. In P. Ciancarini, & M. Wooldridge (Eds.), *Agent-oriented Software Engineering, LNAI Volume 1957*. Berlin: Springer.

Zhong, C., & DeLoach, S. A. (2006). An Investigation of Reorganization Algorithms. In H. R. Arabnia (Ed.), *International Conference on Artificial Intelligence, ICAI 2006, v. 2* (pp.514-517). *Las Vegas:* CSREA Press.

KEY TERMS

Exchange: Sets of actions that two or more agents perform together in a coordinated way, so that objects or services provided by ones are made available to the others that need them.

Link: A set of standard interaction processes, that pairs (or, more generally, subsets of agents) in a multiagent system may be assigned to, in order to help the system to fullfil some internal or external function.

Multiagent System Organization: The structure inherent in a multiagent system, constituted essentially by roles and exchange links between roles, defining standard behaviors and interaction processes to be followed by the agents, in accordance with the way they were assigned to the roles.

Organizational Development: A process through which the structure of a multiagent system organization improves its quality and strength. Organizational development is essentially a qualitative process, with possible quantitative effects on the organization structure.

Organizational Dynamics: The set of rules that govern the temporal changes in of the organization of a multiagent system.

Organizational Growth: A process through which the structure of a multigent system organization increases the number of its roles and links. Organizational growth is essentially a quantitative process.

Role: A set of standard behaviors, that agents in a multiagent system may be assigned to, in order to help the system to fullfil some internal or external function.

Service: A coordinated set of actions that an agent performs in order to satisfy a specific need of another agent or set of agents.

ENDNOTES

[1] In this book, see Chapter XVIII "A Framework for Dynamic Agent Organizations" by Fatima and Wooldridge for another approach to organization dynamics building on methods for dynamical task and resource allocation.

[2] In this book, for the issue of modularity in the description of organizations, see Chapter VI "A Formal Framework for Organizational Modeling and Analysis" by Popova and Sharpanskykh, where a formal hierachical approach to organization description is presented.

[3] The separation between organization and population structures raises a series of problems concerning the relationships between individuals and the roles they play in the organization, and between the official organizational interactions that the individuals perform for the correct playing of their organizational roles, and the private, non-official, social interactions that they perform between each other while (and often in spite of) playing those roles. The study of such problems concerning the relationships between the organizational and the population levels from the point of view of the PopOrg model are out of the scope of the present chapter, but see Chapter X "Grounding

Organizations into the Mind of the Agents" by Castelfranchi, for a survey and analysis of concerns which seem to be close to ours.

4   In the cases where several scales of exchange values are considered, a correspondence relation between such scales is required. Otherwise, the agents will have no means to reach a common understanding about the correctness of their respective evaluations.

5   We assume that all steps in a stage occur simultaneously.

6   Whenever possible we write $bal(\alpha, \beta, t)$, $\mathbf{R}^t_{l_{\alpha\beta}}, \mathbf{S}^t_{l_{\alpha\beta}} \mathbf{T}^t_{l_{\alpha\beta}} \mathbf{V}^t_{l_{\alpha\beta}}$, and $r^\tau_{l_{\alpha\beta}}$, $s^\tau_{l_{\alpha\beta}} t^\tau_{l_{\alpha\beta}} v^\tau_{l_{\alpha\beta}}$, and analogously for the exchange stage $\text{II}_{\alpha\beta}$, leaving implicit the reference to the exchange process e.

7   Since the PopOrg model focuses on the extensional aspects of a MAS organization, the treatment of the intensional aspects of the agents' actions is out of the scope of the model. See Chapter IX "A Logic for Agent Organizations" by Virginia and Frank Dignum for a logical treatment of the extensional aspects of the actions (effects, dependencies, etc.) and of the extensional issues related to the organizational aspects of the performance of such actions (organizational responsibilities, etc.).

8   See (Costa & Dimuro, 2008), for previous work where the organization structure does not consider the periodicity of the exchange processes that define links.

9   We are considering here the case of informal organizations, that is, organizations that individual agents establish among them to systematically coordinate their informal interactions. Morality is an essential aspect of such organizations, as the moral judgements that agents make about each other behaviors are important for the persistence of such organizations.

10   We note, immediately, the unnecessarily strong requirement imposed by such tentative formulation, that the return service be realized immediately after the first service was performed.

Chapter XVIII
A Framework for Dynamic Agent Organizations

Shaheen Fatima
Loughborough University, UK

Michael Wooldridge
University of Liverpool, UK

ABSTRACT

This chapter presents an adaptive organizational policy for multi-agent systems called TRACE. TRACE allows a collection of multi-agent organizations to dynamically allocate tasks and resources between themselves in order to efficiently process and incoming stream of tasks. The tasks have deadlines and their arrival pattern changes over time. Hence, at any instant, some organizations could have surplus resources while others could become overloaded. In order to minimize the number of lost requests caused by an overload, the allocation of resources to organizations is changed dynamically by using ideas from microeconomics. We formally show that TRACE has the ability to adapt to load variations, reduce the number of lost requests, and allocate resources to computations on the basis of their criticality. Furthermore, although the solution generated by TRACE is not always Pareto-optimal, TRACE has the properties of feasibility and monotonicity that make it well suited to time-constrained applications. Finally, we present experimental results to demonstrate the performance of TRACE.

INTRODUCTION

In a multiagent system two or more agents join together to achieve goals that individuals on their own cannot, or to achieve them more efficiently (Rosenschein & Zlotkin 94, Faratin, Sierra, & Jennings, 98, Kraus, 01, Falcone & Castelfranchi, 01). It is well recognized that the ability of a multiagent system to dynamically reorganize its structure and operation at run-time is highly valuable for many application domains. For example, consider a multiagent information retrieval system with a number of information repositories. Access to these repositories is provided by information agents. Users request these agents for information, the agents access the repositories and use the available computational resources to process requests. In most practical cases, these requests have two main characteristics: deadlines, and an arrival pattern that is unknown a priori and varies with time. Here the resources used to carry out requests are limited, so they must be used optimally. Thus, such dynamic environments require the multiagent system to operate under a fluctuating load, schedule requests before their deadline, and allocate resources optimally.

Thus maximum possible requests must be processed with available resources. Since the load is time varying, some parts of the system may receive more requests than others and have a higher demand for resources. So the key problem is to develop a method that allows the system to reorganize itself (i.e., allocate resources dynamically in accordance with their demand) in order to adapt to a changing environment. A lot of research effort has been devoted to developing such methods (Waldspurger Hogg, Huberman, Kephart, & Stornetta, 92, Wellman, Birmingham, & Durfee, 96, Clearwater, 96, Wlash & Wellman, 99, Sandholm & Lesser, 01).But there is lack of a single method that addresses all the three issues of deadlines, fluctuating loads, and efficiency. In order to overcome this shortcoming, we present a comprehensive framework that copes with deadlines and a fluctuating load and also addresses the issue of efficient allocation of resources. Note that the objective of this chapter is not to focus on operating systems related issues such as 'serializeability' or 'deadlock management'. These have been dealt with at length in distributed and real time operating systems (Douglass, 02, Tanenbaum & Steen,04). The main objective of this chapter is to focus on developing a market based protocol for resource allocation that works at a higher level than operating systems.

The proposed method is called TRACE (Task and Resource Allocation in a Computational Economy). In TRACE, a request is a task. TRACE is made up of two components: a task allocation protocol (TAP) and a resource allocation protocol (RAP). As agents have different capabilities, it is necessary for them to cooperate effectively. The task allocation protocol (TAP) allocates tasks to agents through a process of negotiation. The changes in load are handled by the resource allocation protocol (RAP), which uses ideas from microeconomics. The main focus of this chapter is the RAP although we give a brief overview of the TAP.

This chapter makes two extensions to the RAP proposed in (Fatima, 01). First, our new version of the RAP has the properties of feasibility and monotonicity So the reallocation of resources (in Fatima:01) can take place only after the RAP terminates normally. In contrast, the feasibility property of the new RAP allows reallocation to take place even before its normal termination. This has the advantage of speeding up the allocation process. Furthermore, since the RAP also has the property of monotonicity, the solution it generates after every iteration improves with the number of iterations. Second, this chapter also provides a comprehensive analysis of the properties of the RAP.

THE SETTING

We formally define the terms used in TRACE and the problem it aims to solve.

Organizations: We have a multiagent system, M, structured as a set of k organizations $M = \{O_1, \ldots, O_k\}$. Each organization is a set of agents: organizations have no internal structure. Different organizations contain mutually disjoint sets of agents. We denote the set of all agents by $AG = \{a_1, \ldots\}$. The members of an organization $O_i \in M$ are denoted membs(O_i), so membs(O_i) $\in$ AG. We write membs(M) to denote members of MAS, so membs(M) = $\bigcup^k_1$ membs(O_i). In each organization, member agents are of two types: *permanent agents* (that are permanently assigned to an organization) and *marketable agents* (that may be temporarily re-assigned to another organization). Intuitively, permanent agents represent the capital of the organization, and marketable agents represent the labour. If $O_i \in M$ is an organization, then we denote the permanent agents in O_i by perm(O_i), and the marketable agents in O_i by mark(O_i) we require that perm(O_i) $\cap$ mark(O_i) = and that perm(O_i) $\cap$ mark(O_i) = membs(O_i).

Goals: Permanent agents receive requests that specify a *goal* and a deadline for completing the goal. The TRACE system assigns a priority to each goal. Let G={g_1,...} denote the set of all goals that can arrive at MAS. There is a set of goals G(O_i) $\in$ G. that arrive at the organization O_i. Each goal, g $\in$ G has four attributes: a deadline, a priority, a set of tasks that comprise the goal, and a plan for achieving the goal. GP(g)$\in$N denotes the priority of a goal, GD(g)$\in$N its deadline, GT(g) the set of tasks that comprise g, and GR(g) the plan for g. The deadline for a goal is specified in the request for it. The priority of a goal denotes its importance; the higher the priority, the more critical it is. The priority of each goal is pre-defined by TRACE and is always fixed.

A goal is composed of a set of tasks that must be carried out in a given order. These tasks, together with an ordering, form the plan for achieving the goal. The task dependencies specify the order in which tasks must be executed. We describe plans more formally after describing tasks. Each permanent agent has a plan library with a plan for each goal. This library is stored in the agent's domain knowledge. Thus, for the goal specified in a request, an agent obtains the plan from its plan library. In TRACE, a task is the smallest unit of activity executed by a single agent. A group of agents may work together on a goal but a task is carried out by a single agent. Let T={t_1,...} denote the set of all tasks. The set of tasks that comprise a goal g is GT(g)$\in$T.

If a permanent agent, *a*, cannot achieve a goal in isolation, then *a* asks other agents in its organization for help. These agents are assumed to be benevolent, so that if they have the capability and the opportunity, they will agree. Agent *a* allocates tasks to other agents within its organization using the TAP. Thus while requests for goals arrive at permanent agents, tasks may be allocated either to permanent or marketable agents through the TAP.

Tasks: At every time step, agents may be allocated a set of tasks. Each task, t $\in$T has four attributes: a priority, a duration, a set of actions that comprise it, and a plan for achieving the task. Let TP(t)$\in$N be the priority of task *t*, TD(t)$\in$N its duration, TA(t)$\in$N the set of actions that comprise *t*, and TR(t) the plan for achieving *t*. A task can be a component of more than one goal. The priority of a task is therefore not an inherent attribute of the task but is assigned the priority of the goal of which it is a part. For a goal request, the permanent agent determines the start time for each constituent task on the basis of the goal deadline, the ordering of tasks and the duration for each task. The ordering and the duration for each task are obtained from the agent's domain knowledge.

The duration of a task indicates the number of time steps required to carry the task out. We model time via the natural numbers, N, and assume that every agent uses the same model, and in addition, that every agent has access to a global system clock. For our present work we assume that all the agents have the same processing speed, so the duration of a task is the same irrespective of the agent that carries the task out.

Plans: We now define plans for goals GR and plans for tasks TR more formally. Let GR denote the set of all plans over the set T of tasks and TR denote the set of all plans over the set, AC of actions. In our framework, plans for goals can be constructed from tasks and actions by means of parallel and sequential composition. An action is the elementary form of activity performed by an agent.

Schedules: Agents each have a set of capabilities and a schedule. An agent's capabilities are a subset of T; we denote the capabilities of agent $a \in AG$ by cap(a), so cap(a)$\in$T. If $a \in AG$ and $t \in T$ t then agent a has the capability to carry out task t iff $t \in$cap(a), Agents differ in their capabilities due to a difference in their knowledge of tasks. An agent has the knowledge to complete a task t if it knows the sequence of actions that must be carried out in order to achieve t. Thus, in TRACE, all the agents can process all types of tasks provided they have the required knowledge. An agent's capabilities can be changed by changing its domain knowledge.

As stated earlier, a permanent agent, a, that receives a goal request can accomplish it individually or with other members of its organization. A team is a group of members within an organization that cooperate to achieve a goal. Within the team, a takes the role of the team organizer and the other agents take on the role of team members. If a permanent agent cannot complete a goal either individually or as a team, then the goal is decommitted (i.e., rejected because its deadline cannot be met). The term decommit is used to mean rejecting a goal that had previously been accepted (but not yet begun execution) in order to accommodate a new higher priority request. One of the main goals of our work is to minimize the number of decommitted goals.

An agent's schedule defines what tasks the agent is working on and when. Tasks on an agent's schedule represent commitments (Cohen & Levesque 90) that the agent has about the future. Let TO denote a set of quads of the form <t,g,p,a> such that $g \in G$, $t \in GT(p)$, p=GP(g) and the request for g arrives at agent a. Formally, a schedule is a function from time points to quads in TO. We denote the schedule of agent $a \in AG$,by sched(a), so sched(a) is a (partial) function sched(a) $N \in TO \cup \{\epsilon\}$. Agents are only allowed to be committed to tasks of which they are capable. Also, an agent cannot process more than one task at any given time.

The system proceeds in a series of rounds; at every round, an agent receives tasks to process, and must decide how to process them. After deliberation, the agents update their internal schedule, and in particular, decide what task to work on for that round. If an organization finds that it has goals than it cannot achieve, then it can acquire labour from other organizations in order to achieve them. This labour comes in the form of the marketable agents—not permanent agents. Labour is obtained for a single round.

Complexity: It is worth noting that the task scheduling problem TRACE is attempting to solve is computationally hard (Fatima:01).

THE TRACE SYSTEM

A MAS in TRACE is a set of computational organizations. An organization (see Chapter I "The Role of Organization in Agent Systems" by V. Dignum for other definitions of an organization) has three components: i) a set of permanent agents, which are assigned to the organization indefinitely; ii) a set of marketable agents, which may be temporarily hired by other organizations to make up shortfalls in labour; iii) a distinguished agent called *resource manager* (RM), which has the responsibility of determining resource needs (in the sense of marketable agents) for its organization, and of obtaining labour from other organizations when required.

Since arrival pattern of requests changes with time, some organizations may get few requests and require few resources, while others may get more requests and require more resources to complete them. To begin, no agent knows when or what requests it will receive. However, as time progresses, the agents observe the arrival pattern of requests and dynamically change the allocation of resources to organizations in accordance with the arrival pattern.

The allocation of tasks to agents in an organization is done by the TAP and the allocation of resources to the organizations is done by the RAP. Task allocation is done by means of negotiation (Smith, 80). Resource allocation is done using a micro-economic approach (Arrow & Hahn, 71) because such an approach gives a Pareto-optimal. An allocation is said to be Pareto-optimal if no organization can be made better off without making some other organization worse off. Under this condition, the resources in the system are used as well as can be. solution. Before describing the protocols we explain the knowledge agents have.

Agents have two types of knowledge: domain knowledge and organizational knowledge. Domain knowledge includes the plans for goals and tasks. The domain knowledge for tasks, denoted KT, is a set of triples. Each triple indicates the task, the duration for the task, and a plan for it. The domain knowledge for goals is a set of triples that contain the goal, its plan, and priority.

Let $KG(O_j) \in KG$ and $KT(O_j) \in KT$ be the domain knowledge for goals that may arrive at organization O_i and the corresponding tasks. $KG(O_i)$ is the knowledge for goals in $G(O_i)$ and $KT(O_j)$ denotes the corresponding task knowledge. The RM and all the permanent agents of organization O_i have $KG(O_i)$ and $KT(O_i)$. But the marketable agents of O_i have only the domain knowledge for tasks. The domain knowledge of the RM and permanent agents is fixed and does not change, while the domain knowledge is allocated to marketable agents dynamically by the RAP and changes after every allocation depending on the organization to which the agent is allocated.

The organizational knowledge for O_i, $KO(O_i) \in AG$, is the set of agents, both permanent and marketable, that belong to O_i. Permanent agents are allocated to an organization indefinitely. But as marketable agents are allocated dynamically to organizations, $KO(O_i)$ changes after every reallocation. Thus organizations in TRACE exist at a logical level. By changing the agents' organizational knowledge, the agents that comprise an organization can be changed. However, the physical structure of the MAS remains unchanged. The organizational knowledge for O_i is stored with all the permanent agents and the RM of O_i.

THE TASK ALLOCATION PROTOCOL

The task allocation protocol used in TRACE is based on the Contract Net (Smith:80b). It is used to determine an allocation of tasks to agents within the organization. This involves finding suitable team members and the time at which the tasks can be executed. Due to lack of space only a high level description of the TAP is presented here. In order to find team members and arrive at a commonly agreed time with them, an agent a that receives a request for a task t determines if it has the capability to carry out the task (i.e., if $t \in cap(a)$) before the deadline $dl(t)$ of the task. If not, it generates a proposal for others to carry out the task, and sends an announcement to all agents in its organization. If these agents can process the task, they send a bid. If the proposed time is not acceptable, the prospective team member sends a bid with a modified time. If the organizer finds the modified time acceptable, then it agrees in principle to the task, otherwise it may propose some other time and this process repeats until a mutually agreed time is found.

During task allocation, any conflicts with existing commitments are resolved on the basis of priorities. Lower priority tasks are either rescheduled to accommodate a more critical task, or decommitted altogether if deadlines make rescheduling impossible. Whenever an agent drops an existing commitment to accommodate a higher priority request, it informs all organization members. When a task is decommited, the manager of that task increments a counter, which indicates the number of decommitted tasks. All task managers periodically send this value to their respective RMs. In addition, all marketable agents calculate the percentage time they remain idle during a certain period. This information is also passed on to the respective RMs, which then perform reallocation.

THE RESOURCE ALLOCATION PROTOCOL

Resource allocation has long been studied by economists, resulting in the development of elegant normative models that describe how resources in an economy can be optimally shared (Arrow & Hahn, 71, Mas-Colell & Whinston, 95). There are two basic microeconomic approaches, (Hurwicz, 73): price-directed and resource-directed. The advantage of the latter is that if the initial allocation is feasible (i.e., the total amount of resources allocated equals the amount available), so too are later allocations. Also, it has the property of monotonicity (i.e., successive iterations of the algorithm result in increasing system-wide utility) (Ho, Servi, & Suri, 80). Hence we use the resource directed approach for our RAP.

The RMs periodically determine the resource needs of their respective organizations. Each period is called a reorganization cycle. In TRACE, the MAS is organized as a market economy comprised of overloaded organizations that have a demand for agents and under-loaded organizations that have a supply of idle agents. Reorganization is the process of supplying idle agents to organizations with a demand for them. Reorganization changes the number of agents in an organization, and their domain and organizational knowledge. Also, if the total demand over the entire MAS exceeds the total supply, reallocation is done to minimize the decommitment of high priority goals. Each RM performs the following steps at the end of each cycle.

1. Obtain information about demand for resources from agents of its organization. The demand for resources in the $(t+1)$ cycle, C_{t+1} is determined on the basis of the demand for the previous cycle, C_t.
2. Compute the equilibrium allocation (using the resource-directed approach).
3. Transfer the relevant domain knowledge to the newly allocated agents.
4. Notify the permanent agents of its organization about the new allocation.

We first briefly describe the resource-directed microeconomic approach for determining the equilibrium allocation (Ho, Servi, & Suri, 80). In this approach, an arbitrary initial allocation of resources is made. The allocation is then iteratively changed. During each iteration, each organization computes the marginal utility of the resource it needs, given its current allocation of the resource. The marginal utility of the organization O_i, denoted $\mu(O_i)$, is the increase in utility due to the allocation of an additional unit of that resource. These values are then sent to other organizations and the average marginal utility is determined across all the organizations. The allocation of resources to organizations is then changed such that organizations with an above average marginal utility receive more resources while organizations with a below average marginal utility receive less of the resource. When the marginal utility is almost equal for all the organizations, the resulting allocation is in equilibrium and is Pareto-optimal (Arrow & Hahn, 71). Since our aim is to minimize the decommitment of high priority goals, we use priority as a measure of utility; the higher the priority of a goal, the higher the utility of achieving it. The utility to an organization is the sum of utilities of goals achieved in a given cycle. A more precise statement of the RAP follows.

Step 1: At the end of each reorganization cycle, agents in an organization convey the following two items of information about that cycle to their respective RMs.

Information about the decommitted goals: The permanent agents send this information because only they act as team organizers. This information is used for reallocation of marketable agents (see step 2) and for the dynamic distribution of domain knowledge to them (see step 3).

Information about the idle time: This is used to identify idle agents. Marketable agents convey this information because only these agents can be reallocated. Note that the TRACE is aimed at cooperative problem-solving scenarios, so the agents do not lie to their RM Each RM determines the demand for more agents on the basis of the above information. The MAS is reorganized for cycle, C_{t+1}, on the basis of requests received in the previous cycle, C_t on the assumption that the arrival pattern of requests for C_{t+1} will be the same as that for C_t. Thus, if the number of goals decommitted by an organization (say O_i) is zero for a cycle, and η agents remain idle, then the number of agents O_i required for the next cycle is $|membs(O_i)| - \eta$, where $|membs(O_i)|$ is the number of permanent and marketable agents in O_i. But if the number of goals decommitted in O_i is greater than zero and there are no idle agents, O_i has a demand for additional agents in order to achieve the decommitted goals. This demand is determined by the RM on the basis of its information about the time required to complete the decommitted goals (given in the domain knowledge) and their deadlines. Let D_i denote the demand at O_i i.e., the number of agents required by O_i in a given cycle. Let AL denote the allocation list that represents the current allocation of marketable agents to the k organizations. This is a k element list in which the ith element denotes the set of marketable agents allocated to organization O_i.

From this information, each RM finds the mean priority (MP_i) of goals decommitted by its organization, the number of additional agents (D_i) required to handle the decommitted goals, and the set (I_i) of idle agents in its organization, and sends it to all the other RMs. Each RM compiles three lists: i) a list (MP) of k elements; the ith element (MP_i) denotes the mean priority of goals decommitted by O_i, ii) a list (D) of k elements; the ith element (D_i) is the demand for agents in O_i and iii) a list (I) of k elements; the ith element (I_i) is the set of idle agents in O_i. Each resource manager sends MP_i, D_i, and I_i to every other resource manager. The equilibrium allocation is then determined as follows.

Step 2: Based on the number of decommitted goals and the number of idle agents in a given cycle, we define the following three scenarios for an organization. In the first scenario (S_1) the number of decommitted goals is greater than zero and the number of idle agents is zero. The load on such an organization is more than its processing capability and there is a demand for additional agents in order to achieve all the decommitted goals. In scenario (S_2) the number of decommitments and the number of idle agents are both zero. The load on such an organization matches its processing capability and there is neither a demand for additional agents nor a supply of idle agents. Finally, in scenario (S_3) the number of decommitments is zero and the number of idle agents is greater than zero. Such an organization has a supply of idle agents. The RAP reallocates idle agents from organizations in scenario S_3 to those in scenario S_1.

TRACE is in equilibrium (note that we have not shown the convexities of agent's preferences. This is because, for large economies, it has been shown in (Mas-Colell & Whinston, 95) that nonconvexities of agent's preferences are no obstacle to (near) existence of equilibrium) when one of the following conditions is true: there is no demand for agents in any of the k organizations (i.e., there is no organization in scenario S_1 and each element of D is zero), or none of the organizations has idle agents (i.e., there is no organization scenario S_3 and all the elements of I are empty sets, although D may contain non-zero elements) and all organizations have the same marginal utility. The equilibrium allocation is found as follows. Beginning with the current allocation as the initial allocation, each RM goes through the following steps to arrive at the equilibrium allocation.

While there is demand for agents and also supply of idle agents do:

2.3   From MP determine the organization, O_x, that has the highest mean priority of decommitments, i.e., the highest marginal utility.

2.3   Let I denote an element of I_y, where *y* is an index into I such that. I_y is non-empty. Reallocate I to organization O_x.

2.3   Update D and I.

These steps are performed iteratively until the termination condition (either there is no demand for agents or there is no supply of idle agents) is reached and the MAS is in equilibrium. Now the RMs transfer relevant domain knowledge to the newly allocated agents as follows.

Step 3: The above steps compute the equilibrium allocation of agents to organizations. However, these agents may lack the domain knowledge required to process the requests at the organization. So the RM transfers this knowledge to the newly allocated agents. This dynamic distribution of knowledge enables effective use of available computational resources; an agent that is idle but lacks the knowledge required to execute tasks can acquire that information as indicated above.

Step 4: The RMs finally notify the permanent agents of their respective organizations about the equilibrium allocation. After reorganization, all permanent agents update their organizational knowledge.

Subsequently, the TAP refers to this changed organizational knowledge to select team members for tasks. Thus, as stated previously, organizations in TRACE exist at a logical level and are represented as organizational knowledge with all the permanent agents and the RMs.

PROPERTIES OF RESOURCE ALLOCATION PROTOCOL

The following theorems show that TRACE has the following properties: i) feasibility of allocation, ii) monotonic reduction in the number of decommitments, iii) reduction in the decommitment of high priority goals from one cycle to the next, iv) adaptiveness, v) efficient use of resources, and vi) efficiency of allocation.

Theorem 1: The allocation is feasible at the end of every iteration in the computation of the equilibrium allocation.

Proof: Each iteration reallocates a single marketable agent from an organization in scenario S_3 to an organization in scenario S_1. The sum total in allocation therefore remains zero at every iteration (see step 2 of the RAP). ∎

Note that step 2 of RAP terminates when the equilibrium allocation is found. However, since the allocation remains feasible after every iteration in the computation of the equilibrium solution, the computation can be stopped after any iteration in order to speed up the process of reallocation. Although stopping the computation prematurely saves time, it may not result in a Pareto-optimal allocation.

Theorem 2: If the arrival pattern of requests for cycle C_{t+1} remains the same as that for C_t at all the organizations, each iteration in the computation of the equilibrium allocation results in a strict monotonic decrease in the total number of decommitments in MAS in C_{t+1} relative to C_t.

Proof: Each iteration reallocates a marketable agent from an organization in scenario S_3 (say O_i) to an organization in scenario S_1 (say O_j). At the end of the first iteration, O_i gets an extra agent while O_j loses an idle agent. If the arrival pattern of requests for the cycle C_{t+1} remains the same as that for C_t, Oi decommits fewer goals in C_{t+1} relative to C_t. On the other hand the number of decommitments in O_j remains zero both in C_{t+1} and C_t. The sum total of decommitments in Oi and O_j therefore decreases. Each successive iteration further reduces this sum. Each iteration therefore results in a strict monotonic decrease in the total number of decommitments in MAS. ■

Theorem 3: If the arrival pattern of requests for cycle C_{t+1} remains the same as that for C_t at all the organizations, at the end of each iteration, the mean priority of goals decommitted in each organization either decreases or remains the same in the cycle C_{t+1} relative to C_t.

Proof: Each iteration reallocates a marketable agent from an organization (say O_j) in scenario S_3 to an organization (say O_i) in scenario S_1 and has the highest mean priority of decommitments. Since O_i gets an extra agent, it decommits fewer goals in C_{t+1}. Since the TAP decommits low priority goals in order to accommodate high priority ones, the mean priority of decommitted goals in O_i is reduced in C_{t+1}. The number of decommitments and hence the mean priority of decommitted goals in O_j is zero, both before and after reallocation. ■

Theorem 4: If the load on organization O_i exceeds its processing capability (i.e., the number of decommitments in O_i is greater than zero) in C_t creating a demand for D_i additional agents, the equilibrium allocation increases the processing capability of O_i by adding D_i additional agents to it in C_{t+1} provided MAS has D_i idle agents in C_t that can be allocated to O_i.

Proof: It is straightforward to verify this from step 2 of the RAP. ■

Theorem 5: The RAP reduces the average number of agents required by an organization under varying load, relative to static allocation.

Proof: Let R^t_i denote the number of marketable agents required by organization O_i in C_t in order to achieve all the goals and let AL^t_i denote the number of agents allocated to O_i in C_t. Also, let AL^{max}_i denote the maximum value of AL^t_i over n consecutive cycles. The average number of agents allocated to O_i during the n cycles is $(\sum^n_{t=1} AL^t_i)/n$. In order to achieve the same level of performance as the dynamic allocation scheme of the RAP, a static allocation scheme would require AL^{max}_i agents to be allocated to O_i throughout the n cycles. ■

Theorem 6: The equilibrium allocation is Pareto-optimal if, at the end of allocation, there is no organization in scenario S_1.

Proof: The computation for equilibrium allocation terminates under one of two possible conditions: there is no organization in scenario S_1, or there is no organization in scenario S_3. For the first condition, it is clear that all the organizations have sufficient number of agents to carry out all the goals successfully and the number of decommitments is zero at every organization. All the organizations therefore have the same (i.e., zero) marginal utility and the allocation is Pareto-optimal. For the second condition, i.e., there is no organization in scenario S_3, the allocation may not be Pareto-optimal. This is because two or more organizations may be in scenario S_1 and have different values for the mean priority of decommitted goals. This results in a non Pareto-optimal allocation since the organizations may have different marginal utilities. ∎

EXPERIMENTAL RESULTS

In order to evaluate the effectiveness of TRACE, a number of experiments were carried out. These serve to quantify its ability to reduce the number of decommitments and adapt to changes in computational load by reorganizing the MAS, and make effective use of resources. The system was implemented in C, and the behavior of the system was studied by randomly varying the computational load across different organizations in the MAS.

Reduction in decommitments: The first experiment was done to measure the reduction in the number of decommitments made by the system. Each organization of the MAS was assumed to have 10 permanent agents and the number of marketable agents was 10 times the number of organizations.

Figure 1. A graph of load against time for four organizations in a typical run of TRACE

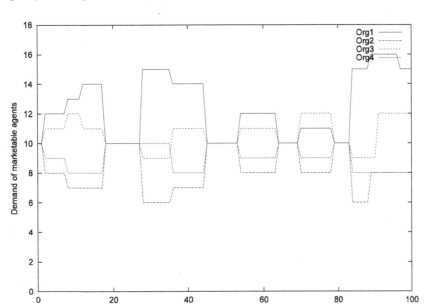

Table 1. TRACE scales up: the percentage reduction in decommitments remains stable as the numbe of organizations grows

Number of organizations					
	4	8	16	32	64
Percentage Reduction	74.12	75.98	74.30	75.10	74.10

The system was allowed to run for 100 reorganization cycles by gradually varying the computational load in each organization for every cycle Figure 1 shows a fragment of a typical run.

As a control, the experiment was repeated without using the TRACE RAP (i.e., by simply dividing the marketable agents equally among the organizations, and keeping the number of agents in each organization constant throughout). From these two results the percentage reduction in the number of decommitments using the reorganization method was determined. The results of this study are summarized in Table 1.

A desirable characteristic of open MAS is the ability to scale well to large systems. The simulation results as shown in Table 1 were obtained by increasing the number of organizations from 4 to 64. Note that in this experiment the number of agents increases with the number of organizations (we had 10 permanent agents in each organization, and the total number of marketable agents was 10 times the number of organizations). The number of requests was increased in the same proportion. Basically, the conditions to which an organization is subjected are the same but the number of such organizations has been scaled up.

Figure 2. A graph of agents demanded (solid line) and agents allocated (dotted line) against time during a typical run of TRACE

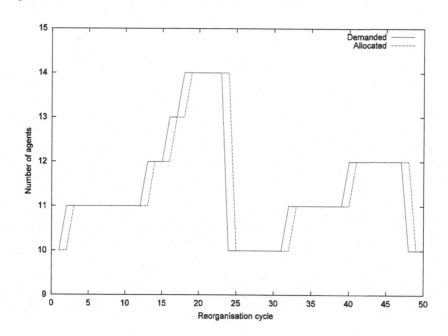

This increase, however, did not affect the percentage reduction in decommitments. This indicates that with respect to reduction in decommitments, the proposed reorganization approach scales well to large systems.

Adaptiveness of the MAS: The main objective of TRACE is to make the MAS adaptive to variations in load. Figure 2 shows the variation in number of marketable agents demanded over 50 cycles in one organization and the agents acquired by it over 50 cycles through the RAP. As the number of decommitments in a cycle increases, the number of new agents in the next cycle increases correspondingly. For instance, in reorganization cycle 2, when the requirement for agents increased from 10 to 11, the number of additional agents in the next cycle increases correspondingly. Similarly, a decrease in the number of decommitments results in a decrease in the number of agents. These results demonstrate the ability of the MAS to adapt to load variations.

Efficient use of resources: In Figure 2, The average number of agents over 50 cycles is 12. In order to achieve the same level of performance as in TRACE, a MAS with constant number of agents would require 14 permanent agents (the maximum number of agents required by one organization). Thus the proposed approach, (which requires around 12 agents on an average), is more economical in terms of resource usage.

RELATED WORK

A number of methods have been proposed for handling load variations in multiagent systems. These can be classified into two types: those that (like our work) use a microeconomic approach and those that do not (for instance (Scerri, Farinelli, Okamoto, & Tambe, 05). We focus on microeconomic approach based methods because they help in getting Pareto optimal allocations. For instance, Spawn (Waldspurger, 92) uses market-based methods to utilize idle computational resources in a distributed network of workstations. In Spawn, each problem-solving request needs to determine its requirement for resources and participate in an auction if necessary. But resource management in TRACE is done only by the RMs. This makes the reorganization process simpler, and also reduces the time required to compute the equilibrium allocation. Also, Spawn does not address the issue of deadlines while TRACE does. Finally, our RAP, unlike Spawn, has the properties of feasibility and monotonicity that make it well-suited to time constrained problem-solving.

Market mechanisms were also studied in (Sandholm & Lesser, 01) for task allocation to self-interested agents. This is analogous to the decommitments in TRACE. This work differs from TRACE in the following ways. First, TRACE is a combination of the contract net protocol (Smith, 80b) (for task allocation to cooperative agents) and the resource-directed microeconomic approach for resource allocation. On the other hand, (Sandholm & Lesser, 01) is based on the contract net protocol and (more importantly) is aimed at self-interested agents. The second difference is that (Sandholm & Lesser, 01) is not targeted towards handling load fluctuations in different parts of the MAS while TRACE is. A microeconomic approach has also been used in (Kurose & Simha, 89, Wellman, Birmingham, & Durfee, 96, Wlash & Wellman, 99), but these models do not address the issues of deadlines and fluctuating load while TRACE does.

CONCLUSION

This chapter presents an adaptive organizational policy for multiagent systems called TRACE. TRACE is comprised of a task allocation protocol (TAP) and a resource allocation protocol (RAP) that work together in time constrained environments with fluctuating load. We showed that the TAP has the ability to adapt to load variations, reduce the number of lost requests, and efficiently allocate resources. Although the solution generated by the RAP is not always Pareto-optimal, it has the properties of feasibility and monotonicity that make TRACE well suited to time-constrained applications.

REFERENCES

Arrow, K., & Hahn, F. (1971). *General competitive analysis*, San Francisco, CA: HoldenDay.

Clearwater, S. H. (Ed.). (1996). *Market-based control: A paradigm for distributed allocation*, World Scientific.

Cohen, P., & Levesque, H. (1990). Intention is choice with commitment. *Artificial Intelligence, 42*, 213-261.

Douglas, B. (2002). *Real time design patterns: Robust scalable architecture for scalable systems*, Addison Wesley.

Falcone, R., & Castelfranchi, C (2001). The human in the loop of a delegated agent: The theory of adjustable social autonomy. *IEEE Transactions on Systems Man and Cybernetics, 31*, 406-418.

Faratin, P., Sierra, C., & Jennings, N. R. (1998). Negotiation decision functions for autonomous agents. *International Journal of Robotics and Autonomous systems, 24*, 159-182.

Fatima, S., & Wooldridge, M. (2001). Adaptive task and resource allocation in multiagent systems. *Proceedings of the Fifth International Conference on Autonomous Agents,* (pp. 537-544).

Ho, Y., Servi, L., & Suri, R. (1980). A class of center-free resource allocation algorithms. *Large Scale Systems, 1*, 51-62.

Hurwicz, L. (1973). The design of mechanisms for resource allocation. *American Economic Review, 63*, 1-30.

Kraus, S. (2001). *Strategic negotiation in multi-agent environments*. Cambridge, MA: The MIT Press.

Kurose, J., & Simha, R. (1989). A microeconomic approach to optimal resource allocation in distributed computer systems. *IEEE Transactions on Computers, 38*, 705-717.

Mas-Colell, A., & Whinston, M. (1995). *Microeconomic Theory*. Oxford University Press.

Rosenschein, J., & Zlotkin, G. (1994). *Rules of Encounter*. MIT Press.

Sandholm, T., & Lesser, V. (2001). Levelled commitment contracts and strategic breach. *Games and Economic Behavior, Special Issue on AI and Economics, 35*, 212-270.

Scerri, P., Farinelli, A., Okamoto, S., & Tambe, M. (2005). Allocating tasks in extreme teams. *Proceedings of the Fourth International Conference on Autonomous Agents and MultiAgent Systems*, (pp 727-734).

Smith, R. (1980). The contract-net protocol: High level communication and control in a distributed problem solver, *IEEE Transactions on Computers, 29*, 1104-1113.

Tanenbaum, A. S., & Steen, M. Van (2004). *Distributed systems: Principles and Paradigms*. Pearson Education.

Waldspurger, C., Hogg, T. Huberman, B. A., Kephart, J., & Stornetta, W. (1992). Spawn: A distributed computational economy. *IEEE Transactions of Software Engineering, 18*, 103-117.

Walsh, W., & Wellman, M. (1999). Efficiency and equilibrium in task allocation economies with hierarchical dependencies.*Proceedings of the Sixteenth International Joint Conference on Artificial Intelligence*, (pp 520-526).

Wellman, M., Birmingham, W., & Durfee, E. (1996). The digital library as a community of information agents. *IEEE Expert, 11*, 10-11.

KEY TERMS

Goal: A goal is composed of a set of tasks that must be carried out in a given order.

Marketable Agents: Agents that may be temporarily re-assigned to another organization.

Permanent Agents: Agents that are permanently assigned to an organization.

Resource Manager: Agent responsible for resource allocation.

Schedule: A set of tasks that may be executed in parallel or sequentially.

Task Manager: Agent responsible for task allocation.

TRACE: Task and resource allocation in a computational economy.

Chapter XIX
Dynamic Specifications for Norm–Governed Systems

Alexander Artikis
National Centre for Scientific Research "Demokritos", Greece

Dimosthenis Kaponis
Imperial College London, UK

Jeremy Pitt
Imperial College London, UK

ABSTRACT

We have been developing a framework for executable specification of norm-governed multi-agent systems. In this framework, specification is a design-time activity; moreover, there is no support for run-time modification of the specification. Due to environmental, social, or other conditions, however, it is often desirable, or even necessary, to alter the system specification during the system execution. In this chapter we extend our framework by allowing for "dynamic specifications", that is, specifications that may be modified at run-time by the members of a system. The framework extension is motivated by Brewka's "dynamic argument systems"—argument systems in which the rules of order may become the topic of the debate. We illustrate our framework for dynamic specifications by presenting: (i) a dynamic specification of an argumentation protocol, and (ii) an execution of this protocol in which the participating agents modify the protocol specification.

INTRODUCTION

A particular kind of Multi-Agent System (MAS) is one where the member agents are developed by different parties, and where there is no direct access to an agent's internal state. In this kind of MAS it cannot be assumed that all agents will behave according to the system specification because the agents act on behalf of parties with competing interests, and thus they may inadvertently fail to, or even deliberately choose not to, conform to the system specification in order to achieve their individual goals. A few examples of this type of MAS are Virtual Organisations, electronic marketplaces, argumentation (dispute resolution) protocols, and negotiation protocols. MAS of this type are often classified as 'open'.

We have been developing executable specifications of open MAS (Artikis, 2003; Artikis, Sergot & Pitt, 2003; 2007); we adopt a bird's eye view of these systems, as opposed to an agent's own perspective whereby it reasons about how it should act. Furthermore, we view agent systems as instances of *normative systems* (Jones & Sergot, 1993). A feature of this type of system is that actuality, what is the case, and ideality, what ought to be the case, do not necessarily coincide. Therefore, it is essential to specify what is permitted, prohibited, and obligatory, and perhaps other more complex normative relations that may exist between the agents. Amongst these relations, we place considerable emphasis on the representation of *institutionalised power* (Jones & Sergot, 1996) — a standard feature of any norm-governed system whereby designated agents, when acting in specified roles, are empowered by an institution to create specific relations or states of affairs (such as when an agent is empowered by an institution to award a contract and thereby create a bundle of normative relations between the contracting parties). We encode specifications of open MAS in executable action languages from the field of Artificial Intelligence (Giunchiglia, Lee, Lifschitz, McCain & Turner, 2004; Kowalski & Sergot, 1986).

Our executable specifications may be classified as 'static', in the sense that there is no support for their run-time modification. In some open MAS, however, environmental, social or other conditions may favour, or even require, specifications modifiable during the system execution. Consider, for instance, the case of a malfunction of a large number of sensors in a sensor network, or the case of manipulation of a voting procedure due to strategic voting, or when an organisation conducts its business in an inefficient manner. Therefore, we present in this chapter an infrastructure for 'dynamic specifications', that is, specifications that are developed at design-time but may be modified at run-time by the members of a system. The presented infrastructure is motivated by Brewka's 'dynamic argument systems' (Brewka, 2001) — argument systems in which, at any point in the disputation, participants may start a meta level debate, that is, the rules of order can become the current point of discussion, with the intention of altering these rules.

Our infrastructure for dynamic specifications allows protocol participants to alter the rules of a protocol *P* during the protocol execution. *P* is considered an 'object' protocol; at any point in time during the execution of the object protocol the participants may start a 'meta' protocol in order to decide whether the object protocol rules should be modified: add a new rule-set, delete an existing one, or replace an existing rule-set with a new one. Moreover, the participants of the meta protocol may initiate a meta-meta protocol to decide whether to modify the rules of the meta protocol, or they may initiate a meta-meta-meta protocol to modify the rules of the meta-meta protocol, and so on.

We chose an argumentation protocol based on Brewka's reconstruction of a theory of formal disputation to illustrate our infrastructure for dynamic specifications: the object and meta protocols are all argumentation protocols. In other words, at any time during a debate the agents may start a meta level argument to change the rules that govern their debate. The argumentation protocol was chosen for the sake of providing a concrete example. In general, the object protocol may be any protocol for open MAS, such as a protocol for resource-sharing, coordination or e-commerce; similarly a meta protocol can be any procedure for decision-making over rule modification (voting, negotiation, and so on). This issue is further discussed in the final section of the chapter.

The remainder of this chapter is organised as follows. First, we briefly review the Event Calculus, the action language that we employ to formalise system specifications. Second, we review our static specification of an argumentation protocol (extensively presented in (Artikis, Sergot & Pitt, 2007)). Third, we present a dynamic specification of the argumentation protocol and an infrastructure for modifying the argumentation protocol specification at run-time. Fourth, we present an execution of the protocol, demonstrating how the agents may alter the protocol specification. Finally, we compare our work to Brewka's account and to other research on dynamic protocol specifications, and outline directions for further research.

THE EVENT CALCULUS

The Event Calculus (EC), introduced by Kowalski and Sergot (1986), is a formalism for representing and reasoning about actions or events and their effects in a logic programming framework. In this section we briefly describe the version of the EC that we employ. EC is based on a many-sorted first-order predicate calculus. For the version used here, the underlying time model is linear and it may include real numbers or integers. Where F is a *fluent* (a property that is allowed to have different values at different points in time), the term $F = V$ denotes that fluent F has value V. Boolean fluents are a special case in which the possible values are true and false. Informally, $F = V$ holds at a particular time-point if $F = V$ has been *initiated* by an action at some earlier time-point, and not *terminated* by another action in the meantime.

An *action description* in EC includes axioms that define, amongst other things, the action occurrences (with the use of happens predicates), the effects of actions (with the use of initiates and terminates predicates), and the values of the fluents (with the use of initially and holdsAt predicates). Table 1 summarises the main EC predicates. Variables (starting with an upper-case letter) are assumed to be universally quantified unless otherwise indicated. Predicates, function symbols and constants start with a lower-case letter.

Table 1. Main predicates of the Event Calculus

Predicate	Meaning
happens(Act, T)	Action Act occurs at time T
initially($F = V$)	The value of fluent F is V at time 0
holdsAt($F = V$, T)	The value of fluent F is V at time T
initiates(Act, $F = V$, T)	The occurrence of action Act at time T initiates a period of time for which the value of fluent F is V
terminates(Act, $F=V$, T)	The occurrence of action Act at time T terminates a period of time for which the value of fluent F is V

The following sections present a logic programming implementation of an EC action description expressing our argumentation protocol specification.

AN ARGUMENTATION PROTOCOL

In this section we briefly present an argumentation (dispute resolution) protocol based on Brewka's account (Brewka, 2001) of Rescher's theory of formal disputation (Rescher, 1977). A detailed description of this protocol, which we call RTFD*, and a formalisation in the action language $C+$ (Giunchiglia, Lee, Lifschitz, McCain & Turner, 2004) can be found in (Artikis, Sergot & Pitt, 2007). In this chapter we present a formalisation of RTFD* in the Event Calculus because this action language has proven to be more appropriate for supporting run-time activities (see (Artikis, 2003; Artikis, Sergot & Pitt, 2007) for a discussion about expressing protocol specifications in $C+$ and the Event Calculus).

There are three roles in the protocol: proponent, opponent and determiner. The protocol commences when the proponent claims the topic of the argumentation — any other action does not count as the commencement of the protocol. The protagonists (proponent and opponent) then take it in turn to perform actions, such as claiming, conceding to, retracting or denying a proposition. Each turn lasts for a specified time period during which the protagonist may perform several actions (send several messages) up to some specified limit. After each such action the other participants are given an opportunity to object within another specified time period. In other words, *Ag*'s action *Act* is followed by a time period during which *Ag* may not perform any actions and the other participants may object to *Act*. The determiner may declare the winner only at the end of the argumentation, that is, when the specified period for the argumentation elapses. If at the end of the argumentation both the proponent and opponent have 'accepted' the topic of the argumentation (in a sense that will be made clear later), then the determiner may only declare the proponent the winner. If, however, the proponent does not accept the topic then the determiner may only declare the opponent the winner. Finally, if the proponent accepts the topic and the opponent does not, the determiner has *discretion* to declare either of them the winner. It may also have an *obligation* to decide one way or the other, depending on which version of the protocol we choose to adopt.

Table 2. Main actions of RTFD*

Action	Textual Description
claim(Protag, Q)	*Protag* claims Q
concede(Protag, Q)	*Protag* concedes to Q
retract(Protag, Q)	*Protag* retracts Q
deny(Protag,Q)	*Protag* denies Q
declare(Det, Protag)	*Det* declares *Protag* the winner of the disputation
objected(Ag)	*Ag* objects to an action

Table 2 displays the main actions of RTFD* whereas Table 3 presents a number of the fluents of the EC action description expressing the RTFD* specification. *Ag* is a variable expressing protocol participants, *Protag* expresses protocol protagonists, *Det* denotes the agent occupying the role of determiner, *Q* denotes the propositions that protagonists may claim, concede to, retract or deny, and *Act* represents a claim, concede, retract or deny action. The fluents of the EC action description are inertial. The semantics of the actions and the utility of the fluents will be explained in the following sections.

Physical Capability

The *system events* of the RTFD* specification are the timeouts — these are issued by a global clock. A type of timeout event is used to denote the turn of each participant. When RTFD* commences (this happens when the proponent claims the topic of the argumentation) a global clock starts 'ticking'. The first timeout signals the end of the proponent's turn and the beginning of the opponent's turn to 'speak', by setting *turn = opponent* (see Table 3 for a description of the *turn* fluent). The next timeout signals the end of the opponent's turn and the beginning of the proponent's turn, by setting *turn = proponent*, and so on.

The remaining actions of the RTFD* specification are those performed by the protocol participants (see Table 2). It is a feature of RTFD* that an agent may object to the actions of another participant. The action *objected(Ag)* represents that an objection has been made by agent *Ag*. We abstract away details of how an objection is transmitted within the specified deadline (recall that every action *Act* is followed by a time period during which no action may take place apart from an objection to *Act*). Instead, each 'step' of RTFD* corresponds to a claim, concede, retract, deny, or declare action by one of the participants together with an indication of whether that action was objected to by one or more of the other participants. For example:

Table 3. Main fluents of the RTFD specification*

Fluent	Domain	Textual Description
turn	*{proponent, opponent, determiner}*	the turn to 'speak'
role_of(Ag)	*{proponent, opponent, determiner}*	the role *Ag* occupies
premise(Protag, Q)	{t, u ,f}	*Protag* has an explicit, unconfirmed, or no premise about *Q*
accepts(Protag, Q)	Boolean	*Protag* accepts *Q*
objectionable(Act)	Boolean	*Act* is objectionable
pow(Ag, Act)	Boolean	*Ag* is empowered to perform *Act*
protocol	*{initial, executing, idle}*	the protocol is at the initial state, executing, or idle

happens(*objectedClaim(Protag, Q), T*) ←
    happens(*claim(Protag, Q), T*),
    happens(*objected(Ag), T*)   (1)

represents a claim that Q by *Protag* that has been objected to by some other participant. Similarly,

happens(*notObjectedClaim(Protag, Q), T*) ←
    happens(*claim(Protag, Q), T*),
    $\forall$ *Ag* not happens(*objected(Ag), T*)   (2)

expresses a claim that has not been objected to ('not' denotes 'negation by failure' (Clark, 1978)). The object mechanism is beyond the scope of this chapter; for an extensive discussion about this issue see (Artikis, Sergot & Pitt, 2007).

We have chosen to specify that any protagonist is always capable of signalling a claim, concede, retract, deny, and object action, and the determiner is always capable of signalling a declare and object action. The effects of these actions are presented next.

At the initial protocol state the protagonists have no premises, that is, the value of every *premise(Protag, Q)* fluent is f. The protocol commences with the proponent's claim of the topic. The effects of a claim are expressed as follows:

initiates(*notObjectedClaim(Protag, Q), premise(Protag, Q)* = t, *T*) ←
    holdsAt(*premise(Protag, Q)* = f, *T*)   (3)

Rule (3) expresses that *Protag*'s claim of Q leads from a state in which *Protag* has no explicit premise that Q (that is, *premise(Protag, Q)* = f) to a state in which it does have an explicit premise that Q (that is, *premise(Protag, Q)* = t), on the condition that no (other) agent objects to the claim. An objection is only effective in blocking the effects of a claim if it (the objection) is well-founded (in a sense to be specified below). If the objection is not well-founded then it does not block the effects of the claim (though it might have other effects, such as exposing the objecting agent to sanctions). We therefore add the constraint:

initiates(*objectedClaim(Protag, Q), premise(Protag, Q)* = t, *T*) ←
    holdsAt(*objectionable(claim(Protag, Q))* = false, *T*),
    holdsAt(*premise(Protag, Q)* = f, *T*)   (4)

Boolean fluents *objectionable(Act)* are used to represent that an objection to *Act* is well-founded.

Suppose that protagonist *Protag* claims a proposition Q. Opponent *Protag'* may respond to *Protag*'s claim by conceding to, or denying the claim. If *Protag'* does neither then we say that *Protag'* has an 'unconfirmed' premise that Q, denoted by *premise(Protag', Q)* = u. The value of a premise fluent is set to 'unconfirmed' as follows, for every pair of distinct protagonists *Protag* and *Protag'*:

initiates(*notObjectedClaim(Protag, Q), premise(Protag', Q)* = u, *T*) ←
    holdsAt(*premise(Protag, Q)* = f, *T*),
    holdsAt(*premise(Protag', Q)* = f, *T*)   (5)

initiates(*objectedClaim(Protag, Q), premise(Protag', Q)* = u, *T*) ←
    holdsAt(*objectionable(claim(Protag, Q))* = false, *T*),
    holdsAt(*premise(Protag, Q)* = f, *T*),
    holdsAt(*premise(Protag', Q)* = f, *T*)   (6)

In other words, *Protag*'s claim of *Q* leads (subject to possible objections) to a state in which *Protag'* has an unconfirmed premise that *Q*, provided that *Protag'* does not already have a premise that *Q* (that is, provided that the value of *premise(Protag', Q)* is f). If *Protag'* already has a premise that *Q* (that is, *premise(Protag', Q)* = t) then its premise does not become unconfirmed, and it does not need to respond to *Protag*'s claim.

A response to claim is a concession or a denial; consider the effects of a concession:

initiates(*notObjectedConcede(Protag, Q), premise(Protag, Q)* = t, *T*) ←
    holdsAt(*premise(Protag, Q)* = u, *T*)   (7)

initiates(*objectedConcede(Protag, Q), premise(Protag, Q)* = t, *T*) ←
    holdsAt(*objectionable(concede(Protag, Q))* = false, *T*),
    holdsAt(*premise(Protag, Q)* = u, *T*)   (8)

Similarly we may express the effects of a denial and a retraction in terms of the protagonists' premises. Regarding declarations, a *declare(Det, Protag)* action signals *Protag* the winner of the dispute (subject to objections). (For more details on the effects of the protocol actions see (Artikis, Sergot & Pitt, 2007)).

We now turn our attention to objections: when is an objection to an action *Act* effective in blocking the effects of *Act*, that is, when is *Act* objectionable? When the agent that performed *Act* did not have the 'institutional power' to perform *Act*. An account of institutional power in the context of the argumentation protocol is given next.

Institutional Power

The term institutional (or 'institutionalised') power refers to the characteristic feature of organisations/institutions — legal, formal, or informal — whereby designated agents, often when acting in specific roles, are empowered, by the institution, to create or modify facts of special significance in that institution — *institutional facts* — usually by performing a specified kind of act. Searle (1996), for example, has distinguished between *brute facts* and institutional facts. Being in physical possession of an object is an example of a brute fact (it can be observed); being the owner of that object is an institutional fact.

According to the account given by Jones and Sergot (1996), institutional power can be seen as a special case of a more general phenomenon whereby an action, or a state of affairs, *A* — because of the rules and conventions of an institution — counts, in that institution, as an action or state of affairs *B* (such as when sending a letter with a particular form of words counts as making an offer, or banging the table with a wooden mallet counts as declaring a meeting closed).

We use the concept of institutional power in the argumentation protocol specification as follows. We say that, for example, sending a *claim(Ag, Q)* message while having the institutional power to make a claim, counts, in the argumentation protocol, as a non-objectionable claim, that is, a claim whose effects cannot be blocked. If, however, the claim is uttered by an agent without the power to make the claim, then this action will be objectionable and, therefore, its effects will be blocked by an objection issued by another agent. The same applies to the remaining protocol actions.

The institutional power to make a claim, for instance, is formalised as follows:

holdsAt($pow(Protag, claim(Protag, Q))$ = true, T) ←
$\quad$ holdsAt($premise(Protag, Q)$ = f, T),
$\quad$ holdsAt($protocol = executing, T$),
$\quad$ holdsAt($role\_of(Protag) = Role, T$),
$\quad$ holdsAt($turn = Role, T$) $\hspace{3cm}$ (9)

According to the above rule, *Protag* is empowered to claim Q if: (i) *Protag* does not have a premise that Q, (ii) the protocol is 'executing', that is, it is neither in the initial state nor has it finished, and (iii) it is *Protag*'s turn to 'speak'. The power to make a claim at the initial protocol state, and, in general, to perform the remaining protocol actions, is formalised in a similar manner.

As mentioned above, performing an action without the corresponding institutional power constitutes this action objectionable; an objectionable claim, for instance, as defined as follows:

holdsAt($objectionable(claim(Protag, Q))$ = true, T) ←
$\quad$ holdsAt($pow(Protag, claim(Protag, Q))$ = false, T) $\hspace{2cm}$ (10)

Similarly we define when the remaining protocol actions are objectionable.

The specification of the procedural part of the argumentation includes a specification of permitted and obligatory actions, as well as sanctioning mechanisms to address the performance of forbidden actions and non-compliance with obligations — see (Artikis, Sergot & Pitt, 2007). We do not present here this aspect of the procedural part of the argumentation, and the logic of disputation (although a brief discussion about this logic will be presented later). The protocol specification presented so far is

Figure 1. An infrastructure for run-time protocol modification

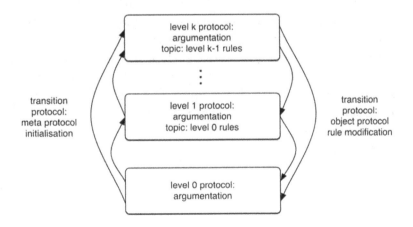

sufficient for illustrating the infrastructure for changing the protocol specifications at run-time, which is the aim of this chapter.

A DYNAMIC ARGUMENTATION PROTOCOL

Being motivated by Brewka (2001), we present an infrastructure that allows protocol participants to modify (a subset of) the rules of an argumentation protocol at run-time. More precisely, we consider the argumentation protocol as an 'object' protocol; at any point in time during the execution of the object protocol the participants may start a 'meta' argumentation protocol in order to potentially modify the object protocol rules: add a new rule-set, delete an existing one, or replace an existing rule-set with a new one. The topic of the dispute of the meta protocol is the proposed rule modification of the object protocol. Moreover, the participants of the meta protocol may initiate a meta-meta protocol to modify the rules of the meta protocol, or they may initiate a meta-meta-meta protocol to modify the rules of the meta-meta protocol, and so on — see Figure 1. In general, in a k-level infrastructure, level 0 corresponds to the main (argumentation) protocol while a protocol of level n, $0 < n \leq k$, is created, by the protocol participants of level m, $0 \leq m < n$, in order to debate over the protocol rules of level $n-1$.

Each protocol level has its own protocol state; for instance, agent Ag_1 may occupy the role of proponent in level 0 and the role of opponent in level 1 (role-assignment in meta protocols will be discussed in the following section), Ag_2 may be empowered to claim q in level 0 but have no powers in level 2, it may be the opponent's turn to 'speak' in level 1 and the determiner's turn to 'speak' in level 3, and so on. In order to distinguish between the protocol states of different protocol levels, we relativise the protocol rules according to the protocol level. More precisely, we add a parameter in the representation of actions and fluents, expressing the protocol level PL, as follows: $claim(Protag, Q, PL)$, $objected(Ag, PL)$, and so on for actions, $turn(PL)$, $objectionable(Act, PL)$, and so on for fluents.

The rules of an argumentation protocol are divided into two categories: 'core' rules, that is, rules that are always part of the protocol specification, and 'replaceable' rules, that is, rules that may be deleted, or replaced by other rules, under certain circumstances, during the protocol execution by means of a meta protocol. Consider, for example, the 'silence implies consent' property of the presented argumentation protocol. This property can be summarised as follows: a protagonist that does not explicitly respond to a claim by the other protagonist is assumed to concede to the claim. We may specify the rules expressing this property as replaceable, that is, the protocol participants may choose to include this property in, or exclude it from, the protocol specification at any point in time during the protocol execution.

The rules that are part of a protocol at a given time are called 'active' (clearly, core rules are always active during a protocol execution) whereas all other rules are called 'inactive' (this is similar to what is called 'external time of norms' — see, for example, (Marín & Sartor, 1999)). Protocols of different levels may not have the same set of active rules. For example, at a particular point in time t a replaceable rule-set tagged as 'sic', expressing the silence implies consent property, may be active in level 0 and level 2 but inactive in level 1; this is expressed as follows:

holdsAt($active(sic) = [0,2]$, t)

The $active(R)$ fluent expresses the protocol levels in which a rule-set R is active. To illustrate the meaning of the $active$ fluent consider the following example:

holdsAt(*accepts(Protag, P, PL)* = true, *T*) ←
    holdsAt(*active(accept)* = *List, T*),
    PL ∈ *List*,
    holdsAt(*premise(Protag, Q , PL)* = t, *T*),
    implies(Q, P)   (11)

holdsAt(*accepts(Protag, P, PL)* = true, *T*) ←
    holdsAt(*active(sic)* = *List, T*),
    PL ∈ *List*,
    (holdsAt(*premise(Protag, Q , PL)* = t, *T*) ;
     holdsAt(*premise(Protag, Q , PL)* = u, *T*)),
    implies(Q, P)   (11')

Rules (11) and (11') provide simple, alternative formalisations of the conditions in which a protagonist 'accepts' a proposition — the determiner declares the winner of the dispute according to what is accepted by both protagonists. The first two conditions of these rules express whether these rules are active in a protocol level. Rule (11) is tagged as 'accept'; according to this rule, *Protag* accepts P in a protocol of level *PL* if: (i) the 'accept' rule is active in level *PL*, (ii) *Protag* has an explicit premise that Q in level *PL*, and (iii) P is a (classical) logical implication of Q. The *implies* are simply suitably chosen atemporal predicates[1]. Rule (11') incorporates the silence implies consent property: a protagonist accepts all logical implications of each of its explicit *and unconfirmed* premises — recall that *premise(Protag, Q, PL)* = u expresses that *Protag* has an unconfirmed premise that Q in a protocol of level *PL*, that is, *Protag* has not responded to a claim that Q made by the other protagonist in level *PL*. (';' expresses disjunction.) Given rules (11) and (11'), a protocol of level n exhibits the silence implies consent property if the rule tagged as 'sic' is active in this level; if the 'accept' rule is active, on the other hand, this property is not incorporated in the protocol level.

Apart from adding, deleting and replacing rule-sets, protocol participants may also modify the values of certain components of the protocol specification. In the argumentation protocol example, participants may change at run-time the number of turns that each protagonist may take, and the duration of a turn.

In order to modify the protocol rules of level n (for example, to replace the 'accept' rule with the 'sic' rule), that is, in order to start a protocol of level $n+1$, the protocol participants of level n need to follow a 'transition protocol' — see Figure 1. We present an example specification of a transition protocol next.

Transition Protocol

For the sake of an example we have specified a very simple transition protocol: a protocol protagonist of level n proposes a modification of the rules of this protocol level (or of the rules of level $n+m$). If the protagonist is empowered to propose such a change then the protocol of level $n+1$ (or $n+m+1$) begins; otherwise the proposal is ignored. Clearly, in more realistic scenarios the transition protocol would be more complicated. For instance, a protagonist's proposal for rule modification should be seconded by another participant, say the determiner, before the meta protocol commences, or a protagonist's proposal could initiate a meta protocol even if the protagonist is not empowered to make the proposal, provided that no other agent objects. Moreover, a proposal for rule modification may not necessarily initiate a meta protocol — the proposal may be accepted by the participants resulting in the immediate application of the rule modification. Such transition protocols could be formalised similar to the argumentation protocol presented so far, or other interaction protocols presented elsewhere (Artikis, 2003).

In this simple example we have specified the power to propose a rule-set replacement as follows:

holdsAt(*pow(Ag, propose(Ag, replace(OldRule, NewRule), PL', PL))* = true, *T*) ←
$\quad$ *PL'* ≥ *PL*,
$\quad$ (holdsAt(*role_of(Ag, PL)* = *proponent, T*) ;
$\quad$ $\quad$ holdsAt(*role_of(Ag, PL)* = *opponent, T*)),
$\quad$ holdsAt(*protocol(PL' + 1)* = *idle, T*),
$\quad$ holdsAt(*active(OldRule)* = *List, T*),
$\quad$ *PL'* ∈ *List*,
$\quad$ holdsAt(*active(NewRule)* = *List$_2$, T*),
$\quad$ *PL'* ∉ *List$_2$* $\hfill$ (12)

The above rule states that a protocol participant *Ag* of level *PL* is empowered to propose to replace an *OldRule* rule-set, from level *PL'*, with a *NewRule* one if:

- *PL' = PL*, that is, *Ag* proposes a rule modification in the protocol that currently participates, or *PL' > PL*, that is, *Ag* proposes a rule modification in a meta protocol.
- *Ag* occupies the role of proponent or that of opponent in level *PL*. In other words, in this example specification the determiner is not empowered to propose a modification of the protocol rules.
- There is no protocol taking place in level *PL'+1*. In this example, only one protocol may take place in each level. Therefore, an argumentation protocol for modifying the rules of level *PL'*, that is, a protocol of level *PL'+1*, may commence only if there is no other protocol of level *PL'+1* taking place.
- The *OldRule* rule-set is active in level *PL'*.
- The *NewRule* rule-set is inactive in level *PL'*.

The power to propose the addition or deletion of a rule-set is formalised in a similar manner.

In a more realistic scenario the power to propose a rule modification would probably have additional conditions. For instance, a rule-set should only be replaced by an 'interchangeable' rule-set (it should not be possible, for example, to replace a rule-set expressing the conditions in which an agent is permitted to perform an action with a rule-set expressing the conditions in which a proposition is accepted by a protagonist). In some systems an agent would not have the power to propose a rule modification (or the power to accept or second a rule modification, in more complex transition protocols) that would create a (type of) protocol inconsistency. In other systems an agent may be empowered to propose a rule modification that leads to a protocol inconsistency — the acceptance or not of the proposed modification would be decided based on the arguments of the proposing agent presented in the meta level. Moreover, inactive rule-sets proposed to become active may come from a specified rule library, thus allowing only for pre-determined protocol changes, or agents may propose the addition of completely new rule-sets. (Vreeswijk (2000), for instance, allows for pre-determined protocol changes whereas Brewka (2001) allows for any type of protocol change. There is no comment, however, in the latter approach on the issue of creating protocol inconsistencies.) The formalisation of examples taking under consideration these issues is an area of current research.

The effect of a 'successful' proposal for rule modification in level n, that is, the effect of proposing a rule modification in level n while having the power to make the proposal, is the initiation of a protocol of level $n+1$. The topic of the latter protocol is the proposed rule modification (for example, which rule-set should be replaced by which), the agent that made the proposal occupies the role of proponent, the other protagonist occupies the role of opponent, and the determiner remains the same. The fact that an agent may successfully start a protocol of level $n+1$ by proposing a modification of the protocol rules of level n, however, does not necessarily imply that the rules of level n will be modified. It is only if the agent that successfully proposed the modification is declared the winner of the argument of level $n+1$ that the rules of level n will be modified. Consider the following rules expressing the outcome of a protocol of level $n+1$ that took place in order to replace the *OldRule* rule-set with the *NewRule* rule-set in level n:

initiates(*endTimeout(PL)*, *active(NewRule)* = *NewList, T*) ←
    holdsAt(*topic(PL)* = *replace(OldRule, NewRule), T*),
    holdsAt(*winner(PL)* = *Winner, T*),
    holdsAt(*role_of(Winner, PL)* = *proponent, T*),
    holdsAt(*active(NewRule)* = *List, T*),
    NewList := List ∪ *{PL - 1}*   (13)

initiates(*endTimeout(PL)*, *active(OldRule)* =*NewList, T*) ←
    holdsAt(*topic(PL)* = *replace(OldRule, NewRule), T*),
    holdsAt(*winner(PL)* = *Winner, T*),
    holdsAt(*role_of(Winner, PL)* = *proponent, T*),
    holdsAt(*active(OldRule)* = *List, T*),
    NewList := List \ *{PL - 1}*   (14)

Rule (13) states that an *endTimeout(PL)*, that is, the last timeout of level *PL*, results in activating the *NewRule* rule-set in level *PL-1* if: (i) the topic of the argument of level *PL* was the replacement of the *OldRule* rule-set with the *NewRule* one, and (ii) the winner of the argument of level *PL* was the agent occupying the role of proponent. If the winner was the opponent or there was no declared winner, then the *NewRule* rule-set would not have been activated in level *PL-1*. Similarly, rule (14) states that an *endTimeout(PL)* results in making the *OldRule* rule-set inactive in level *PL-1* if the two aforementioned conditions hold.

ANIMATION

In order to illustrate the proposed infrastructure for dynamic specifications, in this section we animate an example run of a 2-level argument system. A part of the narrative of events of this run is displayed in Table 4 (*oTimeout(PL)* denotes a timeout initiating the opponent's turn to 'speak' in level *PL*; similarly *pTimeout(PL)* and *dTimeout(PL)* denote, respectively, timeouts initiating the proponent's and the

Table 4. A sample run of RTFD*

Time	Action
0	*claim(agent₁, murderer(jack), 0)*
	...
14	*claim(agent₁, on(blood, shoe), 0)*
14	*objected(agent₂, 0)*
15	*oTimeout(0)*
18	*claim(agent₂, illegal_info(on(blood, shoe)), 0)*
30	*pTimeout(0)*
31	*concede(agent₁, illegal_info(on(blood, shoe)), 0)*
45	*oTimeout(0)*
46	*propose(agent₂, replace(sic, sic_ill_info),0,0)*
49	*claim(agent₂, replace(sic, sic_ill_info), 1)*
	...
77	*dTimeout(1)*
78	*declare(det, agent₂, 1)*
93	*endTimeout(1)*
	...
135	*endTimeout(0)*

determiner's turn to 'speak' in level *PL*). This narrative is motivated by Brewka's (2001) case study of a dynamic argument system. In the example presented here the argumentation protocol includes a single replaceable component, rule (11'), expressing that the propositions a protagonist accepts are determined by the silence implies consent property. Rule (11') is initially active in all protocol levels.

Given that the RTFD* specification is expressed as a logic program, we may query our implementation to determine the system state current at each time and protocol level (for instance, which roles each participant occupies, what premises each protagonist has, what powers each participant has, which actions are objectionable, and so on). We will discuss next the system states of the run displayed in Table 4.

The protocol of level 0 commences with the claim of *agent₁*, occupying the role of proponent, that Jack is a murderer, that is, the topic of the argument of level 0 — see time-point 14 in Table 4 (recall that the last parameter of an action is the protocol level in which the action is performed). At time-point 14 *agent₁* makes a claim that there is evidence, victim's blood on Jack's shoe, that convicts Jack as the murderer. The evidence, however, was obtained illegally. Therefore, at the same time *agent₂*, occupying the role of opponent, objects to *agent₁*'s claim. *agent₂*'s objection is unsuccessful in blocking the effects of *agent₁*'s claim because the claim is not objectionable: *agent₁* is empowered to make the claim at that time since it does not have an explicit premise that there is victim's blood on Jack's shoe, the protocol is executing, and it is *agent₁*'s turn to 'speak' (see rule (9)). The effects of *agent₁*'s claim are that *premise(agent₁, on(blood, shoe), 0)* = t and *premise(agent₂, on(blood, shoe), 0)* = u (see rules (4) and (6)). Consequently, according to rule (11'), currently active in level 0, expressing the conditions in which a proposition is accepted, both protagonists accept *on(blood, shoe)*. At time-point 15 a timeout takes place initiating *agent₂*'s turn to 'speak'. *agent₂* does not deny *agent₁*'s claim that there is victim's blood on Jack's shoe; however, *agent$_2$* claims that the presented evidence was obtained illegally. *agent$_1$* concedes to this claim when it is its turn to 'speak' (at time-point 31) since, according to rule (11'), *agent$_1$*'s concession does not change the fact that *on(blood, shoe)* is accepted by both protagonists.

In order to change what is accepted, *agent$_2$* proposes a modification of the rules of level 0; it proposes to replace rule (11') tagged as 'sic' with the rule below, tagged as 'sic_ill_info':

$$\text{holdsAt(} \textit{accepts(Protag, P, PL)} = \text{true, } T) \leftarrow$$

$$\text{holdsAt(} \textit{active(sic\_ill\_info)} = \textit{List, } T),$$

$$PL \in \textit{List},$$

$$(\text{holdsAt(} \textit{premise(Protag, Q , PL)} = \text{t, } T) ;$$

$$\text{holdsAt(} \textit{premise(Protag, Q , PL)} = \text{u, } T)),$$

$$\text{holdsAt(} \textit{illegal\_info(Q)} = \text{false, } T),$$

$$\textit{implies(Q, P)} \tag{11''}$$

Rule (11'') is a variation of the silence implies consent property that considers illegally obtained evidence: *Protag* accepts evidence and its implications, put forward by itself or by the other protagonist *Protag'* (and not challenged by *Protag*), provided that the evidence is not illegally obtained. *illegal_info* are suitably chosen fluents.

agent$_2$'s proposal, at time 46, for modifying the rules of level 0 is 'successful' because *agent$_2$* is empowered to make the proposal at that time (see rule (12)): the modification concerns the protocol level in which *agent$_2$* currently participates, *agent$_2$* occupies the role of opponent in level 0, the 'sic' rule is active and the 'sic_ill_info' rule is inactive in that level. The result of the 'successful' proposal is the commencement of a protocol of level 1, in which *agent$_2$* occupies the role of proponent (since it initiated this protocol), *agent$_1$* occupies the role of opponent, and the determiner remains the same. (Notice that, at the same time, *agent$_2$* occupies the role of opponent and *agent$_1$* that of proponent in level 0.) At time-point 49 *agent$_2$* claims the topic of the protocol of level 1 which is the replacement of the 'sic' rule with the 'sic_ill_info' one. Following the argument in level 1 (on the modification of the rules of level 0), the determiner of level 1 declares *agent$_2$* the winner; since *agent$_2$* is the proponent of level 1 the proposed rule modification is applied in level 0, that is, the 'sic_ill_info' rule becomes active and the 'sic' one becomes inactive in level 0 (see rules (13) and (14)). (Notice, however, that the 'sic' rule is still active in level 1.) As a result, at time-point 94, after the last timeout of level 1, the values of the fluents *accepts(agent$_1$, on(blood, shoe), 0)* and *accepts(agent$_2$, on(blood, shoe), 0)* are not true, that is, no protagonist accepts that there is victim's blood on Jack's shoe.

It should be noted that the example presented above, in which the rule modification had retroactive effects, was chosen simply for illustration purposes. Clearly, there exist other examples in which the effects of a rule modification need to be applied only after the modification. Both alternatives may be expressed with the use of the Event Calculus.

In Brewka's example argument system (Brewka, 2001) the protocol of level 0 is modified in the following way in order to deal with illegal evidence: every action performed by a protagonist that has put forward illegally obtained evidence is considered objectionable as long as the protagonist does not retract the illegal evidence. This constraint may be incorporated in our formalisation by modifying our specification of objectionable actions. In general, there are several ways to deal with illegal evidence; the presented formalisation is but one example.

CONCLUSION AND FUTURE RESEARCH DIRECTIONS

We presented a specification of an argumentation protocol in which the logic of disputation/argumentation (from which inferences are made to determine the winner) and the procedural part of the argumentation (that defines the conditions in which an agent is empowered, permitted, obliged to perform an action) were separated out from the mechanism by which either the argumentation logic or the argumentation procedure can be changed.

In the development of the static specification of the argumentation protocol (Artikis, Sergot & Pitt, 2007) we were mainly concerned with the formalisation of the procedural part of the argumentation. Like (Brewka, 2001) and (Gordon, 1994; 1995; Prakken, 2001; 2005) we adopted a 'public protocol semantics' (Prakken, 2006), that is, we made no assumptions about the participants' internal architectures. We refined Brewka's distinction of possible and legal actions — we distinguished between physical capability, institutional power, and permission (and obligation). Moreover, unlike Brewka, we have been concerned with the *execution* of our protocol specifications. Indeed, in the previous section we presented an execution of an example protocol specification; protocol participants may query at any point in time our executable specification in order to inform their decision-making. A more detailed comparison of our work with Brewka's account and related research from the argumentation field, from the standpoint of *static* argument systems, however, may be found in (Artikis, Sergot & Pitt, 2007).

In this chapter we were concerned with the run-time modification of the protocol specification. As Brewka (2001) points out, the need to allow for argumentation protocol rule modification at run-time by means of argumentation has already been identified in the literature (see, for example, (Loui, 1992)). A main difference of our work from Brewka's *dynamic* argument systems lies in the fact that we place emphasis on the transition protocol that is used to move from an object protocol to a meta protocol. We provided a concrete formalisation of a simple example transition protocol, distinguishing between successful and unsuccessful attempts to initiate a meta protocol. Moreover, we outlined alternative formalisations of more complex transition protocols and formalised a simple procedure for role-assignment in a meta level. In Brewka's simple example of a dynamic argument system a protocol participant may always successfully initiate a meta protocol; furthermore, there is no discussion about role-assignment in the meta level.

Vreeswijk (2000) has also investigated forms of meta argumentation. The starting point for this work was two basic observations. Firstly, that there are different protocols appropriate for different contexts (for example, quick and shallow reasoning when time is a constraint; restricted number of counter-arguments when there are many rules and cases; etc). Secondly, that 'points of order', by which a participant may steer the protocol to a desired direction, are standard practice in dispute resolution meetings. Vreeswijk then defined a formal protocol for disputes in which points of order can be raised to allow (partial) protocol changes to be debated. A successful 'defence' meant that the parties in the dispute agreed to adopt a change in the protocol, and the rules of dispute were correspondingly changed.

As mentioned earlier in the chapter, Vreeswijk allowed only for pre-determined protocol changes. Unlike our work (and Brewka's work), meta argumentation was restricted to a single meta level. Moreover, there was no treatment of a 'transition protocol', that is, there was no formalisation of a procedure with which a participant could (attempt to) initiate a meta argument.

The example presented in our chapter included a single replaceable component— a 'partial protocol specification' in the terminology of Vreeswijk (2000). We could have formalised as replaceable other types of rule-set, such as the rule-sets expressing objectionable actions, permitted actions, obligatory actions, and so on. The decision concerning the classification of a rule-set as replaceable or core is application-specific.

When deciding to classify a rule-set as replaceable, one should consider the possible effects of making this rule-set inactive. As discussed earlier in the chapter, the replacement of a rule-set with another one may create a type of protocol inconsistency — for instance, objecting to an objectionable action may no longer block the effects of this action, a participant may be forbidden and obliged to perform an action, and so on. Moreover, it may be required that a rule modification respects a set of protocol properties, such as 'soundness' and 'fairness' (see, for example, (McBurney, Parsons & Wooldridge, 2002; Prakken, 2001; Vreeswijk, 2000) for definitions of argumentation protocol properties). A way of verifying the effects of rule modification, by means of proving protocol properties, can be found in (Artikis, Sergot & Pitt, 2007).

The infrastructure presented here for dynamic specifications included an argumentation protocol in each level (see Figure 1). In principle, any protocol of level n, $n > 0$, could be any procedure for deciding whether or not to apply a rule modification (the protocol of level 0 is the main (argumentation) protocol). We could have, for instance, an infrastructure for dynamic argumentation protocol specifications in which some or all n level protocols ($n > 0$) are voting protocols, that is, agents take a vote on, instead of debating about, a proposed rule modification. The realisation of such an infrastructure (see (Pitt et al, 2006) for a preliminary voting protocol formalisation), and in particular, the formalisation of a transition protocol leading from an argumentation protocol to a voting protocol, is an area of current work.

Apart from replacing an argumentation protocol of level n ($n > 0$) with a voting protocol, say, one could even replace the main argumentation protocol, that is, the protocol of level 0, with any type of protocol for open MAS (resource-sharing, negotiation, coordination, and so on). In this way it would be possible to have an infrastructure for dynamic resource-sharing protocol specifications, for instance. Such a setting requires suitable transition protocols that lead from level 0 (resource-sharing, for example) to level n, $n > 0$ (argumentation or voting).

On the topic of dynamic specifications for MAS, Bou, López-Sánchez & Rodriguez-Aguilar (2007; 2008) have presented a mechanism for the run-time modification of the norms of an 'electronic institution'. These researchers have proposed a 'normative transition function' that maps a set of norms (and goals) into a new set of norms: changing a norm requires changing its parameters, or its effect, or both. The 'institutional agents', representing the institution, are observing the members' interactions in order to learn, with the use of case based reasoning, the normative transition function, so that the norms that will enable the achievement of the 'institutional goals' in a given scenario will be enacted.

Unlike Bou and colleagues, we do not necessarily rely on specific agents to (learn and) apply the modification of norms. In our case, any agent may (attempt to) adapt the system specification via meta protocols (argumentation, voting, negotiation or some other protocol). This does not exclude the possibility, however, that, in some applications, specific agents are given the institutional power to directly modify the system specification (without argumentation, voting, etc).

Chopra and Singh (2006) present a way of adapting protocols according to context, or the preferences of agents in a given context. They formalise, in the action language $C+$ (Giunchiglia, Lee, Lifschitz, McCain & Turner, 2004), protocols and 'transformers', that is, additions/enhancements to an existing protocol specification that handle some aspect of context or preference. Depending on the context or preference, a protocol specification is complemented, at *design-time*, by the appropriate transformer thus resulting in a new specification.

Like Chopra and Singh, we have used the action language *C+* to express protocol specifications for open MAS (see, for instance, (Artikis, 2003; Artikis, Sergot & Pitt, 2003; 2007)). Unlike these researchers, we are concerned here with the *run-time* adaptation of a protocol specification and, therefore, we have developed an infrastructure (meta protocols, transition protocols) to achieve that.

Chopra and Singh, and Bou and colleagues, express protocols in terms of 'commitments' or obligations (here the term 'commitment' refers to a form of (directed) obligation between agents, and is *not* used as an alternative term for 'premise'). It is difficult to see how an interaction protocol for open MAS can be specified simply in terms of commitments in this sense. At the very least, a specification of a protocol's constitutive norms is also required.

The OMACS (Organisational Model for Adaptive Computational Systems) model (DeLoach , 2008; DeLoach, Oyenan & Matson, 2008) is another approach for dynamic MAS. In OMACS, an agent-based organisation is represented by sets of agents, goals, roles, capabilities, and constraints, an assignment of goals and roles to agents, and a set of evaluative functions (for instance, *achieves*, *capable*, *possesses* and *potential*), that define how well a role achieves a goal, how well an agent can play a role, and so on. Given a trigger event, such as a change in the agents' capabilities, agents employ pre-compiled strategies or on-the-fly computed strategies, to adapt various aspects of an organisation, such as the assignment of roles to agents. The aim of adaptation is the maximisation of the value of the *organisation assignment function* that expresses the quality/efficiency of an organisation.

OMACS concentrates mainly on re-organisation from the perspective of a functional assignment — the assignment of goals and roles to agents — whereas we emphasise, like Bou and colleagues, a different perspective, aimed at a achieving a mapping form norms to norms, that is, the rules which regulate, among other things, the process of performing such a functional assignment. The outcome of the mapping still needs to be evaluated, though, as re-organisation is evaluated in OMACS. One way of evaluating our dynamic specifications, is by examining whether certain protocol properties (such as the ones mentioned earlier) hold. Another way is discussed at the end of this section.

Identifying *when* to adapt a system specification during the system execution, as done in OMACS, for instance, with respect to agent availability, preferences, goals, capabilities, and so on, and in the work of Bou and colleagues with respect to the 'institutional goals', is a fundamental requirement for adaptive systems. This requirement has not been addressed by our work.

We have been concerned with a particular aspect of 'adaptation': the run-time modification of the 'rules of the game' of norm-governed systems. Clearly, there are other aspects of adaptive/dynamic systems, such as, for instance, the run-time modification of the (trading, and other) relationships between agents, the members of a system, the assignment of roles to agents (as done, for instance, in OMACS), and the goals of a system. (Hoogendoorn, 2007; Hoogendoorn, Jonker, Schut & Treur, 2007; Horling, Benyo & Lesser, 2001; Martin & Barber, 2006; Costa & Dimuro, 2008; Shoham & Tennenholtz, 1997) are but a few examples of studies of adaptive systems.

To aid the evaluation process of a system with dynamic specifications, we have been working towards the development of a model (Kaponis & Pitt, 2006), based upon the mathematical theory of Metric Spaces, that allows for quantification of a system's 'degrees of freedom', that is, the replaceable rule-sets. Use of the model allows for a human or machine evaluator to evaluate a system by considering the distance of the system's 'specification position', calculated with the use of the system's degrees of freedom, to a given point in the specification space (say, a desirable specification point or subspace). The distance is calculated with the use of a metric function. In addition to the model, we are developing software tools that largely automate the application of the model on a given system.

REFERENCES

Artikis, A. (2003). *Executable Specification of Open Norm-Governed Computational Systems.* Ph.D thesis, University of London, London.

Artikis, A., Sergot, M., & Pitt, J. (2003). Specifying electronic societies with the Causal Calculator. In F. Giunchiglia, J. Odell & G. Weiss (Ed.), *Proceedings of Workshop on Agent-Oriented Software Engineering* (pp. 1-15). Springer.

Artikis, A., Sergot, M., & Pitt, J. (2007). An executable specification of a formal argumentation protocol. *Artificial Intelligence, 171*(10-15), 776-804.

Bou, E., López-Sánchez, M., & Rodriguez-Aguilar, J. (2007). Towards self-configuration in autonomic electronic institutions. *Proceedings of Workshop on Coordination, Organization, Institutions and Norms in agent systems. LNCS 4386*, pp. 220-235. Springer.

Bou, E., López-Sánchez, M., & Rodriguez-Aguilar, J. (2008). Using case-based reasoning in autonomic electronic institutions. *Proceedings of Workshop on Coordination, Organization, Institutions and Norms in agent systems. LNCS 4870*, pp. 125-138. Springer.

Brewka, G. (2001). Dynamic argument systems: a formal model of argumentation processes based on situation calculus. *Journal of Logic and Computation, 11*(2), 257-282.

Chopra, A., & M, S. (2006). Contextualizing commitment protocols. *Proceedings of Conference on Autonomous Agents and Multi-Agent Systems (AAMAS)* (pp. 1345-1352). ACM.

Clark, K. (1978). Negation as Failure. In H. Gallaire & J. Minker (Eds.), *Logic and Databases* (pp. 293-322). Plenum Press.

Costa, A. R., & Dimuro, G. P. (2008). A Minimal Dynamical MAS Organization Model. *To appear in this volume.*

DeLoach, S. (2008). OMACS: A framework for adaptive, complex systems. *To appear in this volume.*

DeLoach, S., Oyenan, W., & Matson, E. (2008). A capabilities-based model for adaptive organizations. *Autonomous Agents and Multi-Agent Systems, 16*(1), 13-56.

Giunchiglia, E., Lee, J., Lifschitz, V., McCain, N., & Turner, H. (2004). Nonmonotonic causal theories. *Artificial Intelligence, 153*(1-2), 49-104.

Gordon, T. (1994). The pleadings game: An exercise in computational dialectics. *Artificial Intelligence and Law, 2*, 239-292.

Gordon, T. (1995). *The Pleadings Game: An Artificial Intelligence Model of Procedural Justice.* Kluwer Academic Publishers.

Hoogendoorn, M. (2007). Adaptation of organizational models for multi-agent systems based on max flow networks. *Proceedings of International Joint Conferenece on Artificial Intelligence (IJCAI)*, (pp. 1321-1326).

Hoogendoorn, M., Jonker, C., Schut, M., & Treur, J. (2007). Modelling centralized organization of organizational change. *Computational & Mathematical Organization Theory, 13*(2), 147-184.

Horling, B., Benyo, B., & Lesser, V. (2001). Using self-diagnosis to adapt organizational structures. In J. Muller, E. Andre, S. Sen & C. Frasson (Ed.), *Proceedings of Conference on Autonomous Agents* (pp. 529-536). ACM Press.

Jones, A., & Sergot, M. (1993). On the characterisation of law and computer systems: the normative systems perspective. In *Deontic Logic in Computer Science: Normative System Specification* (pp. 275-307). Wiley and Sons.

Jones, A., & Sergot, M. (1996). A formal characterisation of institutionalised power. *Journal of the IGPL, 4*(3), 429-445.

Kaponis, D., & Pitt, J. (2006). Dynamic Specifications in norm-governed open computational societies. *Proceedings of Workshop on Engineering Societies in the Agents' World (ESAW)*. Springer.

Kowalski, R., & Sergot, M. (1986). A logic-based calculus of events. *New Generation Computing, 4*(1), 67-96.

Loui, R. (1992). *Process and policy: Resource-bounded non-demonstrative argument.* Technical Report, Washington University, Department of Computer Science.

Marín, R., & Sartor, G. (1999). Time and norms: a formalisation in the event calculus. *Proceedings of Conference on Artificial Intelligence and Law (ICAIL)* (pp. 90-100). ACM Press.

Martin, C., & Barber, K. (2006). Adaptive decision-making frameworks for dynamic multi-agent organizational change. *Autonomous Agents and Multi Agent Systems, 13*(3), 391-428.

McBurney, P., Parsons, S., & Wooldridge, M. (2002). Desiderata for agent argumentation protocols. In C. Castelfranchi & L. Johnson (Ed.), *Proceedings of Conference on Autonomous Agents and Multi-Agent Systems (AAMAS)* (pp. 402-409). ACM Press.

Pitt, J., Kamara, L., Sergot, M., & Artikis, A. (2006). Voting in multi-agent systems. *Computer Journal , 49*(2), 156-170.

Prakken, H. (2000). On dialogue systems with speech acts, arguments and counterarguments. *Proceedings of Workshop on Logics in Artificial Intelligence , LNAI 1919*, pp. 224-238.

Prakken, H. (2001). Relating protocols for dynamic dispute with logics for defeasible argumentation. *Synthese, 127*(1-2), 187-219.

Prakken, H. (2005). Coherence and flexibility in dialogue games for argumentation. *Journal of Logic and Computation, 15*, 1009-1040.

Prakken, H. (2006). Formal systems for persuasion dialogue. *Knowledge Engineering Review, 21*(2), 163-188.

Rescher, N. (1977). *Dialectics: A Controversy-Oriented Approach to the Theory of Knowledge.* State University of New York Press.

Searle, J. (1996). What is a speech act? In A. Martinich (Ed.), *Philosophy of Language* (3rd Edition ed., pp. 130-140). Oxford University Press.

Shoham, Y., & Tennenholtz, M. (1997). On the emergence of social conventions: modelling, analysis and simulations. *Artificial Intelligence*, 139-166.

Vreeswijk, G. (2000). Representation of a formal dispute with a standing order. *Artificial Intelligence and Law*, 205-231.

KEY TERMS

Action Language: A formalism for representing and reasoning about actions or events and their effects.

Dynamic Specifications: Specifications that may be modified during the system execution.

Institutional Power: A feature of a normative system whereby designated agents, when acting in specified roles, are empowered by an institution to create relations or states of affairs of special significance within the institution.

Normative System: A system in which actuality, what is the case, does not necessarily coincide with ideality, what ought to be the case.

Open Multi-Agent System: A system in which: (i) there is no access to internal architectures of the agents, (ii) there is no guarantee of benevolent behaviour, and (iii) it is not possible to predict the agents' interactions.

ENDNOTE

[1] This is a very simple formalisation of the logic of disputation that suffices, however, for presenting a simple example; more complicated formalisations of this logic are out of the scope of this chapter.

Chapter XX
Interactions Between Formal and Informal Organizational Networks

Marco Lamieri
Institute for Scientific Interchange Foundation, Italy

Diana Mangalagiu
Management and Strategy Department, Reims Management School, France
Institute for Scientific Interchange Foundation, Italy

ABSTRACT

In this chapter we present a model of organization aimed to understand the effect of formal and informal structures on the organization's performance. The model considers the interplay between the formal hierarchical structure and the social network connecting informally the agents emerging while the organization performs a task-set. The social network creation and evolution is endogenous, as it doesn't include any function supposed to optimize performance. After a review of the literature, we propose a definition of performance based on the efficiency in allocating the task of a simulated organization that can be considered as a network-based problem-solving system. We analyze how the emergence of a stable process in decomposing tasks under different market conditions can alleviate the rigidity and the inefficiencies of a hierarchical structure and we compare the performance of different hierarchical structures under variable environment conditions.

INTRODUCTION

The relation between the organizational architecture and performance has long been of concern to economists (Sah & Stiglitz, 1986; Bolton & Dewatripont, 1994). Their emphasis has been on efficiency, defined as being optimal when interactions are minimized. Traditional economics sees interactions in organizations from an economizing on coordination, transaction or information costs perspective. Interactions are considered as distracting valuable resources (time, attention, energy, equipment, etc.) from productive use itself (Williamson, 1985) and therefore interaction mechanisms are to be minimized. Interactions are seen as "allocative" and are used to coordinate events, functions, businesses, etc. such that these fit together and fit with predefined rules while minimizing the resources consumed to ensure the fit. They are determined by the mode in which the hierarchy and the division of labor are structured and they form an unbroken line from the top managers to the operative employees. As a result, the economics literature on organizations has mostly focused on hierarchies: by connecting N nodes together with the minimum required number of $N - 1$ links and creating a chain of command that is only $L \sim logN$ links in depth, hierarchies are almost as efficient as possible. Hierarchies require each node to interact directly with, on average, b other nodes where $b << N$ and is generally called the "span of control" (Dodds et al., 2003). Numerous studies studied the optimality of hierarchical organizational networks for exerting control, performing decentralized tasks, making decisions, and accumulating knowledge (Van Zandt, 1998; Hart & Moore, 1999; Garicano, 2000; Visser, 2000).

This traditional economics view on organizational interactions holds true in product manufacturing-oriented organizations, in which the transaction costs are low compared to the production costs, strict hierarchical decomposition of tasks into independent units being possible. But in today's knowledge intensive organizations, of highly transactional nature (North & Wallis, 1994), strict decomposition is not anymore possible and allocative interactions are not sufficient for explaining organizational performance. In such organizations, in addition to formal interaction of allocative nature, informal relations are important. These informal interactions can be categorized of being "generative" to the extent that they help individuals in organizations to generate new capabilities, gain new knowledge and insight in a way that allow individuals to handle complex situations (Morieux et al., 2005).

In the last decade, a growing attention has been devoted to informal interactions taking place in organizations. Empirical evidence (Nohria, 1992; Johanson, 1999; Cumming, 2004) has shown that in many organizations, informal interactions are even the primary means by which employees find information, solve complex problems and learn how to do their work. Moreover, informal networks existing in an organization and participating actively in the handling of practices can influence the formal, hierarchical design of the organization, leading to a co-evolution between formal and informal organizational networks (Volberda & Lewin, 2003).

Theoretical studies (Zander & Kogut, 1995; Garicano, 2000) have been also devoted to the role played by the informal interactions and network-related mechanisms in the behavior and capabilities of organizations. Most of them are based on the knowledge-based theory of the firm, where organizations are viewed as social communities specializing in efficient knowledge creation and transfer (Zander & Kogut, 1995). In this view, informal interpersonal networks emerge as a major component of the knowledge transfer process. Other studies, such as Uzzi (1997) focus on the association between informal network structure and organizational performance.

Under these circumstances, the main problem facing an organization is not efficiency, which is a static concept, understood roughly as being maximized when minimizing the number of costly links needed to support a specified task. When the organizational objectives become more various and less specified it not longer makes sense to speak of optimum or efficient solutions. The question is rather if the problem solving technique is robust, i.e. produces workable answers in changing task environments. The robustness, being seen as a highly dynamic efficiency, on the one hand, should protect individuals from being overwhelmed by the direct and indirect effects of changing and unpredictable patterns of collaboration; and on the other hand, should protect the organization as a whole from disintegration in cases where failures occur. The interplay between formal and informal structures in organizations, involving allocative and generative interactions remains unclear. It has been studied in terms of adaptation (Siggelkow & Levinthal, 2003; Lewin et al, 2004) and lately of co-evolution between formal and informal networks (Volberda & Lewin, 2003; Jacobides, 2005), but it is not fully captured by organization theories and methods.

The chapter is organized as follows: after a brief introduction describing the general perspective and objective of the chapter, we provide the background of the relation between organizational architecture, interactions and performance. We review the literature and the current issues on the interaction between the formal (hierarchical) and informal organizational networks and on the formation of organizational routines in hierarchical structures. We introduce the different views on efficiency and robustness and how they relate to the organizational performance. Then we discuss the insight the agent-based modeling approach can bring to the understanding of these issues. We present an agent-based model of hierarchical organizations we have developed considering the interplay between the formal hierarchical structure and the social network connecting informally the agents emerging while the organization performs a task. We present the different components of our model: the role and capabilities of individual agents, the different structures of interactions contributing to the organizational dynamics and the characteristics of the environment in terms of complexity and stability. Next, we introduce our experimental results in terms of comparative performances of organizational structures and specific impact of the environment on organizational performance. We investigate how the interaction between formal and informal organizational structure influences the organizational performance, if and how the informal relations between agents can alleviate the rigidity and the inefficiencies of a hierarchical structure and what organizational structures perform better under different environment conditions in terms of stability, complexity, and competitiveness. Finally, we provide concluding remarks and future research directions.

BACKGROUND

In this section we introduce the main definitions and concepts needed for understanding the interactions taking place between individuals in organizations in order to capture the complex dynamics, structures, routines and performance of organizations.

The theoretical background we refer to starts with Simon's legacy on bounded rationality, routines, near decomposability of problems and formal vs. informal interactions. We give a brief overview of organizational theories considering organizations as complex systems, we introduce of the concepts of bounded rationality, satisficing and routines. Then we discuss the possibility of decomposing complex systems, recalling the distinction that Simon (1962) made between decomposable and non-decomposable problems.

Organizations as Complex Systems

The first to introduce the basic models of the firm economics theory were the French neoclassical economist Cournot (1863), followed by the political economist Marshall (1880). They examined the behavior of the firm in terms of inputs, production methods, output and prices assuming that profit maximization is the goal of the firm. Since then, most traditional economists consider that sales maximization or market share, combined with satisfactory profits, is the main purpose of large corporations. From an economics point of view, a group of individuals is considered to constitute an organization if the group has an objective or a performance criterion that transcends the objectives of the individuals within the group (Van Zandt, 1998). In this context, the interactions among agents are seen from an economizing on coordination, transaction or information costs perspective. Interactions are distracting valuable resources (time, attention, energy, equipment, etc.) from productive use itself (Williamson, 1985) and therefore interaction mechanisms are to be minimized. Interactions are seen as allocative and are used to coordinate events, functions, businesses, etc. such that these fit together and fit with predefined rules while minimizing the time, energy, etc. consumed to ensure the fit. They are determined by the mode in which the hierarchy and the division of labor are structured and they form an unbroken line from the top managers to the operative employees. As a result, interactions define the formal structure of the organization in terms of boundaries, internal design, and functioning and the organization is seen as decomposable.

Bounded Rationality

Adaptive behavior has been widely used in economic modeling until the early seventies. It is usually seen as the simplest outcome of boundedly rational decision processes, as opposed to the optimizing behavior that characterizes substantively rational agents. Economic theory, as is taught in Graduate Schools, is populated of agents who are rational in the sense of perfectly optimizing and only constrained by their environment (which they are assumed to know either perfectly, or in a probabilistic way). These agents have a goal (for example maximization), and always attain this goal within the constraints they face (production possibilities and demand conditions). This framework remains unchanged when agents are faced with uncertainty, that is usually tackled by assigning probabilities to different states of the world, i.e. modifying the set of constraints within which the agent's behavior is still the best possible one. The flow of new information is managed in a completely mechanical way for example by updating prior probabilities according to Bayes' theorem.

With the rise of the rational expectations revolution, a growing number of economists showed their dissatisfaction with substantive rationality. It was claimed then that this particular notion of rationality is not the one adopted by other social sciences as psychology or sociology. These sciences label a behavior as rational not so much according to the outcome (attainment of the constrained optimum) but according to the process that yields a particular decision. This kind of rationality is called bounded or procedural, and following Simon (1955) "is usually studied in situations in which the subject must gather information of various kind and process it in different ways in order to arrive at a reasonable course of action, a solution to the problem".

The shift of focus from the outcome to the process of choice has a straightforward and powerful implication, i.e. the need of accounting for the computational burden of a problem solving procedure.

In a few years a massive amount of experimental evidence showed that even in extremely simple problems agents did not behave according to the rules of substantive rationality. They seemed to look for good satisficing solutions, as opposed to 'optimal' solutions, and furthermore their reaction to the availability of new information was far from following the rules of Bayes' theorem. In other words, even when an optimal solution was in principle clearly available, the computational cost associated with it induced agents to limit themselves to a satisficing one, proving the point of the advocates of bounded rationality.

According to Simon (1955), the decision process is a system for processing information that has a limited processing power. A typical agent's cognitive process can be divided into three steps:

1. First, agents acquire knowledge. They extract information from one problem situation and store it to help them solving similar problems in the future.
2. Then, the learning process takes place through a mix of trial and error and the agents get insight in trying to reach solutions. Past experience and error are continuously used in the process of problem solving in order to improve the chances of getting a good solution.
3. Finally, agents try to generalize their solutions to single problems in order to use them as a forecasting tool. They learn to associate observed patterns to already solved problems, in order to speed the solution of new problems.

Among the studies trying to give empirical grounding to this theoretical construction, there is the interesting work by Egidi & Marengo (1995), where the emergence of "routines" is tested using a laboratory experiment. In this experiment, a two-persons card game is played by a large number of pairs, whose actions are stored in a computer's memory. In order to achieve the final goal, each player must discover his sub-goals, and must coordinate his action with the partner's one. The game therefore involves the division of knowledge and cooperation among players, and gives rise to the emergence of organizational routines. The authors suggest that the organizational routines, i.e. the sequences of actions leading to the realization of the final goal, cannot be fully memorized because of their variety and number. Moreover, it is shown that players do not possess all the knowledge needed by an hypothetical supervisor to play the best strategy: they generally explore only a limited part of the space of the potential rules, and therefore learn and memorize a simple, bounded set of personal meta-rules.

These meta-rules, also called "production rules" in cognitive sciences, are of the form "if Condition then Action". Each Condition can concern either the game configurations or the partner's action. In the former case, the identification of an appropriate "Action" depends on the sub-goals exploration. In the latter case, it depends on the recognition (or discovery) of interaction rules; in this eventuality the production rule embodies a dynamic and possibly cooperative reaction to the partner's action. Organizational procedures (routines) therefore emerge as the outcome of a distributed process generated by personal production rules.

Organizational Structure

Organizational structure is the way in which the interrelated groups of individuals are constructed, the main concern being to ensure effective communication and coordination. Please see also Chapter II "Modeling Dimensions for Agent Organizations" by Coutinho et al. From this very broad definition, we can analyze an organizational structure along four different dimensions as introduced by Chang & Harrington (2006).

1. The allocation of information, which refers to how information moves between the environment and the organization. This dimension describes how agents receive information from the environment and how this information moves within the organization, in brief "who reports to whom". This "hierarchy" may have a fairly stable component in it, as it might be described by the rules of communication laid out in the organizational chart. This is what is called a "formal structure"

in the model we present later in this chapter. Such flows of information can be considered as an endogenous aspect of the organizational model that describes how information is distributed in the organization.

2. The allocation of authority, which is who makes the decisions. There are two critical aspects associated to the allocation of authority, modularity and decentralization. An organization may have to perform many sub-tasks in solving a problem and a key structural issue is how these sub-tasks are combined into distinct modules, which are then re-integrated to produce an organizational solution. The degree to which a problem can be efficaciously modularized depends on the nature of the task. Two classic structures that represent alternative modular forms are the M form where all of the sub tasks associated with a particular product line are combined and the U form where all similar sub-tasks are combined. With this allocation of tasks, there is still the issue of which agents ultimately make the decisions. In the context of a hierarchy, to what degree is authority centralized in higher levels? Is authority matched with who has the best information? The formal authority may differ from the real authority (or power) as noted by Aghion & Tirole (1997). If an agent with decision-making authority relies heavily on the information provided by other agents, then the real authority may lie with those providing the information. The allocation of information and real authority are thus intertwined. The hierarchy can be defined as a network in which every node is connected with (at least) "a parent node with sub- or super-ordination within different social domains". For example, Galam (2005) introduces a model where any top-level agent directly depends on the choices of the bottom-level agents. Other models describe an organization as a network of layers "sharing a common goal" of optimization, having "the same horizontal position of power and authority" (Reihlen, 1996). This concept named "heterarchy" in opposition to hierarchy and used to create flexible organizational configurations was introduced by McCullogh (1945). A heterarchy "permits different elements of an organization to cooperate whilst individually optimizing different success criteria".

3. The organizational norms and culture. Agents' behavior in an organization is somehow influenced by the organization's past and this past is embedded in what is called norms or culture, as described in March (1991). The presence of the culture embedded in organizations is often modeled as a reinforcement process and leads to "path dependency" in the evolution of the organization.

4. The motivation. Agents may be modeled as having preferences (e.g. income level, effort) and these preferences translate into behavior depending on the incentives present in the organization.

Organizational Routines

Early concepts of routines emphasized a fixed pattern of individual behavior in response to a defined stimulus. Using a computational metaphor, March and Simon (1958, pp.142) state that "most behaviors, and particularly most behaviors in organizations, are governed by performance programs". A set of activities is routinized when the choice has been simplified by the development of a fixed response to defined stimuli. If the search process has been eliminated, but a choice remains in the form of a clearly defined and systematic computing routine, according to March and Simon (1958), the activities are still routinized. The idea of a fixed response to a given stimulus, accompanied by the absence of search, provides the foundation upon which much subsequent theorizing about routines has been based. More recently, Ashforth & Fried (1988) used the concept of an event schema to argue that routines are sustained by the cognitive structures of organizational agents. Nelson & Winter (1982) introduced a wide variety of metaphors for routines: routines as genes, routines as memory, routines as targets for control, replication, and imitation. The definition of routine introduced by Nelson and Winter (1982) expands on March and Simon's (1958) notion of a fixed response to include patterns of behavior that function as a recognizable unit in an evolutive way. For an exhaustive survey on organizational routines, see Feldman and Pentland (2003).

Near Decomposability

Considering the level of complexity in organizations, there are simple structures consisting of only few components that interact either minimally or linearly and complex structures in which one component may affect and be affected by many others. An example of a simple structure is a production system in which the co-ordination structure is imposed by technical or organizational constraints and one component controls the flow. In this case, the events occurring within the system can be described straightforwardly: first we look at what is done by one part and then how this affects the next. An example of a complex structure is a production system in which the structure of the connections among the units is variable. In this case, as the level of complexity of the system increases it may become difficult to identify interdependencies among components. In such cases, attempting to understand the operation of the entire machine by following the activities in each component in a brute force manner is liable to be futile (Bechtel, 1993).

Decomposability, defined as a way to manage complexity and to govern interdependencies among parts within a system (Langlois, 2000), allows the subdivision of the overall structure (or task) so that it becomes manageable and the system intelligible. Separating the sets of variables with the higher internal interdependence and the lower connection with other system variables reduces the reciprocal influence between components. Thus, the value of overall performance of a decomposable system depends very little on the interactions among its components. This means that by optimizing each single component we reach the (global) optimal solution. In a non-decomposable system it is difficult to reach the optimal solution through local and independent adjustments.

Nearly decomposable structures, instead, are those characterized by weak but not necessarily negligible interactions. In such cases, the value of overall performances highly depends on the interaction among system components. Moreover, the optimization of each subsystem (independently) rarely leads to the global optimum. Simon (1962, 1991) argues that essentially all complex systems share the feature of having a near decomposable architecture. Indeed, they are characterized by a structured ordering of successive sets of subsystems that is organized into hierarchical layers of parts in such a way that interactions among elements belonging to the same parts are much more intense than interactions among elements belonging to different parts. By "intense" interaction we mean that the behavior of one component depends more closely on the behavior of other components belonging to the same part than on components belonging to other parts or that this influence happens on a shorter time scale (effects propagate faster within a part than among parts) or that the influence is more widespread (within a sub-unit almost all elements interact, whereas interactions among elements belonging to different sub-units are more scarce) (Egidi & Marengo, 2002).

Organizations can be characterized as near decomposable systems when through division of labor, divisionalization and hierarchical decomposition of tasks, individuals within a hierarchical sub-unit have closer, more widespread, more intense and more frequent interactions than individuals belonging to different sub-units.

If we consider the outcome of a process where all the relations are important and the decomposition of the problem is bounded by interaction, a near decomposable system is more efficient than a "mechanical" decomposable problem. The agent-based model we present later in this chapter tries to address this issue. The economics addresses this issue through the transaction cost theory (Williamson, 1975), which heavily relies on Simon's bounded rationality theory. The transaction cost theory advances that the process of decomposition of economic activities is limited by the availability of coordination mechanisms, which can efficiently coordinate sub-units. Another explanation is more cognitive in nature and springs directly from Simon's work on problem solving and bounded rationality (Simon, 1962). Problem solvers faced with problems whose complexity outweighs their bounded computational capabilities are forced to work on conjectural decompositions of the problem into sub-problems. On the one hand, such decompositions are necessary heuristics for computationally limited individuals, as they reduce to a collection of sub-problem of more manageable size problems whose complexity largely defeats their computational capabilities. Moreover, very often some of these sub-problems may already be familiar to the problem solvers or at least display some analogies with known problems. However by treating sub-problems as independent or quasi-independent some existing interdependencies are almost inevitably ignored and sub-optimality, biases, systematic mistakes are almost inevitably introduced (Egidi & Marengo, 2002). This is a fundamental source of sub-optimality due to bounded rationality and computational constraints: it is a source which relates to limitations to bounds in the representational capabilities of individuals, organizations and society and sets a clear constraints on the efficiency of the division of labor and knowledge.

Informal and Formal Networks

Earlier in this chapter we have seen that allocative interactions and the implementation of predefined rules cannot fully explain the organizational behavior in an increasingly complex environment and that informal interactions help individuals in organizations to generate new capabilities, gain new knowledge and insight. Informal networks are self-generated, self-organized and self-managed inter-relationships between organizational agents. Such interrelationships form the foundations of effective and efficient flows of information, experience, knowledge and ideas. In essence, these informal networks work as an "informal division of labor", upholding the view that performance relies significantly upon a formal recognition of the informal organization (Morton et al., 2004).

A growing body of organization and management theory and research on the informal organizational networks supports the idea of interrelationships that enhance or constrain access to valued resources (Krackhardt & Hanson, 1993; Ibarra, 1993; Heckscher & Adler, 2005; Heckscher, 2007).). The informal network can traverse functions and divisions to facilitate more rapid outcomes and coordination between formal teams and integrators. This creates new problems for leadership, which must foster and manage differentiated systems of relationships through network design.

Although the interplay between formal and informal structures in organizations, involving allocative and generative interactions has been increasingly studied in the last decade, it is yet to be fully captured by the organization theories and models. Empirical evidence (Nohria, 1992; Burt, 2000; Cumming, 2004) show that in many organizations, informal networks are the primary means by which employees find information, solve complex problems, and learn how to do their work. Indeed, informal networks or communities nested in an organization and participating actively in the handling of practices can influence the formal, hierarchical design of the organization. There are also theoretical attempts to understand this dynamics. Most of them are based on the knowledge-based theory of the firm, where organizations are viewed as social communities specializing in efficient knowledge creation and transfer (Zander, 1995). In this setting, informal interpersonal networks emerge as a major component of the knowledge transfer process. Other studies focus on the association between informal network structure and organizational performance (Uzzi, 1997). Other studies on the role of the informal organizational networks have focused on awareness and recognition (Morton et al., 2004) and on the ways the informal networks can actually be manipulated or exploited in order to improve organization's performance. Firms using concurrent engineering, for example, recognize the value of informal communication in product development and often collocates project team members to facilitate a positive environment for more rapid exchange of ideas and information (Baker, 1992; Backhouse & Brookes, 1996). However, this strategy is not without its difficulties. The expertise that made project team members attractive in the first place can be diluted over lengthy periods of collocation. Team members also have varying degrees of skill in informal communication and may not address the importance of developing personal networks.

Agent-Based Models for Organizations

One way of addressing the organizations' complexity issues is by designing and analyzing computational models (Agent-Based Models or ABM). This approach has caught the attention of a number of scholars in organizational science (Burton & Obel, 1995; Carroll & Burton, 2000; Lomi & Larsen, 2001; Nissen et al, 2006) and is increasingly making significant contributions to management practice. As they are becoming validated, calibrated and refined, computational simulation models of organizations are increasingly used as organizational design tools for predicting and mitigating organizational risks or as "virtual synthetic experiments" (Levitt, 2004; Lin et al, 2006).

The agent-based models view organizations as collections of agents, interacting with one another in their pursuit of assigned tasks. An ABM doesn't need to answer the question of "the organization's utility function" as it is sufficient to instantiate agents and let organizational behavior emerge from the interaction of agents amongst themselves and with the environment and measure the organization performance (Bonabeau, 2002). In this framework, the performance of an organization is seen most of the time as being determined by the structure of interactions among agents, which define the lines of communication, allocation of information processing tasks, distribution of decision-making authorities, and provision of incentives (Chang & Harrington, 2006). It may involve the frequency or the average time to reach a particular target (a global optimum, for example) or the accuracy of the organization's decisions or solutions performed. Organizations are considered as complex, non-linear, dynamic and highly interactive systems. The organizational dynamics is the result of an adaptive behavior both at the individual level and at the structural level of agent (Carley & Svoboda, 1996).

One computational approach to organizations focuses on the simulation of organization in order to recreate reality, to perform "what if" analysis, to model stocks and flows of resources, information and other variables in supply chains and enterprises and study the evolution of actual organizations. *PowerSim*[1], *Stella*[2] and *Java Enterprise Simulator*[3] are examples of this approach (please see also Chapter IV "OMACS: A Framework for Adaptive, Complex Systems" by DeLoach and Chapter VIII "Structural Aspects of Organizations", by Grossi and F. Dignum).

A number of agent-based model development platforms such as *Swarm*[4], *StarLogo*[5], *Agentsheets*[6], *AGR*[7], *MOISE+*[8] and *OperA*[9] allow rapid specification, simulation and analysis of multi-level agent-based system models. Such development platforms are beginning to be used for designing project and program organizations.

Other approaches focus on the organization formation (Stacey 1995, McKelvey 2004, Axtell 1999) or on the adaptation and evolution of existing organizations (Carley et al, 1999; Miller, 2001; Dupouet & Yildizoglu, 2003). The processes of self-organization and emergence at play in organizations have specificities that are tied to the context in which they take place. Routines and power relations that constrain and resist nascent processes structure organizations. As a consequence, self-organization and emergent changes find themselves embedded in, and constrained by a relatively rigid strategic and organizational context.

Commercial-grade modeling tools such as *Organizational Consultant* (Burton & Obel, 2004) is designed to diagnose and repair organizational misfits in terms of contingency theory findings for an organization. *SimVision_R,* based on the Virtual Design Team research prototype for designing the micro-work processes and organization structure of projects, programs, and matrix organizations (Jin and Levitt, 1996) and *Brahms* (Sierhuis et al, 2007) are other examples of computational modeling and simulating tools for team and group communication and work processes and practices.

ORGANIZATIONAL PERFORMANCE

Organizational performance is one of the most important constructs in organizational science and the most important measure of the success of a business firm. Organizational performance also means different things to different stakeholders and the extent of the emphasis placed on various dimensions of performance is contingent on the environment in which an organization operates.

Academically, organizational performance is the ultimate dependent variable of interest for those concerned with just about any area of economics: accounting is concerned with measuring performance; marketing with customer satisfaction and market share; operations management with productivity and cost of operations, organizational behavior with employee satisfaction and structural efficiency; and finance with capital market response to all of the above. March & Sutton (1997) found that roughly 28% of articles in the Strategic Management Journal, the Academy of Management Journal and the Administrative Science Quarterly included some measure of organizational performance.

In the business policy literature there are two major streams of research on the determinants of firm performance. One is based primarily upon an economic tradition, emphasizing the importance of external market factors in determining firm success. The other line of research builds on the behavioral and sociological paradigm and sees organizational factors and their fit with the environment as the major determinants of success. Business performance at the corporate level is widely assessed in the economic tradition by the return, through changes in the price of the stock and dividends, to shareholders. However, corporate level performance analysis, whether for strategic or public policy purposes, is inappropriate in many instances because of the heterogeneity of the firms' operations. The strategic business units in a firm are often very diverse. Profitability analysis grouping these entities together yields few of the insights needed for strategic or public policy decision-making. Because of this heterogeneity, the profitability analysis is often advocated and undertaken at the business unit level, based on accounting data. In particular, the accounting measure, return on investment (ROI), is widely regarded as the most useful measure and ultimate "bottom line" test of business performance (Reese & Cool, 1978). It is used both as an objective of management and as a dependent criterion variable to evaluate the effect of various factors on performance. Other better indicators do exist but all of them share a common approach measuring the performance based on accounting books and stock returns.

We are interested in a completely different performance definition: we would like to measure the organizational performance in term of organization efficiency using a behavioral and sociological paradigm and see organizational factors and their fit with the environment as the major determinants of success. Please see also Chapter VIII "Structural Aspects of Organizations", by Grossi and F. Dignum for alternative ways of defining organizational performance. Industrial organization economics has proven extremely useful to researchers of strategy content in providing a basic theoretical perspective on the influence of market structure on firm strategy and performance. While there is a range of specific models, major determinants of firm-level profitability include: characteristics of the industry in which the firm competes; the firm's position relative to its competitors; and the quality or quantity of the firm's resources.

Organizational performance can, of course, be considered at a disaggregated level, as for example in studies of the direct costs of producing a particular product using a specific technology or of efficiency in performing a particular task (March and Sutton, 1997). Identifying the causal structure of organizational performance phenomena on the basis of the incomplete information generated by historical experience is problematic. Any observation-based organizational history is rife with resolute ambiguities that can frustrate the efforts of statistical and interpretive imagination to identify causal links among historical events.

Perhaps even more than their economist counterparts, organizational researchers have developed a wide variety of models of performance. While the organization behavior and theory literatures are rich in the breadth and depth of their studies of organization structures, systems, and people, the variety of conjectures and empirically tested models makes aggregation difficult. For example, just determining the appropriate construct of performance or effectiveness involves measures ranging from employee satisfaction to shareholder wealth (Goodman and Pennings, 1977; Cameron, 1986). In broad terms, this stream of research suggests that managers can influence the behavior of their employees (and thus the performance of the organization) by taking into account factors such as the formal and informal structure, the planning, reward, control and information systems, their skills and personalities, and the relation of these to the environment. That is, managers influence organizational outcomes by establishing 'context', and that context is the result of a complex set of psychological, sociological, and physical interactions. The difficulty in working with such multifaceted models lies in developing, collecting and aggregating appropriate measures (Bonoma, 1985). Many constructs within the literature are difficult to measure and those, which are relatively easier to capture, are often at the micro (individual) level. For example, can we say that a firm on the whole is bureaucratic just because it has several levels to its hierarchy? Can a firm be over-differentiated in one area and under differentiated in another? In contrast, firm performance is an aggregate phenomenon.

Theory or empirical evidence of linkages to performance abounds within each paradigm. But surprisingly little has been done to integrate the two and evaluate the relative effect of each on firm profitability.

Interactions Between Formal and Informal Organizational Networks: A Computational Agent Based Model

The work described below addresses this issue of performance measurement at the structure-level using an agent based computational model. Our aim is to bridge the gap between the economic definition of performance and the organizational stream of research outlined in the previous section. We propose an agent based computational model shaped to capture the intra-firm production process as a generative interaction among workers and managers. We introduce a dynamic definition of performance that tries to grasp the interaction between the formal and informal networks of relations within the firm. The use of agent-based simulation allows us to consider the simulated organization as a virtual laboratory and we can test different scenario and hypotheses. We test our definition of performance against different scenarios: how the performance of the firm is affected by the structure of the market and how it is affected by the organizational structure and how the distribution of workers' skills affects their workload in order to define the possible reallocation of sub-tasks within the organization.

An organization has an output say, a set of practices and delivers some measure of performance. Performance may be measured by profit (or some analogous criterion) or may involve specifying a particular target (for example, the global optimum). In the later case, the performance can be measured by the frequency with which an organization reaches the target or, if eventually it will always reach it, the average time it takes to do so (Chang & Harington, 2006). An organization's employees may have different goals than those of their manager. Fortunately, an ABM needs not answer the question of "what is an organization's utility function" as it is sufficient to instantiate agents and let organizational behavior emerge from the interaction of agents amongst themselves and with the environment. By building an organization with a bottom-up approach, we can avoid taking an anthropomorphic view to complex entities such as organizations. The main questions traditionally driving the modeling of organizations have largely been normative. What is the optimal form of organization for achieving an organization's goals? More generally, what is the relationship between environmental properties, organizational structure, and organizational performance? An important question is how a hierarchically ordered economic system emerges and how the decomposition of tasks in different hierarchical structures can lead to different performances.

The Organizational Environment: Efficiency vs. Robustness

An empirical comparison in terms of ROA (returns on assets), ROE (returns on equities), market value and sales growth against the 1000 firms considered in Forbes' Annual Report on American Industry found that although the portfolio of excellent firms performed above average, they were significantly less successful than the top 250 firms identified by Forbes (Aupperle et al, 1986). Similarly, in a study based on survey data, a portfolio of 41 of the excellent firms was compared to the lower and upper halves of a performance ranked sample of Fortune 1000 firms matched for industry and sales volume (Venkatraman & Ramanujam, 1986). The excellent companies were significantly higher performers (based on sales growth, net income growth, market share change and ROI) than the lower group but significantly worse than the upper group on all these measures ($p<0.01$) except sales growth for which the result was not significant. These doubts were confirmed by the subsequent performance of the excellent firms. Indeed, in the period 1981-1986 a portfolio of 29 of the excellent firms provided a return 1% above the S&P500 average, while 39 'un-excellent' companies, chosen for their poor performance on the 6 dimensions used by Peters and Waterman, provided a return 12% above the average (Clayman, 1987). Recent studies such as Devinney et al (2005) confirm these results.

The poor performance of the excellent companies demonstrates the difficulties of using arbitrary combinations of measures to evaluate 'performance' and reliance on managers affected by 'recency' bias to be involved in determining 'excellence'. The standard economic measures of performance described earlier do not consider that, under conditions of environmental uncertainty, hierarchies are extremely prone to cascading breakdowns because the failure of nodes near the top of the hierarchy effectively severs large sub-networks from the main organization, thereby impairing global coordination and than performance as a consequence. A long line of work in organizational sociology in which issues such as the interaction between an organization and its environment (Burns & Stalker, 1961; Thompson, 1967), the role of uncertainty in necessitating communication (Burns & Stalker, 1961; Lawrence & Lorsch, 1967), and the importance of adaptability to innovation and crisis management (Burns & Stalker, 1961; Krackhardt & Stern, 1988; Kelly & Stark, 2002) have frequently been emphasized. Some authors operationalize the performance of organizations in ambiguous environments in terms of robustness extending optimality approach form the economics literature on firms.

The Proposed Model

The proposed definition of performance is grounded on the complexity framework and, in order to grasp a part of the complexity of the organizations and the interaction among simple agents, we propose a theoretical computational agent based model. This approach leads to a definition of performance that is not analytical but emerges as the outcome of a simulation model considering the interplay between two views of an organization: a formal and an informal structure. Each structure is modeled as a network, where the nodes represent the agents. This organizational structure can be seen as a distributed network-based problem-solving system (see also Chapter XXII "Organizational Self-Design in Worth-Oriented Domains" by Kamboj and Decker for alternative ways of organization seen as a problem-solving system).

The formal structure is the organizational hierarchy. This view is static and represents the functional division of work. The coordination is seen as an allocation of an order within a pre-existing set of resources or activities. In the formal structure, each agent has control on the agents below her and can modify this structure by deleting or creating ties.

The informal structure defines the personal relations within the organization and influence the way the organization performs a task. It is dynamic, emerges from the generative interactions during the task performing and it affects the performance of the simulated organization.

Both views are modeled as networks where nodes represent the agents and links represents the relations between agents as in Figure 1.

Figure 1. Example of a simulated organization as the interplay of a formal and informal network

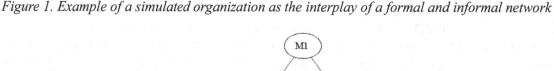
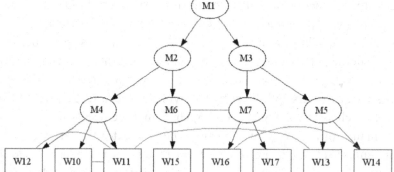

The agents are bounded rational, with cognitive and informational constraints and they have only a partial view of the organization. Each agent is autonomous, has skills and learning capabilities, accumulates experience and is able to perform a part of a task. The agents either improve their skills while performing tasks (learning by doing) or decrease them due to a forgetting mechanism. The agent' skill set is a set of abilities and a position in the hierarchical structure. We consider a population of agents $A = \{a_1, a_2, \ldots, a_n\}$ characterized by heterogeneous professions. The profession is the formal competence of the agent related with her position. The agents at the upper level in the hierarchy can perform a part of the task (if they have the required profession) or they can allocate the tasks to lower level agents in case they are skilled to perform it or, as last option, passes the task to someone upper in the hierarchy that follows the same procedure. The performance of an agent is defined as the aggregate performance of the agents below her.

We consider an exogenous environment $E(T,FN,SN)$, which sends tasks $T_1, T_2 \ldots T_n$ to the organization. A task $T = \{s_1, s_2, \ldots, s_m\}$ is a sequence of steps s to be performed, represented by integers drawn from a distribution. Performing each step requires a specific profession $P(s)$. In an indirect way, the task-set describes the environment; for a firm, the task is a metaphor of the market in terms of demand size and products differentiation.

There are some assumptions on tasks' execution that are needed in order to define the simulation dynamics:

1. task steps are sequential: if the first step has not been performed, it cannot move to the second step;
2. task value is drawn from Uniform and Normal distributions with different parameters.

The algorithm defining the dynamics of the model is quite simple and can be summarized as follows:

1. At each time step, an agent a_1, chosen at random, receives a task T_1 from the environment.
2. The agent a_1 receiving the task performs its first step s_1 if her profession fits the one required by the first step (s) of the task T_1.
3. Agent a_1 looks for another agents a_2, connected to her through the informal network $IN(A)$, able to perform the next step.
4. If step 3 cannot be performed, agent a_1 sends the task to the next higher level in the formal network $FN(A)$ where the upper-level agent allocates it to another agent.

Table 1. Example of task set

Task Set T
$T_1 = \{10, 11, 13, 14\}$
$T_2 = \{11, 15, 13, 22\}$
$T_3 = \{15, 17, 13, 14\}$
$T_4 = \{11, 16, 10, 13\}$

5. The process continues iterating steps from 1 to 4 until all steps $s_1 \ldots s_m$ of task T_1 have been performed. If one step of the task cannot be performed by the organization, the whole task is rejected. Task rejection occurs when the task arrives at the top agent in the hierarchical levels either directly from the environment or pushed up within the organization and no agent below her is able to perform one or more steps of the task.

6. At the end, the task T_1 is completed or rejected by the organization and a new task T_2 arrives from the environment, the process start again from step 1.

At the beginning of the simulation, a formal structure is set; no predefined informal structure is assumed and the ties in the informal structure are created over time. The probability at each time tick to create an informal link between agent a_i and agent a_j is defined as:

$$P_c = N\left[\mu = \frac{1}{D_{FN}\left(a_i, a_j\right)}; \sigma = 1 \right]$$

where $D_{FN}\left(a_i, a_j\right)$ is the distance, in the formal network *FN*, between agent a_i and agent a_j. The probability P_c is a normal distribution centered on the reciprocal of the distance $D_{FN}\left(a_i, a_j\right)$. This algorithm has been shaped in order to capture the difficulty to of workers to get in touch with manager in a higher hierarchical position. This feature is justified by the cognitive cost of maintaining a social relation within an organization, this cost being expressed both in time needed to keep the relation alive and cognitive effort. In this respect, the hierarchical organization is created in order to filter and limit the number of people reports to each manager; in the same spirit this algorithm attach a lower probability to create a social tie with a high level manager. The informal structure is dynamically shaped by an evolutionary algorithm that reinforces the links used the most frequent and lowers the strength of the less used links. If an informal link is too weak, it is removed according to a threshold defined exogenously by the parameter γ. The simulations shown in the next sections describe experiments testing the sensitivity of the model to γ. Links connecting upper-level agents are general and can serve different tasks, while lower-level links are more task-specific. Once new informal links are established, agents use them to pass tasks thus increasing organization's performance since there is no cost associated with passing the task through informal links.

The informal structure is a metaphor of a problem decomposition process. This model describes the subdivision of the overall structure of a task T so that the latter steps s becomes manageable and the system intelligible. Through decomposition, reciprocal influence among components is reduced and is solved by the formal structure and the informal structure. This resulting performance of the simulated organization can be obtained directly by separating sets of operations with the higher internal interdependence (steps).

The emergence of clusters in the informal network describes isolated sub-systems that can be left to specialized decision units without affecting the final outcome of the system. The performance of the organization in this sense is related both with the opportunity to decompose the task in separated subtasks and to allocate them to subsystems (clusters of agents connected in an informal network).

The tasks that pass through the hierarchical structure can be considered as residual operations not completely decomposed. The execution of such tasks cannot be completed within a single informal cluster of agents (we can imagine it operating as single offices within a division) because one or more skills required are not present in the informal cluster. In this case, the task needs to be re-allocated by a manager to an agent not connected with the cluster. This decomposition process has a cost and follows the rules imposed by the organizational structure. The processing cost associated with the decomposition is high considering the coordination needed among the different levels of the organization, while the processing cost for the emerging informal structure is negligible considering that the processing of the task is all performed without the necessity of further coordination.

In our setting, we consider two sets of parameters: the characteristics of the agents with respect to their skills and the characteristics of the tasks. As far as the organization is formalized with this model, the definition of performance we consider is straightforward and we try to keep it as simple as possible. In order to compute the proxy of the performance of the organization in this setting, we use four simple indicators that can be computed at the task level and a simple proxy of productivity that can be computed at the agent level.

Completion Time Γ

This is the simplest measure of performance proposed in the model and it considers the number of simulation time ticks needed to perform all the steps in the task. This value is a raw proxy of the processing cost of the task but it does not decompose the effect of the hierarchical organization efficiency from the effect of the informal network efficiency. The value can be decomposed in the number of transaction trough the formal network and the number of transaction trough the informal network.

$$\Gamma = \Gamma_{FN} + \Gamma_{IN}$$

The higher this value, the higher the production process cost determined by both hierarchical task allocation inefficiency and informal task-decomposition inefficiency.

Hierarchical Transaction Number Γ_{FN}

The number of transitions through the formal network Γ_{FN}, this measure is a proxy of the efficiency of the informal allocation of activity within the organization. The lower this value, the better the organization is able to decompose the task in sub-tasks that can be performed in informal cluster of agents without the need of further coordination by managers. Higher this value is smaller is the hierarchical coordination efficiency.

Task Completion Cost $C(T_s)$

The cost C of performing step s of task T by agent a, given the organization's structure, is defined as:

$$C(T_s) = C_p(a_s) + C_t(a_{s-1}, a_s)$$

This cost C is divided in two components:

Table 2. Formal structures used in experiments

Structure	Flat	Balanced	Unbalanced
Level 1	1 Agent	1 Agent	1 Agent
Level 2	12 Agents	4 Agents	3 Agents
Level 3	72 Agents	16 Agents	11 Agents
Level 4		64 Agents	6 Agents
Level 5			64 Agents

$$C_p\left(a_s\right)=\frac{1}{S_{a_s}}$$

$$C_t\left(a_{s-1},a_s\right)=\frac{1}{\min\left(\Theta_{a_s},\Theta_{a_{s-1}}\right)}$$

where $C_p\left(a_s\right)$ is the cost of performing step s by agent a considering her skill S in step s. In the second formula, C_t is the transaction cost for the task moving from agent a_{s-1} to agent a_s and Θ_a is the hierarchical position (level) of agent a.

The effect of workers' skills on the cost component C_p is negative $\frac{\partial C_p}{\partial S}=-1/S_{a_s}^2$, and the increase of one unit of skill leads to a reduction in the performing cost associated.

The cost component C_t is affected by the formal structure of the organization: the lower the average distance among agents, the lower the coordination cost associated with moving the task between two agents.

Agent Productivity Φ

In order to better understand the organization's dynamics, we define also the agent's a productivity in performing the task T:

$$\Phi\left(a,T\right)=\frac{\rho\left(T,a\right)}{L\left(T\right)}$$

where $\rho\left(T,a\right)$ is the number of steps of task T processed by agent a and $L(T)$ is the length of the task (the number of step to be performed). This measure is affected both by the number of steps in the task (and indirectly by the environment) and by the formal and informal structure of the organization. We are expecting to have distributions close to a normal distribution. A centered productivity distribution shows an efficient allocation of resources, while a positive skewed productivity (the right tail is longer and the mass of the distribution is concentrated on the left of the figure) signals a structural inefficiency where few workers are performing many steps while a higher density of worker are low-productive.

Experiments and Results

In our experiments we considered three different organizational structures as described in Table 2. For each structure, we run two different sets of experiments:

Figure 2. Number of transitions through the formal network without informal structure creation for Normal(μ = 8, σ = 1) and Uniform(μ = 0, σ = 15) distributions; balanced, unbalanced and flat structures

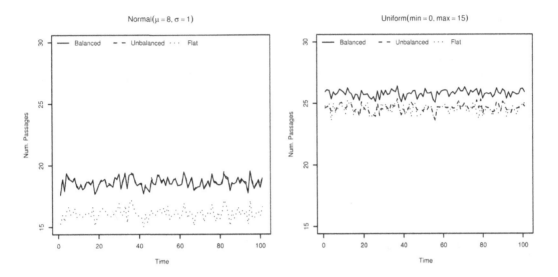

Figure 3. Costs using the formal network without informal structure creation for N(μ = 8, σ = 1) and U(μ = 0, σ = 15) distributions; balanced, unbalanced and flat structures

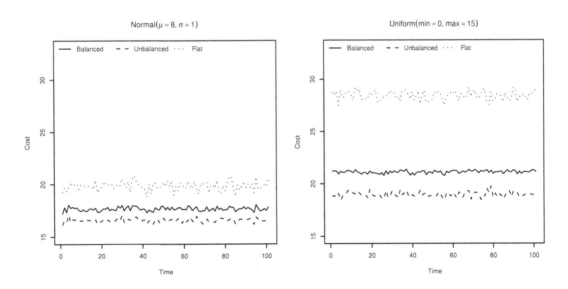

- Considering only the formal network without any informal link creation;
- Considering both the formal and the emerging informal network.

We run different experiments considering task-set values distributions: two normal $N(\mu = 8, \sigma = 1)$, $N(\mu = 8, \sigma = 3)$ and one uniform distribution $U(\min = 0, \max = 15)$. The normal versus uniform distribution of task-set mimic different environments: the normal with σ = 1 reflects the most "stable" environment while the uniform distribution mimics a more "fluctuating" environment. Our aim is to test the performance sensitivity to different environment.

For all the experiments we used some fixed parameters in order to compare the results from different experiments:

- Population: 85 agents
- Task set parameters:
  - Task length: 10
  - Task set domain: [0,15]
  - Task batch size: 100
- Network evolution parameters:
  - Ties reinforcement rate: 0.1
  - Ties decay rate: 0.001
  - Ties destruction threshold: 0.1

Organization Performance without Informal Structure

In this first experiment, we considered only the formal network without any informal network creation. The idea is to define a benchmark for further experiments. By definition, the hierarchical structure is

Figure 4. The informal network emergence

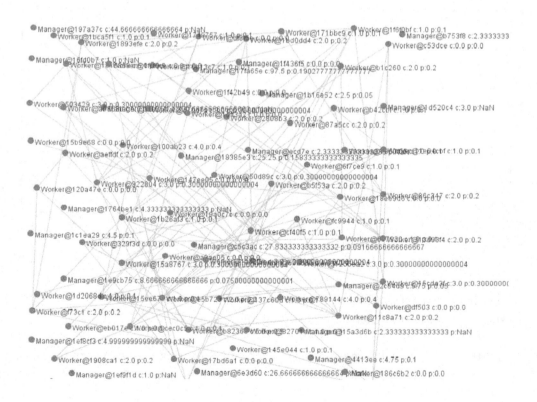

Figure 5. Number of formal transitions and costs with and without informal network (average of the three considered structures)

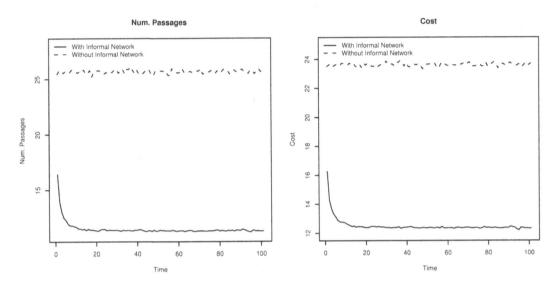

organized in a tree and sub-trees form, where the agents with similar professions are grouped in the same sub-tree.

In this experiment, the average number of transitions needed for performing heterogeneous task-sets (uniform task-set distribution) is sensibly higher than for performing homogeneous task-sets (normal task-set distribution), for the three different organizational structures (Figure 2). This is due to the difficulty faced by the organization to face fast-changing environments that requires tasks very different one from the other. In this thought environment a rigid hierarchical organization faces its limits and in order to solve tasks that require skills from different branch of the firm a formal escalation to manager is often required. If we think to a steel production company the task required to be performed (like a new order of a given amount of steel) are often very similar and a rigid structure can easily and efficiently perform such task focusing on problem decomposition and high vertical specialization of workers. As soon as the task required to be performed become heterogeneous (think for example to a business consulting company that is required to solve strategic business problems) a rigid hierarchical structure is not efficient any more. In the latter case a flat structure with small flexible working teams can do a better job. As the average distance between nodes is lower in a flat structure than in a balanced one, the average number of transitions is also lower. The unbalanced structure is an intermediate condition: when performing a homogeneous task-sets, the number of transitions is similar to the one corresponding to the balanced structure, while when performing a heterogeneous task-sets, the number of transitions is similar to the to the one corresponding to the flat structure.

In terms of cost, the balanced and unbalanced structures show similar costs regardless of task-set distribution. The flat structure involves often transitions through high-level agents, thus significantly increasing the costs despite a lower number of transitions (Fig. 3). The flat structure is affected by the task-set distribution. When performing an homogeneous task-set, tasks with similar steps can be managed in the same department without transitions through high-level managers. When performing a heterogeneous task-set, many tasks need escalation to high-level agents and, considering that in the flat structure the escalation always involves the top-agent, the differences in term of costs are increased.

Figure 6. Number of informal network transitions

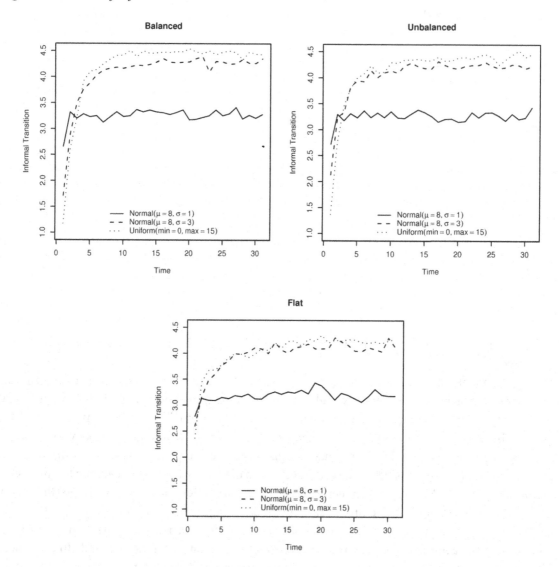

The Emergence of Informal Networks

In a second experiment, we consider both formal and informal structures. The emergence of informal cluster of agents is evident in the model. In an initial period the informal links are unstable and change frequently due to the underlying reinforcement process. After this short initial period (10 time ticks), links are starting to emerge and converge toward a stable shape. For all of the three considered structures the emergent network stabilizes and we illustrate this stabilization process for the unbalanced structure in Figure 4. This figure is showing agents (workers and managers, in red dots) with the associated skills (s) and productivity (p). The network connecting agents is the informal network emerged during the simulation after 10 ticks. The boldness of the lines is proportional to the power of the tie as described by the evolutionary algorithm creating the social network: light ties are seldom used and they are going

Figure 7. Number of formal transition considering the three different structures with informal structure

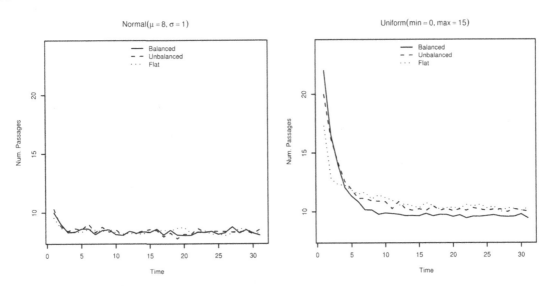

to disappear, while bold ties has been used often to transmit tasks and have been reinforced. The shape of the social network, after the initial simulation period of approximately 10 ticks, becomes stable (as shown also in Figure 6).

The informal network can facilitate the coordination among agents in the process. The new ties are increasing the connectivity of the network, decreasing the average path length of the graph and increasing the clustering coefficient. This dynamics implies an increasing efficiency of the organization over time, decreasing both the number of transition needed to perform the tasks and the costs as shown in Figure 5.

The speed of informal links creation increases with the homogeneity of the task-set as shown in Figure 6. When stabilized, the process decreases on average both cost and average number of transitions and also the variance of the cost and number of transitions.

Counter intuitively, we observe that that the higher the task heterogeneity, the more links of the informal structure are used for performing the task. In a changing environment there is an "over-creation" of links that quickly disappear. These links are used for specific tasks, which in the long run are not needed anymore, because of the high task-set heterogeneity.

The main finding of the model shows that, while without the informal structure there are significant differences in term of costs and number of transitions between the three structures simulated, when the informal structure emerges these differences become very small. The evolving process is smoothing the inefficiency embedded in the structures and is minimizing the cost and the number of transitions as clearly visible comparing Figure 6 (with informal links) and Figure 2 (experiment 1, without informal links).

The first case is very sensitive to the organizational structure. On the opposite, if we consider semi-decomposable problems, and we take into account learning agents able to create an informal network, we can see that the organizational structure become less relevant in affecting performances.

Even if the emergence of a formalized process alleviates the difference in performance between structures, the distribution of agent's performance is still very different between structures as shown

Figure 8. Productivity distribution's histograms

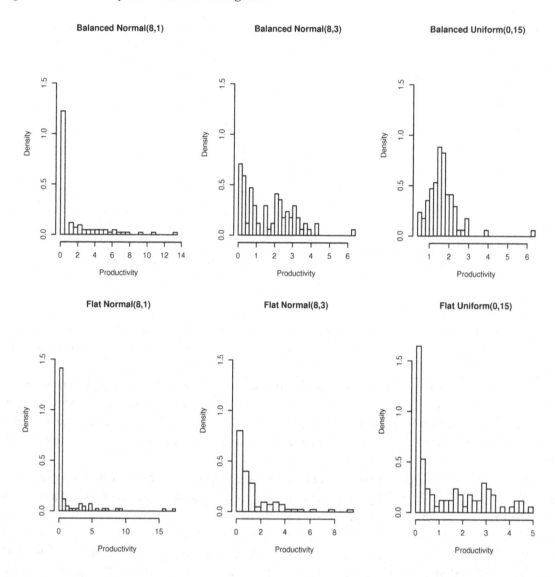

in Figure 8. The most interesting case is the uniform task-set, where the productivity, in the case of a balanced structure is close to Gaussian, while for the flat structure is still very asymmetric. This asymmetry highlights that most of the agents have a very low productivity (almost zero) and few of them are productive. In this sense, the balanced structure looks more "rational", and the workload of the agents is more equally distributed.

CONCLUSION AND FUTURE RESEARCH DIRECTIONS

In this chapter we presented an agent-based model of organization considering the interplay between the formal hierarchical structure and the social network connecting informally the agents emerging while the organization performs a task-set. In the model, the informal structure creation and evolution is endogenous, as no function supposed to optimize performance is included in it. The aim of this model is to understand the effect of formal and informal structures on organization's performance.

After a review of the literature, we proposed a definition of organizational performance based on the efficiency in allocating the task of our simulated organization that can be considered as a network-based problem-solving system. We defined three measures of performance: starting from the simple number of simulation time ticks needed to perform all the steps in the task (Γ), decomposed in the effect of the formal hierarchy on the performance (Γ_{FN}) measured as the number of formal escalations to higher level in the organization needed to perform the task. The task completion cost $C(T_s)$ is decomposed in the cost of performing a single step of the task by the agent (C_p), that is related with agent's skills, and the cost associated with formal and informal coordination needed to complete the steps in the task (C_p).

In order to test the simulated organization' performance, we implemented three different hierarchical structures: a flat, a balanced and an unbalanced structure. There is not an optimal structure of problem decomposition for any of the tested environments and the results show that each structure is the most efficient considering specific environmental conditions.

The emergence of informal network among agents in the organization is a process that takes place through a reinforcement mechanism that facilitates the coordination among agents in the process. The emergence of a stable informal structure can alleviate the rigidity and the inefficiencies of a hierarchical structure minimizing costs and number of transitions.

The formal structure alone is very sensitive to the decomposability of the problem. When we consider semi-decomposable problems, and we take into account learning agents able to formalize routines into processes, we observe that the organizational structure become less relevant in affecting performances.

The stability of the environment is a crucial point affecting the evolution of the informal network, the agent's productivity and the time required by the organization to fit it through the formalization of routines. An unstable environment leads to a higher number of informal links creation / destruction and higher adaptation costs, related also with high cognitive cost of the agents adapting to it. In both environments, when a stable informal shape is reached, different structures show no significant differences in performance but only differences in agents' productivity distribution.

This chapter shows how computational modeling can be used to investigate the organizational performance. This approach has the advantage to let us consider formal and informal coordination within the organization modeled as a network. The drawback is that the proposed measure of performance cannot be derived analytically and it is difficult to test empirically with real world data.

The future directions of this research are heading in both these directions. First, we intend to derive a simplified definition of performance that, even if connected with the model results, let us derives it analytically. Second, from this simplified definition of performance we intend to test our theoretical predictions about the effect of organizational structure on performance using empirical data. The empirical data needed to fit this model are both macro (economic performance of the organization, formal structure and information about the specific industry the organization is operating in order to model the environment) and micro (workers and manager's behaviors, agent's skills) at the agent-level. The economic information about the firm performance can be extracted from balance sheets and the stylized description of the industry can be obtained from public available information. For example, we are envisaging using data on consumption and production at the product level defined as 6-digits ATECO code for every industry provided by the Italian Statistical Institute. The most difficult part is obtain information about agents' skills and behaviors: we believe that the best way is using surveys, often made by consulting firms in order to assess a organizational change.

One important stream of research, particularly fruitful using AB model, is devoted to test policy implications. As soon as the model will be empirical grounded it could be used also for policy analysis. On one side, we will test the effect of different organizational structures performing what-if analysis on performance. We will test the effect of the entrance of the organization in a neighboring industry: from a modeling perspective it means to consider the introduction of new tasks to be performed and how this change impacts the organization's efficiency and performance. A second important policy test that can be performed with the model is evaluating an exogenous shock in the environment. For example, the European Union integration and the emergence of a common market is changing firms' behavior: the environment is becoming much more competitive in Europe and the integration due to the introduction of a common currency is shaping new scenarios. In many industries, the competition among firms is moving back from prices to quality and efficiency. As an example, in the service sector a competitive advantage is not only a lower price but also a higher service level standard (we can think about mobile communication industry where a loss of connectivity in a given area is a big issue or the missing adoption of a new high speed technology can lead to important market share losses). A purely economic evaluation of competitive advantage of firms based on price and marginal cost is not well suited anymore to this context. Both the task to be performed and the economic cost associated with the task need to be carefully tested in the new environment. Extending this model towards a multi-organization model and a production chain network, the ideas carried by this research can bring insight on the effect on of new institutional scenarios on a given industry or a given country.

REFERENCES

Aghion, P., & Tirole, J. (1997). Formal and real authority in organizations. *Journal of Political Economy, 105*, 1-29.

Ashforth, B. E., & Fried, Y. (1988). The mindlessness of organizational behaviors. *Human Relations, 41*, 305-329.

Aupperle, K. E., Acar, W., & Booth, D. E. (1986). An Empirical Critique of In Search of Excellence: How Excellent are the Excellent Companies? *Journal of Management, 12*, 499-512.

Axtell, R. (1999). *The emergence of firms in a population of agents: Local increasing returns, unstable Nash equilibria, and power law size distributions*. CSED Working Paper, Economic Studies, The Brookings Institute.

Backhouse, C. J., & Brookes, N .J. (Eds) (1996). *Concurrent Engineering: What's Working Where*. Design Council, Gower, Aldershot.

Baker, W. (1992). The network organization in theory and practice. In Nohria, N., Eccles, R.G. (eds.), *Networks and Organizations: Structure, Form and Action*. Boston, MA: Harvard Business School Press.

Bechtel, W., & Richardson, R. C. (1993). *Discovering complexity: decomposition and localization as strategies in scientific research*. Princeton, NJ: Princeton University Press.

Bolton, P., & Dewatripont, M. (1994). The firm as a communication network. *The Quarterly Journal of Economics, 109*(4), 809-839.

Bonabeau, E. (2002). Agent-based modeling: Methods and techniques for simulating human systems. *PNAS, 99*(3), 7280-7287.

Bonoma, T. V. (1985). Case research in marketing: opportunities, problems, and a process. *Journal of Marketing Research, 22*(May), 199-208.

Burns, T., & Stalker, G. M. (1961). *The Management of Innovation*. London: Tavistock Publications.

Burt, R. (2000). *The network structure of social capital*. In Sutton, R. and Staw, B. (Eds.), Research in Organizational Behavior (pp. 325-433), JAI Press, Greenwich, CT.

Burton, R., & Obel, B. (1995). The Validity of Computational Models in Organization Science: From Model Realism to Purpose of the Model. *Comp. and Math. Org. Theory 1*(1), 57-71.

Cameron, K. (1986). A study of organizational effectiveness and its predictors. *Management Science, 32*(1), 87-112.

Carley, K., Prietula, M., & Lin, J. (1999). *Design versus cognition: The interaction of agent cognition and organizational design on organizational performance*, Vol. Evolving societies: The computer simulation of social systems, Conte, R and Chattoe, E. (eds).

Carley, K., & Svoboda, D. (1996). Modeling organizational adaptation as a simulated annealing process. *Sociological Methods and Research,* 138-168.

Carroll, T., & Burton, R. M. (2000). Organizations and Complexity: Searching for the Edge of Chaos. *Computational & Mathematical Organization Theory, 6*(4), 319-337.

Chang, M. H., & Harrington, J. (Ed.) (2006). *Agent-based models of organizations*. In *Handbook of Computational Economics, 2: Agent-Based Computational Economics*, Tesfatsion, L. & Judd, K. (Eds.), Publisher North-Holland, Handbooks in Economics Series.

Clayman, M. (1987). In search of excellence: The investor's viewpoint. *Financial Analysts Journal*, May/June.

Cummings, J. N. (2004). Work Groups, Structural Diversity, and Knowledge Sharing in a Global Organization. *Management Science, 50*(3), 352-364.

Delmastro, M. (2002). The Determinants of the Management Hierarchy: Evidence from Italian Plants. *International Journal of Industrial Organization, 20,* 119-137.

Devinney, T. M., Richard, P. J., Yip, G. S., & Johnson, G. (2005). *Measuring Organizational Performance in Management Research: A Synthesis of Measurement Challenges*. Australian Graduate School of Management, September.

Dignum, V. (2004) *A model for organizational interaction: based on agents, founded in logic*. PhD thesis, Utrecht University.

Dodds, P. S., Watts, D. J., & Sabel, C. F. (2003). *Information exchange and the robustness of organizational networks*, Working Paper, ISERP, Columbia University.

Dupouet O., & Yildizoglu, M. (2003). *Organizational Performance in Hierarchies and Communities of Practice*, WEHIA, Kiel, Germany, 28-30 May.

Egidi, M. (1995). *Routines, hierarchies of problems, procedural behaviour: Some evidence fom experiments*, Technical Report 9503, Computable and Experimental Economics Laboratory.

Egidi, M., & Marengo, L. (2002). *Cognition, institution, near decomposability: rethinking Herbert Simon's contribution*. Technical report, University of Trento, Computable and Experimental Economics Lab Working Paper.

Feldman, M. S., & Pentland, B. T. (2003). Reconceptualizing organizational routines as a source of flexibility and change. *Administrative Science Quarterly, 48*, 94-118.

Ferber, J., Gutknecht, O., & Michel, F. (2004). From agents to organizations: an organizational view of multi-agent systems. In *AOSE IV: 4th Intern. Workshop*. LNCS Vol. 2935, 443-459. Berlin: Springer.

Galam, S. (2005). Stability of leadership in bottom-up hierarchical organizations. *Journal of Social Complexity, 2*(2), 62-75.

Garicano, L. (2000). Hierarchies and the organization of knowledge in production. *Journal of Political Economy, 108*(5), 874-904.

Goodman, P. S., & Pennings, M. (1977). *New Perspectives on Organizational Effectiveness*. San Francisco, CA: Jossey-Bass.

Hart, O., & Moore, J. (1999). *On the Design of Hierarchies: Coordination versus Specialization*. NBER Working Paper n°. 7388, Cambridge, MA.

Heckscher, C. (2007). *The Collaborative Enterprise: Managing Speed and Complexity in Knowledge-Based Businesses,* Yale University Press.

Heckscher, C., & Adler, P. A. (2005). *The Corporation as a Collaborative Community*. Yale University Press.

Hübner, J., Sichman, J., & Boissier, O. (2002). A model for the structural, functional, and deontic specification of organizations in multiagent systems. In *Advances in Artificial Intelligence: 16th Brazilian Symposium on AI*, SBIA'02, LNAI Vol. 2507, 118-128. Berlin: Springer.

Ibarra, H. (1993). Network centrality, power, and innovation involvement: Determinants of technical and administrative roles. *Acad. Management J., 36*(3) pp. 471-501.

Jacobides, M. G. (2005). *The Inherent Limits of Organizational Structure and the Unfulfilled Role of Hierarchy: Lessons from a Near-War*, July, SSRN.

Johanson, J.-E. (1999). Formal structure and intra-organisational networks. An analysis in a combined social and health organisation in Finland. *Scandinavian Journal of Management. 16*, 249-267.

Kelly, J., & Stark, D. (2002). Crisis, recovery, innovation: Learning from 9/11. *Environ. Plann. A, 34*(9), 1523-1533.

Krackhardt, D., & Hanson, J. R. (1993). Informal networks: the company behind the chart. *Harvard Business Review, 71*(4), 104-110.

Krackhardt, D., & Stern, R. N. (1988). Informal networks and organizational crises: An experimental simulation. *Social Psychology Quarterly, 51*(2), 123-140.

Lamieri, M., & Mangalagiu, D. (2006). *Efficiency and evolution of hierarchical organizations.* In *Physik sozio-okonomischer Systeme (AKSOE) Proceedings*, Dresden, 27-31 March 2006.

Langlois, R. (2000). *Modularity in technology and organization*, Technical report, paper presented at the conference on Austrian Economics and the Theory of the Firm, August 16-17, Copenhagen Business School.

Lawrence, P. R., & Lorsch, J. W. (1967). *Organization and Environment.* Boston: Harvard Business School Press

Lewin, A. Y., Weigelt, C. B., & Emery, J. D. (2004). Adaptation and Selection in Strategy and Change: Perspectives on Strategic Change in Organizations. In Poole, M. S. & Van de Ven, A. H. (eds.) *Handbook of Organizational Change and Innovation.* Oxford: Oxford University Press.

Levitt, R. E. (2004). Computational Modeling of Organizations Comes of Age. *Journal of Compuational and Mathematical Organization Theory 10*(2), 127-145.

Lin, Z., Zhao, X., Ismail, K., & Carley, K. M. (2006). Organizational design and restructuring in response to crises: Lessons from computational modeling and real-world cases. *Organization Science, 15*, 598-618.

Lomi, A., & Larsen, E. R. (2001). *Dynamics of Organizations: Computational Modeling and Organization Theories.* Menlo Park, CA: American Association of Artificial Intelligence.

March, J. (1991). Exploration and exploitation in organizational learning. *Organization Science, 2*, 71-87.

March, J., & Simon, H. (1958). *Organizations.* New York: Wiley.

March, J. G., & Sutton, R. I. (1997). Organizational performance as a dependent variable. *Organization Science, 8*(6), 698-706.

McCullogh, W. (1945). A heterarchy of values determined by the topology of nervous nets. *Bulletin of Mathematical Biophysics 7*, 89-93.

McKelvey, B. (2004). *A "simple rule" approach to CEO leadership in the 21st century in Complexity theory and the management of networks.* P. Andriani & G. Passiante (eds.), Imperial College Press.

Morieux, Y., Blaxill, M., & Boutenko, V. (2005). Generative Interactions: The New Source of Competitive Advantage. In *Restructuring Strategy: New Networks and Industry Challenges*, Cool, K.-O., Henderson, J.-E., & Abate, R. (eds.), Blackwell, Malden, MA.

Morton, S. C., Brookes, N. J., Smart, P K., Backhouse, C. J. & Burns, N. D. (2004). Managing the informal organisation: conceptual model. *International Journal of Productivity and Performance Management, 53*(3), 214-232.

Nelson, R. R., & Winter, S. (1982). *An evolutionary Theory of Economic Change*, Cambridge, MA: Harvard Univ. Press.

Nissen, M. E., Orr, R. J., & Levitt, R. E. (2006). *Streams of Shared Knowledge: Computational Expansion of Organization Theory*. Working Paper, Center for Edge Power, Naval Postgraduate School.

Nohria, N. (1992). Introduction: Is a network perspective a useful way to studying organisations. In Nohria and Eccles (Eds.), *Networks and Organisations: Structure Form and Action*. Boston MA: Harvard Business Scholl Press.

North, D., & Wallis, J. (1994). Integrating institutional change and technical change in economic history: a transaction cost approach. *Journal of Institutional and Theoretical Economics*, pp. 609-624.

Reese, J. S., & Cool, W. R. (1978). Measuring Investment Center Performance. *Harvard Business Review. May-June, 56*, 28-46.

Sah, R. K., & Stiglitz, J. E. (1986). The architecture of economic systems: hierarchies and polyarchies. *Amer. Econ. Rev., 76*(4), 716-727.

Sierhuis, M., Clancey, W. J., & Van Hoof, R. (2007). Brahms: A multi-agent modelling environment for simulating work processes and practices. *International Journal of Simulation and Process Modelling, 3*(3), 134-152.

Siggelkow, N., & Levinthal, D. A. (2003). Temporarily Divide to Conquer: Centralized, Decentralized, and Reintegrated Organizational Approaches to Exploration and Adaptation. *Organisation Science, 14*, 650-669.

Simon, H. A. (1955, February). *A behavioral model of rational choice. The Quarterly Journal of Economics, 69*(1).

Simon, H. A. (1962). The architecture of complexity. *Proceedings of the American Philosophical Society 106*(6), 467-482.

Simon, H. A. (1991). Organizations and markets. *Journal of Economic Perspectives, 5*(2), 25-44.

Stacey, R. D. (1995). The Science of Complexity: An Alternative Perspective for Strategic Change Processes. *Strategic Management Journal, 16*, 477-495.

Terna, P. (2006). *An agent based model of interacting and coevolving workers and firms*. Technical Report, Agent Based models: From analytical models to real life phenomenology, ISI, Turin, Italy.

Thompson, J. D. (1967). *Organizations in Action*. New York: McGraw Hill.

Uzzi, B. (1997). Social structure and competition in interfirm networks: The paradox of embeddedness. *Administrative Science Quarterly, 42*, 35-67.

Van Zandt, T. (1998). *Organizations with an endogenous number of information processing agents*. In *Organizations with Incomplete Information, chapter 7*. New York: Cambridge University Press.

Visser, B. (2000). Organizational Communication Structure and Performance. *Journal of Economic Behavior & Organization, 42*, 231-252.

Volberda, H. W., & Lewin, A. Y. (2003, December). Co-evolutionary Dynamics Within and Between Firms: From Evolution to Co-evolution. *Journal of Management Studies, 40*, 2111-2136.

Venkatraman, N., & Ramanujam, V. (1986). Measurement of business performance in strategy research: A comparison of approaches. *Academy of Management Review 11*(4), 801-814.

Williamson, O. (1975). *Markets and Hierarchies: Analysis and antitrust implications*. The Free Press.

Williamson, O. (1985). *The Economic Institutions of Capitalism*. New York: Free Press.

Zander, U., & Kogut, B. (1995). *Knowledge and the speed of the transfer and imitation of organizational capabilities: An empirical test. Organisation Science, 6*(1), 76-92.

ADDITIONAL READING

Aldrich, H. (1999). *Organizations Evolving*. Sage Publications, London.

Axtell, R., Axelrod, R., Epstein, J. M., & Cohen, M. D. (1996). Aligning simulation models: A case study and results. *Computational and Mathematical Organization Theory, 1*(2), 123-141.

Barr, J., & Saraceno, F. (2002). A computational theory of the firm. *Journal of Economic Behavior and Organization, 49*, 345-361.

Baum, J. A. C. (eds.) (2002). The Blackwell Companion to Organizations. Oxford: Blackwell Publishers.

Baum, J. A. C., & Singh, J. V. (eds.) (1994). *Evolutionary Dynamics of Organizations*. New York: Oxford University Press.

Bouchard, V. (2005). Models of emergence in the business firm. *21ˢᵗ EGOS Colloquium*, June 30 - July 3, Berlin.

Chakravarthy, B. S. (1986). Measuring strategic performance. *Strategic Management Journal, 7*, 437-458.

Dessein, W. (2002). Authority and communication in organizations. *Review of Economic Studies, 69*, 811-838.

Dow, G. K. (1990). The organization as an adaptive network. *Journal of Economic Behavior and Organization, 14, 159*-185.

Egidi, M. (2003). Decomposition patterns in problem solving. *Experimental 0309003*, EconWPA.

Egidi, M., & Marengo, L. (1993). Division of Labour and Social Coordination Modes : A simple simulation model. In N. Gilbert (Editor) *Simulating Societies*, UCL Press.

Epstein, J. M. (2003). *Growing adaptive organizations: an agent-based computational approach*. The Santa Fe Institute, Working Paper 03-05-029.

Ethiraj, S. K., & Levinthal, D. (2002). *Search for architecture in complex worlds: an evolutionary perspective on modularity and the emergence of dominant designs*. Wharton School, University of Pennsylvania.

Gino, F. (2002). *Complexity measures in decomposable structures*. Technical report, EURAM (European Academy of Management) Conference on Innovative Research in Management, May 9-11, Stockholm, Sweden.

Holmstrom, B .R., & Tirole, J. (1989). *The theory of the firm*. In Schmalensee, R., Willig, R. D. (eds.), *Handbook of Industrial Organization, vol. I.* Elsevier, Amsterdam.

Levinthal, D. (1997). Adaptation on rugged landscapes. *Management Science, 43*, 934-950.

Levinthal, D., & March, J. G. (1981). A model of adaptive organizational search. *Journal of Economic Behavior and Organization, 2*, 307-333.

Maskin, E., Qian, Y., & Xu, C. (2000). Incentives, information, and organizational form. *Review of Economic Studies, 67,* 359-378.

Milgrom, P., & Roberts, J. (1992). *Economics, Organization and Management*. Englewood Cliffs, NJ: Prentice Hall.

Miller, J. H. (2001). *Evolving information processing organizations*. In Lomi, A., Larsen, E.R. (eds.), *Dynamics of Organizations: Computational Modeling and Organization Theories*. Menlo Park, CA: AAAI Press/The MIT Press.

Nelson, R. R. (1994). The co-evolution of technology, industrial structure and supporting institutions. *Industrial and Corporate Change, 3.*

Peters, T. J. & Waterman, R. (1982). *In Search of Excellence*. New York: Harper and Row

Prietula, M. J., Carley, K. M., & Gasser, L. (1998). *Simulating organizations: Computational models of institutions and groups*. Cambridge, MA: The MIT Press.

Radner, R. (1993). The organization of decentralized information processing. *Econometrica 61*, 1109-1146.

Reihlen, M. (1996). *The logic of heterarchies making organizations competitive for knowledge based.* Technical report, Universitat Koln Seminar fur Allgemeine Betriebswirtschaftslehre, Betriebswirtschaftliche Planung und Logistik.

Rivkin, J. (2000). *Imitation of complex strategies. Management Science, 46*, 824-844.

Rivkin, J., & Siggelkow, N. (2003). *Balancing search and stability: interdependencies among elements of organizational design. Management Science, 49*, 290-311.

Rojas, E. M., & Mukherjee, A. (2003). Modeling the Construction Management Process to Support Situational Simulations. *Journal of Computing in Civil Engineering, 17*(4), 273-280.

Winter, S. G. (1986). *The research program of the behavioral theory of the firm: Orthodox critique and evolutionary perspective.* In Gilad, B. & Kaish, S. (eds.), *Handbook of Behavioral Economics, Volume A: Behavioral Microeconomics*, Greenwich, CT: JAI Press.

KEY TERMS

Allocative Interactions: Are used to coordinate events, functions, businesses, etc. such that these fit together and fit with a pre-existing scheme while minimizing the time, energy, etc. consumed to ensure the fit (Morieux et al, 2005).

Bounded Rationality: A term for the phenomenon that cognitive blinders prevent people from seeing, seeking, using, or sharing relevant, accessible, and perceivable information during decision-making. The bounded rationality phenomenon challenges traditional rationalist perspectives and suggests that the rationality of actual human and company behavior is always partial, or 'bounded' by human limitations. This concept recognizes that decision making takes place within an environment of incomplete information and uncertainty. Herbert Simon pointed out that most people are only partly rational, and are in fact emotional and irrational in the remaining part of their actions. They experience limits in formulating and solving complex problems and in processing (receiving, storing, retrieving, transmitting) information (Companion to Organizations, J. Baum Eds., Oxford Blackwell, UK, 2002).

Generative Interactions: Interactions are generative to the extent that they allow for the emergence of new capabilities to handle complexity, notably the increased complexity of signals from the environment. They are used to gain additional knowledge and insight. The value of interactions is rising because their generative function has become the solution to increasingly challenging organizational problems that go far beyond coordination needs (Morieux et al, 2005).

Hierarchical Structure: A pyramid-shaped system that arranges the relations between the entities within an organization in a top-down way. Power, responsibility and authority are concentrated at the top of the pyramid and decisions flow from the top downwards. The pyramid can be more steep or more flat. A steep pyramid has many layers of management, a flat organization has relatively few (Companion to Organizations, J. Baum, 2002).

Near Decomposability: According to H. Simon basically all viable systems, be they physical, social, biological, artificial, share the property of having a near decomposable architecture: they are organized into hierarchical layers of parts, parts of parts, parts of parts of parts and so on, in such a way that interactions among elements belonging to the same parts are much more than interactions among elements belonging to different parts. By "intense" interaction is meant that the behavior of one component depends more closely on the behavior of other components belonging to the same part than on components belonging to other parts (i.e. the cross-derivatives are larger within a part). This kind of architecture can be found in business firms, where division of labor, divisionalization, hierarchical decomposition of tasks are all elements which define a near decomposable system: individuals within a hierarchical subunit have closer, more widespread, more intense and more frequent interactions than individuals belonging to different subunits. But a very similar architecture can also be found in most complex artifacts (which are made by assembling parts and components, which in turn can be assemblies of other parts and components, and so on), in software (with the use of subroutines, and even more so in object-oriented programming) (Egidi and Marengo, 2006).

Organizational Performance: Comprises the actual output or results of an organization as measured against its intended outputs (or goals and objectives). It is a broad construct which captures what organizations do, produce, and accomplish for the various constituencies with which they interact.

Specialists in many fields are concerned with organizational performance including strategic planners, operations, finance, legal, and organizational development (Companion to Organizations, J. Baum Eds., Oxford Blackwell, UK, 2002).

Routines: In the economics and business literatures, the notion of organizational routine has come to stand for regularity in economic activity. The concept of organizational routine is used to capture repetitive, stable activity leading to behavior patterns or recurrent interaction patterns. However the term is used also refering to some cognitive representation such as rules and cognitive. "We will regard a set of activities as routinized, [then,] to the degree that choice has been simplified by the development of a fixed response to defined stimuli. If search has been eliminated, but a choice remains in the form of clearly defined and systematic computing routine, we will say that the activities are routinized" (March and Simon 1993, page 142).

Satisficing: In economics, satisficing is a behavior which attempts to achieve at least some minimum level of a particular variable, but which does not necessarily maximize its value. The most common application of the concept in economics is in the behavioural theory of the firm, which, unlike traditional accounts, postulates that producers treat profit not as a goal to be maximized, but as a constraint. Under these theories, a critical level of profit must be achieved by firms; thereafter, priority is attached to the attainment of other goals. The word satisfice was coined by Herbert Simon as a portmanteau of "satisfy" and "suffice". Simon pointed out that human beings lack the cognitive resources to maximize: we usually do not know the relevant probabilities of outcomes, we can rarely evaluate all outcomes with sufficient precision, and our memories are weak and unreliable.

Span of Control: Refers to how relationships are structured between leaders and subordinates in organizations. It represents the number of people/subordinates that can be effectively managed by one manager. The optimal Span of Control is dependent upon the nature of the work of the subordinates, the skills, capabilities, experience, seniority, qualifications of the managers and subordinates, the use of information technology, the detail at which work rules and procedures have been formalized and are known by the subordinates, the applied management style and the desired depth of the hierarchy in an organization (Companion to Organizations, J. Baum Eds., Oxford Blackwell, UK, 2002).

Section VII
Applications

Chapter XXI
Personal Assistants for Human Organizations

Steven Okamoto
Carnegie Mellon University, USA

Katia Sycara
Carnegie Mellon University, USA

Paul Scerri
Carnegie Mellon University, USA

ABSTRACT

Intelligent software personal assistants are an active research area with the potential to revolutionize the way that human organizations operate, but there has been little research quantifying how they will impact organizational performance or how organizations will or should adapt in response. In this chapter we develop a computational model of the organization to evaluate the impact different proposed assistant abilities have on the behavior and performance of the organization. By varying the organizational structures under consideration, we can identify which abilities are most beneficial, as well as explore how organizations may adapt to best leverage the new technology. The results indicate that the most beneficial abilities for hierarchical organizations are those that improve load balancing through task allocation and failure recovery, while for horizontal organizations the most beneficial abilities are those that improve communication. The results also suggest that software personal assistant technology will facilitate more horizontal organizations.

INTRODUCTION

Intelligent software personal assistants (SPAs) are one of the most exciting applications for organizational multi-agent systems. A software personal assistant (SPA) is an agent that acts to support a user in a human organization by automating individual tasks and facilitating coordination with other members of the organization. Recent and current research has looked at developing SPAs for a diverse range of domains, including emergency response and military teams, office environments, factory floors, and even outer space. The envisioned SPAs possess a wide range of abilities, such as scheduling joint activities (Dent et al, 1992; Garrido & Sycara, 1996; Modi et al, 2004), sharing key information (Wagner et al, 2004), monitoring and reminding individuals of key timepoints (Chalupsky et al, 2001), filtering incoming communication (Maes, 1994), assisting in negotiation decision support (Li et al., 2006), and even ordering lunch (Chalupsky et al, 2001).

Software personal assistants stand to benefit from multi-agent organization research in two ways. First, as large-scale, complex multi-agent systems, SPA deployments are natural candidates for organization-centric engineering approaches to manage control and coordination complexity. As SPA-enabled organizations become more commonplace, the need for an organization-centric approach will only become more apparent, because SPA interactions between different organizations will require that these systems operate flexibly, robustly, and securely as open systems. Secondly, no matter what engineering approach is chosen for an SPA system, the SPAs will be situated in human organizations with specific organizational constraints, and thus the SPAs must be able to represent and reason about those constraints in order to operate successfully and transparently. The representation and reasoning of organizational structures and norms is currently one of the hottest areas of agent organization research (Grossi et al., 2007; Vasconcelos et al., 2007).

While significant technical challenges remain in developing SPAs, many of these issues are the subject of recent and current research and will not be discussed extensively in this chapter. Instead, we will focus on the crucial issue of how human organizations will be affected by the use of this technology, which has gone largely unexamined. This represents a significant gap in the current research, as it is likely that SPAs will have a revolutionary effect on the way human organizations operate, just as previous information technology innovations such as personal computers, corporate databases, and e-mail revolutionized the way organizations operate. In addition, the issue of which of the many envisioned SPA abilities are most useful for improving the efficiency and effectiveness of an organization is only poorly understood. This is a possibly costly oversight, as history is replete with examples of technological innovations, including early SPA systems, that have unexpected and even undesirable impacts when coupled with existing organizational practices and behaviors.

Our goals for this chapter are three-fold: first, to develop a conceptual framework that can be used to quantifiably evaluate proposed SPA technologies; second, to quantify the impacts proposed SPA abilities will have on existing organizations, in order to provide input to SPA designers on which abilities are most promising to pursue; and third, to explore how organizations may best be redesigned to leverage the SPA technology, in order to provide input to SPA adopters on how to best apply the technology. The approach taken in this chapter lies at the crossroads of agent organization modeling and computational organization theory. We develop a computational model of the organization. This methodology of computational modeling is similar to that used for quantifying performance in organizational theory (Carley 1994; Prietula & Carley, 1998). We evaluate the impact different proposed SPA abilities have on the behavior and performance of the organization. Because SPAs frequently affect detailed work activities, and their broader influence on the organization is unclear, we must model the organization at a fine-grained level of detail, capturing, for example, communication paths, decision making, etc., in order to see their effects. To that end, we have created an abstract simulation environment that takes proposed organizational models and tasks to be performed by the organization and computes key properties of task execution, including how well and how quickly the organization performed the task and how robustly it handled individual failures. The simulation captures important aspects of the operation of the organization, such as non-determinism and cognitive limits of individual members of the organization, but abstracts away domain level details, making it feasible to evaluate many instances of organizations.

One of the major difficulties in evaluating SPA abilities is that they are still an area of ongoing research. Because one of our goals is to provide input to SPA designers before the SPA capabilities have been fully developed, it is not possible to directly model the specific mechanisms by which SPAs will operate. Instead, we abstract away the details of the SPA mechanisms and instead use the effects of those mechanisms on the behavior of individual humans to determine the impact on the organization. For example, instead of directly modeling the specific ways in which SPAs will increase the rate at which humans can make effective decisions, we instead model the SPAs' impact as increasing the decision making rate within the organization, with the understanding that any SPA mechanism that has the same effect will have similar effects on organizational performance. This allows us to evaluate the many proposed SPA abilities without having to solve the hard and open problems required to implement those abilities for different organizational contexts. By referencing ongoing projects and previously published literature, we have identified a set of key abilities that are being developed, including information sharing, task allocation, automated monitoring and supervision, communication management, joint activity coordination, decision support, and recovery from unexpected failures. Using our computational model of the organization, we evaluate the impacts of different SPA abilities individually and in combination.

When embracing a new technology, organizations will first deploy it in lieu of existing technologies or practices, then gradually adapt to better utilize the new technology. This can have a transformative effect on the way organizations are structured and operate. For this reason, it is not sufficient to merely study the impact SPAs will have on existing organizations, but also to see how organizations might change and adapt in the presence of SPAs to best leverage the technology. In order to investigate this, we compare the designs of organizations before and after SPA deployment to see which structures and SPA abilities are most beneficial. Our results indicate that the most beneficial SPA abilities for horizontal, decentralized organizations are those that facilitate improved communication, while for hierarchical, centralized organizations, the most beneficial SPA abilities are those that improve load balancing through task allocation and failure recovery.

BACKGROUND

Research on SPAs has generally focused on developing SPAs for a wide range of environments, including office settings (Chen & Sycara, 1998; Modi et al, 2005; Payne et al, 2002), disaster response domains (Schurr et al, 2005), and military operations (Lenox et al, 2000b; Wagner et al, 2004), rather than on studying their impact on human organizations. This research into developing SPAs can be roughly partitioned into three categories. The first category focuses on technical issues underlying specific abilities, using techniques such as Markov decision processes (Varakantham et al., 2005), constraint satisfaction and constraint optimization (Modi, 2004; Maheswaran et al., 2004), and decision trees (Mitchell, 1994). Performance evaluations in these approaches tend to focus solely on the performance of the SPA (measured by computation time, learning accuracy, etc.), and completely ignore the human user or the organization.

The second category considers the interaction between an SPA and its user. This research focuses on developing and evaluating different user interfaces for SPAs, taking into account factors such as (McCrickard & Chewar, 2003; Horvitz, 1999). This usually involves human experiments interacting in which a user interacts with a prototype SPA. While these studies consider the cognitive capabilities and limitations of a human user and how these can be affected by an SPA, they consider only the *individual* performance of a single user and its SPAs, instead of the organizational performance of an SPA-enabled organization. However, results from these studies are complementary to the approach taken in this chapter, as they quantify the effects SPAs have on individual performance, while we begin with the impacts SPAs have on individual performance and quantify the effect this has on the collective performance of the organization as a whole.

The third category includes systems of agents that have actually been built and tested in assisting humans (Chalupsky et al, 2001; Lenox et al, 2000a; Sycara & Lewis, 2004), and is a far smaller category than the other two. These studies also involve experiments with human subjects, but several subjects interact with the system at a time, assisted by their respective SPAs. This is closest in spirit to our objective, however, these experiments are generally very limited in size and scope, and frequently are not conducted on the true end-users of the technology. This is natural because of the impracticality of deploying a full SPA system in a large organization. In the largest and longest-running SPA experiment to date, an SPA system (the "Electric Elves") was built and deployed in an office environment and used for several months (Chalupsky et al., 2001). However, even this system was operated with fewer than 10 users. While experiments such as these are important for the eventual development and deployment of SPAs in the workplace, they are impractical for large scale tests and are inherently restricted to testing existing SPA technology.

Computational organization theory has focused specifically on the human and organizational performance factors that SPA-oriented research has largely ignored. This research area uses computational models of human organizations to answer questions of organizational behavior and performance (Carley & Prietula, 1994; Prietula et al., 1998). It is widely accepted as a practical way to conduct experiments on large scale human organizations, especially using "what-if" analysis to consider the effects hypothetical changes will have on organizational behavior (Carley, 1995). This approach has been used to evaluate the effects of different forms of information technology on specific organizations (Levitt et al. 1994; Majchrzak & Finley, 1995), but these approaches require a detailed model of how the information technology works, which is not practical in the case of yet undeveloped SPAs.

One aspect of SPA design that has been neglected is the explicit representation and reasoning about organizational concepts. For example, while the Electric Elves project was generally considered a success, the SPAs were observed to have several serious shortcomings, because they had not been designed with an organizational awareness (Tambe et al., 2006). Instead, machine learning methods were used to generalize rules to guide their operation, and in many cases the learned rules violated the norms of the human organization in which they were situated. The system designers included ad hoc rules in an attempt to repair this shortcoming, but were only partially successful.

Although the approach taken in this chapter is agnostic as to the specific engineering methodology used for SPAs, we recognize that an organization-centric approach to agent control could solve many of the issues that plagued the Electric Elves project by providing the SPAs with the ability to reason about the organizational norms in choosing its actions. Even if an agent-centric design process of the SPAs system as a whole was used, SPAs could still greatly benefit from the formal organizational languages (Grossi et al. 2007; Serrano & Saugar, 2007) and organizational frameworks (Dignum et al., 2004) in order to adhere to the norms of the human organizations in which they are situated. For a more detailed exposition on how SPAs may be made organizationally-aware, please see Chapter XIII "Autonomous Agents Adopting Organization Rules," by van der Vecht.

The approach presented in this chapter uses organizational models in a different way than they are conventionally used in multi-agent systems. The conventional usage (which is also reflected in most of the other chapters of this book) is to use organizational models to provide organization-centric control of a distributed agent system, while remaining agnostic about the evaluation methodology. In contrast, an organizational model is used in this chapter to simulate the operation of a human organization in order to evaluate the organizational performance, while remaining agnostic about the control methodology. It is important to note that these two approaches may be used complementarily; the approach presented in this chapter is certainly capable of evaluating organization-centric SPA systems, but it is also capable of evaluating agent-centric SPA systems, which is a key advantage, as most SPA systems to date have been designed from an agent-centric perspective.

Other recent research efforts have focused on evaluating the organizational performance of multi-agent systems (Grossi et al., 2006; Horling, 2006). An organizational design language expressing quantitative relationships that exist between organizational elements was provided in (Horling, 2006), along with a framework for quantifying various organizational performance characteristics. In (Grossi et al., 2006), aspects of organizational performance are determined by examining graph theoretic properties of the structure of the organizational model. This allows several general measures of performance to be made, but relies on an explicit organization-centric model of control and the performance measures are static with respect to the organizational structure. While these works present important advances in moving from agent-centric to organization-centric performance evaluation, they are both focused on pure agent organizations, instead of specifically addressing hybrid organizations such as an SPA-enabled organization. Preliminary work on understanding the impact of software personal assistants was described in (Okamoto et al., 2006).

The adoption of information technology by organizations generally follows three phases (Carley, 1996). In the first phase, the new technology is used as a simple substitute for existing technologies and practices. In the second phase, the organization members adjust their behavior as they become more familiar with the properties of the new technology. Finally, in the third phase, the organizational structure is changed to better fit the new behavior. Three notable and well-studied technologies that have adhered to this general progression are electronic marketplaces (Malone, 1987), e-mail (Yates & Orlikowski, 1992; Garton & Wellman, 1993), and corporate databases (Carley, 2002).

Electronic marketplaces initially replaced existing intra-organization coordination procedures between different divisions, thereby reducing costs (Malone, 1987). As these savings were realized, usage of electronic marketplaces increased. Finally, the coordination costs were sufficiently reduced that many organizations chose to outsource the work previously done in-house, and use electronic marketplaces for inter-organizational coordination.

Similarly, e-mail was initially used as a replacement for telephone calls and written memoranda (Yates & Orlikowski, 1992). This combined the asynchronous and permanent nature of memoranda with the speed and interactivity of telephone calls. This led changes in organizational behavior, including status equalization and often an increased volume of communication through e-mail as organizations moved through the second phase of adoption (Garton & Wellman, 1993). Finally, in the third phase organizations were restructured to take advantage of the new communication potential of e-mail, with less centralized, less hierarchical structures (Garton & Wellman, 1993; Ahuja & Carley, 1998).

It is generally assumed that information technology reduces coordination costs and improves organizational performance, an assumption that is supported by the studies of electronic marketplaces and e-mail. However, it has also long been observed that information technology may have a negative effect on organizational performance (Ackoff, 1967). A study of corporate databases provides a more recent cautionary warning (Carley, 2002). In this case a database was deployed to increase the retention and accessibility of organizational knowledge that had previously been retained only by a handful of experts in the organization. The initial phase of adoption led to a shift in reliance from these experts to the database system. However, in the second phase, people stopped updating the database, assuming that someone else would, leading to an eventual loss of organizational knowledge. This highlights the point that it is essential to account for the interactions between a proposed technology and the organization's dynamics in order to avoid deleterious effects.

APPROACH

In this section we elaborate on the general approach to evaluating the impact of SPAs on human organizations. We will also provide a concrete example for which we will later provide results. Because direct experimentation with real SPA-enabled organizations is impractical, we construct computational models of human organizations to evaluate organizational performance, a technique which has become widespread in the field of organization theory (Carley & Prietula, 1994; Prietula et al., 1998). These models consist of three complementary components: the task model, which represents the problem being met by the organization; the model of individual actors, which represents how human actors operate individually; and the model of the organization, which represents how human actors interact to collectively dictate the behavior of the organization. As with any abstraction, there is a fundamental trade-off between the fidelity of the model and the practicality of evaluation. The aspects to abstract are specific to the kind of organization being represented as well as which features are of interest to the evaluator. For example, in an office environment between peers, social features such as fairness and reciprocity are important determinants of actor behavior, while their effect may be negligible in military settings where soldiers are drilled to simply execute their orders.

Once we have a computational model of the organization without SPAs, we consider the effects of SPAs on the organization. We do not explicitly represent SPAs in the organization, but instead model their effects as changes in organizational constraints and parameters. For example, the proposed ability of SPAs automating communication between actors (Chalupsky et al., 2001) may be modeled as a reduction in the communication delay between actors from the baseline value without SPAs. This approach avoids directly implementing the abilities of SPAs (a substantial area of research in its own right) as well as providing an opportunity for published experimental results from that field to we included in the organizational model.

As an example of this general methodology, we consider organizations that are configured to achieve a particular large scale task, where there is an existing, known plan for achieving that task. Examples of such scenarios include a disaster response effort or a military operation. These kinds of domains are extremely challenging to the people operating in them, because the environment is highly dynamic with frequently tight windows of execution for tasks, and people have limited access to incomplete information, often with slow and unreliable communication. For example, in a military operation, soldiers on the ground must often rely on synchronous radio transmissions through human communications operators, who relay information to commanders and other soldiers participating in the operation, which can result in information being delayed or distorted. The same characteristics that make these domains so challenging to current organizations also present a number of promising opportunities for SPAs to improve organizational performance by addressing these limitations.

In these domains, actors typically execute hierarchical plans. In our work, we represent an organization of human actors that execute a hierarchical plan similar to hierarchical task networks such as TAEMS (Lesser et al., 2004). Note that a "hierarchical plan" denotes different levels of plan abstraction and does not necessarily imply that the plan will be executed by a hierarchical organization. Indeed, in our experimental evaluations, we consider horizontal and distributed organizational structures executing these plans, in addition to traditional hierarchical organizational structures.

Under these plans, the actors perform a variety of heterogeneous tasks and communicate in order to make decisions. The basic structure is that the organization must make a number of decisions, represented as decision tasks. Each decision requires a specific set of information as input, and this information is acquired by successfully executing sensing tasks. This abstraction describes a wide range of real-life organizations, from military units that detect and eliminate enemy threats, to businesses that identify customer needs and reallocate investments. In this chapter we focus specifically on abstractions of domains such as military operations or disaster response scenarios.

There are a number of assumptions that govern the behavior of actors in this model. Each task is assigned statically to a single actor, who is responsible for performing that task within a fixed window of time, which is known to the actors. While actors may be assigned many tasks with overlapping execution windows, the actors are limited in the number of tasks that they can perform simultaneously, reflecting well-known cognitive limitations of humans. Each task has a fixed duration, and that once begun, the task must be performed for its entire duration without interruption. Attempts to perform a task may fail, with the failure occurring randomly during the duration of execution, and a failed task cannot be attempted again.

In order to reduce the effect of task failures on plan success, there are redundant, pre-determined contingent tasks (or contingencies) built into the plan. Non-contingent tasks (both sensing and decision tasks) are termed primary tasks, with a specific, known contingency that is to be executed if the primary task fails. Contingencies can also provide redundancy for other contingencies, so that for each primary task, there may be a sequence of contingencies to be invoked in order, in case of successive task failures. Such a sequence of tasks (beginning with the primary task) is termed a task chain, and for each task chain the organization has as a subgoal that one task be successfully completed in that chain, with preference given for tasks earlier in the chain. For each task chain, the responsibility for ensuring that the subgoal is achieved is invested in a manager role, which is statically assigned to one of actors. Managers have the sole power of authorizing the execution of contingencies.

Actors gain information through the successful completion of sensing tasks. This information must then be communicated to the decision makers that use the information. An actor assigned a decision task can only perform that task if it has all the required information. Actors can only transmit information along predetermined, bidirectional communication links, and are bounded in the number of communication links they can maintain. Communication is assumed to be point-to-point, multi-hop with each hop taking a fixed amount of time.

We do not explicitly represent SPAs in the organization, but instead model their effects as changes in organizational constraints and parameters. For example, the presence of SPAs may be modeled by decreasing the communication delay from a baseline for an organization without SPAs. In the rest of this section we formally model an organization and the human actors that comprise it.

Formally, a human organization O is a tuple

$$O = \langle A, T, I, Prov, Req, Window, Dur, Cap, Fail, G, delay_c, M, d \rangle$$

with the following components:

- $A = \{ a_1, a_2, ..., a_m \}$: the set of *human actors* in the organization.
- T: the set of tasks to be performed by the actors. Tasks are partitioned in two orthogonal ways:
  - $T = T_P \dot{\cup} T_C$
    - $T_P = \{t1, t2, ..., t_n\}$: the set of *primary tasks* to be performed.
    - $T_C = \bigcup_{t_i \in T_P} C_i$: the set of *contingencies* to be performed in case of task failures.
  - $T = T_D \dot{\cup} T_S$
    - T_D: the set of *decision-making tasks* that require information to be performed.
    - T_S: the set of *sensing tasks* that provide information when successfully performed.
- $I = \{ I_1, I_2, ..., I_l \}$: the set of information produced by sensing tasks and used by decision tasks.
- $Prov: T \rightarrow P(I)$: the information provision function mapping (sensing) tasks to the set of information provided by successfully completing the (sensing) task.
- $Req: T \rightarrow P(I)$: the information requirement function mapping (decision-making) tasks to the set of information required to perform the decision-making task.
- $Window: T \rightarrow [0,\infty) \times [0,\infty)$: the execution window function mapping tasks to the earliest and latest times that the task can be performed.
- $Dur: T \rightarrow [0,\infty)$: the duration function indicating how long each task takes to perform.
- $Load: T \rightarrow [0,\infty)$: the load function indicating how much cognitive load each task requires.
- $Cap: A \times T \rightarrow [0, 1]$: the capability function indicating how well actors perform each task.
- $Fail: A \times T \rightarrow [0, 1]$: the failure function indicating the probability actors will fail at performing each task when attempted.
- G: the undirected graph with actors as vertices and edges indicating possible communication paths between actors.
- $delay_c$: the communication delay.
- M: the assignment matrix of primary tasks and contingencies to actors. Each primary task or contingency must be assigned to exactly one actor.
- d: the deadline by which time all decisions must be made in order for the organization to succeed.

For each primary task $t_i \in T_P$, there exists 0 or more contingencies, $C_i = \{c_i^1, c_i^2, ..., c_i^{ki}\}$. The contingencies are pre-determined backup tasks that are invoked in case of task failure, and are ordered by preference. Hence contingency c_i^1 must be performed if primary task t_i fails, and contingency c_i^2 must be performed if contingency c_i^1 fails, and so on. The set of all contingency tasks is written as T_C.

Several of the model components represent the abilities and limitations of the actors, although there is no explicit model cognitive model of the human actors. The abilities of the actors are represented by the capability function, *Cap*, which incorporates and abstracts the many features of task execution to provide a numerical score for how well each actor performs each task. This function incorporates both the cognitive and physical abilities of the actors used in performing tasks. The *Dur*, *Load*, and *Fail* functions represent some of the limitations of the actors.

The results obtained using this model will be dependent on the fidelity of the model to the actual organization being represented. One point of concern is the parameters (such as *Cap*, *Dur*, etc.) that represent individual actor abilities. There are several ways to determine values for these parameters. Case studies of similar organizations, if available, can be used to supply the values directly. Models of human cognition, such as ACT-R (Anderson, 1993; Byrne, 1999) or SOAR (Laird et al., 1987), can also be used to derive the parameter values for individual actors. Because the organizational model does not require a specific cognitive model of the actors, any available or applicable such model may be used to determine the parameter values. When the specific details of the organization are not known (or when a general class of organizations are under consideration), a range of parameter values should be considered.

Organizational Structure

The undirected graph G in the specification of the organization describes the structural communication links that exist between members of the organization. The vertices of G are the actors in A. An edge between $a_i \in A$ and $a_j \in A$ indicates that a_i can communicate with a_j. There are two cases where an actor must communicate with another actor. The first case is when an actor supplies information to another actor, i.e., a path must exist between two actors a_i and a_j if $M(a_i, t) = 1$ and $M(a_j, t') = 1$ and $Prov(t) \cap Req(t') \neq \emptyset$. The second case occurs when an actor fails at its task, and the fact of this failure must be communicated to the manager of the task chain, who then authorizes execution of the contingency.

Because many contingencies may not actually be performed, some of the edges in G (namely those which only transmit information for those tasks) may not actually be used. Moreover, even those edges that are on paths required for primary tasks may not be used if the actor performing the task fails, since a contingency would then be invoked. Hence we distinguish between two graphs, G and G'. We refer to G as the potential structure graph, since it must contain all edges that could be required for any possible combination of tasks and contingencies. G', on the other hand, is called the instantiated structure, and only contains those edges that are actually being used given the current set of tasks and contingencies.

Human cognitive limitations restrict the number of contacts a person can effectively maintain. We model this as constraints on the potential structure graph G. In particular, we bound the degrees of the actors in G such that for all $a \in A$, $degree(a) \leq max_{deg}$. Cognitive limitations also impose constraints on the structure of G', given by max'_{deg}. As tasks are executed and contingencies invoked, the links in G' change. If the degree of an actor in G' exceeds its maximum bound, that actor is said to experience communication overload, and is unable to use the communication links that exceed the bounds. Here we assume that the bound is $max'_{deg} = 1$, which models the standard synchronous communication prevalent in human organizations today: actors can only communicate with a single other actor at a time, and both parties must be engaged in conversation in order for communication to occur.

For this domain we chose to model the organizational structure as a graph of the possible communication links in the organization. While this modeling choice was motivated by the specific domain of interest, the approach of using a graph to represent possible actions between organization members is quite general and powerful. For more information, please see Chapter VIII "Structural Aspects of Organizations" by Grossi and F. Dignum.

Execution

The actors attempt to perform primary sensing tasks assigned to them in M. For any primary task failure, contingencies are invoked as described earlier. If an actor succeeds at a sensing task t_s (whether it is a primary task or contingency), the actor gains information $Prov(t_s) \subseteq I$. This information has an associated quality which we denote by $Qual: I \rightarrow [0, 1]$. For all $I_j \in Prov(t_s)$, we let $Qual(I_j) = Cap(a, t_s)$.

The actor then transmits the newly learned information to all neighbors as defined in G. These neighbors store the information in their personal knowledge bases and also in turn propagate the information to their neighbors.

When an actor assigned a decision-making task gains all the information required to make the decision, either from other actors or by performing the sensing tasks itself, it attempts to perform the decision (which can fail). If the actor succeeds, the decision is made with a quality that depends on both the capability of the decision-making actor and the quality of the provided information, and the organization then gets a reward for making the decision. This reward is denoted $Reward: T_P \cap T_D \rightarrow |$ and is defined in the following way. For a decision-making task t_d successfully performed by actor a, reward is given by:

$$Reward(t_d) = Cap(a, t_d) \left(\sum_{I_j \in Req(t_d)} Qual(I_j) \right)$$

where $Qual(I_j)$ is as defined above. The total reward earned by the organization will be one measure of organizational performance, as described next.

Organizational Performance

The performance of an organization is complex and multi-attributed. There are many possible measures of performance, such as privacy (Maheswaran et al., 2005), resource usage (Lenox et al., 2000b), and volume of communication (Chalupsky et al., 2001). In this work, we focus on the following three specific measures.

- *Success rate.* This is a measure of how well the organization handles individual failure and is calculated as the fraction of the time the organization makes all the decisions represented in T_D before the deadline d.
- *Reward.* This is a measure of how well the organization makes decisions when it succeeds, and is calculated as

$$\sum_{t_d \in T_D \cap T_P} Reward(t_d)$$

- *Speed.* This is a measure of the organization's efficiency and is calculated as the difference between the deadline time *d* and the time at which the last task finishes execution.

The overall objective function used for performance is a weighted sum of these three measures.

MODELING PERSONAL ASSISTANTS

The SPAs are not directly represented in our model. Instead we model their effects on the constraints of the human actors in the model. We do not model aspects such as social comparison or reciprocity as motivating factors for the SPAs, because these are concepts from agent societies between peers, while the SPAs in our organizations exist solely to assist their human users and are subservient to them. The abilities of SPAs are generally being designed to overcome perceived cognitive limitations of humans that are thought to limit the performance of organizations. In this section, we describe three such limitations and the models of SPA abilities -- communication management, contingency management, and decision support -- that might overcome these limitations.

Many other SPA abilities (and corresponding cognitive limits) might have been modeled. We focused on this initial set because there was active research in the field on developing these abilities. SPA abilities related to communication management include processing incoming e-mail (Maes, 1994) and asynchronously conveying information previously transmitted by walkie-talkie (Wagner et al., 2004). Transferring responsibility of tasks (Wagner et al., 2004; Schurr et al., 2005) is an SPA ability related to contingency management. Integrating dynamic information and providing users with suggestions (Mitchell et al., 1994; Lenox et al., 2000b) has been studied as a way of SPAs providing decision support to users. This research has focused on developing the SPA abilities and not on the effect of the SPA abilities on organization performance. Furthermore, the question of how the organization can change to better utilize the abilities has not been addressed.

Our choice of selected SPA abilities was also restricted to those most suited to the special purpose organizations that are the focus of this chapter. Future work will expand the scope of SPA abilities, including those where there is not yet active research.

Communication Management

Utilizing SPAs to improve communication is one of the most obvious and heavily researched SPA abilities (Maes, 1994; Malone, 1987). The rate at which decision-makers in an organization can effectively make decisions is limited by two key factors: (i) their ability to get the appropriate information to make required decisions and (ii) their innate processing speed for making those decisions. While wired and wireless networks can convey information at amazingly fast rates compared to human communication speeds, in most cases people are still required to input information and subsequently process received information. The input and output times are subject to human limitations and are fast becoming (if they are not already) a major bottleneck in intra-organization communication, one which could be alleviated by SPAs.

The cognitive load of managing incoming information and directing outgoing information is also a significant constraint that may be relaxed by SPA technology. Specifically, a decision-maker may be able to handle input from a greater number of members of an organization and hence, either get more direct access to required information or make more decisions. For example, the CEO of an organization needs information from many parts of the organization to make key strategic decisions. However, it is cognitively and organizationally infeasible for a person to directly receive input from a large number of people (Carley, 1995). Hence, in the case of the CEO, that information must pass through a small number of department heads, both delaying the information and potentially distorting it. Conversely, suppliers of information are limited in how many others they can provide information to, requiring organizational structures that channel information and introduce delays and distortion. SPA technology could allow information suppliers to more directly communicate with the decision-makers requiring their information.

We modeled three distinct effects that SPA-enhanced communication could have. Firstly, SPAs could directly reduce communication delay by relieving input and output transmission bottlenecks. This is modeled as a reduction in communication delay. One effect of this change in the organization is that it may reduce the frequency of communication overload in synchronous communication, because active links are present in G' for less time. The second effect SPAs could have is in providing asynchronous communication between actors, modeled as setting $max'_{deg} = max_{deg}$. This has a major effect in eliminating communication overload, even if actual communication delay does not change. The third effect that SPAs could have is in reducing the cognitive load of managing incoming information from others in the organization and directing outgoing information to others, so that actors can maintain a greater number of communication links. The effect of this directly impacts the possible organizational structures and is modeled by increasing the value of max_{deg}.

Task Contingency Management

In addition to reducing communication overload, an SPA may manage contingencies in order to prevent its actor from being cognitively overloaded by tasks. Instead of invoking contingencies only when a domain-level failure is suffered, the SPA may monitor the actor's current status and workload and automatically invoke contingencies for any tasks that would overload the actor. This monitoring can be done in a variety of ways, for example by tracking the user's position via GPS or other method (Chalupsky et al., 2001; Wagner, et al. 2004). We assume that actors schedule their pending tasks in order to avoid overload if at all possible, deferring tasks with the most time remaining. When a task can no longer be deferred (due to impending deadlines, for example), the actor invokes the contingency. While this gives maximum flexibility to the actor, it also reduces flexibility for the contingent actor, because it has less time to execute the contingency.

With SPA-managed task contingencies, an actor's SPA automatically invokes contingencies as soon as a potential overload is detected. This gives the contingent actor more flexibility, but may invoke contingencies that did not have to be invoked, which can lead to reduced redundancy in the plan. Thus SPAs also monitor whether their user can subsequently perform tasks for which contingencies were previously invoked; if this occurs, the SPAs transfer responsibility for the task back to the user.

Similar approaches have been developed or proposed for SPAs in other environments (Chalupsky, 2001; Decker & Sycara, 1997a; Maes, 1994). Intuitively, these SPA capabilities should make the organization more robust to individual failure. Managing contingencies or assigning roles has been a key area of research, but this is the first work that attempts to quantify the benefit of such a capability on an organization and understand how the organization may change to leverage this capability.

Decision Support

As introduced above, a key cognitive constraint on humans in an organization is the number of decisions that can be effectively made in a limited amount of time. SPAs could relax this constraint in a variety of ways, e.g., taking over routine tasks to provide more time for decisions (Dent, 1992; Garrido, 1996; Schurr 2005), or retrieving, collating, and presenting information in a way that speeds up the actual decision-making process (Decker, 1997b; Maes, 1994; Lenox et al., 2000b). Without reference to specifically how it is done, in the computational model of the organization, we consider two possible effects of SPA decision support. In the first possible effect, SPAs simply allow a person to effectively make more decisions in the same period of time by decreasing the duration of decision tasks. In the second possible effect, SPAs reduce the cognitive load of each decision task, allowing a person to make more decisions simultaneously, without affecting the duration of any single decision task.

EXPERIMENTAL SETUP

In the experiments presented here we were primarily interested in domains such as disaster response scenarios or military operations in which a large number of actors are deployed in a dynamic environment, uncertain environment. Many of the choices for organizational constraints reflect this interest. For example, in the chaos following a natural disaster, many tasks will have fairly high failure rates and small execution windows, as buildings continue to burn and collapse, etc. In addition, communication will be dependent on synchronous radio transmissions relayed between people with fairly long delays to obtain or transmit information. In such an environment, the people executing the tasks will generally not have the time or resources to find other recourses if the communication infrastructure breaks down due to overload.

We evaluated a large number of organizations with a variety of organizational structures through simulation. The basic experimental setup was as follows:

- 80 human actors.
- 176 total primary tasks and contingencies.
  - 16 primary decision tasks, each requiring information provided by 3 distinct sensing tasks.
  - Each decision task has 1 contingency.
  - Each sensing task has 2 contingencies.

We tested three basic types of organizational structures: regular hierarchies, rings, and random structures. Regular hierarchies are obviously hierarchical structures, but the rings and random structures were inherently horizontal organizational structures. In a regular hierarchy, the actors form a complete n-ary rooted tree, where n is the span of control. We tested hierarchies with spans of control of two, three, and four, denoted by RH2, RH3, and RH4, respectively. Every actor in a regular hierarchy has one upward link and a fixed number of downward links, so this structure is invariant to changes in max_{deg}. Note, however, that for a regular hierarchy with span of control n to be allowed at all, max_{deg} must be greater than or equal to $n+1$.

Regular hierarchies are used as representatives of traditional hierarchical structures common to human organizations, and as such, there are several additional constraints on the operation of an organization with such a structure. Firstly, information must always flow upward through the hierarchy, so that decision makers are always ancestors of the actors with sensing tasks. This greatly constrains the assignment of tasks based on the structure. Secondly, control flows downward, so that managers are always ancestors of the actors assigned to the tasks being managed.

In a ring structure, the actors form a cycle. If actors can link to more than two other actors (i.e., max_{deg} > 2), actors also form links at regular intervals across the ring to minimize the average path length to every actor. In the extreme, this leads to G being fully connected (when max_{deg}). We consider rings with actors having three, four, and five neighbors, denoted by Ring3, Ring4, Ring5, respectively. Ring structures are used as representatives of flat, peer-to-peer organization.

The third type of structure considered is the non-hierarchical random graph. Links were added randomly between actors so that each actor has a fixed number of communication links, if possible. We considered random graphs where each actor has three, four, and five neighbors, denoted by Rand3, Rand4, and Rand5, respectively. Like the ring, this is envisioned as a flat, peer-to-peer organizational structure, and is included primarily as a reference for the other structures.

The organizations tested consisted of two parts, the organizational structure and the task assignment. We generated a large number of organizational structures and used different task assignment algorithms on each of the structures in order to generate the organizations we used for evaluation. Because the task assignment problem is NP-hard in general, we used a heuristic algorithm to assign the tasks for regular hierarchies and ring structures. This algorithm greedily assigns tasks to actors while balancing the assigned load on each actor so that the chance of cognitive overload is reduced. In addition, care is taken to ensure that information from sensing tasks can reach the decision makers, with preference given so that the distance the information much travel (and hence the delay incurred) is minimized, if possible. The additional requirements of regular hierarchies described above impose additional constraints on the task assignment. A completely random allocation was used for random graph structures.

For each organization generated (i.e., organizational structure coupled with task assignment), we simulated the operation of the organization 100 times. The fraction of simulated runs in which the organization successfully completed the plan was used as an approximation of the success rate. The average reward and speed over successful runs were used as approximations to the organization's reward and speed, respectively. If an organization did not succeed at all in the 100 runs, all three metrics received a score of 0.

The next section will describe the experimental results of the baseline performance without SPAs and performance with SPAs modeled as various relaxations of the baseline constraints. The baseline configuration used the following settings:

- Sensing task durations chosen randomly as 10±1 for primary tasks, 15±3 for the first contingency, and 20±5 for the second contingency.
- Decision durations were chosen randomly as 5±1.
- Sensing task windows were [0, 50] for the primary task and first contingency, and [25,100] for the second contingency.
- Decision task windows were [0, 100].
- Probability of failure was chosen uniformly at random from [0.01, 0.40] for each task.
- Deadline: $d = 100.0$.

- Communication delay: $delay_c = 2.0$.
- $max_{deg} = 4$. This setting allows the RH2, RH3, Ring3, and Ring4 organizational structures in the baseline configuration.
- Synchronous communication: $max'_{deg} = 1$.

EXPERIMENTAL RESULTS

The Figures in this section show *performance averages* for different organizational structures. These give a rough measure for how well organizations of that structure tend to perform, and are calculated in the following way. The success rate performance average is the average of the success rates for all organizations of that structure and assignment algorithm. The reward and speed performance averages were calculated as the averages of the reward performance and speed performance, respectively, of all organizations of that structure and assignment algorithm with non-zero success rate. Hence the reward and speed performance averages include the performance of only those organizations that succeed at least some of the time. This indicates how much reward organizations receive or how quickly organizations complete the plan when they succeed.

Baseline Results

The baseline raw performance averages for the RH2, RH3, Ring3, Ring4, Rand3, and Rand4 structures are shown in Figure 1. The RH4, Ring5, and Rand5 structures are *not* presented here, as they violate the baseline constraint $max_{deg} = 4$, but they will be presented for comparison below with the results of SPA-managed communication. In Figure 1, the different organizational structures are plotted on the *x*-axis, while the *y*-axis shows the raw, normalized performance averages for each of the three components. The reward performance average, shown in red, is greater for ring structures than for regular hierarchies. This is because the additional constraints on task assignments in the regular hierarchies restrict the pool of actors that can be assigned the task, resulting in less capable agents being assigned. Organizations with the RH2 structure also have a greater reward performance average than those with the RH3 structure, because the same constraints become tighter as the span of control increases. How-

Figure 1. Baseline performance averages

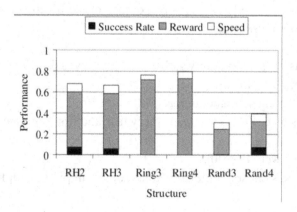

ever, even the regular hierarchies have greater reward than the random graphs, showing that they are able to assign tasks to agents with above average capability.

The bottom component, which is not visible for Ring3, Ring4, and Rand3, is the success rate performance average. The Figure indicates that the success rate is low for regular hierarchies (with less than a ten percent success rate for RH2 and RH3) and random structures (less than a ten percent success rate for Rand4), and zero for the ring structure. One possible reason for this is suggested by the small speed performance averages, shown as the top components in the Figure. Such small values indicate that the organizations, when they succeed, do so very close to the deadline. Most of the time, the organization exceeds the deadline and hence fails the plan.

The organizations tend to exceed the deadline for different reasons, depending on the structure. In ring structured organizations, the average path length between actors tends to be longer than in regular hierarchies. This results in communication that is so slow that information does not reach decision makers until after the deadline, especially when contingencies are invoked, as they tend to be performed by actors that are farther from the decision maker. In regular hierarchies, the tree structure coupled with the requirement that communication flows upward create a bottleneck in communication as information from successfully completed tasks and failure notices for failed tasks overload the communication capacities of actors further up the hierarchy. This prevents information from reaching decision makers quickly, as well as prevents contingencies from being invoked in a timely manner. The RH2 structure has a slightly higher success rate than the RH3 structure because its smaller span of control makes it less likely that actors suffer communication overload. As a result, the RH2 structure also has a greater speed performance average than the RH3 structure. The Rand3 structure suffers many of the same problems as the ring structures, but Rand4 performs surprisingly well because random graphs tend to have short paths between all nodes with multiple redundant paths.

Results of SPA Effects on Communication Management

The effect of reducing the communication delay in the organization through SPAs is shown in Figure 1(b)(c)(d). The communication delay is varied on the *x*-axis, with the baseline value of $delay_c = 2.0$ on the far right. On the far left of the *x*-axis is the ideal case of instantaneous communication, when $delay_c = 0$. At this point, there is no delay for communication no matter what distance it must travel, and there is no communication overload because communications links are active for effectively no time. Thus the performance of the organizations when $delay_c = 0$ are independent of any communication-related issues.

The impact of different communication delays on the success rate performance averages is shown in Figure 2. While all organizational structures improve as the communication delay is decreased, there is a threshold effect with ring structures where performance increases dramatically, far faster than observed with hierarchies. Ring structured organizations typically fail because communication takes too long; contingencies are not authorized until after their execution windows have passed, and decision makers do not receive required information until after the deadline. The threshold effect occurs because for sufficiently short communication delay, rings are able to communicate in a timely fashion and these failures are avoided. This is further seen in comparing the Ring4 structure to the Ring3 structure. Because Ring4 has a greater number of cross links and hence shorter average paths between actors when compared to Ring3, it also can tolerate higher communication delays, showing a

Figure 2. Performance averages with SPAs that reduce communication delay; (a) Success rate; (b) Reward; (c) Speed

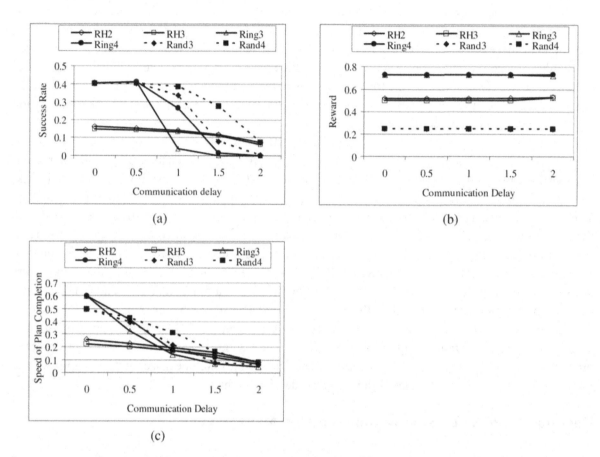

(a)

(b)

(c)

much greater improvement in success rate from a delay of 1.5 to a delay of 1.0 compared to the Ring3 structure, which largely thresholds at a delay between 1.0 and 0.5.

The success rate of the regular hierarchies also improves with reduced communication delay, as can be seen in Figure 2(a). However, it is very interesting to note that regular hierarchies, while starting from much greater success rates than ring structures at the baseline communication delay value, do not improve as much as ring structures do. Even with instantaneous communication shown at the far left of the *x*-axis, regular hierarchies still succeed only around 15% of the time. This shows that the lower success rates of hierarchical organizations are due to reasons other than communication delay and overload.

The random graphs had higher success rates than the ring structures for moderate values of communication delay. This is because random graphs tend to have shorter paths between actors, which reduces the impact of communication delay.

Decreased communication delay has no effect on the reward obtained by organizations, as shown in Figure 2(b). The ring structures clearly obtain more reward when successful than the hierarchical structures, due to the greater flexibility in assigning tasks to ring structures. Both of these structures obtain more reward than the random structures, finding agents of above average capability to execute tasks.

Figure 3. Performance averages with SPAs that provide asynchronous communication and reduced communication delay; (a) Success rate; (b) Speed; Reward performance averages are omitted as they are not significantly different from the synchronous baseline and reduced communication delay cases

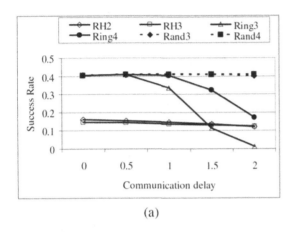

(a)

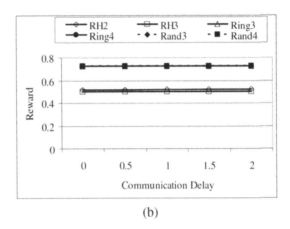

(b)

Figure 2(c) shows the effect of communication delay on the speed performance averages. Regular hierarchies improve linearly with decreased communication delay, as the reduced time spent communicating leads to faster plan execution. The relatively low maximum achieved for regular hierarchies when $delay_c = 0$ when compared to that of ring and random structures indicates that even when communication delay and overload are removed, regular hierarchies suffer from other limitations that restrict their ability to quickly perform tasks. The most significant of these (as we will see later) is cognitive overload that arises because the hierarchical constraints on task assignments restrict cause actors to be more heavily loaded than in the ring structure. In contrast, ring structures greatly improve their speed even faster than would be expected by a simple linear speed up, as seen with regular hierarchies and random graphs. The reason for this (as we shall see shortly) is that the shorter communication delay reduces communication overloads, and so task execution is sped up as decision tasks and contingencies that had been waiting for information or authorization at longer communication delays are able to execute earlier.

The effect of asynchronous communication on organizational performance, in conjunction with reduced communication delay, is shown in Figure 3. Figure 3(a) and Figure 3(b) show success rate performance averages and speed performance averages, respectively, with asynchronous communication and varying amounts of communication delay. Reward performance averages with asynchronous communication are unchanged from those seen in the synchronous baseline and reduced communication cases, and are omitted. Because asynchronous communication removes communication overloads, the data shown in Figure 3 indicate the extent to which communication factors other than communication overload affect organizational performance.

Figure 3(a) shows that the greatest communication factor limiting regular hierarchies from succeeding are communication overloads. At the baseline communication delay, regular hierarchies with asynchronous communication achieve plan success almost twice as often as they do with synchronous communication. Decreasing the communication speed in addition to this also improves the success rate linearly, but the gains that can be obtained by this are not as great as those obtained by using asyn-

Figure 4. Performance averages for SPAs that increase the number of potential communication links each actor can have; (a) Success rate; (b) Speed

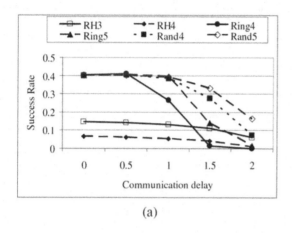 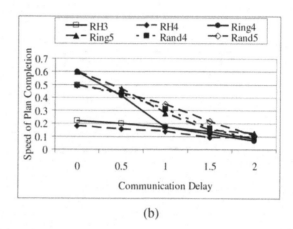

(a) (b)

chronous communication. This suggests that for SPAs being designed for hierarchical organizations, it may be more beneficial to provide asynchronous communication than to simply increase the rate at which synchronous communication can occur.

Communication overloads are also a significant problem in the ring structures, especially at higher communication delays, as indicated in Figure 3(a) by the greatly improved performances of Ring4 at the baseline communication delay of 2 and Ring3 at delay of 1.5. However, Ring3 continues to perform very poorly with a communication delay of 2, because the long delay still prevents actors from effectively communicating even without communication overloads. Overall, the threshold effect of reduced communication delay on the success rate of ring structures is much less pronounced than it was for synchronous communication. Part of the reason for this is that with synchronous communication, reduced delay affects both communication-related causes of failure, whereas with asynchronous communication, it only affects how quickly information is transmitted in time for decision tasks and contingencies to be executed. From Figures 2(a) and 3(a) it can be seen that the dramatic threshold

Figure 5. Performance averages; (a) with SPA-managed task contingencies; (b) without SPA-managed task contingencies

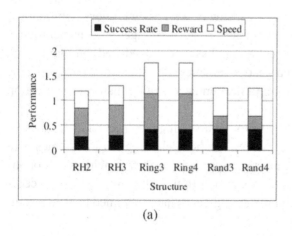 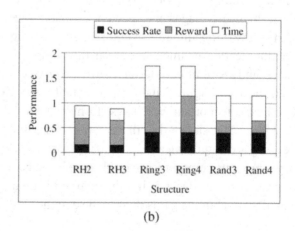

(a) (b)

behavior in synchronous communication occurs primarily when the communication delay has been reduced sufficiently for communication overload no longer to be a major cause of plan failure.

Of all the structures, random graphs are the most affected by communication overload. Figure 3(a) shows that the success rate performance averages of random graphs are essentially maximal with asynchronous communication, even for the baseline delay. This strongly suggests that asynchronous communication facilitates flat, decentralized organizational structures.

Figure 3(b) shows that with asynchronous communication, both regular hierarchies and random graphs demonstrate linear speedup with decreased communication delay. Ring structures also have a speedup that is much closer to linear than it was with synchronous communication.

Figure 4 shows the effect of using SPAs to manage communications so that the number of communication links each actor can effectively maintain is increased to five. This allows three new organizational structures, a regular hierarchy with span of control 4 (RH4), a ring with 5 neighbors per actor (Ring5), and a random graph with 5 neighbors per actor (Rand5). Figure 4(a) shows the effect on success rate

Figure 6. Performance averages with SPAs that reduce decision load; (a) Success rate; (b) Speed

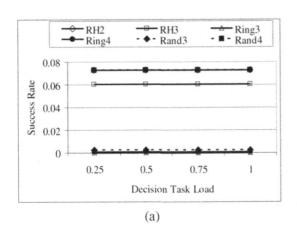

(a)

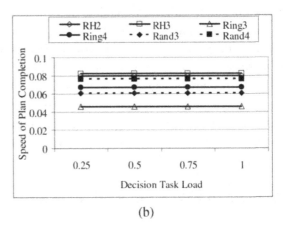

(b)

Figure 7. Performance averages with SPAs that reduce decision duration; (a) Success rate; (b) Speed

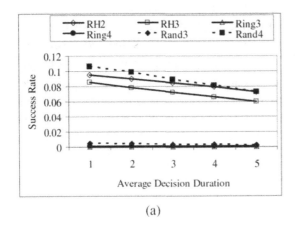

(a)

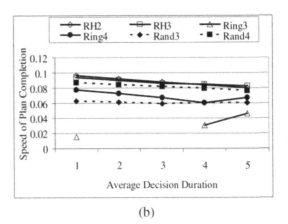

(b)

and Figure 4(b) shows the effect on speed of completion. For comparison, each Figure includes the structures with one fewer neighbor per actor (RH3, Ring4, and Rand4). Again, there is no significant change in reward, so that is omitted.

From Figure 4(a) it is clear that adding an additional communication link benefits ring and random structures by allowing faster communication and a greater number of redundant paths, while it harms regular hierarchies because the hierarchical task assignment constraints causes actors to be too heavily loaded to complete all of the requisite tasks before the deadline. Thus even when there is instantaneous communication, RH4 performs very poorly. The effect on speed performance averages in Figure 4(b) are similar to those seen previously, with improvement for ring and random structures and a loss of performance for the regular hierarchy.

Results of SPA Effects on Task Contingency Management

Figure 5(a) shows the performance averages when SPAs allow flexible contingency invocation to prevent cognitive overload. In order to see the potential impact of flexibly and robustly reducing cognitive overload, these results were obtained with a communication delay of 0, so that there were no communication-related causes of failure. For comparison, the performance averages with synchronous communication with delay 0 and no SPA-managed task contingencies is shown in Figure 5(b). From a comparison of Figures 5(a) and 5(b), it is apparent that SPA-managed contingencies greatly increase the success rate performance averages of hierarchical organizations, but have no effect on ring and random structures. This strongly suggests that if SPAs are being developed for a hierarchical organization, task contingency management is one of the most important capabilities to be taken into consideration. However, the performance of the regular hierarchies is still less than that of the ring structures, which suggests that hierarchical organizations with enhanced communication technologies that effectively eliminate communication delay may reap additional benefits by switching to a less centralized organizational structure.

Results of SPA Effects on Decision Support

Figure 6 shows the effect of SPAs that provide decision support by reducing the cognitive load of decision tasks. The other organization parameters are set to the baseline configuration. The load of decision tasks is varied on the x-axis. The baseline value of load of 1 is shown on the far right of the x-axis. As can be clearly seen, changing the decision task load has no effect on performance.

Figure 7 shows the effect of SPAs that provide decision support by reducing decision task durations. This has more of an effect on the organizational performance. Figure 7(a) shows that decreasing decision duration linearly increases the success rate of the organization, because faster decisions make it more likely that the organization will meet the deadline. Figure 7(b) shows that decreasing the decision task duration also tends to have a very slight increase on the speed performance average. Because success rates were so low for this setting, there was a larger amount of noise than usual, especially for ring structures.

CONCLUSION

Software personal assistants hold great promise to revolutionize human organizations by automating routine tasks and improving coordination between people. Despite various research prototypes and applications, SPA technologies have not yet been able to enter the workplace. We believe that this is due to remaining unsolved technical problems, such as SPAs inferring human intentions, mutual understandability of user and agents, and the unknown impact of introducing SPAs. This chapter is a first step toward addressing this last issue.

In this chapter we developed a conceptual framework and computational model to quantify the impact that various software personal assistant capabilities will have on the performance of human organizations. We found that the type of capabilities that are most beneficial depend on the organizational structure. For hierarchical organizations, SPA capabilities to manage cognitive and communication overload were most important, while for decentralized, flat organizations, SPA technologies that increased the speed of communication were the most helpful. This suggests that SPA designers should consider the appropriate set of SPA technologies depending on the target application, as they would confer the greatest benefits on the organization when deployed. However, the immediate application of SPAs to an organization is only the first phase of their adoption. Our results showing that flat, decentralized organizations perform best overall in the presence of SPAs suggests that over time, even hierarchical organizations may become less centralized in an effort to greater leverage the enhanced communication and coordination offered by SPAs.

ACKNOWLEDGMENT

This research was sponsored in part by AFOSR grant FA9550-07-1-0039 and in part by the U.S. Army Research Laboratory and the U.K. Ministry of Defence and was accomplished under Agreement Number W911NF-06-3-0001. The views and conclusions contained in this document are those of the author(s) and should not be interpreted as representing the official policies, either expressed or implied, of the U.S. Army Research Laboratory, the U.S. Government, the U.K. Ministry of Defence or the U.K. Government. The U.S. and U.K. Governments are authorized to reproduce and distribute reprints for Government purposes notwithstanding any copyright notation hereon.

REFERENCES

Ahuja, M., & Carley, K. M. (1998). Network structure in virtual organizations. *Organization Science, 10*(6), 741 – 757.

Ackoff, R. L. (1967). Management misinformation systems. *Management science, 14*(4), B147 – B156.

Anderson, J. (1993). *Rules of the mind.* Hillsdale, New Jersey: Lawrence Erlbaum Associates.

Byrne, M. D. (1999). ACT-R/PM and menu selection: Applying a cognitive architecture to HCI. *International Journal of Human-Computer Studies, 12*, 439 – 462.

Carley, K. M., & Prietula, M. J. (Ed.). (1994). *Computational Organization Theory.* Hillsdale, New Jersey: Lawrence Erlbaum Associates, Inc., Publishers.

Carley, K. M. (1996). Communicating new ideas: The potential impact of information and telecommunication technology. *Technology in Society, 18*(2), 219 – 230.

Carley, K. M. (1995). Computational and mathematical organization theory: Perspective and directions. *Journal of Computational and Mathematical Organizational Theory, 1*(1), 39 – 56.

Carley, K. M. (2002). Computational organization science: A new frontier. *Proceedings of the National Academy of Sciences of the United States of America, 99*(10), 7257 – 7262.

Chalupsky, H., Gil, Y. Knoblock, C., Lerman, K., Oh, J. Pynadath D. V., Russ, T. A., & Tambe, M. (2001). Electric Elves: Applying agent technology to support human organizations. In *Proceedings of the Thirteenth Conference on Innovative Applications of Artificial Intelligence* (pp. 51 – 58). AAAI Press.

Chen, L., & Sycara, K. (1998). WebMate: A personal agent for browsing and searching. In *Proceedings of the 2nd International Conference on Autonomous Agents* (pp. 132 – 139).

Dent, L., Boticario, J., Mitchell, T., Sabowski, D., & McDermott, J. (1992). A personal learning apprentice. In William Swartout (Ed.), *Proceedings of the 10th National Conference on Artificial Intelligence – AAAI-92* (pp. 96 – 103). MIT Press.

Decker, K., & Sycara, K. (1997a). Intelligent adaptive information agents. *Journal of Intelligent Information Systems, 9*(3), 239 – 260.

Decker, K., Pannu, A., Sycara, K., & Williamson, M. (1997b). Designing behaviors for information agents. In *Proceedings of the First International Conference on Autonomous Agents* (pp. 404 – 412).

Dignum, M.V., Vázquez-Salceda, J., & Dignum, F.P.M. (2004). OMNI: Introducing social structure, norms and ontologies into agent organizations. In P. Bordini & et al. (Eds.), *Programming Multi-Agent Systems* (pp. 183-200). Heidelberg: Springer.

Garrido, L., & Sycara, K. (1996). Multi-agent meeting scheduling: Preliminary experimental results. In *Proceedings of the Second International Conference on Multi-Agent Systems.*

Garton, L. E. & Wellman, B. (1993). Social impacts of electronic mail in organizations: A review of the research literature. (Tech. Rep. KMDI-HP-93-13). Toronto, Canada: University of Toronto, Knowledge Media Design Institute.

Grossi, D., Dignum, F., & Meyer, J.-J. C. (2007). A formal road from institutional norms to organizational structure. In *Proceedings of the Sixth International Conference on Autonomous Agents and Multiagent Systems.* New York: ACM.

Grossi, D., Dignum, F., Dignum, V., Dastani, M., & Royakkers, L. (2006). Structural aspects of the evaluation of agent organizations. In *Proceedings of the Fifth International Conference on Autonomous Agents and Multiagent Systems.* New York: ACM.

Gurbaxani, V., & Whang, S. (1991). The impact of information systems on organizations and markets. *Communications of the ACM, 34*(1), 59 – 73.

Horling, B. (2006). *Quantitative organizational modeling and design for multi-agent systems.* Doctoral dissertation, University of Massachusetts at Amherst.

Horvitz, E. (1999). Principles of mixed-initiative user interfaces. In *Proceedings of CHI '99, ACM SIG-CHI Conference on Human Factors in Computing Systems* (pp. 159 – 166). ACM Press.

Laird, J. E., Newell, A., Rosenbloom, P. S. (1987). SOAR: An architecture for general intelligence. *Artificial Intelligence, 33*(1), 1 – 64.

Lenox, T., Hahn, S., Lewis, M., Payne T., & Sycara, K. (2000a). Agent-based aiding for individual and team planning tasks. In *Proceedings of the International Ergonomics Society/Human Factors and Ergonomics Society 2000 Congress.*

Lenox, T., Hahn, S., Lewis, M., Payne, T., & Sycara, K. (2000b). Task characteristics and intelligent aiding. In *Proceedings of the 2000 IEEE International Conference on Systems, Man, and Cybernetics* (pp. 1123 – 1127).

Lesser, V., Decker, K., Wagner, T., Carver, N., Garvey, A., Horling, B., Neiman, D., Podorozhny, R., Nagendra Prasad, M., Raja, A., Vincent, R., Xuan, P., & Zhang, X. Q. (2004). Evolution of the GPGP/TAEMS domain-independent coordination framework. *Autonomous Agents and Multi-Agent Systems, 9,* 87 – 143.

Levitt, R. E., Cohen, G. P., Kunz, J. C., Nass, C. I., Christiansen, T., & Jin, Y. (1994). The "virtual design" team: Simulating how organization structure and information processing tools affect team performance. In Carley, K. M. & Prietula, M. J. (Eds.), *Computational Organization Theory.* Hillsdale, New Jersey: Lawrence Erlbaum Associates.

Li, C., Giampapa, J., & Sycara, K. (2006). Bilateral contract negotiation decisions with uncertain dynamic outside options. *IEEE Transactions on Systems, Man and Cybernetics, Part C.: Special Issue on Game Theoretic Analysis and Stochastic Simulation of Negotiation Agents, 36*(1), 31–44.

Maes, P. (1994). Agents that reduce work and information overload. *Communications of the ACM, 37*(7), 30 – 40.

Majchrzak, A. & Finley, L. (1995). A practical theory and tool for specifying sociotechnical requirements to achieve organizational effectiveness. In Benders, J. J., De Haan, J., & Bennett, D. (Eds.), *Symbiotic approaches: Work and technology.* London: Taylor and Francis.

Malone, T.W., Yates, J., & Benjamin, R. I. (1987). Electronic markets and electronic hierarchies. *Communications of the ACM, 30*(6), 484 – 497.

Malone, T.W. (1985). *Organizational structure and information technology: Elements of a formal theory* (CISR WP No. 130, Sloan WP No. 1710-85, 90s WP No 85-011). Cambridge, Massachusetts: Massachusetts Institute of Technology, Sloan School of Management, Center for Information Systems Research.

Maheswaran, R. T., Tambe, M. Bowring, E. Pearce, J. P., Varakantham, V. (2004). Taking DCOP to the real world: Efficient complete solutions for distributed event scheduling. In *Proceedings of the Third International Conference on Autonomous Agents and Multiagent Systems.* New York: ACM.

Maheswaran, R. T., Pearce, J. P., Varakantham, P., Bowring, E., Tambe, M. (2005). Valuations of possible states (VPS): A quantitative framework for analysis of privacy loss among collaborative personal assistant agents. In *Proceedings of the Fourth International Conference on Autonomous Agents and Multiagent Systems*. New York: ACM.

McCrickard, D. S. & Chewar, C. M. (2003). Attuning notification design to user goals and attention costs. *Communications of the ACM, 46*(3), 67 – 72.

Mitchell, T. M., Caruana, R., Freitag, D., McDermott, J., & Zabowski, D. (1994). Experience with a learning personal assistant. *Communications of the ACM, 37*(7), 80 – 91.

Modi, P., Veloso, M., Smith S., Oh, J. (2004). CMRadar: A personal assistant agent for calendar management. In *Proceedings of the Sixth International Workshop on Agent-Oriented Information Systems* (pp. 134 – 148).

Myers, K., Berry, P., Blythe, J., Conley, K., Gervasio, M., McGuinness, D., Morley, D., Pfeffer, A., Pollack, M., Tambe, M. (2007). An intelligent personal assistant for task and time management. *AI Magazine*, 2007.

Okamoto, S., Scerri, P., & Sycara, K. (2006). Toward an understanding of the impact of software personal assistants on human organizations. In *AAMAS '06: Proceedings of the Fifth International Joint Conference on Autonomous Agents and Multiagent Systems* (pp. 630 – 637). New York: ACM.

Payne, T., Singh, R., & Sycara, K. (2002). Browsing schedules: An agent-based approach to navigating the semantic web. In *Proceedings of the First International Semantic Web Conference* (pp. 469 – 474).

Prietula, M. J., Carley, K. M., & Gasser, L. (Ed.). (1998). *Simulating Organizations*. Menlo Park, California: AAAI Press/The MIT Press.

Schurr, N., Marecki, J., Tambe, M., Scerri, P., Levis, J.P., & Kasinadhuni, N. (2005). The future of disaster response: Humans working with multiagent teams using DEFACTO. In *Proceedings of the AAAI Spring Symposium on Homeland Security*.

Serrano J. & Saugar, S. (2007). Operational semantics of multiagent interactions. In *Proceedings of the 6th International Joint Conference on Autonomous Agents and Multiagent Systems*. New York: ACM.

Sycara, K. & Lewis, M. (2004). Integrating agents into human teams. In E. Salas & S.M. Fiore (Eds.), *Team Cognition* (pp. 203 – 233). Erlbaum Publishers.

Sycara, K. & Zeng, D. (1996). Coordination of multiple intelligent software agents. *International Journal of Cooperative Information Systems, 5*(2,3), 181 – 212.

Tambe, M., Bowring, E., Pearce, J. P., Varakantham, P., Scerri, S., Pynadath, D. V. (2006). Electric elves: What went wrong and why. In *Proceedings of the AAAI Spring Symposium on "What Went Wrong and Why"*.

Varakantham, P., Maheswaran, R., & Tambe, M. (2005). Exploiting belief bounds: Practical POMDPs for personal assistant agents. In *Proceedings of the Fourth International Conference on Autonomous Agents and Multiagent Systems*. New York: ACM.

Vasconcelos, W., Kollingbaum, M. J., & Norman, T. J. (2007). Resolving conflict and inconsistency in norm-regulated virtual organizations. In *Proceedings of the Sixth International Conference on Autonomous Agents and Multiagent Systems*. New York: ACM.

Wagner, T., Phelps, J., Guralnik, V., & VanRiper, R. (2004). COORDINATORS: Coordination managers for first responders. In *AAMAS '04: Proceedings of the Third International Joint Conference on Autonomous Agents and Multiagent Systems*. Washington, D.C.: IEEE Computer Society.

Yates, J., & Orlikowski, W. (1992). Genres of organizational communication: A structurational approach to studying communication and media. *Academy of Management Review, 17*(2), 299-326.

ADDITIONAL READING

Bowring, E., Tambe, M., & Yokoo, M. (2005). Optimize my schedule but keep it flexible – distributed multi-criteria coordination for personal assistants. *AAAI Spring Symposium on Persistent Assistants: Living and Working with AI.*

Decker, K., Sycara, K., & Williamson, M. (1997). Intelligent adaptive information agents. *Journal of Intelligent Information Systems*, 9, 239 – 260.

He Q., Sycara, K., & Finin, T. (1998). Personal security agent: KQML-based PKI. In *Proceedings of the 2nd International Conference on Autonomous Agents* (pp. 377 – 384). New York; ACM.

Hinds, P. & Kiesler, S. (1995). Communication across boundaries: Work, structure, and use of communication technologies in a large organization. *Organization Science, 6*(4), 373 – 393.

Lenox, T., Hahn, S., Lewis, M., Payne, T. R., Sycara, K. (2000). Task characteristics and intelligent aiding. In *Proceedings of the 2000 IEEE International Conference on Systems, Man, and Cybernetics*, pp. 1123 – 1127.

Nourbakhsh, I., Lewis, M., Sycara, K., Koes, M., Young, M., & Burlon, S. (2005). Human-robot teaming for search and rescue. *IEEE Pervasive Computing, 4*(1), 72 – 78.

So, Y. P. & Durfee, E. H. (1996). Designing tree-structured organizations for computational agents. *Computational and Mathematical Organization Theory, 2*(3), 219 – 246.

Yates, J., Orlikowski, W. J., & Okamura, K. (1999). Explicit and implicit structuring of genres in electronic communication: Reinforcement and change of social interaction. *Organization Science, 10*(1), 83 – 103.

KEY TERMS

Actor: The human members of the organization. The actors are the entities that are actually executing tasks and are explicitly represented in our model. The actors may be assisted by software personal assistants, which relieve various cognitive and communication constraints.

Cognitive Load: The amount of an actor's cognitive facilities that is required to perform a task or set of tasks. People are inherently limited in the amount of cognitive load they can bear, and thus relieving cognitive load is one of the major goals for a successful software personal assistant design.

Communication Overload: A person's inability to engage in an excessive number of simultaneous communication acts. Communication overload arises because people have bounded capacities for processing communicated information. This is primarily a problem with synchronous communication.

Decision Task: A task that requires information generated by successfully executing sensing tasks. A decision task cannot be executed until all requisite information has been acquired.

Organizational Structure: The set of relationships among organizational members constraining their possible actions. In this chapter we consider communication structures that restrict with whom an organization member can communicate. We consider hierarchical, tree-based structures as well as horizontal structures, namely rings and random structures.

Primary Task: A task that is not a contingency of any other task. Executing a primary task is the preferred way to achieve an organizational goal, while contingencies are less preferred but allow the organization to cope with failure.

Sensing Task: A task that generates useful information when successfully completed. The generated information can be used in a decision task.

Software Personal Assistant (SPA): An agent that supports a human user by automating routine individual tasks and facilitating coordination with other members of the organization. The effect of a software personal assistant on its user is to relax various cognitive and communication constraints. To be fully effective, software personal assistants must be aware of the organization in which they are situated.

Task Contingency: A task to be executed in the event another task cannot be successfully completed. Each task has at most one, unique and specific contingency that is known in advance. A contingency may in turn have its own contingency to be executed in event of failure. Contingencies represent pre-planned backup or alternative ways to achieve an organizational goal.

Chapter XXII
Organizational Self–Design in Worth–Oriented Domains

Sachin Kamboj
University of Delaware, USA

Keith S. Decker
University of Delaware, USA

ABSTRACT

This chapter presents an approach to organizational-self design (OSD), a method of designing organizations at run-time in which the agents are responsible for generating their own organizational structures. OSD is especially suitable for environments that are dynamic, albeit slowly changing. Such environments preclude the use of static, design-time generated, organizational structures, and yet contain certain characteristics and conditions that change slowly, if at all, and these characteristics can be harnessed for the purposes of creating stable organizational structures. This chapter extends the existing approaches to OSD by applying them to worth-oriented domains – that is, domains in which problems are represented using TÆMS based task structures. This chapter presents our OSD primitives and framework and discusses some interesting future lines of research.

INTRODUCTION

Multiagent systems are increasingly being used to solve a wide variety of problems in a range of applications such as distributed sensing, information retrieval, workflow and business process management, air traffic control and spacecraft control, amongst others. Each of these systems has to be designed at two levels: the micro-architecture level, which involves the design of the individual agents, and the macro-architecture level, which involves the design of organizational and social aspects of the system. In this book, we are primarily concerned with the macro-architectural, organizational design of the multiagent system.

At the organizational level, the multiagent designer is primarily concerned with issues such as the number of agents needed to solve the problem, the task structure (i.e. the breakup of the problem into subgoals), the task and resource assignments to the individual agents and the coordination mechanisms to be used. These issues can be resolved by choosing an organizational structure and by instantiating that structure with actual agents. The organizational structure consists of roles that the agents play and the manner in which they interact with other agents in the system. The instantiation consists of selecting the number of agents needed in the system and the assignment of roles and resources to the individual agents.

The organizational structure employed directly influences the effectiveness of the organization in solving the problem at hand, the resources needed by the agents and the cost of coordinating the activities of the individual agents. Hence, the organizational design is a very important part of the multiagent system design. However, there are few good rules and formal mechanisms for designing effective organizations for computational agents that are general enough for a wide range of agent systems. For example, consider the question of the number of agents needed in the system. If too few agents are available, the system will be overloaded and will not be able to perform optimally. If too many agents are used, resources may be wasted and contention for the limited resources amongst the agents will increase.

The macro-architectural design is further complicated by the fact that there is no best way to organize and all ways of organizing are not equally effective (Carley and Gasser, 1999). Instead, the optimal organizational structure depends both on the problem at hand and the environmental conditions under which the problem needs to be solved. In some cases, the environmental conditions may not be known a priori, at design time, in which case the multiagent designer does not know how to come up with the suitable organizational structure. In other cases, the environmental conditions may change requiring a redesign of the agents' macro-architecture. Hence, it is not obvious that a static design-time approach to an organizational structure is feasible in a significant number of cases. At the opposite end of the spectrum, systems may be designed to create a new, bespoke organizational structure for every problem instance. The most popular example of such a one-off task allocation approach is the Contract Net protocol (Smith and Davis, 1978). Such an approach brings with it a different set of inefficiencies and belies the fact that while many real environments have dynamic components, there are also commonalities in the structure of problem instances that can be taken advantage of through proper organizational structuring.

Organizational Self-Design (OSD) (Corkill and Lesser, 1983; Ishida et al., 1992) has been proposed as an approach to designing organizations at run-time in which the agents are responsible for generating their own organizational structures. We believe that OSD is especially suited to the above scenario in which the environment is semi-dynamic as the agents can adapt to changes in the task structures and environmental conditions, while still being able to generate relatively stable organizational structures that exploit the common characteristics across problem instances.

In our approach, problem solving requests arrive at the organization continuously at varying rates and with varying deadlines. To gain utility, the agents in the organization need to solve the problems by their given deadlines. We start off with an initial organization consisting of a single agent that is solely responsible for all the problem solving activities. As new problem solving requests arrive, the agent checks to see whether it can complete the request by the given deadline. If not, the agent spawns off a new agent that is responsible for some subpart of the main problem, thus parallelizing the solution to the problem. If an agent is free for an extended period of time, it may decide to combine with another agent to save computational resources. Hence, we propose two organizational primitives that are responsible for generating the organizational structure: spawning and composition. These organizational primitives are further described in Section 4.

We use TÆMS as the underlying representation for our problem solving requests. TÆMS (Lesser et al., 2004) (Task Analysis, Environment Modeling and Simulation) is a computational framework for representing and reasoning about complex task environments in which tasks (problems) are represented using extended hierarchical task network structures (Chen and Decker, 2005). The root node of the task structure represents the high-level goal that the agent is trying to achieve. The sub-nodes of a node represent the subtasks and methods that make up the high-level task. The leaf nodes are at the lowest level of abstraction and represent executable methods – the primitive actions that the agents can perform. The executable methods, themselves, may have multiple outcomes, with different probabilities and different characteristics such as quality, cost and duration. TÆMS also allows various mechanisms for specifying subtask variations and alternatives, i.e. each node in TÆMS is labeled with a characteristic accumulation function that describes how many or which subgoals or sets of subgoals need to be achieved in order to achieve a particular higher-level goal. TÆMS has been used to model many different problem-solving environments including distributed sensor networks (Decker, 1997), information gathering (Lesser et al., 2000), hospital scheduling (Decker and Li, 2000), emergency medical services (Chen and Decker, 2005), and military planning. (Zimmerman et al., 2007; Wagner, 2004). An example of a TÆMS task structure is shown in Figure 1 and a formal model of TÆMS is presented in Section 3.

Our primary intellectual contribution in this work is the application of organizational self-design to worth-oriented domains, the most complex class of problems. Extending OSD to worth oriented domains allows us to generate different organizational structures that make different quality/cost tradeoffs based on the organizational design constraints specified and the performance criteria being optimized. Such

Figure 1. A TÆMS task structure. The polygons (labeled A – D) represent tasks and the circles (labeled A – E) represent executable methods. The + iconography indicates a SUM CAF while ▽ represents a MIN CAF. The arrows represent NLEs – the thick arrow represents hard constraints such as ENABLES (represented by a solid arrow from J to I) and DISABLES (represented by a broken arrow from H to E). The thin arrows show soft constraints such as FACILITATES (solid arrow from K to F) and HINDERS (broken arrow from D to E). Method characteristics and other details are omitted.

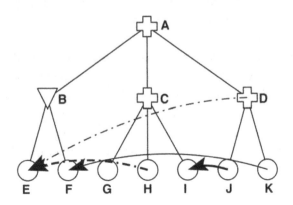

tradeoffs are not possible in task-oriented and state-oriented domains. Another positive side-effect of using TÆMS to model the domain problem is that it allows us to model uncertainties in the execution of tasks and to diminish the effects of these uncertainties on the performance of the organization.

Unfortunately, various researchers (Horling 2006; Nair, 2003) have shown that the problem of finding an optimal organizational structure is intractable for all but the simplest of problems and organizations. For example, Horling, 2006 proves that instantiating a valid organization from a set of templates, at compile-time, is an NEXP-Complete problem. Hence, we do not try to generate an optimal organization at run-time nor do we make any guarantees about the performance of our generated organizations. Instead, we attempt to generate satisficing organizations that are able to complete the input problem instances before their deadlines.

We are hoping that our research in this area might offer key insights to the design of organizations for worth-oriented domains. In particular we are hoping to come up with a general-purpose theory for organization in such domains.

The organization of the rest of this chapter is as follows: In Section 2 we describe other approaches to OSD. This is followed by a formal description of our task and resource model in Section 3. We, then, provide a more detailed description of our approach in Section 4. Finally, we evaluate our approach in 5 and present some future research directions in Section 6.

BACKGROUND AND RELATED WORK

The concept of OSD is not new and has been around since the work of Corkill and Lesser on the DVMT system (Corkill and Lesser, 1983), even though the concept was not fully developed by them. More recently Dignum et al., 2004, have described OSD in the context of the reorganization of agent societies and attempt to classify the various kinds of reorganization possible according to the reason for reorganization, the type of reorganization and who is responsible for the reorganization decision. According to their scheme, the type of reorganization done by our agents falls into the category of structural changes and the reorganization decision can be described as shared command.

Our research primarily builds on the work done by Ishida et al., 1992, in which they use OSD in the context of a production system in order to perform adaptive work allocation and load balancing. In their approach, they define two organizational primitives – composition and decomposition, which are similar to our organizational primitives for agent spawning and composition. The main difference between their work and our work is that we use TÆMS as the underlying representation for our problems, which allows, firstly, the representation of a larger, more general class of problems and, secondly, quantitative reasoning over task structures. The latter also allows us to incorporate different design-to-criteria schedulers (Wagner and Lesser, 2000).

Horling et al., 2001, present a different, top-down approach to OSD that also uses TÆMS as the underlying representation. However, their approach assumes a fixed number of agents with designated (and fixed) roles. OSD is used in their work to change the interaction patterns between the agents and results in the agents using different subtasks or different resources to achieve their goals. Later work (Horling and Lesser, 2005) by the same group describes a language (ODML) for modeling, analyzing and predicting, at design time, the effect of an organizational structure. However, it is not clear how their approach can be applied to OSD at runtime.

We also extend on the work done by Shehory et al., 1998, on Agent Cloning, which is another approach to resource allocation and load balancing. In this approach, the authors present agent cloning as a possible response to agent overload – if an agent detects that it is overloaded and that there are spare (unused) resources in the system, the agent clones itself and gives its clone some part of its task load. Hence, agent cloning can be thought of as akin to agent spawning in our approach. However, the two approaches are different in that there is no specialization of the agents in the former – the cloned agents are perfect replicas of the original agents and fulfill the same roles and responsibilities as the original agents. In our approach, on the other hand, the spawned agents are specialized on a subpart of the spawning agent's task structure, which is no longer the responsibility of the spawning agent. Hence, our approach also deals with explicit organization formation and the coordination of the agents' tasks which are not handled by their approach.

Other approaches to OSD include the work of So and Durfee, 1993, who describe a top-down model of OSD in the context of Cooperative Distributive Problem Solving (CDPS) and Barber and Martin, 2001, who describe an adaptive decision making framework in which agents are able to reorganize decision-making groups by dynamically changing (1) who makes the decisions for a particular goal and (2) who must carry out these decisions. The latter work is primarily concerned with coordination decisions and can be used to complement our OSD work, which primarily deals with task and resource allocation.

TASK AND RESOURCE MODEL

To ground our discussion of OSD, we now formally describe our task and resource model. In our model, the primary input to the multi-agent system (MAS) is an ordered set of problem solving requests or task instances, $<P_1, P_2, P_3, ..., P_n>$, where each problem solving request, P_i, can be represented using the tuple $<t_i, a_i, d_i>$. In this scheme, t_i is the underlying TÆMS task structure, $a_i \in N^+$ is the arrival time and $d_i \in N^+$ is the deadline of the ith task instance[1]. The task t_i is not "seen" by the MAS before the time a_i, i.e., the MAS has no prior knowledge about the task t_i before the arrival time, a_i. In order for the MAS to accrue quality, the task t_i must be completed before the deadline, d_i.

Furthermore, every underlying task structure, t_i, can be represented using the tuple $<T, \tau, M, Q, E, R, \rho, C>$, where:

- T is the set of tasks. The tasks are non-leaf nodes in a TÆMS task structure and are used to denote goals that the agents must achieve. Tasks have a characteristic accumulation function (see below) and are themselves composed of other subtasks and/or methods that need to be achieved in order to achieve the goal represented by that task. Formally, each task T_j can be represented using the pair (q_j, s_j), where $q_j \in Q$ and $s_j \subset (T \cup M)$. For our convenience, we define two functions SUBTASKS *(Task)*: $T \to P(T \cup M)$ and SUPERTASKS *(TÆMS node)*: $T \cup M \to P(T)$, that return the subtasks and supertasks of a TÆMS node respectively[2].

- $\tau \in T$, is the root of the task structure, i.e. the highest level goal that the organization is trying to achieve, with respect to this problem instance. The quality accrued on a problem is equal to the quality of task τ.

- M is the set executable methods, i.e., $M = \{m_1, m_2, ..., m_n\}$, where each method, m_k, is represented using the outcome distribution, $\{(o_1, p_1), (o_2, p_2), ..., (o_m, p_m)\}$. In the pair (o_l, p_l), o_l is an outcome and p_l is the probability that executing m_k will result in the outcome o_l. Furthermore, each outcome, o_l is represented using the triple (q_l, c_l, p_l), where q_l is the quality distribution, c_l is the cost distribution and d_l is the duration distribution of outcome o_l. Each discrete distribution is itself a set of pairs, $\{(n_1, p_1), (n_2, p_2), ..., (n_n, p_n)\}$, where $p_i \in \Re^+$ is the probability that the outcome will have a quality/cost/duration of $n_l \in N$ depending on the type of distribution and $\sum_{i=1}^m p_l = 1$.

- Q is the set of quality/characteristic accumulation functions (CAFs). The CAFs determine how a task group accrues quality given the quality accrued by its subtasks/methods. For our research, we use four CAFs: MIN, MAX, SUM and EXACTLY_ONE. For example, if the CAF of task T is SUM, then the quality of T is the sum of the qualities of its subtasks. See Decker, 1995, for formal definitions.

- E is the set of (non-local) effects, i.e. $E = \{e_1, e_2, ..., e_n\}$, where each effect, $e_i = <\alpha, \beta, \delta>$. Here, $\alpha \in (T \cup M)$, is the source of the non-local effect, $\beta \in M$, is the sink method of the non-local effect and d, is a temporal function that computes the characteristics of the sink given the characteristics of the source. Again, see Decker, 1995, for formal definitions.

- R is the set of resources.

- ρ is a mapping from an executable method and resource to the quantity of that resource needed (by an agent) to schedule/execute that method. That is $\rho(method, resource) : M \times R \to N$.

- C is a mapping from a resource to the cost of that resource, that is $C(resource) : R \to N^+$

We also make the following set of assumptions in our research:

1. The agents in the MAS are drawn from the infinite set $A = \{a_1, a_2, a_3, ...\}$. That is, we do not assume a fixed set of agents — instead agents are created (spawned) and destroyed (combined) as needed. In practice, such agents might be drawn from an underlying computing grid/cloud.

2. All problem solving requests have the same underlying task structure, i.e. $\exists t \forall_i t_i = t$, where t is the task structure of the problem that the MAS is trying to solve. The underlying task structure of the problem instances will henceforth be referred to as the global task structure. We believe that this assumption holds for many of the practical problems that we have in mind because TÆMS task structures are basically high-level plans for achieving some goal in which the steps required for achieving the goal—as well as the possible contingency situations—have been pre-computed of-fline and represented in the task structure. Because it represents many contingencies, alternatives, uncertain characteristics and run-time flexible choices, "the same underlying task structure" can play out very differently across specific instances.

3. All resources are exclusive, i.e., only one agent may use a resource at any given time. Further-more, we assume that each agent has to "own" the set of resources that it needs—even though the resource ownership can change during the evolution of the organization.

4. All resources are non-consumable.

ORGANIZATIONAL SELF-DESIGN

Organizational Structure

In our approach, organizations are represented using an organizational structure that is primarily composed of roles and the relationships between the roles. One or more agents may enact a particular role and one or more roles must be enacted by every agent. The roles may be thought of as the parts played by the agents enacting the roles in the solution to the problem and reflect the long-term commitments made by the agents in question to a certain course of action (that includes task responsibility, authority, and mechanisms for coordination). The relationships between the roles are the coordination relationships that exist between the subparts of a problem.

Also note that the organizational design is directly contingent on the task structure of the problems being solved (the global task structure) and the environmental conditions under which the problems need to be solved. Here, the environmental conditions refer to such attributes as the task arrival rate, the task deadlines and the available resources.

To form or adapt their organizational structure, the agents use two organizational primitives: agent spawning and composition. These two primitives result in a change in the assignment of roles to the agents. Agent spawning is the generation of a new agent to handle a subset of the roles of the spawning agent. Agent composition, on the other hand, is orthogonal to agent spawning and involves the merging of two or more agents together — the combined agent is responsible for enacting all the roles of the agents being merged. Hence, OSD can be thought of as a search in the space of all the role assignments for a suitable role assignment that minimizes or maximizes a performance measure.

In order to participate in the organization, and to apply these primitives, the agents need to explicitly represent and reason about the role assignments and must maintain some organizational knowledge. This knowledge is represented in each agent using a TÆMS task structures, called the local task structure. Hence, we define a role as a local task structure. These local task structures are obtained by rewriting the global task structure and represent the local task view of the agent vis-a-vis its role in the organization and its relationship to other agents. Hence, all reorganization involves rewriting of the global task structure. However, note that the global task structure is NOT stored in any one agent, i.e. no single agent has a global view of the complete organization. Instead each agent's organizational knowledge is limited to the tasks that it must perform and the other agents that it must coordinate with — it is this information that is represented using the local task structures.

To allow the agents to store information about other agents in the task structure, we augment the basic TÆMS task representation language presented above by adding organizational nodes (O). Like TÆMS nodes, organizational nodes come in two flavors (i.e. $O = (T_O \cup M_O)$): (a) organizational tasks, (T_O), which are used to aggregate other organizational nodes; and (b) organizational methods, (M_O), that are used to represent either organizational knowledge or organizational actions that have some fixed semantics. To differentiate organizational nodes from "regular" TÆMS nodes (i.e. nodes that are in $T \cup M$), we will refer to non-organizational nodes as domain nodes (denoted as D). We define the following organizational nodes:

1. **Container-Nodes:** $\Sigma \subseteq T_O^3$, are aggregates of domain nodes and organizational nodes. Formally, $\Sigma = \{\sigma_1, \sigma_2, ..., \sigma_q\}$ where each $<\sigma_i = t_i, s_i>$. In this context $t_i \in \{ROOT, CLONE, COORDINATION\}$ is the type of the container and determines its purpose; and $s_i \subset (D \cup O)$ is the set of subtasks/nodes in that container.

2. **Non-Local-Nodes:** $\Delta \subset M_O$, are used to represent a domain node in some other agent's local task structure. Non-Local-Nodes are used to represent nodes in the global task structure that the agent knows the identity (label) of but does not know the characteristics (e.g. quality, cost duration) of [4]. Formally, $\Delta = \{\Delta_1, \Delta_2, ..., \Delta_n\}$; each Δ_i can be represented using a set consisting of a single element, $\eta \in \{LABEL(d) | d \in D\}$ that encapsulates the identity of an existing domain node.

3. **Clone Selectors:** $S_C \subset M_O$ are used to select amongst the clones of a node. The purpose of a selector node within a clone-container is to enable one or more of the clones, so that the enabled nodes can be "executed" by their agents owning those clones. See Section 4.1 for a more detailed formal description.

4. **NLE-Inheritors:** $N \subset M_O$, are methods whose sole purpose is to transfer the non-local effect from a non-cloned node to a cloned node or vice versa. See Section 4.1 for the rationale behind these nodes.

To allow for a change in an agent's organizational knowledge, we define three rewriting operations on a local task structure, which are described below. However, before any of these rewriting operators can be applied, we need to create an aggregator node (s), called a root node for storing "extra" organizational nodes that are created by the rewriting operations and that can not be affixed to any other part of the task structure. Recall, that we start off with a single agent whose local task view is equivalent to the global task view, t. Hence, the created root node will be $\sigma_1 = <ROOT, \{t\}>$. This node is shown on the left of Figure 2a.

Breakup: The rationale behind the breakup operator is to divide the workload of an agent so that parts of it can be assigned to a new agent during the spawning process. If the workload of an agent consisted only of independent executable methods (M), this would be a simple case of picking some subset of M for the spawned agent. However, in our problem domain, methods are (recursively) aggregated into tasks using CAFs and may have interrelationships (NLEs) with other tasks and methods. Hence, executable methods cannot be executed in isolation without considering all the interdependent effects of that execution.

Hence, when a spawning agent divides a local task structure, A into two subparts B (for itself) and C (for the spawned agent), it still needs to maintain some knowledge about the tasks/methods in C while, at the same time, allowing the spawned agent to have as much autonomy as possible about the execution of C. Specifically the agent will need to know about the subset of nodes in C that are interrelated to the nodes in B, either through NLEs or through subtask relations. We will call this subset the *related set*, of B. Similarly, the spawned agent will need to know some information about the nodes in B that are interrelated to the nodes in C through NLEs (i.e. the related set of C).

Furthermore, to allow for the maximum autonomy of both the spawning agent and the spawned agent, we limit this knowledge to consist of (1) the identity (label) of the nodes in the related set and (2) the relationship (i.e. subtask or NLE) through which they are related. Once the agent has been spawned, the two agents can negotiate a coordination mechanism for the relationship (for details see Section 4.2).

This knowledge will be preserved by creating non-local nodes (Δ's) to replace the nodes in the related set. During the breakup rewriting operation, the NLEs will be altered to point to/from the non-local nodes instead of the domain nodes in the *related sets*. These non-local-nodes will be added to the root-node. This process is illustrated in Figure 2a and the algorithm for the breakup operator is shown in Algorithm 1.

Merging: The idea behind the merging operator is to allow two agents to be composed into a single agent. Hence, merging involves combining two different local task structures from two different agents to form one local task structure.

Two requirements for the merging operation are (a) merging should be the exact inverse of breakup, i.e. if A is a task structure that was broken into B and C, merging B and C should give A; and (b) merging should be associative, i.e. the resultant local task structure formed after merging should not depend on

Figure 2. Figure showing the three task structure rewriting primitives. The ◇ nodes represent non-local nodes, that are the responsibility of some other agent. The ⊔ node (Node C(C)) is used to represent a clone container; the ⊥ node (Node S(C))is used to select which clone to "start", while the × nodes represent the NLE-inheriting-methods.

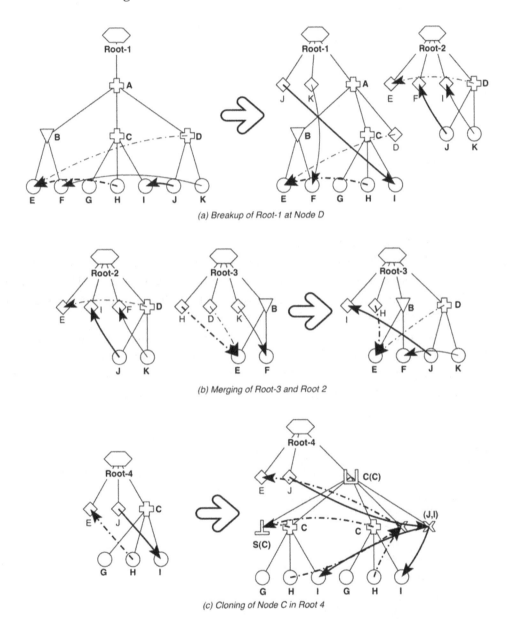

(a) Breakup of Root-1 at Node D

(b) Merging of Root-3 and Root 2

(c) Cloning of Node C in Root 4

the order in which the constituent local task structures were combined. Stated in another way, if using n breakup operations on a root node, σ, generates n local task structures ($\{\sigma_1, \sigma_2,..., \sigma_n\}$), then n merging operations on these task structures, *in any order*, should regenerate σ. Furthermore, note that there is no requirement that merging take place only between task structures that were previously broken up.

An example of a merging operation is shown in Figure 2b and the algorithm for the merge operator is shown in Algorithm 1. In order to fulfill these requirements, firstly, the domain nodes in the two local task

Algorithm 1.

Algorithm 1 BREAKUP ($\tau \in \Sigma$, $\upsilon \in D$)

1: $\bar{\tau} \Leftarrow$ DESCENDENTS(τ) $-$ DESCENDENTS(υ)
2: $\bar{\upsilon} \Leftarrow$ DESCENDENTS(υ)
3: **for all** { $N \mid N \in$ NLES(τ) } **do**
4:    **if** (SOURCE(N) $\in \bar{\tau}$ and SINK(N) $\in \bar{\upsilon}$) **or** (SOURCE(N) $\in \bar{\upsilon}$ and SINK(N) $\in \bar{\tau}$) **then**
5:       $x \Leftarrow$ GETNONLOCALNODE(SOURCE(N))
6:       $y \Leftarrow$ GETNONLOCALNODE(SINK(N))
7:       $M \Leftarrow$ COPYNLE(N)
8:       REPLACENODE(N, SOURCE(N), x)
9:       REPLACENODE(M, SINK(N), y)
10:   **end if**
11: **end for**
12: $x \Leftarrow$ GETNONLOCALNODE(υ)
13: REPLACENODE(τ, υ, x)
14: **return** CREATEROOTNODE(υ)

---

structures, σ_1, σ_2, have to be merged to form the same graph structure as in the global task structure. This is done in lines 4–8 of the algorithm. Furthermore, any non local nodes that might exist in DESCENDENTS(σ_1) that have corresponding domain nodes in σ_2 have to be eliminated and vice versa. This is done in lines 11–15 of the algorithm. Finally, any two non-local nodes that have the same identity should be merged into a single non-local node (lines 9–11) or formally $\exists \Delta_1, \exists \Delta_2 \mid (\Delta_1 = <\eta_1> \;\wedge\; \Delta_2 = <\eta_2> \;\wedge\; \eta_1 = \eta_2) \Rightarrow \Delta_1 = \Delta_2$.

Cloning: When we discussed the breakup operator above, we said that the rationale was to use it to "*divide the workload of an agent so that parts of it can be assigned to a new agent ...*". However, a precondition for applying the breakup operator is that number of executable methods in the root node, σ, (of the local task structure) of the spawning agent, A, should be greater than 1; ($\mid$ |{ $x \mid x \in$ DESCENDENTS(σ)

Algorithm 2.

Algorithm 2 MERGE ($\tau \in \Sigma$, $\upsilon \in \Sigma$)

1: Let $\upsilon \Leftarrow <ROOT, S_\upsilon>$
2: **for all** {$y \mid y \in$ DESCENDENTS(υ) } **do**
3:   $x \Leftarrow$ FINDNODE(τ, LABEL(y))
4:   **if** NULL(x) **then**
5:      DELETENODE(υ, y)
6:      **if** $y \in S_\upsilon$ **then**
7:         ADDNODE(τ, y)
8:      **end if**
9:   **else if** ($x \in \Delta$) **and** ($y \in \Delta$) **then**
10:      MERGENODES(τ, x, y)
11:   **else if** ($x \in D$) **and** ($y \in \Delta$) **then**
12:      DELETENODE(υ, y)
13:   **else if** ($x \in \Delta$) **and** ($y \in D$) **then**
14:      REPLACENODE(τ, x, y)
15:   **end if**
16: **end for**
17: **return** τ

$\wedge\ x \in M\}| > 1$). This precondition exists because it makes no sense for A to spawn off a new agent, B, and assign it the one and only executable method that agent A was executing — effectively freeing up A but creating a just as much overloaded agent, B.

To overcome this restriction, we introduce a cloning operator that is responsible for making two copies, $< c_1, c_2 >$ of a substructure, $v \in D^s$ so that the root task, t can be broken up at node, v, and the breakaway part, c_2, be allocated to a new agent. Hence, the cloning operator is always meant to be used in association with the breakup operator and the breakup operation should come after the cloning operation.

An example of the cloning operator is shown in Figure 2c and the algorithm is described in Algorithm 3. To clone a node, v in a root task, τ, we first create a new container node, $\sigma_c = < CLONE, \{v\}>$, called a *clone container* and replace v in τ with σ_c. The clone container will be used to "hold" all the created clones.

Next we need some mechanism to select amongst the clones, that is, when a new task instance arrives, we have to pick one of the clones (and by inference, one of the owning agents) to run that instance. To do this, ideally, we need to create a clone selector $s_c \in S_c$ method and add *enables* NLEs from s_c to both c_1 and c_2. Then method s_c has to be executed before any of the clones can be run and it can selectively enable one or more of the clones. However, the TÆMS formalism defined in Decker, 1995 does not specify the semantics of an enablement from a method to a task and we allow the clones (c_1 and c_2) to be tasks as well as methods. Rather than add semantics for the enablement between a method (the clone

Algorithm 3.

Algorithm 3 CLONE ($\tau \in \Sigma$, $\upsilon \in D$)
1: $\overline{\tau} \Leftarrow$ DESCENDENTS(τ) – DESCENDENTS(υ)
2: $\overline{\upsilon} \Leftarrow$ DESCENDENTS(υ)
3: $\phi \Leftarrow$ CREATECLONECONTAINER(υ)
4: **for all** $\{x \mid x \in \overline{\upsilon}\}$ **do**
5: $\quad y \Leftarrow$ COPYNODE(x)
6: $\quad$ ADDNODE(ϕ, y)
7: **end for**
8: **for all** $\{N \mid N \in$ NLES(υ) $\}$ **do**
9: $\quad$ **if** SOURCE(N) $\in \overline{\tau}$ **then**
10: $\quad\quad x \Leftarrow$ CREATEINHERITINGNODE()
11: $\quad\quad$ ADDNODE(ϕ, x)
12: $\quad\quad L \Leftarrow$ COPYNLE(N)
13: $\quad\quad M \Leftarrow$ COPYNLE(N)
14: $\quad\quad$ REPLACENODE(N, SINK(N), x)
15: $\quad\quad$ REPLACENODE(L, SOURCE(L), x)
16: $\quad\quad$ REPLACENODE(M, SOURCE(M), x)
17: $\quad\quad y \Leftarrow$ FINDNODE(ϕ, SINK(M))
18: $\quad\quad$ REPLACENODE(M, SINK(M), y)
19: $\quad$ **else if** SINK(N) $\in \overline{\tau}$ **then**
20: $\quad\quad$ { Similar to the source }
21: $\quad$ **end if**
22: **end for**
23: ADDNODE(ϕ, υ)
24: **return** ϕ

selector) and a task (the clone nodes), we achieve the same effect by (a) creating a disables NLE from the clone to the clone selector, s_c, and (b) always selecting s_c for execution in the scheduler. Since all the clones disable s_c, the only way to satisfy the task structure would be to run s_c before any of the clones. s_c can then selectively send results to the chosen clones.

Finally, there might be some NLEs in the clones c_1 and c_2 that have a source or destination as a non-clone node. (Formally, $\{ e \in E \mid [\text{SOURCE}(e) \in \text{DESCENDENTS}(c_j) \wedge \text{SINK}(e) \in (\text{DESCENDENTS} (\sigma) - \text{DESCENDENTS}(c_j))$ $\vee [\text{SINK}(e) \in \text{DESCENDENTS}(c_j) \wedge \text{SOURCE}(e) \in (\text{DESCENDENTS} (\sigma) - \text{DESCENDENTS}(c_j))] \}$).

Such NLEs that transcend clone boundaries have to be handled carefully in order to (a) preserve their original semantics and (b) allow the presence of clones to be transparent to the non-clone nodes. In order to achieve this effect, we create special methods called *NLE-Inheritors*, (N). These methods are simply conduits for the effects from the cloned nodes to the non-clone nodes.

In addition to being used for load balancing, another advantage of the cloning operator is that it can be used to increase the robustness capacity of an agent by having multiple agents work on the same task simultaneously. However, the details are outside the scope of this chapter (See Kamboj and Decker (2008) for details).

These operators result in the rewriting of a local task structure. In the case of agent spawning, the spawning agent, A, selects a node, $v \in D$ for breakup, runs the breakup operator to divide its local task structure into two parts, $< \sigma_1, \sigma_2 >$, and then spawns a new agent, B, with σ_2 as its local task structure.

For agent composition, on the other hand, composing agent, A with a local task structure σ_1, selects another agent, B with a local task structure σ_2, to compose with. Agent A then sends a message to Agent B requesting composition. Agent B then calls the merging operator to merge σ_1 and σ_2 to form a single local task structure, σ. Agent B can now be killed and the composition operation is now compete.

Coordinating the Agents

We allow various coordination mechanisms to be used with our approach. Coordination between the agents is also achieved by rewriting the local task structures of the agents. Recall that a newly spawned agent will have local tasks structure consisting of domain nodes and organizational nodes. The organizational nodes consist of, amongst other things, non-local-nodes (Δ) that represent domain nodes in other agents. These non-local nodes form coordination points between the agents and will be overwritten with coordination nodes corresponding to the selected coordination mechanism.

To select a coordination mechanism, (1) the newly spawned agent starts off a negotiation phase in which it send a mechanism proposal for all the non-local-nodes to the agents that own the corresponding domain nodes; (2) the other agents can either accept the coordination mechanism or they can send a counter-proposal. This exchange is repeated until both the agents commit to the same coordination mechanism or until all the coordination mechanisms are exhausted, in which case the default coordination mechanism is chosen.

Whereas many coordination mechanism can potentially be supported by our approach, we have currently only implemented the send-results/wait-for-results mechanism[6]. In this mechanism, each agent executes methods independently of the other agents and sends a result to the other agents as soon as they become available. If to execute a method, an agent needs results from another agents, it simply waits for those results. The addition of this coordination mechanism to the local task structures is shown in Figure 3. In the future, we would like to implement more complicated coordination mechanisms.

Figure 3. Figure showing the addition of coordination nodes to the task structure. The Π node represents a coordination task. The $|\Rightarrow$ methods (Nodes H and D) involve sending results to the specified nodes while the $\Rightarrow|$ method (Node K) indicates that the agent needs to wait for a result from whatever agent is processing that node. The $\square$ node is added to allow Node B to wait for the preceding node, while the $\triangleright$ node is used to start the succeeding nodes.

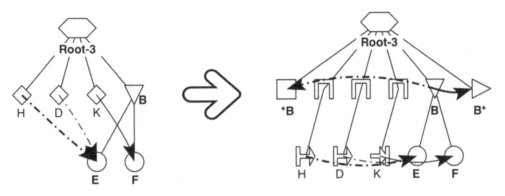

Detecting the Need for Organizational Change

As organizational change is expensive (requiring clock cycles, allocation/deallocation of resources, etc.) we want a stable organizational structure that is well suited to the task and environmental conditions at hand. Hence, we wish to change the organizational structure only if the task structure and/or environmental conditions change. Also to allow temporary changes to the environmental conditions to be overlooked, we want the probability of an organizational change to be inversely proportional to the time since the last organizational change. If this time is relatively short, the agents are still adjusting to the changes in the environment - hence the probability of an agent initiating an organizational change should be high. Similarly, if the time since the last organizational change is relatively large, we wish to have a low probability of organizational change.

To allow this variation in probability of organizational change, we use simulated annealing to determine the probability of keeping an existing organizational structure. This probability is calculated using the annealing formula:

$$p = e^{\frac{-\Delta E}{kT}}$$

where ΔE is the "amount" of overload/underload[7], T is the time since the last organizational change and k is a constant. The mechanism of computing ΔE is different for agent spawning than for agent composition and is described below. From this formula, if T is large, p, or the probability of keeping the existing organizational structure is large. The probability of organizational change, q, can be calculated using the formula, $q = 1 - p$. Note that the value of p is capped at a certain threshold in order to prevent the organization from being too sluggish in its reaction to environmental change.

Agent Spawning

Agent spawning should only occur when the agent doing the spawning is too overloaded to complete the tasks in its task queue by their given deadlines. The obvious question then is: *"How can the agents know when they are overloaded?"*

One way in which the agents could detect overload would be to wait till they fail to complete their tasks on time (i.e. an agent could wait till the deadline on a task in its task queue is exceeded). Two problems with this approach are:

1. An agent executing a method may, on a single run at any given time, take significantly longer to finish it than normal. That is, the missed deadline may be a one-time occurrence. This is because, usually, there is some uncertainty in the time needed to execute a method[8]. Hence, missing a deadline on the current execution run does not automatically imply that the agent is overloaded or that it will consistently miss deadlines in the future.

2. The overload diagnosis only occurs after the agents have already failed to execute tasks in their task queue. Ideally, we would prefer to diagnose and prevent task failures before they actually occur.

The first problem can easily be rectified if the agents wait for a certain percentage of the tasks in their respective task queues to fail before spawning off new agents. However, this solution does nothing to address the second problem.

To have a more proactive approach to organizational structuring, we use two different items of information as described below:

Meta-Information about the task: By meta-information, we mean the information about the characteristics of a task. For our purposes, we make use of three pieces of meta-information about the tasks being attempted:

*   the *min time* or the absolute minimum time that agent must have in order to have a non-zero probability of completing the task;
*   the *expt time* or the expected time needed to complete the task; and
*   the *g_min time*[9] or the minimum time needed to guarantee task completion, in the absence of failures. (That is, the time needed to have a probability of 1 of completing the task, in the absence of failures).

To understand the difference between the three, consider an executable method that has two outcomes, the first of which takes a minimum of 3 cycles and a maximum of 5 cycles to execute and the second of which takes a minimum of 5 and a maximum of 7 cycles to execute. Now, the agent needs at least three cycles to have a non-zero probability of completing this executable method, which would be the case if the executable method had the first outcome and took only 3 cycles to achieve it. Hence the *min time* is 3. Also, the agent needs at least 7 cycles to guarantee task completion[10] — hence the *g_min time* is 7. The *expt time* would be the amount of time it takes to complete the method on average and would depend on the probability of the two outcomes.

Formally, let

Outcomes(Method): M → {(o,p) | o is an outcome of M ∧ p is the probability of outcome o}

be a function that returns the outcomes of a method and *DurationD (Outcome): O → {(m,q) | m ∈ N ∧ q ∈ ℜ⁺},* be a function that returns the duration distribution of outcome, *O*. Then:

- $min(m \in M) \leftarrow \min_{(o,p) \in Outcomes(m)} \left[\min_{(m,q) \in DurationD(o)} m \right]$

- $expt(m \in M) \leftarrow \sum_{(o,p) \in Outcomes(m)} p * \left[\sum_{(m,q) \in DurationD(o)} (m*q) \right]$

- $g\_min(m \in M) \leftarrow \max_{(o,p) \in Outcomes(m)} \left[\max_{(m,q) \in DurationD(o)} m \right]$

The meta-information for a higher-level node (task) depends on both the CAF of the task and the meta-information of its subtasks. Formally, if CAF(Task) : T → {MIN, MAX, SUM, EXACTLY_ONE} is a function that returns the characteristic accumulation function of a task, then this meta-information can be recursively computed from the meta-information of the subtasks using the formulas

$$min(t \in T) \leftarrow \begin{cases} \sum_{t_j \in SUBTASKS(t)} min(t_j) & \text{if } CAF(t) = \text{MIN} \\ \min_{t_j \in SUBTASKS(t)} min(t_j) & \text{if } CAF(t) = \{\text{SUM, MAX, EXACTLY\_ONE}\} \end{cases}$$

$$expt(t \in T) \leftarrow \begin{cases} \sum_{t_j \in SUBTASKS(t)} expt(t_j) & \text{if } CAF(t) = \text{MIN} \\ soh_{t_j \in SUBTASKS(t)} expt(t_j) & \text{if } CAF(t) = \{\text{SUM, MAX}\} \\ avg_{t_j \in SUBTASKS(t)} expt(t_j) & \text{if } CAF(t) = \text{EXACTLY\_ONE} \end{cases}$$

$$g\_min(t \in T) \leftarrow \begin{cases} \sum_{t_j \in SUBTASKS(t)} g\_min(t_j) & \text{if } CAF(t) = \text{MIN} \\ \min_{t_j \in SUBTASKS(t)} g\_min(t_j) & \text{if } CAF(t) = \{\text{SUM, MAX,} \\ & \text{EXACTLY\_ONE}\} \end{cases}$$

The effective time available for completion of a task: The time available for completion of a task is computed by assuming that all tasks are equally important, that all tasks need to be executed and that the total time available needs to be equally divided amongst all the outstanding tasks.[11] If these assumptions hold, we can compute the time available using the steps given in Algorithm 4. Refer to Figure 4 for an example demonstrating the use of these steps.

Given these two pieces of information, the agent using Algorithm 5 to determine if agent spawning is necessary. The crux of this algorithm is the *for* loop on lines 4 and 7, which compares the effective time available for a task, $t_{avail}(Task_i)$, against $min(Task_i)$. If the former is smaller, the agent is guaranteed to fail on the current task and the agent immediately spawns off a new agent (line 5). If, on the other hand, $t_{avail}(Task_i)$ is greater than $min(Task_i)$ but less than $g\_min(Task_i)$, the agent uses simulated

Algorithm 4.

Algorithm 4 Algorithm to compute the effective time available for a task
1: Let $\text{AT}(t_i) \rightarrow N^+$ be a function that returns the arrival time of a task t_i.
2: Let $\text{DT}(t_i) \rightarrow N^+$ be a function that returns the deadline of a task t_i.
3: Fig. 4b: Divide the total time into consecutive time slices bounded by the arrival times and deadlines of each task
4: Let $\text{START}(ts_i)$ and $\text{END}(ts_i)$ be two functions that respectively return the starting and ending times of a time slice , ts.
{ Fig. 4c: Compute the time available per task for each time slice }
5: **for** each time slice, ts_i **do**
6:     $n[ts_i] \Leftarrow$ number of outstanding tasks in time slice i
7:     $d[ts_i] \Leftarrow \text{END}(ts_i) - \text{START}(ts_i) + 1$
8:     $t_{avail}[ts_i] \Leftarrow d[ts_i] / n[ts_i]$
9: **end for**
{ Fig. 4d: Compute the total effective time available for each task }
10: **for** each task, t_j in the task queue **do**
11:     $MySlices \Leftarrow \{ ts \mid \text{AT}(t_j) \leq \text{START}(ts) \text{ and } \text{END}(ts) \leq \text{DT}(t_j) \}$
12:     $t_{avail}[t_j] \Leftarrow \sum_{ts_i \in MySlices} t_{avail}[ts_i]$
13: **end for**

Algorithm 5.

Algorithm 5 Algorithm to determine if agent spawning is necessary
1: Let $T_{curr} \Leftarrow$ be the current time (the time instance at which this algorithm is run)
2: **for** $Task_i$ in $OutstandingTaskQueue$ **do**
3:     Let $t_{avail}(Task_i) \Leftarrow$ be the effective time available for $Task_i$, computed using Algorithm 4.
4:     **if** $t_{avail}(Task_i) < min(Task_i)$ **then**
5:         SPAWNAGENT()
6:     **else**
7:         **if** $min(Task_i) < t_{avail}(Task_i) < g\_min(Task_i)$ **then**
8:             SPAWNAGENT() with probability, p, calculated using the annealing formula, with $$\Delta E = \frac{1}{\alpha[t_{avail}(Task_i) - min(Task_i)] + (1 - \alpha)[g\_min(Task_i) - min(Task_i)]}$$ where α is a constant
9:         **else**
10:             do nothing
11:         **end if**
12:     **end if**
13: **end for**

annealing to calculate if a new agent should be spawned, with ΔE computed as shown in Equation 1. The reasoning behind computing ΔE like this is that if $t_{avail}(Task_i)$ is less than $g\_min(Task_i)$, there is some probability of the agent failing $Task_i$ due to a lack of time.

The probability of keeping an existing organizational structure in this case should then be proportional to (and ΔE should be inversely proportional to[12]): (a) the difference between the effective time

Figure 4. Figure demonstrating the steps required to compute the effective time available for completion of a task on an example task queue with four outstanding tasks. Tasks 1, 2, 3 and 4 have arrival times of 1, 2, 3 and 3 respectively. The deadlines for the four tasks are, in order, 5, 6, 5, and 8.

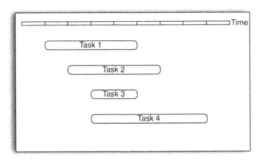

(a) The four outstanding tasks represented on a timeline.

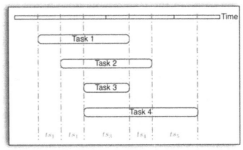

(b) The total time is divided into consecutive time slices, bounded by the arrival time and deadline of the tasks.

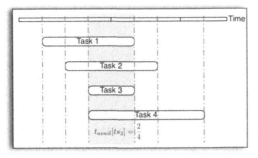

(c) The time-available-per-task is computed for each time slice.

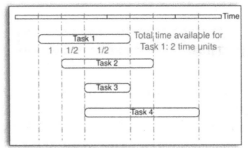

(d) The time available for a task is computed by summing up the time-available-per-task for each time slice in which the task appears.

available, $t_{avail}(Task_i)$, and $min(Task_i)$; and (b) the difference between $g\_min(Task_i)$ and $t_{avail}(Task_i)$, with α being a constant used to determine which of the terms (a) or (b) gets to dominate the calculation. We use former term, Term (a), because the closer $t_{avail}(Task_i)$ is to $min(Task_i)$ the greater the chance of the agent failing a task. We use the latter term, Term (b), because the greater the value of this difference, the greater the disparity between two outcomes of the method — one that takes a large amount of time and one that takes a smaller amount of time.

Note that since agent spawning is triggered by an indication that the agents might fail on the tasks in the task queue as opposed to actual failure on a task, the agents can be thought to have a proactive approach to organizational design.

Agent Composition

Agent composition is exactly orthogonal to agent spawning as agent composition only occurs when the agents are underloaded. In such a situation, some of the agents will be sitting idle waiting for tasks to arrive. These idle agents will either be utilizing resources while waiting, or more likely, will have resources allocated to them that could be used elsewhere in the system. An example of the former case is when agents are using CPU cycles while waiting (busy waiting). An example of the latter case is when agents have been allocated network bandwidth that is being unused while the agents are sitting idle. In either case, there is an inefficiency in the allocation and use of resources. In such cases, it makes sense to combine some of the free agents with other agents thus freeing unused resources.[13]

To calculate if agent composition is necessary, we again use the simulated annealing equation. However, in this case, ΔE is computed differently and is proportional to the amount of time for which the agent was idle. In particular, $\Delta E = \beta * Idle\_Time$, where β is a constant and $Idle\_Time$ is the amount of time for which the agent was idle. If the agent has been sitting idle for a long period of time, ΔE is large, which implies that p, the probability of keeping the existing organizational structure, is low. Since agent composition only occurs after the agent is already idle (and hence already wasting resources), the agents can also be thought to have a reactive approach to organizational design.

Hence, organizational design in our agents is both proactive (in the case of agent spawning) and reactive (in the case of agent composition). This combination of proactive and reactive behavior gives our agents the ability to complete as many tasks as possible, as the agents react quickly to bad news (inability to complete the outstanding tasks) and slowly to good news (the agents are underloaded).

EVALUATION

To evaluate our approach, we ran a series of experiments that simulated the operation of both the OSD agents and the Contract Net agents on various task structures with varied arrival rates and deadlines. At the start of each experiment, a random TÆMS task structure was generated with a specified depth and branching factor. During the course of the experiment, a series of task instances (problems) arrive at the organization and must be completed by the agents before their specified deadlines.

To directly compare the OSD approach with the Contract Net approach, each experiment was repeated several times — using OSD agents on the first run and a different number of Contract Net agents on each subsequent run. We were careful to use the same task structure, task arrival times, task deadlines and random numbers for each of these trials.

We divided the experiments into two groups: experiments in which the environment was static (fixed task arrival rates and deadlines) and experiments in which the environment was dynamic (varying arrival rates and/or deadlines).

The two graphs in Figure 5, show the average performance of the OSD organization against the Contract Net organizations with 8, 10, 12 and 14 agents. The results shown are the averages of running 40 experiments. 20 of those experiments had a static environment with a fixed task arrival time of 15 cycles and a deadline window of 20 cycles. The remaining 20 experiments had a varying task arrival rate - the task arrival rate was changed from 15 cycles to 30 cycles and back to 15 cycles after every 20 tasks. In all the experiments, the task structures were randomly generated with a maximum depth of 4 and a maximum branching factor of 3. The runtime of all the experiments was 2500 cycles.

Graphs 6a, 6b, 6c and 6d show the variation in the various measured characteristics over time for a randomly chosen experiment under static environmental conditions for a range of performance characteristics. Similarly, graphs 7a, 7b, 7c and 7d demonstrate the performance of the various groups of agents under dynamic conditions.

Figure 5. Average performance for all experiments: Graph comparing the average performance of the OSD organization with the Contract Net organizations (with 8, 10, 12 and 14 agents). The error bars show the standard deviations.

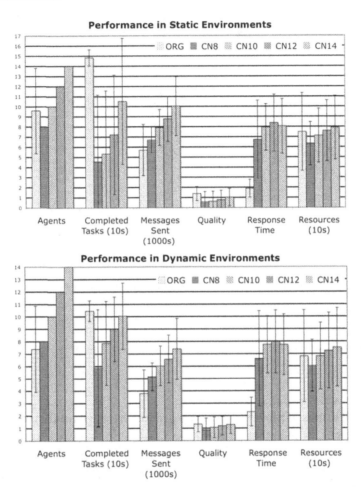

We tested several hypotheses relating to the comparative performance of our OSD approach using the Wilcoxon Matched-Pair Signed-Rank tests. Matched-Pair signifies that we are comparing the performance of each system on precisely the same randomized task set within each separate experiment. The tested hypotheses are:

1. **The OSD organization requires fewer agents to complete an equal or larger number of tasks when compared to the Contract Net organization:** To test this hypothesis, we tested the stronger null hypothesis that states that the contract net agents complete more tasks. This null hypothesis is rejected for all contract net organizations with less than 14 agents (static: $p < 0.0003$; dynamic: $p < 0.03$). For large contract net organizations, the number of tasks completed is statistically equivalent to the number completed by the OSD agents, however the number of agents used by the OSD organization is smaller: 9.59 agents (in the static case) and 7.38 agents (in the dynamic case) versus 14 contract net agents[14]. Thus the original hypothesis, that OSD requires fewer agents to complete an equal or larger number of tasks, is upheld.

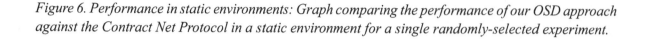

Figure 6. Performance in static environments: Graph comparing the performance of our OSD approach against the Contract Net Protocol in a static environment for a single randomly-selected experiment.

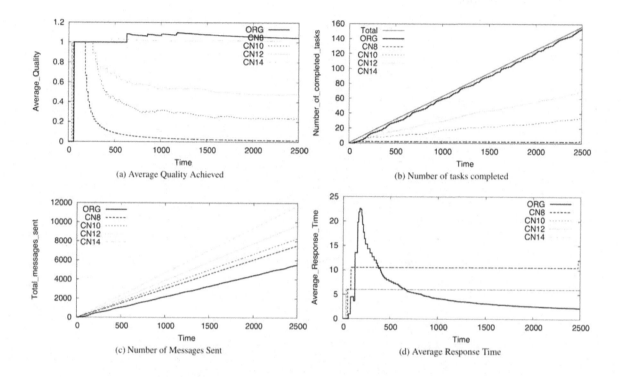

2. **The OSD organizations achieve an equal or greater average quality than the Contract Net organizations:** The null hypothesis is that the Contract Net agents achieve a greater average quality. We can reject the null hypothesis for contract net organizations with less than 12 agents (static: $p < 0.01$; dynamic: $p < 0.05$). For larger contract net organizations, the average quality is statistically equivalent to that achieved by OSD.

3. **The OSD agents have a lower average response time as compared to the Contract Net agents:** The null hypothesis that OSD has the same or higher response time is rejected for all contract net organizations (static: $p < 0.0002$; dynamic: $p < 0.0004$).

4. **The OSD agents send less messages than the Contract Net Agents:** The null hypothesis that OSD sends the same or more messages is rejected for all contract net organizations ($p < 0.003$ in all cases except 8 contract net agents in a static environment where $p < 0.02$)

Hence, as demonstrated by the above tests, our agents perform better than the contract net agents as they complete a larger number of tasks, achieve a greater quality and also have a lower response time and communication overhead. These results make intuitive sense given our goals for the OSD approach. We expected the OSD organizations to have a faster average response time and to send less messages because the agents in the OSD organization are not wasting time and messages sending bid requests and replying to bids. The quality gained on the tasks is directly dependent on the number of tasks completed, hence the more the number of tasks completed, the greater average quality. The results of

Figure 7. Performance in dynamic environments: Graph comparing the performance of our OSD approach against the Contract Net Protocol in a dynamic environment for a single randomly-selected experiment.

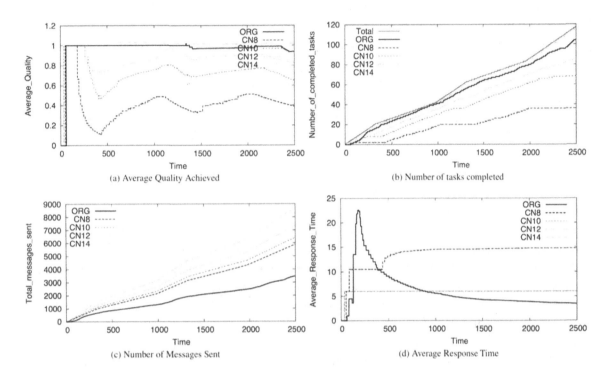

(a) Average Quality Achieved

(b) Number of tasks completed

(c) Number of Messages Sent

(d) Average Response Time

testing the first hypothesis were slightly more surprising. It appears that due to the inherent inefficiency of the contract net protocol in bidding for each and every task instance, a greater number of agents are needed to complete an equal number of tasks.

CONCLUSION

In this chapter, we have presented an approach to OSD – a method of designing organizations at run-time in which the agents are responsible for generating their own organizational structures. Our OSD approach uses two primitives *agent spawning* and *agent composition*, which in association with the three task rewriting operators: *breakup, merge* and *clone* are used to dynamically create and modify the organization at run-time. Furthermore, we have demonstrated how the individual agents can be coordinated and have shown how a need for organizational change can be detected.

We have also compared our OSD approach to the contract net protocol and have shown that the organizations generated by our approach perform better than the contract net organizations as they complete a larger number of tasks, achieve a greater quality and also have a lower response time and communication overhead. Finally, in the next section, we present some interesting future lines of research.

Relation to Other Chapters in this Book

A complimentary approach, the Organization Model for Adaptive Computational Systems (OMACS), to designing dynamic organizations is presented in Chapter IV "OMACS: A Framework for Adaptive Complex Systems" by DeLoach) of this book. The OMACS approach defines an organization in terms of the goals of the organization, the roles needed to achieve those goals, the constituent agents that make up the organization and the capabilities of the constituent agents. The OMACS approach also describes a set of relations/functions (achieves, requires, possesses, etc.) that can be used to map agents to roles and goals so as to maximize an *organization assignment function (OAF)*.

The primary difference between the OMACS approach and our OSD approach is the primary focus of the work - The OMACS approach emphasizes the agents that make up the organization and tries to find a good allocation (one that maximizes the *OAF* function) of agents to the roles and goals of the organization. Our OSD approach, on the other hand, emphasizes the problems or goals that the organization is trying to achieve. The idea behind our approach is that the multiagent designer is primarily concerned with the set of problems that he/she wishes to solve and should not have to worry about the details of the organization that solves those problems. The OMACS approach is more suitable when there are a fixed set of pre-existing agents in the multiagent system whose capabilities are known. Our OSD approach is more geared towards real-world applications in grid/volunteer/cloud computing where a user has a workflow that he/she wishes to enact and OSD can be used for the purposes of task/resource allocation. Our OSD approach also focuses on the mechanism by which the reorganization occurs and we have presented a distributed algorithm that can be used for the task/resource allocation. The OMACS approach allows various reorganization algorithms to be used though most of them are centralized. Another difference between the OMCAS approach and the OSD approach is that the OMCAS approach is more similar to a one-off task/resource allocation scheme like the contract net protocol in that it treats every problem instance as separate and creates a different organization for each.

There are, however, similarities between the OMACS approach and our OSD approach. The TÆMS task representation language is very general and can be used to represent many of the concepts in the OMACS approach. For example, the goals in OMACS are Tasks in TÆMS; the roles are equivalent to the executable methods; and the concept of roles requiring capabilities can be represented by the mapping of executable methods to the set of resources needed for executing the method. Finally, the assignment of agents to roles and goals is done in our approach by "creating" agents that have allocated the desired set of resources on the grid/cloud.

Other chapters in this book that deal with dynamic organizations include Chapter XIX "Dynamic Specifications for Norm-Governed Computational Systems" by Artikis et al. and Chapter XX "Interactions Between Formal and Informal Organizational Networks" by Lamieri and Mangalagiu. The former chapter primarily deals with norms in open systems. In that chapter, the authors describe how the agents might change the *rules of behavior* of the agents in the system. Since our approach does not deal with open systems, we do not discuss norms in our approach (although using different coordination algorithms can capture some of the ideas presented in that chapter). The latter chapter primarily deals with using agent based modeling to study human organizations. Our approach on the other hand is solely concerned with software organizations.

FUTURE RESEARCH

In our future work, we plan to:

1. *Implement other coordination mechanisms and evaluate the relative performance of these mechanisms.* In particular, we would like to answer questions like: (a) Do certain coordination mechanisms preclude the use of certain organizational structures, or vice versa; and (b) What coordination protocols are suitable for an arbitrary type of organizational structure? Towards this end, we will be looking at both commitments made during spawning and mechanisms available during execution of a task instance.

2. *Evaluate the effect of changes in the organizational design constraints on the kinds of organizations that can be generated.*

   Recall that in our approach, we start off with an organization consisting of a single agent. If the agent can't complete the tasks in its task queue by their respective deadlines, the agent spawns off a new agent. Hence, the hard constraint that tasks must be completed by their deadlines is an organizational design constraint, since it directly affects both the formation of the initial organization and the subsequent reorganizations that takes place.

   Our approach can be easily extended to make use of different organizational design constraints (such as desired quality or maximum cost) to guide the organizational formation process. In such cases, instead of having the available time (which might be a function of the number of outstanding tasks in the task queue) guide the formation process, another constraint like, say, the desired quality might be used instead.

   We would like to investigate (a) how changes in the design constraints (such as tightening of deadlines, changes in the maximum cost or number of agents allowed, constraints on the coordination mechanisms permitted, etc) might affect the organization formation process; and (b) how multiple organizational design constraints might be combined together to guide the formation process. It is not entirely obvious how the latter might be attempted as some of the design constraints might conflict with each other and finding a satisficing organization might be non-trivial. Therefore, we would like to investigate all the issues associated with using multiple organizational design constraints

3. *Show how existing workflow languages might benefit from the use of organizational modeling,* especially the kind of modeling being done by our approach. Most existing workflow languages (like Business Process Execution Language for Web Services (BPEL4WS) (Juric, 2006), Grid-Flow (Guan et al., 2005), and Grid Services Flow Language (Krishnan et al., 2002)) are very procedural, in that they describe exactly how workflows are composed of their component subtasks, but do not allow alternatives workflows based on environmental conditions. As argued by (Atlas et al., 2005), such approaches are fairly rigid and are not suitable for dynamic environments.

   We strongly believe that grids and web services would benefit from using a more declarative approach, in which the workflow is represented using TÆMS and an approach similar to ours is used for "executing" these workflows. We would like to use a detailed example to show why this is the case.

REFERENCES

Atlas, J., Swany, M., & Decker, K. S. (2005). Flexible grid workflows using TÆMS. *Workshop on Exploring Planning and Scheduling for Web Services, Grid and Autonomic Computing.*

Barber, K. S., & Martin, C. E. (2001). Dynamic reorganization of decision-making groups. In *AGENTS '01: Proceedings of the fifth international conference on Autonomous agents*, pages 513–520, New York, NY, USA. ACM Press.

Carley, K. M ., & Gasser, L. (1999). Computational organization theory. In Wiess, G., editor, *Multiagent Systems: A Modern Approach to Distributed Artificial Intelligence*, pages 299–330, Cambridge, MA. MIT Press.

Chen, W ., & Decker, K. S. (2005). The analysis of coordination in an information system application - emergency medical services. In *Lecture Notes in Computer Science (LNCS), number 3508*, pages 36–51. Springer-Verlag.

Corkill, D ., & Lesser, V. (1983). The use of meta-level control for coordination in a distributed problem solving network. *Proceedings of the Eighth International Joint Conference on Artificial Intelligence*, pages 748–756.

Decker, K. S. (1995). Environment centered analysis and design of coordination mechanisms. *Ph.D. Thesis, Department of Computer Science, University of Massachusetts*, Amherst.

Decker, K. S. (1997). Task environment centered simulation. In Prietula, M., Carley, K., and Gasser, L., editors, *Simulating Organizations: Computational Models of Institutions and Groups, pages 105–131.* AAAI Press/MIT Press.

Decker, K. S ., & Li, J. (2000). Coordinating mutually exclusive resources using GPGP. *Autonomous Agents and Multi-Agent Systems, 3*(2), 133–157.

Dignum, V., Dignum, F., & Sonenberg, L. (2004). Towards dynamic reorganization of agent societies. In *Proceedings of CEAS: Workshop on Coordination in Emergent Agent Societies at ECAI*, pages 22–27, Valencia, Spain.

Guan, Z., Hernandez, F., Bangalore, P., Gray, J., Skjellum, A., Velusamy, V., & Liu, Y. (2005). Gridflow: A grid-enabled scientific workflow system with a petri-net-based interface. *Concurrency and Computation: Practice and Experience*, 18(10):1115–1140.

Horling, B., Benyo, B., & Lesser, V. (2001). Using self-diagnosis to adapt organizational structures. In AGENTS '01: *Proceedings of the fifth international conference on Autonomous agents*, pages 529–536, New York, NY, USA. ACM Press.

Horling, B ., & Lesser, V. (2005). Analyzing, modeling and predicting organizational effects in a distributed sensor network. *Journal of the Brazilian Computer Society, Special Issue on Agents Organizations*, pages 9–30.

Horling, B. (2006). Quantitative Organizational Modeling and Design for Multi-Agent Systems. *PhD thesis, University of Massachusetts at Amherst.*

Ishida, T., Gasser, L., & Yokoo, M. (1992). Organization self-design of distributed production systems. *IEEE Transactions on Knowledge and Data Engineering*, 4(2):123–134.

Juric, M. B. (2006). *Business Process Execution Language for Web Services: BPEL and BPEL4WS*. Packt Publishing, 2nd edition edition.

Kamboj, S ., & Decker, K. S. (2008). Exploring robustness in the context of organizational self-design. *AAAI 2008 Workshop on Coordination, Organizations, Institutions and Norms in Agent Systems (COIN)*.

Krishnan, S., Wagstrom, P., & von Laszewski, G. (2002). GSFL: A workflow framework for grid services. ANL/MCS-P980-0802.

Lesser, V. R., Decker, K., Wagner, T., Carver, N., Garvey, A., Horling, B., Neiman, D. E., Podorozhny, R. M., Prasad, M. V. N., Ra ja, A., Vincent, R., Xuan, P., & Zhang, X. (2004). Evolution of the GPGP/ TÆMS domain-independent coordination framework. *Autonomous Agents and Multi Agent Systems*, 9(1-2), 87–14

Lesser, V., Horling, B., Klassner, F., Raja, A., Wagner, T., & Zhang, S. X. (2000). BIG: An agent for resource-bounded information gathering and decision making. *Artificial Intelligence*, 118(1-2), 197–244

Lesser, V., Horling, B., Raja, A., Wagner, T., & Zhang, X. (2000). Resource-Bounded Searches in an Information Marketplace. *IEEE Internet Computing: Agents on the Net*, 4(2), 49–57.

Nair, R., Tambe, M., and Marsella, S. (2003). Role allocation and reallocation in multiagent teams: Towards a practical analysis. In *Proceedings of the Second International Joint Conference on Autonomous Agents and Multi-agent Systems (AAMAS-03)*, pages 552–559.

Shehory, O., Sycara, K., Chalasani, P., and Jha, S. (1998). Agent cloning: an approach to agent mobility and resource allocation. *IEEE Communications Magazine*, 36(7), 58–67.

Smith, R. G ., & Davis, R. (1978). Distributed problem solving: The contract net approach. In *Proceedings of the 2nd National Conference of the Canadian Society for Computational Studies of Intelligence*.

So, Y ., & Durfee, E. (1993). An organizational self-design model for organizational change. In *AAAI-93 Workshop on AI and Theories of Groups and Organizations: Conceptual and Empirical Research*, pages 8–15, Washington, D.C.

Wagner, T. (2004). Coordination decision support assistants (coordinators). *Technical Report 04-29, BAA*.

Wagner, T ., & Lesser, V. (2000). Design-to-criteria scheduling: Real-time agent control. *Proceedings of AAAI 2000 Spring Symposium on Real-Time Autonomous Systems, pages 89–96*.

Zimmerman, T. L., Smith, S., Gallagher, A. T., Barbulescu, L., and Rubinstein, Z. (2007). Distributed management of flexible times schedules. In *Sixth International conference on Autonomous Agents and Multiagent Systems (AAMAS)*.

KEY TERMS

Agent Composition: The combining or merging of two agents together to form a single agent responsible for all the activities of the two combined agents.

Agent Spawning: The creation of a new agent to handle part of the workload of the spawning agent.

Global Task Structure: A TÆMS task structure representing the complete problem being solved by the multiagent system. The global task is equivalent to a workflow in grid/cloud computing terminology.

Local Task Structure: A TÆMS task structure that is used to represents the local task view and organizational knowledge of an agent. The local-task structure is used to represent roles and relationships within an agent.

Organizational Self-Design: A method of designing organizations at run-time in which the agents are responsible for generating their own organizational structures.

Organizational Structure: The union of the roles and relationships that exist within an organization. The organizational structure is used to constrain and guide the activities of agents in the organization.

Relationships: The coordination relationships that exist between subparts of a problem.

Roles: The parts played by the agents enacting the roles in the solution to the problem. The roles reflect the long-term commitments made by the agents in question to a certain course of action (that includes task responsibility, authority, and mechanisms for coordination).

TÆMS: Acronym for Task Analysis, Environment Modeling and Simulation. TÆMS is a computational framework for representing and reasoning about complex task environments in which problems are represented using extended hierarchical task network structures.

Task Rewriting: The process of modifying a task structure. Task rewriting is achieved using a set of operators that act on one or more local-task structures to generate new local-task structures. Task rewriting is usually the first step in changing the organizational structure of an agent.

ENDNOTES

[1] N is the set of natural numbers including zero and N^+ is the set of positive natural numbers excluding zero.

[2] P is the power set of set, i.e., the set of all subsets of a set

[3] Currently, $\Sigma = T_O$, that is, the only type of organizational tasks that have been defined are container nodes. However, we might need to add other organizational tasks in the future.

[4] At least initially at the time of breakup. It can however learn these characteristics through some coordination mechanism

[5] Note that we allow both tasks and methods to be cloned

[6] This mechanism is equivalent to the GPGP "DO" Commitment

7   Note that even though we are using the deadlines of the task instances as the primary impetus for organizational change, nothing in our work precludes the use of other performance metrics for detecting a need for organizational change. For example, we could decide to reorganize whenever the quality on the tasks falls below a certain threshold.

8   Recall that in TÆMS, the durations of the executable methods are probabilistic, in that, methods are allowed to have multiple outcomes with different probabilities. Furthermore, each outcome is allowed to take a varying amount of time to complete based on some probability distribution. Hence, we can typically only calculate expected durations, or likely upper and lower bounds on the duration.

9   Note that the *g_min time* is the same as the worst-case execution time (or *wcet*) for executable methods. However, for some task CAFs, this time may differ significantly from the task's worst-case execution time. To see why, consider a task, T, with a SUM CAF and two executable methods A and B. A and B have *g_min times* (*wcets*) of 2 and 7 respectively. Now, the wcet of T is 9, which occurs when the agent decides to schedule both methods A and B. However, the *g_min time* is only 2, since the agent only needs to schedule method A to guarantee a non-zero quality for task T.

10 The reasoning behind the *g_min time* is that the agent cannot control the outcome of a method and, furthermore, has no way of knowing the actual duration of an outcome. This is because an agent can only decide on whether or not to execute a particular method but has no way of influencing or controlling the actual execution of the method. Hence, to guarantee method completion, the agent needs to allocate the maximum amount of time that any outcome of the method might take to complete.

11 These assumptions do not guarantee optimality in any way. Rather it is trivial to demonstrate a case where an agent would gain more quality by ignoring certain tasks. These assumptions have been chosen for simplicity rather than for optimality.

12 Recall that if ΔE is large, p or the probability of keeping an existing organizational structure is low.

13 Another reason for combining agents might be to reduce the coordination overhead associated with the communication delay between the agents. If the communication time is greater than the time saved due to the greater parallelism between the tasks (as a result of having multiple agents), it makes sense to combine some of the agents.

14 These values should not be construed as an indication of the scalability of our approach. However, we have tested our approach on organizations with more than 300 agents, which is significantly greater than the number of agents needed for the kind of applications that we have in mind (i.e. web service choreography, efficient dynamic use of grid computing, distributed information gathering, etc.).

Chapter XXIII
A Formal Petri Net Based Model for Team Monitoring

Olivier Bonnet-Torrès
Beorn Technologies, France

Catherine Tessier
Onera-DCSD, France

ABSTRACT

This chapter focuses on a Petri Net-based model for team organization and monitoring. The applications considered are missions performed by several robots that cooperate in different ways according to the goals to be achieved. Formal operations on the Petri Net representing the mission plan allow the dynamic hierarchy of subteams to be revealed and the agents' individual plans – including the relevant cooperation context – to be calculated. The model also allows several failure propagation ways within the team to be highlighted and local plan repair to be considered. Moreover Petri Nets allow direct implementation, and monitoring and control of the plan at each level of the organization: team, subteams, and individual robots.

INTRODUCTION

Teams of physical agents (robots, UAVs, embedded systems) are more and more considered for missions in dangerous, remote or heterogeneous environments (e.g. search and rescue operations in urban environments). Such teams are usually composed of two to about fifteen robots and may be organized as subteams (e.g. ground and air robots working in pairs) possibly merging or splitting according to the tasks to achieve (e.g. a rendez-vous of two pairs of robots for a four-robot task). A team has to be equipped with methods to reorganize subteams so as to adapt to changes within the team (e.g. robot failure) or within the environment, to new mission goals... Therefore the architecture for controlling such a team must satisfy the following requirements:

- it must be suited to heterogeneous agents;
- it must support the organization of the team as explicit dynamic subteams;
- it must allow the physical agents to operate in real-time;
- it must allow human operators to supervise the mission at any level: team level, subteam level, physical agent level[1];
- it must deal with disruptive events and implement a replanning function.

Each agent is equipped with sensors – in order to collect information as well as to detect events – and actuators – in order to perform actions. Events may be categorized as regular events, e.g. start and stop signals of activities and messages, known disruptive events, i.e. events that are likely to happen but whose occurrence time is unknown, and unexpected events. The problem addressed in this chapter is that of offering a complete, integrated framework for multi-robot missions. Such a framework should address mission preparation as well as execution monitoring and error recovery. Therefore the core issues we are dealing with are the following:

- monitor the teamplan and events at any level within the team: team level, subteam level, physical agent level;
- handle disruptions at the most local level possible within the team in order to avoid their spreading over the whole team or avoid unnecessary replanning;
- limit consequences of unknown events to a local level.

Please see Chapter VI "A Formal Framework for Organization Modeling and Analysis" by Popova and Sharpanskykh for more discussion on a formal framework for modeling and analyzing organizations with constraints.

The chapter will focus on a formal Petri net based model that deals with these issues within an integrated framework. The concepts and mechanisms for representing the dynamics of the team organization will be presented. Then failure handling and local repair will be dealt with.

MULTI-AGENT TEAMS AND PETRI NETS

We will consider that:

- some agents *are coordinated* if these agents interact and at least a part of the interaction is based on information passing;
- some agents *collaborate* if they are coordinated and if they have common goals;
- a *team* is a set of agents that are put together as a necessary structure to pool skills and resources in order to satisfy the goals of a mission through collaboration.

Two classes of approaches for representing and organizing a set of agents may be distinguished:

- bottom-up approaches, that focus on coordination of individual agents;
- top-down approaches, that focus on collaboration within a team.

Goal-Driven Multi-Agent Systems

To complete a mission a system must reach a primary goal. We hence focus on goal-driven agent systems.

An appropriate scheme for missions is hierarchical planning.

Planning in (Thangarajah *et al.*, 2003) develops a bi-partite goal-plan tree: each goal, beginning with the primary mission goal, may be reached by executing one of several plans (OR branching); each (partial) plan may in turn be subdivided into necessary subgoals (AND branching), and so forth. The construction is very close to GraphPlan. The process is improved with identifying positive interactions between goals or plans, thus resulting in an internal, single-agent, (partial) plan-merging construction. Yet the goal-plan tree is a useful construct close to a hierarchical goal decomposition tree.

Multi-agent systems may take several forms (Horling & Lesser, 2005). Among them, coalitions are formed in a bottom-up manner. Societies are built from the top but as hollow structures the rules or constitution of which the agents must comply with. As for teams, they are gathered when designing the mission, in order to achieve a specific goal.

As far as task allocation is concerned, Scerri *et al.* (2005) proposed an approximate decentralized constraint optimization algorithm to solve assignment issues in very wide teams. In such an environment, knowledge of teammate capabilities is imprecise. The model limits each task to be allocated to one agent at a time. Collaborative work is defined through the inter-dependency between tasks, leading to local coalition formation. The approach is promising and the token-based algorithm for committing to some collaborative task is close to Petri net resource management. Xu *et al.* (2005) generalize the notion of token-based algorithm: tokens can hold information, a resource or a task. It applies on a multiple Partially Observable Markov Decision Process (POMDP) model: each agent passes the token according to a POMDP local interpretation of the global team problem. But agents are organized in a "flat" acquaintance network that does not take all advantage of tighter or looser coupling due to joint task performance, e.g. the existence of tighter subteams.

Kotb *et al.* (2007) model robotic agent plans with Petri nets: actions correspond to transitions whereas states are represented by places. Capabilities correspond to units formed around transitions. Aggregating – composing – and sequencing capabilities build plans. Cooperation planning occurs when composing capabilities from two different agents. Sequencing may be performed with dynamic programming. However the approach suffers from a scalability issue both in the number of agents and in task complexity, because of dynamic programming. The approach described by El Fallah-Seghrouchni *et al.* (2004) considers hybrid automata to formalize and execute agents' plans. The automata are generalized into synchronized automata in order to represent the teamplans, but this does not account for teamwork with collaborative actions. It also supposes that a global clock exists, an assumption that is difficult to reconcile with real robots.

In the theory exposed by Köhler *et al.* (2007), the society is constituted using Petri net models. More precisely the social process of entering the society is applied to social units, a notion extensible to actors but also to processes. Any element entering the society can be represented with a Petri net, and is a (socionic) agent, because it is either an actor – the traditional sense of agent – or an object or an idea interacting with other social units. Upon entering the society – being created – all social units adapt themselves to fit the social order. This process is called structuration or self-organization. The society itself can undergo a structuration, meaning that it continually adapts to itself and its contents. The theory has been put into practice and the SONAR architecture has been set up. The Petri nets used are nets-within-nets, i.e. Petri nets whose tokens may be other Petri nets. Firing transitions may cascade to Petri net-token transitions and then a communication channel is synchronized so as to pass some information both ways. It is also a way to coordinate different traditional or socionic agents.

The above mentioned approaches focus on coordinating individual agents. Let us now focus on teams that are already constituted.

Agent Teams

In order to attain a mission goal, SharedPlan, a collaborative multi-agent planning framework (Grosz & Kraus, 1996), is based on the hierarchical decomposition of shared plans into a sequence of recipes to be applied by a team of agents. Tambe's STEAM framework for teamwork (Tambe, 1997) shares some features with SharedPlan, among which a hierarchical decomposition of the mission goal. In STEAM each agent selects an operator, i.e. a reactive behavior implemented with precondition application and terminal rules. The selected operator may involve the whole team or a subteam. In that case a joint intention must be agreed about by the agents. Therefore at any moment the team agrees on a joint intention to achieve the mission and each agent maintains its own hierarchy of joint – if involving a (sub)team – or individual intentions. Contrary to these approaches we do not focus on joint intentions and beliefs. Yet communicating the termination of a durative action is a form of commitment to believe a joint intention is no longer needed.

Sanchez-Herrera & Lopez-Mellado (2004) focus on protocol modeling with nets-within-nets. One of the assumptions of the framework is that the environment is known and can be modeled as a Petri net in which the agent tokens evolve. On the contrary Kaminka & Frenkel (2005) integrate Petri nets for interaction protocol modeling, into the BITE architecture. BITE extends Tambe's work with behavior-selecting teams. It consists in three components: a team (or organization) hierarchy, a behavior graph decomposed as hierarchies and sequences, and a set of interaction protocols for behavior transitions described with Petri nets. In the approach an agent may only have one behavior at a time and thus only appears in one branch of the organization. In (Kaminka *et al.*, 2007) two more components are added: (1) some behaviors for maintaining the preconditions of tasks during their execution, and (2) some protocols that maintain the team cohesion during task execution. The approach solves some of the drawbacks in BITE and aims at improving fault tolerance in the team.

Recovery Systems and Architectures for Multi-Agent Systems

Error recovery is a key issue. The recovery mechanism described by Tambe (1997) is based on monitoring the activity of teammates through maintaining the joint intentions. At the same time each team operator is decomposed into individual operators and if one agent is not able to play its role, i.e. to execute its operator, the team operator is deemed unachievable. In that case replanning consists in substituting the failing agent or subteam. In case of impossibility the repair fails. However some reconfiguration may still be possible.

The approach of Browning *et al.* (2002) focuses on detecting observations contradicting coordinated operations. Genc & Lafortune (2003) suggest Petri net, model-driven diagnosis of systems. Such solutions would require either much knowledge of the environment or a total event system observability, both unrealistic requirements. Constraint satisfaction as used by Kalech *et al.* (2006) is another variant of these models; its complexity lies in the duplication of the agents' states and the combinatorial complexity of finding the right variable to satisfy again the constraint system.

Once the error is diagnosed, the system must recover. For plan-based systems, two main possibilities are offered:

- Cushing & Kambhampati (2005) advocate for rebuilding the plan: all commitments made prior to the failure are kept and replanning must take them into account;
- Drabble *et al.* (1997) suggest that the plan can be repaired: the planning problem is "continuous" and any single, small, localized repair will not disrupt the plan.

Drabble *et al.* (1997) propose substitution or addition repairs only, whereas van der Krogt *et al.* (2005) also include derefinement, the abduction of some parts of the plan in order to avoid a local minimum. Yet, as stated by Fox *et al.* (2006), if repair usually performs better, the choice depends on the domain. The chapter will propose an alternative way to repair and rebuilding.

Multi-agent systems are sometimes being operated in real-world situations. Operational architectures provide support for execution, monitoring and error recovery. Paolucci *et al.* (2000) present an architecture for execution and planning: plans are often deemed invalid by the time they are executed. Therefore interleaving planning and execution provides a valid plan at all times. The architecture is based on a hierarchical decomposition and a hierarchical partial planner: the partial plan is further instantiated when the information is gathered on the field. But interleaving slows down activity execution, since planning is usually more time-consuming.

Ingrand *et al.* (2001) adopt a similar point of view. The architecture is modular and includes procedural execution control, supervision, temporal planning, time-stamping and procedural diagnosis. Linking a procedural controller, that lacks proactiveness, with a supervisor and an interleaved temporal planner absorbs many of the drawbacks of both schemes. Up to now the approach is limited to single agents.

Petri net models have been used, as in (Odrey & Mejia, 2003) in production management. The problem addressed is to recover seamlessly from failures in an open-shop, a workshop with multi-function, interchangeable machines. The architecture is multi-agent and hierarchical: each machine in the shop owns a production agent, a mediator agent and a recovery agent. Machines, their different operations and the internal agents are modeled with interconnected, colored, timed Petri nets. When a failure is detected the recovery agent looks for a partial solution. If impossible it involves other reconfigurators through a contract net. Petri net-based flexible manufacturing systems offer some similarities with mobile robotic agents.

Petri Nets in Planning

As hinted above, Petri nets are not only used for team or plan representation but also as a planning engine. PetriPlan (Silva *et al.*, 2000) is a translation of GraphPlan into a Petri net reachability problem, thanks to integer programming. The approach lacks efficiency because of a one-to-one relation between mutex and Petri nets lock places. TokenPlan (Meiller & Fabiani, 2001), also a Petri net-based planner, improves the GraphPlan algorithm with a possibility to break down the search space, thus accelerating the plan search. Shaw & Bordini (2007) provide another Petri net-based planning framework. It consists in translating the goal-plan tree of Thangarajah *et al.* (2003) into Petri nets. All these approaches only deal with mono-agent systems.

Our proposition will be based on a top-down approach of the multi-agent case, as it is more relevant for the issues tackled in this chapter. It uses the concept of *holarchy*, in the sense of Horling & Lesser (2005), i.e. each agent is either an individual or a group (subteam) of agents. For simplification purposes we will consider the holarchy is equivalent to a team in which aggregated agents are virtual. In particular no assumption is made in the model on implementing aggregated agents. The scalability of the approach depends on these implementation aspects: bandwidth usage and – primarily – the decision mechanism, with regards to agreeing on task completion for instance.

In the remainder the general framework is a mission specified in terms of goals: physical robot agents are operated in order to carry out the goals and they are organized as subteams varying in time according to the tasks to achieve. Even though the experimental framework advocates for a planning system, the chapter will not focus on the planner itself. Many planners may be plugged into the architecture proposed here. Indeed the chapter aims at emphasizing the organization of the team as dynamic subteams, the relationships between the teamplan and the individual agents' plans, as well as the execution, monitoring and local repair processes.

THE TEAM AS A DYNAMIC ORGANIZATION

From Mission Specification to Teamplan

The mission is characterized by an objective to be reached by the agent team. An agent is a physical entity (or a set of physical entities) equipped with resources (sensors, actuators, communication devices) that is implemented to achieve some goals within the mission through services it can offer, therefore contributing to the achievement of the objective. The decomposition of the mission objective gives a hierarchy of goals that must be reached. Some goals involve individual agents (i.e. a robot), other involve composite agents (Shoham, 1993), i.e. subteams or even the team itself. Some temporal constraints may exist on goals or between goals. An elementary goal is such that there exists at least a known recipe to achieve it. A recipe (Grosz & Kraus,1996) is the specification of a course of actions to be performed by an individual or a composite agent resulting in the achievement of a goal; it involves services and duration constraints.

The mission specification, the available recipes and the services the agents can offer are given to a planner that outputs a plan for the whole team of agents (provided a solution exists), choosing one recipe per elementary goal, allocating agents to recipes according to the services they offer, and dealing with temporal constraints. As we focus on the team organization, the planning process itself is out of the scope of this work. The output teamplan is then translated into a Petri net (Figure 1) where each place is associated with an instantiated recipe involving one or several individual agents and each transition is associated with the beginning or the end of a recipe. A marking of the Petri net represents the current state of the teamplan, i.e. the subset of recipes that are being simulated or executed.

Even if this teamplan Petri net is "flat", it is worth noticing that the current structure of the team can be inferred from the structure of the Petri net and its current marking (Figure 1). This is dealt with formally in the next section.

Figure 1. Teamplan

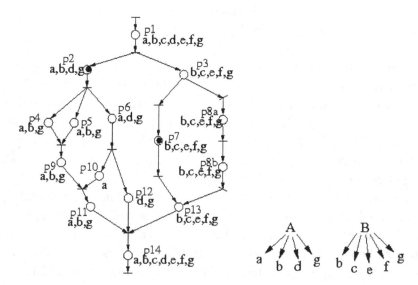

Note: a...g *are the individual agents; marking* $\{p_2, p_{11}\}$ *is the current state of the team: agents* a, b, d, g *are organized as subteam* A *to achieve the recipe associated with place* p_2 *whereas agents* b, c, e, f, g *are organized as subteam* B *to achieve the recipe associated with place* p_{11}; *an individual agent may belong to several subteams, therefore contributing to the associated recipes through different services it can offer provided resource and space constraints are met.*

Agenticity and a Formal Definition of Teamplan

Agenticity

More formally the team X is composed of individual agents $\{x_1, x_2, ..., x_n\}$. It is organized as a hierarchy H_X and each node in the hierarchy is considered as an agent a_i (Shoham, 1993). Let $A = \{a_1, a_2, ..., a_m\}$ be the set of agents in team X. Preliminary properties are that:

1. the team is an agent: $X \in A$, i.e. $\exists p \in [1,...,m], X = a_p$;
2. each individual agent has a counterpart in A: $x_i \in X \Rightarrow \exists j \in [1,...,m], x_i = a_j$.

The father of agent a_i is denoted *father*(a_i). *child*(a_i) is the set of the children of a_i. *child*(.) and *father*(.) are functions and as such can be composed. The hierarchy H_X is an application:

$$A \setminus \{x_1, x_2 ..., x_n\} \rightarrow A$$
$$a_i \mapsto child(a_i)$$

Definition 1. [Agenticity] The *agenticity* of agent a_i with regards to team X is its depth in the hierarchy H_X whose root is the team: $Ag_X(a_i) = depth(a_i, H_X) = (u \mid father^u(a_i) = X)$. The agenticity of agent a_i with regards to any subteam a_j, $a_i \subset a_j$ is its depth in the hierarchy H_{aj} whose root is the considered subteam: $Ag_{aj}(a_i) = depth(a_i, H_{aj}) = (u \mid father^u(a_i) = a_j)$.

Definition 2. [Father agent] The *father agent* of agent a_j is agent $a_k = father(a_j)$ corresponding to the father node in the hierarchy H_X. The father's agenticity is less than the child's by 1:

$$a_j \subset child(a_k) \Rightarrow Ag_X(a_j) = Ag_X(k_j) + 1.$$

Examples

1. The agenticity of an agent pertaining to no subteam is 1 with regards to the team: $X = a_p$, $x_i = a_j$, $\nexists k \in [1,...,m] \setminus \{j,p\}$: $a_j \subset a_k \Rightarrow Ag_X(x_i) = 1$.
2. If all agents belong to the same team, the agenticity of the team is 0 with regards to the agent population:

$$\forall i \in [1,...n], \exists j \in [1,...n]: a_i = x_j \Rightarrow Ag_A(X) = 0, \ A = \{x_i, i \in [1,...n]\} \cup \{X\}.$$

N.B.: the agenticity of an agent can also be defined wrt an agent $a_j \neq X$.
Two ways of extracting parts of the hierarchy are also defined:

Definition 3. [Fork - Twig] A *fork* H_{ai}^1 of root a_i is a sub-hierarchy extracted from H_X whose root is a_i and truncated to agents whose agenticity is 1 wrt to a_i.

A *twig* is a particular case of a fork with all children being individual agents.

The Teamplan Petri Net

Definition 4. [Teamplan Petri net] Let P_X be the teamplan. P_X is a p – and t – time colored interpreted Petri net (David & Alla, 2005; Jensen, 1997):
$P_X = (P, T, T, S, N, C, F_P, F_S, G, F_T, A, E, I, M_0)$ such that (Figure 1):

1. P is a finite set a places p_i, each p_i representing the activity (i.e. an instantiated recipe) associated with an elementary goal;
2. T is a finite set of transitions t_j;
3. $T = A \cup R$ is a set of temporal intervals, with A a set of date intervals and R a set of duration intervals;
4. S is a finite set of arcs s_k;
5. N is a node function from S into $P \times T \cup T \times P$;
6. C is the color set;
7. F_P is a color function from P into C;
8. F_S is an arc expression function from S into $C \rightarrow C^N \times C^N \rightarrow C$, that associates a color transformation with each arc;
9. G is a transition guard function;
10. F_T is a temporal function that associates an interval of R with each place and an interval of A with each transition;
11. A is a set of actions;
12. E is a set of events;

13. I is the interpretation of the net that associates one or several events of E and one or several actions of A with each transition;

14. $\mathcal{M}_0 \in C^N$ is the initial marking of the Petri net.

The token color set C includes the black color c_0 and the set of agenticity forks H_{ai}^1 of root a_i: the color of a token represents a composite agent and its children. In this work, only twigs are used (the child agents of the twigs are individual agents). F_P is the application:

$$P \rightarrow C$$

$$p_i \mapsto H_{ai}^1$$

the color $F_P(p_i)$ of a token within a place p_i is the twig of root the composite agent a_i corresponding to the recipe associated with p_i. Therefore a reachable marking $\mathcal{M}$ of the Petri net is a set of twigs.

The initial marking $\mathcal{M}_0$ in the initial place of the Petri net (place p_1 in Figure 1) is the twig of root X (i.e. the agent representing the whole team).

F_S is a function that modifies the color of a token passing through an arc: for arc s_k from place p_i towards transition t_j, $F_S(s_k) = (F_P(p_i) \rightarrow c_0)$; for an arc s_k from transition t_j towards place p_i, $F_S(s_k) = (c_0 \rightarrow F_P(p_i))$. This allows the guard function G to be simplified: G only allows tokens of color c_0 to enable transitions.

In fact, the way F_S modifies the token color (through the intermediate color c_0) is given by the planning process, i.e. how composite agents are allocated to successive recipes.

Transition t_j may be triggered if:

- the duration associated with each input places of t_j is respected;
- the predicted triggering date is within the time interval associated with t_j;
- all the input places of t_j are marked;
- the events associated with t_j occur when t_j is enabled.

When t_j is triggered, tokens go through t_j as follows:

- the tokens (twigs) of the input places of t_j are removed from the input places and transformed into c_0 tokens through t_j input arc expression functions;
- the events associated with t_j are consumed;
- the actions associated with t_j are triggered;
- c_0 tokens are transformed into twigs through t_j output arc expression functions and are put into the output places of t_j.

This teamplan Petri net allows the plan to be simulated or executed; but as such, it does not highlight the way the team is dynamically organized. Making the teamplan hierarchical will make the dynamic subteam organization explicit. This is the topic of the next section.

Figure 2. Structures within the teamplan

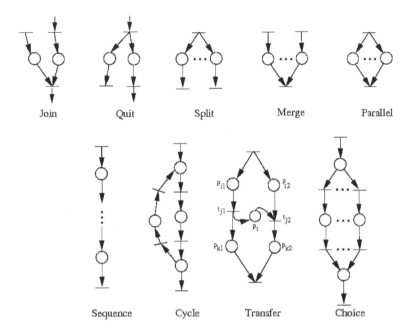

From Teamplan to Hierarchical Teamplan

Structures

The teamplan Petri net bears typical structures (Bonnet-Torrès & Tessier, 2005) (see Figure 2) that correspond to local modifications of the team organization during the mission. The input and output transitions of each structure correspond to the team changing ways of organization.

The join structure allows q agents to join the team. The entering agent (either an individual agent or a composite agent) has an agenticity of 1 wrt the team.

The quit structure allows q agents to quit the team. The leaving agent (either an individual agent or a composite agent) has an agenticity of 1 wrt the team.

The split structure allows creating from a subteam m subteams whose levels of agenticity are increased by 1 wrt the initial subteam.

The merge structure allows fusing m subteams to form a single subteam whose level of agenticity is decreased by 1 wrt the m initial subteams.

The parallel structure is the concatenation of a split and a merge structures.

The sequence structure stands for a sequence of recipes; this structure does not modify the involved agents.

The cycle structure stands for a repeated series of recipes; this structure does not modify the involved agents.

The transfer structure allows transferring q agents from the recipe associated with p_{i1} to the recipe associated with p_{k2}. This is equivalent to collocating a join structure and a quit structure where p_t represents the withdrawing agents on the one side and the arriving agents on the other.

The `choice` structure allows a subteam to choose among r possible recipes. The organization of the team is not modified by this structure.

The structures can be easily extracted from the teamplan Petri net P_X through the incidence matrix I_X of P_X that represents the arcs of the Petri net (Murata, 1989).

Example: let us consider the `transfer` structure. The corresponding submatrix within I_X is the (Figure 3).

Structure Reduction and the Hierarchical Teamplan

In order to make the teamplan hierarchical and therefore make the dynamic subteam organization explicit, we use reduction rules based on the Petri net classic reduction rules (Murata, 1989). Indeed the common use of Petri net reduction rules is to simplify some specific configurations of places and transitions of a large net so as to ease the analysis of the properties of the net. In our case reduction rules allow each structure within P_X to be simplified as a macro-place, thus revealing the organization of agents as subteams.

Example: let us consider a simple structure involving a single possible marking (see Figure 4). Agents x_1 and x_2, as subteam X, perform the recipe associated with place p_x whereas in parallel agent y, as subteam Y, performs the recipe associated with place p_y. This `parallel` structure is reduced to macro-place $p_{x|y}$ meaning that agents x_1, x_2 and y, at a lower agenticity level (i.e. at a less detailed level), work as subteam Z. Nevertheless the fact that subteams X and Y exist is recorded in the hierarchy.

When a structure involves several successive markings, the agent organization corresponding to each marking has to be considered when reducing the structure and building the agenticity hierarchy.

Example: reduction of the `transfer` structure.

A transfer structure is identified through a submatrix $I_{transfer}$ (see Figure 3) within the incidence matrix I_X. The first step is to eliminate the transfer place p_t, thus eliminating (p_t) row within $I_{transfer}$ and keeping a record within places p_{i2} and p_{k1}. The reduced structure then includes two `sequence`

Figure 3. Submatrix for `transfer` *structure*

$$
I_{transfer} =
\begin{array}{c}
\\
\\
\\
(p_{i1}) \\
(p_{i2}) \\
(p_t) \\
(p_{k_1}) \\
(p_{k_2}) \\
\\
\\
\\
\end{array}
\begin{pmatrix}
& & & (t_{j_1}) & (t_{j_2}) & & \\
& & & 0 & 0 & & \\
& & & \vdots & \vdots & & \\
& & & 0 & 0 & & \\
\cdots & \cdots & & -1 & 0 & \cdots & \cdots \\
\cdots & \cdots & & 0 & -1 & \cdots & \cdots \\
\cdots & 0 & & 1 & -1 & 0 & \cdots \\
\cdots & \cdots & & 1 & 0 & \cdots & \cdots \\
\cdots & \cdots & & 0 & 1 & \cdots & \cdots \\
& & & 0 & 0 & & \\
& & & \vdots & \vdots & & \\
& & & 0 & 0 & & \\
\end{pmatrix}
$$

Figure 4. Reduction of the `parallel` *structure, one subteam level is created*

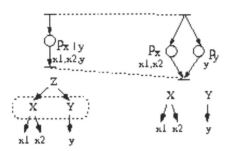

Figure 5. Reduction of the `transfer` *structure The names of the macro-places keep a record of the structure that has been reduced*

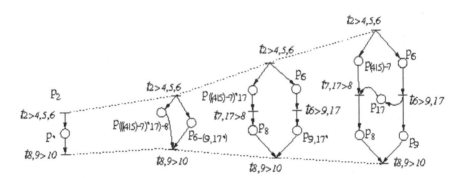

structures that will be reduced to one macro-place each, resulting in a `parallel` structure that will be reduced in turn to a single macro-place (see Figure 5, to be read from right to left).

When the marking of the structure is $\{p_{(4|5)\text{-}7}, p_6\}$, agents a, b and g work as subteam AA on the one hand, and agents a, d and g work as subteam AB on the other hand. In the successive reduced patterns, the hierarchy remains unchanged except for p_*, a macro-place corresponding to the reduction of a `parallel` structure: subteam A is created thus putting together subteams AA and AB.

When the marking of the structure is $\{p_{(4|5)\text{-}7}, p_{17}, p_9\}$, agents a, b and g are within subteam AA, agent a is being transferred from subteam AB to subteam AA, and agents d and g are within subteam AB. As previously, in the successive reduced patterns, the hierarchy remains unchanged except for p_*.

Finally when the marking of the structure is $\{p_8, p_9\}$, agents a, b and g work as subteam AA on the one hand and agents d and g work as subteam AB on the other hand. As previously, in the successive reduced patterns, the hierarchy remains unchanged except for p_* (see Figure 7).

The reduction rules are applied sequentially thus successively creating new agents (subteams) and enriching the agenticity hierarchy, until the whole teamplan is reduced to one single place corresponding to the whole mission and involving the whole team X.

Example (see Figure 6): let us consider the teamplan of Figure 1 with marking $\{p_4, p_5, p_6, p_{12}\}$. This marking corresponds to the one-level agenticity organization with four subteams AAA, AAB, AB and B.

Figure 6. Reduction creating subteams and agenticity levels

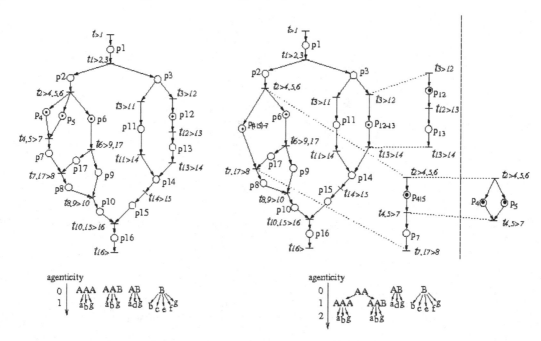

The `parallel` structure composed of places (p_4, p_5) is reduced to macro-place $p_{4|5}$ thus creating subteam *AA* that puts together subteams *AAA* and *AAB*. Then the `sequence` structure composed of places $(p_{4|5}, p_7)$ is reduced to macro-place $p_{(4|5)\text{-}7}$; on the other hand the `sequence` structure composed of places (p_{12}, p_{13}) is reduced to macro-place $p_{12\text{-}13}$, the corresponding hierarchy remains the same.

The whole process is shown on Figure 7 for two different markings.

The Dynamic Organization of the Team

The hierarchical teamplan allows the dynamic organization of the team to be highlighted as each reachable marking of P_X corresponds to an agenticity hierarchy that is revealed when making P_X hierarchical through successive reductions.

Example: let us consider the teamplan of Figure 1 with marking $\{p_4, p_5, p_6, p_{12}\}$.

When transition $t_{4,5>7}$ is triggered, the marking becomes $\{p_7, p_6, p_{12}\}$ and the agenticity hierarchy changes as follows (Figure 7): subteams *AAA* and *AAB* are merged as subteam *AA*.

When transition $t_{6>9,17}$ is triggered, the marking becomes $\{p_7, p_{17}, p_9, p_{12}\}$, and agent a is being transferred from subteam *AB* (Figure 7).

From Hierarchical Teamplan to Individual Plans

The hierarchical teamplan is useful for subteam organization representation and monitoring, but it is indeed necessary to be able to control physical agents (robots). Consequently it is necessary that each individual agent should have its own plan, including a local view on the teamplan:

Figure 7. The agenticity hierarchies corresponding to marking $\{p_7, p_6, p_{12}\}$ and then to marking $\{p_7, p_{17}, p_9, p_{12}\}$

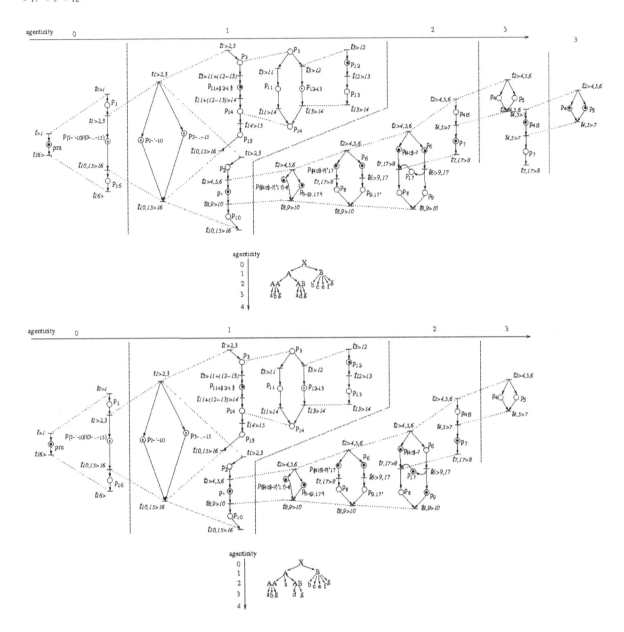

Definition 5. [Individual plan] The individual plan P_{ai} of agent a_i is a Petri net (as defined by definition 4) where all places involve a_i:

$$\forall\, p \in P_{ai}, \exists\, a_j \in A, H^1_{aj} = F_P(p), a_i \in child(a_j).$$

The individual hierarchical plan $\mathcal{P}_{ai}$ of agent a_i is the hierarchical form of individual plan P_{ai}: all the places in $\mathcal{P}_{ai}$ involve a_i or one of its ancestors in the agenticity hierarchy H_X,

$$\forall\, p \in \mathcal{P}_{ai},$$

$$\exists a_j \in A, H_{aj}^1 = F_P(p), \exists u \in N, a_j \in father^u(a_i)$$

The individual hierarchical plan $\mathcal{P}_{ai}$ organizes agent a_i's activities and interactions with the rest of the team. As all agents' activities and interactions are described in the teamplan, there is a formal relation between the teamplan and agent a_i's individual plan. This relation is a projection that is similar to the projection of colored Petri nets on one color (Capra & Cazzola, 2006) or the projection of labeled Petri nets on one object (Cheung & Chow, 2007).

Example: Figure 8 shows the individual plan of agent *d* as a result of the projection of the hierarchical teamplan on agent *d*. The agenticity hierarchy features the ancestors of agent *d* and the brothers of the ancestors, for this particular marking. Indeed the agenticity hierarchy provides an acquaintance network with acquaintance "degrees": an agent may know well some of its counterparts (meaning they directly interact – this is the case for agents *d*, *a* and *g* for this marking (Figure 8)), or more vaguely (meaning they only interact through the hierarchy – this is the case for *d* and agents belonging to subteams *AA* and *B*).

FAILURE PROPAGATION AND TEAMPLAN REPAIR

The Petri net based hierarchical teamplan and its projection on the individual agents are implemented as such (Bonnet-Torrès *et al.*, 2006) within the control architecture of the robots (the implementation itself is beyond the scope of this chapter; please see (Bonnet-Torrès *et al.*, 2006) for further information). Executing the individual plans amounts to playing the associated projected Petri nets. Monitoring the execution can be done at any level of agenticity within the hierarchy. Monitoring includes failure detection, i.e. the detection of events that are likely to invalidate a part of the plan. The detection of

Figure 8. Agent d's individual plan

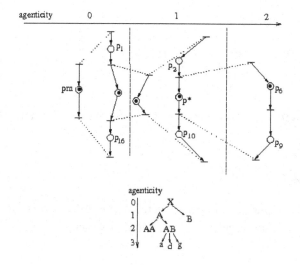

known disruptive events – i.e. events that are likely to happen but whose occurrence time is unknown – is assumed to give information about which robot or which service has failed, whereas unexpected events are assumed to be detected only through a violation of a temporal constraint associated with a transition.

The consequences of a failure, i.e. how the different parts of the teamplan are impaired, are assessed through four failure propagation modes: organization, causality, structure, mission tree.

Four Failure Propagation Modes

Propagation of a Failure through the Team Organization

Let us consider the current state of the teamplan. The immediate consequence of an agent failure is that each current activity involving this agent is impaired. More precisely:

- if the failure affects individual agent x entirely, the activities corresponding to the places whose tokens involve x (i.e. x is one of the twig leaves) are impaired;
- if the failure affects one service σ of agent x, the recipes associated with the marked places and using σ are impaired.

Example (see Figure 9): agent b is detected to have failed during the activity associated with place p_{11}. Activities associated with places p_4 and p_5 are also impaired.

Causal Propagation

The causal propagation of a failure within a structure is the fact that all the downstream places of an impaired place within a structure of the teamplan are also affected.

Figure 9. Propagation through the team organization for the current marking

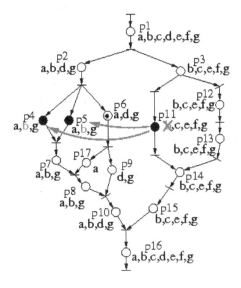

Figure 10. Causal and structural propagations

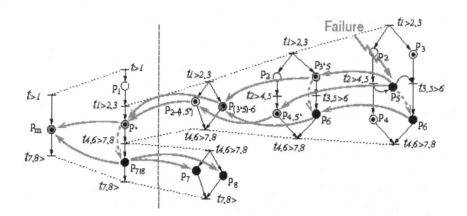

Example (see Figure 10): let us consider a failure affecting place p_5 of the following `transfer` structure. Through causal propagation, the activity corresponding to place p_6 is also impaired.

Structural Propagation

The structural propagation of a failure transfers the consequences of a failure from the affected structure to the corresponding macro-places within the hierarchical teamplan. This means that the subteam of a lower agenticity is also affected. Indeed structural propagation generalizes causal propagation to the team hierarchical organization. Both causal and structural propagations are interwoven and are computed iteratively.

Example (see Figure 10): dashed arrows represent causal propagation whereas plain arrows represent structural propagation. Structural propagation is performed towards the lower agenticity levels, e.g. from p_5 to p_{3*5} and $p_{4,5*}$, then to $p_{2-(4,5*)}$ and $p_{(3*5)-6}$ and p_*; and backwards to the upper agenticity levels, e.g. from $p_{7|8}$ to p_7 and p_8 after the causal propagation from p_* to $p_{7|8}$.

Consequences on the Mission Goal Tree

If a service fails some recipes may not be available any more. Consequently some elementary goals may not be satisfied anymore, and a part of the mission goal tree may become invalid.

Example (see Figure 11): service χ within agent b has failed. Consequently recipes r_{15} and r_{16} cannot be used any more by the planner and subgoal 312, therefore subgoal 31, cannot be satisfied any more. Another subtree will have to be considered to satisfy goal 3, e.g. subgoal 32 with recipe r_{20}.

When called for plan repair, the planner will have to consider services, agents and recipes that are not impaired by the failure, i.e. the mission goal tree without the invalid subtrees.

Figure 11. An impaired goal tree

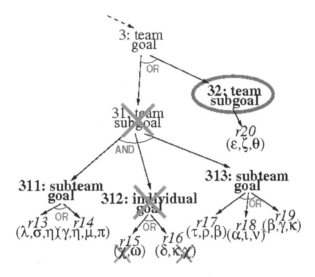

Teamplan Repair

Given the team organization and the consequences of a failure, we aim at repairing the teamplan as locally as possible, through a bottom-up approach. Local repair is based on three rules that are applied successively as heuristics by the planner from the most local to the less local, until a solution is found (provided one solution exists): agent substitution, place substitution, structure substitution. Indeed only a sub-problem of the whole planning problem is given to the planner, i.e. only the parts of the plan that are affected by the failure. The parts of the plan that are not impaired, i.e. the activities of the subteams that are only loosely linked to the impaired agent, can go on with their activity execution while the impaired part is being repaired.

Agent Substitution

The agent substitution heuristic leads to the most local repair for the planner: the recipes corresponding to the impaired places are achieved with other agents offering the same services, provided they are available and the time and resource constraints are met.

Example: agent d has failed in p_6 and is replaced by agent f (see Figure 12 up).

Place Substitution

The place substitution heuristic amounts to changing the recipe, i.e. the elementary goal can still be achieved with a different recipe.

Example: place p_6 is replaced by place p_{34} associated with another recipe or another subgoal involving subteam AB' that features agents a and g only (see Figure 12 middle).

Figure 12. Agent substitution, place substitution, structure substitution

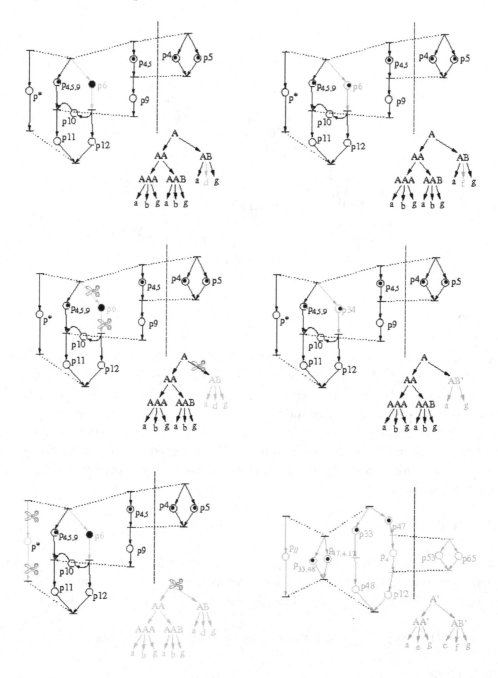

Structure Substitution

When a whole structure is impaired, the structure substitution heuristic replaces the whole structure by replanning the goals involved in the initial structure and under its time constraints.

Example: place p_6 cannot be replaced, therefore the whole structure, i.e. macro-place p_* has to be replaced; p_* is repaired through $p_{//}$ involving a different subteam A' that in turn involves two subteams AA' with agents a, e and g and AB' with agents c, f and g (see Figure 12 down).

Discussion

Provided the failures are limited and there exist spare services, agents or recipes for the mission, local repair is often the most efficient approach as it can be performed in-line while the sound part of the team goes on executing its activities.

Nevertheless local may become somewhat global if an impaired service or agent is involved in several subteams. Moreover local repair is just heuristics for the planner; if they fail, the planner will try to replan the whole part of the mission that remains to be executed. Therefore triggering local or global replanning should be based on the analysis of the consequences of the failure. Please see Chapter IV "OMACS a Framework for Adaptive, Complex System" by DeLoach for more discussion on the adequacy of models and policies for system reorganizations.

CONCLUSION

This chapter has focused on the dynamic organization of a team of robot agents. A formal tool (Petri net) and some of its properties (reduction) are adapted and allow the organization of the team as dynamic subteams to be highlighted within the teamplan, i.e. the re-organization of individual agents as cooperative groups according to activities they have to perform. Moreover at a given time, the current state of an individual agent x's plan features the agents x closely collaborates with, and the other agents as looser acquaintances.

The whole formal model has been implemented within a control architecture for a team of four Pekee indoor robots in a mission involving successive pair subteams. Beyond modeling the organizational structure of the team, the teamplan Petri net allows simulating, executing and monitoring the plan within the same framework and the individual plans allow the real robots to be controlled. Furthermore the hierarchical teamplan allows the human operator to supervise the execution at any agenticity level: team (the four robots as a whole), subteams (pairs) or individuals. The framework is being reused for experiments involving teams from 2 to 12 robots "on the field"[2].

The consequences of a failure within the team are identified formally thanks to the plan structure. Repair is performed as locally as possible through heuristics given to the planner. Some disruptive events have been considered in the experiments (obstacles, camera failure, robot failure) and the results show that, though systematic local organization repair is cheaper than global replanning (fewer recipes reconsidered, fewer replanning nodes), further refinements should be considered:

- according to the failure and its consequences and to the spare resources available, the most *relevant* repair level should be considered as the first heuristics instead of the most *local* one;
- the choice between *local* (or *relevant*) repair and *global* repair should be made according to the mission and team characteristics: indeed the more loosely-coupled the team, the more efficient the local repair.

REFERENCES

Browning, B., Kaminka, G., & Veloso, M. (2002). *Principled monitoring of distributed agents for detection of coordination failure.* International Symposium on Distributed Autonomous Robotic Systems (DARS'02), Fukuoka, Japan.

Bonnet-Torrès, O., Domenech, P., Lesire, Ch., & Tessier, C. (2006). *EXHOST-PIPE: PIPE extended for two classes of monitoring Petri nets.* 27th International Conference On Application and Theory of Petri Nets and Other Models of Concurrency (ICATPN'06), Turku, Finland.

Bonnet-Torrès, O., & Tessier, C. (2005). *From teamplan to individual plans: A Petri net-based approach.* AAMAS'05, Utrecht, The Netherlands.

Capra, L., & Cazzola, W. (2006). A Petri-net based reflective framework for the evolution of dynamic systems. *Electronic Notes in Theoretical Computer Science, 159*, 41-59.

Cheung, K. S., & Chow, K. O. (2007). A Petri net based method for refining object oriented system specifications. *Electronic Notes in Theoretical Computer Science, 187*, 161-172,

Cushing, W., & Kambhampati, S. (2005). Replanning: A new perspective. *International Conference on Automated Planning and Scheduling (ICAPS'05), poster session*, Monterey, CA.

David, R., & Alla, H. (2005). *Discrete, continuous and hybrid Petri nets.* Springer-Verlag.

Drabble, B., Dalton, J., & Tate, A. (1997). Repairing plans on-the-fly. *NASA Workshop on Planning and Scheduling for Space*, Oxnard, CA.

Fox, M., Gerevini, A., Long, D., & Serina, I. (2006). Plan stability: replanning vs. plan repair. *International Conference on Automated Planning and Scheduling (ICAPS'06)}*, Lake District, UK.

El Fallah-Seghrouchni, A., Degirmanciyan-Cartault, I., & Marc, F. (2004). Modelling, control and validation of multi-agent plans in dynamic context. AAMAS'04, New York, NY.

Grosz, B., & Kraus, S. (1996). Collaborative plans for complex group action. *Artificial Intelligence, 86(2)*, 269-357.

Genc, S., & Lafortune S. (2003). Distributed diagnosis of discrete event systems using Petri Nets. *International Conference on Application and Theory of Petri Nets (ATPN'03)*, Eindhoven, The Netherlands.

Horling, B., & Lesser, V. (2005). A survey of multi-agent organizational paradigms. *The Knowledge Engineering Review, 19*(4), 281-316.

Ingrand, F-F., Chatila, R., & Alami, R. (2001). An architecture for dependable autonomous robots. *IEEE workshop on Dependable Robotics*, Seoul, South Korea.

Jensen K. (1997). Coloured Petri nets. Basic concepts, analysis methods and practical use. *Monographs in Theoretical Computer Science*. Springer-Verlag, 2nd edition.

Kotb, Y.T., Beauchemin, S.S., &. Barron, J.L. (2007). Petri net-based cooperation in multi-agent systems. *4th Canadian Conference on Computer and Robot Vision (CVR'07)*, Toronto, ON, Canada.

Kaminka G., & Frenkel I. (2005). Flexible teamwork in behavior-based robots. *AAAI'05 (NCAI'05)*, Pittsburgh, PA.

Kalech, M., Kaminka, G., Meisels, A., & Elmaliach, Y. (2006). Diagnosis of multi-robot coordination failures using distributed CSP algorithms. *NCAI'06,* Boston, MA.

Köhler, M., Langer, R., von Lüde, R., Moldt, D., Rölke H., & Valk R. (2007). Socionic multi-agent systems based on reflexive Petri Nets and theories of social self-organisation. *Journal of Artificial Societies and Social Simulation, 10(1).*

Kaminka, G., Yakir, A., Erusalimchik, D., & Cohen-Nov, N. (2007). Towards collaborative task and team maintenance. *AAMAS'07,* Honolulu, HI.

Meiller, Y., & Fabiani, P. (2001). Tokenplan, a planner for both satisfaction and optimization problems. *AI Magazine, 22(3)*, 85-87.

Murata T. (1989). Petri Nets: properties, analysis and applications. *Proceedings of the IEEE, 77(4)*, 541-580.

Odrey, N., & Mejia., G. (2003). A re-configurable multi-agent system architecture for error recovery in production systems. *Robotics and Computer-Integrated Manufacturing, 19*, 35-43,

Paolucci, M., Shehory, O., & Sycara, K. (2000). *Interleaving planning and execution in a multiagent team planning environment. Electronic Transactions on Artificial Intelligence Journal, 4(1).*

Shaw, P., & Bordini, R. (2007). Towards alternative approaches to reasoning about goals. *5th International Workshop on Declarative Agent Languages and Technologies (DALT'07),* Honolulu, HI.

Silva, F., Castilho, M., & Künzle, L.A. (2000). Petriplan: a new algorithm for plan generation (preliminary report). *IBERAMIA-SBIA'00*, Sao Paolo, Brazil.

Scerri, P., Farinelli, A., Okamoto, S., & Tambe, M. (2005). Allocating tasks in extreme teams. *AAMAS'05,* Utrecht, The Netherlands.

Sanchez-Herrera, R., & Lopez-Mellado, E. (2004). Modular and hierarchical modelling of interactive mobile agents. *IEEE International Conference on Systems, Man and Cybernetics.* The Hague, The Netherlands.

Shoham, Y. (1993). Agent-oriented programming. *Artificial Intelligence, 60,* 51-92.

Tambe, M. (1997). Towards flexible teamwork. *Journal of Artificial Intelligence Research, 7,* 3-124.

Thagarajah, J., Padgham, L., & Winikoff, M. (2003). Detecting and exploiting positive goal interaction in intelligent agents. AAMAS'03, Melbourne, Australia.

Van der Krogt, R., de Weerdt, M., Roos, N., & Witteveen, C. (2005). Multi-agent planning through plan repair. *AAMAS'05*, Utrecht, The Netherlands.

Xu, Y., Scerri, P., Yu, B., Okamoto, S., Lewis, M., & Sycara, K. (2005). An integrated token-based algorithm for scalable coordination. *AAMAS'05*, Utrecht, The Netherlands.

KEY TERMS

Hierarchical Teamplan: A hierarchical Petri net featuring the different subteams within the team. As the marking of the hierarchical teamplan evolves, the dynamics of the subteams is highlighted.

Local Teamplan Repair: Aims at repairing the plan of the team as locally as possible.

Petri Net *(P, T, F, B)*: A bipartite graph with two types of nodes: P is a finite set of places and T is a finite set of transitions. Arcs are directed and represent the forward incidence function $F : P \times T \to IN$ and the backward incidence function $B : P \times T \to IN$ respectively. An **interpreted Petri net** is such that conditions and events are associated with places and transitions. When the conditions corresponding to some places are satisfied, tokens are assigned to those places and the net is said to be marked. The evolution of tokens within the net follows transition firing rules. Petri nets allow sequencing, parallelism and synchronization to be easily represented.

Team: A set of agents that are put together as a necessary structure to pool skills and resources in order to satisfy the goals of a mission through collaboration.

Teamplan Petri Net: A Petri net representing the plan of a team.

ENDNOTES

[1]   Please see Chapter XXI "Personal Assistants for Human Organizations" by Okamoto et al. for more discussion on the impact of computer assistant capabilities on human organizations and Chapter XII "Communications for Agent-Based Human Team Support" by Sukthankar et al. for more discussion on self-organization and teamwork in agent-human hybrid teams.
[2]   http://action.onera.fr/node/63

About the Contributors

Virginia Dignum received a PhD in computer science from the Utrecht University, The Netherlands. Before joining academia in 2003, she worked in consultancy and system development for more than 12 years. Her current research focuses on agent based models of organizations, in particular in the dynamic aspects of organizations, and the applicability of agent organizations to knowledge management. She participates and leads several national and EU-projects, and has more than 50 published articles. She organized several international workshops, was treasurer of AAMAS 2005 and is vice-chair of the Benelux Artificial Intelligence Association.

* * *

Marco Alberti is a research fellow at the University of Ferrara's Department of Engineering. Marco graduated in electronic engineering from the University of Ferrara in 2001 and obtained his PhD in information engineering from the University of Ferrara in 2005. Marco's research interests are abductive logic programming, constraint logic programming, multi-agent systems, and normative systems.

Alexander Artikis is a research associate at the National Centre for Scientific Research "Demokritos", in Athens, Greece. He was awarded his PhD in computing (multi-agent systems) from Imperial College London. His research interests lie in the areas of distributed artificial intelligence, and temporal representation and reasoning. He has been publishing in related conferences and journals, and worked on several national and European projects.

Olivier Boissier received his PhD in computer science at INPG Grenoble in 1993 and his Habilitation à Diriger des Recherches (HdR) at ENS Mines de Saint-Etienne and University Jean Monnet Saint-Etienne in 2003. He is currently professor of Computer Science at the Ecole Nationale Supérieure Mines of Saint-Etienne, France. Olivier Boissier is active in the research and development of multi-agent systems for 15 years. His main research contributions concern: coordination and control of multi-agent systems.

Olivier Bonnet-Torrès is originally an engineer in embedded computing and aerospace systems; he defended his PhD thesis in multi-agent robotics in 2007 at the French Aerospace Lab (ONERA) in Toulouse. Olivier was shortly employed by IBM Germany and worked as a UAV systems engineer at Aurora Flight Sciences and Athena TI in Manassas, VA. He is the co-founder and chief scientist of Beorn Technologies, a company based in Le Mans, France and specialized in applied research for autonomous systems and open-source management and business applications.

Chris Burnett is a PhD candidate currently studying as the Computer Science Department of the University of Aberdeen in Scotland, and at the Robotics Institute at Carnegie Mellon University, PA. He attained his BSc (Hons) in computing science at the University of Aberdeen in 2006. His primary research interests lay is the areas of multi-agent systems, specifically the issue of trust in multi-agent systems.

Cristiano Castelfranchi, is professor of Cognitive Sciences at the University of Siena (Communication Science); director of the Institute of Cognitive Sciences and Technologies of the National Research Council, in Roma. His main contributions are on the cognitive foundations of social phenomena (cooperation, communication, power, norms, autonomy, institutions, social emotions, etc.). Program chair of the first AAMAS conference 2002; general chair of AAMAS 2009; member of JAAMAS and JASSS boards; Fellowship of ECCAI (August 2003) "for pioneering work in the field of AI"; Special award "Mind and Brain" for research in Cognitive Science- University of Turin, 2007.

Christopher Cheong is a lecturer in the school of business information technology at RMIT University, and a PhD candidate in the school of computer science and information technology. His interests lie in the areas of artificial intelligence, intelligent agents, evolutionary computing and software engineering. More specifically, he is interested in applying these interests to the business domain.

Federico Chesani is a research assistant the University of Bologna's Department of Computer Engineering (DEIS). Federico received his PhD in computer science from the University of Bologna in 2007. Federico's research interests include abduction and computational logic, verification techniques and specification languages, applied to multi-agent systems and service oriented computing. Federico is member of the Italian Interest Group on Logic Programming (GULP).

Marco Colombetti is full professor of Computer Science at Politecnico di Milano and at Università della Svizzera italiana. His main research themes are agent communication languages, artificial institutions, semantic web, human communication and interaction. He is member of AI*IA (the Italian Association for Artificial Intelligence) and ISCAR (the International Society for Cultural and Activity Research), and "Associate" of Behavioral and Brain Sciences.

Luciano R. Coutinho received a MSc degree in Informatics from Federal University of Paraíba, Brazil, in 1999. Currently he is assistant professor at Federal University of Maranhão, in São Luís, Brazil, and PhD student at University of São Paulo, Brazil. His research interests include multi-agent systems, agent organizations, ontology engineering and model-driven engineering.

Mehdi Dastani is a lecturer in computer science at the Utrecht University. He is working in the area of multi-agent systems and multi-agent programming for the last ten years and has published many papers on these subjects. He is the general chair of the European Agent Systems Summer School (EASSS), a co-organizer of ProMAS (The International Workshop on Programming Multi-Agent Systems) and multi-agent programming contest. He has been the PC member of various international conferences and workshops such as AAMAS (International Joint Conference on Autonomous Agents and Multi-Agent Systems) and JELIA (European Conference on Logics in Artificial Intelligence).

Keith Decker is an associate professor in the Department of Computer and Information Sciences at the University of Delaware. His research interests include multi–agent systems, computational organization design, distributed planning and scheduling, and bioinformatics. He received his BS in applied math from Carnegie Mellon University in 1984, his MS in computer science from Rensselaer Polytechnic Institute in 1987, and his PhD in computer science from the University of Massachusetts in 1995. He received a NSF CAREER Award in 1998, and a DARPA recognition award in 2006. Decker is on the editorial board for the *Autonomous Agents and Multi-Agent Systems Journal* and is program co-chair for AAMAS 2009.

Scott DeLoach is an associate professor in the Computing and Information Sciences Department at Kansas State University. His research focuses on methods and techniques for the analysis, design, and implementation of complex adaptive systems, which have been applied to both multi-agent and cooperative robotic systems. Dr. DeLoach is best known for his work in agent-oriented software engineering. He is creator of the multi-agent systems engineering methodology (MaSE), its follow-on organization-based multi-agent systems engineering methodology (O-MaSE), and the associated agentTool analysis and design tool. He is on the editorial board of the *International Journal of Agent-Oriented Software Engineering*, has been on over 25 conference and workshop program committees, has in excess of 50 refereed publications, and has advised over 25 graduate students. Dr. DeLoach came to Kansas State University after a twenty year career in the US Air Force.

Frank Dignum received a PhD in 1989 in Amsterdam. Subsequently he set up the computing science department of the University of Swaziland. In 1992 he joined the AI group in IST, Lisbon. From 1993 he started working on agents and electronic commerce at the TUE in Eindhoven. From 2000 he is associate professor at the UU in the area of agent technology. He has published numerous papers and books and organized several workshops and was the local chair of AAMAS 2005.

Shaheen Fatima is a lecturer in the Department of Computer Science at Loughborough University, UK. Her research interests lie in the area of autonomous agents and multi-agent systems, specifically in resource allocation in multi-agent systems using market-based methods, and in agent mediated negotiation for the domain of electronic commerce using techniques from game theory. She has published over thirty articles in the area and served on the program committees of several conferences and workshops.

Jacques Ferber is professor of Computer Science at Montpellier II. He received his PhD degree from Univ. Paris 6 in 1983. His domain of research is about multi-agent systems since 1987, distributed systems and multi-agent simulation. He is author of the book *Multiagent Systems, an Introduction to Distributed Artificial Intelligence*, which has been published in French, English and German. He is member of several editorial boards such as JAAMAS and JAOSE. He co-authored the MadKit platform, widely used for educational and research purposes, and the AGR generic model for organizations. He has published more than a hundred scientific papers in international journals, conferences and workshops about multi-agent systems.

Nicoletta Fornara has an MSc in computer science and a PhD in communication for a work on interaction and communication among autonomous agents in multi-agent systems. She is postdoc researcher and lecturer at Università della Svizzera italiana and at Politecnico di Milano. Her research mainly focuses on the formalization of artificial institutions for the specification of open interaction systems. She is member of the steering committee of the COIN workshop series, she has been in the PC of AAMAS since 2005 and in the PC of other international workshops.

Marco Gavanelli is an assistant professor in computer science at the University of Ferrara's Department of Engineering. Marco obtained his PhD in information science from the University of Modena and Reggio-Emilia. Marco's research interests include logic programming and its applications, abductive reasoning, multi-criteria optimization, constraint logic programming and its integration with operations research, reformulation of problems into SAT. Marco is a coordinator of the interest group on Knowledge Representation and Automatic Reasoning of the Italian Association for Artificial Intelligence (AI*IA).

Joseph A. Gianpapa is a research computer scientist and the project manager for Dr. Sycara's research laboratory in the Robotics Institute, which is within the School of Computer Science at Carnegie Mellon University. He has a MSc from the Language Technologies Institute, also from the School of Computer Science at CMU, and a BA in computer science from Brandeis University. Prior to joining CMU he had designed and developed diverse commercial systems, such as an AI-based system to detect tax evasion and a multi-protocol data communications network gateway for a flagship European airline. His current research interest is in improving agent understanding of human intentions and actions through natural language and non-verbal interactions and observations.

Davide Grossi is postdoctoral researcher at the University of Luxembourg. He has obtained a degree in philosophy at Pisa University and the diploma of "Scuola Normale Superiore" of Pisa in 2003. In 2007 he obtained a PhD in artificial intelligence at Utrecht University. His PhD thesis dealt with the formal aspects of the specification, analysis and design of agent organizations and institutions. His current research interests concern the connection between logic and the theories and methodologies of social sciences.

Sachin Kamboj is a PhD candidate in the Department of Computer and Information Sciences at the University of Delaware. His research interests include multi-agent systems, networking and bioinformatics. He received his BE in computer science and engineering from Rajiv Gandhi Technical University in 2002 and his MS in computer science from the University of Delaware in 2005. He received the Quantum Leap Innovations graduate student excellence award in 2008 and was nominated for a best student paper at AAMAS 2007.

Dimosthenis Kaponis is a PhD student in the Department of Electrical and Electronic Engineering at Imperial College London. His research interests include distributed artificial intelligence and in particular multi-agent systems, mathematical modeling, data mining and information visualization. He is currently working on models and methods for the evaluation of adaptable multi-agent systems.

Marco Lamieri, PhD in computational economics at University of Turin. Currently economist at the Economic Research Department of Intesa Sanpaolo s.p.a. and associate researcher at the Complex Systems Lagrange LAB, Institute for Scientific Interchange Foundation, Turin, Italy. Marco's research field is industrial economics. The selected research methods, besides verbal and statistical analysis, is agent-based computational economics (ACE) with particular focus on model's realism using empirical data. The main research interest is economic dynamics, in particular the dynamics of interactive social processes involving (boundedly) rational, learning agents.

Evelina Lamma received her degree in electronic engineering from University of Bologna, Italy, in 1985 and her PhD degree in computer science in 1990. Evelina is full professor at the Faculty of Engineering of the University of Ferrara, Italy, where she teaches Artificial Intelligence. Evelina's research activity focuses on logic programming languages and their extensions, logic for AI, knowledge representation systems, machine learning, multi-agent systems.

Diana Mangalagiu, professor in Organization Sciences at Reims Management School, France and associate researcher at the Complex Systems Lagrange LAB, Institute for Scientific Interchange Foundation, Turin, Italy, has a background in both "hard" and "soft" disciplines: computer science and artificial intelligence (PhD), microelectronics and instrumentation (MSc), electrical sciences (MSc), sociology (MSc) and organization science (MSc). She specialized in the study and the modeling of social and economic systems, using an interdisciplinary approach combining organization sciences, sociology, economics, physics and computer science. Her research is both theoretical and empirical, aiming at identifying and analyzing the connections between the microscopic fundamental level of the individual agent and collective social phenomena.

Paola Mello obtained her PhD in computer science in 1989 from the University of Bologna, Italy. Since 1994 Paola is a full professor at the University of Bologna's Faculty of Engineering, where she teaches artificial intelligence. Paola's research focuses on theoretical aspects and applications of logic programming languages, artificial intelligence, expert systems, multi-agent systems and Web services. Paola participated in several national and international (UE) research projects in the context of computational logic.

John-Jules Ch. Meyer obtained his PhD in 1985 at the Vrije Universiteit Amsterdam. He was a professor in Amsterdam and Nijmegen from 1988 to 1993. Since 1993 he has been a professor at the computer science department of Utrecht University. Currently he is heading the Intelligent Systems Group. He was the scientific director of the Dutch graduate school in Information and Knowledge-based Systems (SIKS) during1995-2005. He is a member of the IFAAMAS board steering the international AAMAS conferences. In 2005 he was awarded a fellowship of the European Coordinating Committee for Artificial Intelligence (ECCAI).

Steven Okamoto is a doctoral candidate in the School of Computer Science at Carnegie Mellon University. He holds a BSc and a MSc in computer science from the University of Southern California.

Graçaliz Pereira Dimuro graduated in Civil Engineering at UCPel, Pelotas, Brazil, in 1980. MSc and PhD in computer science at UFRGS, Porto Alegre, Brazil, in 1991 and 1998, respectively. Adjunct professor of Computer Science at UCPel, Pelotas, Brazil, since 1998. Graduate students supervisor at the Graduate Programme in Informatics at UCPel since 2005. Main interests: mathematical foundations of computer science, soft computing, mathematical aspects of multiagent systems.

Jeremy Pitt is a Reader in Intelligent Systems in the Department of Electrical and Electronic Engineering at Imperial College London. His research is based on the application of logic to computing and communications, and he has worked on numerous projects concerned with natural language processing, automated reasoning, project management, telecommunications, human-computer interaction, and multi-agent systems. His current research focus is on organized adaptation in agent societies and affective computing and its impact on computer-mediated communication.

Viara Popova is a research fellow at De Montfort University, UK. She received her master's degree in computer science at Sofia University, Bulgaria. She defended her PhD at Erasmus University Rotterdam, The Netherlands in the area of knowledge discovery. She has performed research in a number of areas including modeling and analysis of organizations, machine learning and data mining, supply chain modeling and optimization, organizational performance indicators, etc.

António da Rocha Costa graduated in electrical engineering at UFRGS, Porto Alegre, Brazil, in 1977. MSc and PhD in computer science at UFRGS, in 1980 and 1993, respectively. Adjunct professor of Computer Science at UCPel, Pelotas, Brazil, since 1998. Graduate students supervisor at the Computer Science Graduate Programme at UFRGS since 1993. Director of the Graduate Programme in Informatics at UCPel since 2005. Main interests: foundations of artificial intelligence, theory and applications of multiagent systems, theory of interactive and developmental computation.

Paul Scerri is a systems scientist at Carnegie Mellon University's Robotics Institute. He is involved in a number of research projects in multi-agent systems, including work with teams of unmanned aerial vehicles, intelligent personal assistants, human-agent collaboration and communication networks.

Alexei Sharpanskykh is a postdoctoral researcher at the VU University Amsterdam. He received his master's degree in computer science at the Zaporizhzhya National Technical University (Ukraine), and a PhD degree at the VU University Amsterdam in the area of artificial intelligence. Currently he is doing research in modeling and analysis of multi-agent organizations in the context of a number of projects in the areas of logistics, incident management and air traffic control.

Jaime Simão Sichman received his PhD at INPG, France. He is associate professor at University of São Paulo, Brazil. His research interests are related to agents' organizational models, multi-agent based simulation, and reputation and trust in MAS. He is program co-chair for AAMAS 2009.

Munindar P. Singh is a full professor in the department of computer science at North Carolina State University. Munindar's books include *Multi-agent Systems* (Springer-Verlag 1994), *Readings in Agents* (coedited with Mike Huhns; Morgan Kaufmann, 1998), *Practical Handbook of Internet Computing* (edited; Chapman & Hall, 2004), *Service-Oriented Computing* (with Mike Huhns; Wiley, 2005). Munindar was the editor-in-chief of *IEEE Internet Computing* from 1999 to 2002. Munindar is a founding member of the editorial boards of *IEEE Internet Computing, Journal of Autonomous Agents and Multi-agent Systems, Journal of Web Semantics*, and *Service-Oriented Computing and Applications*. Munindar serves on the founding board of directors of IFAAMAS, the International Foundation for Autonomous Agents and Multi-Agent Systems.

Gita Sukthankar is an assistant professor in the School of Electrical Engineering and Computer Science at the University of Central Florida, and an affiliate faculty member at the UCF's Institute for Simulation and Training. She received her PhD from the Robotics Institute at Carnegie Mellon, an MSc in robotics from Carnegie Mellon, and an BA (cum laude) in psychology from Princeton University. From 2000-2003, she worked as a researcher at Compaq Research/HP Labs (CRL) in the handheld computing group. Dr. Sukthankar's current research is on plan/activity recognition for adversarial games and multi-agent systems.

Katia Sycara is a professor in the School of Computer Science at CMU and a Sixth Century Chair in Computer Science at the University of Aberdeen, UK. She has a PhD in computer science from Georgia Institute of Technology and holds an Honorary Doctorate from the University of the Aegean. She is a fellow of IEEE, fellow of AAAI and the recipient of the ACM/SIGART Agents Research Award. She has (co)authored more than 350 papers and has given numerous talks. She is on the Scientific Advisory Board of France Telecom. She has been founding EIC of the *Journal of Autonomous Agents and Multi-Agent Systems* and on the board of 6 additional journals.

Tiberiu Stratulat is assistant professor at University of Montpellier II, France. He received a PhD degree in computer science from the University of Caen, France, in 2002, and a software engineer degree from "Politehnica" University of Bucharest, Romania, in 1993. His research works are related to the study of the multi-agent interaction using social metaphors. He investigated the use of norms in agent-based systems and proposed appropriate formal models and architectures to support them. He recently co-authored MASQ, an integrating model that allows the extension of AGR model and MadKit framework with institutional concepts.

John Tranier obtained the BSc in computer science (2001), MA in computer science (2003), and PhD in computer science (2007), all from the University of Montpellier II. He is currently a postdoctoral fellow at the LIAFA (Laboratoire d'Informatique Algorithmique: Fondements et Applications), Paris. John Tranier is active in the research and development of multi-agent systems. His main research interests concern the design of open multi-agent systems and the concepts of environment, organization and institution for multi-agent systems.

Catherine Tessier is a researcher at ONERA, the French Aerospace Lab, in Toulouse, France. She received her PhD in 1988 and her HDR (Habilitation à Diriger les Recherches) in 1999. Her research areas include cooperating agents, authority sharing, adaptive autonomy and situation assessment and tracking, mainly in projects involving uninhabited vehicles.

Nick Tinnemeier is a PhD student at the Intelligent Systems Group, Utrecht University (the Netherlands). His research focuses on the development of programming languages for the implementation of multi-agent organizations. Before coming to Utrecht he completed his MSc in computer science at the University of Twente (The Netherlands) in 2006.

Paolo Torroni is an assistant professor of computer engineering at the University of Bologna's Department of Computer Engineering (DEIS). Paolo received his PhD in computer science from the University of Bologna in 2002. Paolo's research interests include using logic in computer science and

AI, declarative and logic programming, hypothetical reasoning, argumentation, semantic web services and agent-based systems. Paolo is a member of the steering committees of the agent-related workshop series CLIMA, DALT and CISWN, and the secretary of the Italian Interest Group on Logic Programming (GULP).

Maksim Tsvetovat is an assistant professor of Computational Social Science at George Mason University. His research is centered on building multi-agent models of social systems, including evolution of conflicts in societies, formation and dissolution of political systems, modeling terrorist organizations and civil conflicts. He has received his PhD from Carnegie Mellon University, where he concentrated on development of models of terrorist organizations.

Bob van der Vecht studied artificial intelligence at the Rijksuniversiteit Groningen. For his master degree (2004) he conducted research on team coordination in Robocup soccer at the SocRob group at IST in Lisbon. He is currently employed by research company TNO, and is doing a PhD at the Universiteit Utrecht. Current work focuses on the relation between autonomy and coordination in the area of multi-agent systems.

Francesco Viganò is assistant researcher at the Università della Svizzera italiana. His research themes are agent communication and formal verification of artificial institutions.

Michael Winikoff is an associate professor in the school of computer science and information technology at RMIT University. His research interests concern notations for specifying and constructing software. In particular, he is interested in agent oriented software engineering methodologies and is co-author of the book *Developing Intelligent Agent Systems: A Practical Guide*, published by Wiley and Sons in 2004.

Michael Wooldridge is a professor in the Department of Computer Science at the University of Liverpool, UK. He has been active in multi-agent systems research since 1989, and has published over two hundred articles in the area. His main interests are in the use of formal methods for reasoning about autonomous agents and multi-agent systems. Wooldridge was the recipient of the ACM Autonomous Agents Research Award in 2006. He is co-editor in chief of the journal *Autonomous Agents and Multi-Agent Systems*, and his introductory textbook, *An Introduction to Multiagent Systems* was published by Wiley in 2002.

Pınar Yolum is an assistant professor at Boğaziçi University, Department of Computer Engineering. Pınar received her PhD in computer science from North Carolina State University in 2003. Pınar's research interests include multi-agent interaction protocols, ontologies, and semantic Web services. Pınar serves on the program committees of international conferences, including International Joint Conference on Autonomous and Multi-agent Systems and International Conference on Web Services.

Index

W